FOCUSING PARTNERSHIPS

FOCUSING PARTNERSHIPS

A Sourcebook for
Municipal Capacity Building
in Public–Private Partnerships

Janelle Plummer

With contributions from
Chris Heymans
Brad Gentry
Richard Slater
Steve Waddell

 Public-Private
Partnerships for the
Urban Environment

Research for
 Department for
International
Development

Earthscan Publications Ltd, London • Sterling, VA

First published in the UK and USA in 2002
by Earthscan Publications Ltd

A catalogue record for this book is available from the British Library

ISBN: 1 85383 838 1

Page design by Brightmark, Pretoria
Typesetting by PCS Mapping & DTP, Gateshead
Printed and bound in the UK by Thanet Press Ltd, Margate, Kent
Cover design by Dierdré Bartie
Cover photographs by Adrian Coad and Guy Stubbs

For a full list of publications please contact:

Earthscan Publications Ltd
120 Pentonville Road, London, N1 9JN, UK
Tel: +44 (0)20 7278 0433
Fax: +44 (0)20 7278 1142
Email: earthinfo@earthscan.co.uk
Web: **www.earthscan.co.uk**

22883 Quicksilver Drive, Sterling, VA 20166-2012, USA

Earthscan is an editorially independent subsidiary of Kogan Page Ltd and publishes in association with WWF-UK and the International
Institute for Environment and Development

A catalogue record for this book is available from the British Library

Library of Congress Cataloging-in-Publication Data

Plummer, Janelle.
   Focusing partnerships : a sourcebook for municipal capacity building in public-private partnerships/Janelle Plummer; with
   contributions from Chris Heymans ... [et al.].
        p. cm.
   Includes bibliographical references and index.
   ISBN 1-85383-838-1
     1. Urban policy. 2. Urban poor—Government policy. 3. Municipal services. 4. Public-private sector cooperation.
   I. Heymans, Chris

HT153 .P65 2002
307.76—dc21

2002000486

This book originates from a research project funded by the UK Department for International Development (DFID). The views expressed
are not necessarily those of DFID

Printed on elemental chlorine-free paper

Acknowledgements

This sourcebook has been prepared with funding from the Department for International Development (DFID), UK, through the Knowledge and Research Programme. It is the result of a two-year research project entitled 'Building Municipal Capacity for Private Sector Participation' carried out by GHK International in collaboration with the University of Birmingham and the United Nations Development Programme (UNDP) Public–Private Partnerships for the Urban Environment (PPPUE) facility.

A number of people contributed to this research stage. I am very grateful to: Andrew Nickson from the International Development Department at the University of Birmingham, UK, who conducted the Latin American case studies in Cartagena and Córdoba; Richard Slater, also from the International Development Department, for jointly authoring the Biratnagar Case study in Nepal, and to Renuka Manandhar and Madan Manandhar from the Nepal Administrative Staff College for their logistical assistance; Godfrey Nhemachena, the Town Clerk of Gweru in Zimbabwe, for his tremendous assistance on the Gweru case study; Chris Magwangqana, the Mayor of Stutterheim, and to Jean Pierre Mas and Marius van Aardt of Water and Sanitation Services South Africa (WSSA), for their fantastic support in the preparation of the Stutterheim case study. I would like to thank all the staff members of the public and private sector organisations that were interviewed and kindly gave up their time to provide the information required. The final preparation of this book drew on these specific case studies and the vast body of literature and knowledge on public–private partnerships available in a range of fields. I would like to acknowledge all those studies that directly and indirectly contributed to the message of this work, the illustrative material and the range of issues included for municipal officials to consider.

I am also particularly grateful to the co-authors and principal contributors to this publication: Chris Heymans, institutional development consultant and public–private partnerships (PPP) policy specialist in South Africa, for authoring Chapter 9 co-authoring Chapters 10 and 12 and his ongoing interest in the development of the book; Brad Gentry from Yale University and a close partner in the knowledge exchange activities of the UNDP PPPUE facility, for co-authoring Chapters 7 and 8 under extreme time pressures; Steve Waddell of Organisational Futures, Boston, for co-authoring Chapter 6 and for his challenging and thoughtful contributions on stakeholders and processes; and Richard Slater for his contribution on municipal capacity in Chapters 11 and 12. The depth of knowledge of these contributors has enriched the information presented in these chapters, and their diverse experience has enhanced the scope of this book. I am indebted to each one.

I would also like to thank Barry Jackson at the Municipal Infrastructure Investment Unit (MIIU), South Africa, Jamie de Jager at the Mvula Trust, South Africa, Ana Hardoy and Ricardo Schusterman at the International Institute for Environment and Development – America Latina (IIED-AL), Buenos Aires, Barbara Evans, Mukami Kariuki and Clarissa Brocklehurst at the Water and Sanitation Program (WSP), in Washington and Nairobi, David Irwin, ADB Advisor to the Kathmandu Metropolitan Corporation and Keshav Sthapit, the Mayor of Kathmandu, in such troubled times, Liliana Miranda and Carlos Grey at Ecociudad, Lima, Peru, Alan Jones at Wessex Water, UK, Chris Ricketson at Halcrow, UK, Gordon Binder and William Reilly at Aqua International Partners, San Francisco, Nadir Ehsan at GHK, London, Adrian Coad, at SKAT, Switzerland and to Marcela Bochetto, Pradeep Kurukulasuriya, Neel Kamath and Mohamed Mukhtar at Yale, the team of students who assisted Brad Gentry. I am most grateful for all contributions to the development of the illustrative material.

At DFID I am grateful to John Hodges for his perspective piece on PPPs, to Peter Roberts, Michael Mutter and to Magdalena Banasiak of the Infrastructure and Urban Development Department for facilitating the research funding that made this book and its dissemination possible. At PPPUE, my thanks to Peter Grohmann, the Global Task Manager for his continuing interest in this endeavour and for facilitating the funding of Brad Gentry's input under the UNDP/Yale collaborative programme. At GHK I would particularly like to thank Jelle Van Gijn for his belief and logistical support.

A special thanks to those who provided comments on the final draft: Richard Batley, International Development Department, University of Birmingham, Ken Caplan, Business Partners for Development, Richard Franceys, IHE and Chris Heymans particularly, for their time and effort; John Kirke and Jamie Simpson of GHK; the urban team at DFID; and also the students from Yale involved in the PPPUE collaborative programme. The comments covered a broad range of issues from a number of differing perspectives. I hope this final version addresses at least some of the important concerns raised.

A special thanks go to Jonathan Sinclair Wilson, Publishing Director at Earthscan, for his interest in this capacity building series; Frances MacDermott, Publishing Manager at Earthscan, for all her tireless work towards such a lengthy publication; and to Rowan Davies for her thorough editing.

Most of all, my thanks go to my family: my husband, Mark Harvey, for his ongoing support without which this endeavour would not have been possible, our wonderful son Tommy for his energy and patience and to our lovely baby Louis for smiling endlessly at the editing stage.

I sincerely hope that the compilation of this material, and the message the book imparts to those responsible for addressing urban governance and poverty reduction bring greater focus to public–private partnerships in water, sanitation and solid waste services and that it in some way contributes to sustainable improvements in the quality of the lives of poor people in developing countries.

My thanks to all those who participated.

Janelle Plummer
January 2002

Contents

List of Boxes

About the Contributors

Brad Gentry is a lecturer at the Yale School of Forestry and Environmental Studies, and Co-Director of the Yale/UNDP collaborative programme on Public–Private Partnerships for the Urban Environment (PPPUE). Trained as a biologist and a lawyer, his research, teaching and professional activities focus on strengthening the links between private investment and improved environmental performance. He has worked on the environmental aspects of private investments around the world and across many sectors, including water, forests, land use and energy. He is the author of many publications, including *Private Capital Flows and the Environment: Lessons from Latin America* (Edward Elgar, 1998). He is now coordinating a 'collaborative learning' course with universities around the world on using public–private partnerships to improve the delivery of urban environmental services.

Chris Heymans, a South African based private consultant, is a governance and institutional development specialist with a particular interest in local government, public policy management and urban development. Holding degrees in political science and economics, he previously worked for different development organisations and lectured at a number of universities. He has worked with government, private and donor organisations and NGOs inside and outside South Africa, and participated in the drafting of a number of Policy Documents, Green and White Papers produced by the post-apartheid South African Government since 1994. As Policy Manager at the Development Bank of Southern Africa (DBSA), he initiated the regular DBSA Development Report, editing the first one, titled *Infrastructure: a foundation for development* in 1998. He also edited the journal, *Development Southern Africa* between 1997 and 1999. In 1999-2000 he assisted South Africa's National Treasury in developing a regulatory framework and operational guidelines for PPPs, and was editor of the National Treasury's *Intergovernmental Fiscal Review* – a comprehensive overview of provincial and local government finances in South Africa – in 2000 and 2001.

Janelle Plummer is an urban poverty specialist working with GHK International. The focus of her work is building local government capacity for more effective urban poverty reduction. She has worked on a range of participatory poverty assessments, and the design and implementation of poverty reduction and services projects in Asia and Africa. Her poverty focus has led her to carry out detailed explorations into how challenging policies such as community participation and public–private partnerships can be implemented within the existing constraints of municipalities in developing countries. She is the series editor of the Municipal Capacity Building Series published by Earthscan and the author of the companion volume *Municipalities and Community Participation: A Sourcebook for Capacity Building*.

Richard Slater is a consultant in governance, public policy and municipal management. He has spent over 15 years with the School of Public Policy, University of Birmingham, as well as working as an independent consultant for a wide range of multilateral and bilateral donors. He also has substantial experience of working on decentralisation and poverty reduction projects in the urban sector in Asia with expertise in project design, implementation and impact assessment. He is currently involved in the design and implementation of major municipal reform projects in Andhra Pradesh, West Bengal and Sri Lanka where he is working closely with GHK International.

Steve Waddell is a researcher-consultant with The Collaboration Works – Organizational Futures, based in Boston (www.thecollaborationworks.com). He has a PhD (sociology) and an MBA. The focus of his work is development of networks, usually of large scale (often global), aiming for complex development outcomes by engaging diverse organisations (usually government, civil society and business). He is affiliated with Boston College, a member of the governing council of the Society for Organizational Learning (www.solonline.org), leader of the Global Public Policy Research Group (www.gppnresearch.org), and an Associate of Simon Fraser University's Centre for Innovation in Management (www.cim.sfu.ca) and SmithObrien (www.smithobrien.com). He can be reached at swaddell@prodigy.net.

Acronyms and Abbreviations

AA	Aguas Argentinas
ADB	Asian Development Bank
AGBAR	Aguas de Barcelona
AGUACAR	Aguas de Cartagena
AMC	Ahmedabad Municipal Corporation (India)
BMC	Biratnagar Sub-Municipal Corporation
BOT	build–operate–transfer
BoTT	build–operate–train–transfer (South Africa)
BPD	Business Partners for Development
CBO	community-based organisation
CD	community development
CEO	chief executive officer
CMIP	Consolidated Municipal Infrastructure Programme (South Africa)
COSATU	Congress of South African Trade Unions
COVAAP	Vigilance Committee for Drinking Water (Peru)
DAS	Departamento de Aguas y Saneamiento (Argentina)
DBOT	design–build–operate–transfer
DBSA	Development Bank of Southern Africa
DCC	Dar-es-Salaam City Commission
DCD	Department for Constitutional Development (South Africa) now DPLG
DFID	Department for International Development (UK)
DPLG	Department for Provincial and Local Government (South Africa)
DSSD	Dar-es-Salaam Sewerage and Sanitation Department
DWAF	Department of Water Affairs and Forestry (South Africa)
EAPP	El Alto Pilot Project (Bolivia)
ECA	export credit agency
EIA	environmental impact assessment
EIB	European Investment Bank
ERSEP	Ente Regulador de Servicios Publicos (Argentina)
ESAP	economic structural adjustment programme
ETOSS	Ente Tripartito de Obras y Servicios Sanitarios (Argentina)
EU	European Union
FINIDA	Finnish International Development Agency
GCC	Gweru City Council
GDP	gross domestic product
GEAR	growth, employment and redistribution strategy (South Africa)
GNLC	Greater Nelspruit Local Council
GNP	gross national product
GNUC	Greater Nelspruit Utility Company (South Africa)
GoSA	Government of South Africa
HH	household
HRD	human resource development
IDP	integrated development plan
IDS	Institute of Development Studies (UK)
IIED	International Institute for Environment and Development

IIED-AL	International Institute for Environment and Development – America Latina
IFC	International Finance Corporation (South Africa)
IFI	international finance institution
ILO	International Labour Organization
IMF	International Monetary Fund
ISD	institutional and social development
JAC	Junta de Acción Comunal
kip	Lao monetary unit
kl	kilolitre
KMC	Kathmandu Metropolitan City (Nepal)
LAPF	Local Authority Pension Fund
LDE	Lyonnaise des Eaux (France) now Ondeo
LED	local economic development
m^3	cubic metres
MCH	Municipal Corporation of Hyderabad (India)
MIIF	Municipal Infrastructure Investment Framework (South Africa)
MIIP	Municipal Infrastructure Investment Plan (South Africa)
MIIU	Municipal Infrastructure Investment Unit
MLGNH	Ministry of Local Government and National Housing (Zimbabwe)
MoU	memorandum of understanding
MSP	municipal service partnership
MSWM	municipal solid waste management
MWSS	metropolitan waterworks and sewerage system (Manila)
NBI	National Business Initiative (South Africa)
NEDLAC	National Economic Development and Labour Advisory Council (South Africa)
NGO	non-governmental organisation
NPR	Nepalese rupees
NWSC	National Water Supply Corporation
O and M	operations and maintenance
ODA	Overseas Development Administration (UK) *now* DFID
POT	Plan de Ordenamiento Territorial (Colombia)
PDR	People's Democratic Republic
PPA	participatory poverty assessment
PPIAF	Public–Private Infrastructure Advisory Facility (World Bank)
PPP	public–private partnership(s)
PPPUE	Public–Private Partnerships for the Urban Environment (UNDP programme)
PSP	private sector participation
R	rand (South Africa)
RDP	Reconstruction and Development Plan (South Africa)
RfP	request for proposals
RfQ	request for qualifications
RoSA	Republic of South Africa
RUPP	Rural–Urban Partnership Programme (Nepal)
SABS	South African Bureau of Statistics
SALGA	South African Local Government Association

SAMWU	South African Municipal Workers Union
SAUR (UK)	Société d'Aménagement Urbain et Rural (UK)
SDF	Stutterheim Development Forum (South Africa)
SEDAPAL	Sanitation and Potable Water Company of Lima
SEP	service expansion plan
SIDA	Swedish International Development Agency
SL	sustainable livelihoods
SSIP	small-scale independent provider
STLC	Stutterheim Transitional Local Council (South Africa)
SUMA	universal service and environmental fee (Argentina)
SW	solid waste
SWM	solid waste management
SWOT	strengths, weaknesses, opportunities and threats
TA	technical assistance
ToR	terms of reference
TShs	Tanzanian shillings
UDLE	Urban Development through Local Efforts (Nepal)
UFW	unaccounted-for water
UNDP	United Nations Development Programme
USAID	United States Agency for International Development
USN	Urban Sector Network
UWS	urban water supply
watsan	water and sanitation
WDC	Ward Development Committee
WPLG	White Paper on Local Government
WSP	Water and Sanitation Program
WSP-AND	Water and Sanitation Program – Andean Region
WSSA	Water and Sanitation Services South Africa
WTP	willingness to pay
ZD	Zimbabwean dollars

Foreword

There is undoubtedly some homework still to do in terms of ensuring that private sector participation can meet the needs of poor people. It is also evident that regardless of the mandate given to the public sector, poor communities are not always at the top of its agenda either. The more prepared the public sector can be before entering into a contract with the private sector, the more likely that the contract will live up to a formidable set of local government and local community expectations.

Through numerous case studies and solid analysis of what works and what doesn't, this book sheds significant light on how to take advantage of the strengths of the private sector. It places private sector participation within the entire picture of urban management, community participation and poverty alleviation programmes, understanding that the demands placed on municipal officials are vast and varied. Boosting the capacity of the public sector to partner serves everyone's interests – whether a private sector company that has just won a contract that more clearly defines the roles and responsibilities of each party; an NGO that is working alongside local government to facilitate service delivery in poor communities and requires the leeway to experiment; or poor communities themselves that require more informed, more conscientious and more responsive governance from their elected officials and civil servants.

Transforming local governments to be more responsive, whether they make use of private sector participation or not, is in some places a very daunting task. Efforts such as this sourcebook which provides simple, accessible guidance based on analysis of numerous case studies are to be applauded. While municipalities are generally prone to say that 'such and such approach may have worked for them, but it won't work for us', this book is not prescriptive – it does not say that 'this worked here and thus it will work there' – and that is part of its beauty. Instead, it provides a series of considerations and tools that will facilitate making both governance and government more effective. It allows municipalities to tailor their approach through more informed analysis of the problems that they face and the options that are possible.

The sourcebook achieves this by providing information on the constituent parts of a service public–private partnership (PPP) concerned with the poor. It discusses *who* is and can be involved in PPPs, broadening the net here to include the potential roles of NGOs and independent service providers as well as the large multinational companies discussed elsewhere. It considers *what* issues partnerships should address, stressing that municipal officials need to understand ingredients if they are to create PPPs that fulfil local objectives. It gives information on the implications of current organisational structures and contractual types but encourages municipal decision-makers to construct relevant PPPs able to respond to local needs and assets. It also looks behind the scenes at the skills needed on the public sector side to initiate, establish and sustain the complexities of a pro-poor PPP.

At WaterAid, we believe in the possibility of a world where basic needs like water and sanitation can be readily accessed. We know that, depending on the context, different stakeholders need to play their rightful role in making this happen. Given their mandate, their scope and their ability to integrate all the different programmes they manage, no group is more important than local governments. With that in mind, we highly recommend this piece of work and look forward to sharing it with the municipalities with which we work.

Ravi Narayanan
Executive Director
WaterAid

Guy Stubbs

Introduction

Until quite recently, municipalities in developing countries formulated and implemented infrastructure and service projects utilising budgets handed down from higher levels of government. Municipal officials, in some cases influenced by political priorities, conceived, designed, constructed and managed projects and then handed over the finished product to other municipal officials for operation and maintenance. While this may not have been considered effective or sustainable, municipal organisations and officials were geared towards this approach and many have the technical capacity to play these roles. Moreover, the status of municipal officials and their relationships to society as a whole reflected their ability to make financial and technical decisions, select contractors and provide services.

However, in the context of the widespread decentralisation and devolution of responsibility to local levels of government, some municipalities have quickly found that they have neither the human nor the financial resources to meet the extent of their obligations. If national-level policy or donor conditionality are not driving change, enlightened or desperate municipal leaders are recognising the potential contribution – mostly the investment contribution – of the private sector. This is resulting in an ever-increasing shift from public service provision to some form of partnership with the private sector. This shift to private sector involvement is perhaps most marked and contentious in the delivery of infrastructure and other basic services.

In less than a decade, the rapid increase in partnership initiatives has meant that there are a number of public authorities and private utilities testing new ways of working together for mutual gain. Yet the outcomes are not yet fully known. The experiences of most projects are often discussed in terms of inputs and outputs, and success is measured against predetermined (but not necessarily substantiated) contractual requirements set down by a public sector that is unfamiliar with this task. While a number of municipal–private partnerships have been in place for a decade, such local partnerships are still relatively rare. Relationships between the private sector and government, particularly municipal government, are thus still in their infancy. Furthermore, while there are many signs of the benefits of the involvement of the private sector, to date there are few, if any, rigorous assessments of the impacts. In the context of increasing private sector involvement, impact assessments are urgently needed to guide policy-makers and stakeholders as to whether or not a partnership with the private sector is indeed always an appropriate solution, under which conditions such partnerships shine, and in which areas they have failed.

To broaden knowledge of partnerships in the context of developing countries, over the last two years a number of agencies, governments and operators have focused efforts on improving their understanding of public–private service delivery to urban poor communities and low-income areas. Within the partnership debate, the need for improved service coverage and higher levels of investment in unserviced or underserviced areas of the city is coming to the fore, because the constraints of delivering to these areas were not adequately understood at the outset of such partnerships. Performance relating to poor areas was not explicitly built into regulatory frameworks, and supporting mechanisms (such as technical options, service gradation and financing arrangements) were not embodied in contractual agreements. As a result, in many cities the private sector has been unable to meet targets. In some cases targets have created perverse incentives, and in other cases the targets themselves are inappropriate and do not reflect the needs of the poor.

This investigation of the delivery of services to the poor through partnerships – and the dissemination of lessons learnt to date – enabled some recent transactions to adopt more appropriate financial, institutional and technical alternatives. While these (mostly) donor-led initiatives may have reached national-level policy-makers, and may have started to influence contract formulation, it is questionable whether municipal government and implementing agencies at the local level have had access to or benefited from these revised approaches. It is unlikely that municipal officials are any clearer on whether or how private sector participation (PSP) can effectively address the needs of the poor. There is certainly little evidence of any capacity building for them to do so.

Yet despite these efforts and the various initiatives in service delivery at all levels of government, the debate over private sector involvement has not always been fully played out. It is of particular concern that many advocates of the private sector's role in basic services have not yet aligned their ideology with the realities of very poor, institutionally weak cities. Although current rhetoric reinforces the point that private sector participation is not a panacea for the service and infrastructure deficiencies prevalent in the South, actions tend to inherently contradict this, sending an unambiguous message that private sector participation is the answer to most ills. Some initiatives with the private sector are being applied in isolation – often in contexts in which other public/community or NGO partnerships may have been more appropriate – provide mounting evidence of the need for more objective assistance to support municipalities (and higher levels of government) in identifying both goals and solutions. Moreover, assistance is also needed to ensure that undertakings with the private sector are effectively targeted.

In the future, it seems vital that advocates begin to recognise that a central aspect of targeting the poor must consist of a greater synergy between the private sector approach (founded in the economic/financial disciplines) and the broader experiences of poverty reduction that lean towards the importance of social capital and sustainable livelihoods. This means that the development of the basic framework of partnerships (the basic tool proposed in this sourcebook) needs to address a number of key issues. Chapter 5, for instance, expands on some of the primary concerns that arise because public–private partnerships (PPPs) to date have done little to acknowledge this experience. On the face of it, private sector participation has cut down the possibilities for or implementation of integrated solutions to poverty reduction – solutions that ensure that unsustainable single sector interventions are avoided. Some argue that, with the efficient formal private sector delivering a service, outcomes will be different from the failed slum-improvement projects of the past. Others are not so sure, and in line with the approach proposed in this book, they advocate the importance of linking sector partnerships closely with other initiatives in order to bring about improvements in livelihood outcomes.

Closely associated with this discussion is the very closed definition normally applied to the 'private' sector. Notwithstanding the opportunities of investment that come with the large-scale formal private sector, in reality, the small-scale private sector is frequently a key stakeholder in service delivery to the poor, and greater emphasis should be given to initiatives that build on such assets. Accordingly, this book, which is concerned with focusing partnerships, provides information on small-scale providers and includes them as an integral part of the term 'private' in the partnership framework.

Ultimately, this book is aimed at capacity building; it is critical that policy-makers and advocates of municipal–private partnerships begin to understand just how onerous all this is. The shift towards private sector participation in so-called public sector functions may be a new area for formal private sector actors, but for the municipalities it is part of a series of structural and procedural changes to municipal service delivery. The capacity of municipal governments to absorb and implement these new policies is, however, rarely supported by a level of capacity building commensurate with the change envisaged.

Prior to the private sector participation tide, perhaps the most fundamental change in recent years has been the shift towards demand-led service delivery – towards **community participation** in the planning, implementation and management of services and infrastructure. This shift came about not least because empirical evidence showed that engineering- or supply-led infrastructure and services provided in poor neighbourhoods resulted in only short-term benefits, and frequently resulted in the poorest groups and households being squeezed out of their newly serviced areas due to market pressures. Donor-funded slum-improvement projects, for instance, received massive capital investments in comparison to normal municipal budgets, and such injections of capital proved unsustainable.[1] The shift towards demand-led service delivery was considered advantageous to service sustainability and beneficial to the users. It is now widely argued that the process itself is empowering, improving the capacity of individuals and groups to participate in their own development.

In some countries, another important shift resulted in holistic approaches towards poverty reduction. Seeking a sustainability not attained through sectoral service improvement projects, urban poverty reduction responses became **multisectoral**, emphasising the linkages between sectors (such as water supply and health promotion). This 'integrated' approach has included, for instance, community development, micro-credit, income generation, basic infrastructure and services, health promotion and education. Environmental service improvements are considered a part, albeit the most capital-intensive part, of the overall poverty reduction framework. Programming for service improvements was then revised to fit into an integrated programme of development.

These demand-led and integrated approaches require very different skills and organisational capacity within municipal government, and tasks to be undertaken by municipal officials need to change dramatically. To promote demand-led infrastructure, officials must bring together various actors in the decision-making process and facilitate rather than dictate. Engineers accustomed to making unilateral decisions, measuring success in terms of inputs and outputs and judging performance in terms of time, quality and cost, are expected to master low-cost options, micro-planning and community maintenance, normally without training or support from the engineering profession. To create an integrated approach to poverty reduction, municipal actors are asked to interact, and organisations are asked to achieve a (hitherto unheard of) level of inter-departmental coordination, and in some cases to accept a reshuffling in departmental status and responsibility. Both approaches require massive attitudinal change – a change that frequently sidelines investment and technical concerns and promotes the concerns of sustainable community development.

Within this framework, a new actor – the **formal private sector** – is introduced into the process of delivering services to a city. Driven by predetermined contractual obligations, programmes and quantitative targets, this policy change demands quite different municipal competencies: understanding alternative forms of contracts, contract preparation, performance monitoring, regulatory frameworks and negotiation. While the process may err towards an engineering-led approach and may be more akin to the technical decision-making of the past, the municipal role in the delivery process is utterly transformed. In most cases, municipal managers and technical officials have been asked to cease being project providers and become managers and monitors. Without adequate capacity building, many have experienced problems and are now, unsurprisingly, accused of micro-managing private sector activities.

Within this multi-layered and somewhat conflicting context, the discussion of **pro-poor private sector participation** has emerged – introducing a partnership arrangement that often means involving communities and informal service providers as well as the formal private sector and is surely, by any standards, a most complex endeavour for municipal government to embark upon. On the one hand, this delivery process is demand-led and participatory, requiring flexibility; and on the other hand, private sector participation is often investment-led (or at least project-led), and characterised by contractual obligations requiring rigidity and predictability. Furthermore, the role of interested stakeholders is more complex (particularly by the potential inclusion of small-scale providers who are often poor themselves) and objectives such as equity and job creation create an infinitely more ambitious agenda.

Seen in this evolving context, such rapid and significant process changes are considerable, even to a private sector organisation in a developed country. Yet in developing countries, shifts such as these have become common aspects of municipal life. The municipality is expected to absorb these changes effortlessly. Change may be necessary and reform a condition of funding, but it is fundamentally constrained by the inertia of the bureaucracy, by inappropriate skills, and perhaps resistant attitudes among staff. For those municipal leaders who come from the long-established tradition of engineering-led service provision and have not had any experience of such changes, the enormity of the challenge must be constantly asserted in order that capacity building initiatives are given greater importance. Until capacity building initiatives become commensurate with the degree of change envisaged, policy frameworks will remain impractical and out of the reach of all but a few large municipal organisations. In this context of rapid change and somewhat conflicting agendas, what does a municipality need to know to formulate, establish and sustain partnerships that are focused on bringing improvements to the poor?

The Capacity Building Purpose

The ultimate aim of this Municipal Capacity Building Series[2] is to promote effective and sustainable forms of service delivery to poor people living in urban areas in the South. While the first sourcebook in this series[3] focused on the important role of communities in this process, this volume considers the current trend towards private sector involvement and the associated capacity issues at the municipal level. The intention is to promote tangible understanding of service partnerships focused on the poor – one which promotes confidence and awareness of this approach to service delivery.

This sourcebook is concerned with the municipal actor, and recognises that involving new actors, introducing new processes and adopting new forms of delivery are not easy changes for local government. The purpose of this book is to provide an exploration into the issues concerning municipal officials. The book seeks to underpin municipal capacity building for focused partnerships by:

- providing a framework for strengthening the capacity of municipal actors to bring about effective service partnerships involving the private sector;
- proposing the key elements of an integrated strategy set in the context of effective governance;
- presenting in detail the key issues involved in the formulation and implementation of meaningful service partnerships; and
- generating a source of illustrative material to enable municipal actors to better understand the main issues and to heed the lessons of their peers.

The research leading to this book has analysed and documented a number of municipal experiences of private sector involvement in the delivery of services and infrastructure.[4] Case studies were drawn from Southern Africa, South Asia and Latin America. Together they provide a range of good and bad practice, illustrating the constraints of context and the importance of learning lessons through the experience of others.

Target Audience

This book is directed at capacity builders: those responsible for municipal capacity building and focused on promoting more effective partnerships involving the private sector in service delivery. Depending on the context, actors responsible for capacity building at the municipal level may come from any one of a number of sectors. The book primarily aims to support the efforts of development agencies, professionals, universities and training institutes in their capacity building endeavours; but it is, of course, available for all municipal managers who are keen to extend their understanding, and policy-makers who may have acknowledged the enormity of the task at the implementation level. Like its forerunner in this Municipal Capacity Building Series, it is hoped that this volume will provide a springboard for capacity builders to undertake a more holistic approach – capacity building in the context of broader poverty reduction and local governance. A forthcoming toolkit is specifically directed at municipal officials.

Scope and Focus

In order to meet these municipal capacity building objectives (and not withstanding these general development goals), the scope of this sourcebook is focused on particular areas of the debate. First, the work is clearly concerned with the implementation of partnerships at the local or **municipal level** of government. This does not deny the importance of policy-making and the influential role of national-level regulatory frameworks and policies on municipal initiatives. These are critical, and are covered in depth elsewhere.[5] However, while this macro level emphasises the importance of getting the preparation right, little support is actually provided for municipalities and other public sector implementing bodies. This book therefore supplements this body of material by addressing the micro level – it looks at how policies are implemented by those who have to implement them.

Second, the research seeks to explore private sector participation in relation to the broader municipal objectives of effective **governance and management**. In the rush towards private sector participation in a particular sector, there seems little encouragement for municipalities to stand back and look at the whole picture. Therefore, the book pursues a theme that links private sector participation with municipal reform, management and poverty reduction.

Third, the work has an **urban** focus. In the context of increasing decentralisation and rapid urbanisation in many parts of the world, this series is concerned with the problems of resource-deficient urban local government. While these deficiencies tend to be amplified in secondary cities and towns, the emphasis here is not on size but on the lessons that are relevant for dissemination to smaller municipalities, where financial and human resources are particularly constrained. It therefore includes reference to larger cities if initiatives seem relevant and replicable. In terms of overall scope, this urban focus includes the peri-urban context. It is often peri-urban areas that lack access to network services and pose major challenges to governments and private service operators.

Fourth, the work promotes an approach to service partnerships that is **inclusive** of a wide range of urban actors (such as non-governmental organisations (NGOs), informal service providers and community organisations) in varying and complex roles. Given that no two contexts are the same, it is therefore unlikely that any solution will fit all situations. This book does not fall into the privatisation camp, which promotes private sector solutions regardless of context and capacity. Instead, it aims to expose the various alternatives, open up the options and promote partnership solutions that are contextually specific and lead to sustainable improvements for the poor.

Most importantly, this work focuses on how partnerships can address the **poor**. It is particularly concerned with those urban contexts overwhelmingly troubled by poverty and service constraints. It is concerned with marginalisation processes, and the political economy of allocating resources and delivering basic services to the poor. While it acknowledges the indirect benefits that reforms can bring, it is also specifically concerned with maximising the potential of direct and targeted improvements for the poor.

Given the primary objective of municipal capacity building in relation to the poor, illustrative material in this book is limited to those physical services that fall within the responsibility of municipalities, and which have the most significant impact on the quality of the lives of the poor in cities. These include **water, sanitation and solid waste**. This is not to deny that some municipalities may not deliver all these services, that some municipalities may have responsibility for other key services affecting the poor such as energy and transport, or that private sector participation in non-basic municipal services often creates a platform for change. It is hoped that many of the descriptions apply to a much broader range of municipal activities, and that the illustrative material can provide pointers for these initiatives.

A number of parameters have defined the scope and boundaries of the work. First, the research and outputs are concerned with partnerships that include actors in the **for-profit** private sector.[6] This limitation does not exclude a role for NGOs – indeed, the book actively promotes such roles – but it seeks to consider the nature of partnerships that involve the complexities of profit, and the benefits that the for-profit sector can bring. Notably, the approach includes the informal sector where possible. Indeed, 'private sector' can refer to the formal or informal sector, international or local, or large or small enterprises. Key definitions are provided in Box 1.1.

1

Box 1.1   Definitions

Private sector participation (PSP)	'PSP' refers to the involvement of the private sector in some form, at some stage in the delivery of services. It is a general term that is used to cover a wide range of private sector involvement including large and small scale, international and local, and the formal and informal sectors.
Public–private partnerships (PPPs)	The term 'PPP' is used in various ways in various contexts. Frequently it implies some form of private investment and transfer of risk to the private sector; but in other countries the stress lies with the concept of partnership and not with the contract or the investment. In this sourcebook we have adopted a broad usage to describe some form of partnership endeavour involving both the public and private sectors (but not excluding the involvement of the third sector, civil society).
Privatisation	This term is used to mean the transfer of ownership to the private sector. Divestiture is beyond the scope of this sourcebook.
Service delivery or service provision	The term 'service delivery' is used in preference to 'service provision', removing the implication that there is a provider and a beneficiary. This is an important distinction.
Pro-poor or poverty focused	'Pro-poor' implies that the overall aim is beneficial for the poor and may be achieved through a range of initiatives, while 'poverty-focused' is used to imply a greater degree of targeting to ensure direct benefits to the poor.
Participation or consultation	These terms have very different meanings in participation literature, and are not used interchangeably. 'Participation' is generally used to refer to a two-way flow of information. It implies a greater degree of influence over the decision-making process and opens up opportunities for more direct involvement in implementation processes. 'Consultation' means that a stakeholder is contacted and their views sought, but the level of engagement and influence may be limited.
Municipal	The term 'municipal' refers to the local level of urban government. It is the municipal level that is frequently and increasingly responsible for urban services and infrastructure. It also often forms the implementation arm of government in cities, and is responsible for executing policy. Water and sanitation services in many countries are delivered through local-level line agencies rather than the municipality itself, and much of the information contained in this book will be of relevance to these organisations as well.
Capacity building	The term 'capacity building' includes a broader understanding of capacity that includes human resource development, organisational development and the regulatory framework. 'Municipal capacity building' refers specifically to organisational and human resource development (HRD) issues, and those regulatory issues that are within the scope of municipal government.

The detailed structure, organisation and sequence of the book are covered in Chapter 2. Each chapter is located within a strategic framework for capacity building. A broad range of detailed illustrative material supplements the text throughout. This is a primary characteristic of this series, a tool developed to make concepts and issues tangible and real for municipal decision-makers. Illustrations are drawn from 15 cities and towns in countries as diverse as Argentina, Bolivia, Chile, Colombia, India, Laos, Nepal, South Africa, Tanzania and Zimbabwe.

Guy Stubbs

A **Strategic Framework** for Municipal Capacity Building

This chapter presents a strategy to develop the capacity of municipalities to understand, formulate and implement public–private partnerships (PPPs) focused on improving services for the poor. This strategy implicitly covers the 'what', 'why' and 'who' of partnerships in the context of poverty, municipal government and outside influences; it also emphasises the importance of linking partnerships with existing urban governance and poverty reduction frameworks. Aspects concerning the poor are inherent in all the components; they are overlaid with a concern for those existing and potential dimensions of partnerships that affect the poor. Underpinning the partnership with receptive, skilled and effective public sector partners is highlighted as being a key aspect of the framework. This chapter provides a framework for capacity building and provides the structure for the remainder of the sourcebook.

Irrespective of location, a strategy for building capacity in private sector participation at the local level of government should aim to rationalise and structure the primary elements and issues into a coherent and comprehensive framework. Such a framework and its inherent divisions can only ever provide a guide, and can only ever represent one approach to the problem. The political and economic context and the institutional, social and cultural norms at the local level will invariably result in changing emphases and highlight specific problems. This framework is therefore presented with the intention that consideration should be given to each and every context as an integral part of its application.

Box 3.1 provides a diagram illustrating the strategic framework for capacity building.

This sourcebook discusses a range of issues and provides a range of illustrations of PPPs. It is aimed at broadening the debate and raising levels of awareness about PPPs – especially as they relate to the poor – through municipal capacity building initiatives. These issues and illustrations are many and varied. No individual municipality is expected to pick up this reference book and implement its contents. Rather, the book it intended to provoke consideration and dialogue about what is possible and relevant in any specific context. The primary elements of the strategic framework are signposted through the repetition of the key diagram, locating each chapter in relation to the strategy and book as a whole.

The illustrative material placed in boxes is intended to be detailed rather than cursory. Each box tells a story of an experience. These boxes can be read individually, by chapter, or by case, with the intention of bringing reality to partnership concepts.

Part 1 • Focusing Partnership Goals

Meeting municipal objectives through partnerships

Locating and linking partnerships in urban governance and management

Contributing to poverty reduction

Part 1 considers what 'focusing a partnership' means. In order to consider PPPs in relation to the urban poor, a municipality needs first to clarify their objectives of improving services and the benefits that a partnership involving the private sector might bring, to consider the way the partnership will be developed and function as a part of city governance, and to consider the mechanisms that will ensure that the partnership contributes to poverty reduction.

☐ **Meeting municipal objectives through partnerships** Chapter 3

In order to focus a partnership effectively, it is necessary to establish whether the partnership approach is appropriate for the purpose of meeting the intended municipal objectives. A fundamental element of capacity building for PPPs, therefore, is the development of an understanding of municipal problems and objectives, and the consideration of whether a partnership approach to service delivery has the potential to meet these objectives. The chapter discusses the

Box **2.1**   Focusing Public–Private Partnerships on the Poor
A Strategic Framework for Building Municipal Capacity

Focusing Partnership Goals

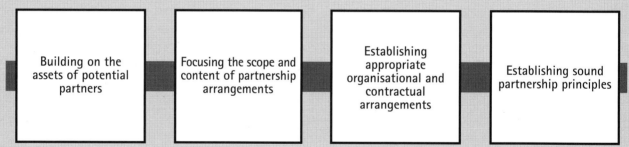

| Meeting municipal objectives through partnerships | Locating and linking partnerships in urban governance and management | Contributing to poverty reduction |

Developing a Partnership Framework

| Building on the assets of potential partners | Focusing the scope and content of partnership arrangements | Establishing appropriate organisational and contractual arrangements | Establishing sound partnership principles |

Enhancing Capacity to Implement Partnerships

| Understanding the operating context of municipal partnerships | Enhancing human resources | Supporting organisational development |

fundamental question asked by many officials – why involve the private sector in municipal service delivery? – and considers the benefits and the key issues that municipalities should look out for. It aims to provide a basis for municipal action that is then filled out by each subsequent element of the framework.

☐ **Locating and linking partnerships in urban governance and management** Chapter 4

Current best practice provides a range of reforms intended to result in the more effective governance and management of cities. These reforms include, for instance, democratic processes, stakeholder participation, financial sustainability and cost recovery, corporatisation, human resource development, accountability and transparency, and so on. The process of developing private sector participation in urban infrastructure and services both influences and is influenced by this dynamic process of reform. Partnerships are not isolated 'projects' but primary aspects of shifting methods of urban governance and management. This element of the framework is introduced to locate the concept of PPPs within a broader understanding of how cities in developing countries are run, to consider where private sector participation fits in this process, and to establish the key linkages between sectors and municipal functions. One of the primary aspects of this discussion concerns the sectoral approach to private sector participation in the context of the multisectoral obligations of municipalities. Few cities have developed an integrated approach to partnerships that recognises the existence of other partnerships or the potential impacts of partnership development on other sectors.

☐ **Contributing to poverty reduction** Chapter 5

In developing countries a majority of the population may live below the poverty line. One of the fundamental issues affecting decision-making in the preparation, design and implementation stages of a public–private partnership concerns the way in which the partnership aligns with and contributes to poverty-reduction initiatives. Unlike other discussions on PPPs and the poor, which start with the contractual mechanisms of PPPs such as tariff design or expansion mandates, the development of a focused partnership framework starts with the needs of the poor and the lessons of decades of poverty-reduction initiatives. Evidence from poverty reduction and sustainable livelihood approaches points towards a number of factors as being critical to sustainable improvements in the quality of life for the poor. This element of the framework promotes understanding of the implications of these lessons, and provides some basic steps for municipalities to follow to ensure that the partnership contributes, as far as is possible, to poverty reduction.

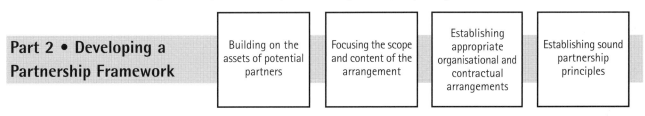

| Part 2 • Developing a Partnership Framework | Building on the assets of potential partners | Focusing the scope and content of the arrangement | Establishing appropriate organisational and contractual arrangements | Establishing sound partnership principles |

Part 2 is concerned with the nature of partnership arrangements. It considers these in terms of the actors that might be involved in the arrangement, the content of the arrangement, the existing vehicles for putting the arrangement in place, and the fundamental parameters underlying an effective partnership.

☐ **Building on the assets of potential partners** Chapter 6

Typically, established PPPs involve only public and private partners, and treat communities as customers or 'end-users'. In the case of water and sanitation at the local level, this generally means that the partnership is bilateral, comprising the municipality (or perhaps the water and sanitation authority) and a large-scale private operator able to bring skills and perhaps investment to the service in question. Yet experience over the last decade clearly shows that involving a range of interested stakeholders and creating an inclusive, transparent process can result in more focused partnerships that are more likely to meet their goals. If partnerships are to develop with an effective focus on the needs of the poor, community-based organisations (CBOs) and NGOs are both important players in the partnership arrangement, and mechanisms need to be developed to formalise, legitimise and/or recognise their role. Involving poor communities in environmental upgrading initiatives provides a solid foundation for the effort, underpinning cost recovery and promoting long-term sustainability. NGOs are often important entry points to poor communities, and they provide key skills in capacity building, hygiene promotion and awareness building; at times, they act as effective mediators between operators and consumers. Other stakeholders are the existing providers of urban services (such as rag-pickers and water-sellers), who may be severed from their incomes by formal changes to delivery mechanisms, and who also offer the capacity to fill gaps for the poor. Donors and external consultants promote and/or underpin the private sector participation (PSP) process in developing contexts. This element of the strategy presents the characteristics of key actors, their potential roles and responsibilities, and the nature of relationships that form or can be formed between these partners – from the early stages of consultation and planning (between the municipality and the community) to the partnership development and implementation stage. This is the 'who' of the partnership framework.

☐ Focusing the scope and content of partnership arrangements   Chapter 7

The 'what' of the partnership framework is described by defining the scope and content of the arrangement. This element of the strategy focuses on enhancing the understanding of key aspects of partnerships focused on the poor. It responds to possible municipal objectives such as physical improvements, social equity, capital investment, economic efficiency and capacity building. It thus includes a wide range of issues that together make up the content of the arrangement: physical issues such as service coverage, options and performance standards; social aspects such as community participation, equity, affordability, choice, payment mechanisms, gender marginalisation and integrated responses; political aspects such as worker re-employment and the impacts on informal services providers; financial and economic aspects such as risk management, financial incentives and cost recovery; and institutional aspects that need to be considered in the creation of a partnership framework that builds capacity for more effective partnerships and more effective institutions. The purpose of presenting these issues as a menu of ingredients in a partnership framework is to encourage municipalities to think through the composition of a partnership in relation to their objectives.

☐ Establishing appropriate organisational and contractual arrangements   Chapter 8

The key aspects of the partnership framework (the scope and content, the potential actors) need to be structured into an appropriate organisational and contractual arrangement. This element of the framework explores possible partnership structures and describes legal instruments (their characteristics and how they may influence the partnership focus). This includes a discussion of the current range of contract options utilised – from service and management contracts to affermage/lease,[1] franchise, concession and build-operate-transfer forms of contract. In addition, it provides a discussion on organisational relationships with small-scale providers and NGOs and considers where the municipality sits in relation to a utility or a joint venture.

☐ Establishing sound partnership principles   Chapter 9

This element of the partnership framework proposes that fundamental principles need to be adopted at the outset, and included in the strategic approach for successful and sustainable preparation and implementation of PPPs. These include the principles of transparency, accountability, specificity, legitimacy, flexibility, equity, participation, clarity, predictability and empowerment. It discusses the importance of these principles and elaborates on their meaning in the context of municipal–private sector partnerships.

| Understanding the operating context | Enhancing human resources | Supporting organisational development |

Part 3 • Enhancing Capacity to Implement Partnerships

Part 3 is focused on the capacity required at the municipal level to bring all this about. In order for the municipality to take forward partnerships focused on the poor, it is necessary to not only consider what the ingredients are and who the players are, but what kind of capacity will lead them there. In essence, this means understanding the key steps in the process of initiating, developing and implementing a partnership. This includes: developing a better understanding of the factors that affect the capacity of the municipality to act; enhancing human resources; and supporting organisational and managerial change.

☐ Understanding the operating context   Chapter 10

The partnership framework does not exist in a vacuum. Like most municipal endeavours, it exists within an operating environment that both influences and is influenced by municipal capacity and action. The primary part of this is the regulatory environment: a key factor in the development of PPPs is the legislative and regulatory structure (whether it is found at the national or provincial level). This has an over-riding influence on municipal capacity and action in relation to PPPs. In addition to the regulatory framework, the political and economic climate will have a significant impact on the possibilities of any partnership, while the policy and administrative context (and the risk of blockages and interference, for instance) will influence how and what can be achieved. Given that, in most contexts, government structures are hierarchical, the operating context is determined by the degree of influence of higher levels of government and the overall role of the municipality in the administrative structure. The strategy for building capacity in municipal-level PPPs highlights the importance of understanding the constraints and limitations of the operating context, to ensure that goals are achievable, viable and sustainable.

☐ Enhancing human resources   Chapter 11

Human resource development is an inevitable and critical component of the strategy to create service partnerships. From the perspective of a resource-deficient municipality, this chapter considers the numerous skill sets that are needed to create a new form of pro-poor partnership, whether they are found in-house or are bought in. Understanding the range of skills required is defined as a competency in itself. Most municipalities, even those in which some resources are available, will lack the skills necessary to meet the new challenge of partnerships involving the private sector and poor communities. This discussion, therefore, presents the skills needed to achieve a partnership focused on the poor. While human resource development will vary significantly along with the arrangement that is envisaged and the existing capacities of the municipality, new competencies are required for PPPs, and municipalities need to be aware of the extent and diversity of these skills. This will enable decision-makers to decide what expertise is needed in-house, and which skills are best bought in from the outside. A particular focus of this chapter is on the skill sets needed to ensure that partnerships address the needs of the poor and converge with other poverty-reduction programmes, and the skills needed for partnering (municipalities are often accused by large and small-scale private enterprises of not knowing how to be partners). This discussion is summarised in a skills framework and is supplemented by a description of methodologies for developing and sustaining skills within the municipality.

☐ Supporting organisational development   Chapter 12

Evidence clearly suggests that the greater the capacity of the municipality, the more effective the partnership. The partnership approach does not remove the need for a municipality to be a well-managed and well-organised institution, capable of playing its role in the management and monitoring of the service-delivery partnership. This element of the strategy focuses on the organisational capacity of the municipality. It considers the key aspects of organisational development necessary to create sustainable partnerships in the context of a heavily bureaucratic and lethargic municipal organisation. It considers organisational constraints and responses in terms of management, systems, structures and finances. It also considers municipal attitudes. Given the nature of municipalities and the scope of municipal functions in developing cities, perhaps the fundamental challenge and change required to launch effective partnerships is attitudinal. The creation of a supportive cadre of officials and politicians is a primary step in the development of municipal PPPs, and in the development of municipal capacity to create and sustain effective PPPs.

Chapter 13 presents a summary of this information in **A Framework for Action.**

Part 1
Focusing Partnership Goals

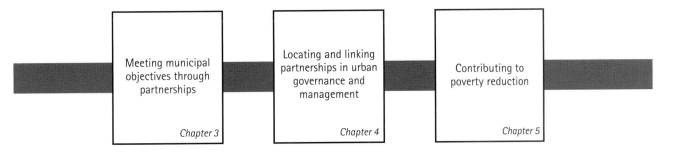

Meeting municipal objectives through partnerships

Chapter 3

Locating and linking partnerships in urban governance and management

Chapter 4

Contributing to poverty reduction

Chapter 5

Chapter 3 **Key Questions**

☐ Why involve the private sector in service delivery?

☐ What objectives can be met through municipal service partnerships?

☐ What trends have resulted in increased private sector participation?

☐ What are the potential benefits and key drawbacks of private sector involvement?

Focusing Partnership Goals

| Meeting municipal objectives through partnerships | Locating and linking partnerships in urban governance and management | Contributing to poverty reduction |

Adrian Coad

Meeting **Municipal Objectives** Through **Partnerships**

It is not surprising that, in many cases, municipalities are still unconvinced by the shift to private sector participation (PSP). For decades, many have accumulated a host of concerns over the whole idea of private sector involvement in basic service provision. Case study evidence suggests that some of this doubt is based on historical precedent – the very mention of 'private sector' conjures up images of monopolies and exploitative practices that ultimately lead to the public sector taking responsibility for basic services. Some of the doubt has been created through misinformation, hearsay and (sometimes inaccurate) assumptions. Other concerns have political foundations – the reluctance to allocate a large portion of municipal budgets and deplete the power of decision-making. Still other concerns are ideological – based on a fundamental opposition to market liberalisation and privatisation trends. However, some hesitations are due to the uncertainties surrounding costs and long-term benefits, particularly for disadvantaged groups.

It would be useful to present a comprehensive range of the objectives and reasons for private sector participation given in the existing literature. The advocacy provided by the World Bank has led to a wealth of literature that asserts the benefits of private sector participation, disseminates experience, and analyses (mostly in economic terms) the experience of private sector participation in both network and non-network services. This body of information forms an important source for municipal capacity building and is frequently cited throughout this book. However, with notable exceptions,[1] there is still little mention of the possible disadvantages and the potential areas of private sector failure, especially in relation to the poor. In the rush towards private sector solutions to service deficiencies, much of the documentation seems to lack a rationale, preferring instead to make definitive policy statements. Many promotional documents produced by donors mix problems with policies and solutions. Other widely available toolkits and guidelines produced for developing countries launch quickly into how private sector participation can be achieved, without providing any justification of why private sector participation may be necessary or desirable. For municipal officials venturing down this path for the first time, a process of justification and clarification is crucial not only to understand the benefits of involving the private sector, but also to highlight the problems that may need to be mitigated.

As the objective of this sourcebook is to assist municipalities in building the capacity to develop public–private partnerships (PPPs) that are beneficial to the poor, an important starting point is to recognise that doubts over the role of the private sector may colour the perspective and capacity of local government to develop effective partnerships. A fundamental step is therefore to consider why the private sector should get involved at all. This chapter outlines municipal problems and possible objectives and opportunities, sets out the key reasons for involving the private sector, and introduces some of the unresolved areas. The details of this debate are an inherent part of the chapters that follow.

This discussion is supplemented by a wide range of perspectives on private sector involvement provided by participants of PPP arrangements. Each respondent was asked the same question: Why involve the private sector in service delivery? Their perspectives bring out some of the issues discussed in this chapter. Juxtaposing Boxes 3.2–3.8 is, however, an attempt to illustrate different views, from the guarded position of an NGO to the confident position of the financier.

The Service Problems of Municipalities

Municipalities in developing countries face an insurmountable task: on this, there is little disagreement. The frequently quoted levels of urban infrastructure deficiency provide ample evidence worldwide of the crises and challenges that face urban managers. However, deteriorating infrastructure and declining service delivery are just the outward signs of the crisis in urban management brought about by a range of external and internal economic, institutional, social, demographic and environmental factors. The rapid rate of urbanisation is well known to municipal managers in Latin America and Asia, and increasingly in sub-Saharan Africa. Growing urban populations place significant pressure on the existing infrastructure in core areas and create a demand for improved service delivery in underserviced marginal and peri-urban areas. Existing infrastructure is often past its prime. Declining economic growth in many parts of the world

Box **3.1**   A Municipal Objectives Framework

Local Governance

| To create a better place for all to live in | To create sustainable, equitable, environmentally sound development |

Economic

- To improve efficiency
- To promote cost effectiveness
- To ensure economic sustainability
- To generate economic growth

Environmental

- To improve availability, quality and reliability of services
- To expand service coverage in poor areas
- To ensure environmental sustainability

Financial

- To promote capital investment
- To enhance cost recovery
- To promote private investment in operations and maintenance

Social

To improve the wellbeing of the poor	To ensure affordability
To improve health, security and safety	To empower the poor and promote choice
To improve equality in service provision	To target vulnerable groups and ensure gender equity
To ensure job and income security	To enhance opportunity for sustainable poverty reduction

Political

To achieve legitimacy	To maintain power over allocation of resources
To ensure a political mandate for private sector participation	To improve voter base through improved municipal functions
To represent constituency interests	To access rent seeking opportunities

Institutional

- To improve skills
- To access new technologies
- To delegate management to skilled organisations
- To institutionalise better management practices

has constrained investment and finance. A chronic deficiency in municipal resources – brought about through mismanagement, inadequate finances or overly-bureaucratic and ineffectual management – has led to overloaded and unmaintained systems. The impact of each factor varies according to the context, but all contribute to the more visible problem of deteriorating services and infrastructure, and are an intrinsic part of the municipal service problem.[2]

From the perspective of the poor, however, the urban problem is not only that services are inadequate, but also that the existing processes of resource allocation have often resulted in the marginalisation of the poor from the benefits of the existing infrastructure and services. This inherent political bias in the decision-making over service provision will not be removed by an increase in private capital investment if that investment is not accompanied by policies and mandates which ensure that the poor benefit.

The description of municipal service problems can be quite complex and the perception of service problems can vary between stakeholders. Within basic service delivery (such as water supply, sanitation and solid waste services), various sector-specific factors, along with demand and supply constraints, often change the nature of the problem. Understanding the complexity of the problem is thus a keystone that leads to clarity in the definition of objectives and greater understanding of the benefits of the private sector. Yet many municipalities have a limited capacity for analysing and articulating physical and institutional problems, and many overlook the ways in which users experience service problems. This lack of skill ultimately affects decision-making and the development of appropriate solutions.

Municipal Service Objectives

It is not surprising that the multiplicity of municipal service problems, and the varying perspectives on these problems, lead to an assortment of objectives and priorities, each relating to the agenda, status and capacity of the stakeholder. In order to determine whether a partnership is successful or is meeting the service needs of the municipality, it is necessary to define the needs that will be addressed, and agree objectives. Objectives that are described in terms of one selected goal, such as 'improved efficiency', provide only a limited description of what the stakeholders in a municipality hope to achieve. Objectives will respond to both strategic and practical concerns, and will be expressed in different terms. They also change over time, and often change as capacity increases. Objectives will vary across the stakeholder groups: the urban poor (as consumers or informal service providers), municipal administrators and politicians, government representatives, and external agents (such as donors and NGOs). There is never just one municipal objective, and it is unlikely that one solution could meet the requirements of all the stakeholders.

In order to present the possible range of municipal service objectives, a framework (illustrated in Box 3.1) attempts to assemble a range of possible objectives from a range of stakeholders. At the top of this framework is the key objective of urban governance – to create a better place in which all may live. The more specific objectives of potential stakeholders are grouped into sectors such as:

- economic objectives (to improve efficiency and generate urban economic growth);
- financial objectives (to create capital investment or transfer risk);
- political objectives (to represent constituents and maintain power over the allocation of resources);
- physical/environmental objectives (to improve the quality of the urban environment);
- social objectives (to improve livelihoods and create greater equity in service provision); and
- institutional objectives (to improve local capacity to manage and govern the city).

Most importantly, this framework includes the specific social or livelihood objectives of poor households and individuals: better access to affordable services, less time spent collecting water, fewer water-borne and faecal-borne diseases and improved access to and security of employment. It also includes the objectives of external agents: e.g., the donor

Box **3.2**   **Why Involve the Private Sector in Service Delivery?**
A Mayor's Perspective

When I campaigned for the position of Mayor of Kathmandu, Nepal, I promised the people that I would rebuild and revitalise the city. Much has been achieved, but there is more to do. Despite the constant efforts of Kathmandu Metropolitan City (KMC) the challenge must involve all of us, and in this regard the private sector, formal and informal, has a role to play. KMC has recognised this and has recently adopted a policy to promote public–private partnerships. This was an important decision. Let us consider why.

Nepal is still a rural country, with over 80% of its population living in scattered settlements, many of which are remote and difficult to access. Population continues to increase at 2.5% per annum and yet suitable land to feed the increasing number of mouths is critically short. The result – migration to urban areas on an unprecedented scale. In 1991 city population was approximately 420,000, but today it exceeds 750,000. In the last 10 years city population has increased at 6% per annum or more, and the demand for urban services has sky rocketed.

Who is to provide these services? Previously this was the responsibility of central government, when the country was a monarchy, but following restoration of multi-party politics in 1991, the government has pursed a policy of decentralisation whereby municipalities are progressively required to take on the thankless task of managing urban areas. The task is enormous and it is true to say that most municipalities in Nepal operate in a state of permanent crisis. Kathmandu is no exception. As soon as we repair a road, a drain, a burst water-pipe or a street light, another just around the corner requires attention. Our infrastructure is old and inadequate, and is in need of constant maintenance. And to make matters worse, more people arrive day by day demanding new services in areas that were once fields and will soon become concrete jungles. 'Ke garne' (What to do)?

We soon realised that our pitiful budget and meagre staff resources were not enough to meet the challenge. All around us people are building houses, companies are constructing offices, development is going on. Why should not these same people invest in the very services that they demand? Why not encourage them to share the burden that the public sector alone cannot bear? There is no shame in this. Municipalities cannot do everything. We should manage of course, but this does not mean that we have to provide all the services ourselves. Instead, we should be like the conductor of a large and varied orchestra, whose musicians hail from all sectors of society. The challenge is to decide which piece of music to play, to ensure that all the instruments are in tune with each other, and that the flute can still be heard above the strident tones of the brass.

In 2000, the Council of Kathmandu Metropolitan City approved a 'Private Sector Participation: Private–Public Partnership Policy of KMC'. This was a landmark decision and the foundation stone for a new era of urban management in the capital city. In accordance with this policy, the private sector is already actively engaged in the provision of urban services and the impact can be seen in marked improvements to the quality and efficiency of the urban environment. In recent years the private sector has:

- taken over management of the bus terminus and will soon invest in expansion of the facilities;
- landscaped and managed open spaces around the town as part of a policy to beautify the city;
- collected the garbage through innovative schemes, often operated by local user groups on a self-sustaining basis;
- managed parking on a systematic basis and collected fees;
- started the collection of vehicle registration fees; and
- assumed the management of pedestrian bridges with a commitment to build more for the benefit of pedestrian safety in an environment in which the number of motor cars is increasing day by day.

In addition, PPP modalities are currently under negotiation to:

- manage markets;
- construct and operate an abattoir;
- construct and operate a solid waste composting and transfer station;
- repair and maintain KMC's fleet of vehicles;
- operate a trolley bus service, as an extension to the existing service;
- construct and operate an underground car park and shopping centre in the heart of the city; and
- construct and operate a cultural centre.

Thus far, experience has been positive. Mutual confidence between the public and private sector is growing, and I anticipate that in the future more and more services will be managed as PPP ventures. I believe that the lessons learned in Kathmandu can be, and are being, applied elsewhere in Nepal, and are applicable to other countries in Asia.

Keshav Sthapit, **Mayor of Kathmandu Metropolitan City**

objective of sustainable, equitable, environmentally sound development and more accountable, transparent forms of local government; and the NGO objective of more equitable services for the poor.

While this broad range of municipal objectives may be ambitious and somewhat idealistic, this comprehensive approach helps municipalities to recognise and prioritise objectives. Through it, it is also possible to see that many past initiatives have focused on only some of these municipal objectives. By stressing the need for increased capital investment and improved efficiency to meet the environmental and physical objectives of service delivery, effort has generally been biased towards economic and financial objectives. Traditional forms of PPPs have prioritised such objectives over the social, political, and institutional objectives that are nevertheless equally important aspects of sustainable service delivery.

Municipal Opportunities

In fulfilling these objectives, municipal managers have a few options before them. In the past, municipal government aimed to provide services almost exclusively through the municipal machinery. Some may have enabled communities and NGOs to become involved in service delivery to fill gaps in delivery to low-income areas, but the role of the formal private sector in municipal functions was non-existent and capital inflow from outside sources was minimal.

So what has changed that enables a new actor to enter into the realm of municipal service delivery? Notwithstanding the critical role of Anglo-American donors in promoting the shift towards the private sector, **globalisation** and **localisation** processes have both been key factors influencing the new municipal agenda. Whereas the processes of globalisation can take some time to reach municipal actors, localisation processes in many countries have been both powerful and unavoidable. Policy change in relation to democratisation and decentralisation to local levels of government, which arose in the 1980s, took hold in the early 1990s. National governments (often pressured by development agencies to bring government closer to the people) instigated a process of handing increased authority and responsibility to local government. In many parts of the world a form of local governance that includes all parts of society has replaced the traditional top–down processes of decision-making and budgetary control.

The decentralisation process has taken various forms with vastly different meanings, from the extremes of the state government of Kerala in India (with its motto 'planning for the people by the people') to the decentralisation processes in Nepal, where the delegation of authority has not been accompanied by the allocation of financial resources and control. Nevertheless, the very process has changed the status of municipalities, along with the location of some decision-making over municipal functions and with it the actors' capacity to approach the delivery of municipal services in new ways. The process of decentralisation, however, has not only brought with it increased responsibility and opportunity for municipalities. In most, if not all cases, it has also led to severe financial deficits. The changing role of the municipality is thus closely aligned with the weakening of finances. Municipalities have been led into a position in which it is not only desirable but also necessary to re-examine the means through which they deliver municipal services.

Simultaneously, the process of globalisation has led to significant increases in international, private capital flows to developing counties, and has introduced the private sector as a key actor in the economies of developing countries.[3] The shift from foreign-aid-based development to privately financed economic growth has occurred because many governments have established a more market-oriented economy, and because many national governments have adopted a liberalised trade regime and an openness to foreign investment. While it is still necessary to ask where this increased private capital has been targeted, it seems clear that this shift in the sources of financing has not been accompanied by a concern for capacity. Despite the opportunities offered in the context of globalisation and increased private capital flows, it is unsurprising that the weakest institutions are often marginalised from these possibilities.[4] Indeed, those chronically deficient municipalities most affected by decentralisation are also those least likely to attract private sector

3

Box 3.3   Why Involve the Private Sector in Service Delivery?
An Operator's Perspective

Through the involvement of the private sector, municipalities are generally anxious to ensure and accelerate the changes that they think are necessary in terms of water and sanitation service delivery. Some of the municipalities around the world provide an excellent service to their customers. Nevertheless, many of them acknowledge that they suffer drawbacks, which inhibit adequate service delivery: bureaucracy, financial constraints, excessive political interference, etc.

Through its various contracts with large municipalities like Buenos Aires, Casablanca, Atlanta, Santiago and Jakarta, and also with smaller municipalities and government departments, Ondeo-Lyonnaise des Eaux (formerly Suez Lyonnaise-des-Eaux) has demonstrated that such inhibitions can be overcome so long as both partners (public and private) are fully committed to the partnership.

Under the above-mentioned conditions, an experienced and competent private partner is able to bring the added value requested to the partnership. It can:

- enable a decision-making culture based on business principles and not on political or bureaucratic considerations;
- motivate and empower the personnel through the implementation of comprehensive training programmes and the introduction of performance management systems;
- align the personnel to a customer-focused approach;
- develop innovative and alternative service delivery options to the low-income communities; and
- establish a sustainable utility through the implementation of cost-effective processes, and also through the injection of the necessary capital investment funding.

The injection of private funding is obviously of great interest to many municipalities. They aim at concentrating their financial resources for capital investment on services such as roads and parks, which don't attract direct revenue and therefore cannot be 'ringfenced'.

Of the various models of PSP, the concession remains the most efficient; the private operator can optimise the total cost by deciding daily how to arbitrate between operating and capital investment costs. The result is that through its optimisation of the service operation, the private operator enables the financial resources to be made more productive, thus increasing the achievable capital investment programme. For example, Aguas Argentinas, the Buenos Aires operator managed by Ondeo, is investing around US$200 million annually, which represents 40% of the company revenue.

In comparison, the privatisation model implies that the operator has to buy existing assets or pay a licence fee, as in the UK, Chile or for some US and Central European companies. In this case, the operator has to bill the customers for the cost of past investments, which doesn't contribute to an improvement in current and future service.

The change to customer-focused and business-orientated services is greatly facilitated when private utilities such as Ondeo, which supply more than 110 million people, can add expertise and experience from their various contracts around the world. As such, Ondeo has considerable expertise through a network of specialists in terms of water services provision to low-income communities. Inexperienced private companies would certainly experience enormous difficulties in bringing affordable and adequate services to such communities, which represent a large proportion of the various metropolis populations.

The establishment of such partnerships with experienced private companies requires sound regulatory frameworks. It also requires fair returns as well as a clear and fair balance of risks between the various parties. This means that the consumers, the decision-makers and the private partner all need to be satisfied.

Jean Pierre Mas, Operations Executive, Johannesburg Water Management (JOWAM)

capital, or able to climb on the ladder of support towards private sector participation – a ladder frequently offered by various external agencies. Whereas grant aid often brought with it technical assistance for institutional strengthening, and thus support to use funding more effectively, private sector funds have mostly been unaccompanied by the capacity development necessary to strengthen the government organisations responsible for decision-making and coordination.

The Benefits

Yet in this context – declining local government resources and the potential of increased private capital flows – many municipalities in developing countries find themselves in an unfamiliar position. Irrespective of capacity, many have recognised that they now might have a choice as to how they will deliver services within the municipality. Many have also realised that they do not have to struggle on their own, but that they need to consider how to reorient past approaches. The redefinition of the roles of the private and public sectors, particularly the private sector crossing into basic service delivery, enables municipalities to explore new solutions to old problems.

So what benefits does the private sector bring to service delivery? Apart from the observation that most municipalities were not succeeding in getting services to the people, the case for formal private sector participation in municipal services is based in the belief that the formal private sector has an inherent financial, economic and management capacity and is thus better placed to deliver urban services.

Notwithstanding the broad range of municipal objectives described above, all but a few municipal officials will assert that the primary constraint facing them is the lack of financial resources. Indeed, some will assert it is the only real constraint on them in achieving their objectives. The cold hard fact, as many managers see it, is a lack of money to maintain and expand services and infrastructure to keep up with the demands of the city. The international private sector creates opportunities for **increased access to capital** for much-needed investment in infrastructure. Certain arrangements involving the private sector in network industries, such as water supply, can lead to an injection of finance made available through the private partner. However, so great is international confidence in the role of the private sector in basic service provision that the commitment to the process itself opens doors to other avenues of finance. Case study evidence clearly suggests that support from the World Bank and the Inter-American Bank, for instance, has been made conditional upon an agreed role for the private sector. Whether or not it is fail-safe, money is the reason that so many economists, treasurers and financiers find the whole prospect of private sector involvement in infrastructure so attractive.

The international confidence accompanying private sector involvement is most likely to be linked to the **economic efficiencies** that private undertakings often bring to their endeavours. To some extent, the majority of attributes cited as the benefits of private sector participation (e.g., better business and personnel management, technical skills and technologies) each fundamentally contributes to the increased efficiency of the operations. Some argue that these benefits themselves are secondary – they simply would not be pursued if they did not lead to a more profitable and efficient operation. Yet, if well structured, the superior **management, skills and technologies** offered by the private sector can also be central to the fulfilment of some institutional strengthening objectives; and if properly focused, the skills and capacity of the private sector to develop new solutions (through research and development initiatives) can lead to innovative options being introduced in low-income areas.

Over and above this simplified understanding of the direct benefits of private sector participation is a range of indirect benefits that are also mostly economic and financial. It is often suggested, for instance, that the **reduction in public expenditure on basic services** and infrastructure releases public finances for welfare expenditure, and that the injection of private sector investment into the urban and national economy **stimulates urban economic growth** and creates secondary distributional effects. When combined, these benefits clearly address a number of financial objectives.

3

Box **3.4**

Why Involve the Private Sector in Service Delivery?
An NGO's Perspective

The Mvula Trust entered into a partnership with the private sector in 1997 to help fulfil a key service-related reconstruction and development target of the new South African government, and since then it has had direct experience of the benefits and drawbacks of private sector participation in the delivery of water and sanitation services.

While Mvula has developed and worked with a participatory model for sustainable service delivery in poor rural areas, it also recognised that a project in South Africa involving the private sector was a feasible option as a delivery vehicle for water and sanitation improvements, and it was decided that we would achieve far more being a part of the process (and looking out for the poor stakeholders) than we would by distancing ourselves from the process.

Of course the benefits of private sector participation vary substantially with different types of contracts, depending on the financial resources that they bring to some projects, but our experience in the build–operate–train–transfer (BoTT) contract in South Africa suggests that the government gained access to improved management capacity through this public–private partnership.

The complex nature of a BoTT concession requires the private organisation responsible to have strong skills in contract administration, programme and project management, coordination and quality control. In addition, the private partners contribute technical knowledge in the planning, designing and monitoring of construction activities. The private sector can also provide guarantees and professional indemnity insurance required for large and capital-intensive contracts – something an NGO cannot do.

The partnership approach also brings an administrative benefit to government. By tendering only once for multi-year engagements, the government cuts down enormously on its traditional role and speeds up the process while maintaining accountability and oversight. As well as increased speed, the BoTT strategy can reduce administrative costs for government.

At the same time, and despite these contributions and benefits, the private partners represent an altogether new type of stakeholder, especially when working on improvements in poor areas. Their results-driven approach is frequently at odds with our work in mobilising and strengthening communities to take on operation and maintenance roles. We often find we are aiming for effectiveness while the hard-nosed private representatives (to varying degrees) are striving for efficiency.

In particular, private partners unfamiliar with poverty-related service improvements do not always grasp the need for social development inputs, or the need to build trust and commitment with communities through participatory processes. Many also do not display the flexibility and technical knowledge for service options that benefit poor consumers. Some would still like to see a supply-led approach adopted, despite the terms of reference.

In many respects, the capacity of the private sector to become involved in the delivery of services to the poor is dependent on individual champions from the private firms involved, and the difficulties seem due to the inflexibility of the private organisations with regard to new circumstances, as well as the over-riding profit motive, which arises from time to time.

Consequently, to function effectively, the partnership and the working environment require clear objectives, policies and principles before any work takes place. For an NGO working with a very different agenda, it is important to establish some rules on transparency. Despite the new management approach, when it comes to their own organisation the private sector can be very closed. But in a partnership involving an NGO, some issues – such as the level of profit – need to be transparent, or the NGO will feel uncomfortable being a party to the process. Similarly, it is important for government not only to set up the regulatory environment and ensure a properly designed contract, but to oversee how and when this is put in place. The private sector works best, and is most cost effective, when the outputs are known and the process from beginning to end can be quantified. More consideration needs to be given to the methodology for the procurement of private partners in ill-defined projects to avoid governments paying through the nose for the service that is being provided.

Jamie de Jager, The Mvula Trust, South Africa

Why Involve the Private Sector in Service Delivery?

Box 3.5

A Low-income Community Perspective

Before piped water services were introduced into a number of low-income areas of Buenos Aires, settlements relied predominantly on fetching water (especially from a nearby meat-packing plant), and water deliveries from a municipal truck. Looking back, the residents had many complaints about these water sources: the water was unsuitable for drinking; women and children spent some four hours fetching water every day, and often suffered back pains and injuries as a result. Two pregnant women described falling as they tried to carry water along muddy roads. The municipal truck delivered water up to three times per week, depending on the condition of the truck and roads. The service was irregular and the overall amount of water delivered was insufficient. Households had to ensure that someone was in the settlement at the time the truck arrived to secure deliveries. On one occasion, an influential politician intervened to ensure that the truck did not deliver water to a community that had failed to support him. Truck drivers often favoured customers who provided bribes, and obtaining water from the truck became the source of frequent disputes among neighbours.

From the perspective of the inhabitants of four informal settlements on the periphery of the metropolitan area, the involvement of the private sector was indispensable to gain access to an adequate water supply. The private operator was to manage the only source of potable water in the area. Research carried out by the NGO, IIED-AL and IIED suggested that the involvement of the private sector could radically improve access to potable water. In addition, residents believed that the intervention of the private utility would resolve a lawsuit between a contractor and the national government, which had prevented the extension of piped water services for more than a decade.

While the research indicated considerable potential for engaging private utilities in improvement efforts, it also demonstrated that switching to a private utility does not in itself solve the problem of improving water and sanitation in low-income areas. Community residents and leaders believe that the primary reason for the success in the four communities can be attributed to the collaborative nature of the approach. The collaborators included Aguas Argentinas (the private utility), local government, CBOs, an NGO and a number of the local residents. Multi-sector collaboration was viewed by most of the residents as the only means through which they could gain access to water and sanitation services, given the infrastructure charges imposed by the utility at that time, and the lack of land titles. The contribution of labour on the part of the communities and of building materials on the part of local government and NGOs helped to overcome the first constraint. The participation of local government was indispensable for convincing the utility to provide services despite unresolved land tenure issues.

The process was not straightforward by any means. Although Aguas Argentinas had expanded its water networks to an area near the four settlements, the company's expansion plan did not include the informal settlements because their inhabitants lacked land ownership. (According to the agreement of the concession, the private operator was exempted from expanding services to areas where land ownership and physical layout were not regularised.) Furthermore, given that the expansion was to be financed through an exorbitant infrastructure charge, it was obvious that low-income groups would not be able to afford it. Thus, the poor were not going to be served. Ultimately, constructive pressure from all parties led to action by Aguas Argentinas to meet the needs of the low-income communities. The company realised that it needed to learn from a direct involvement in informal settlements. An added incentive was that illegal connections were a source of significant water loss, likely to increase with the expansion of the networks and add to political and public relations problems. Simply ignoring the plight of the urban poor was not in keeping with the image the company was trying to project.

As a result of the collaboration, 4500 residents of these settlements gained access to water supply services, and 2400 of these residents gained access to sewerage. No other initiative in these settlements has ever achieved the same widespread support and participation from residents. They testified that access to water represented the most cherished collective experience and brought about fundamental improvements in their living conditions. After decades of organising their daily routines around obtaining water, and still suffering from ill-health due to its insufficiency and low quality, the inhabitants of four low-income settlements in Buenos Aires have, due to private sector involvement, what they perceive to be a sustainable supply of potable water.

3

Box **3.6** ## Why Involve the Private Sector in Service Delivery?
The Water and Sanitation Program Perspective

There is no doubt that in many parts of the world, the reform of existing water and sanitation service delivery arrangements is urgently required. The most stark illustration of this need is the millions of poor and informally settled urban households that lack access to even the most rudimentary safe water and sanitary facilities.

In many places the private sector is already a major supplier of services (ranging from vended water, through latrine-pit emptying and disposal services, to large-scale private or community-based distribution systems). This 'informal', 'small-scale' or 'local' private sector is often critically important for the poor, providing appropriate services and flexible payment arrangements. The sector is often criticised for providing services at high cost (particularly for vended water), but recent research shows that many small-scale operators provide excellent value for money, reliable services and payment arrangements that are more manageable for the poor than those associated with networked systems.

Sometimes policy-makers may decide that a radical increase in the role of the 'formal' private sector is the only politically viable way to achieve the necessary change in performance. However, this strategy will not necessarily generate gains for poor consumers. Recent high-profile transactions in the water sector have tended to place less emphasis than is required on the importance of serving poor people (a significant proportion of potential consumers in most cases). This happened either because it was assumed that efficiency gains would benefit the whole population, or for reasons of political expedience, which caused reforms to be hurried through with insufficient time to consider the nature of the consumer base. Clearly, with a decade of learning behind us, it is time to start a more active engagement early in the reform process to bring the needs of poor people to the forefront.

Once a government is committed to reform it is important that all the options are considered, and their potential to improve access for poor consumers is evaluated alongside considerations of efficiency and increased capital investment.

Why use the private sector? In situations of deteriorating utility performance, the large-scale private sector (often international) may be a vehicle for improved efficiency, increased investment and better cost recovery. These benefits can only be realised if the transaction is well designed, if regulatory control is effective, and if government is willing to step back from the day-to-day provision of services. There is a very significant risk that poorly designed transactions may harm poor consumers. Particular care is needed to ensure that small and local providers are not displaced through careless design of the contract, and that sloppy tariff design does not create disincentives for the operator to connect new poor households.

The local private sector may have a major role to play in operating parts of the water or sanitation system (or entire systems in smaller towns). Local private operators may be well placed to operate public toilets, which often provide excellent services for poor people. Municipalities need to accommodate the potential of these operators, formalise them where appropriate and ensure the right level of regulatory control (to open up the market while securing minimum output standards).

The informal private sector (small-scale, non-profit NGOs and CBOs) is often ignored and frequently harassed, but it is sometimes heavily involved and provides appropriate services (as we have seen). Municipalities have to learn new ways of working with the private operators as partners, again providing a supportive environment.

The objective of reform should always be to improve service delivery, and to secure better, safer and more affordable services for poor people. Private sector participation is not an end in itself, it is one possible way to improve service delivery. In order to be able to select the most appropriate approach, capacity needs to grow: professionals must learn more about the poor, and local government must learn more about the options for effective service delivery, including the private sector.

Mukami Kariuki, Clarissa Brocklehurst and Barbara Evans, The Water and Sanitation Program

We have noted above another fact – that the majority of municipalities have failed to deliver services efficiently. There are exceptions, but these are now quite rare. The cause for these inefficiencies may be related to deficiencies in the sector and the physical context, but more often than not a lack of competition, an overly-bureaucratic process, a lack of business acumen, skills, training and technology, a lack of cost recovery and ongoing political interference have led to chronic inefficiencies. Irrespective of context, those rare examples of well-managed public utilities (and the rarer examples of effective functional departments within municipalities) come about because some or all of these factors have been removed.[5] The private sector approach – within a competitive context – can **remove blockages** that government cannot address.

Yet if we consider the private sector in all its guises, the potential benefits of private sector involvement are far greater. The benefits of the **national private sector** (discussed in Chapter 6) in many ways supplement those that the international large-scale private sector brings. National companies can bring the benefits of local knowledge, understanding of the context of a sector, and local networks to facilitate action.

From their past experience in working within poor communities, **the small-scale private sector** (detailed in Chapter 6) can bring sound knowledge about the capacities and limitations of the poor, understanding of cultural and physical factors affecting specific areas, and a flexibility unachievable in large-scale operations. Evidence suggests that the role of this low-profile private sector actor may be critical in achieving some of the social objectives highlighted earlier, and in mitigating harmful effects of formal private sector involvement. It is therefore important for municipal decision-makers to understand the benefits of all parts of the private sector, and the ways in which each can contribute to a broader concept of private sector participation.

The benefits of private sector participation can also be described in terms of how the private sector impacts upon or measures up to predetermined rights. This argument has been developed in South Africa in relation to eight consumer rights.[6] These are the rights to: the satisfaction of basic needs, to safe products and services, to information, to choice, to be heard, to have access to redress, to consumer education, and to a healthy and sustainable environment. Any service, irrespective of the provider, can be measured according to these criteria.

The Prerequisites

However, the ability of the international private sector to bring financial and economic benefits to bear can be dependent on some quite onerous preconditions. It is usually essential that effective regulatory control is established, that the partnership arrangements provide clarity and predictability, that the process of procurement is transparent, that the agreement is monitored, and that penalties are enforced. All of these preconditions point towards a changing role of the municipality, in particular the capacity of the municipality to provide the level and quality of oversight required.

Irrespective of its form, if the private sector is to deliver benefits to the poor, much of the onus to create a partnership and an environment in which these benefits can come to fruition lies with the municipalities. It is not the private sector's role to look out for the poor. The need for a more strategic municipal vision – to coordinate and integrate the potential assets of the private sector – is paramount, as is the role of the public sector in ensuring adequate regulation and resolving crucial constraints that hinder service improvements, such as land tenure. The public sector must also recognise the role of informal sector providers and other organisations in the development of more inclusive partnerships.

Key Concerns over Private Sector Involvement in Delivering Services to the Poor

The implicit suggestion that private sector participation is biased towards economic and financial benefits leaves queries over other municipal objectives. Although the private sector may intrinsically address the concerns of many municipal

3

Box **3.7** **Why Involve the Private Sector in Service Delivery?**
A Donor's Perspective

In line with the broader trend towards decentralisation, which is shifting infrastructure responsibilities from national to municipal governments, municipal governments with whom DFID are working are, with our encouragement, turning increasingly to the private sector to find solutions. There is ample evidence under our programme to demonstrate that the involvement of the private sector in the delivery of urban services can reduce costs and improve the efficiency and scope of urban services while introducing new capital investment for the provision of services. The changing role of local government from direct service provider to regulating and facilitating the private sector continues to shape our approach in infrastructure service provision, which is increasingly advocating public–private partnerships (PPPs).

Through PPP, the advantages of the private sector – innovation, access to finance, knowledge of technologies, managerial efficiency and entrepreneurial spirit – can be combined with the social responsibility, environmental awareness and local knowledge of the public sector in an effort to solve urban problems. PPP provides a rich menu of ideas and models for local government to choose from, such as management contracts, concessions, franchises, leases, commercialisation and pure private entrepreneurship. Flexibility is the key and needs to be present in the choice of parties to play different roles.

Private provision of services is easiest to apply where consumers can be charged and competition is possible. While the type of private sector competition is dependent on the scale of the investment, the technology required and the maturity of the business sector, it will only be effective if independent regulators have the capacity to protect the public from excessive charges and ensure affordable services to low-income consumers. This applies not only to water supply and sewerage, but also to electricity supply, public transport and commercial refuse collection.

However, even where governments have put in place certain legislative and regulatory instruments as a means of improving the legal and commercial environment, and have introduced a level of economic pricing, they have frequently failed to inspire the confidence that is required to see PPP implemented successfully. Potential investors often see the available financial returns as insufficient to justify the risk.

The issue of municipal capacity needs to be addressed as PPP requires an enlargement and strengthening of the regulatory role of local government to monitor and enforce contracts and protect the interests of the public. Further constraints centre on the inability of local authorities to address the issue of equity around how private sector involvement in municipal service provision can ensure availability and accessibility to the poor, e.g. through safety nets and cross-subsidisation. This can be partly attributed to their failure in recognising possibilities for encouraging partnerships between community-based initiatives and the private sector.

There also exists strong opposition to the increased use of the private sector to provide services due to factors such as political opposition, the inability or lack of interest of the private companies in providing services at affordable prices, the insufficiency of local private sector management skills to provide services efficiently and effectively, etc.

DFID's experience is that donors can help municipalities to access private sector funding and management expertise in a number of ways:

- sensitising key decision-makers to the possibilities offered by PPP;
- helping to restructure utilities to make them open to private investment opportunities;
- advising on enabling legislation;
- assisting with the preparation and letting of contracts and the establishment of appropriate regulatory arrangements;
- helping municipalities attract private sector partners by supporting investments with appropriate arrangements to help mitigate risks; and
- once private sector investors are involved, encouraging partnerships with self-help organisations and NGOs to improve service delivery to the poor.

DFID is currently undertaking support in all these areas, much of it in partnership with other donors. We plan to continue with our work in this area and are particularly keen to build on existing and new partnership arrangements to this end.

J W Hodges, Head of Infrastructure and Urban Development Department, UK Department for International Development

decision-makers, the physical, economic and financial sides are not the only objectives that the range of stakeholders in a municipality seeks. Box 3.1 highlights the importance of social, political and institutional objectives as well.

Meeting broader social and political objectives

Experience to date suggests that the formal private sector may be less adept (and, at the very least, initially is less adept) at fulfilling objectives outside the economic and financial domains. With some exceptions, this is especially true of social objectives. While the formal private sector does bring with it the concept of the 'customer' (rather than the 'beneficiary'), it generally has little experience in the consultative processes and levels of stakeholder involvement that are necessary to fulfil social and political objectives. While there are examples of successful institutional development and/or community capacity building components being included in partnerships, these are exceptions to the norm, and efforts to work with the poor in a developmental way are still in their infancy. This is not, however, a reason to reject private sector involvement, but it is a reason to ensure that key social objectives are fulfilled by raising awareness of their importance, creating a demand for operators with broader social competencies, and including other appropriate actors in the partnership framework. Chapter 6 thus focuses on the various competencies of potential stakeholders, including NGOs, and their role in partnerships focused on the poor.

Creating appropriate solutions

The debate over private sector involvement has also led to queries about the relevance of private sector solutions in quite diverse economic, institutional, social, environmental and political conditions. This argument quite justifiably highlights the fact that a range of objectives in a range of municipal functions would surely produce a range of solutions, and the approach advocated here acknowledges the validity of this argument and the need for contextually specific solutions to be developed. One of the key purposes of a sourcebook about PPPs must be to explore the range of options that involve the private sector, the range of private sector actors and the role of other potential actors. The trends are changing. While many private sector activities and PPPs used to be forced to fit in with predetermined models (in a 'one size fits all' approach), current thinking advocates creating appropriate solutions utilising a range of actors and options. There is therefore significant potential for producing a wide range of responses. This book responds by prioritising an understanding of the elements before leading into a discussion of contracts. Municipalities themselves must understand the ingredients of an appropriate arrangement.

Price increases

There is much debate over the increased costs associated with private sector involvement. Advocates often suggest that, in practice, costs do not increase (see Box 3.8 compared with Box 7.18 in relation to water tariffs in Buenos Aires), or that those costs cannot be attributed to private sector involvement. One argument is that many changes frequently associated with private sector participation are in fact due to implicit or explicit government reform programmes (including pricing reform), and that it is incorrect to blame the private sector for a wide range of changes and impacts which come about because the sector is reformed.[7]

A key issue is the assumption that the private sector increases tariffs. While it is often the case that tariffs increase when the private sector assumes responsibility, it is also a result of the introduction of a cost-recovery policy by government. If the government has the intention of improving efficiency and increasing potential investment, a first step is establishing a commercial operation, and cost recovery is at the heart of that reform. Although they are often carried out simultaneously, it can be argued that private sector participation is a separate decision; the decision leading to higher tariffs could have been associated with a corporatisation process. Advocates also argue that prices may go down, that they are simply adjusted to bring them in line with the real cost of providing that service.

3

Box 3.8 **Why Involve the Private Sector in Service Delivery?**
A Financier's Perspective

About 100 serious ventures in private sector participation in the delivery of water and sanitation services have taken place worldwide over the past decade or so. This is a still a relatively modest phenomenon, though, involving at most about 5% of the urban population in the developing world. Most involve contracts or concessions, not a complete sale of assets, or what I would call a 'true' privatisation. The impetus for private sector involvement in water supply and treatment came not from ideology but typically because the public systems have been grossly inefficient, the finances precarious, and the infrastructure deteriorating. Theft of water is rampant. Rates of leakage and unaccounted-for water in many municipal systems in developing countries exceed 40%, even 60% to 70% in some old systems in Eastern Europe. The norm for well-managed systems is 10%, maybe 15%.

The promise of private sector involvement is real. New sources of funding are essential given that most countries will have to finance the bulk of water service improvements themselves. The assistance available from bilateral and multilateral donors is simply too limited.

The private sector brings more to the effort than money, though. Private contracts, concessions or outright ownership of components of the water sector also can improve incentives for efficiency in husbanding and allocating scarce water supplies. Private entities can reduce waste and unaccounted-for water quite significantly, and can get more productivity from fewer staff than public bodies typically can. And the private sector can bring state-of-the-art technologies to bear.

Notwithstanding Argentina's current economic circumstances, the experience of the private sector in Buenos Aires is instructive. Since 1993, rehabilitation of the existing system has cut water losses from about 40% to about 25%; water supply coverage of the population has increased by 10% without any new water sources; sewerage service has increased by 8%; and despite a recent increase, tariffs are lower than those charged by the public utility before the public–private partnership was formed.

One major hurdle to developing municipal water and sanitation projects involving the private sector, however, has been that they are quite costly to design and package. Standardised concession agreements and other elements of project development for the most part have not been widely adopted, even within the same country. Each project seems unique in its legal and financial underpinnings, making the transaction costs substantial for all parties. Labour unions and others often object to private sector participation, fearing lay-offs, and that can lead to time-consuming litigation.

The willingness or ability to pay the full cost of providing water services in host countries is another barrier to private sector involvement. Water has been heavily subsidised in some places and attempts to get consumers to pay more have met resistance. Customer willingness to pay for the collection and treatment of wastewater is even lower than for water supply.

The tariff – how much to charge for clean water – is often a contentious issue. There is a spectrum of views about water tariffs, ranging from water as a right, whose cost should be subsidised or even free, to water as a good or commodity, the price of which should reflect the true cost of providing it. Without the right tariff structure, a water authority lacks the funds to expand coverage or repair leaking pipes, adopt new methods or collect payments. With tariffs that are artificially low, there is little incentive for consumers to conserve and the resulting use of water is distorted and excessive.

I hasten to add that there are good and bad ways to invite the private sector to play a larger role in meeting the public's water needs. In some places, private sector involvement has meant merely turning over concessions to the same people who operated them previously, now regrouped into a private company and better paid. For others, the shift to private sector delivery has favoured the insiders and those with government connections.

A new discipline and an active role by government are required to ensure that private sector participation meets public objectives. Private investors will require – and governments will be wise to ensure – that transactions are transparent, bidding is conducted in the open and without favouritism, contracts are respected and enforced, agreements and standards are policed, and economic rewards are conditioned on performance. A strong private sector role requires strong and sophisticated government oversight.

William K Reilly, Founder and Chief Executive Officer, Aqua International Partners, San Francisco, USA

From the perspective of the political opponents, consumers and unions, the shift from public sector services to private sector delivery is associated with higher prices, higher costs and lost jobs. They argue that the private sector inevitably results in increased tariffs, as it is often a condition in PPP negotiations. The introduction of a commercial approach to service delivery and the associated cost-recovery reform also means that the utility operator will increase its efficiency in collecting tariffs. This will mean that those poor households that have received a service for free – because they did not pay – will see an end to this implicit subsidy arrangement.

However, in the context of partnerships, cost–benefit is a key issue. Few municipalities have undertaken adequate cost–benefit analyses that realistically compare the costs of public and private provision. This is an essential response in the context of discussions over increased costs. In order to focus partnerships on the poor, the key issue lies in the complex debate over sustainability, including the conditions required for the financial sustainability of the private operator, and those required in order that the poor might be able to make use of the service on a sustainable basis.

☐ The impacts of formalisation

However, other changes to the status quo may be brought about by private partners who are aiming to minimise risk. Many of these changes do not occur in developed contexts, and as a result many international operators and advocates of PPPs have not yet understood social impacts. A particular concern for the poorest groups, for instance, is that private sector investment will only be undertaken in a formal context where risk can be limited by using legal contracts and regulations to form the basis of any action.

However, processes of marginalisation and the very structure of the lives of the poor often places them in an informal context – and this informality has become an important part of their survival and is a key aspect of the way cities work. By its nature, the international large-scale private sector is generally unable to tolerate the informality that characterises their lives. This means, for instance, that the private sector will not work with informal service providers or other informal actors (unless they are formalised). It generally discontinues the practice of illegal connections (often without mitigating action), and is constrained by the illegalities of land and housing. Generally, the private operator will seek a level of formalisation far beyond the reach of the poorest communities.

However, formalisation can also bring benefit to poor households. Not all informal service providers are trustworthy: many exploit the poor householder's lack of access to services, and the regularisation of informal service providers into a lawful local private sector may bring long-term benefit. Although formalisation may ultimately help to remove exploitation, ensure better quality and availability of services, and lead to a greater inclusion of low-income settlements, evidence suggests that there are mixed outcomes for the poor, and it must be recognised that this lengthy process is likely to affect the existing livelihood strategies of the poor, particularly the most vulnerable households and individuals.

Enhancing Potential Benefits

There are both benefits and drawbacks to private sector involvement in service delivery. In order to formulate positive partnerships that are beneficial to the poor, municipalities must see that benefits are maximised and problems mitigated – all in relation to well-considered and prioritised municipal objectives. The approach presented here draws on the opportunities offered by the formal private sector but recognises that the capacity of the formal private sector is limited and that adverse impacts may be produced. It is necessary to ensure that these are each enhanced and mitigated as appropriate through partnership mechanisms. The formation of a partnership that extends the benefits of the formal and informal private sector, supplements these with the skills and resources of other actors, and places all resources in a focused partnership framework, forms the basis of the following chapters.

73600

☐ **Where does private sector participation 'fit' in the context of urban governance and management?**

☐ **How does it link with other municipal functions, partnerships and actions?**

☐ **What factors affect the sequencing of partnership development in a municipality?**

Focusing Partnership Goals

| Meeting municipal objectives through partnerships | Locating and linking partnerships in urban governance and management | Contributing to poverty reduction |

Guy Stubbs

Locating and Linking Partnerships in **Urban Governance and Management**

4

A primary issue often set aside in the development of public–private partnerships (PPPs) for service delivery is that municipal services and the process of their delivery are an integral part of a multifaceted, multifunctional organisation. They do not stand as isolated initiatives but are part of a broader municipal effort. Similarly, the process of changing the approach to service delivery is not an isolated shift, but one that often falls within a much broader set of municipal reforms. The process of developing private sector participation (PSP) in urban infrastructure and services is influenced by, and influences, the entire process of municipal reform.

It is therefore critical to recognise that private sector participation in a service sector, such as water or waste, is not created or implemented in a vacuum. Service partnerships are often the direct concern of municipal government and outcomes are linked to the fulfilment of other municipal obligations. This chapter explores where private sector participation fits in the changing field of local governance and urban management. It first considers the elements of the reform process that are linked with decentralisation. It then considers service partnerships in relation to the multisectoral obligations of municipalities, and the need for strategic service planning to locate and link partnerships into city governance and management.

The Elements of the Reform Process

In practice, the development of partnerships as a means to the delivery of services in municipalities occurs as a part of a larger, all-encompassing municipal reform process. Central to this discussion is the reorientation from top–down urban planning and management to effective urban governance. The concept of local governance involves a variety of local agents in the sharing of power, with municipal government having a coordinating rather than a monopolistic and controlling role.[1]

Yet for municipal government, the shift in policy and attitudes required to achieve good governance is not easy or natural. Apart from the development of a sound democratic basis, approaches to good governance require municipalities to reposition themselves as one of many municipal stakeholders, and to create effective participatory processes with these stakeholders. It requires municipalities to develop an accountability and transparency previously unknown to them. It requires innovative organisational, human resource and financial management. It requires municipalities to reconsider their provider role in all municipal functions, to develop a predictable environment, to consider the potential of all private and civil society stakeholders including informal stakeholders, and to reconsider delivery mechanisms. In practice, it may require strategic change, be it through networking with other municipalities or unbundling functions.

It is important to remind advocates of PPPs in specific municipal services that the key aspects attributed to effective partnerships are in fact a reflection of the principles of better governance.[2] Partnership actors should not assume that accountability and transparency or strategic planning are pursued only for the good of the partnership. In most cases these are broader governance concerns, and PPPs should link into and build on existing efforts, no matter how humble.

Yet the key aspects of good governance are often vital to the development of service partnerships (see Box 4.1). For instance, the formulation and sustainability of partnerships will be dependent on the commitment and mobilisation of councillors and political leaders. Immature political leadership will affect all municipal reform processes and capacity building is an important part of a municipal reform programme. Whereas partnerships can promote capacity building in some areas (e.g., to induct new councillors in PPPs), the development of capable leaders in newly democratised contexts

Box 4.1 Locating Municipal Service Partnerships

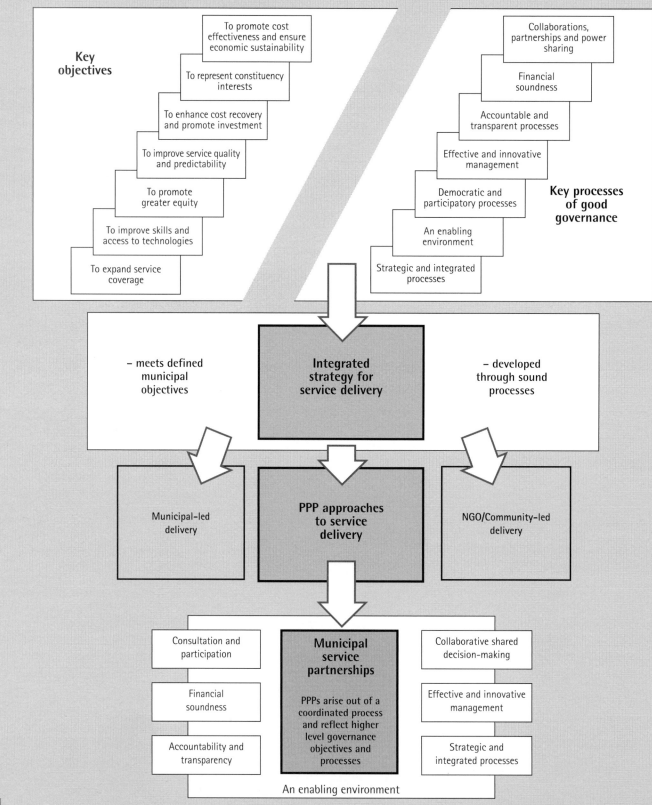

takes time. Partnerships are put at risk when key (non-public sector) actors fail to understand the complexity and susceptibility of new councils.

The processes of democratisation are not limited to electoral democracy; they also include the development of stakeholder participation in municipal decision-making. Whereas some consultative processes are developed purely for the purpose of partnership formulation, in most cases municipalities will have already established vehicles for involving civil society and the private sector in municipal decision-making. Organisational structures may be an important part of this process: for instance, the neighbourhood committees and ward committees in Indian cities are established and legal forums for participatory decision-making. It is important that participatory processes concerning service partnerships build on such structures (addressing, of course, the known deficiencies of that structure).

Municipalities clearly experience growing pains when adopting more open participatory approaches in relation to all decisions, including private sector participation. Administrators accustomed to calling the shots must get used to facilitating rather than controlling. Engineers struggle with redefined roles that undermine their status and power as the providers of technical knowledge. Newly elected politicians must accept that winning a seat does not give them carte blanche in decision-making. All municipal actors must engage in the collaborative spirit and work with other stakeholders.

Best practice in urban management prioritises strategic planning and highlights the importance of holistic and integrated processes and solutions. Yet in the recent past, the sectoral nature of service partnerships has promoted isolated sectoral solutions, and in some cases a lack of coordination has undermined city development strategies. The strategic process must focus initially on the overall picture, and provide a framework for developing specific partnerships in functional sectors. Conversely, establishing an integrated strategy is likely to enhance the benefits to be gained from a service partnership and enable benefits to be targeted.

The strategic vision of municipal services also requires supporting institutional arrangements. Municipalities therefore establish committees, task forces and other dedicated units to coordinate their various departmental interests. If a municipality is keen to pursue partnership options, it must establish the structure with which to do so. This was the approach taken in Kathmandu in Nepal, where a high-level committee, a task force and a secretariat were established to take the private sector participation policy forward (see Box 4.2).

Establishing sound urban management also means that a municipality must address those areas in which it lacks an acceptable level of professionalism. These activities will vary from overall improvements in the technical and managerial capacity of staffing, to the formulation of procedures that promote accountability and transparency, to the introduction of information technologies to assist in administrative functions. Each of these processes affects and will be affected by the formulation and implementation of partnerships. At the same time, the process of establishing a service partnership is in itself characteristic of a more professional organisation, and a willingness to accept change, challenge the status quo and promote better ways of fulfilling municipal obligations. Important aspects of this include the development of an enabling environment and effective financial management.

This reform process is not easy. The natural tendency of governments to resist change, the lack of skills and access to capacity building, the engrained and sometimes corrupt practices of dysfunctional municipalities, the resistance to transparency, and the fear of technology and human resource changes all emphasise the need for massive attitudinal change. The emergence of service partnerships in this context can be both problematic and supportive. 'Learning by doing' is an important capacity building method, and municipal officials may well be convinced by seeing how the private sector works, and the tangible improvements in municipal services. However, the slow rate of change to a more transparent and accountable organisation and the inertia of a municipality can frustrate partnership development. These aspects of organisational capacity building are discussed further in Chapter 12.

4

Box **4.2** ## Municipal Policy Towards Public–Private Partnerships
Kathmandu, Nepal

The most significant private sector participation (PSP) activity in Nepal has developed in Kathmandu. The most recent efforts have focused on the development of a policy framework for private sector participation in the municipal (KMC) functions. Approved by the municipal board, this outlines, in explicit terms, the intention to 'attract the private sector by creating a conducive and trustful environment for their investments by ensuring the maximum facilities that can be given by KMC'. With the support of an Asian Development Bank (ADB) capacity building programme, the KMC has drawn in specialist skills to assist in policy development. It is contemplating a range of different forms of PSP and a number of priority areas.

There are several opportunities for PPP in Kathmandu:

- the expansion of existing urban services and additional necessary services to meet the overall development objective of KMC;
- an increase in the KMC's management capacity through private sector investment for PPP projects;
- the construction and management of basic facilities in health services, education, water supply, solid waste management, commercial complexes, industrial estates and other main services; and
- the development of a market, a bus terminal, a modern slaughterhouse, an underground car park, mass transit along the ring road and many other similar projects.

The priority areas and potential for private sector participation in the KMC and other locally dominated activities are significant. The KMC has identified many potential projects, some of which are already being implemented. Most of these are in the solid waste management area. Other potential activities include construction and/or operation of marketplaces, passenger bus terminals and a slaughterhouse. The priority areas for PSP and PPP activities are urban services, single-function commercial activities and integrated area-development ventures. 'Urban services' are made up of three services, although the KMC is responsible for neither water nor road maintenance. 'Single-function commercial activities' refers to business activities that in other circumstances might be government-regulated commercial private sector activities: abattoirs, passenger bus terminals and parking facilities. All these activities have great potential to recover their investment and operating costs through user fees. 'Integrated area-development ventures' include commercial complexes and industrial estates. These ventures are interesting, because the KMC does not have the resources to provide urban services directly to the area developments. Thus, the developments must build and maintain the services by themselves. Because these new 'enclaves' are self-financing, they are a natural starting point for private sector involvement. The KMC has plans to package such a venture.

There are two types of sub-sectors: service contract sub-sectors (non-capital-investment) and investment sub-sectors (capital-intensive). A single sector, such as solid waste, can comprise both service-contract sub-sectors (street sweeping, collection of solid waste, billing and collection) and investment sub-sectors (recycling, landfill disposal, composting activities). Investment sub-sectors deserve special attention because they bring 'off-budget' funds for capital additionality. It is also challenging to arrange private sector involvement in these sub-sectors because more assurances are required to protect private sector investment.

Criteria have been established for the selection of PPP proposals. These include financial viability, technical and engineering competency, contract and institutional management capacity and project management capacity. Basic standard operating procedures have been developed under this policy framework for PSP transactions. These include feasibility guidelines, procurement guidelines and contracting guidelines that will be made available to the interested private parties for transparent transactions.

The following institutional arrangements have been made by KMC to facilitate the PPP projects:

- A **high-level committee** consisting of representatives from all the political parties within the KMC and other professional associations like the Nepal Bar Association, the Nepal Engineering Association, the chambers of commerce and industries, and Transparency International. The main function of this committee is to formulate PSP policies and to approve the projects for implementation.
- A **PSP task force** including all the departmental heads concerned, experts as required and members of the respective committee. The task force examines the proposal submitted by the private sector minutely and also checks the tender document according to set standards, and then recommends it to the high-level committee for consideration and approval.
- A **PSP secretariat**, which is being established under the private secretariat and protocol office of the mayor. The function of the secretariat is to coordinate and facilitate PSP activities for smooth decision-making within the departments, the high-level committee task force and external private parties.

Through acknowledging the importance of PSP for the overall development and upgrading of the infrastructure and services of Kathmandu, the slogan 'my pride, my legacy and my Kathmandu' will be achieved.

Source: Kathmandu Metropolitan City, 2000

Given the interconnected nature of partnership approaches and current attitudes towards governance and management, it is essential that municipalities understand how partnerships can underpin good governance and how good governance can support partnerships.

Does the development of PPPs support good governance? While the answer given is often an unambiguous 'yes', when examined closely the answer is more likely to be that certain types of partnerships support the processes of good governance, while those that are exploitative or non-consensual clearly do not. To this end, municipalities need to know that they can and should make changes to these partnerships, introduce participatory processes, establish a competitive environment, and ensure the involvement of all stakeholders in creating partnerships that align with their objectives. Municipalities forming new partnerships would be wise to look to those private sector partners with experience in this approach. Among other benefits, this will gradually create a demand for a private sector that is better able to work within the bounds of good governance objectives.

In order for partnerships to support broader governance initiatives, it is important that municipalities and their partners ensure that arrangements do not ignore fundamental principles of reform. This may be a tall order, but in recent years evidence has suggested that a new breed of partnerships can work within these parameters. These new partnerships encourage participatory and consultative processes, engage actors from civil society, promote transparency through awareness building and open policies, and also promote the development of solutions appropriate to a particular context. Yet this has not always been the case: many existing, more traditional PPPs are far from participatory or consultative. Many do not possess the flexibility required for good governance, and many government-sanctioned monopolies have ignored calls for greater competitiveness and transparency.

Does good governance support the development of PPPs? This chapter argues explicitly that the efforts made by urban managers towards good governance are at the foundation of PPPs, and that the development of PPPs is a reflection of these broader efforts. That is not to say that all municipalities pursuing good governance objectives will give the highest priority to private sector participation. Many prefer to pursue collaborations with NGOs and communities first, while others have started with internal reforms, or are focused on establishing more effective and accountable processes.

The Service Obligations of the Municipality

One of the notable characteristics of the various support mechanisms for PPP development is that they focus on one service sector (e.g., water and sanitation, or solid waste). No doubt due to the very different characteristics of different sectors, publications and capacity building forums tend to focus on private sector participation in one sector or another.[3] Yet this approach is far removed from the reality of how towns are managed. In practice, in any one day or electoral cycle municipalities must address the operation, maintenance and (frequently) the replacement of infrastructure for a range of physical services. They must respond to endemic problems and emergencies and address city-wide economic growth as well as targeted poverty reduction. In so doing, many are constantly relying on the revenue of one service sector to subsidise the shortfall in another or to fund activities in a non-earning sector. This is the reality of municipal management when human and financial resources are limited.

Urban management is a complex and multifaceted endeavour. Typically, it includes the planning, management and often the delivery (including operation and maintenance) of a wide range of services to urban residents, businesses and industry. From the perspective of an urban manager, these functions can be disaggregated into:

- basic services with a large public-health impact (e.g. water supply, sanitation, solid waste removal, drainage, health services);

4

Links to Boxes
10.2, 10.5, 10.8

Box **4.3** **Integrated Development Planning**
South Africa

Following the national and local democratic elections in South Africa in 1994–95, local government became a primary vehicle for promoting equity in the reconstruction and development of the country. During the apartheid regime, local government in South Africa created and perpetuated separation and inequity, because the principal legislation that instituted spatial separation was applied at the local level. Recent developments in policy and legislation on the role of local government in South Africa are therefore driven not only by the need to bring the government closer to the people, but also by the need to reverse the policy and planning of the past and redefine the nature and objectives of local government.

The White Paper on Local Government (WPLG) creates the policy framework for municipal governance to promote local government; it specifies social development and economic growth should be prioritised, as should the promotion of the role of community in the design and delivery of municipal programmes. It also stresses the need for services to be affordable and integrated with other forms of service and housing provision. It explicitly recommends that municipalities look at alternatives for accelerating the delivery of basic services, and cites public–public, public–private and community partnerships as options for consideration.

Decisions about the mechanisms and actors that should be involved in service delivery are implemented through an integrated development plan (IDP) and the integral Municipal Infrastructure Investment Plan (MIIP), which sets out how the municipality will achieve service delivery targets. The IDP is the primary tool for local government planning in local, strategic and holistic development interventions, i.e. for municipal councils to instigate participatory planning processes with civil society and private sector stakeholders to articulate their short-, medium- and long-term goals. As such, through the IDP municipalities develop a strategy to achieve their development objectives, including the mobilisation of resources and capacity and the desired approach to service delivery (and partnerships for services).

The IDP process establishes the specific development programme, sets a budget to enable the programme to be implemented, monitors and evaluates how well it is implemented, and allows for an ongoing process of change and improvement. Several important activities make up the IDP process:

- assessing the current situation in the municipal area;
- assessing the needs of the community;
- prioritising these needs in order of urgency and importance;
- setting goals to meet these needs;
- devising strategies to achieve the goals within a set timeframe;
- developing and implementing projects and programmes to achieve key objectives;
- setting targets so that performance can be measured;
- budgeting effectively with limited resources; and
- monitoring and reassessing the development programme.

The key process requirement in the IDP is participation. In all local government activities, participation is a key aspect of the democratic process and is seen as the key to all aspects of developmental local government – it is the link that ties it together. It is particularly important, especially in public–private partnerships, that municipalities ensure that new arrangements for the delivery of services and the creation of infrastructure do not sacrifice the principles of governance, participation and poverty eradication that are at the heart of our post-apartheid local governance system.

The optimal use of funding for infrastructure requires careful long-term planning. Within the IDP, municipalities in South Africa are advised to develop infrastructure investment plans that take account of all sources of funding. An infrastructure investment plan helps to plan for long-term financial sustainability, and to ensure that service levels are affordable. Although the choice about the level of service remains with the municipality concerned, the Consolidated Municipal Infrastructure Programme developed at the national level recommends that levels of service be matched to household income to ensure affordability in the long term. The infrastructure investment plan also assists with prioritising potential projects. It indicates and programmes future infrastructure needs to ensure systematic development in the area. Based on current and projected indicators of need and growth, it aims to synchronise infrastructure and housing delivery.

The process envisaged therefore facilitates an integrated approach to municipal management – one that has the potential to bring public–private partnerships under the same umbrella as local economic development. In practice, the incorporation of public–private partnerships has not been developed to any significant extent, but policy presents clear opportunities for coordinating environmental and social interventions and for linking formal, informal, large- and small-scale enterprises in the development of service partnerships.

Sources: Plummer 2000a; USN, 1998; RoSA, no date

- city-wide non-basic services required to promote and maintain economic growth and productivity (e.g. electricity, transportation, civic infrastructure, economic development activities);
- poverty reduction activities focused on the poorest groups in the city (education, income generation, micro-credit and savings services);
- other social services needed for social development and promoting equity (emergency services, women's development activities, youth development activities); and
- recreation services (sports facilities, parks and gardens, cultural and entertainment facilities).

With limited resources, municipalities aim to balance all these needs and perform all these functions to keep political, institutional and social forces in check. In the pursuit of efficiency and effective management practices, it is considered good practice for municipalities to 'ringfence' the accounts for each municipal service. This enables financial reporting to show all the costs – including those (such as staff costs or vehicle repair) that are often hidden in normal municipal accounting procedures, informs municipal decision-making and creates a transparent process through which cross-subsidisation takes place. However, isolating water and sanitation services or solid waste into freestanding cost centres or partnerships does have significant implications for the overall management of the city. Given their sheer size within municipal budgets and operations and their capital-intensive nature, the isolation of these services can place much greater strain on other sectors. It can also lead to an unintended prioritisation of these sectors over others (because the private firm has to be paid). More often, municipalities subsidise welfare activities from the water account on an ad hoc basis and the separation of water and sanitation activities into a freestanding partnership entity will require them to adopt more strategic and transparent systems.

In relation to the poor, one of the primary concerns of isolating physical service provision in discrete partnerships is the separation of important physical activities from multisectoral poverty reduction programmes. The lessons of earlier poverty reduction responses draw attention to the importance of integrated approaches (see the detailed discussion in Chapter 5). Yet a hard fact of life is that much of the capital put into poverty reduction programmes is required for construction activities, and this core investment facilitates many of the economic, social and human development activities undertaken in poor areas. In well-considered initiatives, these were carefully programmed in relation to each other to bring about maximum benefit. Yet typically, and even in those instances in which municipalities micro-managed private sector activity, the introduction of private sector participation in service delivery has diminished the municipality's concern for integrating activities.

A primary issue to be addressed in the development of service partnerships is how the proven benefits of integrated urban management can be reconciled with the benefits of separating services for specific partnership initiatives. Municipalities need support to work through a service planning stage, to effectively programme related activities and to take on a central coordinating role – one made all the more difficult because the processes of delivery are many and varied.

Partnerships also require a municipality to play a significantly more considered, strategic role than they had to when they could improvise on their own. Involving other stakeholders and introducing long-term commitments demand more strategic planning, and better understanding of the linkages and implications of each and every service as a part of an integral package. In South Africa, the development of the integrated development planning (IDP) approach (see Boxes 4.3 and 4.4) attempts to create a strategic and participatory planning process within municipalities, one that effectively locates municipal service partnerships and links them to all other inputs and outcomes. The fundamental difference between the IDP and previous planning tools is that it encourages municipal government to integrate its planning, budgeting and monitoring, and create a holistic rather than a piecemeal process. The IDP now ensures, for instance, that engineering departments do not prepare plans for infrastructure in isolation from housing or social development departments. This kind of strategic planning is also reflected in the innovative approaches taken by the Kerala State Government in India under the People's Planning Campaign.

4

Links to Boxes
6.22, 8.5, 9.1, 9.3

| Box 4.4 | **PSP as Part of a Wider Restructuring Process**
Johannesburg, South Africa

The metropolitan government of Johannesburg embarked on a comprehensive restructuring process to recover from a dire crisis in the late 1990s. The initiative, known as Igoli 2002, contains many aspects that reflect the key ingredients of partnership with actors outside the municipality. It shows the role of external pressures (the financial crisis), the importance of forward planning, the need to engage key stakeholders, and the range of options that can be utilised to support effective service delivery. Private sector partnerships form just one aspect of this approach. Most importantly, the authority embarked upon a process of integrated reform through which a system of change could be established, and links made between key functions.

The city's financial predicament made headlines in 1997–98. Following rent and service charge boycotts against apartheid in the 80s and early 90s, a culture of non-payment developed in Johannesburg, and in the context of continued urban poverty non-payment for rates and services is a problem. This led to cash shortfalls and the need to delay and negotiate extended payment terms to major suppliers of services like electricity and water. Funds and reserves were increasingly used to finance debt, leading to a reliance on loans and cash generated by operating activities to sustain the municipality. Small but persistent overspending on the budget further drained its cash liquidity.

Attempts to relieve the pressure through foreign borrowing were blocked by the national Department of Finance in 1998. Financing was then obtained from the Development Bank of Southern Africa to sustain operating cash flows and to prevent defaults on loans from major creditors. The bank demanded that corrective action be taken to ensure that future financial distress would be avoided. A committee of councillors and external consultants took action to control expenditure and instil budgetary discipline.

Longer-term planning was clearly necessary, and the different municipalities within the metropolitan area were involved in drafting Igoli 2002, which was finalised in November 1998. The plan represents a fundamental departure from the conventional, bureaucratic, municipal management paradigm in Johannesburg, aiming to build delivery partnerships with the private sector, reduce the functional scope of the metropolitan area's activities and draw a clear distinction between service delivery and regulatory functions across the administration.

The key elements of the plan include:

- creating public utilities for water, sanitation and electricity. The utilities will raise capital funding, introduce new management practices and improve performance and efficiencies. With the council as the shareholder and regulator, the utilities will focus on service delivery, and will be able to make contracts with private service providers.
- Creating agencies to manage roads and stormwater, drainage, parks and cemeteries, and introducing business principles and efficient management practices into the management of these services. The agencies operate as contractors, which allows for greater accountability and the introduction of performance incentives. Legally they are able to engage in partnerships with private and non-governmental service agencies.
- Privatising a small number of assets not considered to be core business, including stadiums, Metro Gas and the Rand Airport.
- Corporatising certain functions such as the zoo, the civic theatre, the bus service and council-owned farms. These facilities thus remain under council control, but are managed as separate corporate agencies.
- The core administration of the council is split into a central administration, which performs the 'client' function, and a regional administration, which performs the 'contractor' function. It thus performs an important regulatory role.
- A labour relations plan and a change management programme has been developed, to form the basis for introducing changes and negotiating with stakeholders, especially within the municipal structure.

The creation of the utilities has taken major effort involving a range of legal and institutional challenges. By 2000–01, the cash position of Johannesburg had improved substantially and it was anticipating a budget surplus.

Sources: Chris Heymans; DBSA, 2000

Effective service planning also requires the municipality to engage in effective monitoring, feedback and revision. While all stakeholders engage in the rhetoric of monitoring, most have little experience of it, are unaware of what is required and have not usually engaged in meaningful feedback. Few initiatives provide examples of revision processes that have effectively reoriented activities to ensure optimum targeting and impact. If partnership options are pursued, municipalities can build in capacity building for effective monitoring to ensure that the process is achieving the required focus.

Urban Management Implications for Service Partnerships

Many of the key issues and responses emerging in newly formulated partnership approaches focused on the poor are central developmental concerns – they are not related to just one service sector. Yet many partnerships tend to assume that these processes are established for the partnership alone. For instance:

- **Subsidies and tariffs**   Decision-making over subsidies and tariffs is linked to municipal government decision-making about the level and targeting of poverty reduction interventions. Deciding on water subsidies in isolation from sewerage, drainage, health and education is not feasible, particularly when finances are constrained. Policy is required to determine prioritisation and resource allocation. At the local level, the tariff structure can be a complex concern that is affected by the political decision-making of municipalities (and higher levels of government) in relation to different services, community groups and localities.
- **Demand-responsiveness**   Awareness of the factors affecting service demand and affordability, and the development of flexibility in service delivery mechanisms, are crucial in effective urban management. The poor constantly balance their service needs as part of their overall livelihood strategy, which undergoes constant adjustment to suit the changing household circumstances. The cost of different service options, for instance, needs to be considered in terms of individual household strategies and city-wide municipal capacity.
- **Land tenure**   The lack of tenure security is a primary structural problem affecting the livelihoods of the poor. The security and safety of women and the ability of the poor to earn an income and obtain credit are affected, as are physical services. Government (at all levels) has land management responsibilities that includes improving tenure security for a vast number of poor households. Partnerships involving the private sector obviously raise the profile of tenure issues, as investment in infrastructure will be curtailed until settlements are deemed legal; but tenure is a strategic urban management and poverty reduction issue loaded with political and social implications.
- **Informal service providers**   The formalisation of the informal sector is a city-wide concern forming part of the economic development strategy of the city. Efforts to legalise particular service providers must be seen in the dynamic and interdependent context of a wide range of informal service providers. Intervening in established processes may affect the livelihoods of the poor significantly. Enforcing standards of water quality, for instance, may put small-scale providers out of business and deprive poor households of water. Parallel activities may be required to mitigate any negative impacts of change.
- **Community participation and empowerment**   The capacity of the community to participate meaningfully in development is not restricted to one project or one specific period of time. Many community-based initiatives start in one sector and ultimately contribute to an overall process of community development. Ideally, mechanisms for participation should be a part of a programme of activities that are effectively integrated or linked over time. They should take into consideration the different capacities of individuals and communities, the demands placed on their time and the assets at their command.

The Partnership Learning Curve

Despite the argument that service partnerships are a part of broader management activity, in practice, municipalities will still have to create partnerships on a sector-by-sector basis, and so many are interested to know how to go about the

4

Links to Boxes
9.4, 9.5, 10.4, 11.3, 11.4, 12.7

Box 4.5   Building Experience in Private Sector Participation
Gweru, Zimbabwe

The process of involving the private sector in municipal functions in Gweru originated in 1995, with a national capacity building programme for local government managers to expose them to and familiarise them with the benefits of commercialising a range of municipal functions. This initiative was a direct result of the national economic reform programme led by the World Bank, and while the emphasis lay on commercialisation, it clearly included the possibility of delegating management to the private sector. This paved the way for local authority functions to be privatised. All 22 local authority managers in the country were then asked to propose commercialisation options within their own municipalities.

By September 1996, the Gweru Town Clerk notified the national government of Gweru's intention to move forwards with the commercialisation/privatisation of 20 municipal functions. These included water and sanitation services. Not least because of the previous capacity building efforts, the council welcomed the proposals made by the Town Clerk. It is interesting to note that the process of introducing the private sector in Gweru focused on effective urban management. It was not applied to just one sector, but was seen as a new approach to the management of the city. The urban management decision was to commercialise as many services as were appropriate and possible.

The second important characteristic of the Gweru process at this stage was that there was no fixed agenda or adherence to one option. Of the first three functions that were commercialised (distilleries, theatres and security services), each was approached in a very different manner. The distillery operations were reorganised into a commercial enterprise, wholly owned by the council; a lease arrangement was established for the theatre; and security services are managed through annual service contracts. Thus the drive towards the commercialisation of municipal functions was a key part of the development of healthy municipal finances, and one of the notable characteristics of town management prior to any private sector participation in water and sanitation services.

The experience of three of these sectors is described below.

Theatre (lease contract)   Prior to the management contract, the city theatre had been run by the Housing and Community Services Department of the Gweru City Council (GCC), with approximately eight staff. It had an annual loss of approximately US$20,000 at 1995 prices. In 1996 the GCC approached the Gweru Theatre Guild to take over the management for a 10-year period. The theatre assets remain with the council, and the guild pays the council an annual fee of ZD 12,000. The guild is responsible for fee collection, and retains all the profits. Since commercialisation, theatre services for the community have improved and the council receives a small leasing fee rather than a significant loss.

Security/enforcement services (service contract)   A cost–benefit analysis carried out in 1996 showed that the private sector could deliver security services at a lower cost and more effectively than the municipality. As a result, the GCC tenders security services on an annual basis to local companies. The chief security officer monitors performance. Indicators of improved effectiveness include: a decrease in the number of break-ins at municipal buildings, an increase in the number of arrests; and fines for violating municipal by-laws. The GCC continues to provide some security services to ensure the ongoing employment of security guards, but it has placed a moratorium on staff recruitment and intends to create service contracts for all similar services in the future.

Liquor undertaking (corporatisation)   The Gweru liquor undertakings were commercialised in 1997. They now form a registered company that is wholly owned by the council, but is autonomous and has an independent board of directors. Before corporatisation, liquor undertakings made a substantial loss that drew unnecessarily on council resources. In 1996, the estimated net loss was US$490,000. This was turned around when it was taken over by skilled private sector managers. In 1999, the annual profit was approximately US$200,000; in 2000, profit was estimated to be in the order of US$750,000. Dividends are now paid to the council.

The experience and success of these initiatives created an environment in which the GCC felt that it was able to embark on a more ambitious move towards private sector involvement in the water and sanitation sector. The Town Clerk stresses that all the officials and politicians experienced a steep and helpful learning curve through these first initiatives, and that by 'extending the barriers' in other sectors the council gained invaluable experience in stakeholder consultation. The Gweru case provides an illustration of a municipality that gradually and deliberately developed a process of involving private sector actors in a range of sectors, in a variety of ways. Each initiative is freestanding, but forms a part of an overall strategy. In terms of outcome the degrees of success vary, but all sectors, with the exception of solid waste, have experienced large-scale improvements in efficiency and service.

Source: Plummer and Nhemachena, 2001

sequencing of partnerships within the municipality. For instance, should certain services be reorganised before others? Which service should come first? What dictates the order? Should contentious services be left until stakeholders are more accustomed to the idea? Are lessons from one service partnership transferable to another?

Many contextual factors have determined municipal decision-making to date and case study experience does not suggest that there is an obvious pattern. Analysis does, however, suggest some simple pointers for municipal consideration. These include the following:

- **Politicians develop confidence when they see partnerships work** Experience in one or two services can give political decision-makers the drive and resolve to promote further private sector involvement in other sectors. The success of small initiatives with service contracts, management contracts and corporatisation (see Box 4.5 on Gweru) can move the partnership agenda forwards significantly. In Gweru, councillors gradually realised that they were being supported because voters could see improvements in service, and the councillors could boast that these were being achieved at a lower cost. Administrators were convinced by the financial gains and reduced risk.

- **There is a steep learning curve associated with PPPs** Municipal management teams develop organisational capacity and noticeable skills simply by having been through a process of developing partnerships. This capacity brings substantial benefit to service partnerships organised thereafter. Skills and confidence are vital to the early stages of project formulation. In particular, the appointment of consultants, the processes of tendering and negotiation, and the finalisation of contracts are all transferable skills.

- **Attitudinal barriers are removed as partnerships develop** Developing positive attitudes towards the private sector among municipal and civil society stakeholders takes time. The gradual process of involving the private sector in a number of services in Gweru proved that receptive attitudes could be developed quite quickly once assumptions were addressed and the fear of corrupt practices alleviated. Accountability and transparency were central to achieving a 'change-friendly' environment.

- **The nature of the service – whether it is a basic or non-basic service – affects the decision-making process** Many municipalities will opt for smaller, non-critical service partnerships first, but if the national policy encourages municipalities to resolve basic services such as water supply they may opt to develop partnerships immediately in a basic, network service. The diverse characteristics of network and non-network services are thus another aspect for consideration. Network services will be of interest to large international operators, whereas non-network services such as solid waste and some sanitation services may attract local and national investment. Many municipal officials have expressed their fear of the international private sector, and prefer to work with national businessmen before embarking on more ambitious processes with more skilled partners.

- **The scope of the service may affect the timing of private sector involvement** Smaller functions may not create fewer labour problems, but are critical steps towards more ambitious arrangements, testing reactions and building capacity. Evidence suggests that they may be basic services, such as on-site sanitation, which can be 'unbundled' into a discrete service package.

All of these issues – the reform process, the multisectoral function and the learning organisation – are central to understanding where partnerships and partnership development are 'located' in urban governance and management.

Establishing a Process of Strategic Service Planning

Locating a partnership in the context of municipal objectives and reform requires a partnership to emerge from a structured, strategic planning process that takes in the considerations discussed above, and sees partnerships within the broader sphere of urban management and governance. This may be obvious and easily achieved in some contexts, but

4

Box **4.6**   Strategic Planning in the Development and Implementation of Partnerships

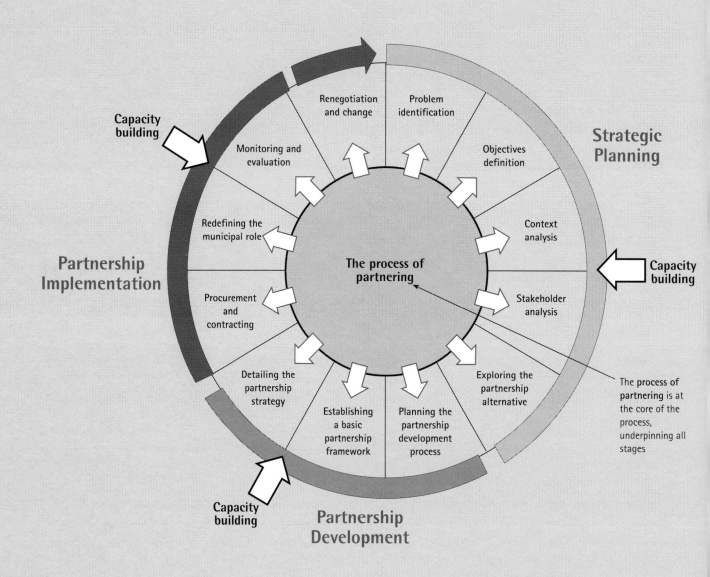

Capacity building

Strategic Planning

Renegotiation and change

Problem identification

Monitoring and evaluation

Objectives definition

Redefining the municipal role

Context analysis

The process of partnering

Capacity building

Partnership Implementation

Procurement and contracting

Stakeholder analysis

Detailing the partnership strategy

Exploring the partnership alternative

Establishing a basic partnership framework

Planning the partnership development process

The process of partnering is at the core of the process, underpinning all stages

Capacity building

Partnership Development

not in all. Chapter 12 presents some of the key issues concerning the strategic management process and the development of municipal procedures.

Chapter 2 has already stressed the importance of understanding municipal problems and objectives. A simplified strategic planning process that precedes the development of a partnership can be conducted within the municipality by undertaking a number of key steps:

- identifying the problems to be solved;
- defining service objectives;
- analysing the key factors influencing service delivery;
- understanding the opportunities and constraints of potential stakeholders and their roles in service delivery; and
- investigating partnership alternatives and coordinating a system of service delivery.

The strategic planning process will thus involve the formulation of municipal objectives and the development of a strategy to service delivery that responds to an analysis of the stakeholders and the context. This should include a strategy for focusing the partnership on the poor. This strategic process creates a platform for decision-making linked into broader municipal management, service delivery and poverty reduction goals. This will mean, for instance, that the proposed strategy for water and sanitation services might be developed alongside a strategy for solid waste management or energy. The aim is to ensure that a coherent pattern of infrastructure development occurs – one that recognises opportunities, constraints and livelihood implications as well as community and municipal capacities.

To supplement this discussion, Chapter 5 focuses on the importance of developing partnership approaches that actively contribute to poverty reduction. Chapter 6 provides an in-depth discussion of the range of actors involved in partnerships that follow a good governance approach.

Chapter 5 **Key Questions**

☐ **How does a municipality contribute to poverty reduction through a public–private partnership?**

☐ **What are the key steps in creating a strategy that focuses partnerships on the poor?**

☐ **Do current approaches towards public–private partnerships do enough?**

☐ **What lessons of poverty reduction can be included in the development of partnerships?**

Guy Stubbs

Contributing to Poverty Reduction

Do Public–Private Partnerships Currently Do Enough?

When international agencies first started promoting private sector involvement in municipal services, the inefficiency of the public sector in delivering urban services was the fundamental cause of concern. As a result, support – and publications – in the early to mid-1990s mainly focused on the benefits of private sector participation (PSP) and how it could be achieved. In this context, the delivery of services to low-income areas was part of the problem to be solved and was addressed through the development of policy, regulatory frameworks and contract provisions in relation to tariffs, expansion mandates and network upgrades. At this time, consideration was not explicitly given to the diversity of the customer base in developing countries or, more specifically, to the complex set of issues concerning delivery to the poorest households. The very shift to private sector involvement in the delivery of basic services required a fundamental reorientation and this occupied the debate in its earliest years.

Since that time, a number of factors have led to greater consideration being given to the poor in the development of public–private partnerships (PPPs) in service delivery. The primary multilateral advocate of private sector participation in these early years, the World Bank, has accrued significant experience in PPPs in a range of sectors (electricity, water and sanitation, telecommunication), and those involved in the formulation and monitoring of this process have seen the need for solutions that more effectively reach the poor. Simultaneously, and adding weight to this direction, the World Bank has itself introduced a more explicit policy focus on poverty reduction in its client countries.

Recently, therefore, many of the Bank-led discussions about private solutions to infrastructure provision for the poor have been developed by organisations and individuals already committed to private sector participation in service delivery. They bring with them a wealth of knowledge about the particulars of policy, regulations, incentives, and tariff structures, all of which are core concerns for PPPs. The approach generally adopted is to draw first on the key elements and lessons of existing contracts. The result of this investigation and the current direction of pro-poor PPPs for infrastructure is that the overall shape of the partnership is being manipulated but its basic structure remains the same. Some would argue that only the trimmings have been changed.

In relation to water and sanitation services, this approach has been taken further by two other important (and related) organisations: the Business Partners for Development[1] initiative focusing on the water and sanitation sector, and the broader Water and Sanitation Program.[2] Both seek to create a shift in the way the PPP works (see Boxes 6.20 and 6.21). With the cooperation of operators, the public sector, NGOs and donors, each has developed or been working with a range of pilot projects that have stretched the boundaries of standard contracts, extended actor roles and created innovative processes. Through these initiatives a number of core issues concerning the poor have been rethought, and alternative technical, financial and institutional solutions are currently being considered. In particular, the role of NGOs is being reconsidered and extended into PPPs, approaches to condominial systems are now being tested, discussions on tariff structures and subsidies are addressing impacts on the poor, and the issues surrounding expansion mandates and service standards are being explored. Each of these avenues of investigation is developed further throughout this sourcebook.

Notwithstanding the increasing interest in extending the boundaries of PPPs, to date these are isolated initiatives. Most approaches to PPPs are still based on standard models and assumptions, and these determine the limits to which PPPs can contribute to poverty issues in the urban environment. They include, for instance, the assumption that the poor obtain indirect benefits when city-wide operations are more efficiently and skilfully delivered (there is little focus on negative impacts); that PPPs are developed in single service sectors; and that PPP arrangements conform to one of the pre-established PPP contract types.

5

Box **5.1** Potential Impacts of Infrastructure Improvements

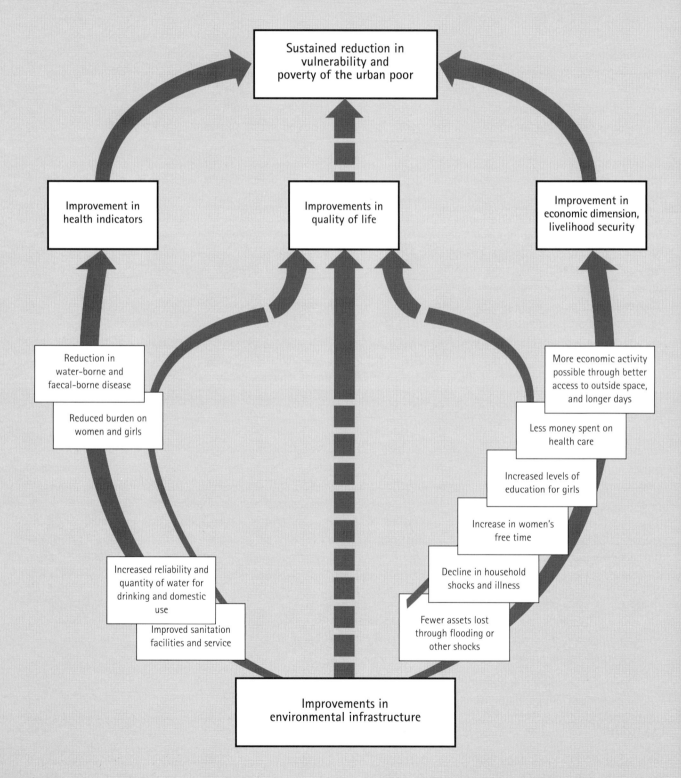

Sources: Adapted from Amis, 2001; Plummer, 2000b

Is this enough? In the context of broader municipal responsibilities and the shift to local governance (described in Chapter 4), municipalities must ask whether the application of a standard partnership model is appropriate. Does it enable them to meet poverty reduction goals? Can they expect more? Should they strive for more? Can their objectives be met by squeezing and adapting the traditional PPP paradigm?

For those primarily focused on urban poverty reduction, one of the problems with the existing approach towards private sector participation in municipal service delivery is that it takes PPP delivery models developed in the North and applies them in the South. Without questioning the possible benefits of private sector participation or discouraging private sector investment in developing countries, it is wise to explore whether these Northern models are well constructed for the prevailing context of poverty and capacity deficiency found in municipalities in developing countries. Can the basic parameters of the partnership be focused on maximising the potential for the poor, rather than making do with what can be achieved within existing constructs? Can the scope be defined in relation to the needs of the poor rather than defining the scope in relation to a contract type?

Another cause of disquiet is that the vast range of lessons that have been learnt through decades of urban poverty projects have seemingly been cast aside in the rush towards the partnership approach. Many PPPs have been developed by economic, financial, legal and engineering experts, who are knowledgeable in the mechanics of contracts but quite inexperienced in the nature and scope of the social and institutional problems of impoverished cities in developing countries. Few have drawn on the vast knowledge that has been developed in the course of implementing decades of service delivery projects with poor communities.

In order to consider the potential of private sector participation in the delivery of services to the poor, it is helpful to stand back from current approaches, models and contract types. Rather than asking how a model contract can be adapted to suit the poor, this chapter focuses on how service delivery processes can be **constructed** to best respond to the needs of the poor. In looking towards the private sector, it suggests that municipalities should be exploring strategic change more fully and promoting deliberate contributions to existing poverty reduction objectives. It requires forward planning and action to ensure that the foundations of the partnership framework are more appropriately defined, both in themselves and in relation to other poverty-focused activities. This discussion, therefore, considers how a municipality might go about developing a poverty strategy for a partnership, and highlights the key ingredients of that strategy. Drawing on the lessons of poverty reduction processes and policy, it proposes ways in which municipalities can integrate private sector participation in a livelihoods approach to poverty reduction.

Ideally, a framework for focusing a service partnership on the poor grows out of a broader municipal poverty strategy and participatory initiative. If municipalities do not have an established poverty strategy, steps can be taken to locate partnerships within the broader agenda of poverty and poverty reduction by:

- developing better understanding of the characteristics of poverty;
- defining the needs and objectives of the poor in relation to services;
- identifying the key processes that underlie a partnership involving the poor;
- identifying the key issues of concern to local communities and households; and
- identifying the key stakeholders and assets that support existing livelihoods.

Establishing a Sound Basis for a Poverty-focused Partnership

The following section describes some of the key actions municipalities can take to develop partnerships that contribute to poverty reduction goals. The lessons discussed below, while not comprehensive, point towards the types of changes

5

Links to Box
7.5

| Box **5.2** | **Differing Experiences of Poverty**
A South–East Asian Profile |

The following household stories illustrate the differing experiences of urban poverty in Vientiane Laos. The stories are supplemented by poverty wheels that portray the key cause–effect parameters. A simple comparison in the wheels illustrates both the different experiences and recurring themes of poverty.

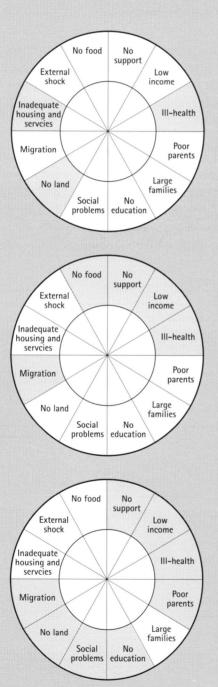

Insecure tenants

Madame A is around 30 years old. She is married with two children and is pregnant. Three years ago she and her family were evicted from a house in Sihom and moved to Thong Khankham. There they occupy a timber and corrugated-iron-clad house on stilts. Their rent is around 10,000 kip.* The house was empty before they moved in as it was considered uninhabitable. It is the innermost house in this area, on the lowest, most waterlogged ground. the house sits in a mix of flood-waters, sewage and solid waste. To reach the house the family picks its way along 10 metres of rotting timber. The insanitary and damp environmental conditions around the house cause Madame A to worry for the health of her children. Her eldest son had malaria recently. They continue to live there because it is cheap, they have no jobs and cannot afford anything else.

An abandoned migrant

Madame M is 62 years old. She migrated from China in 1960 when she was 15 years old, and her young baby died during the journey. When she settled in Laos she was given Laotian nationality. Her husband has left her and is remarried. Madame M lives by herself in a tiny hut. She is alone and homesick, and would like to return to China. Her monthly income is 60,000 kip. She collects and eats vegetables that grow in the neighbourhood, and sometimes buys rice and fish. She used to sell noodle soup, but people did not pay. Her income now comes mainly from cleaning and washing for other households.

Her hut has a sheet-metal roof, and as it is not raised, during the wet season the hut is constantly flooded. The pathway to her house is narrow and very muddy. She does not have an electricity or water connection. Instead she uses a candle for light and buys water from neighbours. Her house is behind that of a rich family who constantly pressurise her to move. She says she settled there first and will never move. She has nowhere else to go.

Although she has been severely sick several times, she does not visit the doctor. When she has nothing to eat, a neighbour or the village authority provides her with cash or rice. She never borrows money because she knows she can not pay it back. Madame M once saved 30,000 kip but lost it in the national lottery. She believes her poverty is caused by her lack of ideas about how to make what is needed for her daily life; she also believes that she inherited it from her forefathers.

A beggar and drug user

Madame X is from an ethnic minority in the rural areas of Laos. Her husband fled to France and she has been alone for 30 years. She lived in several places in Vientiane and then moved to Nong Chan; she will soon have to move again. When she first came to the city she sold herbal medicine, and sewed cement bags together for rice farmers to use in rice harvesting and processing. She is illiterate; she worked on a farm and never went to school. She has no family to rely on and now she begs in the market. She gets around 13,000 kip per day. She smokes heroin to relieve her pain.

* kip = Lao monetary unit

Source: Adapted from Plummer, 2000b

that the PPP must embrace if future solutions are to bring about maximum benefit to poor urban dwellers. The lessons of participation, capacity building, integration, variability and diversity, gender marginalisation and the role of existing service providers are useful examples of service delivery focused on the poor. This chapter does not stand alone, however; key poverty-related issues are detailed in each of the chapters that follow.

Developing a Better Understanding of the Characteristics of Poverty

The degree to which those within the administrative and political arms of a municipality understand the scope and nature of the poverty within their jurisdiction varies considerably. In-depth understanding of the poor is patchy, and officials' confidence in their own knowledge is often exaggerated. Needless to say, the introduction of the private service operators to contexts in which there is little knowledge or understanding of the needs and dominating characteristics of poverty is unlikely to bring about changes in the quality of the lives of poor people. It is futile to speak of pro-poor private sector participation without such knowledge. Disempowered communities, a weak NGO sector, uninformed or powerless municipal officials and a lack of political will together create a bias that is impossible to counter.

Before formulating a service partnership (as with any activity targeting the poor), a municipality must first consolidate and/or confirm its understanding of the nature of poverty and poverty responses in the city. Evidence from poverty reduction programmes suggests that a process that promotes understanding of the community and the dynamics of their neighbourhoods, lanes and households is a key aspect of successful interventions. It is not only necessary to know how many poor people there are and where they live, but to understand who the poor are, the nature and varying capacities of households, and the role and capacity of individuals within those households. It is necessary to understand how households and individuals survive. Experience suggests that this step is frequently omitted from partnership development, and it is included here to remind municipal officials that the partnership approach does not preclude the need for an adequate understanding of poor communities' needs.

☐   Locating service needs in relation to livelihoods

For a municipality focused on improving services to the poor, the first stage is to develop this understanding of the poor's livelihoods, to develop links into poor communities that enable information to be channelled and institutional knowledge to be developed. Participatory poverty assessments and livelihood analyses are effective participatory processes through which governmental and non-governmental actors can develop knowledge about the livelihoods of poor communities. Such studies involve the poor in identifying their own problems and needs, or the assets that structure their livelihoods.

A primary purpose of this targeted information collection is to ascertain the specific nature of poverty for a full range of inhabitants, from the robust to the vulnerable. This includes the nature of livelihood strategies and how various types of households cope in a crisis. To this extent it should examine various trends and stages in the lives of the poor. It should expose the inter-relationships between the various dimensions of poverty and thereby highlight causal links between service and non-service problems. The process should provide an assessment of the structure, dynamics, severity and characteristics of poverty in a community and within households. Such information is essential if investment, interventions and interactions are to be targeted and effective in alleviating poverty. These approaches differ from other demand-assessment methods[3] in that they are qualitative, inclusive and open.

Carried out effectively, qualitative assessments can form the basis of community participation within the partnership and delivery process. Participatory action should not only give a voice to powerful, elite members of the community (who are normally men) but also empower the weaker and more vulnerable groups to express *their* perception of *their* poverty.

5

☐ Understanding existing supply mechanisms

The information collected through this analysis should also include the various forms of support that the poor can access. For instance, NGOs may have established effective credit and savings groups, which would form useful models for poor communities. Rag-pickers may have organised themselves into cooperatives and created effective micro-enterprises for tertiary-level solid waste removal. Water-sellers may have successfully scaled up their deliveries to new peri-urban areas. The municipality may have developed effective community liaison; health workers may have achieved some success with mother and child clinics.

The research should also identify the gaps in current supply and find out how they are filled by the poor. How do the poor get their water when there is no network supply, or when standpipes are broken? How do women and children find safe and private spaces to wash and defecate? Where do poor households dump their rubbish, and what are the impacts (on, for example, health)? Knowledge about gaps and supply mechanisms is crucial to an understanding of the impacts of change, and the potential roles of communities, NGOs and the private sector. They provide further details of the context, the people and how they manage. Understanding existing access arrangements is often crucial to ensure that the partnership arrangement does not produce unintended impacts and to initiate solutions that mitigate negative impacts.

Defining the Objectives of the Poor in Relation to Services

This process of needs identification described above enables a municipality to clarify specific objectives relating to the poor. Most importantly, it enables poor communities to become directly involved in prioritising objectives. Clearly, a service partnership is not successfully focused on the poor if poor communities and households have not placed priority on the need for that service, and do not prioritise household expenditure on it. Municipal managers who have a clear understanding of objectives are more able to create appropriate solutions than those who are unprepared and led by the availability of solutions (such as private sector investment) rather than by the nature of the problem.

Of course, the definition of objectives is a skill and requires capacity. It is likely that poor people do not express their needs and objectives in a form that all actors understand, and that some municipal officials will not understand the importance of their objectives. Whether directly or through NGOs and other agents, it is the municipality's – not the private sector's – responsibility to ensure that objectives and priorities are properly translated and incorporated into municipal action plans for service delivery.

Identifying Key Processes that Underlie a Partnership Involving the Poor

Over recent decades, grassroots organisations, governments and local and international donors have learnt a vast range of lessons about poverty and poverty reduction. These lessons are essential to the development of more effective and sustainable poverty reduction programmes, policies and pilots. It is not the purpose of this book to dwell on detailed lessons; the goal here is to consider how partnerships can be focused and how to optimise the contribution of a PPP.

To this end, the following discussion focuses on six key lessons: community participation; capacity building; integrated (multisectoral) poverty reduction responses; as well as the importance of understanding variability and diversity; gender marginalisation and enhancing existing assets. It describes the lessons learnt to date, and asks whether these have been or can be taken into the arena of private sector participation. Accompanying this text are boxes illustrating the tools and techniques that can assist in this process.

The demand-responsive, participatory approach

Perhaps the foremost lesson of poverty reduction activities concerns the process of delivery – specifically, ensuring that the decision-making over the nature and scope of services (or other interventions) responds to the demands of the poor themselves, and not to the factors and stakeholders that determine supply. In relation to basic service delivery, the importance of facilitating service improvements that are demand-led cannot be overestimated. Decades of improvements to slums and squatter settlements have proved unsustainable because infrastructure was provided to low-income residents through a process that did not involve them in decision-making.

In order to establish the level of service demand, a variety of tools and techniques were developed that enabled governments, agencies and funders to know what the urban poor needed and how it could best be delivered. Experience showed that the poor must become participants in rather than beneficiaries of the process, and that development processes must be designed with in-built flexibility to ensure that participation could be achieved. The participation of poor communities is essential to ensure efficacy and sustainability in project ends, and to maximise the benefits of project means.[4]

Despite the wide dissemination of the benefits of involving communities in development, and the few initiatives that are currently including communities, a vast number of PPPs have been and continue to be developed without this participation. Notwithstanding the work of more recent innovative pilots conducted on a small scale, most PPPs in water and sanitation (and many in solid waste) developed over the last decade have excluded the poor from the process. Operators argue that they respond to consumer demand. Low-income groups, like their middle- or high-income urban neighbours, are treated as customers, but most do not differentiate between the poor and the non-poor. Few have taken account of the fundamentally different nature of a poor customer base, and many are unfamiliar with the characteristics of (and constraints on) poor households. Even among those municipalities experienced in and aware of the benefits of community participation, many have not effectively merged private sector participation with community participation in service partnerships.

Yet those innovative PPPs (see, for example, Boxes 7.3 and 7.6) that have incorporated communities into the delivery process expose the benefits that participation brings. At the same time they draw attention to the need for operators to change standardised methods: to adapt to differing levels of demand within a community, and to provide different levels of service or means of payment. They also draw attention to the possibility for increasing community involvement to reduce costs, and increasing ownership by providing labour to the operator and overseeing simple construction tasks.

The critical role of communities in PPPs focused on the poor is developed in detail in Chapter 6.

Capacity building

The capacity of communities to maximise the potential of development processes and inputs is often limited by the lack of education, their disempowered position and a lack of familiarity with participatory processes and decision-making. If this is the case, a key challenge to be met in the early stages of partnerships is the development of a strategy for addressing the weak capacity of the community (particularly the women) and the formulation of appropriate and contextually specific mechanisms for their involvement. A capacity building strategy should address both skills development and organisational capacity. Individual training must address a number of key areas: confidence building, literacy, legal literacy, micro-credit and, where appropriate, technical skills for service delivery. Poor men and women need skills to work in teams and to negotiate with operator/government representatives and other interest groups. Groups need management and accounting skills, and improved capacity to access information. In some cases the dynamics of a group and its leadership will also change and with that a shift in the way a neighbourhood prioritises service (or other) needs is likely to occur.

The development of appropriate, effective and meaningful community participation can be achieved through a process of capacity building and support. Experience suggests that it is essential to build capacity:

- within the community, to build understanding of the potential of community involvement and to create mechanisms through which the community can play an effective and meaningful role;
- within the partnership (based on an understanding of the potential role of the community and the mechanisms for establishing effective interfaces with the poor); and
- with those individuals and teams that work directly with poor communities.

In addition, evidence clearly points to the importance of creating effective organisations at the community level (and institutional arrangements at other levels) to structure community involvement. Group formation is dependent, inter alia, on existing organisations, existing capacities, gender relations and social dynamics. Various lessons stress the distinct possibility of the non-poor capturing the benefits when community groups are not representative or are dominated by the non-poor elite. Experience has shown that disaggregating the community into smaller groups (women's groups, user groups and other vulnerable people's groups) to initiate participation and build confidence at the outset can strengthen its ongoing capacity to participate and establish sustainable benefits.

In PPPs a key part of the development of participatory processes is the consideration of how the poor interact with partnership representatives. The private sector and government may both need significant support and a great deal of attitudinal change. Building capacity in implementing pro-poor, gender sensitive, participatory methods can be achieved through activities targeted at three levels: decision-makers, management and implementation staff.

In order to support the capacity building process, and underpin the partnership objectives and the efforts of those working with communities, supporting structures (be they NGOs or other forms of expert support) are often key aspects of the delivery process. The exact configuration of this support is dependent on the institutional assets of actors in any given situation.

☐ Integrated poverty responses

Participatory poverty assessments undertaken in urban contexts in developing countries indicate that the urban poor suffer from a wide range of interlinked problems relating to low income, poor health, illiteracy, insanitary physical conditions, disempowerment and so on. Poverty interventions have, increasingly, attempted to address this interlinked nature. The experience of various environmental improvement projects has proved that the benefits of water, sanitation, drainage and solid waste programmes, for instance, are maximised by conducting these improvements within an integrated programme. Improving services on their own often creates unsustainable interventions,[5] but improving services at the same time as empowering communities and individuals, increasing income-earning opportunities, facilitating credit, promoting hygiene and health, and/or underpinning education activities empowers communities to access the environmental improvements.

Seen in the context of poverty reduction processes, one of the primary problems caused by sectoral private sector participation in service delivery is that it puts aside the lessons that have been learnt about integrated poverty reduction responses, tertiary level infrastructure interventions, and the need to address the multidimensional problems of poverty in an integrated way.

Yet experience in PPPs to date has done little to acknowledge this experience. One of the important implications of the private sector taking over water and sanitation delivery particularly, is that this ringfencing process removes an important aspect of the multisectoral approach to poverty reduction – the money. While *community development* may be at the heart of participatory approaches to poverty reduction, and *income generation activities* promote sustainability, *infrastructure development* has often provided the financial foundation – the springboard – for other activities. Once the delivery of infrastructure and services has been isolated through a PPP, convergence of poverty reduction activities has rarely been established.

Whereas the single-sector approach proceeds with a solution pertaining to one sector (water and sanitation, solid waste or electricity) and creates linkages within that sector (e.g., between middle-income and low-income areas, subsidies, etc.), the multisectoral approach to poverty reduction creates linkages around the poor's needs (e.g., water supply, health promotion, housing upgrades, income generation, community development). In some rare cases, non-physical interventions such as hygiene promotion, community development and credit facilities have been taken on by the private operator and a degree of synergy achieved around sustainable service delivery. Such was the case in El Alto, where the operator agreed to participate in a pilot scheme that would rapidly increase the number of households connected to the network (see Box 7.6). In this case, the operator saw the benefit of community participation and hygiene promotion, as these would increase the ability of households and communities to make use of the water and sanitation services. It also recognised and responded to the poor's need for financial support to fund the costs of connections and in-house installations.

While evidence tells us that urban poverty reduction is more effective when an integrated approach is adopted – i.e., that purely physical improvements are often unsustainable in low-income communities – evidence also suggests that private sector participation in urban infrastructure improvements can be more effective because a range of efficiencies and benefits can be brought to bear to produce broader and more immediate improvements. Yet it is also likely that private sector participation can reduce the scope for *direct* multisectoral poverty reduction initiatives. In order to maximise the integration of poverty responses when a private operator is involved, municipalities must therefore ensure that the formulation and management of a service delivery partnership is carried out in the context of other linked poverty responses. They have a responsibility to facilitate integration and to work with all partners to nominate the stakeholder that is most able to perform a specific role. In order to focus partnerships on the poor, municipal decision-makers must perform a coordinating role ensuring that, at the strategic, planning and implementation levels, the activities of PPP service delivery are linked into other activities.

Responding to the variability and diversity of the poor

Another important lesson of poverty reduction, particularly relevant in the context of partnership development and cost recovery, is that the poor's ability to make use of a service varies. Their use of a service generally increases and decreases in relation to a range of dynamic factors and livelihood assets. Poor people develop complex strategies to ensure their survival in a crisis, or simply to cope with seasonal variations in their poverty. These might include a variety of mechanisms to increase income and strategies that result in the reduction of household expenditure. In particular, the economies that poor households make by cutting down on education, health care and food, and cutting back on the utilisation of services. Participatory assessments are useful in explaining the composition of these strategies and the importance of reducing household expenditure in services during a crisis.[6]

This variability is an important issue in the design of new approaches to service delivery. In essence, the degree of access and the need for improved water and waste services will change over time. Service delivery approaches must respond to the poor's need to upgrade during plentiful times, and to downgrade during lean times. Interventions that do not provide the poor with the flexibility to change service demand and expenditure, but result in fixed outgoings, reduce the range of strategies that the poor can employ to cope with their poverty. Irrespective of the standard of service they receive, this will increase, not decrease, the vulnerability of the poorest.

Box **5.3**   Simplified Disaggregation of Low-income Communities
Biratnagar, Nepal

Links to Boxes
6.7, 9.2, 12.5

	Very poor	Middle poor	Poor
Income	• Ranges from 0 to NPR* 900	• NPR 1500–2000	• NPR 2000–3000
Possible employment	• Unemployed, irregular or seasonal employment, one wage earner • Domestic staff, child labour, destitutes, occasional labour • Women and children work	• Daily waged employment, no security, one wage earner • Sweepers, domestic staff, vendors, rickshaw pullers, labourers, bus conductors • Women work (perhaps at home)	• Semi-skilled but poorly paid, perhaps supplemented by part-time work of second wage earner, one member regular secure employment • Carpenters, masons, unskilled government or factory workers
Social circumstances	• Extended families with up to 17 members • Marginalised groups • Girls marry at 12–14 years	• 8–10 members in household • Some marginalised groups especially tribal groups and scheduled castes • Girls marry at 12–15 years	• 7–8 members in household Less likely to be marginalised, can access assistance • Girls marry at 14–17 years
Food	• Have little to eat • One meal per day rice/curry with green chilli • (Male) earner takes meal first	• Two meals per day • Rice/dhal/curry with chilli • Women may miss meals to save	• Two meals per day • Some chicken/mutton and rice/dhal/ curry or chapati • All family members eat, may give to the very poor
Cooking fuel	• Use animal stools and straw made locally	• Collect firewood, dry bushes etc	• Collect firewood, dry leaves of sugar cane and bushes, some have kerosene stoves
Clothing	• Get clothes from other people and beg for cloth	• Obtain second-hand clothes from bazaars at special festivals	• Obtain second-hand clothes for children to wear to school
Education	• Only a few go to school up to fifth standard	• Up to 35% boys and 25% girls go to school up to grade 5	• Both boys and girls go to school (approximately 50%) up to grade 5
Health care	• May go to government hospitals • Traditional medicines • No support structures to rely on	• May go to government hospitals • Can't afford/rarely buy medicines, rely on support structures	• Government hospitals/clinics • Buy medicine, borrow if necessary, just manage
Credit/Debt	• No confidence in borrowing or lending. Cannot obtain loans, beg in an emergency	• Borrow from neighbours in an emergency	• Borrow from local merchants at 36–60% per month
Housing	• Homeless or temporary (huts bamboo, straw or plastic)	• Temporary shelter	• Semi-permanent dwelling of permanent materials
Tenure	• No security as tenants or owners, encroach on government land	• Some rent	• Some have forms of land titles and security of tenure • Some rent
Water	• No access to potable water, or 50-metre walk to communal supply	• Access via communal standpipe	• Access via communal tube well
Sanitation	• No access to latrine, use road/ riverside etc	• Access to communal latrine or use roadside, field	• May share facilities (pit latrine)
Lighting	• Rely on street lighting at night and kerosene lamps	• Kerosene lamps • Illegal connections • Neighbours' connections	• Some have illegal connections or simple globe, or some form of line connection from a neighbour

* NPR = Nepalese rupees (NPR 1 is approximately equivalent to US$0.013)

Source: Plummer and Slater, 2001

It is also necessary to recognise that there is a great diversity in the capability, vulnerability and capacity of low-income groups. Urban areas, communities, neighbourhoods, households and individuals experience different levels of poverty and are affected in very different ways. Low-income communities are often said to be 'poor', as if there is only one idea of 'poor'; but in practice, urban poor communities are heterogeneous, and poverty responses must respond to the diversity of their problems, needs and priorities. Box 5.3 provides an income/assets-based picture of this diversity in the context of Nepal.

Various poverty assessments show that a significant difference between the poorest urban dwellers and their slightly-less poor and better-off poor neighbours lies in the way households prioritise service needs and fund service expenditure. The very poor spend no money whatsoever on water, sanitation or solid waste services; the middle-poor spend some on water, and none on sanitation or solid waste, and they cut back on water expenditure in a crisis. The better-off poor are willing and able to pay for water and solid waste services, but do not always prioritise sanitation services. They are likely to maintain this expenditure through difficult times, but cut back in emergencies. They have more choice about the adaptations they make and are thus less vulnerable. This is developed further in Box 6.14.

A range of urban poverty initiatives have emphasised the importance of assessment processes that give a voice to all the members of the community and respond to the variability and diversity of their needs. Lessons emphasise that while service provision may be improved, the access various groups and individuals have to these services will remain unequal without mechanisms that redress marginalisation. Most large-scale private sector interventions envisage the low-income group as homogenous, or as a geographically defined area requiring one common solution. These attitudes can be even more entrenched than they were in previous methods of municipal provision. Few have begun the process of disaggregation, which recognises the varying capacities of the poor. Yet the small-scale private sector often works effectively with this diversity, giving poor householders a choice of service and financial options.

Responding to gender biases and marginalisation

Experience also shows that gender affects the perception of key problems and service deficiencies. It is well established that women are the managers of waste, for example, and of water for domestic use. If male household members have water provided for them on a daily basis and do not participate in its collection, they are unlikely to prioritise it. If the girls and women are the collectors, as is typically the case, they are more than familiar with the problems of waiting times, distances and heavy loads. They are also able to define the impact of inadequate water on other aspects of their lives: teenage girls, for example, who leave school early to queue for water; women and children who are unable to use communal toilet facilities at night due to the threat of rape or violence; or female market vendors who risk travelling long distances in the early hours of the morning to wash vegetables.

However, typically it is the male elite that has the loudest voice within a community and the service needs of poor women are neglected. The political, cultural and social marginalisation of women in many societies means that development processes must find appropriate ways to give space to women to allow them to express their perspectives and participate meaningfully in delivery processes. At a later date they should be asked to provide feedback on the impact of interventions.[7] Conventional PPPs have not yet acknowledged or incorporated the large range of gender issues that affect service delivery. The gender aspects of poverty-focused PPPs are introduced in Chapter 7.

Identifying the key stakeholders and assets that support existing livelihoods

The poor depend on a range of actors for their services. Evidence from a wide range of poverty focused activities in various sectors has shown that building on the potential of established support systems (such as NGOs), established

5

Links to Boxes
3.5, 6.13, 7.2, 7.3, 7.11, 7.18, 8.12, 9.8

| Box **5.4** | **Integrated Poverty Responses**
Buenos Aires, Argentina

Looking back on our 10 years of work in Barrio San Jorge in Buenos Aires (see also Box 7.3), we realise that our main challenge has been to support the rekindling of community action and organisation, and in so doing, to support the reconstruction of social capital based on the promotion of solidarity and reciprocity between neighbours. The activity of IIED-AL in Barrio San Jorge throughout the last decade has maintained one overall objective: to improve living conditions by means of the organisation and participation of the inhabitants in a comprehensive development process. This approach implies a questioning of the traditional government and NGO approaches to poverty reduction in Argentina, which are generally short-term, sectoral and top-down programmes and projects.

Our work in Barrio San Jorge was based on two main strategies: the promotion of a more integrated and long-term approach, which builds on continuous and complementary improvements, and the involvement of stakeholders, who were identified as individuals, groups, organisations or institutions whose interests could be affected by the initiatives.

The first strategy stemmed from the acknowledgement that the inhabitants of Barrio San Jorge (and other informal settlements) have multiple and diverse needs and problems. Virtually all are rooted in a common cause: poverty. Most are closely inter-related. The development of a more integrated approach to these needs has not led to the need to implement projects in every sector, but to the development of an integrated perspective in every initiative in which we were involved. This perspective was based on the recognition of the intersectoral nature and effects of all the interventions; an examination of their coordination can often ensure that they complement and reinforce each other. The building-material bank is an example of this approach. This not only supports housing improvement but was used to give advice about construction techniques and design. It also served to disseminate information about the relationship between habitat and health. It also developed a credit system to allow the inhabitants to purchase materials on credit, which helped them to learn how to manage credit. The building materials warehouse was also essential for storing materials for the water and sewerage project.

Another advantage of having many initiatives in different sectors was the availability of different funding sources, as many external funders will only consider providing support for particular sectors. This also meant that if one initiative was interrupted, it was possible to continue with others. Achieving continuity is important in maintaining community organisation. The inhabitants of Barrio San Jorge have experienced several interventions animated by political interests – mostly before a local or provincial election – which, after a short period, became of little value or even useless. The extension of water supplies from the nearby factory, which had been carried out in part because of the political aspirations of the factory's president, was an important achievement, but the lack of standpipe maintenance created drainage problems and pools of stagnant water. On one occasion, the main street of Barrio San Jorge was filled with soil and levelled, but the soil was not compacted, and after the first rain shower it became so muddy that it restricted the use of motor vehicles for several days, just before an election. Such interventions have a short life and the inhabitants take over the maintenance and repair, despite their limited resources.

The continuity of actions and the achievement of tangible results have been crucial to the community and its morale. For instance, the mother and child centre encouraged a growing interest from small groups of residents who supported the initiative – mostly women – in initiating new activities. After groups had laid pipes for water and sewerage, others went on to lay pavements. The inhabitants of Barrio San Jorge needed support not for one or two development projects but for continuous actions that supported a long-term development process.

Our second strategy consisted of working in partnership with the different actors involved in the development process, i.e., not just community groups but also local and provincial government agencies, other NGOs, the private sector and donors. The interaction with such a wide range of organisations taught us several lessons:

- it is important to establish where and with whom common goals can be developed.
- Partnerships with any stakeholders are time-consuming exercises in persuasion, lobbying and bargaining to make different views, rationales and priorities compatible.
- Negotiations with local actors produce important results; at the same time, partnership also implies taking considerable risks and having to bear the consequences.
- The development of partnerships with other organisations is important, but given the unpredictable performance of some organisations, experience suggests the need to analyse costs and benefits.

Source: Schusterman and Hardoy, 1997

delivery mechanisms (such as water tankers or independent waste collectors) and established relationships, can be quite critical in enhancing the success of new interventions, safeguarding against impacts on the most vulnerable groups, and facilitating immediate improvements and interim arrangements. The large-scale private operator thus becomes one partner among many, working towards solutions that meet social as well as physical and financial objectives.

A number of actors play a variety of roles in a focused partnership arrangement. Together they will be able to respond to the specific needs of the poor and take up those processes that promote poverty reduction. The development and implementation of a partnership framework should therefore include communities and their representatives, such as the NGOs and small-scale service providers on which they currently rely. This enables the meaningful participation of poor communities at planning and implementation stages. Depending on the organisations and resources in a specific context, it may involve a number of linked and coordinated actors and organisations offering the skills and resources needed to address the key livelihood aspects affecting service sustainability in poor areas. The role of the potential partners involved in arrangements focused on the poor are developed in Chapter 6.

The Sustainable Livelihoods Approach

A 'livelihood' comprises the capabilities, assets (including both material and social resources) and activities required for a means of living. A livelihood is sustainable when it can cope with and recover from stresses and shocks and maintains or enhances its capabilities and assets both now and in the future, while not undermining the natural resource base.[8]

During the 1990s, a significant number of the lessons described in this chapter about poverty responses were acknowledged and consolidated into policy-making through the development of a comprehensive approach to poverty reduction, referred to as the sustainable livelihoods (SL) approach.[9] In essence, the SL approach aims to provide a cohesive methodology for poverty reduction that focuses on the livelihoods and vulnerability of the poor. It builds on and resembles, but simultaneously challenges, many previous development approaches. At its core is the understanding that people must be placed at the centre of any development initiative.[10]

The SL approach includes and promotes the development of PPPs in service delivery. It highlights the importance of transforming structures, and specifically emphasises the need for a range of governmental, non-governmental and private actors to work together in the pursuit of poverty reduction. This is based on the lesson that all too frequently, existing (and transforming) structures do not always work to the benefit of the poor,[11] and that the processes that frame the livelihoods of the poor systematically restrict them and their opportunities for advancement.[12] In close association, the SL framework promotes the transformation of processes, which result in effective structures. This is to be established and sustained by the development of enabling frameworks, incentive systems, regulatory environments, and formal processes that encourage private sector activity; and by considering the informal practices and power relations that frame relationships between the poor and other actors.

The purpose of introducing the SL framework here is to consider it as a mechanism through which municipalities and other actors can bring a poverty focus to a service partnership. The SL framework, its principles and core concepts provide a useful starting point for the creation and re-creation of partnerships that aim to contribute to poverty reduction. Because it provides an analytical framework for integrating ideas and methods, it is an ideal tool for municipalities to use in formulating a structured and systematic approach to poverty reduction in which people, not outputs, are the focal points. Municipalities and other actors can use it to both plan new partnerships that work to the benefit of the poor, and to review existing partnership arrangements. These principles and their implications on service partnerships are illustrated in Box 5.5.

5

Box 5.5   Incorporating the Principles of Sustainable Livelihoods in PPPs

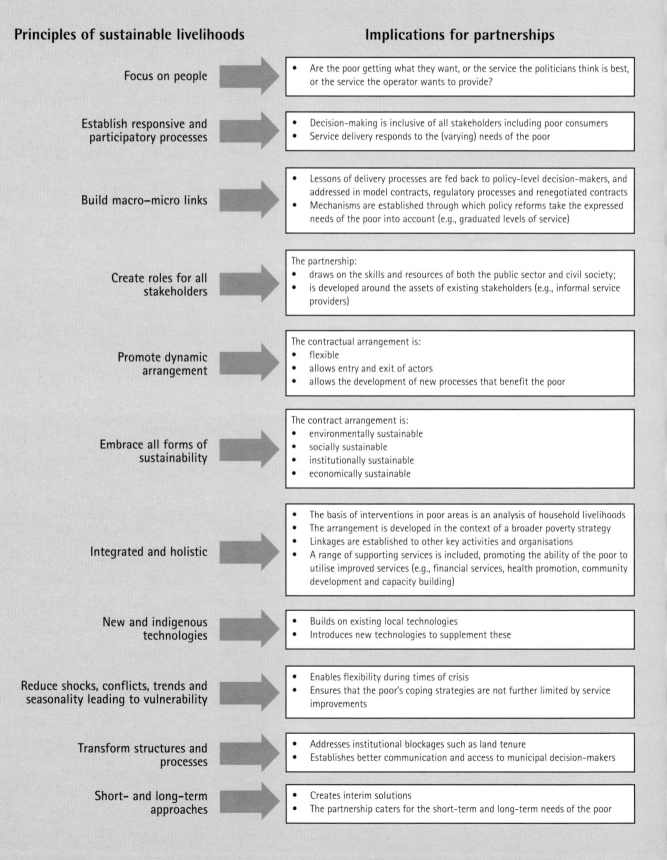

Principles of sustainable livelihoods	Implications for partnerships
Focus on people	• Are the poor getting what they want, or the service the politicians think is best, or the service the operator wants to provide?
Establish responsive and participatory processes	• Decision-making is inclusive of all stakeholders including poor consumers • Service delivery responds to the (varying) needs of the poor
Build macro–micro links	• Lessons of delivery processes are fed back to policy-level decision-makers, and addressed in model contracts, regulatory processes and renegotiated contracts • Mechanisms are established through which policy reforms take the expressed needs of the poor into account (e.g., graduated levels of service)
Create roles for all stakeholders	The partnership: • draws on the skills and resources of both the public sector and civil society; • is developed around the assets of existing stakeholders (e.g., informal service providers)
Promote dynamic arrangement	The contractual arrangement is: • flexible • allows entry and exit of actors • allows the development of new processes that benefit the poor
Embrace all forms of sustainability	The contract arrangement is: • environmentally sustainable • socially sustainable • institutionally sustainable • economically sustainable
Integrated and holistic	• The basis of interventions in poor areas is an analysis of household livelihoods • The arrangement is developed in the context of a broader poverty strategy • Linkages are established to other key activities and organisations • A range of supporting services is included, promoting the ability of the poor to utilise improved services (e.g., financial services, health promotion, community development and capacity building)
New and indigenous technologies	• Builds on existing local technologies • Introduces new technologies to supplement these
Reduce shocks, conflicts, trends and seasonality leading to vulnerability	• Enables flexibility during times of crisis • Ensures that the poor's coping strategies are not further limited by service improvements
Transform structures and processes	• Addresses institutional blockages such as land tenure • Establishes better communication and access to municipal decision-makers
Short- and long-term approaches	• Creates interim solutions • The partnership caters for the short-term and long-term needs of the poor

A Poverty-focused Partnership

A poverty-focused partnership is thus an integral part of a broader strategic approach to poverty reduction. If possible, it should originate from an overall poverty strategy and be developed to link closely with other parallel actions. This means that municipalities must facilitate the coordination necessary to achieve this approach.[13] The first responsibility of the municipality is to define the needs and objectives of the poor. A range of processes, actors and actions (illustrated in Box 5.6) are central to poverty-focused partnerships.

Perhaps the most fundamental shift requires all partners to recognise that **people, rather than the service, are at the centre** of the initiative. Any one service or service partnership is just a portion of an overall response to poverty, and must be envisaged as a contribution that needs to be coordinated. A single sector partnership is never a holistic response: it always requires interaction with other parts. It is impossible to avoid the fact that water supply or any other service is just one dimension of improved physical wellbeing, and improved physical wellbeing is just one livelihood outcome. Benefits will be maximised if service delivery initiatives are undertaken in relation to other livelihood outcomes.

It is also necessary to ensure that any potential **negative impacts** on livelihoods are identified at the outset, and that mechanisms are built into the partnership framework to mitigate these effects. For instance, an ill-conceived partnership approach can affect vulnerable groups who cannot afford the service. Tenants might have to suffer higher household expenditures even though they have not been party to the decision-making. Women might have to reprioritise household finances to make payments; informal service providers (such as rag-pickers and water-sellers) may lose their livelihoods.

Accordingly, an important corollary to the approach proposed here is the need for **skilled urban management** – management practices that bring together very different actors, like the poor and the private sector, and emphasise the importance of integrated and strategic approaches to urban management and city development. This is not about the private sector role so much as the strategy and construction of the approach, and the capacity of the municipal or public sector body to assemble an arrangement that has a strategic intention and the capability of addressing the needs of the poor.

A second important corollary is that the **donor sector**, so active in the field of PPPs, must promote greater convergence of the approaches they advocate. If PPPs are to become effective in meeting the needs of the poor, they must be linked to the livelihood responses to poverty.

A third important corollary is that the **private sector needs to build capacity**. Despite the confidence of some international private operators, their capacity to work with the poor is often quite limited. Greater competency and new attitudes in the private sector will make for more sensitive partners, better able to grasp and work towards poverty reduction goals. In order to sit at the table with other partners working directly with the poor, the private sector requires more skills, many of which can be learnt by exploring the lessons of poverty reduction.

The implementation of a new approach to PPPs will not always be easy. As this book promotes a revised approach to PPPs, it is essential to confront constraints to such changes and to consider how any change might be achieved. Accordingly, for a municipality to succeed in bringing about a focused partnership arrangement:

- the approach and methodology must be **realistic**. It is necessary for advocates and implementers to acknowledge the vast differences that lie between policy formulation and the reality of bringing together public sector constraints and private sector interests.
- The framework must be open, **inclusive** and comprehensive, so that all potential avenues of exploration are represented even if they seem overly ambitious at the outset.

Box **5.6**   A Strategic Approach to Focusing Partnerships on the Poor

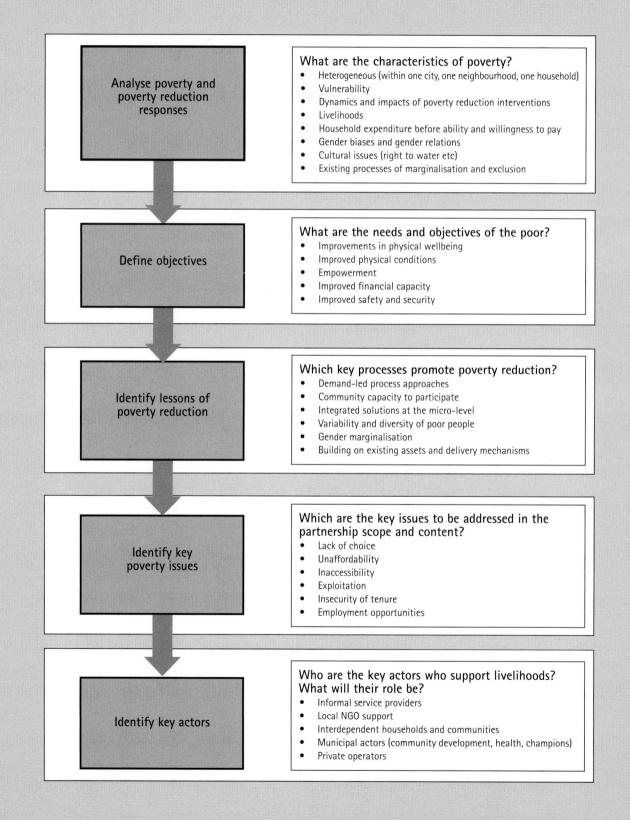

What are the characteristics of poverty?
- Heterogeneous (within one city, one neighbourhood, one household)
- Vulnerability
- Dynamics and impacts of poverty reduction interventions
- Livelihoods
- Household expenditure before ability and willingness to pay
- Gender biases and gender relations
- Cultural issues (right to water etc)
- Existing processes of marginalisation and exclusion

Analyse poverty and poverty reduction responses

What are the needs and objectives of the poor?
- Improvements in physical wellbeing
- Improved physical conditions
- Empowerment
- Improved financial capacity
- Improved safety and security

Define objectives

Which key processes promote poverty reduction?
- Demand-led process approaches
- Community capacity to participate
- Integrated solutions at the micro-level
- Variability and diversity of poor people
- Gender marginalisation
- Building on existing assets and delivery mechanisms

Identify lessons of poverty reduction

Which are the key issues to be addressed in the partnership scope and content?
- Lack of choice
- Unaffordability
- Inaccessibility
- Exploitation
- Insecurity of tenure
- Employment opportunities

Identify key poverty issues

Who are the key actors who support livelihoods? What will their role be?
- Informal service providers
- Local NGO support
- Interdependent households and communities
- Municipal actors (community development, health, champions)
- Private operators

Identify key actors

Introducing change can be remarkably straightforward when the will is in place, but it also requires capacity. What can seem radical in one context can be seen as a simple practical change in another. The key objective is to bring about a shift in approach – in arrangements, processes and actors – that will most effectively meet the livelihood outcomes defined by the poor. The concept of appropriateness is central to this end. A solution that has a sound basis and is allowed to evolve is more likely to bring about the required result than a solution that is inappropriately imposed.

Part 2
Developing a Partnership Framework

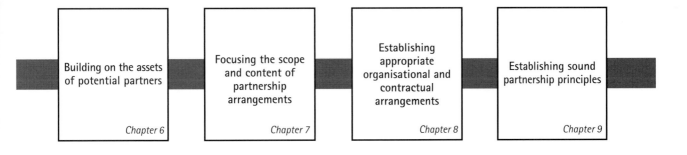

Building on the assets of potential partners

Chapter 6

Focusing the scope and content of partnership arrangements

Chapter 7

Establishing appropriate organisational and contractual arrangements

Chapter 8

Establishing sound partnership principles

Chapter 9

Chapter 6 Key Questions

- ☐ Who are the potential actors in a partnership?

- ☐ Which actors can assist in achieving better targeting of poor communities?

- ☐ What are the characteristics of the private sector, the municipality, the civil society sector and consumers?

- ☐ How do relationships work in practice?

- ☐ How is effective partnering achieved?

Developing a Partnership Framework

| Building on the assets of potential partners | Focusing the scope and content of partnership arrangements | Establishing appropriate organisational and contractual arrangements | Establishing sound partnership principles |

IIED–AL

Building on the Assets of Potential Partners

Janelle Plummer and Steve Waddell

In the pursuit of partnerships focused on achieving sustainable service improvements for the poor, municipalities must explore and expand their knowledge of the opportunities for partnering. While this book explicitly includes the private sector as a potential partner for municipal service delivery, the focus on partnerships for the poor opens up the question about which other actors should be involved in a reconstructed approach. Building on the previous discussions that highlight the importance of integrated approaches to urban management and poverty reduction, this chapter therefore considers the potential of each of the three organisational sectors (government, the private sector and civil society) in partnerships developed at the municipal level.

This chapter outlines the nature and diversity of each potential actor, their characteristics and potential roles, and the challenges they face in working together towards the delivery of services in poor urban contexts. In succession, it disaggregates these aspects in relation to municipalities, the private sector and civil society, and then considers the important roles of external agents (such as donors and specialist consultants).

In particular, this chapter considers the different types of private sector actors involved in service delivery in low-income areas. It describes the large-scale international operators generally associated with public–private partnerships (PPPs), the national level of the private sector, and the small-scale service providers, often overlooked in the PPP framework. This attempt to disentangle the various types of stakeholders within a sector is then adopted in relation to civil society, and the discussion considers some of the key stakeholders from civil society (NGOs, consumers, employees and trade unions).

The chapter argues that there are distinct and fundamental characteristics of each organisation and that effective partnerships combine the key attributes of these actors to respond effectively to the service needs of the poor. It also acknowledges that building partnerships between such different stakeholders is not easy, and stresses that it is necessary for municipal officials – and all prospective partners – to build a better understanding of the potential attributes of each stakeholder.

Municipal Government

The nature and diversity of municipalities in service delivery

While it is clear that municipalities differ significantly in terms of capacity, attitudes and functions, it can also be argued that most display certain fundamental characteristics, which are very different from those of private sector or civil society actors. Municipalities have powers of enforcement and taxation (although these are often modest compared to other government levels). They have particularly important leadership powers, through which they can convene various actors and build collective visions. On the other hand, they are often burdened by bureaucratic procedures and political interference, and undermined by a lack of human and financial resources. Many are content with the status quo, or lack the power they need to act; some have never exercised their power because they are dominated by a culture of apathy and resistance to change. These are all fundamental characteristics affecting the effective delivery of urban services.

It is likely that municipalities will need to embark on a process of change if they are to involve other stakeholders effectively and move away from providing services themselves. In order to understand the nature of the change required, it is first necessary to identify the strengths and weaknesses of the municipalities – to assess their capacity to enter into effective and sustainable partnerships with both the private sector and the various actors making up civil society. This analysis will expose the attitudes, issues and concerns harboured by municipalities in relation to the private sector, for instance, and thus earmark some potential partnership difficulties. Conversely, an understanding of a particular municipality's strengths, and the capacity it has shown to innovate, may help to define some of the opportunities and attributes that it will bring to a partnership.

Links to Boxes
7.17, 8.6, 9.6, 11.1, 12.1

Box 6.1 **Municipal Capacity and the Changing Municipal Role**
Stutterheim, South Africa

The municipality of Stutterheim, located in the Eastern Cape of South Africa, first adopted a 10-year affermage contract* for the delivery of water and sanitation services in 1993, prior to the democratic elections in South Africa. The contract was formed with Aqua Gold (now WSSA, a joint venture between Northumbrian-Lyonnaise International and a local company, Group 5). The shift towards the private sector as a vehicle for the delivery of municipal services of all types came at a time when the local council was dominated by businessmen who were keen to streamline the municipality and delegate the responsibility for service functions to private sector companies. In the case of water and sanitation, the intention was to delegate the management of all water and sanitation responsibilities. In the apartheid context of segregation in South Africa, this included the provision of all water supply and sewerage services to the people living within the 'white' areas of the town, and the provision of bulk water and the treatment of sewerage effluent for the segregated township areas. It is important to note that the political arm of the council provided the driving force for the partnership arrangement.

After the national and local elections in 1994–95, Stutterheim Council was amalgamated with the administration that had previously been responsible for providing services to the township areas. Despite this vast change and a six-fold increase in population under the municipal jurisdiction, the new Stutterheim Transitional Local Council (STLC) chose to establish in-house capacity to deliver water and sewerage to the underserviced parts of the municipality and not to contract the private operator to extend its operations. At the instigation of WSSA, this decision has been revisited a number of times. There is no question that WSSA would prefer to deliver all services at all levels in all parts of the municipality. The current arrangement does not optimise efficiency of service delivery, and WSSA is criticised for being involved in a contract that appears to perpetuate unequal services. Nevertheless, the council has consistently chosen to retain responsibility for delivering and upgrading some tertiary-level water and sanitation services, believing this to be a more cost effective in the low-income areas of the municipality.

At the outset, the council was supported, not led by, the executive arm of the municipality. The partnership was developed in the isolated context of water and sanitation without consideration of the roles and responsibilities for other related initiatives. The role of procurement was passed on to a national engineering consultant and the process was carried out in accordance with standard contracting procedures. However, soon after the contract was established, the old (white-only) council was replaced by a council – democratically elected by all citizens – with different priorities. More focused on the social aspects of their constituency, less experienced in management, and beset by the turnover in key engineering staff, the council has never been able to properly manage or monitor the partnership arrangement or implementation process. The contract itself does not define responsibilities well, and the lack of a regulator in South Africa has resulted in repeated problems over the allocation of costs and responsibilities.

The partnership does not form part of a strategic planning or integrated development approach, and the council has failed to establish any connection between the water and sanitation partnership and economic development activities with the poorer groups in the town (despite the fact that water and sanitation services represent some 12% of the council annual budget and there is a mandate for integrated development planning; see Box 4.3). The municipality plays no substantial coordinating role.

At the time the partnership was established, there was little concern for the mechanics of public consultation or the explicit involvement of stakeholders in the decision to enter into a partnership arrangement. The council had a mandate to manage the town and was not concerned with building a consultative approach or obtaining explicit approval for a decision on delegating management. Effective town management was, however, a key issue, and the council envisaged a key role for the private sector in attaining this end.

The case of Stutterheim provides an illustration of a partnership arrangement that is, to some extent, misread by municipal decision-makers. It also provides an illustration of an arrangement where partnership objectives and roles need to be reoriented to meet the new demands and visions of the post-apartheid council. The primary concerns expressed by council officials in Stutterheim, and echoed by the private operator, concern the capacity of the municipality to act as an equal party in the contract (see Boxes 11.1 and 12.1). This lesson is relevant for all municipalities, particularly those, like Stutterheim, which are managed by political representatives who had no involvement at the partnership formulation stage. Among other messages, it highlights the need for ongoing capacity building throughout the duration of a contract if the political wing of a municipality is to act as an effective decision-making partner, able to optimise its own role and the role of the private sector in changing circumstances.

* See Chapter 8 for more detail on leases and affermage contracts

Source: Plummer, 2000a

Municipal attitudes towards poor communities and NGOs are also primary indicators of how they will behave, and the decisions their leaders will make. While some have experience of participatory processes, few have embraced the strategic change that would promote community participation as an inherent process in the formulation and delivery of services. While the traditional model of the municipality as provider has been obscured by community participation in some situations, rarely has it been transformed.

It is also notable that those municipalities that have pursued associations with both the private sector and the community in water, sanitation or waste services have generally kept these approaches quite separate. With notable exceptions, few have attempted to bring the experience of working with civil society into a PPP. Evidence suggests that this is because the municipal goals of involving the private sector aim to solve financial and institutional deficiencies, while initiatives involving civil society aim to target poverty more directly. These two sets of problems have not generally been unified in the problem analysis or the response. One of the key aspects of a PPP focused on the poor is the integration of all initiatives into an innovative, holistic solution.

The characteristics of municipalities

Like national and provincial/state levels of government, municipalities display a number of common and distinguishing characteristics.[1] In democratic contexts, the primary interest of the elected leaders is political; councils are ultimately controlled by voters, and by higher political bodies. The level of political control is convincingly illustrated in South Africa where, despite apparent autonomy at the local level of government, the decision-making of elected officials at the municipal level is often determined by national-level political mandates.

Often, where local level democracy is less mature, the interests of the municipality are still determined by the executive arm, and are often bureaucratic. A municipality might be concerned with maintaining the status quo and resisting any change likely to harm existing status and hierarchies. Many contexts demonstrate how these political and administrative interests conflict, and the impacts of a resistant municipal executive on the implementation of new or challenging policies. Municipal administrators' primary concern is not the electorate, but higher levels of management whose concerns are often self-reinforcing.

In theory, municipalities obtain their power through legislative, regulatory and enforcement frameworks, and their authority to tax. However, under-resourced local governments, often secure their power through their roles as providers and patrons, and ultimately through the control they have over the allocation of municipal resources. This is particularly relevant in relation to municipal services such as water supply, sanitation and solid waste disposal, as municipal officials often have the ability to determine who gets the service, when they get it, and how much they get. The voting power of the poor does not always bring about a better outcome if politicians exclude marginalised groups or fail to act sincerely on their behalf.

Municipalities bring their important rule-making capacity to partnerships. However, they usually have many established procedures (or rules) to address situations that are very different from those with partnership strategies. One of the great concerns of constituents is that procedures can also fuel a lack of transparency. Some argue that overly bureaucratic procedures have masked the fact that decades of officials have obtained personal rewards from dubious decision-making. Moreover, dependence on historic and unnecessary procedures is also a primary reason for failure in partnerships and inefficiency. It is not the existence of rules that is in question, but the need to ensure that the rules and procedures by which a municipality functions are changed to create a partnership-supportive environment.

In particular, building partnerships requires a different approach than the usual one to rule-making, with a fully predetermined procedural framework that defines the relationships between actors. While municipalities have a critical

6

Box **6.2**   Municipal Roles in Service Partnerships

(a) Municipality as provider: the traditional cluster of roles

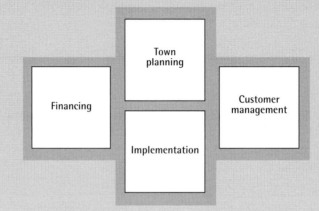

(b) The municipal partner in a standard PPP: an amended cluster of roles

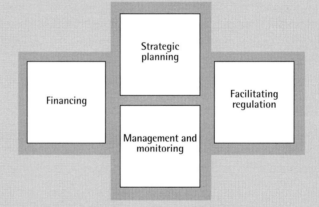

(c) Municipal roles in a focused partnership: an expanded cluster of roles

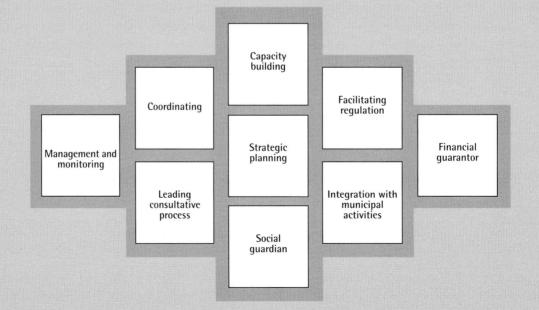

role in bringing their rule-making capacity to develop a partnership-supportive framework, much of the framework evolves as the partnerships evolve.

Democratically elected municipalities are also concerned with very different timeframes than are potential private sector or civil society partners. Their interest in political power means that they make decisions according to a timeframe determined by elections.[2] Service delivery programmes are often lengthy, and private sector partners look for contract durations commensurate with risk and investment. Yet the election timeframe can be quite short. In some states in India, for instance, mayors are elected on an annual basis, and councillors are elected every three years. This forces politicians to focus on short-term, visible results each and every year, often abandoning strategic plans that lead to sustainable long-term improvement. In relation to partnerships, the effects of such short-term thinking on long-term contracts can be detrimental to implementation processes.[3] In order to combat this effect, it is critical for the partnership process to acknowledge this concern, and produce short-term results that can also be achieved within an election cycle.

☐ The potential roles of the municipality

Municipal partners are in a unique position in partnership arrangements for service delivery. On the one hand they are very dependent on the private sector for investment, cost efficiencies and/or know-how, and on the community for its willingness to play the game, pay its tariffs and participate in operations and maintenance. On the other hand, as the initiators of potential partnerships, municipalities have enormous power. At the outset they are able to determine and direct strategy. They determine, for instance, the extent, nature and scope of the partnership, the actors involved, and the requirements for consultation and community participation. They determine how much of the service mandate to delegate, for how long, in what manner and to whom. While the private sector inevitably builds a stronger presence, at the later stages the municipality oversees the implementation process. The municipality determines the requirements for expansion and service standards, and sets the initial agenda for a pro-poor framework.

Evidence also suggests, however, that municipalities behave very differently with different kinds of partners (e.g., established international operators versus informal small-scale providers), and thus assume very different roles in different service sectors. They exhibit much more self-assurance in working with private enterprise in low-technology activities such as solid waste or septic-tank cleaning than in network service arrangements such as water supply, where they often lack the confidence and skill needed to perform allocated roles (see Box 6.1).

Box 6.2(b) illustrates the different roles that may be played by the municipality in service partnerships. Some roles are obligatory and should be performed by the municipality; others may be dependent on the competencies and comparative advantage of other actors that may become involved.

- **Strategic planning**   A primary role of the municipality in a poverty-focused partnership is to ensure that activities are integrated, efforts converge and investment is targeted. While it is necessary to have collaborative processes, ultimately this planning role cannot be delegated.
- **Management and monitoring**   The management and monitoring role of a municipality will vary according to the service, the type of arrangement and the contract. It is likely that its operational role will be reduced, but it needs to redirect its skills and time towards monitoring the performance of other partners.
- **Financing**   The municipality is likely to be responsible for the development of a financial strategy for raising both operating and capital costs, and for executing the strategy.
- **Regulation**   Where the external operating context does not provide an adequate regulatory framework, municipalities will need to decide how the arrangement is regulated and facilitate these arrangements. (For a detailed discussion on regulation, see Chapter 10.)

6

| Box **6.3** | The Changing Municipal Role in Solid Waste Management |
| | Hyderabad, India |

The municipality in Hyderabad, Andhra Pradesh, India, has established itself as a well-run organisation able to work effectively in community development, and to work with the district to resolve land tenure issues and to create sustainable improvement in the low-income areas of the city. Although the city does not at this time have a democratically elected council, the municipal corporation has successfully embarked on a process of contracting-out solid waste management in the city, radically changing its role from that of service provider to one in which it works with small-scale private sector organisations to manage waste within the city.

The Municipal Corporation of Hyderabad (MCH) has a sound history of drawing in private sector resources to resolve urban management issues. In the 90s, innovative land-sharing initiatives undertaken with the MCH and poor communities assisted the municipality in resolving some difficult tenure and service problems in core areas of the city. In this exercise, the municipality took on the role of facilitator, aiming to bring together the disparate interests of a private landowner with those of a poor community, to bring about a sustainable solution to squatting in the city.

In 1994 the MCH attempted its first initiative with private sector contracting in the vast task of covering a city where 2000 metric tons of waste are generated daily. The process of shifting from 'provider' to 'monitor' has not been straightforward. Early efforts proved unsuccessful because the municipality did not provide the supervision necessary to ensure contractors met performance standards without attempting to cut corners. The municipality has undergone a steep learning curve, learning lessons through mistakes and experience. This underlines the importance of monitoring and of establishing contracts that can be effectively monitored.

In 1994, the MCH opted for a system that required the contractor to fix its rates for sweeping, collecting and transferring waste. This approach – covering 10% of the city – resulted in the contractors simply bidding low to win contracts, and then employing insufficient staff to carry out the work. As a result, the MCH altered its approach in 1996 to enable easier monitoring. This system was based on a payment per load, which was thought to constitute an incentive for the private sector to clean the area to a higher standard. This system covered 25% of the city. Contractors bid per load (per ton), and the contract was awarded to the tenderer with the lowest bid. Keen to increase the quantities of garbage collected, contractors picked up rubbish from areas outside their allocated zones.

In 1998 the MCH introduced a new programme – which they called the 'unit system' – in which 55% of the municipal area was to be the responsibility of private contractors working on one-year service contracts. For its part, the municipality introduced a process of systematic monitoring . This is carried out twice daily by the conservancy department (assistant medical officers and the sanitary inspectors) of the MCH and the local communities. A public complaints line was established and the council thus continues its role in customer management.

Yet despite the success of this system, the MCH has struggled with its new role in relation to labour. In the midst of strikes, squats and absenteeism, senior municipal officials entered into lengthy negotiations with the unions. Although the MCH was flexible in some respects to change, in the main, little room was given to the union. The MCH relied on its status, and its reputation for strict tactics, to establish union support.

While the contract stipulates that workers are to be employed in accordance with the Minimum Wages Act, this has been difficult to enforce. The MCH is aware that contractors attempted to underpay staff (approx 800–900 rupees fewer than the unit rate established by the MCH) in order to increase their own profit. Therefore, the MCH introduced severe penalties to discourage this practice across the city. The lack of feedback from workers is obviously a drawback, so senior officials have introduced random checks and have cancelled numerous contracts when they established beyond doubt that the practice of underpaying was taking place.

Source: personal Interview, June 2000; Zerah, 1999

In the poverty-focused approach to service partnerships, these four roles are extended (see Box 6.2(c)) to include roles that are vital in ensuring effective and sustainable benefit to poor households and communities.

- **Coordination**   The municipality must ensure that appropriate stakeholders are involved, that their roles are clear, and that as disputes arise there is a process for resolving them.
- **Consultation and participation**   Municipalities have a responsibility to lead a process of consultation and encourage the active participation of all primary and secondary stakeholders.
- **Social guardian**   The municipality has an important role in ensuring that equity concerns are addressed. One of the primary municipal responsibilities is to facilitate a supporting mechanism for the poor, so that their voice is heard within the partnership. A municipality may draw on the services of an NGO, depending on the local situation.
- **Capacity building**   Typically, all actors will require some capacity building to work effectively in a partnership. Municipalities will have to decide how this capacity building will be achieved and ensure that the partnership arrangement accommodates it.
- **Integration with municipal activities**   Many established partnerships address only one specific service. A key municipal role is to establish linkages and integration with other poverty responses and urban management functions.

A municipality will need to clearly identify the key municipal roles that cannot be delegated, those that – on balance – are best played by them, and those that can be delegated with ease.

☐   Constraints affecting the municipal role in partnerships

Municipalities are thus challenged with the new and unfamiliar roles of enabler and facilitator, and very different approaches to the roles of manager and monitor. Various officials and political representatives within a municipality will display different interests and capacities. A municipality's capacity to perform these roles is therefore determined by individual, municipal, partnership and external constraints. These include:

- overly bureaucratic procedures, inappropriate to partnerships;
- inadequate skills and managerial capacity;
- inappropriate political interference;
- resistance to change;
- inter-departmental competition;
- inappropriate incentive structures; and
- mistrust and scepticism over private sector incentives and NGO approaches.

The human resource and organisational issues affecting their capacity to perform these roles are addressed in Chapters 11 and 12.

The Private Sector

☐   The nature and diversity of the private sector

The term 'private sector' can be used to mean many things. In discussions of PPPs, the term 'private sector' often implicitly refers to multinational companies – large, profit-oriented organisations that operate across borders and report to shareholders. However, the development of private sector involvement in poverty-focused service delivery can and should denote a far broader vision of the private sector – one that includes a range of actors delivering services. The primary characteristic of the private sector is not size, scope or capacity. The key distinguishing characteristic is that individuals, organisations, businesses or enterprises act in the pursuit of profit.

6

Box 6.4 Disaggregating the Private Sector

	Formal/large scale		**Informal/small scale**
	International companies	National companies	Micro-enterprises / Small-scale independent providers / Informal providers
Competencies	• Technical expertise • Financial resources • Management expertise	• Technical expertise • Management expertise • National knowledge • Local legitimacy	• Local knowledge • Innovation with local resources
Benefits	• Inflow of finances, skills and technologies • Managerial experience • Innovation	• Building national capacity and expertise • Local networks • Government links	• Generating local socio-economic development impact • Creating community ownership • Powerful development impact if properly engaged
Market interests	• Large-scale projects • Market entry • Limited risk	• Medium-scale projects • Secondary cities • Working in consortia	• Filling gaps in service supply • Flexible commercial opportunities requiring limited investment • Relatively high risk, but small size • Poor households • Inaccessible, marginal areas • Peri-urban areas
	• Water supply	• Solid waste • Water supply in consortia	• Tertiary level: water supply, sanitation services, and solid waste collection
Political issues	• (Generally) outside the web of local politics: might be less corruptible	• Generally very dependent upon local politics and individuals	• Outside the political system and therefore less valued and less influential
Other issues	• Driven simply by contracts • Profits taken out of country • Inevitably promote an international culture national values	• Driven by national pride • Profits more likely to stay in country • Culturally more likely to support	• Driven by need for personal income • Profits usually retained in community • More likely to meet very poor's requirements

With regard to the delivery of municipal services, it is useful to consider three different types of enterprise: international, national and small-scale (formal or informal) local enterprise. Although all of these types involve the pursuit of profit, their scales of operations are almost always associated with the distinct competencies and benefits that they bring to a partnership. Within each typology there is undoubtedly further diversity; the categories are not discrete but operate as a continuum, and PPPs may include one or all of these categories in a collaborative effort. The categories are summarised in Box 6.4.

The term 'private sector', in relation to municipal service delivery, therefore covers a vast range of profit-making organisations – large and small, formal and informal, in a range of sectors. One end of the private sector spectrum is represented by large international water companies such as Ondeo-Lyonnaise des Eaux, Vivendi and Thames Water. The other end is represented by the water-vendor with a cart, selling water by the container. In the solid waste sector, the national operators with compactors and large-scale landfill and recycling facilities are contrasted with the small-scale rag-picking cooperatives or itinerant waste-buyers, whose self-employed recycling activities are the basis of their livelihoods. In between these extremes lies a set of profit-making enterprises/organisations whose capacities and interests are all potentially relevant to the different types of water and waste services.

☐ The characteristics of international business

In recent years, large international companies (also known as multinationals, transnationals, international corporations) have begun to participate in the delivery of a number of basic urban services, including energy, telecommunications and water and sanitation services. Municipalities are attracted to partnering with multinationals in order to obtain investment, efficiency and skills (see Chapter 3), but fundamentally aim to improve municipal services and build local capacity. Business goals are to make profits and develop new markets on a permanent basis.

International private companies are usually engaged in municipal service provision because they can provide three types of resources:

1. professional management expertise in improving service efficiency and quality;
2. technical expertise that a municipality (particularly a small municipality) cannot sustain, and the expertise developed through international research and development; and
3. capital for investment in equipment and infrastructure costs.

The potential contribution of these companies cannot be ignored, even by the most sceptical observer. The Argentine, Colombian and South African contexts, as well as many others, all expose the operating efficiencies and improved service quality that can result from effective private sector involvement.[4] International business often (but not always) brings its own capital, and its presence increases international investor confidence. This has significant impact on a municipality's capacity to fulfil its function. In the case of Colombia in 1995, the World Bank made it clear to Cartagena that private sector involvement was a prerequisite for Bank financing of the water and sanitation sector in that city. This swayed the incoming mayor to renegotiate the existing agreement with Aguas de Barcelona. As a result, the World Bank and the Inter-American Development Bank invested substantial funds in the sector.

What are the characteristics of multinational companies, and what do they bring to service partnerships? The multinationals involved in water and sanitation services, for instance, are characterised by the commercial nature of their operations, by their size, by their market share, by the experience, knowledge and technical know-how they have in the sector, by their access to capital and by the level of international confidence in their capacity.

Box **6.5**   Market Share of Multinational Watsan Operators in Low- and Middle-income Countries

Multinationals	Market share* (Private company share by population served)	Example contract locations
Ondeo (formerly Suez Lyonnaise des Eaux) including WSSA, Northumbrian and Aguas de Barcelona	41%	• Cartagena, Colombia • Palmira, Colombia • El Alto, Bolivia • BOTT, South Africa • Stutterheim/Queenstown/Fort Beaufort, South Africa • Johannesburg, South Africa • Buenos Aires, Argentina • Cordóba, Argentina
Vivendi (Generale des Eaux)	29%	• Pilot in KwaZulu-Natal, South Africa • Tucuman, Argentina • Tunju, Colombia • Monteria, Colombia • Bogota, Colombia (water treatment plants) • Brazil • Malaysia • Mexico City • Havana, Cuba
SAUR (SAUR UK)	9%	• Dolphin Coast, South Africa • Maputo, Mozambique (+ 4 towns) • MoU Gweru, Zimbabwe • Vietnam (Hanoi and Bay of Along) • Cote d'Ivoire • Senegal • Conakry, Guinea • Mendoza • Central African Republic
Thames Water RWE	9%	• Jakarta, Indonesia • Rancagua, Chile • Shanghai, China • Izmit, Turkey
United Utilities	3%	• Tallinn, Estonia • Bielsko Biala, Poland • Sofia, Bulgaria • Manila, The Philippines
Anglian Water	2%	• ESVAL – Region V, Chile • Brusque STW, Brazil • SmVAK, VAKJC, Beroun, Czech Republic • Bangkok, Thailand • Lima Land, Manila, The Philippines • Hexian, China
Azurix**	3%	
Others	4%	

* Market share (of the private sector share) in low- and middle-income countries
** This table was compiled before the collapse of Enron

Sources: Franceys, 2001; Operators and operator websites

Unlike its municipal partners, who are largely driven by political motives, the large-scale international business sector is primarily interested in financial incentives. It is controlled by owner-stakeholders and driven by profit goals. Private partners gain their power because they can access and provide finance for a partnership, and by their superior skills and knowledge base, augmented by their increased access to information at the local level.

While municipal partners are characterised by their adherence to municipal procedures, the international private operator is concerned with the (bilateral) contract established for the purposes of the partnership. When that contract describes inputs and outputs, the private sector approach focuses on these obligations, rather than outcomes. Evidence from two partnerships in South Africa indicates that the operators managed their roles within the partnerships strictly in accordance with the contracts – even where this was not the most effective approach – and their decision-making was driven by adherence to rules. This hindered other partners from pursuing more general partnership objectives concerned with long-term sustainability, and suggests that an outcome-based approach would have been more effective.

The international operator is concerned with two timeframes. The overall duration of a contract determines the financial decisions and actions of the operator. In many of the older water and sanitation concession arrangements, it has become clear that the programming of expansion mandates to poor areas is seen in the overall contractual context, and thus poor areas that are costly to upgrade have been programmed last. Yet at the same time, every business works within predetermined business cycles, and actions are often tailored to suit quarterly or annual profit reports to shareholders.

While total private sector involvement is still limited in absolute terms, their market share is certainly increasing (the comparative market share of the largest water companies operating in developing countries and the location of some of their primary operations are indicated in Box 6.5). Due to the attraction of the mega-cities and large urban agglomerations of the South, there is an increasing trend for international operators to set up national offices in countries that are heading towards private sector policies. Many have become involved in small initiatives to establish a foothold in the market, and to learn the idiosyncrasies of the operating context.

While a few international companies currently control the water and sanitation market in developing countries, there is also substantial evidence that each operator has a slightly different set of requirements and interests. Accordingly, each brings different competencies to the municipal function. An early finding of the research leading to this book was that international water operators have very different levels of interest in, capacity for and commitment to delivering services to the poor. While some show an outward commitment to poor consumers, and are exploring innovative tools and techniques to improve service coverage, others indicate that they do not adjust the level of service or the mechanisms for payment, nor do they consider labour-based technologies in their delivery to poor consumers. One operator representative was dismayed by the idea of the poor as active participants in the development process, and another by the argument that low-income areas and poor communities are diverse and may require individual solutions. Municipal officials involved in selection processes must be aware that international operators are not all the same, and do not have the same interests and expertise.

Analysis of the objectives of a handful of water and sanitation multinationals shows that company mandates focus on business, consumer satisfaction, efficiency and environmental sustainability. The inclusion of environmental sustainability in their mission statements is a reflection of their Northern roots. Yet, despite the fact that in developing countries over 50 per cent of consumers might be living at or below the poverty line, only one or two have included reference to improving services for the poor in their mission statements, or to formally recognising the social dimensions of their function.[5]

The core competencies of international operators generally lie with building physical infrastructure, and with undertaking operation and maintenance in 'developed' settings – those with substantial institutional and social infrastructures. This

Box **6.6**   Working in Low-income Areas
The Rationale and Approach of an International Water and Sanitation Operator

One of the most common and often unanswered questions concerning private sector participation in service delivery to the poor in developing countries is why the private sector would want to get involved at all. On the face of it, the returns are low, the risks are high, the problem is complex and the opportunities elsewhere are plentiful. The following discussion, relating to water and sanitation services, describes some of the key issues raised by an international private water and sanitation operator.

While many international private operators have not shown any interest in entering the water and sanitation market in developing countries, many have and there is an increasing trend towards do so. Box 6.5 outlines the market share of the largest companies as a percentage of the share currently attributed to the private sector. Yet the total private share is still low: unofficial estimates suggest it may be as low as 5%. Given that over 2 billion people lack access to safe drinking water, and nearly 3 billion lack access to sanitation, in the eyes of business, a significant market remains untapped.

Given the opportunities offered by increasing globalisation and liberalisation of trade regimes, international companies are entering this market to meet the objectives of their shareholders; their fundamental motivation is not charity but business. *'The water services company acts within the framework of a commercial system and [sometimes] intervenes to the detriment of other types of water provision, since these communities always have access to water one way or another, legally or otherwise.....[We] must offer a wide industrial perspective, especially as our long-term mandates involve strong commitment to operations whose results may only be achieved in the long term, and by adopting a customer-oriented approach. A large private operator has the ability to develop comprehensive concepts incorporating all the necessary technical, institutional and financial components for developing sustainable management methods for water and sanitation in disadvantaged areas...'*

Despite the opportunities for the private sector, the problems of delivering water and sanitation (and other services) in low-income areas are marked. Lyonnaise des Eaux, for instance, has identified three main problems in addressing water and sanitation requirements in poor neighbourhoods. Without question, the first of these is the complex problem of land ownership and control. Private operators need to evaluate each case separately in terms of technical and political impacts to determine the risks and opportunities. For the private operator, land regularisation is necessary before the installation of urban service networks. Second is the problem that connection costs are too high relative to the ability to pay. This may be due to expansion costs being passed on to the (poor) unconnected consumers, or it may be due to the excessive installation costs and the difficult nature of the land that the poor often occupy.

The third critical problem for international private operators looking to work in poor areas in developing countries is that customer management costs are too high. This may be due to:

- a high percentage of unpaid bills;
- a high rate of unbilled or fraudulent consumption;
- a low level of individual consumption by users (small bills and high collection costs); and
- high network maintenance costs.

Lyonnaise des Eaux has proposed that the key to unlocking service delivery to the poor is recognising that there are no ready-made (generic) solutions appropriate to all contexts. Its research and development cell stresses that thorough preliminary investigation underlies the process of entering the market, particularly in poor areas, and that each situation must be analysed on a case-by-case basis and addressed through tailor-made responses.

Following its experience in diverse contexts, Lyonnaise des Eaux has recognised that it needs to:

- understand and classify the local conditions (institutional, population and technical);
- understand the commercial aspects relating to charging and collection:
    - the types of assessment and measurement of consumption;
    - the period within which charging and collection should be made;
    - the tariff structure (whether it is progressive, uniform, regressive or according to the level of service); and
    - the method of collection;
- clarify the commercial aspects of investment financing (e.g., by immediate or staggered payments, grants, or external financing);
- clarify the technical aspects of water supply (resources, supplying); and
- clarify the technical aspects of sanitation (on-site systems, collection, final treatment).

Source: Suez Lyonnaise des Eaux, 1998

also includes clear and well-supported policy, financing and regulatory structures; processes of consultation and planning engaging large numbers of community and other organisations; and the presence of sophisticated professionals among the municipal and other groups that they work with. The degree to which international operators have successfully 'Southernised' their operations varies greatly but, even at best, is far from complete.

Multinational interest and roles in developing countries are affected by a number of factors. First, they are concerned with the enabling environment. Chapter 10 provides a description of the key policy, political, economic, legislative/regulatory and administrative factors that affect the development of service partnerships. They are concerned with risk, incentive structures, and cost recovery. One key issue associated with risk arises over the amount of capital investment and the time allowed for repayment; although long durations of concessions give longer periods in which to recapture costs, they also mean an increase in exposure to the risk of major political changes.

Incentive structures can be useful to clarify expectations, but companies also require information to enable them to establish possibilities and limits. The issue of cost recovery is often closely associated with risk, and arises when tariff issues are discussed. The company wants to know that there will indeed be a revenue stream that will provide sufficient repayment.

The potential role of the multinational service provider will be dependent on:

- the demands of the public sector actors;
- municipal capacity;
- ability to pay international rates;
- the risks of the operating context; and
- the local risks the private sector is prepared to take (e.g., risk on operations and maintenance but not on capital investment).

Typically, the role of the formal private sector enterprise may be that of contractor, operator, monitor, manager, lessee, part-owner or financier. The water multinationals traditionally take on standard water production, treatment and distribution tasks in the project cycle such as planning, construction, strategic and practical management, technical design, operation and maintenance and customer management. They may also take on non-traditional tasks such as capacity building and the delivery of non-physical services, usually in collaboration with local organisations. Many international companies argue that if there is a demand for a service then they can provide it, but many others have proved that this is not always successful, and that they are better off sticking to their core functions.

The characteristics of national business

There is a great deal of variation in the level of sophistication of business in developing countries, but at their core, the nationally owned medium- to large-scale businesses working in water and waste services in developing countries display the same characteristics as international operators, although on a smaller scale. They are fundamentally concerned with profit, controlled by their owners and driven to improve efficiency in order to decrease costs and increase profit margins. They have access to investment capital, normally varying with the industry and scale of the business, and some will have access to national capital markets to fund expansion.

Yet in many ways, nationally owned and managed businesses are a far cry from the large international operators that benefit from state-of-the-art management, technical expertise and experience, and access to greater resources. These large operators provide greater comfort to financial backers or donors. Many national business managers are less skilled than government leaders; many have enjoyed little or no competition for decades, and have thrived on just one or a few

Links to Boxes
5.3, 9.2, 12.5

Box **6.7**   ## A National Solid Waste Operator
Biratnagar, Nepal

Following the disappearance of the private operator Americorp's managing director from Biratnagar (see Box 9.2), a national consulting engineer, SILT, established itself as a committed and stable partner in municipal solid waste management in Biratnagar. The arrangement under which the operator now undertakes solid waste services in Biratnagar is a complex agreement with the Biratnagar sub-municipal corporation. It comprises the spurious initial contract, a number of informal agreements and an additional service contract. While many aspects of the Biratnagar case are unusual and unlikely to be widely replicated, the very existence of this PPP is instructive to municipalities as it describes the sort of irregular partnerships that can develop. It also describes the formation of a national solid waste management business expanded from traditional engineering consulting services.

Given its history of both international and national operators, the Biratnagar case addresses a number of issues in relation to these different actors. It illustrates, for instance, the sort of inappropriate technical and financial options that might be proposed by international operators inexperienced in the specific needs and problems of developing cities. The initial scheme proposed for Biratnagar offered a technically inappropriate and financially unviable proposition, and there is little question in hindsight that it was unsuitable in the socio-economic context of Biratnagar. Based on figures provided by the UN, Nepal appears to have one of the lowest rates of urban solid waste generation (at 0.50 kilograms per capita per day), and this is expected to increase only marginally by 2025 (World Bank, 1999). Despite this, the original operator suggested, and the council accepted, a proposal relevant for the waste generation rates of highly developed cities in the North. One of the simple lessons of the Biratnagar case thus relates to the lack of viability of high-technology proposals and the high levels of investment proposed at the outset. The national operator was quick to amend the proposal to include more appropriate solutions for the landfill site, the compactors were replaced by simple tractor trailers, and the household containers have been simplified. Knowledge of what is financially and technically viable in the Nepalese context has been a critical element in the sustainability of the initiative.

The Biratnagar case also demonstrates that the capacity of national level private operators can be limited. Neither the municipality nor the operator have had experience in managing an integrated solid waste management programme. Both parties have had to learn from experience and experiment with systems and procedures. The main capacity deficiencies have been concerned with contract formulation and negotiation, technical analysis of waste management operations, financial analysis and management, integrated waste management practices, public consultation processes, alternative waste management systems, the role of NGOs and CBOs, and community participation in waste operations.

As a result, the mayor of Biratnagar argues that the current scope and content of the partnership is probably limited in the medium to long term. He argues that the national operator does not have the resources and technical capacity to undertake all the waste-related activities required by the city. However, in relation to the existing service, there is also some question over the capacity of the operator to replicate the initiative and significantly increase the scale of the operation. In particular, the makeshift and ad hoc nature of the operations (seen in the proposal for leasing a site for a compost plant from a friend) and the personal attention paid to each facet of the operation by the general manager, suggest that significantly greater coverage and replication may not be achieved without increased systematisation.

While the operator is not skilled in working with the poor and the various dimensions of poverty reduction, it is noticeable that the scale of its operations has enabled it to develop small-scale and ad hoc initiatives with the poor where it sees a potential benefit to its operations. Be it in a small way, its ability to adopt new processes and involve new actors is a particular dimension of the way the initiative has developed. The primary area of concern in relation to the poor is the terms and conditions of the employment of (poor) individuals. In many partnerships one of the key benefits of the private sector is the ability to promote and sustain better work practices. While it may be argued that conditions are not worse than municipal conditions, it is also notable that the national private sector operator has not promoted or felt any obligation to improve health and safety arrangements for workers.

The partnership arrangement is a complex one filled with uncommon practices. Yet despite this, the mayor reports that the majority of councillors are quite satisfied with the performance of the partnership, and that the council is in favour of further private sector initiatives in service delivery. From an objective viewpoint, however, there would appear to be fundamental problems with this solid waste initiative that are not being addressed by municipal decision-makers. Foremost among these is that the partnership, under the current terms, is unviable and unsustainable for the operator.

Source: Plummer and Slater, 2001

clients who are highly dependent upon inter-personal relationships. In the context of municipal service delivery, with the clear exception of solid waste management in Latin America, experience is limited.

Despite this, and for many other reasons, there is a growing trend towards national private sector participation (PSP) in municipal service delivery. This participation appears to arise where national enterprises are included in large consortiums as local partners (often as a tender condition); where international companies will not risk local economic conditions; and where enterprises are expanding their competencies to fill gaps in an existing market. To some extent, the first circumstance applies to water supply, and the latter to non-network (including both solid waste and sanitation) waste services.

In the case of solid waste management, there is a vast range of successful national businesses of various scales operating and managing solid waste services in cities in developing countries. Indeed, while there is an increasing interest from international operators – keen to enter lucrative and established markets, or keen to merge urban water and sanitation with solid waste activities – the norm in municipal solid waste management over the last few decades has been for contracts to be won by national companies. In Latin America and the Caribbean, where many large cities have undertaken large-scale contracting-out, 40–50 per cent of the urban population is served by private operators.[6]

Other companies have arisen through expansion from one business to another, often in response to market demand. This is exemplified by the initiatives of a pipe-manufacturer-turned-network-installer in Warangal in India,[7] and SILT in Nepal. Originally a consultant engineering firm, SILT expanded its activities into solid waste management in Biratnagar and, later, Kathmandu. While this was originated in dubious circumstances (see Box 6.7 describing the fraudulent conduct of the international operator), the initiative has sustained itself due to the level of local knowledge, the (forced) low level of investment and an unambitious approach to sweeping, collection and transfer activities. On the other hand, SILT has struggled because of the lack of finance, skilled management and experience in the service sector, and because of an overly ambitious contract that inexperience led it to sign.

Working alone, the national private sector – whether of a large or a medium scale – can offer opportunities that municipalities might not be able to realise with international operators. Since the success of national companies is closely associated with national economic and business performance, they often have a greater commitment to projects. Typically, they do not require guarantees, are willing to take on more risk, and are willing to work in lower-profile locations – perhaps even in less lucrative secondary cities – than their international counterparts. While they may bring fewer skills and lower levels of investment, their contribution may provide a sound basis, and a more level playing field, on which to launch a private sector partnership.

In the delivery of municipal water and sanitation services, by far the most common involvement of national businesses is in consortia comprising international operators. National businesses bring a number of key benefits to such consortia, and many international operators place a great deal of value upon having a well-established and astute local partner. Benefits include:

- knowledge of the local context, problems and idiosyncrasies, including local traditions and etiquettes;
- local contacts and networks – who's who and how the system works;
- local legitimacy that enables better interaction with government; and, frequently,
- better knowledge of the technical viability of project solutions.

In South Africa, the association between the national construction company G5 and Ondeo-Lyonnaise has resulted in a successful international and national profile. The national partner brings local legitimacy that allows the partner to interact with government as a constituent as well as a business. It can also lead to greater confidence on the part of

Links to Boxes
6.15

Box 6.8   Water Tanker Service Delivery in Peri-urban Areas
Lima, Peru

The participation of small-scale independent providers, together with a successful community mobilisation programme on the periphery of Lima, has contributed to a significant upgrade in the quality, quantity and reliability of water supply to poor residents of the informal settlements.

In the late 80s, poor households in the municipality of Villa María del Triunfo obtained water from tankers informally providing urgently needed water to the rapidly expanding hillside settlements in the outlying areas of the city. The only option was for residents to pay high prices for untreated water delivered by water tankers. The settlements were riddled with water- and faecal-borne diseases and skin complaints because of the poor water quality and arid conditions. In 1990, an outbreak of cholera prompted the government to take action and an agreement was made to channel EU (Spanish) aid finance into a potable-water supply programme. This programme comprised a number of physical improvements, as well as social and institutional development components.

The most innovative characteristic of the programme was the creation of a tri-sector partnership involving the municipality, the communities and the private water-tanker drivers. The decision to include previously exploitative small-scale providers recognised that this fleet of ad hoc tankers represented an asset and not a liability to be discarded. The design of the programme for safe water thus strategically included these small-scale water suppliers as a vital link in the arrangement. Efforts were then made to regulate the quality and price of the water supply to ensure that the system became fair, viable and sustainable.

Perhaps the most significant step in this process was the formalisation of the water tanker provision, through registration as small businesses and the development of tanker driver associations. The new system requires that the tanker drivers obtain treated water from one of the four official pumps provided for this purpose by SEDAPAL (Sanitation and Potable Water Company of Lima). Although sometimes insufficient in quantity, this water is of the same quality as that supplied to the city network. The tanker drivers pay the utility per tanker. The tankers are annually contracted by the COVAAPs (the community management organisations) to provide regular water to the water reservoirs, built as a storage facility, to which a small independent network is then constructed. The tanker drivers are paid a fixed amount agreed by the community and regulated by the municipality.

These small enterprises vary. Some are single owner-drivers; others are local businessmen with 5–10 tankers, employing 10–20 workers. They have invested US$6000–9000 per vehicle. In order to ensure ongoing work, the businesses maintain their tankers regularly (although there is some concern about the hygiene standards). At the city level, monitoring of the service is carried out by the Directorate of Environmental Health (DIGESA) in the national ministry, which monitors the quality of water supplied at the pump and the conditions of the tankers, and issues an authorisation for water transportation. The municipality regulates and monitors the service at the local level.

Initially operated for some years in the informal sector, the tanker enterprises were brought under the umbrella of the programme in 1996. This required them to become registered businesses and perform in accordance with the standards established by the programme and the municipality. A key characteristic of these businesses is their lack of managerial and administrative capacity. They have had no opportunities for developing skills in formal accounting and management or technical proficiency. Consequently, they noticeably lack a knowledge of their responsibilities as water distributors and in relation to taxation and fees.

Although the tanker drivers argue that there is not much difference in their profitability (and they must pay taxes), establishing themselves as formal sector businesses has improved their access to credit, enabling them fund expansion of the businesses. It has also allowed them to expand their client base to include commercial businesses, not just the COVAAPs in the local settlements. They have also been able to create jobs for unskilled and semi-skilled local workers. They argue that the main benefit of the arrangement for them is their legitimacy, primarily reflected in their being able to purchase good quality water from SEDAPAL, and thus ensure their own sustainability as service providers.

Apart from the benefits for these SSIPs, the people of the peri-urban areas of Lima have been the primary stakeholders to benefit from the initiative (in all its facets), including the partnership with the water tanker drivers. A good quality service now reaches the households in the marginal areas (both in terms of terrain, distance and informality) of Lima. Over 300,000 people now have improved access to safe and adequate drinking water. The process of community empowerment in this context is described in Box 6.15.

Source: Ecociudad/GHK, 2001

government that the partnership is serious, since the national business keeps a much greater proportion of its business within the country and will be heavily affected by non-performance.

Involvement in non-exploitative partnerships[8] clearly benefits national businesses. Not only are such partnerships lucrative (and present risks that are acceptable to international businesses), but the transfer of management know-how and environmental technology can be invaluable in preparing the national business for independent activities elsewhere. Governments often seize these advantages, and actively promote consortia that involve national companies as a strategy to build the capacity of their national business sectors.

The characteristics of small-scale and informal service providers

In many parts of the world, small-scale independent providers (SSIPs), and those who often work within the informal sector – have long been the providers of water and waste services to large sections of urban populations.[9] Municipalities have, at least implicitly, relied on the range of services that this private sector group has provided, be it water supply through tankers (see Box 6.8), sanitation services by way of vacuum trucks or manual latrine cleaners, or solid waste services through local sweepers and small collection vehicles (see Box 6.9). Despite this important role, municipalities have done little to influence the development of these operations, for good or ill. On the one hand, these independent providers fill gaps in municipal service provision, and their services are in urgent demand. On the other hand they are ignored. Their informality, the vast differences in their standards of service, the constraints of the regulatory context, and the fact that they generally deliver to politically marginalised and perhaps illegal settlements, means that it is easier to overlook their existence than work with them in the supply process.

In terms of the private sector debate, it is notable that small-scale independent providers have been delivering a fully private service to high numbers of poor households for decades. However, rarely do we witness a partnership arrangement in which the municipal (or line) agency is responsible for the urban service, and rarely do we see any official recognition of the role independent providers play within the city. In contrast to the increasing attention being paid to municipal labourers – often a subject of great concern in the formulation of PPPs – the impacts of formal private sector involvement on independent providers are rarely addressed. On the contrary, SSIPs often have their investments expropriated by newly-appointed concessionaires without compensation (see Box 7.11 illustrating the *aguateros* in Paraguay).

In many cases, the important role played by small-scale independent providers in developing cities has been overlooked in the push to attract the capital investment and managerial skills that come with large-scale operators and long-term contracts. However if municipalities are to work successfully towards an overall poverty strategy, it is absolutely essential that they recognise the complementary roles of these smaller private entrepreneurs. The poverty analysis and the technical analysis of existing services should therefore include a detailed assessment of the existing role and impacts of small-scale service delivery to the city and to poor communities in particular. With this information in hand, municipalities are in a better position to devise arrangements that build on local capacities.

Box 6.10 outlines some of the types and characteristics of small-scale independent providers working in water, sanitation and solid waste services in developing cities. They provide a diverse collection of services in a highly competitive market. Activities tend to focus on activities in the secondary and tertiary sectors (with the exception of borehole operators, or the few small-scale private networks) as small-scale independent providers tend to operate in distribution and collection at the local level; there is a clear distinction between water, sanitation and waste service providers. They rarely provide services in more than one sector.

The small-scale enterprise is typically an informal, independent, subsistence, self-employed or family-based arrangement, managed on a day-to-day basis and providing a service that requires low levels of investment. Most have developed in

6

Box 6.9   A Micro-enterprise Profile
Billy Hattingh Solid Waste, South Africa

The Billy Hattingh solid waste removal scheme came about in 1992–93, prior to the South African democratic elections as a result of the relationship between Billy Hattingh (BHA), a local entrepreneur, and two local banks. The objectives of the initiative were to assist in the development of micro-enterprise among black communities in South Africa, to improve environmental conditions for poor communities, to strengthen the communities served, and more generally, to promote the growth of the small and medium enterprise sector in South Africa. The strategy for realising this objective has focused on establishing innovative solid waste micro-enterprise in otherwise unserved urban communities (formerly township areas). The initiative assists unemployed but interested individuals from the previously disadvantaged groups, to work towards the development of an effective and profitable business.

The scheme relies on a facilitator to seek interested local authorities (such as Tygerberg and Greater Alberton) to enter into a tri-partite partnership arrangement. This contractual arrangement is between the facilitator (at the outset BHA, now Tedcor), the municipality and the selected solid waste entrepreneur. The aim of this arrangement is to provide a formal structure for local waste services, underpinned by a formal connection to an established entrepreneur. Once a local authority and a community were selected, a steering committee was formed (consisting of local civic leaders, the municipality and Billy Hattingh). This committee is responsible for the selection of the entrepreneur. Candidates must be unemployed and resident in the community to be served, and that they must be willing and able to employ local labour in the business.

Local banks have undertaken to provide financial support for all approved projects facilitated by BHA. The financial support includes a loan for a truck, tractor or trailer and a 30m³ storage container, as well as other necessary appliances and equipment. Maintenance and repairs are carried out by the supplier of the equipment or by a dealer approved by Billy Hattingh. BHA is responsible for the monthly reporting and for ensuring proper financial management of each micro-enterprise. This includes ensuring not only that the loan financing is successfully obtained and repaid, but also that all taxes, personal contributions, compensations, insurances and so on are separately accounted for and used solely for this purpose.

Following a competitive tender, the entrepreneur signs a contract with the municipality undertaking to provide a service in a defined area, and the municipality pays a monthly fee directly to the operator. The municipality retains responsibility for the service and the collection of service payments from residents. The term of the service contract is normally five years. The contract provides strict performance standards outlining the services to be provided, including that the entrepreneur shall collect all waste deposited in designated waste containers from every collection point within the designated area once a week; provide a litter-picking service; sweep and remove all debris and sand from all surfaced roads, footpaths and sidewalks etc.; and that the entrepreneur should deliver and collect waste bags without containers. The liaison committees responsible for monitoring performance include municipal representatives, BHA (now Tedcor), the entrepreneurs and community development forums, and as such communities have been given a defined role in the delivery process.

In order to ensure that entrepreneurs have the capacity to fulfil all the tasks associated with their enterprise, BHA provides training and development services and in the past has provided the technical and financial training necessary. This capacity building is a critical phase in the overall process, improving skills in business management, personnel management, industrial relations and waste and transport management. This training has been developed to suit the nature of micro-enterprise operations.

All stakeholders – communities, council officials, the entrepreneurs, trade unions and the financing banks – have provided positive feedback on the initiative. In Khayelitsha (on the outskirts of Cape Town), prior to the introduction of the initiative by the Tygerberg council, the lack of door-to-door collection and frequent removal of waste from communal skips, combined with illegal dumping and indifferent communities and workers, had resulted in very poor environmental conditions. At this time the cost of a far inferior service was in the order of US$0.30 per service per month, and this has been reduced to US$0.18. Since the micro-enterprise scheme was launched, conditions have improved radically, service is reliable, communities are working in support of a clean neighbourhood, residents are proud to invite people to their homes, former dump sites have been converted into taxi ranks and parks, and the people employed through the initiative are empowered and are now able to provide adequate incomes for their households. The success of the scheme has spread, and a number of councils have entered the scheme, meaning that a large number of solid waste micro-enterprises have been established.

Source: personal interviews with Tedcor; Sindane, 2000

response to demand; they must win their customers' loyalty, maintain their equipment effectively to maximise their efficiency, and innovate and adapt in order to stay in business in a competitive market.[10] As a result they are often knowledgeable about users' ability and willingness to pay, and about the specifics of local conditions – what works and what does not. With the exceptions of those who operate exploitative monopolies, a characteristic of SSIPs is the demand-responsive nature of their service.

Conditions obviously vary according to context, but in terms of water supply, small-scale independent providers frequently work in the expanding peripheral areas of cities. These areas are settled informally and are rarely served by networks. These marginalised poor communities and households require small quantities of water for domestic (and sometimes agricultural) use. They find ways to pay for it, and it is now well established that they are often willing to pay, or have to pay well over the price paid by the non-poor for their water supply. The consumption patterns and the preferences shown by consumers reinforce the need for flexibility, as the livelihood strategies of the poor adjust in accordance with varying incomes and expenditures. Small-scale service providers also serve non-poor customers residing outside the network area, and poor communities in core areas of the city. Many of the inner areas of cities have no access to water due to the unaffordable nature of water connections, the illegality of the settlements, the marginal nature of the land, or the political difficulties of accessing network supply. In a range of Latin American, Asian and African cities, evidence suggests that the ISPs operate a competitive water distribution market for the poor, and they work in parallel with, but rarely in association with the monopolistic, large-scale, private or public sector water operators.

Levels of sanitation services vary considerably throughout the South. Even within Africa, the extensive networks of Southern African cities, such as those found in Zimbabwe, stand in stark contrast to East Africa, where most cities lack sewerage networks. For the overwhelming majority of poor citizens, access to clean and effective sanitation services is limited (generally more limited than water), and SSIPs fill the gaps in this provision. As with solid waste, workers in sanitation services (often called 'conservancy workers' when employed by the government) tend to be very poor themselves; they operate vacuum trucks for the cleaning of septic tanks, or clean latrines manually to remove sludge. The work is poorly paid, has a low status and is detrimental to their health. Other entrepreneurs have established public toilet (or shower) facilities which, apart from providing a service to the general population, provide a safe alternative facility for women and girls, otherwise accustomed to squatting in unsafe neighbouring areas at night.

Solid waste services provided by SSIPs include sweeping, door-to-door collection, area collection by handcarts, rag-picking and recycling. Often, the poor provide these services to the non-poor or better-off poor, who are willing to part with small sums to avoid having to undertake these tasks themselves. Evidence in Hyderabad and Bangalore in India concerning CBOs that arrange for poor householders to collect waste indicates a demand for lane-level solid waste services, and shows that mechanisms can be arranged for payment. In each case, householders paid the waste collector a small monthly fee for the service.

Evidence suggests that a number of factors, closely linked to the informality of SSIPs, constrain their inclusion in government-initiated partnership arrangements. These include:

- lack of inclusion of SSIPs as stakeholders in the strategic approach to the partnership;
- lack of legal provision for SSIPs, even in the context of policies encouraging private sector participation;
- drive to formalise business activity, which can put small-scale operators under financial stress (if taxation systems are biased and they do not have the financial management support necessary to undertake their trade in the formal sector);
- lack of access to credit or a sound financial base;
- fear that their efforts will be expropriated in the future;
- lack of capacity of their customer base (e.g., low levels of literacy, unemployment and the lack of physical wellbeing and empowerment), which makes their clientele vulnerable to crisis;

Box **6.10**   Independent Service Provider Profiles

	Who are the independent service providers?	Benefits for the poor	Constraints on PPPs
Water services	• Standpipe operators • Water-carters (handcarts, donkey-drawn carts) • Water tankers • Water resellers • Private borehole operators • Small network operators	• Fill a service gap left by formal providers • Flexibility and adaptation to local conditions • Technical approaches suitable to the community and location • Economic options suitable to the community and location • Employment comes from the community • Money for the service stays close to the community • Local entrepreneurial talent is developed	• Legal uncertainty • Lack of recognition of their contributions • Risk of investment being expropriated by the concessionaires • Usually they are unorganised, which means many relationships (rather than one with a larger company) must be managed
Sanitation services	• Latrine cleaners • Public toilet operators • Vacuum truck operators • Sludge treatment plant operators	• Flexibility and adaptation to local conditions • Technical approaches suitable to the community and location • Economic options suitable to the community and location • Employment comes from the community • Money for the service stays close to the community • Local entrepreneurial talent is developed	• Risky investment, particularly if large-scale private operators are likely to displace them from the market • Legal uncertainty • Lack of recognition • Work conditions harmful to health • Usually they are unorganised, which means many relationships (rather than one with a larger company) must be managed
Solid waste services	• Sweepers • Collectors • Drivers • Rag-pickers	• Service areas that cannot be serviced by conventional city-wide methods • Cost effective • Affordable • Flexible • Employment comes from the community • Money for the service stays close to the community • Local entrepreneurial talent is developed	• Often not effectively integrated into the city-wide system • Often suffer from the lack of access to micro-credit (and technical assistance) • Usually they are unorganised, which means many relationships (rather than one with a larger company) must be managed

- lack of land tenure in the areas serviced by the SSIPs, which means that the type of service they provide is limited;
- lack of coordination between SSIPs in addressing blockages;
- lack of SSIP associations that can effectively interact with large-scale operations; and
- lack of business management skills.

Despite these impediments, SSIPs bring substantial benefits to cities and to poor communities. For instance, they typically:

- reach the households that formal service providers have failed to reach;
- reach physically marginal areas (e.g., flooded marshlands, steep hillsides) that are not served by networks or formal providers due to technical constraints on network infrastructure and/or a lack of land tenure;
- are flexible and can provide, either individually or through market forces, the type of service that customers demand (and can afford);
- adapt to changing circumstances to ensure they make a profit;
- are particularly knowledgeable about the constraints of local conditions and communities; and
- are often efficient due to the high density of the settlement.[11]

It is important for municipal officials to note that SSIPs already play a role in service provision in their cities. Where they are not exploitative, small-scale providers that fill gaps in existing services represent a significant resource that frequently meets the differentiated needs of poor consumers. Sectoral reform that focuses on increasing private sector involvement should recognise that small-scale providers are an essential part of this sector. The strategy developed for service partnerships should consider, through unbundling approaches, how SSIPs are brought into the partnership in the short, medium and long term, the formal and informal relationships between these partners, and the impacts of this change on the poor. Understanding of what SSIPs provide and why is a key starting point. Over time strategies may also need to define mechanisms for assisting these service providers to find new areas of employment or enhance their businesses, whether through skills training, income generation activities or the development of alternative approaches.

Potential roles of the private sector

Given the diversity of the individuals and organisations included in the term 'private sector', it should be no surprise that there is a huge number of potential roles for the sector. In relation to water and sanitation services or solid waste management, municipalities can test whether the private sector – in its broadest sense – has the capacity to carry out technical roles, such as design, construction, operation and maintenance, whether it has the financial resources to bring revenue (for long-term investment or ongoing operations) to the partnership, and whether it has the managerial and operational skills to take on overall operational and customer management. Municipalities must also investigate the capacity of the private sector to engage in participatory processes and generally work with poor communities in the city.

Challenges to effective private sector engagement

Although evidence reveals the substantial benefits of engaging the private sector, there are some particular challenges to its effective participation. These often arise out of using the formal private sector for tasks that are beyond its core competencies, and out of the difficulty of constructing effective interfaces between the stakeholders. Unlike small-scale providers, international and national private sector enterprises may not:

- have experience of and empathy with the poor;
- have staff who are skilled in working with poor, heterogeneous urban communities;
- feel comfortable with the divergent characteristics of municipal or civil society partners, and prefer instead to go it alone;

Links to Boxes
3.4, 6.12, 6.26, 7.21, 8.13

Box 6.11   The Roles of an NGO in a Water and Sanitation Partnership
South Africa

The mission of the Mvula Trust (see also Box 3.4) is to improve the health and welfare of poor and disadvantaged South Africans by increasing their access to safe and sustainable water and sanitation services. Its strategy is to support the development of good practice in the sector by testing and advocating sustainable models of cost-effective delivery and management. In 1997, Mvula Trust entered a consortium as the institutional and social development (ISD)-lead service provider for the build, operate, train and transfer (BoTT) contract for the delivery of water to poor peri-urban and rural villages in the Eastern Cape of South Africa. The provision for this ISD role, termed 'organisational development', was included from the outset in the Terms of Reference (ToR) as one of the key roles in the partnership arrangement and delivery process.

Under the BoTT arrangement, the ISD tasks for which Mvula Trust is responsible include:

- *Establishing sustainable community-based organisations.* Community leadership is considered a critical dimension of the BoTT approach. This task area is aimed at establishing effective communication channels between the community, the municipality and service providers. It is achieved through the structuring and organisation of a project steering committee and village water committee, and by working with local government to ensure that communication between community organisations and the council are established and effective. Mvula Trust appoints specialist community workers to adapt participatory methods with each individual community to enhance existing organisations and to facilitate decision-making regarding services.

- *Facilitating agreements and cost recovery mechanisms.* The ToR for the ISD services links the establishment of effective CBOs to the customer service agreements that are necessary for the works to proceed. ISD workers are responsible for working with communities to explain proposals, make revisions and ultimately sign off the customer agreement. The ISD provider is also responsible for building awareness in cost recovery. This area of work involves liaison with the community to establish agreement on overall costs and the development of options with the community for the payment of tariffs. Mvula Trust is also charged with the identification of poor households unable to afford tariffs, and with setting recommendations for how tariffs will be covered to ensure that they are included in the benefits of the improved service.

- *Providing health and hygiene promotion.* Utilising participatory methods, and starting with an analysis of existing health patterns, baselines, identification of primary health problems and health-related behavioural changes, the health promotion activities are developed around one key behaviour that undermines health in the community. The work thus includes identification, planning, implementation, monitoring and evaluation. Indicators are framed in terms of increased knowledge of health and hygiene issues within the communities.

- *Undertaking monitoring and evaluation.* This programme aims to monitor and evaluate the outcomes of BoTT activities in each community during the operation and maintenance phase of the works. Utilising participatory methods, the ISD team identify problem areas related to the water supply scheme and suggest solutions and recommendations for refurbishment.

- *Developing the water service provider role.* The development of a water service provider (WSP) as a long-term organisation to operate the water system is the primary mechanism for the delivery of service improvements. The ISD team plays a key role in establishing the development of the WSP and the institutionalisation of the WSP in the community. Allied to this is capacity building to ensure that the proposed WSP is able to carry out the role defined in the national regulatory framework. This includes, for instance, customer liaison, management and cost recovery.

- *Facilitating labour procurement.* This component of the work aims to promote local employment through the procurement of labour from each community. The ISD provider role facilitates this process by strengthening the established CBOs (in this case the Project Steering Committee) to act as brokers in the procurement of manual labour for construction works, and by supporting the community in its liaison with the contractor. Communities are expected to form a labour desk and formulate business plans in accordance with BoTT procedures. Capacity building is provided to ensure that nominated labour desk members from the community are familiar with the tasks involved and the procedural limitations of the work.

- *Building local ownership.* The contract provides for the hiring and training of previously disadvantaged individuals and companies to carry out the works, and for them to gradually gain share ownership in the management company.

The Mvula experience of facilitating these ISD activities has been mixed. The emergence of disagreement within the partnership arrangement – especially where partners have not appreciated the importance and implications of community-based approaches – has created ongoing problems for Mvula in achieving the sustainability it places high on its agenda.

Source: Developed from RoSA, 2000b

- appreciate the need for time to undertake participatory processes; or
- appreciate the social and cultural differences between international corporations and local settings, and between business and society.

In particular, the private sector often has difficulty with methodologies that involve poor householders and communities as decision-makers and participants. There is an underlying belief that 'business knows best'. With the right operator, and if approached creatively with support from other actors, these differences may be important sources of innovation.

Civil Society Actors

Over the last decade, the role of civil society in development initiatives has gained increasing acceptance, and this shift has been taken up in a few PPPs focused on the poor. These initiatives have recognised the central place of consumers, the critical supporting role of NGOs and the important political role of trade unions. While these are just three actors in a wider range of civil society individuals and organisations, they perform greatly differing roles in the formulation of partnerships and are therefore discussed in detail below.

Non-governmental Organisations

☐ The characteristics of non-governmental organisations

There is as much diversity in the NGO sector as in the municipal and private sectors, discussed above. International, national and local NGOs, with vastly different mandates, display very different levels of skills and experience, and thus offer very different competencies to service-oriented partnerships. Some are staffed by social and technical professionals, some by volunteers, and others by a mixture of the two – all in an effort to bring benefit to others.

Despite this massive diversity, when compared with the public and private sectors, NGOs also reveal a set of fundamental and unique characteristics (see Box 6.23). Unlike the private sector, which is driven by a profit motive, the primary interest of (legitimate) NGOs working with the poor is social.[12] Many organisations (large and small, international and local) work without profit, generally undertaking their role with the purpose of promoting justice and equity and improving the quality of the lives of vulnerable and marginalised groups in the society. Adhering to ideology is often an important characteristic of such organisations – many struggle with their roles and the validity of certain actions. In the main, their work is carried out for public rather than private benefit.

Like private sector companies, the scope, skills and overall capacity of NGOs will largely determine the roles they can perform within a partnership, and just as with private sector companies, many municipalities are wary of NGOs and their roles with the community, particularly when past relationships and experiences have been ineffective and confrontational. Many will not be clear about the benefits that the NGO sector can bring to a service partnership. Yet over recent decades, poverty reduction projects in a number of sectors have exposed the benefits of NGO involvement in replicating initiatives.

NGOs work to a timeframe that is very different from that of the public and private sectors. Their over-riding concern with the sustainability of service improvements often makes their vision long term. This is often reflected, for instance, in their commitment to the time element of effective participatory processes. In practice, this ideal vision is often affected by the short-term and tenuous nature of their funding. Only well-established NGOs are usually able to work within a timeframe that brings about their sustainability objectives.

Primary assets of many NGOs include their dedication and capacity to work in diverse and often difficult situations with few resources. Because of these characteristics, many NGOs working with urban poor communities build a level of trust

Box **6.12**   Key Issues for NGOs: The Experience of The Mvula Trust
South Africa

Links to Boxes
3.4, 6.11, 6.26, 7.21, 8.13

The Mvula Trust has been involved in the institutional and social development component of BoTT for four years. During this time it has identified a number of important issues that jeopardise its ongoing involvement in PPP approaches to the delivery of water and sanitation services to the poor. Foremost among these are:

- *The lack of commensurate objectives and vision.* One of the fundamental areas of conflict for an NGO working with private sector partners is the diverse nature of their goals. If the objectives, vision, and organisational mandates of the private sector and the government cannot converge, Mvula doubts that the arrangement will be sustainable or will meet its own policy objectives. Experience to date in the BoTT suggests that the main areas of disquiet are those that the NGO prioritises. These include, for instance, participatory methodologies, sustainability, handover and replicability. Mvula has found that these goals frequently conflict with the efficiency objectives of the private sector, but it asserts that this efficiency is short term, and needs to be reconsidered in terms of the long-term sustainability of the outputs. In the lead up to BoTT, the project preparation stage did not provide opportunity for partners to air their concerns and agree approaches at the outset. Mvula emphasises the importance of establishing non-negotiable items at the outset. In this situation it is possible to resolve problematic issues or withdraw from the arrangement.

- *The problem of transparency.* One of the areas that Mvula finds untenable is that the project itself promotes transparency and accountability, but the private sector is unwilling to present arrangements in a transparent manner. The Mvula experience with communities in BoTT suggests that its own reputation is put at risk because the consortium is not willing to openly declare expenditure, income and profit, and is not willing to subject itself to transparent monitoring and performance evaluation. From the Mvula perspective, this is essential not only to ensure that the principle of transparency is equally applied to all aspects of the partnership and service, but to ensure that Mvula is not unknowingly involved in exploitative practice.

- *The issue of profit.* A key policy question facing the Mvula Trust is how it should address profit, and how to determine an acceptable level of profit. It is widely accepted that the private sector brings with it a profit incentive, and that profit brings with it efficiency. Improved efficiencies are a key goal of the private sector to ensure that it is able to decrease costs and improve its profits. However, the lack of transparency with regard to profit places the NGO partner in a consortium in which the private sector partners may have increased their profit margin to a level that the NGO finds exploitative and unacceptable. Second, the NGO is carrying a large portion of the responsibility but the profit is being absorbed by the private sector organisations. (In the BoTT consortium, all other lead service providers are shareholders in the consortium, but Mvula Trust declined the opportunity to be a shareholder out of concern that it could negatively influence or compromise its role.) Mvula currently functions on a non-profit basis within the BoTT. It is currently considering whether such activities should subsidise the advocacy and policy work it undertakes as a core function and/or whether BoTT should be used as a source of finance to create an organisation that is sustainable for 5–10 years.

- *The learning and knowledge agenda.* In order to meet the Mvula mandate for effective learning and dissemination of best practice, it is necessary for partners to subject the partnership arrangement to objective evaluation. Such a commitment has not been forthcoming and as a result there is no adequate monitoring of private sector partner performance, which would enable problems to be aired and resolved, and lessons to be learnt and disseminated.

- *Planned internal decision-making.* It may be inevitable that opposing views will be formed within the NGO, especially where decision-making at the highest levels of management is overtaken by bidding processes at the local level. In Mvula, a division arose between those who adopted a purist approach aimed at maintaining the integrity of the community-based method of delivery, and the PPP camp, which adopted a practical approach aimed at improving services for large numbers by partnering others to provide services. While the advocates of the practical approach argue that they had a social responsibility to be involved, to influence the agenda and to bring about the best possible solutions, there is nevertheless an unhappy air about the association with the partnership consortium.

- *Acceptable company policy.* Mvula Trust is concerned that its partners should uphold the same ethical work practices that it does.

Source: Interview with Jamie de Jager, Mvula Trust, March 2001

with the poor that is rare for a government agency or private sector company. Much of the work carried out by NGOs focuses on incremental service improvements, and typically this is based around community mobilisation and capacity building. Compared with the public and private spheres they generally show superior skill in communication and thus they are frequently, but not always, ideal facilitators for action at the neighbourhood level.

International NGOs working in service delivery, such as WaterAid, are strong organisations with their own networks at the funding and local levels, and are frequently involved in both policy and implementation. Many international organisations are still opponents of PPPs, but increasingly they are entering and enriching the debate with their perspective. Despite their caution, many have recognised that widespread improvements to urban living conditions can only be brought about through widespread replication of local initiatives, and the overall capacity of the bulk supply. Too many times they have installed taps to find there is no water to flow through them, or organised solid waste collection to find there is no effective city-wide disposal.

Local NGOs are usually involved in the direct implementation of projects and provide valuable, trusted links to poor neighbourhoods. Many will be part of a local civil society network. The linkage between levels, however, is highly variable.[13] In urban areas, the mandates of many NGOs will be centred on one particular concern: advocacy, literacy, micro-credit, health or children's welfare, for instance. Many will have dedicated themselves to this issue and have established credibility and specialist expertise. A primary problem arising in relation to the delivery of services is that the NGOs best placed to work with particular communities may not always have the technical skills to work effectively in physical service provision. This issue of technical knowledge and the ability to communicate options to the poor is becoming increasingly important. Some NGOs expand their scope of work and develop this capacity, but this is not always successful or sustainable, because it is highly dependent on individual skills and attitudes.

☐ The potential roles of non-governmental organisations in service partnerships

The role of the NGO in partnership arrangements for service delivery is therefore generally associated with communities, particularly poor communities. The efficacy with which NGOs can perform roles will vary according to the capacity and interest of the organisation and specific individuals, and according to whether or not it has an established relationship with a community. The first book in this Municipal Capacity Building Series[14] proposed that the potential roles of NGOs include mediation, facilitation, coordination, capacity building, community development, dispute resolution and post-project sustainability. These and other key roles are discussed in relation to service partnerships below.

■ Project formulation and development

NGOs can make a very important contribution to the initial formulation and development of partnerships and service improvement projects in low-income areas. For instance:

- NGO advice in project formulation often leads to more appropriate service responses. Community decision-making is dependent on capacity and communication. Experience suggests that communities making decisions over service options are facilitated by NGO involvement, as NGOs are more familiar with community capacity and needs.
- NGOs can provide knowledge about the appropriate programming and sequencing of activities in relation to capacity building, and can assist in the effective coordination of social, institutional and infrastructure-related activities.
- NGOs often have experience that enables them to understand the role of SSIPs in service delivery, and may be able to facilitate institutional arrangements that bring SSIPs into partnerships rather than marginalise them.
- NGOs will probably be best equipped to understand a community's own resources – such as labour and finances – and how to integrate these into the overall formulation and development of the arrangement.

Box 6.13   Factors Affecting NGOs: The Experience of IIED
Buenos Aires, Argentina

Links to Boxes
3.5, 5.4, 7.2, 7.3, 7.11, 7.18, 8.12, 9.8

In Buenos Aires, the local NGO IIED-AL has been involved in poverty reduction activities, and specifically the improvement of water and sanitation services in Barrio San Jorge, for nine years. IIED-AL involvement in service upgrading originated because the government and line agencies did not have the resources or incentive to undertake works in the *barrios* of Buenos Aires. The network installed in the *barrio* functioned (and was funded) independently.

In 1993, when the Aguas Argentinas (AA) become the concessionaire for water and sanitation network services in Buenos Aires, it did not immediately look to the low-income areas to expand their coverage. Typically, the barrios are informal and poor communities without legal land tenure, living in irregular settlement patterns. Under the contract, AA was responsible for serving only the periphery of the settlement, and then only to legally recognised buildings. However, when AA recognised that it was necessary to start to address the specific problems of low-income settlements, the Barrio San Jorge provided a unique opportunity. In this *barrio*, AA found three important conditions: a small network had been constructed, NGOs and CBOs were established locally and working together on community development, and the municipality was willing to support the operator's involvement.

From its perspective, IIED-AL felt it would be prudent to work with the concessionaire to improve water and sanitation services for the poor, and to promote replication across the *barrios* of Buenos Aires. The question became 'how' not 'whether' it would be involved. How else were water and sanitation services to the *barrios* going to be improved? How could AA be assisted in working in low-income areas to the mutual benefit of all parties (the communities, the concessionaire and the government)?

The collaboration between AA and IIED-AL functioned on a number of levels; the NGO had two different arms. IIED-AL perceived the arrangement to be somewhat precarious because it had no ongoing contractual arrangement with the operator. In the first stage in 1995, IIED-AL and the community transferred the newly constructed independent water and sanitation network in Barrio San Jorge to AA in exchange for a connection into the city-wide system (the construction cost of the network was US$150,000). Following this, IIED-AL undertook short-term contracts (directly with AA) to undertake specific pieces of work. It was involved, formally and informally, in a number of activities such as promotion of activities in low-income settlements; environmental and social assessments; capacity building of Aguas Argentinas managers; sensitisation of AA staff to work in low-income settlements; explaining the codes of working in low-income settlements; and supporting the community development cell established in AA with an IIED-AL representative.

The experience of working with the private sector has been mixed. On the one hand it has been problematic. A level of mistrust and scepticism clouded the perspectives of both parties. The process introduced some risk into the well-established IIED-AL organisation and activities. At times, its reputation was threatened as colleagues in the NGO sector (with little exposure to such private–NGO links) saw IIED's association with Aguas Argentinas as questionable. Many NGOs perceive IIED-AL as working 'for' and not 'with' Aguas Argentinas. This has undermined important collaborations with other NGOs and IIED's role in the local NGO network. Departing from its established activities, IIED had to embrace a number of challenges to work with AA, a process which temporarily destabilised the organisation. Despite these difficulties, IIED-AL concluded that it was worthwhile to help promote the process of institutionalisation of community issues and low-income approaches in a privately-operated utility – especially one responsible for water and sanitation services until 2023.

Benefits then became evident. The partnership activities with IIED-AL undoubtedly helped AA to extend services to low-income areas. The lack of explicit extension mandates to low-income areas meant that the operator could opt to delay such improvements for years. The work with IIED-AL, and the confidence this has lent to AA, has meant that more poor people are receiving services (and improvements to the quality of their lives) at an earlier stage, and perhaps more than would otherwise have been intended. AA has also gained the confidence to work with other NGOs, CBOs and consultants.

Various lessons have emerged from the IIED-AL experience, each of them instructive for local authorities seeking to focus partnerships on the poor and looking to the NGO sector for support to this end. These include:

- Recognising the conflict many NGOs could face if they are to enter into formal or informal associations with the private sector. It is not a simple or natural step for them to take. Many NGOs will resist such a move, and this link may not be possible in the short term.
- Considering the nature of the contractual relationship with the concessionaire. NGOs invest their reputation in such a venture. For NGOs with a poverty reduction mandate, this must be accompanied by some commitment from the operator that its work will be used to the benefit and not the detriment of the poor.
- Considering, in the long term, how NGOs will be compensated for work that supports the concessionaire. It is essential for NGOs to be involved in, and agree, as many provisions as possible before the contract is signed. Without this it becomes a powerless partner.

Source: Developed with IIED-AL

☐ Capacity building

Most CBOs that play a meaningful role in development processes have been empowered through the capacity building work of NGOs or external agents. NGOs can enhance community skills in leadership, literacy, public speaking, teamwork etc., such that communities are able to formulate and articulate decisions confidently in unfamiliar environments. At an organisational level, capacity building activities by NGOs may mean making an organisation or activity financially sustainable (for instance, the day-to-day operation and maintenance of a communal water-tap). In some partnerships, this may mean that the NGO takes on a role in ensuring that the CBO is formalised. In the BoTT in the Eastern Cape in South Africa (see Boxes 6.11 and 6.12), the NGO Mvula Trust is one of the partners of the contracting consortium, and they are specifically responsible for institutional and community development.

By and large, business organisations with their profit-maximisation goals are comparatively heavy-handed at working with communities, and are not interested in their capacity. The capacity building role of an NGO may also include capacity building for the partners. The lack of skills in relation to social and institutional dimensions, and in terms of interacting with poor communities, suggests there is a critical need for greater flows of information from competent NGOs to the private sector. This requires a society-friendly environment and a desire on the part of the other partners to learn.

☐ Community interface

NGOs are normally suited to interfacing with the community.[15] In service delivery projects where the private sector becomes involved in low-income areas, skilled community workers must carry out interactions with the community. The private sector is often heavy-handed in this regard, and while some municipalities have built this capacity through recent experiences with community participation, the NGO sector may still be best placed to take on this role. NGOs can particularly assist in forming a bridge at the early stage by building trust and confidence. Locally established NGOs are often the entry point for communities and can facilitate the process while all the parties become familiar with one another. In some partnerships this role is extended and the NGO becomes the regular conduit for all discussions with communities. Participatory information collection is a key starting point. While this may result in consistency and increased trust between other partnership members, this can place the NGO in an impossible position – especially when it is the bearer of bad tidings or fundamentally disagrees with the message it must impart. For example, in the South African BoTT project, Mvula Trust was opposed to the introduction of pre-paid meters for poor communities, but was contractually obliged to discuss proposals with the community.

☐ Awareness building

A primary role of an NGO in a partnership is helping communities to understand processes and options. This includes building awareness of the various roles and relationships of the partners under the contract, and of the broader legislative framework. It should include information and awareness that enhances choice. Institutional relationships are often complex and can provide a shield of protection. In consortium arrangements, it is vital that poor communities know who is responsible for which tasks, and that these organisations are accountable to them.

☐ Advocacy

Even with improved awareness, a poor community may still not have the capacity to act as an equal partner at the outset, and an NGO can help represent and explain their interests and perspectives. While this may lead to conflict and disagreement over some central issues, the ultimate goal of sustainable service delivery is more likely to come about if communities are adequately represented in the partnership. In this respect the NGO plays an important advocacy role.

| Box 6.14   Disaggregating Service Consumers

	Destitute	Very poor	Poor	Non-poor
Water supply				
Primary interest	• Survival	• Basic service	• Affordable service	• Service at lowest cost
Livelihood requirements	• Access	• Flexibility	• Better service • Flexibility	• Reliability
Primary constraints	• Homelessness	• Insecure tenure • Occupy most marginal land	• Possible insecurity of tenure	• None
Capacity to pay*	• No	• Basic rates, with flexibility in payments	• Basic rates, probably most of the year	• Yes
Capacity/willingness to participate	• No	• Yes, with support	• Yes, maybe dominant	• No willingness
Level of service required**	• Communal, free	• Varies, but likely to change constantly.	• Immediate access, maybe household connection	• Household connection
Sanitation services				
Primary interest	• Survival	• Basic service	• Affordable service	• Service provided at lowest cost
Livelihood requirements	• Access	• Access	• Close access	• Hygiene
Primary constraints	• Homelessness	• Insecure tenure • Occupy marginal land	• Lack of land for sanitation facilities	• None
Capacity to pay	• No	• Basic rates, would not prioritise as for water	• Basic rates, probably most of the year	• Yes
Willingness to pay	• No	• No	• Some households	• Yes
Willingness to participate	• No	• May not prioritise	• May not prioritise	• No willingness
Level of service required**	• Communal, free	• Varies, but likely to change constantly	• Immediate access, choice in service level	• Household connection
Solid waste services				
Primary interest	• None	• Basic service	• Basic service	• Household removal
Livelihood requirements	• No waste	• Little waste, not prioritised	• Some waste, but rarely prioritised, flexibility	• Hygiene
Primary constraints	• Homelessness	• Interest • Dumping creates public health hazard	• Interest • Dumping creates public health hazard	• None
Capacity to pay	• No	• Basic rates, would not prioritise at all	• Basic rates	• Yes
Willingness to pay/ participate	• No	• Some households (capacity building)	• Some households (capacity building)	• Some pay • None participate
Level of service required**	• Communal, free	• Free	• Basic service	• Household service

* Willingness to pay will vary much more significantly and is not included here
** Level of service required often expressed differently by men and women

☐ Service provider

The NGO may also be well placed to take on other poverty reduction activities that reinforce and supplement physical interventions in communities. The importance of hygiene promotion, for example, is well established as an important linked activity. NGOs are often best placed to conduct related activities in relation to community capacity building. In some cases, this may lead to the formation of a community NGO or CBO (such as a cooperative) to take over tasks at the neighbourhood level.

☐ Cost recovery

Perhaps one of the most difficult issues for NGOs is the promotion of cost recovery. It must be linked to issues of fairness and service sustainability. Some NGOs find it difficult to work with cost recovery on principle, while others are concerned more with fairness in allocating costs and determining what is affordable. Frequently, an NGO is the most appropriate actor to work with communities to develop a culture of willingness to pay for a service to ensure sustainability.

☐ Monitoring and evaluation

Closely associated with their roles as advocates for communities, NGOs can perform important roles in monitoring and evaluating progress and impacts at the local level. They are probably best equipped to implement participatory monitoring approaches with communities, and can provide an important role in representing communities for some regulatory issues.

☐ Conflict resolution and arbitration

The role of the NGO as a community interface is frequently extended to that of arbitrator when disputes arise between the private sector and community organisations. This can place NGOs in a situation where there is a conflict of interest, irrespective of their contractual relationships.

☐ Funding channel

Some NGOs have the skills and experience to take on the role of a funding channel. This is likely to be on a small scale; few partnerships envisage the NGO as the conduit for large-scale infrastructure projects, and few NGOs have sufficient project-management or business capacity to handle these projects. They may, however, be the most trusted agents for handling money for community development.

☐ What are the primary challenges for non-governmental organisations working in partnerships?

The process of working with the public and private sectors is neither straightforward nor natural for most organisations in the NGO sector. In many recent policy discussions, assumptions have been made about the capacity and willingness of NGOs to participate in and lend their support to pro-poor initiatives. Many are not able or willing to do so. The mandates and attitudes of many NGOs are so far removed from the private sector that they will shy away from entering such arrangements, while others have acknowledged that the poor will benefit from the role such partnerships can perform. And, as in the private sector, many NGOs have only limited capacities.

The challenge for capable NGOs and for other partners seeking NGO support is to address and resolve the conflicts associated with:

- divergent ideologies, project objectives, methods and work practices;
- mistrust and scepticism built up prior to partnership approaches;
- conflict resolution between communities and private operators;

6

Box **6.15**   Community Mobilisation and Management
Lima, Peru

Links to Box
6.8

One of the notable characteristics of the EU-funded programme established to improve water supply to the outlying areas of Lima, was the role the community adopted. The empowerment process led to it becoming the consumer and the client of the water tanker delivery service (see Box 6.8), and to more generally take responsibility for the management, operation and maintenance of its own water supply system.

Following some successful pilot work undertaken independently by the NGO Ecociudad in the early 1990s, a potable water supply project (the APPJ project) was developed with assistance from the EU with a budget of US$15 million. The primary objectives of the programme were: to establish a sustainable and reliable water supply for the marginal urban settlements of Lima, through the physical construction of reservoirs and the installation of local distribution networks through the settlements; the integration of water tanker supply system in a large number of areas; and to participate fully as key stakeholders through the mobilisation of the community, able to take on a management role upon completion.

Civil society is both the beneficiary and the organiser/supply manager of the process. With technical and capacity building support from local NGOs, communities first assist in the construction of the reservoir and network by providing unskilled labour for digging trenches and the construction of standpipes. They then form water committees called COVAAPs in each sector in which a reservoir is built.

The COVAAP (Vigilance Committee for Drinking Water) is ultimately responsible for the management of the water supply system. It must be formed by the end of the construction phase to take on the responsibility for management, operation and maintenance. The COVAAPs act as community-based water suppliers. Those requiring water to be transported to their reservoirs purchase water from the tanker drivers (at a price capped by the municipality) and this water is sold via the distribution network to each household.

There are a number of distinctive models for these 'water committees' depending on their access to water and the decision-making process of the community, but where there is no other source, they have a private–civil society contract with the water tankers. They all act as profit-making enterprises, but one sub-contracts to the private sector, and the other conducts the distribution process itself.

In the private COVAAP model, as seen in Huaycan (with a 3400-metre network, 40 communal standpipes and 50m^3 reservoir), the operation of the infrastructure and services is contracted to an association of water tanker drivers for a one-year period. It pays a monthly fee of US$58 to the local water committee and undertakes to provide an agreed service to the inhabitants of the area. Water is sold to the households, by the container, via a water attendant employed by the contractor. The COVAAP agrees the tariff at which water is sold for the duration of the contract. This water supply system is provided at a tariff that is 20% cheaper than other community models.

In the community COVAAP model, water tankers are contracted by the COVAAP to supply the water to the reservoirs. COVAAP then takes responsibility for the administration of the system, the maintenance of the system (both the standpoints and the reservoir), and for selling the water from the standpoints to the consumers in its area. The COVAAP is comprised of representatives of the local committees, central authorities, the community promoters and the public works committee promoted by the NGO, and a community representative. Because this model gives the community control over the supply process, it is the most commonly adopted model. A second community COVAAP model obtains the water directly from the SEDEPAL network.

The NGOs play a critical role in capacity building and facilitating communities, as well as a primary service provider role. This includes, for instance:

- executing the construction works;
- promoting the organisation and participation of the local communities in performing their roles;
- providing training on the administration and management of the water system;
- facilitating and managing the labour provided by the community for the construction process;
- organising local capacity building to mobilise communities; and
- organising health promotion activities with the communities.

Currently in its final stages, the initiative has resulted in the completion of 250 micro-projects (each serving 120 households), providing water to some 300 households and a total population of over 1.5 million. Total community contribution via a labour input is estimated at a value of US$3 million.

Source: Ecociudad/GHK, 2001

- funding mechanisms and availability;
- publishing and disseminating partnership experiences;
- profit margins and transparency;
- relegating interaction with NGOs to middle management, and marginalising them from decision-making processes;
- understanding the timeframe needed for institutional and social development;
- the concern for long-term impacts and effectiveness compared with short-term efficiency; and
- internal conflicts over reputation, credibility and compromise.

In order to promote NGO involvement, municipalities formulating partnerships need to identify incentives that will attract potential NGO partners. NGOs need to be reassured that they will be given equal priority and status so that their voices will be heard (see discussion in Chapter 8 highlighting the implications of contracts and structured relationships). They need to see that mechanisms are in place to ensure that partnerships are community-friendly and exhibit a social commitment (e.g., financial commitment to monitoring and evaluation, policy debate, dissemination of best practice), and that the partnership reveals a commitment to capacity building and sustainability. As such, many will argue that key process and content agreements (such as community participation) should be acknowledged at an early stage.

Consumers

☐ The nature and diversity of consumers

Increasingly, initiatives aimed at improving urban services recognise the importance of disaggregating the consumer base, targeting efforts to meet a range of consumer needs and obtaining payment reflective of both the cost of the service standard they receive and their ability to pay. There are at least two types of consumers of basic services in the urban context of developing countries. In the first instance, a fundamental distinction needs to be made between the haves and the have-nots. Non-poor and poor consumers display vastly different service needs and marked differences in capacities that profoundly affect their requirements and their participation in neighbourhood and city-wide delivery processes.

In the main, it is expected that the non-poor should remain detached from the practical implementation aspects of service delivery, pay their bills without incident and behave as informed consumers. However, it is clear that such expectations are inappropriate for poor consumers, and the distinct consumer sub-groups need different structural and process solutions. In the past, this challenge was often avoided. Operators met contractual obligations and prioritised service upgrades for non-poor consumers, as they posed the lowest risks. Alternatively, many projects failed to meet objectives because they made little differentiation between the wealthy and the poor in the organisation of the delivery process and the partners involved. Business approaches have been applied inappropriately in poor communities, or alternatives have been experimental, ad hoc or out-of-contract initiatives.

The fundamental differences between non-poor and poor consumers must be understood in terms of physical, social, political, institutional and economic factors. The most visible is the marginalisation of poor consumers within the city. Although many marginalised and poor households are situated beyond the areas that are geographically defined as slums or squatter settlements, the vast majority are concentrated in underserviced areas on marginal land, often without security of tenure. Typically, network services have not been extended to these areas. Water supply may be communal or illegally obtained, sanitation services may be rudimentary and threatening to personal health and safety, and solid waste services may be non-existent or may not be prioritised. Unlike their wealthier urban neighbours, poor residents often lack access to education, health care and income-earning opportunities. They have been marginalised from the benefits of economic growth elsewhere. Their social status is inevitably low, exacerbated by their inadequate and often unhygienic living conditions. They are generally politically marginalised; they lack access to information and are excluded from most decision-making structures.

Links to Boxes
8.8, 10.7

Box 6.16   Community Collaborations
Córdoba, Argentina

Following the introduction of a water concession in Córdoba (see Box 8.8), in 1998 the Municipality of Córdoba collaborated on a number of small pilot projects aimed at connecting poor communities much sooner than was envisaged under the long-term plan for extending the piped network. The pilot projects were carried out as tri-partite arrangements between the municipality, which contributes finance, the water operator, Aguas Cordobesas, which contributes technical assistance, and the community, which contributes voluntary unskilled labour. They have been funded by an investment grant from a special local development fund and a federal job creation scheme, under which long-term unemployed men are able to get work in unskilled labour.

Relying on clandestine connections to the piped network, the households of Barrio Estación Flores commonly experienced water shortages and low pressure, and many residents became dependent on water purchased from private tankers. Attempts to obtain legal connections to the network had repeatedly failed, so in 1999 an ad hoc committee, Ente Promotor, was created to access a US$48,000 grant from the municipal fund in order to connect to the piped network. Despite internal problems between this ad hoc water committee and the established CBO, which wished to control the fund, bids were invited, a selection process held and the municipality approved a grant transfer to the committee. The work was carried out using the voluntary labour of the community. Aguas Cordobesas provided an inspector of works. A total of 550 households in 16 blocks were connected with 4500 metres of pipes. The work took longer than originally envisaged because of the need to ensure that all households dug trenches outside their homes. Delays were also caused by disagreements over who was responsible for trenches across streets and crossroads.

The committee was successful in reducing the overall cost of the project by ensuring that appropriate materials were used (such as small-diameter pipes) and arguing for lower cost for lower levels of service. (The final cost of the works came in 10% under budget, and was equivalent to just US$78.36 per household connection – less than one-quarter of the standard connection charge of US$350 (including water meter), levied by Aguas Cordobesas on households in the city for work carried out directly by its own contractors.

A second example is provided by Barrio Quebracho, a community of 640 households that has acquired a health clinic, primary school and community centre by the efforts of the residents themselves, without any government support. Up until the pilot scheme was launched, municipal and private water tankers supplied households and there were no illegal connections. The typical monthly household water purchase was three 4000-litre units at US$10 each, giving a total expenditure of US$30. Because of the recession, the male unemployment rate in mid-2000 was over 75%. An ad hoc committee was established in 1998 and accessed a US$100,000 grant from the municipal fund. This committee was accountable to the municipality's Department of Community Participation. Two private companies placed bids to supply materials. The municipality purchased the materials from the winning bidder on behalf of the community and these supplies were then deposited. Work was successfully completed by the end of 1999. Aguas Cordobesas supplied two foremen to supervise the work of local residents, which consisted of digging the trenches outside their respective homes, and a number of unemployed labourers taken on for the construction period. 6000 metres of pipe were laid to a depth of 1.2 metres, all using labour-based construction techniques.

For many years, households in Barrio San Ignacio had been supplied with water by illegal connections to the piped network. An ad hoc water committee was formed in 1998 and a US$70,000 grant was obtained from the local development fund in order to purchase materials. In mid-1999 some 40 local men employed under the federal job creation programme, Plan Trabajar, began work under the technical supervision of Aguas Cordobesas. However, political divisions within San Ignacio soon led to disputes between the local community organisation and the ad hoc water committee over the management of the project. Accusations arose concerning alleged misuse of the municipal grant. When the Plan Trabajar programme came to an end in December 1999, residents refused to complete the work by providing voluntary labour. By mid-2000 the project was paralysed, with only half of the work completed.

The results of these small-scale collaborations have been mixed. Two experienced delays caused by conflicts over the control of funds. The ingredients of the successful projects were that the community participated in the project by supplying voluntary labour, the leadership employed transparency in the management of grant aid, a non-political approach was followed that encouraged the participation of community members in the project, and a centralised leadership was willing to reprimand members who were unwilling to make their own personal contribution to the communal effort.

Source: Adapted from Nickson, 2001b

On the other hand, non-poor consumers generally have some level of access to services, have jobs and regular income, and enjoy a higher social status – all enabling them to access the services they need. Working with the wealthy is good for business because they can afford a highly transactional relationship in which they simply pay someone to provide a service. Research in many industries has demonstrated that business processes and products can be too expensive for the poor.

The characteristics of consumers and community-based organisations[16]

The discussion earlier in this chapter draws attention to the heterogeneity of urban communities, the diversity of groups and households within the low-income bracket and the interdependence exhibited between households for services. It stresses the problem of capacity and the need for capacity building if poor consumers are to be able to pay for services and exercise rights. When considering the relative characteristics of consumers as actors in the partnership, it is essential that the poor are not considered as one homogeneous group, but are disaggregated to acknowledge their different vulnerabilities, capacities and coping strategies. Recognition of this diversity (and the need for proper assessments) will inevitably challenge some widely held views – among private operators particularly – that the poor can be viewed as one consumer type (a type that often only reflects the needs and capabilities of the most vocal members of the community). Box 6.14 sets out some of the characteristics of able and marginalised groups. It points towards a massive variation in the problems, needs, capacities and willingness of service consumers in poor urban contexts.

As individuals, consumers are simply a multitude of voices. In a PPP, individuals' resources and importance can seem minor, yet as a group they are a force and asset to be taken seriously; disaggregated consumer voices form a group that collectively may represent a market that it is possible to work with. In order for such voices to be heard, it is necessary for consumers to form interest groups or user groups to interact with other partners. In many poor urban areas these groups may be established CBOs with broad development agendas (neighbourhood committees, lane committees, people's organisations or women's groups, for instance) or a group that is developed to address a specific municipal service concern (an infrastructure committee, a water committee, a solid waste committee etc.). These two types of groups have fundamentally different attributes but the success or failure of an existing or newly formed committee will depend on the degree to which it represents the marginalised as well as the vocal elite. This requires mechanisms that ensure that the whole community is included, and capacity building to ensure the members are empowered to participate in a meaningful way.[17]

As vehicles of accountability, CBOs are important at all income levels. However, for poor people whose voices are not usually heard, effective CBOs can be critical in interacting with service suppliers. As aggregate groups, organised CBOs (perhaps working with NGOs) and networks of CBOs can:

- provide a vehicle for low-income consumers to articulate their needs and requirements;
- promote contextually specific solutions suitable to particular areas;
- influence construction, operation and maintenance and cost-recovery approaches;
- promote a livelihoods (rather than sectoral) agenda;
- create momentum for change; and
- encourage suppliers to meet (sometimes very) low levels of demand.

The potential roles of poor consumers

The potential roles of consumers in the delivery of water and waste services in urban areas are dependent on individual household capacity and collective organisational capacity. The disaggregation of consumer categories and representative organisations in relation to their resources and competencies is essential to ensure that roles are appropriate.

Links to Boxes
6.18, 12.2

Box **6.17**   **Community Shareholding and Empowerment**
Nelspruit, South Africa

In 1996, when Nelspruit, the capital of Mpumalanga province in South Africa, decided to embark on private sector participation in water supply and sanitation, it faced a number of challenges. The specific developmental purpose was to extend water infrastructure and services to those underserviced, but it was also necessary to empower the local community and ensure their participation in the process of delivery. The municipality came up with a number of innovations in a public-private partnership. These included community shareholding in the concessionaire company, a dedicated development fund that would benefit from the returns on the project and that would focus on local economic development, and systematic attempts to build skills among the labourers involved in the project.

First, a creative arrangement for community shareholding mixes the expertise of the private service provider with local knowledge and interests. At the core of this arrangement is a special-purpose company created by the winning bidder, Biwater, to act as concessionaire. To begin with, 26% of the shares in this company, the Greater Nelspruit Utility Company (GNUC), were owned by Biwater Operations, a South African subsidiary of the British water operator Biwater; 64% were owned by Biwater Capital, the company's Dutch subsidiary; and 10% were owned by SIVUKILE, a community-based consortium of local civic, youth and women's organisations.

But the contract provides for changes – subject to a due process of approval by the municipal council – that would facilitate a growing share for SIVUKILE, as well as for employees. The contract requires that Biwater Operations must, throughout the contract term, hold a significant share of 26%, but the Biwater Capital shareholding can change, especially in the interest of community empowerment. This therefore provides for an organisational structure for community involvement in the short term, with the prospect of majority ownership in the longer term. The aim is for SIVVUKILE to eventually own 51% of the GNUC, with Biwater owning 49%. One of the functions of SIVUKILE is education and training on a large scale, based on the specific opportunities offered by the project.

Biwater's participation in the utility company enables the latter to meet various financial commitments in terms of the contract, such as a substantial performance guarantee, to grow in line with the consumer price index; contract implementation fees paid at the signing of the contract; and concession fees, to be paid annually to the municipality. The company also brings international expertise, gained from its involvement in 55 countries, to the management of water services in the poor areas of Nelspruit. SIVUKILE, in turn, brings a knowledge of the community, and links with key stakeholders, to the project. It provides also a vehicle for gaining skills through the association with Biwater.

GNUC assumed responsibility for operation, management and maintenance, and for obtaining the capital investment necessary for the expansion of services as detailed in the contract. The GNUC then sub-contracted Biwater Operations as an operator, and is able to enter into sub-contracts to ensure the execution of the project. The principles of this sub-contracting are slanted towards empowerment of local small contractors and the use of local labour.

Apart from the shareholding arrangement, local empowerment is also facilitated through a community development fund, to which the consortium must contribute some of its returns. The amount to be contributed by the service provider will rise in line with consumer price inflation. Part of the agreement is that, wherever possible, preference will be given to emerging contractors. The focus is therefore on small, medium and micro-enterprises as vehicles for local economic development. The chairperson of SIVUKILE, Dr Patrick Maduna, emphasised that this fund's activities would be focused on the community as a whole, and not on individual gains. He believed that a community focus would also enhance the empowerment of individuals.

Empowerment also occurs through contract conditions aimed at building local labour skills. The contract covers the interests of municipal employees affected by the arrangement, and seeks to maximise their benefits in the interests of the broader community. Training and staff development feature prominently, and provision is made for equity schemes. The latter will enhance local shareholding automatically as the project grows and continues.

Monitoring functions are the responsibility of the council, and it will have a continuing role (with the GNUC) in setting tariffs, and controlling the quality and the levels of capital investment proposed by the GNUC to meet its performance requirements. As the elected representatives of the local community, this role holds the potential to help ensure optimal local benefit, and adherence to the contract conditions aimed at community shareholding and empowerment. The institutional arrangements are therefore structured so as to engage local stakeholders in the concession company, and to ensure that benefits are derived from the project for the community and workers.

Sources: Kotze, Ferguson and Leigland, 1999; NBI, 2000b

☐ Participants in decision-making

The most important role of the consumer is as a participant in the decision-making process. Yet despite consumer capacity to innovate, this is the role most often ignored in top–down supply approaches. In people-focused approaches, consumer participation in decision-making at the project formulation stage helps to build ownership and to ensure that solutions, for example service levels, are aligned more closely to needs, and that costs and cost-recovery approaches are more cognisant of livelihood strategies. This runs contrary to the traditional view that a 'universal' approach – in which all households, irrespective of capacity, are provided with direct connections – is inevitable. These decisions are generally made by the council and operator, and not by the people. In order to reinforce the important role of the consumer, it is necessary to introduce mechanisms for this engagement (for instance, participatory processes, representatives on steering committees and regulatory boards), and to bring about attitudinal change among other stakeholders. Box 6.17 provides an illustration of community shareholding in Nelspruit, South Africa.

☐ Participants in the construction process

Some poor groups may prefer to reduce the costs of services by contributing labour, and becoming directly involved in the construction process. In a number of innovative projects such as the one at El Alto, big water operators are recognising the importance of community labour as a means to increase the number of service subscribers, and for promoting ownership of installed infrastructure. These communities pay a lower connection fee if they provide labour for the digging of trenches. In other schemes, such as that at Córdoba, communities themselves have initiated schemes so that they benefit, much earlier than intended, from the service upgrade under the concession arrangement. While this is still not always the case (some large international operators openly admit they do not wish to get involved with unskilled labour), the case of El Alto, described in Box 7.6, illustrates how successful such community construction efforts can be.

☐ Participants in the management, operation and maintenance of installed services

Effective community organisations (as illustrated by the Lima case in Box 6.15) may take on operation and maintenance roles for basic facilities and equipment. They may also see the benefit of assuming management roles, especially where facilities are communal. Management may include a role in billing and revenue collection. Such arrangements are often formalised through the development of consumer cooperatives or NGOs structured for this purpose. Where this is carefully planned, it can result in far better cost recovery than that achieved by operators. In Port-au-Prince in Haiti, for instance, a successful NGO initiative was scaled up to provide 100,000 poor households with access to communal standpipes. Water committees were formed and took responsibility for determining requirements, facilitating construction, hiring the standpipe operator, resolving community grievances and organising maintenance. With community agreement they have developed a system in which they charge more than the operator's price and reinvest the profits in other community services. Their visible success has led to an institutionalisation of committees and the empowerment of all the communities involved.

☐ Participants in cost recovery

An increasing focus on payment from the poor for services has often become synonymous with their participation. There is much discussion about how the poor can and do pay for their services. However, one of the lessons of poverty reduction projects and community participation in service delivery projects is that participation means decision-making first, and payment second. Requiring the poor to pay without involving them in the decisions that lead to those services is inappropriate. In this context, developing cost recovery within poor communities can be introduced in a number of ways, through communal or individual approaches. These are explored further in Chapter 9.

6

Box 6.18　A Story of Labour Relations
Nelspruit, South Africa

Links to Boxes
6.17, 12.2

The municipality of Nelspruit has had to engage in complex and extended negotiations with trade unions about the water services concession with a private consortium, aimed at extending coverage to the town's poor areas. The protracted negotiations brought to the fore the need for due consultation with labour, and the complexities of negotiation with unions, especially in situations where trade unions are well organised and institutionally well established. Even though the project has gone ahead, it remains the source of much controversy and trade unions question its appropriateness and successes.

When the local council announced in 1996 its intention to explore PSP options, it obtained cooperation from the local branch of the South African Municipal Workers Union (SAMWU). The early drafts of proposed project documents all attempted to assure workers that their employment conditions would not be jeopardised, and included an extensive section on workers' rights, labour conditions, employment equity and recognition of collective bargaining laws and procedures. In part the council consulted the local union as a stakeholder, while in part South Africa's labour legislation compelled it, as an employer, to engage in such elaborate interactions with organised labour.

The local unions briefed their national office about these developments, and soon the latter became an integral part of the process. At national level, the union officials were in principle opposed to the partnership, and their terminology reflected a categoric opposition: they branded it 'privatisation', profit-seeking that showed scant concern for service provision to the poor.

The differences between the municipality and SAMWU became so fierce that the council suspended negotiations with the preferred bidder in late 1996. The provincial government established a team of provincial politicians to engage with the different parties, and in February 1998 a 'water summit' was held, involving the council, provincial politicians and trade union officials. SAMWU's approach here attempted to make PSP a fallback option, with public provision being the preferred option. The council concluded that this offered no meaningful solution to their capital financing needs. By April the differences were still not resolved, and the council decided to re-enter its talks with the preferred bidder, without union agreement.

A series of meetings followed between the national government department responsible for local government, the South African Local Government Association (SALGA), and the national leadership of the Congress of South African Trade Unions (COSATU), to which SAMWU is affiliated. A framework agreement was concluded in late 1998, presumably as a guide to the conditions under which partnerships at the municipal level would be acceptable to labour, government and organised local government. However, differences about the authority and meaning of the agreement soon became apparent, as COSATU insisted that no partnerships should proceed unless approved by a newly formed sectoral forum established under the terms of the agreement, whereas the government and SALGA insisted that the agreement had not made partnerships subject to such approval.

Nelspruit did submit its draft contract however, and the national department's legal advisor argued the case for it was consistent with the agreement. Although union officials continued to object to this, the council decided to go ahead with the process and the contract was signed in April 1999.

Subsequently, union officials have continued to question the arrangement, and there have also been a number of reports by trade union sources claiming that the private service provider is not honouring the contract. Occasionally, public exchanges still occur, and labour sources insist that infrastructure extension is slow, services are unreliable and costs are escalating. These claims are denied by the council and the service provider.

The opposition from SAMWU and COSATU must be placed in a national context. They see this scheme as a pilot for their national anti-privatisation campaign, fought on a number of fronts nationally by COSATU. Therefore, the resistance to the Nelspruit proposals must be viewed in conjunction with resistance to similar strategies against national privatisation and partnerships, as well as private sector participation in other municipalities.

This makes negotiations very difficult for the local council, and also increases the risk for the private operator. In each partnership negotiation process, an assessment must made of whether national trends have this effect, and whether the council will gain more from engaging in the partnership than from succumbing to the external pressure. It also underscores the importance of gaining external support from higher levels of government to help create an environment conducive to PSP.

Sources: Kotze, Ferguson and Leigland, 1999; NBI, 2000

The challenge for consumers in partnerships

The traditional government-led approach to service delivery often makes government itself responsible for representing consumers' interests – in fact, a distinction between the two is not often made, and this is why consumers, especially poor consumers, have been the recipients of services prescribed by officials. Given the undeniable fact that municipalities have their own interests as well, substantial conflicts arise when government is responsible for setting the rules of the game as well as representing consumers. The case studies throughout this book demonstrate ongoing confusion about the distinction between government and consumers, largely because consumers are not organised as a distinctive voice. The Gweru case (see Box 9.5), however, demonstrates through its extensive consultation process that the municipality understood that it could not simply assume that it represented consumers' interests, and to some extent (with the exception of the issue of service standards), it set out to understand the interests of numerous stakeholders including consumers, and act as a broker of interests.

The two fundamental constraints to incorporating consumers into service partnerships are their lack of organisation and skills. As long as consumers remain uncoordinated, individual voices with no understanding of municipal service provision issues, there is no way to meaningfully include them in a partnership. Creating an inclusive organisation – that is operationally and financially viable for the long term – brings many benefits. Perhaps the most important one is that it builds a legitimate role for the people who use the services. This facilitates the development of appropriate solutions and increases the commitment to pay for the services. Poor communities lack capacity, however, and a significant challenge for partnerships is to ensure that skills and organisational development are established to enhance the capacity of these consumers.

Despite the potential value of CBOs, they have their own problems. One is that they may not focus upon representing their communities, but rather only on specific people or factions within a community. This raises the importance of building their capacity to be more open, and also of engaging – and building – other potentially important organisations such as women's groups. Recognition of the heterogeneity of the consumer group suggests that municipal service partnerships should use different approaches for the poor and the non-poor, and that this should be clarified in partnership agreements. This is not easy, however, given that both municipalities and the private sector have established working practices that do not always make this distinction, and do not always allow other actors to enter the partnership. CBOs and NGOs can play an important role in ensuring the sustainable delivery of services and should be included as partners. With notable exceptions, this is a challenge few projects have yet to accept.

Employees and Employee Representatives

The shift towards the increased participation of the private sector in municipal services is frequently concerned with the impact on existing municipal employees. Increasingly, the tendering of contracts emphasises the importance of worker re-employment and worker terms and conditions, and requests specific proposals as to how each bidder would address these issues. Depending on the arrangement, a shift to private sector involvement may result in a new management, a new employer and new roles for workers in service provision.

In many countries, there is no formal (legislative) barrier to simply discharging employees but the vast majority of municipalities still suffer from overstaffing. Most prudent municipalities, however, believe that employees deserve due consideration and fairness; in others, substantial political reasons lead municipalities to address employees' concerns. Moreover, there are simple implementation issues to factor into the decision-making process. Some current employees will have a critical role in ensuring that the process of reorganising municipal service delivery is smooth. Consequently, both private operators and municipalities are likely to want to build an agreement with employees as a prerequisite to the final contract.

6

Box 6.19   Multilateral Initiatives
PPIAF, The World Bank

The Public-Private Infrastructure Advisory Facility (PPIAF) is a multi-donor technical assistance facility aimed at helping developing countries improve the quality of their infrastructure through private sector involvement. Launched in July 1999, PPIAF was developed on the joint initiative of the governments of Japan and the UK, working closely with the World Bank. PPIAF is owned and directed by participating donors, which include bilateral and multilateral development agencies and international financial institutions. PPIAF was built on the World Bank Group's Infrastructure Action Program and has been designed to reinforce the actions of all participating donors. PPIAF is managed by a small Program Management Unit in the World Bank.

PPIAF pursues its mission through two main mechanisms. First, it channels technical assistance to governments in developing countries on strategies and measures to tap the full potential of private involvement in infrastructure. Second, it identifies, disseminates and promotes best practices on matters related to private involvement in infrastructure in developing countries.

PPIAF can finance a range of country-specific and multi-country advisory and related activities in the following areas:

- framing infrastructure development strategies to take full advantage of the potential for private involvement;
- building consensus for appropriate policy, regulatory and institutional reforms;
- designing and implementing specific policy, regulatory and institutional reforms;
- supporting the design and implementation of pioneering projects and transactions; and
- building government capacity in the design and execution of private infrastructure arrangements and in the regulation of private service providers.

PPIAF assistance can facilitate private involvement in the financing, ownership, operation, rehabilitation, maintenance or management of eligible infrastructure services. Eligible infrastructure services comprise roads, ports, airports, railways, electricity, telecommunications, solid waste, water and sewerage, and gas transmission and distribution.

All of PPIAF outputs fall within the following categories:

- *Infrastructure development strategies:* studies intended to guide governments on options for expanding private sector involvement in infrastructure. This includes national, sub-national and sectoral studies within a country.
- *Consensus building:* activities aimed at building consensus among stakeholders for appropriate policy, regulatory and institutional reforms.
- *Policy regulatory and institutional reforms:* advice on the design and implementation of specific reforms, including studies and drafting of instruments.
- *Pioneering transactions:* support to the design and implementation of particular projects or transactions that are pioneering in some important respect, reflect some measure of innovation, and offer potential demonstration effects.
- *Capacity building:* activities aimed at building government capacity in the design and execution of private infrastructure arrangements and in the regulation of private service providers.
- *Global best practice:* activities focusing on the identification, promotion and dissemination of best practice to the international community in general, rather than to a specific country, on matters relating to private sector involvement in infrastructure in developing countries.

For small proposals (involving PPIAF support of US$75,000 or less), applications are evaluated on a rolling basis and the Program Management Unit will aim to notify proponents of the outcome of the evaluation within two weeks of submission. For medium and large proposals (involving PPIAF support of over US$75,000), applications will be batched on a quarterly basis and the Program Management Unit will aim to notify proponents of the outcome of the evaluation within six to eight weeks of the submission deadline. If a proposal is rejected, an explanation will be provided to the proponent.

Applications for PPIAF support can come from any source. In the case of country-specific activities, however, the beneficiary government must approve all requests for support. An application form for PPIAF support can be downloaded or completed on-line through the PPIAF website (www.ppiaf.org) or can be ordered from the Program Management Unit. Proposals will be assessed against the criteria specified in PPIAF's charter, which is available on the website or can be requested from the Program Management Unit. Those criteria include consistency with PPIAF's mission, government commitment, additionality, donor coordination, value for money, and environmental and social responsibility. Contact details are provided in Appendix A.

Source: Adapted from the PPIAF website, www.ppiaf.org

The nature of employee workforces

Municipal service employees are usually either professional/managerial staff or unskilled and semi-skilled employees (such as sweepers, collectors, conservancy workers, labourers), of whom there can be large numbers. The former are usually small in number, usually without collective representation (a union or association), and have more transferable and desirable skills. It is also likely that they will be informed to some extent, and will have formed a view on whether or not they are in agreement with the shift to a private sector operator. The less skilled employees typically work in poor conditions, with facilities, equipment or clothing that usually inadequately reflect health and safety concerns. In many developing countries conditions are extremely bad. Income levels are also extremely low. A sweeper in Nepal in the case illustrated in Box 6.7, for instance, earns approximately US$25 per month.

In most situations, a local government-workers' union or association will represent their interests. However, their characteristics can vary greatly. Sometimes they are simply 'management unions', under the effective control of management. In some contexts, such as in Nepal where trade unions are in their infancy, workers are represented by weak organisations. In other highly politicised contexts such as South Africa, the trade unions are key stakeholders in partnership negotiations. National and public sector unions have had a key role in defining the approach to municipal services, and private sector approaches can only occur after direct municipal delivery options have been considered. In some cases, local unions have gone along with private sector participation plans, but were later over-ruled by national bodies that opposed the new arrangements in principle.

The potential roles of employees

Employees and representative organisations can be included as key participants in any service redesign process. They have several potential roles in the reorganisation of municipal services. The following section considers the role of employees in developing a new service arrangement.

Opposers

Depending upon the local context, employees can successfully oppose changes in the arrangement of municipal services. Within unions, there are at least two groups of concerned people: union staff and union members. If the union is somehow simply dissolved, union staff will be without a job. Given that they are the intermediaries between management and employees, this can heavily influence the negotiations. However, recognising that the basic goal of a union to improve the welfare of its members is usually taken seriously, staff's concern for impacts upon the union's members – often reinforced by employee members at the negotiating table – must be taken seriously. The ability of employee representatives to reach an acceptable agreement will almost always involve a membership vote.

Cautious supporters

Although the union's focal concern is its members' welfare, union members in municipal services are generally from poor communities. Moreover, employees are also consumers of municipal services and are perhaps among the most knowledgeable about the problems with service delivery. Therefore, once their own employment concerns are addressed, if they are convinced that the change will result in improved services they may become supportive of it.

The Gweru case study demonstrates what is potentially possible when employees are fully engaged and a positive process can be established. All employees were guaranteed jobs on terms at least as favourable as those they had with the municipality (the municipality stopped employing unskilled labour five years ago and is thus no longer overstaffed), and many foresaw more opportunities in terms of personal and career development with the international business partner than with the municipality. This led to cautious support for the changes. Attaining positive outcomes depends on the

Box **6.20**   The Role of the Donor
El Alto, Bolivia

Links to Box
7.6

In February 1997, at the request of the government of Bolivia and prior to a concession contract being awarded for the delivery of water and sanitation services in Le Paz-El Alto, the Water and Sanitation Program – Andean Region (WSP-AND) launched the El Alto pilot project in partnership with SIDA (the Swedish International Development Agency). When Aguas del Illimani was awarded the concession later the same year, it joined the partnership and the pilot project became known as IPAS (Peri-urban Initiative for Water and Sanitation). The collaboration involves a range of actors, coordinated by IPAS and funded by various institutions and agencies. The following table outlines the roles of each partner.

Partner	Institution	Role in the El Alto pilot project	Financial contribution
Aguas del Illimani (ADI)	Private sector	• Infrastructure expansion (40% of the contribution) • Social intervention (60% of the contribution)	US$4.4 million (81.5%)
Ministry of Basic Services and Housing	Government	• Initiated and supports the project; assesses replicability in Bolivian cities	
Municipalities of La Paz and El Alto	Government	• Oversees implementation; ensures compliance with building standards	
Prefecture	Government	• Coordination between La Paz and El Alto	
Centro Interdisciplinario de Estudios Comunitarios (CIEC)	NGO	• Identified neighbourhoods for the pilot project	
Consultant anthropologists	Private sector	• Contracted by the operator to study consumption needs/patterns in low-income areas	
Caja de Los Andes Mutual La Primera	Micro-credit institutions	• Credit for connections and internal installations	
Neighbourhood organisations – Juntas Vecinales	Community	• Each neighbourhood chooses its own technical and financing options	
Swedish International Development Agency (SIDA)	Bilateral agency	• Funds an expert in condominial system	US$900,000 (16.7%)
Water and Sanitation Program – Andean Region (WSP-AND)	International partnership with multi-donor funding	• Provides technical assistance (institutional strengthening and documentation) and monitors the project	US$160,000 (1.8%)

The role of external agents was critical to the emergence of an innovative and pro-poor solution. As a technical support agency, it was envisaged that the WSP would facilitate the transfer of know-how on low-cost water and sewerage systems to Bolivia from neighbouring Brazil (see Box 7.6). The WSP thus provided the technical capacity to take the PPP in new technical and social directions, and SIDA provided the funding needed to support the development process.

Over the four-year involvement, the role of WSP in El Alto has evolved. Initially it provided expertise to the partnership, filling skill gaps to ensure that the initiative moved forward. A small team of WSP technical staff and social mobilisers, all recruited within Bolivia, worked hand-in-hand with the operator and communities to establish a supportive context, and a technical expert familiar with the Brazilian model was brought to Bolivia to provide the technical knowledge and long-term experience of the condominial approach being replicated. This focus shifted towards transferring skills to ensure the sustainability of the initiative once inputs were complete. Many of the WSP staff now work for the operator.

More recently, WSP has been working with the government of Bolivia to introduce policy and a regulatory framework that will allow the condominial approach to be replicated. By establishing a successful pilot in a difficult location, the partnership has proven that alternative forms of service delivery can increase the access of the poor to services, and WSP have facilitated capacity development at policy level necessary to introduce a new regulatory framework embracing appropriate technical and social norms and standards. As an independent (non-private sector) actor, the role of WSP thus moved from downstream practical inputs to upstream strategic inputs – a role that might in the future bring widespread benefit throughout Bolivia.

Source: Personal communication with Barbara Evans, WSP; WSP, 2001b; WSP, 2001c

early and regular engagement of employees; this is advisable whether the unions are strong or not. The sooner employees are involved, the better the prospects of finding a workable arrangement. Business partners must be sensitive to the need to address the legitimate concerns of employees. Some business partners simply will not be sensitive, and this can be verified by their past practice and interviews. Municipalities will need to decide whether this is the sort of organisation they want as a partner.

☐ Creative innovators

In some locations, the role of employees has sparked discussions that have led to more creative solutions than originally contemplated. One option is for establishing employee-owned businesses, to free them of government administrative traditions that often suppress entrepreneurial energy. Often this requires new managers who can build an entrepreneurial environment and have experience with private sector management. In Cartagena, an extremely modest form of this was demonstrated by employees having a small percentage ownership in the new business. In the BoTTs in South Africa, processes have been established for consultants and organisations from traditionally marginalised communities to build substantial share ownership of the service consortia over several years.

Although this type of approach poses some complexities, it has the added benefit of creating organisations that are more aligned with employees' interests (and possibly consumers'), and present options for greater equity. As locally owned organisations, they keep the wealth they generate in the community, and present an opportunity to strengthen the local private sector.

☐ The challenge for employees in service redesign

There is a basic challenge to both initiators of service redesign and employees: how to develop a mutually respectful role when the initiative will inevitably be very disruptive for employees. It is natural for initiators to view employees as a problem, since the current employee structure stands between their idea and its realisation; and there is a natural tendency for employees and their representatives, concerned with their jobs and the impacts of change, to react defensively.

It is essential, therefore, to introduce processes though which employees, employee representatives and employers can learn about each other's concerns and views, and about potential opportunities within the partnership framework. Employees who take a simple oppositional position face public anger when they are perceived as a privileged status quo interest group. Employers who push ahead regardless of legitimate employee concerns face the same problem. It is imperative for both parties to spend some time exploring and defining options to address their respective concerns.

External Agents

☐ International donors and funding agencies

International donors frequently play a key role in driving partnerships involving the private sector. Donor interest in partnerships for the delivery of infrastructure and services has certainly increased significantly over recent years, and the focus has settled on, inter alia, water and sanitation services and solid waste management. Support for partnership formation comes through:

- sectoral reform programmes, focused on creating an enabling or encouraging framework for private sector participation (through policy development and regulatory frameworks);

Links to Box
6.27

Box **6.21**   Business Partners for Development
A Global Initiative

Sustainable development is a global imperative, and strategic partnerships involving business, government and civil society may represent a successful new model for the development of communities around the world. Business Partners for Development (BPD) is an informal network of partners who seek to demonstrate that partnerships among these three sectors can achieve more at the local level than any of the groups acting individually. Among the three groups, perspectives and motivations vary widely, however, and reaching consensus often proves difficult. Different work processes, methods of communication and approaches to decision-making are common obstacles. But when these tri-sector partnerships succeed, communities benefit, governments serve more effectively, and private enterprise profits. The result is a win-win-win situation, which is the ultimate aim of BPD and its divisions, or 'clusters'.

One of four sector clusters within the BPD framework, the Water and Sanitation Cluster, aims – through focus projects, study and the sharing of lessons learnt – to improve access to safe water and effective sanitation for the rising number of urban poor in developing countries. Focus projects are the mainstay of the cluster's work. They yield lessons that inform project fieldwork, help the cluster measure the partnership's efficacy, and identify priority research areas, including technology and terrain, land tenure and non-payment culture. Through focus projects, the cluster seeks to illustrate that – by pooling their unique assets and expertise – tri-sector partnerships can truly provide mutual gains for all. Governments can ensure the health of their citizens with safe water and effective sanitation, while apportioning the financial and technical burden. Corporations can showcase good works while ensuring financial sustainability over the long term, and communities can gain a real voice in their development.

Lessons from the Focus Projects

The Water and Sanitation Cluster's eight focus projects respond to the specific demands and conditions of the communities they serve. As a result of these dynamics, each project's objective is a work in progress. They include: a drinking water supply and sewer system in the El Pozón quarter, Cartagena, Colombia; water supply improvements to Marunda District, Jakarta, Indonesia; restructuring public water service in shanty towns, Port-au-Prince, Haiti; developing water supply and sanitation services for marginal urban populations, La Paz and El Alto, Bolivia; innovative water solutions for underprivileged districts, Buenos Aires, Argentina; sustainable water and wastewater services in underprivileged areas, Eastern Cape and Northern Province, South Africa; management of water services, Durban and Pietermaritzburg, South Africa; and upgrade and expansion of local water networks, Dakar, Senegal.

The secretariat has determined that the best way to learn from the focus projects is through a three-angled line of inquiry. The iterative and complementary approaches are as follows:

- *Sector-by-sector analysis.* The workshop series provides an example whereby each sector was brought together to conduct its own SWOT (strengths, weaknesses, opportunities and threats) analysis of working in partnership with the other two sectors. The actors from the different sectors approach the partnerships in different ways. They have different expectations, fears, capacities, skills and strengths. As the theory suggests, these combine with their other sector counterparts to enhance the projects. Though initial findings are fairly straightforward to an outside observer versed in these types of relationships, the most critical factor is overcoming the stereotypes of different sector counterparts. It proves critical to make concrete assessments of the contributions that individual sectors make, and to build up their confidence in making these contributions.
- *Theme-based review.* This approach attempts to address the impact of the tri-sector relationships on specific project components or project themes. In 2000, a survey was commissioned of the way the partnerships impact on cost recovery in poor areas. Perhaps as testimony to the infancy of the partnership approach, the analysis at the local level of how the partnerships were impacting on specific themes should be deepened. The cluster continues to encourage the partners and partnerships to clarify their working relationships. It also intends to use their experiences to make recommendations to others embarking on a similar tri-sector approach. Activities for 2001 in this area include research and surveys on partnership and alternative approaches to service provision, partnership and land tenure; partnership and regulatory frameworks; and partnership and education/awareness campaigns.
- *Local-level analysis.* This project-by-project or partnership-by-partnership analysis has resulted in the drafting of internal partnership analysis reports that have attempted to document the successes, impacts, challenges and wider contexts of each individual project. The challenge for the secretariat with this approach is that the partnerships are actually living organisms that change on a daily basis. Structures put in place and definitions of roles, responsibilities and budgets are all influential in (and also significantly different between) the eight focus projects. Equally, external events, changes in staff, findings in the communities and other externalities have an impact on the way the partners work together.

Source: Business Partners for Development, Water and Sanitation Cluster

6

- private sector development programmes;
- infrastructure development; and
- municipal reform and decentralisation processes.

These international development programmes are created by agencies that are extensions of governments, in development terms. Notwithstanding the internal agendas of bilateral donors, donor interests in partnership formation may be driven by their interest in:

- promoting the role of the private sector in economic development and reducing the role of the state;
- mobilising private sector investment in the context of decreasing aid flows;
- creating a more efficient, predictable and conducive environment of aid funding and technical assistance;
- promoting institutional change in key sectors;
- promoting private sector participation in service delivery to the poor; and
- promoting efficient, equitable development.

Over the past decade, a number of agencies – the World Bank in particular – have provided direct assistance in the formulation of partnerships, and have made their own funding conditional upon private sector involvement (see Box 7.12 on Cartagena). This direct action has been supported by extensive policy formulation and analysis, and research into the key financial and economic aspects of existing transactions. A number of service sectors, including energy, water and sanitation and solid waste, have produced toolkits to provide guidance on basic issues and processes.[18]

More recently, however, donors have begun to merge their interest in private sector development with poverty reduction mandates. The World Bank and the Water and Sanitation Programme (WSP) have led this process through a number of global initiatives, conferences and workshops (see Box 6.19 for a description of the work of Public–Private Infrastructure Advisory Facility).[19] In the water and sanitation sector, WSP will soon publish guidelines for the development of pro-poor transactions. Donor activity is by no means limited to these examples. The UNDP PPPs for the Urban Environment (PPPUE) initiative promotes local skill development through a global learning network, and local government capacity building in three selected countries (Nepal, Namibia and Uganda).

In many of the most innovative partnerships that have tackled delivery in poor areas, donors have played a central role. Indeed, the importance of the donor as a fourth partner in public–private–civil society initiatives should not be underestimated. It raises questions of sustainability as reliance on the technical assistance takes hold, and replicability as the donor performs key social and institutional roles.

In El Alto, for instance, WSP and the Swedish International Development Agency (SIDA) have been involved in influencing the agenda from the outset (see Box 6.20). WSP objectives are primarily concerned with community capacity building and developing an approach for replication. To this end they have worked with the operator Aguas del Illimani to develop a condominial sewerage approach and then to institutionalise the lessons learnt. WSP employed three or four technical staff. While the project is currently learning from early decisions, the pilot has provided a model of integrated, participatory planning and implementation, empowered communities and introduced alternative technologies.

The role of donors in partnership development includes:

- provision of funds for technical assistance;
- gap-filling, where the competencies of the actors do not correspond with project objectives;
- general guidance on options, particularly in relation to poor areas;
- definition and dissemination of best practice; and
- facilitation of new initiatives as a part of broader sectoral reform.

6

Box 6.22   The Role of Consultants in Restructuring Water and Sanitation Services
Johannesburg, South Africa

Links to Boxes
4.4, 8.5, 9.1, 9.3

In common with most emerging economies, water and sanitation services in South Africa are politically sensitive. While the benefits of successful structural change in the water sector are significant and wide ranging, the consequences of failure can be very serious. With such high stakes it is important that client organisations make the best use of the expertise and experience available from specialised consultants with a track record of similar projects. When the Greater Johannesburg Metropolitan Council adopted its IGOLI 2002 plan for restructuring municipal functions (see Boxes 4.4 and 8.5), and determined that a private operator would be procured to manage and operate the new utility, the council recognised the importance of consultants and undertook an international procurement for suitable international experts to act as lead consultants for the water and sanitation restructuring process.

The contract was won by a joint venture led by the Halcrow Group of the UK, with VKE Consulting Engineers and Malani Padayachi and Associates of South Africa. HKC Investments (financial analysts) and the Palmer Development Group (operations modelling) joined the lead consultancy team at a later stage.

The lead consultants' role included:

- preparing the transition programme;
- defining the role and terms of reference for other consultants, assistance with procuring and managing consultants;
- advising the transition manager on strategic issues;
- designing the management contract, and managing the procurement process for the private operator;
- preparing the bid data room;
- preparing the pre-qualification shortlist and evaluating the bids;
- operational and financial modelling, and feasibility analysis; and
- preparing the initial strategic business plan.

An early task of the lead consultants was to identify the need for additional consultants and to assist in their procurement. In total, 16 separate specialist consultancy firms were engaged during the process, including international legal counsels, local legal advisors, accountants, engineering consultants, communications consultants, human resource consultants and information technology/revenue consultants.

In Johannesburg, instead of the typical lump-sum contract for consultancy services, the council appointed the lead consultants on a time-scale basis, with packages of work being contracted-out as the project progressed. This flexible approach worked well for both council and lead consultants, and was almost certainly considerably cheaper than a lump sum would have been.

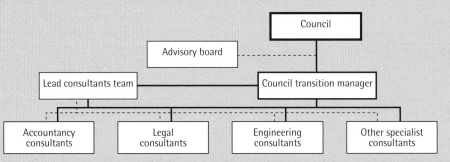

While the success of the process owed a great deal to the council's leadership and the flexible approach of the transition manager, the structure and approach adopted by the council had a number of clear advantages. The lead consultant's role was that of a true advisor to the transition manager. This person was involved in the detail of the issues, and in the development of ideas, and was responsible for driving the process. This resulted in much greater ownership of the solutions by the council. The lead consultants were engaged with flexible terms of reference that recognised that the scope and extent of services was difficult to define at the start. They were able to respond to events in a flexible and efficient way. In addition, sub-consultants were contracted directly to the council, but the management and coordination of consultants was shared between the transition manager and the lead consultants; and by procuring the sub-consultants individually, the council was able to select the best specialist firms for the tasks. This would not have been possible with a traditional consultancy approach, in which the client organisation must accept the team assembled by the winning consultant.

Chris Ricketson, Halcrow Group, UK, lead consultants to the Greater Johannesburg Metropolitan Council

However, with the exception of the pilot work of the Business Partners in Development (BPD) Water and Sanitation Cluster see (Box 6.21), WSP and some work by the Inter-American Development Foundation, there are few initiatives in which donors have actively pursued the potential of combining the public, private and civil sectors. The agenda of many donors clearly promotes PPPs, but in the past has fallen short of addressing poverty issues or promoting a place in the partnerships for civil society. This is an emerging area of interest.

☐   Specialist consultants

Few municipalities will have all the skills necessary to prepare and complete a complex partnership with the formal private sector, and most municipalities in developing countries are probably best advised to seek specialist expertise in the development of partnerships with international and national private firms and organisations (such as WSP). As such, a primary external agent frequently involved in the development of partnerships is the 'expert' who is brought in to a municipality to provide specialist skills, guide the process of partnership development, and/or supplement skills in particular technical areas. Both logic and evidence suggest that the role of the consultant is critical in the formulation of long-term partnerships involving the private sector.

The long duration of some arrangements, such as concessions, suggests that it is pointless (and overly ambitious) to expect municipalities to develop in-house expertise in defining a partnership arrangement – especially if this process happens only once every 20–30 years. Buying this expertise at key points in the process is more cost efficient, and allows municipalities to focus on developing in-house skills for other functions.

Second, some of the skills required in partnership development are extremely detailed in nature. Experts who do nothing else but prepare or negotiate water and sanitation contracts bring extensive specialised experience. Apart from their ability to identify and deal with the critical issues assertively, their involvement levels the playing field – ensuring that the experience in project formulation and negotiation of private operators is matched by a similar level of expertise on the public sector side. Evidence from Gweru, for instance, shows that the role of the consultant was important in building the confidence of the council and task force to carry out their tasks and make decisions, and the presence of an independent, donor-funded specialist was seen as an important mechanism for promoting transparency and assuring the public that the process did not involve corrupt practices.

The inclusion of consultants in the process does not eliminate the fact that municipalities must develop a general level of awareness and understanding of partnerships and their implementation. Nor does the hiring of consultants remove the burden of management from municipal staff. The use of external expertise must be carefully planned, effectively coordinated and meaningfully absorbed into the decision-making process.

In those countries inexperienced in privatisation processes, and where detailed skills are required, it will be necessary to bring in international advisors. This can be a costly process requiring external funding support. In some rare cases in which municipalities are well managed and financed, the cost of specialists might be accepted and absorbed into the transaction cost. However, for the vast majority, the question of appointing external consultants brings with it the question of funds. Donors and funding organisations such as the United States Agency for International Development (USAID), SIDA and the South African Municipal Infrastructure Investment Unit (see Box 10.2) have filled this gap in some municipal initiatives, providing both funding and advice on the identification and appointment of advisors. Yet, to procure this support, municipal managers must have contacts and awareness of such processes, and this is not always the case for those that need the support most.

The potential roles of advisors in the development of partnership arrangements will depend on the primary objectives established by municipalities. Some may appoint advisors from the outset to assist in the overall planning and development process (see Box 6.22). In addition, others may be appointed to advise on:[20]

Box **6.23**   Comparing the Attributes of Potential Actors

General sectoral attributes

	Government	Business	Civil society
Primary interest	• Political	• Economic	• Social
Primary form of power	• Legislation, taxation and enforcement	• Money	• Traditions and values, voting power
Primary goals	• Stable civil society	• Wealth creation	• Establishing rights
Framework for assessment	• Legality	• Profitability	• Justice, equity
Primary form of organisation	• Governmental	• For profit	• Non-profit
Stakeholders controlling action	• Voters/rulers	• Owners	• Communities and members
Primary basis for establishing relationships	• Rules	• Transactions	• Values
Framework for organisation	• Administering	• Managing	• Developing
Primary timeframe	• Election cycles	• Profit-reporting/ business cycles	• Sustainability/regeneration cycles

Source: Adapted from Waddell, 2000

Potential attributes in a municipal partnership

	Municipality	International business	Small-scale providers	NGOs
Primary interest (in the partnership)	• Political • Financial • Physical/ Environmental	• Economic • Financial	• Economic • Financial	• Social • Physical/Environmental
Forms of power (in the partnership)	• Regulatory control • Hierarchy/status • Tradition • Payment	• Money	• Local knowledge	• Values • Reputation
Primary goals (in the partnership)	• To maintain the status quo • To improve the environment	• To create profits • To generate more work opportunities	• To make a living	• To improve the quality of life in poor communities
Framework for assessment	• Legality • Political recognition • Individual profitability	• Profitability	• Profitability	• Equity
Primary form of organisation	• Bureaucratic	• For profit	• For profit	• Non-profit
Stakeholders controlling action	• Voters • Senior management	• Owners/managers	• Their clients	• Communities • NGO leaders
Primary basis for establishing relationships	• Procedures	• Transactions	• Job	• Values
Framework for organisation	• Administering	• Managing	• Operational	• Developing
Primary timeframe	• Election cycle	• Profit-reporting/ business cycle	• Immediate job	• Sustainability/funding cycle

- social issues (the capacity of poor consumers, impacts on workers, social impacts);
- economic and regulatory issues (market structuring, promotion of competition, tariff design, regulatory mechanisms, monitoring, economic instruments);
- legal issues (legislation and regulations, bidding documents, the drafting of contracts);
- technical issues (assessments, specifications and contract requirements);
- environmental issues;
- financial issues (projections, bankability, documentation and sales promotion); and
- the contract negotiation process.

It is important that municipalities build the capacity to effectively appoint and work with advisors. They must take responsibility for the selection by understanding which skills and experience they need. Although experience in the South is now increasing, there is a risk that specialist consultants will not be experienced in issues concerning the poor (and frequently models used in middle- and upper-income countries have been inappropriately recommended). Care should be taken, and donor support enlisted, to ensure that consultancy teams are balanced, include social expertise and have experience in the South.[21]

Once funding is identified, the process of appointing advisors is an important municipal task, involving the preparation of terms of reference, tendering, evaluation procedures and contracting their services. This World Bank toolkits on water and sanitation[22] outline the method of 'packaging' advisory contracts (be it through consortium or individual contracts) and of structuring fees (be they output based or percentage based), and provides indicative terms of reference for legal counsel, engineering consultants and financial advisors.

Partnering

☐ Comparing assets of potential actors

The potential actors in service partnerships (described above) all fit within one of the three organisational sectors: the public sector, the private sector and civil society.[23] In order to maximise the potential of a partnership, the municipality must aim to develop an understanding of the comparative attributes of these potential partners. The framework illustrated in Box 6.23 presents the characteristics described earlier and juxtaposes fundamental differences.[24] While any specific organisation will not perfectly reflect these qualities at all times, the framework provides an analytic tool for comparing the assets of potential partners.

The comparative table sets out the characteristics and allows further consideration of the relative strengths and weaknesses of each organisational sector in relation to the poor. In a competitive environment, business is good at maximising efficiency, and civil society is particularly good at working with poor communities striving for equity. These characteristics arise from the fundamental attributes that distinguish organisations in one sector from those in another.

In relation to water, sanitation and solid waste services (as well as energy and telecommunications) there has been an increasing shift from an approach that only included one organisational sector – the municipality or another public agency – to one where municipalities and the private sector have joined forces in public–private organisational partnerships. In so doing, the arrangement draws on a much wider range of competencies and skills relevant for service delivery and offsetting the weaknesses inherent in each organisational sector. Yet the comparative table, and evidence from service partnerships, tell us that there are still gaps in the traditional public–private package – gaps that can be filled by drawing in the competencies of the civil society sector. Box 6.24 illustrates the development of this process and

6

Locating Partners in the Service Delivery Process
Changing Roles and Relationships

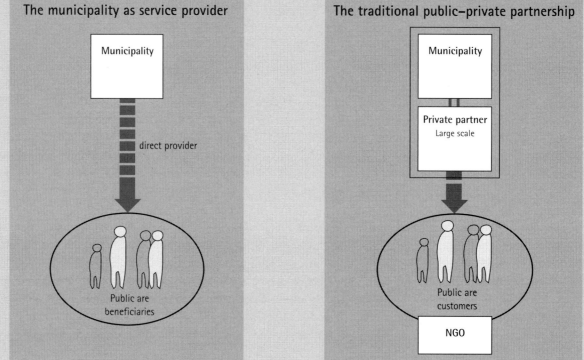

The municipality as service provider

Municipality

direct provider

Public are
beneficiaries

The traditional public–private partnership

Municipality

Private partner
Large scale

Public are
customers

NGO

NGOs often support communities
outside primary partnership

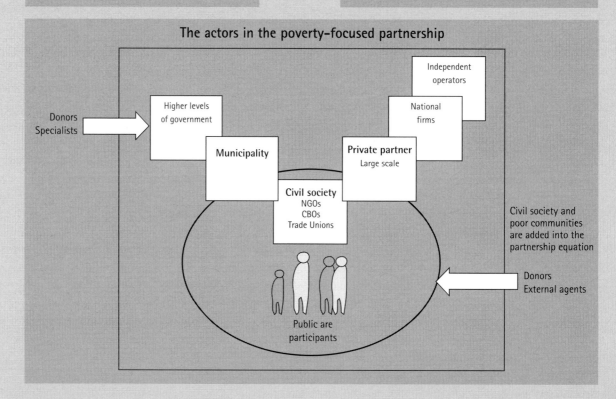

The actors in the poverty-focused partnership

Donors
Specialists

Higher levels
of government

Independent
operators

National
firms

Municipality

Private partner
Large scale

Civil society
NGOs
CBOs
Trade Unions

Civil society and
poor communities
are added into the
partnership equation

Donors
External agents

Public are
participants

the increasing inclusion of various actors within service delivery partnerships. In the development of innovative inclusive approaches to municipal services, the key for municipalities lies in the creation of an approach that taps the strengths of each sector and offsets their inherent weakness through the allocation of roles and a decision-making structure.

Fulfilling municipal objectives

Integrating the competencies from each sector thus forms the basic rationale for partnering. When these attributes and competencies are considered in relation to a municipality's core objectives, it is possible to see the very different contributions the organisations from different sectors can best make towards each objective. Box 6.25 provides a basic framework that enables a municipality to consider the specific competencies, attributes and capabilities of potential partners in relation to municipal objectives (illustrated in Chapter 3 and discussed in detail in Chapter 7), and to see that a combination of these core competencies is likely to get much closer to fulfilling these objectives than if any one of these partners acted alone. A municipality can therefore begin to design a contextually specific partnership based on the assets that each partner brings to the table.

As we have seen, economic and financial objectives can be largely solved through the inclusion of the private sector's core competencies. The private sector brings a focus on efficiency, profit and programme to the partnership, and it is concerned with maintaining its comparative edge and business reputation. At the same time it may have access to capital assets, is often able to mobilise capital, and focuses on financial viability at the outset and throughout the process. Its very presence, as we have seen, promotes confidence for investment and donor support (and vice versa). An NGO, on the other hand, through its ideology and work practices is often less concerned with economic realities and is rarely able to raise the kind of capital needed for network services. Municipalities need massive organisational and management restructuring and skills development to create commercial operations that enable them to meet these economic and financial objectives, and in so doing become quasi-private entities.[25]

Yet when the focus shifts to political objectives, the municipality itself holds most of the cards for meeting them, through an ultimate power of veto and control over the allocation of resources, and the ability to convene stakeholders. To some degree they can be supported by NGOs, who are able to mobilise community support by building awareness and understanding of the benefits of particular approaches. One of the great attributes of the private sector is often its ability to sidestep unwanted political interference.

In relation to social objectives, NGOs have detailed knowledge of the poor and vulnerable groups, experience in delivering services to low-income areas, and an understanding of demand-led participatory processes. They also have a reputation for justice and equity, and their established relationships with poor communities often facilitate community understanding and ownership of delivery mechanisms. While municipalities will have varying degrees of experience (often dependent on the strength of the NGO sector), the private sector has rarely developed this experience. Despite private sector protestations that it can simply develop the skill, evidence suggests that civil society organisations can assist in mediation and are central to the success of community mobilisation.

Municipal institutional and environmental objectives cover a variety of issues, and each sector has a fundamental role in their fulfilment. The municipality itself offers important capacities in meeting institutional objectives: without its political will and its role as the champion of change, it is unlikely that a reform process can be initiated. To municipal capacity building, the private sector contributes a focus on effective management and coordination, and often, knowledge-transfer skills, while the NGO partner might contribute to the institutional objectives by building the capacity of community organisations.

6

All these objectives contribute to more effective service delivery. However the most explicit municipal objective is often to improve the quality, reliability and sustainability of services. While municipalities have a competency in this area, the rapid deterioration of urban infrastructure in developing countries points towards greater need. Together with the efficiency focus described above, the private sector brings specialised skills and knowledge, new technologies and advanced management approaches. In many situations, the NGO sector will bring experience of delivering tertiary-level services and a focus on sustainability. These competencies should then be supported by municipalities, allowing them to focus their attention on legal issues such as the resolution of property rights and the regularisation of informal providers.

Yet despite the generic validity and usefulness of this framework, in practice it is important to recognise that since municipal objectives are diverse and the core competencies of partners will vary in any given context, the allocation of roles may create partnerships with very different structures and sectoral arrangements. Municipalities should not be trying to commit the private sector or NGOs to specific predetermined roles, but instead they should look at the comparative assets of the actors available, and allow the boundaries between actors to shift in relation to competencies. The core competencies framework is a very helpful starting point in establishing where these attributes lie.

Relationships in Practice

The nature of relationships in practice

Relationships between partners are difficult to manage and take time to develop. The different assets of each organisational sector that forms the rationale for partnering come with other differences that are also sources of potential conflict. It is critical that these differences should not be eliminated or somehow suppressed, since once they disappear the rationale for partnering also disappears. Rather, the differences must be coordinated and integrated to work together.

Achieving a good working relationship requires addressing stereotypes. NGOs are assumed by others to be difficult to work with because of the importance they place upon core community values; the private sector is often thought of as being concerned only with profit; and municipalities, as governing agents, are often considered to be inflexible and bound by 'red tape'. These stereotypes, while having some truth, tend to emphasise negative characteristics observed by external parties to the exclusion of positive ones.

Conflicts arise in partnerships when there is a chronic imbalance in the capacities and powers of the partners, and when there is little recognition of the contribution each partner makes. Conflict may arise from the sheer scale and competency of a private sector organisation in relation to a municipality, or simply from the different power bases and competencies of organisations. For example, the private sector's self-confidence and technical expertise can often intimidate others. Its superiority in particular aspects can lead it to act arrogantly. Imbalance creates fear, and fear can lead to conflict. Level playing fields must be created. In Stutterheim (see Box 6.1), the newly elected councillors perceived this imbalance in a partnership, and their relative incapacity in the face of a strong private sector partner led to a weakening of communication channels and ultimately to a breakdown in trust and confidence between the private sector operator and the council.

Another critical element of relationships between sectoral organisations is the role of individuals. Individuals can make or break relationships. At least at the beginning, most successful partnerships are built around the drive and effectiveness of key individuals, and many falter when these individuals depart. Alternatively, some individuals may be the reason that projects do not progress. For example, corrupt municipal officials can colour the perception of a municipality. In such circumstances, primary motives/interests are not political, but personal; the primary form of power is not the law, but status; the municipality is not concerned with legality, but levels of personal compensation for leading officials; and the primary goal is not development, but maintaining existing hierarchies and the social status of officials.

The other important characteristic of relationships between partners is that they are dynamic. As capacity increases, partnering capacity improves and mutual recognition emerges, the nature of the partnership, and the various relationships within it, will develop. Such change may create effective sustainable partnering, or it may be resisted, or it may result in the dissolution of the partnership.

☐ Developing and sustaining relationships

The ideal partnership is based on shared decision-making and mutual commitment. While this may be self-evident, its implications for the structure of the partnership and behaviour of the partners is not always well understood or accounted for. It is necessary to heed the following lessons:

- **Take a learning approach** Relationships work best when actors are willing to learn about one another and about how to work together. In practice, municipal, private and civil society actors do not naturally learn from each other.
- **Ensure extensive up-front discussion** For organisations (and individuals) to become familiar with one another, it is necessary to explore capabilities, and the different uses of words and meanings.
- **Expect mistakes** Mistakes will always arise, and accountability should include identifying lessons and revisions to the process. The learning approach greatly facilitates handling conflicts when they inevitably arise.
- **Clarify individual objectives and build mutual commitment to them** Partnerships necessarily focus upon a collective objective, but, in practice, partners each have their own objectives as well. A company that does not reach profit targets, an NGO not responding to equity concerns, or a municipality incapable of working with its constituency are not effective partners. Collective evaluation processes should be put in place to measure performance regularly and identify ways to address variations.
- **Design around current and potential comparative competencies** Assessments should be made about the competencies that are present, those that are needed, and how to fill the gap. The core competencies framework for organisational sectors can be useful for guiding this analysis and action planning.
- **Treat difference as an opportunity** Differences are sources of frustration, but when a traditional business better understands the livelihoods of the poor and an NGO better understands engineering complexities and management approaches, better system construction and maintenance processes can be developed.

☐ The mechanisms of interaction

Lessons from innovative partnerships suggest that interaction can be assisted by the following:

- **Building collective partnership capacity and trust** Partners must display trust and commitment to the process and the ends. Mechanisms (such as group workshops) that help each organisation to understand how the others work and their respective objectives are useful tools in building a working relationship, and enable individual organisations to clarify their own objectives and key concerns.
- **The role of individual champions** In practice, the partnership depends on the willingness and flexibility shown by individuals. Key individuals can create an effective working relationship; when supportive or unsupportive individuals change, the dynamic of the partnership changes.
- **Inclusive, formal structures for decision-making** In large complex partnerships, to ensure the weaker stakeholders have a voice and can influence decision-making, formal vehicles (steering groups, working committees, evaluation committees etc.) must be formed at strategic and operational levels, include all formal partners, and create openings for informal stakeholders. In smaller arrangements where scale, mandate, time and expectation are less ambitious, projects might be sustained through ad hoc arrangements.
- **Transparency within the partnership** Transparency within the partnership is essential to build trust and commitment. Specific mechanisms for communicating, sharing information, monitoring and evaluation, and

6

Box 6.25 Aligning Sectoral Competencies with Municipal Objectives

Supportive attributes/Competencies of potential partners

	Municipal	Private sector	Civil society
Economic objectives	• Balancing fees in relation to other services • Ensuring value for money	• Efficiency-focused • Profit-focused • Business reputation • Programme-focused	• Distribution of economic benefits (and work) to poor communities
Financial objectives	• Access to donor funding/soft loans • Some have access to bond markets • Can determine cost recovery policy • Mandate to create regulatory environment	• Capital mobilisation • Capital assets • Focus on financial viability • Generate confidence in potential lenders	• Able to enhance cost recovery in poor areas • Realistic assessments of ability to pay • Access to donor funding • Enhances ability to create cost-effective solutions
Political objectives	• Can determine allocation of resources • Can lead stakeholder consultation	• Ability to clarify costs and financial implications of political choices	• Able to build trust in poor communities
Physical/ environmental objectives	• Knowledge of existing infrastructure and operations • Can determine performance standards • Control land tenure arrangements	• Specialised technical knowledge and skills • Access to new technologies	• Able to enhance entry to underserviced neighbourhoods • Able to promote understanding of service options • Able to promote sustainability focus • Knowledge of poor communities and vulnerable groups • Able to promote empowerment and build community capacity • Able to steer coordinated responses
Social objectives	• Local knowledge • May have knowledgeable community development staff • Control land tenure arrangements • Worker re-employment		• Detailed knowledge of poor consumers • Delivery of services to low-income areas • Concern for vulnerable groups • Relationships with poor communities • Concerned with values and justice • Demand-focused
Institutional objectives	• Mandate to instigate change	• Managerial capacities • Can promote improved access to technology and skills	• Mobilisation of community organisations

* Objectives are outlined in Chapter 3

partnership reviews help to create this explicitly, but an implicitly straightforward and open approach needs to be adopted within the partnership.

- **Appropriate contractual mechanisms**   Contracts are necessary as formal mechanisms to define relationships, but their successful application will depend upon parties understanding that they are in a process of ' co-production'– one where they are mutually dependent in finding optimal solutions for all concerned, and making the outcomes successful for all. Partnerships that depend solely upon contracts are bound to fail, as parties will focus upon following the letter of the contract rather than its intent.
- **Building independent capacity**   The building block approach to developing stakeholder capacity (discussed in Chapter 5) allows stakeholders to separately identify issues and opportunities before having to articulate them in a broader forum.
- **Clear definition of roles and responsibilities**   Defining responsibilities at the outset is critical in establishing an even partnership platform where each partner brings their specific skills to the table. There needs to be a process to ensure that these roles are explicitly understood and acknowledged by each partner, and that a sense of value is placed on the contribution of social and technical inputs. Flexibility is also required to enable changes in roles and relationships between partners.
- **Ensuring strong relationships to parent organisations**   A primary difficulty is establishing a balance between the partners' commitment to the partnership and conflicting commitments to their parent organisation. Internal mechanisms need to be established to keep relations within organisations sound: many partnerships have floundered when the partnership cell becomes marginalised from its own organisation.
- **Developing mechanisms to measure success**   Mechanisms to measure the different objectives of each partner need to be created in relation to overall partnership targets.

A range of mechanisms (both processes and structures) can be established to formally support the partner relationships. These must arise from the trust and confidence that should lie at the foundation of the partner relationships.

The Process of Partnering

The process of partnering concerns the development of effective stakeholder relationships. Evidence suggests that there are a number of keys to a successful partnership – e.g., time, stakeholder engagement and capacity building – and each is dependent on the others. At the outset, this means ensuring that all the stakeholders that can be engaged, are engaged in the process of design and development. Local partners, be they private sector or NGOs, may play a key role in the early stages.

The process of partnering is important in all partnerships, but especially in those requiring extended relationships. The large-scale, long-term and complex nature of some partnership arrangements requires ongoing relationship building to involve all stakeholders in working together towards the agreed objectives and to ensure 'learning by doing'. It is inevitable that each partner's expectations, roles and capacities will change. Hence, partnership strategies and frameworks must be flexible, and they should prioritise learning and partnership capacity building.

Relationships will also change in form and extent over the duration of the partnership. Partnering should not be envisaged as a static process that always requires the same inputs, involvement and commitment from all partners. Rather, it should be seen as a process that changes as needs and capacities change. The process should encourage appropriate and evolving relationships.

In the early stages of developing a service partnership, the question is not what type of partnership, but whether there should be a partnership at all. Municipalities will need to involve stakeholders from civil society, in particular, in the

6

Box **6.26** Diversity of Partner Objectives
BoTT, South Africa

Links to Boxes
6.11, 6.12, 7.21, 8.13

One of the primary hurdles being experienced in the South African BoTT partnership in the Eastern Cape is that the partners in the consortium have vastly different objectives and there has been no explicit or conclusive process to develop some sort of convergence and common ground. As a result, the partnership has continued but with significant partnering problems, and has not functioned as effectively as it might have.

The partners argue that the whole initiative to date has been sustained because individuals in the key organisations have facilitated the process. The following table provides a summary of the divergent objectives (as given by each partner), the roles of the main partners in the consortium and the various risks each perceives.

Partner	Role	Objective	Risk
The consortium manager (Amanz' Abantu Services)	• Project management • Client/community liaison/local government • Representation of lead service provider • Accountability/client, stakeholders and shareholders • Overall implementation and responsibility • Contract management/development	• Service delivery • Business development • Meet shareholder expectation	• BoTT fails/is perceived to fail • Reputation • Linked to single contract • Technical/financial/social
Construction contractor (Group Five)	• Construction as per design and specification	• Customer satisfaction • To provide water on time, to specification • Employment (local labour) • Profit	• Rising costs/lower returns • Resources and continuity • Budget constraints
Operations and maintenance (O&M) operator (WSSA)	• Ensure sustainability through appropriate implementation of O&M and cost recovery	• To improve client base – profit/turnover • To meet client objectives/satisfaction • Empowerment • Human resource development • Development of rural skills	• Reputation/image • Profitability/sustainability • Continuity of work • Customer perception/expectation demand • Risk/liability linked to overall performance
Technical consultant (Ninham Shand/FST)	• Design services (design/planning/monitoring etc.)	• To profit financially	• Professional liability • Non-payment for work • Reputation • Risks linked to consortium performance • Rework (waste)
NGO – institutional and social development (Mvula Trust)	• ISD implementation • Advocacy/policy debate • Research and development	• To create an environment for disadvantaged companies and individuals to work in • To develop models for sustainability • To represent the community client	• Reputation (name) • Compromise values • Unclear messages/instructions

Source: Unpublished BoTT document

processes of problem identification and objective definition, in exploring the factors that currently affect service delivery, and in understanding the current methods of formal and informal service provision. Encompassing consumers (particularly poor consumers), trade unions and NGOs will inevitably result in more targeted solutions. Promoting the widest possible understanding of the problem, the potential solutions and their impacts on individuals is vital to the development of an approach that benefits all parties. A variety of tools and techniques will be necessary to establish this participation. The participation of the poor can be ensured through the participatory assessment of their livelihoods. This will involve individual, group and community interactions.

Once it is agreed that a partnership approach is appropriate, it is necessary to engage stakeholders in a structured process of discussion, feedback and decision-making to determine the basic framework of the partnership and the process to be undertaken to operationalise it. The process of defining the principles, purposes and key elements of the partnership will need to be undertaken with as many potential partners as possible. It will require engagement with individual organisations in small forums, and then in larger forums, to agree a collective way forward.

Ideally, formulating a strategic approach to PPPs should involve potential private sector partners and national and local private stakeholders, as their views on financial viability will keep the process in check; it will also introduce them to the municipal objectives. However, if a medium- to long-term arrangement involving the international private sector is envisaged, it is unlikely that the potential partners would be present through this process, and municipalities should ensure that the private sector viewpoint, at the very least, is well represented through consultants or other advisors, and that specific forums are established to discuss plans and obtain feedback from private firms. The process of procurement discussed above will also involve a large number of stakeholders. Here, it is essential that transparency be achieved by establishing an open and inclusive process with communities and tenderers.

Once partners are selected, relationships need to be developed and fostered. It is not sufficient to leave the process of partnering to chance. Group workshops that familiarise each partner with the assets and capacities of other partners, and joint definition of roles and responsibilities, are essential parts of establishing sustainable relationships. Capacity building sessions to this end should be planned for and instigated. Yet municipalities should be aware of the fundamental conflict between establishing definitive contracts for private sector partners, and creating the flexibility needed to ensure that relationships and roles are appropriate and able to evolve. Preparation is often the key, especially in understanding the potential of NGOs and small-scale providers that may complicate the large-scale private sector partner's vision of its own role. It must be made aware of the type of broad partnership involving civil society that is envisaged, and be given the opportunity to explain its position and approach from the outset. Phasing is one easy way of developing commitment and establishing relationships without necessarily incurring the additional long-term cost of early uncertainties.

Municipalities should also recognise that consultation and participation are not the same, and the partnership framework should reflect this understanding. While community participation will vary with the context – including social, cultural, political, historical and institutional factors – it should be taken to mean that partners/stakeholders are involved directly in decision-making events and that decisions can be affected by their contribution. Effective participation is difficult to achieve, especially where stakeholders have different capacities. Effort should be made to identify those marginalised from the process, and to involve them through targeted initiatives. Moreover, care must be taken to make participants clearly accountable for their roles; hence the part they play must be as clear as possible and quite specific about the value they are supposed to add.

6

Links to Box
6.21

Box **6.27**   The Experience of Partnering
KwaZulu-Natal, South Africa

One of the eight pilot projects included in the BPD initiative is located in the KwaZulu-Natal province in South Africa. This PPP pilot was established in early 1999 with the development of a collaborative agreement between the municipalities of Durban and Pietermaritzburg, Umgeni Water (the regional water board), the Mvula Trust (an NGO dedicated to the improvement of water and sanitation services for poor communities), Vivendi Water (an international water utility with experience in the operation and management of municipal water and waste water services) and the Water Research Commission (a national body sponsoring research on water-related issues). The overall budget for the KwaZulu-Natal project is approximately US$2 million, and derives from the contributions of the partners who undertake to provide human and financial resources as well as third party funding for the NGO partner.

The primary objective of the partnership is to better understand the dynamics and potential impacts of tri-sector partnerships and to draw up some guidelines for future implementation. The idea is to demonstrate that tri-sector partnerships between business, civil society and government at all levels provide benefits to all three parties, that they can be much more widely used, and that they can be successful in small- or large-scale projects. During the three years of the project, the partners are working on six pilot areas, which cover a broad range of typical situations encountered in poor urban and peri-urban zones, and they are focusing on the provision of adequate, acceptable and affordable levels of water and sanitation services, community education about water conservation, health and hygiene, operation and maintenance, customer management and the involvement of the communities in the achievement of these objectives.

While the mood during the preparatory stage of the pilot was cautious – the memorandum of understanding that forms the contractual basis for the partnership took nine months to discuss and agree – the partnership has developed substantially during the three-year implementation. Most PPPs do not rely on mutual exchange, but are bound by contractual relationships typical of commercial arrangements. This BPD KwaZulu-Natal pilot project provides evidence of a more genuine partnership involving a wide range of partners skilled in very different areas.

In the KwaZulu-Natal Project the management structures serve to clarify expectations on the part of each of the partners. An outsider's initial glance reveals a fairly wide sense of fluidity and candour. Again, the different organisations do not have a history of working together – allowing time to speak the same language has proved to be a crucial element of the project's development. According to the partners themselves the strength of their relationships has emerged from the time that project partners spent getting to know each other.

The partnership appears to be responsive and is evolving, though not without questions about the role and expectations of Mvula Trust. Mvula's role appears to have changed from being a partner with the over-arching responsibility for the community side of the project, to that of a partner with responsibility for managing the community side of the project. As the partners have become used to working with each other, some cross-over has emerged: Vivendi gets involved in education issues and Mvula gets involved in customer management, and thus the contractual relationship has an informal flexibility to it.

The partnership is one of shared responsibility with a voluntary agreement between the parties to share the overall responsibility for implementing tasks, and to be jointly accountable. Most importantly, the initiative has benefited from the genuine spirit of collaboration that has grown progressively. There now seems to be an unambiguous recognition of the need to strengthen the partnership concept with tri-sector teamwork in addressing each of the specific difficulties of service delivery in poor areas. The experience suggests that a well-functioning partnership may not only mean that each partner fulfils its expected role (e.g., the NGO handles community liaison and education, the public sector is involved in law-making and regulatory functions, and the private sector ensures service provision and financing). The free and open discussions that take place within and outside the task team meetings, and the trust built up over time, have allowed the partners' perspectives to change. None of the partners believe that they have the monopoly on social or technical matters; a joint effort prevails.

The lessons learnt in the KwaZulu-Natal pilot are that the partnership's strength stems largely from internal trust and confidence between the partners. This has given it a great deal of momentum. However, in order to build upon this, tangible results need to be generated and then communicated appropriately. Indicators (whether project or partnership based) can help the partners to do this. There is now a real recognition that by pooling their unique assets and expertise, the three sectors can truly provide mutual gains for all. Governments can ensure the health of their citizens with safe water and effective sanitation while sharing the financial and technical burden. Private companies can improve their performance while ensuring financial sustainability over the long term, and communities can gain a real voice in their development.

Source: Adapted from the KwaZulu-Natal report to steering committee

6

A Final Note on Partners

Driven by the quest for finance and improved efficiency of municipal services, the fundamental shift toward PPPs often places equity and poverty-related service issues in second place. This has naturally led to a focus upon business alone as the key partner for municipalities, and a lack of recognition of the important role of civil society in establishing partnerships that fulfil all objectives, and are holistic in nature. The efficiency focus has been reinforced by the comparatively strong voice and sophistication of the business sector. In contrast, civil society is still emerging in many locations and often lacks the confidence and experience needed in large ambitious partnerships.

From one perspective, changes in the approach to municipal service delivery can be seen as representing an increasingly sophisticated understanding about the roles and competencies of different types of organisational actors. The development of this approach requires municipalities and other potential partners to overcome ideological barriers. Most importantly, the partnership framework must prioritise discussions about who is to be involved and what roles and relationships are to be established.

Chapter 7 **Key Questions**

- ☐ How can objectives be met through the partnership arrangement?

- ☐ What is the potential scope of the arrangement?

- ☐ What issues should be addressed through the content of the arrangement?

- ☐ How can the scope and content focus on pro-poor outcomes?

| Building on the assets of potential partners | Focusing the scope and content of partnership arrangements | Establishing appropriate organisational and contractual arrangements | Establishing sound partnership principles |

Developing a Partnership Framework

Eric Tranchant/Vivendi

Focusing the **Scope and Content of** Partnership Arrangements | **7**

Janelle Plummer and Brad Gentry

The success or failure of a municipal service partnership to focus on the poor will depend not only on the development of a well-functioning partnership team (see Chapter 6), but on the scope and content of the partnership arrangement. In the past, traditional forms of public–private partnerships (PPPs) neglected to address the needs of poor communities in the scope of work defined at the outset. While many municipalities may have been very aware of the key issues affecting service delivery to the poor, this knowledge was not applied to the partnership framework; the agenda often reflected private sector knowledge of the problem and not the knowledge of local stakeholders.

The purpose of this chapter is to promote understanding of the vast range of issues that can be included in a partnership framework focused on achieving direct benefits for the poor. In order to help municipalities to create effective and targeted partnerships, we present and discuss a menu of key elements, describe alternatives and options, and highlight the known implications of the scope and content of partnerships.

There is of course no such thing as a perfect partnership arrangement – any more than there are perfect municipal institutions – and the aim here is not to provide a set of non-negotiable elements that make up an idealised framework. Each municipality will have different problems and requirements and will emphasise different elements; each will have a different capacity to take various parts forward. For a municipality, the key goal in defining the partnership framework must be to fulfil as many of its agreed objectives as possible.

The range of potential objectives proposed in Chapter 3 therefore provides a useful structure for considering the content of a partnership framework (see Box 7.1), particularly the classification of elements into physical, social, political, economic, financial and institutional aspects. Inevitably, many elements relate to more than one objective and many are inextricably linked, but a key reason for considering the scope and content in terms of different kinds of objectives is to **encourage municipalities to build partnerships that respond to their own needs** and to provide a framework through which they might consider all the various dimensions of a poverty-focused partnership.

Of course, the degree to which municipalities will actually be able to achieve their goals depends on the scope of their authority and the results of their negotiations with potential partners and users. As to the scope of their authority, if national or provincial governments establish the rules for tariffs or environmental quality, then municipalities will have to operate within those limits. As to the negotiations, if the private sector firms do not believe they will profit from the partnership arrangement, or if the users do not believe the services they will receive are worth the fees they will pay, then the arrangement will falter before it begins. How these tensions play out in particular partnership arrangements varies across locations and over time and is strongly affected by initial municipal decision-making.

The Physical/Environmental Aspects of the Arrangement

The physical/environmental aspects of a partnership framework will depend on the service in question and the requirements for change. In the main they will relate to improving:

- the extent of service;
- the type (or level) of service; and
- the quality of service.

Service Coverage

In addition to improving the performance of the system, municipalities often seek to develop partnership arrangements

7

Box 7.1   Achieving Objectives
Key Elements of Partnership Arrangements

	Objective	Framework implications – content	Framework implications – process
Physical/ environmental	Better quality service	• Environmental standards	e.g.
	Better service coverage	• Service coverage • Service options – alternative technologies	• Alternative delivery mechanisms • Payment mechanisms
	Environmental sustainability	• Affordability • Appropriateness • Service options	• Demand-responsive
	Effectiveness	• Scope of arrangement	• Inputs of range of actors
Social/political	Improved wellbeing	• Service coverage and quality • Opportunities for income generation • Integrated activities • Linkages to broader poverty responses	• Demand-responsive • Gender-responsive
	Affordability	• Tariffs/subsidies • Service options • Builds on existing assets	• Demand-responsive
	Security/safety		• Tenure security
	Improved equity	• Service coverage and quality for the poor • Incentives to deliver to the poor • Employment of workers • Awareness building	• Demand-responsive • Gender-responsive
	Empowerment	• Community capacity building • Informal sector capacity building	• Participation • Organisation, mobilisation • Inputs of range of actors
	Job security and promoting income generation	• Employment of workers • Role of informal sector	• Inclusive processes
Financial/ economic	Capital investment	• Investment incentives • Investment options	
	Operating investment	• Delegation of operations and management • Financial incentives • Remuneration (fees/profits)	
	Cost recovery	• Customer finances • Tariffs and subsidies	
	Efficiency	• Delegation of operations and management	
	Cost effectiveness	• Competition (monopolies/exclusivity) • Transaction costs • Risk management	
	Economic sustainability	• Cost recovery – tariffs and subsidies • Affordability	• Demand-responsive
	Urban growth generation	• Capital investment	
Institutional	Delegated management	• Delegation of operations and management	
	Access to technology	• Skills transfer • Technology transfer	• Capacity building processes
	Good governance	• Partnership decision-making structures	• Accountable and transparent processes • Participation

that explicitly expand system coverage. This expansion leads to the fulfilment of all types of municipal objectives: physical, political, social, economic, financial and institutional (see Box 7.1). At the simplest level, a partnership framework (and then the tender and contract documents) can include requirements for the partnership to extend the services to specified areas over a specified period of time. This is often referred to as the 'expansion mandate'. For example, the water and sanitation arrangement in Buenos Aires, illustrated in Box 7.3, originally required that water supply connections be increased from 70 to 100 per cent and sewerage connections be increased from 58 to 95 per cent over a 30-year period.

Service expansion can create opportunities. For the private sector, new consumers are added and revenues are increased; for the municipality, customer satisfaction improves, potentially increasing the pool of satisfied voters; for consumers, community involvement in service expansion can reduce costs and increase effectiveness,[1] access is improved and development opportunities can build local capacity for other poverty reduction activities. At the city-wide level, improved services and infrastructure may also open up new areas for economic development.

Executing expansion mandates, however, often introduces a host of difficult issues to be resolved within the partnership framework. These include, for instance, that:

- public or private financing for the expansion may be difficult, time consuming and expensive to obtain;
- more detailed information on the existing delivery system and alternative solutions for expansion may come to light as the partnership proceeds, requiring the renegotiation of specifications and agreement on revised timetables for construction;
- the constraints of land tenure may require political and administrative action;
- water supply upgrade may need to be coordinated with sanitation upgrade, ensuring that large amounts of water are not provided without adequate drainage and sewerage; and
- the costs of connection may be out of the reach of poorer groups.

Targets for expanding service coverage to poor areas will generally need to be accompanied by agreed (and enforced) timetables and incentives. In some of the first PPPs established the complexities and costs of expansion in poor areas were given a low priority; operators simply met coverage targets by carrying out work in less onerous, less risky and less costly areas first. To avoid this pitfall, expansion mandates over long periods, such as 30 years, should probably be further defined with short- and medium-term targets (e.g., 10 per cent in two years, 30 per cent in four years etc.) and specific identification of areas within the city where expansion should occur. This then needs to be enforced. While this was established in the case of the Buenos Aires' PPP, the lack of clarity and enforcement power on the part of the regulator has now muddied the definition of the expansion mandate (see Box 7.2).

In municipalities where there is a chronic deficiency in network services,[2] the framework should also define the interim arrangements for better service provision. A pro-poor arrangement will not leave people without any services for an extended period, but should recognise the need for staged improvements and temporary (short- or medium-term) solutions. In relation to water and sanitation, this may involve ensuring reliable, good quality communal water supplies or toilet facilities, or tanker water and septic tanks in the short- to medium-term. Some poor communities will require incremental upgrading whether or not household connections are going to reach them eventually. This is discussed further in the following section on service options.

As a part of the partnership preparation and strategic planning discussed in Chapter 4, consideration of service coverage requirements will be influenced by an examination of the broad range of ways in which people currently access services. The statement that a neighbourhood 'does not have water supply' is naïve: most households will have devised means to obtain water and dispose of waste, albeit informally or illegally.

Box **7.2** **Service Coverage**
Buenos Aires, Argentina

Links to Boxes
3.5, 5.4, 6.13, 7.3, 7.11, 7.18, 8.12, 9.8

The Buenos Aires concession arrangement established in 1993 for 30 years covers the federal capital and 17 municipalities with a population of about 9.3 million. Prior to the concession, only 70% of the population were connected to the water network and 58% to the sewerage system. The shortfall was most acute in the poorer, suburban areas, where only 55% of the 5.6 million inhabitants had water and 35% sewerage connections. Most of the 30% of the population without connections were living at or below the poverty line, and relied on water from shallow contaminated wells.

In its original form, the concession contract required 1 million inhabitants to be added to both the water supply and sewerage system every 5 years for the first 15 years. In the first 5 years, the coverage of water and sewerage services was to be raised to 86% and 66% respectively. In 15 years, 95% coverage of water services and 83% of sewerage services is to be achieved. By the end of the concession period (30 years), the concessionaire should achieve 100% water supply and 95% sewerage services. The concessionaire is also to expand the wastewater treatment system to ensure treatment of 93% of sewage throughout the concession area. The concession agreement thus included a specific mandate for expansion, implicitly including poorer neighbourhoods (although the contract is worded so that only legal settlements are included). The concessionaire was required to provide potable water and sanitation services, and to ensure the continuity, regularity and quality of those services, based on an agreed set of standards and schedules.

Reflecting precise geographical expansion targets in different zones, the service expansion plan (SEP) identified the necessary works and actions for achieving the required service standards. In the past, the sequencing of service expansion, even with OSN, the public water utility, had been determined by cost and technical expediency. However, IIED-AL worked with Aguas Argentinas to reorient the selection criteria with the aim of addressing deficiencies in the most critical areas – those with greater social and environmental need. It is notable that the plan included areas that were too remote to make network connection feasible. This introduced proposals for coverage that combined non-conventional systems and alternative water sources with traditional methods of service expansion, and required far greater flexibility than that specified in the original contract and set down by the regulator.

The feasibility for network expansion in disadvantaged neighbourhoods was thus revised to include:

- technical feasibility, which included the proximity to potable water sources, land tenure status, physical conditions (flooding, health risks) and settlement regularity;
- social variables;
- social feasibility, such as the capacity of community organisation, social stability, social capital and literacy/education levels, as well as income and unemployment levels; and
- institutional feasibility, particularly the political and institutional structure, coordination and level of civil society participation.

Despite the conditions of the original contract and the requirements of the regulatory structure, Aguas Argentinas has shown that it is willing to reorient its approach to service expansion (see Box 7.20 describing the implications of this on tariffs). The inclusion of participatory processes with communities and NGOs, and the attempts to adopt technological innovations and coordination with municipalities in targeted areas, have actually enabled it to address physical and environmental restrictions in poor settlements located on marginal land (landfills, floodplains and contaminated land) not suitable for traditional network systems. It has enabled the company to plan more strategically and reduce investment costs for expansion into remote areas in the future. The approach to service coverage has also facilitated its work in low-income communities, and ensured its security by working with communities and promoting ownership of the new services, maintenance and promoted cost recovery rates. The inclusion of local government in the process, together with NGOs, CBOs and the operator, creates a promising context for sustainability, should this collaboration be extended into the future delivery process.

Yet the expansion targets originally established are no longer well defined. Aguas Argentinas has successfully negotiated contract amendments that have blurred its actual expansion mandate. The renegotiation of the requirements of the five-year period 1998–2003, carried out in January 2001, actually released it from its expansion targets. In the current context – which changes at a rapid pace – expansion is a matter of investment, in which there is an assumption that expansion will reach the poor. The political manoeuvring that occurs beyond the contract will no doubt continue to affect the scope and location of improvements. Municipalities are vying for assistance and offering various formal waivers and informal incentives to encourage work to be carried out in their areas.

Sources: Mazzucchelli et al, 2001; Water and Sanitation Program, 2001a; Gentry, 1998; Loftus and McDonald, 2001

Examination of existing delivery mechanisms will help in identifying the local assets to be included in partnership arrangements, such as the water tankers in Lima or the rag-pickers in Hyderabad. It will also help to determine whether existing arrangements are exploitative and could be improved through increased regulation. The critical point is that strategies for service expansion must be developed in such a way as to increase, not decrease, the choices the poor can make and to build on the assets they have already established.

This analysis will include informal providers, and information on these providers should be as detailed as possible in order to understand why the poor have opted for that service (Do they have a choice? Or does that provider offer conditions not available elsewhere?) An analysis should document annual costs and quality, the method of delivery, the details of the way the service is used, and the cost of the current provision.

Existing services may be communal or shared. The increasingly common practice of removing such existing services in efforts to achieve certain universal standards of service might be financially advantageous (to the private operator) and politically acceptable, but it often results in reduced choice or access for the poorest and most vulnerable. Efforts to extend coverage to areas currently serviced by communal supplies need to address the implications and effects of removing the only supply available to poorest households. In particular, incremental improvements can be achieved through phased construction programmes and graduating improvements to the levels of service.

The other primary means by which the poor gain access to basic services is through illegal or unlawful means (e.g., obtaining water and electricity through illegal connections and disposing of waste through illegal dumping). Private operators are generally quick to ascertain how much unaccounted-for water is actually being used in low-income neighbourhoods (often by the non-poor as well). Unlike the government, which might have turned a blind eye to these practices, the private sector is unlikely to tolerate them. In order to achieve cost efficiency these illegal connections may be removed or metered. If the illegal connection is simply destroyed, it will either reappear one night or a community will be left without access to water, until it finds another way. Municipalities should try to broker a deal and create community solutions with neighbourhoods that are illegally tapping into water supplies (for instance, fixing a community contribution that guarantees supply until upgrades are agreed and implemented).[3]

Service expansion into poor areas will include consideration of the following factors (discussed in greater detail below):

- the existing infrastructure and service assets;
- the physical constraints of land;
- the existing land tenure arrangements;
- the role of existing, perhaps informal, service providers;
- the levels of service that poor consumers are demanding and the options for incremental improvements;
- the cost of improved services; and
- the impacts of expanded coverage on households in poor communities.

The problems of service expansion are accentuated where partnership arrangements are targeting poor areas. While many of the problems are common to service delivery, irrespective of the operator, many others are created by the complexities of the incentive structures inherent in PPPs. Policy-makers must recognise that municipalities may need support to introduce expansion mandates that meet a pro-poor agenda; municipal leaders should seek specialist support to assist them in achieving municipal objectives.

Land tenure and network extension in informal settlements

One of the foremost issues affecting network service coverage to poor areas is the extent of tenure security that

Box 7.3   A Story of Land, Community Mobilisation and Network Extension
Buenos Aires, Argentina

When the Integral Improvement Programme of Barrio San Jorge in Buenos Aires was launched in an assembly held in the settlement, some 150 people attended – the largest number of inhabitants attending any meeting in recent years. The government required the organisation of the community and the creation of a formal, legally recognised entity in order to integrate the programme and fulfil the necessary procedures to achieve land tenure in the *barrio*. Accordingly, elections were held in Barrio San Jorge for the first time: all residents voted for candidates in their block, and 16 residents were democratically elected to represent the interests of whole community. They constituted a Neighbourhoods Commission, which is the first organisation committed to prioritise the neighbours' main needs over the interests of external political, religious and aid groups.

Although the commission arose not so much as a community initiative but more in response to a demand from the government, most elected candidates and representatives had taken part in activities supported by the institutions working in Barrio San Jorge. This commission formalised a process of building community organisation that had been in progress through small, continuous and diversified initiatives during the previous three years. Thus, in Barrio San Jorge, the community organisation was neither the result of a pure bottom–up process controlled by the population nor a top–down process controlled by external agents, but rather a combination of the two.

Members of the commission and staff from provincial and local government, IIED-AL and other institutions working in Barrio San Jorge took part in a one-week workshop on participatory neighbourhood development. The workshop was run by the German government's technical assistance agency (GTZ), which applied the 'ZOPP' participatory learning methodology to elaborate an integral development plan for the settlement. Among a large number of ambitious goals set for the programme, priority was given to the improvement of infrastructure, basic services and environment and, in particular, the transfer of land ownership from the government to the inhabitants.

Some months later, the commission developed into the cooperative Nuestra Tierra ('Our Land'). Its name expressed the reason it had been founded and its main concern. The cooperative obtained massive support from the inhabitants, since 85% of the families were members, and most began to pay a minimum quota towards its running costs. Both the emerging community organisation and our [the IIED-AL] team put most of their efforts and hopes in land transfer. The emphasis on land regularisation became one of the main strengths of the cooperative for motivating the community. But it was also one of its main weaknesses, as time passed and the hopes of achieving the transfer of land were discouraged by the endless bureaucratic procedures.

Although the intended goal was not met, the cooperative and IIED-AL accomplished one important advance. The provincial government earmarked the site occupied by Barrio San Jorge for housing programmes for the actual settlers, which virtually eliminated the risk of eviction. Nevertheless, the failure to formally complete the transfer of land ownership eroded much of the trust of the community in the cooperative, and also left a heavy burden of frustration among its members.

During this period, the cooperative had begun to be recognised by most inhabitants as the institution of reference for the needs and problems that could not be addressed by individual households. The cooperative became involved in many everyday activities, such as the repair of the water pump, the permanent demand to the nearby factory to not interrupt the supply of water, or the provision of bulbs for public lighting. Other initiatives sought to improve living and environmental conditions, including campaigns for garbage collection, the construction of wire baskets in which households could place their garbage for collection by garbage trucks, and constant pressure on the municipal government to ensure that the waste trucks came to collect the garbage and to provide the machines to clean ditches. IIED-AL supported these and some other actions through a daily presence in the settlement and continuous work with the community to promote the active participation of its members.

Given the fact that the water supply network that the cooperative and IIED-AL were to install would operate much more easily if supplied by the conventional water distribution system, when the newly privatised water company Aguas Argentinas was extending the potable water network to an area close to Barrio San Jorge, increasing pressure was brought to bear on the company to extend its system to the *barrio*.

Links to Boxes
3.5, 5.4, 6.13, 7.2, 7.11, 7.18, 8.12, 9.8

Unlike most community initiatives, in which the inhabitants were invited to meetings in the 'House of the Barrio', in this case the cooperative and IIED-AL went out to meet the people. The strategy stemmed from the idea that if the community did not reach out to the community organisation, the organisation should reach out to the community. Open meetings were held in all the streets of the neighbourhood. At these meetings, members of the cooperative and IIED-AL explained technical aspects of the project and proposed a form of organisation for the implementation, based on the lessons provided by the pilot test. Many inhabitants overcame their fear and reticence about taking part in a community activity by coming to those meetings. When some of them expressed scepticism and mistrust about the project, suggesting that it could be a new unfulfilled 'promise', we [IIED-AL] sought to persuade them with the [achievements already made] we had: 25 houses having access to water and sanitation, hundreds of pipes and cesspits stored in the building material bank, a group of hired workers laying the main pipeline, and many years of permanence in the settlement, sharing not only achievements but also frustrations. We made no promises. The success of the project depended essentially on linking community forces and working together.

Although there was no certainty that the operator would provide water, a group of neighbours decided to take the initiative in their street. The following weekend, three groups of neighbours laid the pipelines in their streets. From those initial groups, the impulse spread all over the settlement. Many streets had to postpone their contribution to the installation of the pipes, as the technicians were not able to assist more than three streets at the same time. With such community mobilisation, it was possible to provide pipelines for 250 houses in three months. This should be compared to the pilot test, when it had taken six months to provide a pipeline for 25 houses. Given the lack of any decision by Aguas Argentinas, IIED-AL contracted a company to drill a well from which to draw salty water for the piped water network. The work became unnecessary, one week later, when Aguas Argentinas confirmed that an extension of the piped potable water system would reach Barrio San Jorge.

Since April 1995, most of Barrio San Jorge's inhabitants have had running potable water within their home. Many have started to improve their bathrooms and kitchens, buy sanitary devices, and fix tiles on the floors and walls. There used to be dozens of buckets in evidence in and around most houses, and now they are no longer there. It also seems that health problems have diminished considerably. According to doctors in the local health centre, health problems associated with poor-quality and inadequate water, and back pains associated with fetching water, have decreased sharply. According to teachers from the local school, the school-children now enjoy more hygienic conditions.

The involvement of the new elected local government and the private water company in the last phase of the project allowed an agreement to be reached for ensuring the maintenance of the network. Aguas Argentinas took over the operation, maintenance and repair of the system, while the families have to pay it at a fixed rate. This was the first experience for this company of working in partnership with a low-income community, an NGO and a local government. The firm also acknowledged the merits of the innovative technology applied within Barrio San Jorge and it is currently applying the same methods in other low-income settlements.

The participation of the community broadened both quantitatively and qualitatively throughout the decade, partly in response to the different approaches taken by IIED-AL and partly because of the characteristics of each project. At the outset, when the team working in Barrio San Jorge had a more assistance-oriented approach, participation was based on limited consultation with the community. When the proposal of some mothers to build a child centre was approved by the church, the group was consulted about its needs and expectations, and two projects were presented for selection.

Subsequently, at the time of formulating a long-range comprehensive programme for the improvement of the settlement, elected representatives of the community took part in the diagnosis of problems, the identification of working objectives and the planning of activities. They also began to become involved in many negotiations with provincial and municipal government, private companies and local donors. In the water supply and sewerage project, almost all street-based groups within the *barrio* negotiated with IIED-AL for changes, such as adopting organisation models and systems which matched their preferences better than those proposed by technical staff, as well as providing labour for project implementation.

Source: Extract from Schusterman and Hardoy, 1997, reprinted with permission

households and neighbourhoods possess at the time infrastructure proposals are being formulated. Irrespective of the source of funding (whether it is a donor agency, NGO or private sector organisation), informal settlements are often marginalised by improvement programmes because their illegal status makes them a risky undertaking. Physical infrastructure may be expropriated, bulldozed, or left to decay if communities are evicted. The concern is exacerbated with private sector financing, because private sector firms not only sink funds into network costs but also expect a return from that investment through a developed customer base. Moreover, as the potential customers and 'financiers' of the service, the poor themselves often deem the risk of insecure tenure too great. Many poor householders are not prepared to pay the capital costs of water and sanitation connections and few will invest in upgrading internal facilities and fittings if they risk eviction, no matter what quality of life and hygiene improvements such investment may bring.

The partnership framework for water and sewerage network services targeting the poor must include a strategy for resolving land tenure constraints. Without this, those poor groups – already marginalised because they lack property rights – become further marginalised because they cannot access the benefits of improved service delivery. Municipalities stating their commitment to pro-poor partnerships are deceiving themselves and others if they have not addressed how the key issues surrounding tenure will be overcome. Coordinating and facilitating land tenure is one role that municipalities cannot delegate. For some settlements, the process is relatively straightforward if the political will is there. The key to unlocking the barriers may lie in tackling the paperwork in a bureaucratic environment. For others, it will require extensive debate and agreement with other government departments (railways, roads, and district and state departments are often involved due to the encroachment on land they own). However, municipalities must set a precedent by resolving tenure issues on munical-owned land before expecting higher levels of government to follow suit.

The resolution of tenure problems occupying private land is obviously more difficult. Whereas some municipalities have instigated land-sharing proposals with private landowners to provide land titles to residents in some core areas of developing cities, these initiatives are few and far between.[4] Land acquisition is rarely an option, and resettlement – particularly from core areas to the periphery – is increasingly frowned upon by donors because of the harmful effects on the poor (e.g., decreased job opportunities and increased travel time). The process of resolving land tenure is also inherently part of a broader land-management process burdened with political wrangling and consequence.

However, some well-focused leaders and champions of change are able to come to agreements that suit a range of stakeholders, thereby facilitating expansion of private sector activities in poor areas of the city. The difficulties of resolving tenure insecurity for the poor are not just partnership issues: they belong to a broader urban management mandate, affecting all aspects of the lives of the poor (see Chapter 5). Nevertheless, they strongly influence the ability of the partnership to meet coverage objectives, and past service improvement initiatives do provide pointers for the municipality to address tenure problems within the partnership arrangement. For instance:

- understanding when the poor have de facto security[5] but not the title deeds due to administrative delays;
- facilitating quicker action to grant title deeds once barriers are removed;
- providing medium-term security (e.g., permission to reside for 10 years) to create a predictable context for the poor and for service providers to make appropriate decisions; and
- creating interim stages of tenure that build confidence and enable other service options to be considered.

Service Options

In extending the service coverage to poor areas, many municipalities consider partnerships to be pro-poor, and many arrangements rely on the expansion mandate to address inequalities in access to services. In many cases, the delivery of new water, sanitation and waste services will improve the quality of people's lives. Yet it is a municipal responsibility to consider whether or not, in any particular context, it is indeed that simple. In particular, consideration needs to be given to affordability of new services and then to the type (or level) of service to be provided. The one-service-for-all ethos often referred to as 'universal coverage' is not the right one for all contexts, and increasingly experience suggests that 'service gradation' is the only way that the poor are going to be able to access better services. As discussed in Chapter 5, a lack of service options often removes the choice available to the poor, undermines livelihood strategies and increases the vulnerability of the poorest groups.

The municipality will not need to consider only the political issue concerning different levels of service. Other social and physical factors will influence the service options to be provided, and these factors will become apparent through the initial context and poverty assessment. In many arrangements, improving services immediately and to the same standards as those provided for existing customers is often hindered because the poor often occupy the most **marginal land** (e.g., steep hillsides or low-lying land) and the cost of installing infrastructure in these areas is prohibitive.

At a micro-level, households on the most **inaccessible** plots within a poor area (which are often occupied by the poorest households) may have to pay the highest connection costs (distances are likely to be greater, for instance), and in many cases the costs of networked services become unaffordable. The partnership arrangement will need to be flexible enough to account for the needs of the more vulnerable households. Also, households within an urban community will generally display a range of capacities, and these will vary at different times. Some will be very poor, at times destitute; some will manage on a humble income; and some will be hovering close to the poverty line. These **heterogeneous** groups will generally demand significant flexibility and variability including different levels of service and the ability to change the service they buy.

One of the primary characteristics of urban poor communities is their level of **interdependence**. Some households (not just tenants) rely entirely on other poor households that do have services to act as their suppliers (e.g., water supply, toilets and/or electricity) (see Box 7.5). While this relationship may be, and frequently is, exploitative, it also often meets a need for flexibility. The introduction of household water and sewerage connections to a community will fundamentally change the informal systems established, and will bring with it advantages and disadvantages. While many householders will benefit enormously, other more complex impacts may result. For instance:

- householder-suppliers who can afford the connection will pass on its cost to the buyers – their poorer neighbours, who can least afford it;
- the buyers do not opt for the higher payment and the seller cannot then afford the connection and tariff – the service becomes less affordable;
- the poorest households raise money for the connection (by going into debt with better-off neighbours); or
- landlords pass on the connection costs to tenants in the form of increased rent. This generally exacerbates problems for the poorest tenants and creates a cycle of evictions and rent increases.

The decision-making process must ensure that all residents are able to express their preferences. All too often, consultation is limited to those on whom the poorest are dependent.

☐ Appropriate technologies

The use of appropriate technologies (such as condominial systems or on-site sanitation) has developed as a feasible way of improving services in poor areas. Despite some resistance, a few municipalities and private operators are now realising that if they are to create partnership arrangements that meet the needs of the poor, they too will have to build on previous experience with alternative technologies and move away from their preferred high levels of services. They are recognising they need to look toward solutions driven by the availability of local resources and capacity, and appropriate to the physical conditions. The technical discussion is beyond the scope of this sourcebook, but municipalities are encouraged to explore appropriate technologies developed in their own contexts and to seek support from organisations that have focused on developing pro-poor solutions through alternative, appropriate technologies.[6]

Box **7.4**   Sample Performance Measurement Indicators

Water and sanitation services – performance monitoring

Measure	Sample indicators
Service quantity	• Water supplied per person per day/by percentage of population served/sewage collected per day/percentage of effluent treated
Service quality	• Raw water quality/seasonal variations/laboratory facilities available/pollution loading/sampling frequency
Customer satisfaction	• Quality and quantity of water provided/complaint response/time for resolution of complaints/quality of collection services provided
Operational efficiency	• Water losses/treatment capacity available versus that required
Financial performance	• Costs per unit of water delivered or collected/staff-to-revenue ratio/service cost per customer served/debt-to-equity (assets) ratio
Labour	• Personnel per quantity/volume of water supplied/technically trained staff per length of pipe or customers served
Environmental controls	• Chemical usage per unit of water supplied/percentage compliance with environmental requirements
Development indicators	• New connections versus needed connections

Source: Urban Services Environmental Rating System, www.teriin.org/users

Solid waste collection* – performance monitoring

Measure	Indicator
Cleanliness of service	• Existence of litter/clandestine waste /waste in drains • Regularity and frequency of collection service • Cleanliness around and cleaning of communal containers etc.
Safe disposal	• Waste quantity delivered at official site/clandestine dumping
Customer satisfaction	• Perception/WTP/willingness to keep to collection requirements
Worker productivity	• Number of workers/waste collected per worker per shift /absenteeism
Vehicle productivity	• Number of vehicles in service/waste quantity collected per shift and per vehicle per day/vehicle downtime
Recycling achievements	• Types/quantity of secondary material recycled
Environmental controls	• Exhaust emission/sump tank/control of litter from vehicles/vehicle washing
Health and safety controls	• Use of gloves/respiratory masks/uniforms • Tools for loose waste/medical checks/vaccinations • Size of load/vehicle condition/accidents/accident cover
Labour practices	• Wages paid/overtime paid/medical expenses/holiday allowances/work breaks/hiring and termination procedures
Hazardous waste segregation	• Refusal to collect hazardous waste/provision of special collection
Fuel consumption	• Consumption fuel records/maintenance/route rationalisation
Reliability	• Downtime of vehicles/number of accidents/worker strikes/absenteeism
Communication	• Notification of service problems/radio accessibility/ease of locating
Finance	• Payment of government property, income, VAT, corporate taxes/regular payment of fair wages and benefits to workers

*Similar measures are available for measuring landfill operations

Source: Cointreau-Levine and Prasad Gopalan, in Cointreau-Levine, 2000

Condominial network designs for water and sewerage services, for instance, were pioneered in Brazil during the 1980s. They involve routing water and sewerage networks across pavements and yards instead of down the middle of streets. What effectively happens is that instead of giving each *individual house* a connection to the trunk line, each *block of houses* has a single connection to the trunk line (as if the block were an apartment building that had been laid on its side). For a number of reasons, this approach substantially reduces the cost of network expansion. First, there is a saving in the length of network required to serve a given number of houses, because it is no longer necessary to run a pipe from the middle of the street into each dwelling. Second, there is a reduction in the diameter of pipe needed. Third, pipes can be buried at a shallower depth because there is no need to protect them from the weight of passing vehicles.

A number of examples point towards the types of service options envisaged in various services:

- The use of **condominial water and sanitation networks** in El Alto reduced system costs and enabled the operator to meet expansion targets. An engineering solution was adopted to reduce the length, diameter and depth of the network required by routing distribution pipes across pavements and backyards (see Box 7.6).
- In Lima, the public sector operator facilitated a system of supplying water to peri-urban areas by providing bulk water through water tankers delivered to purpose-built reservoirs on steep hillsides. The existing informal (and exploitative) **tanker drivers** were treated as an asset in the clean water programme initiative – an asset to be integrated and regularised into the partnership – rather than being dismissed and seeing the service undermined (see Box 6.8).
- In the Billy Hattingh solid waste initiative in South Africa, a network of **small-scale entrepreneurs** working with tractor/trailers has provided waste collection services in many low-income urban areas (see Box 6.9).

Promoting service options is a critical aspect of focusing the content of the partnership framework on the poor. The terms 'service option' and 'levels of service' imply decision-making by the supplier of the service. If a PPP is to become focused on bringing benefits to the poor, the conceptualisation needs to be targeted at people, not at the service itself, and the goal should be to provide service options to meet service needs.

Quality of Service

Typically, the delivery of infrastructure and services in poor cities is plagued by problems. Both the poor and non-poor have access to inadequate services, which may be infrequent, irregular, unreliable, insanitary and insufficient. In relation to solid waste, poor-quality service may involve littering and dumping in the streets and drains and around neighbourhood or zonal collection points. In relation to water, a low-quality service means that potable water is non-existent, that service is not high enough, is infrequent or unpredictable, or that deteriorating infrastructure results in massive water loss. For sanitation, inadequate quality of service may involve untreated effluent being fed back into rivers and streams, or low collection levels leading to overflowing septic tanks or insanitary operations.

A primary physical objective of municipalities is thus to improve the quality and reliability of services, and the partnership framework needs to describe the scope and content of that improvement. Decision-making over the quality of service will be closely associated with the service coverage and levels. In the first instance municipalities will need to have worked out – in relation to costs – the quantity, quality, frequency, reliability etc. that would fulfil stakeholder objectives.

However, in the context of delivering services to the poor, some service standards will need to be defined in relation to the service demanded, and not some predetermined level. The early stages of developing a service strategy will therefore involve the determination of standards that are appropriate for different groups. In some cases these will be universal (for instance, the quality of drinking water), but in other cases the poor may opt for a different service standard than the non-poor (for instance, less frequent refuse collection, shared taps or on-site sanitation), and the scope for minimum service standards (and the potential options) must be clearly defined at the outset.

Box **7.5**   **Community Interdependence**
Vientiane, Laos

Links to Box
5.2

A participatory poverty assessment (PPA) carried out in Vientiane, the capital of the Lao People's Democratic Republic, successfully disaggregated the problems and characteristics of poverty and described the different ways that the urban poor in Vientiane experience their poverty. The purpose of this information was to better understand how to formulate the poverty focused components of a donor-funded urban service programme. The following provides an illustration of the type of information that determines approaches to pro-poor service delivery. It is likely that very different solutions would have been developed without this understanding.

One of the predominant characteristics of the underserviced areas of urban Vientiane – where many of the poor have congregated – is that these neighbourhoods are heterogeneous. That is to say, the communities in these areas are made up of households with a variety of incomes and livelihoods and the most impoverished and vulnerable households live beside households whose livelihoods are more secure. This has a number of important implications. First, the poor not only have diverse incomes but very different experiences of poverty and vulnerability. Consequently, and unsurprisingly, they have very different priorities. While the 'better-off poor' prioritise housing, services and infrastructure to improve the quality of their lives, the very poor prioritise more fundamental needs such as food, land and jobs. For the purpose of demand-led services and infrastructure improvements this means that there are very different demands within each community, and very different levels of affordability and willingness to pay (WTP). The destitute and very poor are concerned with survival and do not prioritise service improvements. Another, 'middle-poor', group prioritises certain services and may be able to afford minor improvements. However, the income and expenditure analysis suggests that the better-off groups can afford to spend more of their income on the running costs (and capital costs) associated with improved levels of service. It is evident that the some of the better off households are currently paying between 6 and 12% for services. It is therefore evident that a significant number of the households living in the underserviced areas of Vientiane would benefit from and can afford project interventions that enable them to obtain access to better levels of service.

However, this heterogeneity has also resulted in significant numbers of households relying on other members of the community. When very poor households suffer from external shocks, such as fires, illness or retrenchment, it is often the better-off neighbours who provide sources of support. The very poor rely on the better-off households for food and services. Most obtain water not from communal sources, but through hoses that connect into the taps of these better-off neighbours. Many obtain electricity by extension leads connected to neighbours. A significant number appear to rely on their neighbour's toilet facilities, whatever they may be. To this extent, services are delivered by low-income private suppliers who have developed an effective and efficient market role. While it is a profitable business approach, dependence may become patronage for the very poor in a crisis.

However, this patronage has another face and better-off households are also seen to exploit the poorer households and use service provision as a source of income for themselves. They profit from their investment in metered service connections by acting as informal suppliers of water and electricity and providers of sanitation facilities. Some of these households are the source of high-interest loans for the poorest households in a crisis, a welcome source of funds which incapacitates the poorest even further.

The interdependency of the very poor households on the better-off poor means that it is very likely that changes to the levels of service and cost recovery mechanisms will impact on the lives of those who currently do not have that service at all. Interventions cannot be targeted at these better-off households without an impact on other more vulnerable households, especially if cost recovery is involved. In this situation, those making the decisions over household-level improvements are not necessarily the ones who will experience the impacts or shoulder the cost. It is very common, for instance, for landlords to pass on the costs they incur to their tenants through increased rents. It is highly likely that households with connections and facilities that take up the opportunity to make service improvements will pass these costs on to their 'service tenants and customers'. This creates increased insecurity for poorer tenants when they have to move. Project interventions should recognise that the very poor are key stakeholders in the improvements of service to the better-off poor, and that improvements may create instability and vulnerability in the poorer groups.

It is also clear from individual household interviews that another scenario exists. In some cases the service suppliers, like some landlords, will be relatively poor themselves, and will rely on the income they receive to supplement income from other sources. Some households, such as female-headed households, may have a water connection dating from a time when they were less vulnerable, and they sell water as a coping strategy. In such cases, providing alternative possibilities for their customers will affect the mechanisms they have developed to survive.

Given the interdependent structure of these communities, it is likely that changes to the service provision of one group will have knock-on effects on other poor groups. These may not all be positive. It is therefore essential that the formulation of micro-level interventions addresses the neighbourhood as an interconnected grouping, a linked system of neighbourhood delivery. *Service delivery solutions will need to be developed that address neighbourhood clusters as integrated groupings of poorer and better-off households.* Given that these processes will be demand-led, this will mean ensuring that mechanisms are introduced which enable the poorest to be heard. Such a holistic approach will ensure that benefits are maximised and negative impacts are addressed.

Source: Plummer, 2000b

The development of the scope and content of the partnership framework will then need to define these specific service goals. This is often achieved through the definition of performance standards that create a basis for determining the acceptability of the service provided or the tasks performed. Depending on the objectives, standards to be defined may include service frequency, quantity, efficiency and productivity, quality, reliability, and expected costs. Many of the performance standards expected of an operator will conform to a norm (national or international) or a goal, but in practice performance standards are simply a means by which a municipality can assess, for instance, whether waste is being collected and transferred at regular intervals, whether complaints are addressed in a timely manner, whether drinking water is of an acceptable quality and accessibility, or whether the level of unaccounted-for water is within an acceptable limit.

Consumers and municipalities should determine the levels of service that are important to them in different sectors. As a starting point for analysis, reference can be made to the international efforts under way to develop common indicators of performance for urban services. These can also provide a useful checklist for any particular municipality's effort to determine locally important performance targets. In the broader picture, the hope is that such consistent measures can then be used to compare performance across service providers and locations, increasing the pressure on operators to perform well.

Performance monitoring aims to measure the performance of services on an ongoing basis to encourage the efficient use of available resources. Performance targets and measurements may be expressed differently depending on the scope of the final arrangement. Some examples of these are indicated in relation to different contract types in Chapter 8. In general, however, best practice recommends that the monitoring of performance should focus on determining whether the outcomes/targets have been met, not constraining operators by prescribing the methods they must use to do so.

Agreement and enforcement of such levels of service will give private partners powerful incentives to ensure that the partnership arrangement leads to improved performance. It is therefore necessary to agree the measurement system – the indicators of performance. The specific indicators will vary from sector to sector – water supply, sanitation, solid waste, energy. Examples of indicators for water and sanitation utilities are provided in Box 7.4, along with those for solid waste operations. At the outset, the definition of the performance standards must be agreed. If agreed, they are then incorporated into a legally binding contract or regulatory requirements. If the standards are not met, action can be taken to enforce legal requirements and public pressure can be brought to bear.

Social Aspects of the Arrangement

If a partnership aims to improve the physical and social wellbeing of poor urban households and communities, the scope and content of the arrangement and the method of carrying out tasks will need to be tailored to suit the requirements of poor users. The primary social aspects of the partnership arrangement described here supplement and extend the discussions on participatory processes and service options. They include:

- equity and access to improved services;
- integrating service delivery;
- gender targeting of service delivery; and
- fair treatment of workers.

Equity and Access to Improved Services

The objective at the heart of a partnership focused on the poor is to address inequalities in service provision. The problem of unequal access to basic services creates and results in the physical, political and social marginalisation of poor

Box **7.6**   Enhancing Service Affordability
El Alto, Bolivia

Links to Box
6.20

In 1997 the Bolivian government, as part of its strategy to provide all households in poor peri-urban areas with high-quality water and sewer connections, awarded a 30-year concession for the operation of services in the La Paz–El Alto metropolitan areas to Aguas del Illilmani, a consortium headed by Lyonnaise des Eaux. A major objective of the concession contract was to improve access to water and sewerage services in El Alto (see Box 6.20), where about 60% of the population lives beneath the poverty line, and about 40% beneath the extreme poverty line. The ambitious expansion targets for the first four years of the concession in El Alto included reaching 100% water coverage and making 38,000 new sewerage connections.

The very high levels of poverty in El Alto raised particular concerns about the affordability of the new water and sewerage services. The average monthly household income is US$122 (equivalent to US$0.80 per capita per day), compared with connection costs of US$229 for a conventional water connection and US$276 for a conventional sewerage connection. This prompted a search for ways to reduce the cost of services to these low-income households, and as a result the El Alto Pilot Project came into being (see also Box 6.20). The El Alto Pilot Project (EAPP) combined a number of innovative components. In order to reduce the cost of providing service connections, condominial network designs were adopted and built by means of community labour. In order to maximise the benefits of these new connections, hygiene education and micro-credit facilities were provided to support households in the construction of their own bathrooms and related sanitary installations.

Drawing on technical lessons learnt in Brazil over the last two decades, the condominial network system provides residential connections through a secondary and tertiary network aimed at reducing installation time and cost. Both water supply and sewerage pipework is planned and constructed along the front or rear of household plots and under pavements rather than roads – always in locations where access in straightforward and pipework lengths can be reduced. Costs are reduced by minimising the length of pipe used, the size of pipe specified, and the depth at which it is located underground. One of the key characteristics of the condominial alternative is that the approach can be adopted without detriment to the quality of service. Analysis of the EAPP experience suggests that savings in the length and diameter of pipes are of the order of 10–20%, while savings in the volume of soil excavation as a result of shallower trenches are of the order of 45–75%. These physical savings translate into overall financial savings of the order of 24% for the sewerage service and 40% for the water service, when the condominial engineering design is implemented using conventional contractors. One of the key characteristics of the condominial alternative is that the approach can be adopted without detriment to the quality of service.

Connection costs can be further reduced if community labour is used in constructing the condominial branches of the network. The decrease in the overall scale of the works to be undertaken increases the opportunity for community involvement in the implementation process. Residents can provide labour for the excavation and filling-in works carried out at the installation and maintenance stages. In El Alto, community participation reduced the network expansion costs by a further 26% for the sewerage service and 10% for the water service, bringing the overall cost reduction of condominial design plus community participation to 50% for both services.

It is necessary, however, to account for the additional costs of social intermediation associated with community participation. In El Alto, a team of social workers was recruited to engage with the community, explain the project, assist in organising condominial units, train them in the necessary construction techniques and supervise the construction process. This was achieved through capacity building workshops and individual visits to each participating household. Each household contributed about one personweek to constructing the network and attending the associated workshops. The total cost of this social intermediation to the utility came to US$8 per household per service, while the household's time can be valued at around US$20. When these costs are added to the network expansion costs, the overall cost saving achieved falls from 50% to around 40% for both the water and sewerage services.

Notwithstanding these costs, this approach not only succeeded in reducing connection costs but also increased the proportion of households connecting to the sewerage service to 75%, compared with 66% in a control neighbourhood. Since its inception in 1998, the EAPP has provided condominial water connections to 1977 households in eight neighbourhoods of El Alto, and condominial sewerage connections to 4050 households in nine neighbourhoods.

As experience elsewhere suggests, the provision of piped water and sewerage services to low-income neighbourhoods is a particularly challenging problem. On the one hand, the costs of such services are often prohibitively high for poor families. On the other hand – even when networks can be extended – households do not necessarily benefit fully from the services if they do not connect or do not change hygiene practices once connected. The peculiar cultural, geographical and social circumstances of El Alto make it – if anything – an acid test for the condominial approach.

Sources: Water and Sanitation Program, 2001b; Water and Sanitation Program 2001c; Foster, 2001

households. Chapters 5 and 6 described how equity in service delivery is inevitably affected by the capacity of poor households themselves, the support they receive from other organisations and the individual and group capacity building integrated into the delivery process. Throughout this chapter, we present a broad range of elements within the partnership framework, such as how quality of service and service coverage each affect the access the poor have to better services. The following section proposes that improving affordability, considering alternative payment mechanisms and increasing choice are also key steps in achieving greater equity.

☐ Affordability

While many service projects over recent decades assumed that the poor could not afford to pay for their services, this notion has now been replaced with a widespread belief that the poor can pay, do pay, are willing to pay, and sometimes pay quite dearly for services. As a result, partnerships are being developed based on the understanding that 'the poor' have the capacity to pay for formal, regular service provision. While this would appear to be the case for some poor households, it is important for service arrangements to reflect a more precise understanding – to recognise the different capacities of poor people, and to acknowledge the different practices and priorities that exist within low-income communities.

Poverty assessments repeatedly show that some poor groups are prepared to pay high prices for their water, even if it is of low quality, simply because the supply (and payment methods for that supply) is flexible. Altering service consumption is often a primary aspect of livelihood strategies and an important means of survival during a crisis. One of the key risks for the poor as they enter the realm of formal water and sanitation provision is the loss of flexibility that informal (although sometimes substandard) services offer them. Informal vendors allow the poor to opt in and out of a service in a way that the formal networked systems – public or private – do not.

The belief that the poor can afford and are willing to pay for services also needs greater examination. In many cases their 'willingness' reflects their need and their lack of choice. For a household surviving on US$50–100 per month, there is an opportunity cost associated with paying for services. Such people may pay for water at the cost, for instance, of schooling or health care. Municipalities need to improve understanding of household expenditure.

We also know that some poor households do not pay, obtaining water for free through illegal connections or from relatives. We know that the poor frequently change the pattern of their consumption as part of their livelihood strategies. Affordability and willingness-to-pay studies promoted in partnership toolkits are a crucial stage of the partnership development – but, as mentioned in Chapter 5, information collection should be carried out in the context of a broader livelihood analysis. A qualitative and quantitative poverty assessment will expose, inter alia, how much the poor currently pay for service provision. It will also reveal the following.

- The source of the service (e.g., an SSIP, a communal supply managed by the community), and the service alternatives currently available to poor households (such as illegal connections, sharing with neighbours, dependency on relatives).
- The frequency of payment (including seasonal variations in service use and payments), the flexibility of payment conditions (including the penalties and enforcement mechanisms), and the options available in a time of crisis (e.g., buying drinking water, using natural sources for washing).
- The percentage of household income spent on each service and the opportunity cost of that expenditure (e.g., women reducing food intake, girls not attending school); what would they spend their money on otherwise?
- How many of the poor can be categorised as being 'able to pay', how this is to be defined, the trends among different poor groups, the differences between willingness to pay and having no choice but to pay, and the links between affordability and other characteristics.
- The factors affecting service affordability (seasonal unemployment, flooding, sickness, marriage).

| Box **7.7** | **Alternative Payment Mechanisms**
Cartagena, Colombia

Barrio Nelson Mandela, located in the extreme east of Cartagena, is probably the poorest peri-urban settlement in the municipality. It arose following a series of land invasions in the early 1990s, primarily by displaced persons fleeing from the civil war, and it was formally recognised in December 1993. By mid-2000 it had an official population of over 30,000 (5500 households) grouped in 24 sectors. Unofficial estimates put the population at around 50,000. Barrio Nelson Mandela is not legally incorporated within the municipal administration, but has a special status outside the administrative system of *comunas*.

According to the 1997 urban planning legislation that created the Plan de Ordenamiento Territorial (POT), the responsibility of municipalities to provide water and sanitation is confined to the legally defined 'urban area' within the municipality. By placing Barrio Nelson Mandela outside that area, the municipality was effectively denying its responsibility for service provision to the settlement. This means that, in practice, some responsibility for water and sanitation in Barrio Nelson Mandela lies with the departmental government and not the municipality. Because of this legal impediment, AGUACAR, the private operator (see Box 7.12), argues that it cannot invest in Barrio Nelson Mandela, as it still falls outside the urban sanitation area to which it must extend coverage under the terms of the 1995 contract. For that reason, one of the main demands of residents is for Barrio Nelson Mandela to be relocated within the urban area, by granting it the status of a new *comuna*. Similarly, community organisations in the settlement are not recognised as fully fledged community organisations, because these may only exist in the legally defined urban sanitation area of the municipality. Instead, residents have established their own communal housing committees (Juntas de Viviendas Comunitarias), but these do not have the same clout as community organisations in negotiations with the municipality.

Until recently, Barrio Nelson Mandela residents obtained water mainly by illegal connections but also from water tankers supplied on an infrequent basis by AGUACAR. A maze of irregular plastic pipework criss-crosses the community, which is built on the side of a steep hill. This has led to sharp conflicts between residents over responsibility for cut-offs, diversions and problems of low pressure. During 1999, AGUACAR held discussions with community leaders in search of an interim solution to the water needs of the residents until the vexed issue of the legal status of Barrio Nelson Mandela could be resolved.

However, AGUACAR decided it would begin to supply water legally to the settlement, but in a collective fashion, thereby avoiding the legal technicality that forbade individual connections in an area outside the urban sanitation area. From the viewpoint of the private partner, this had the short-term benefit of recouping part if not all of the revenue that was previously lost through illegal connections. It also had the long-term benefit of encouraging a 'payment culture' among residents, as a stepping stone towards the eventual introduction of individual household connections. From the viewpoint of residents it had the advantage of ensuring a more regular water supply. It was also hoped that it would put an end to the perennial problem of extensive leakages at the top of the hill where water was tapped from the mains supply and associated very low pressure for residents at the bottom of the hill. This occurred because the illegal connections had been made with small diameter pipe that could not resist high pressure. The legalisation of these connections now meant that residents were willing to invest in replacing this narrow diameter pipework with a secondary network of larger diameter pipework.

The non-traditional system of collective payment for water was introduced in January 2000. Water supplied to the settlement is now measured by 10 separate macro-meters, each of which corresponds to the location of the previous illegal connections to the mains pipe. The coverage of each macro-meter ranges from a low of 120 households to a high of 1188 households. In each case the households are billed collectively. The leaders of the respective community organisations are responsible for collecting payment of a standard monthly contribution by each household. This amount is calculated by simply dividing the collective bill by the number of households. In the first half of 2000, households were typically paying a monthly average of around US$1.2 for 7–8 cubic metres, somewhere in the order of 2–3% of the prevailing monthly household income of around US$40.

The system of collective payment by use of macro-meters has some potential disadvantages. First, there are commercial establishments in Barrio Nelson Mandela (e.g., a private health centre) that consume large amounts of water. But under the communal billing system, they pay the same as a private household Second, there is considerable resale of water, which continues to date because of low pressure in outlying parts of the settlement. Under the communal billing system, residents who re-sell water are charged the same as those who do not, even though their consumption and capacity to pay are much higher. Third, some householders simply refuse to contribute to the communal bill. In the Edén sector, 6 households out of a total of 75 had refused to pay the communal charge ever since it was introduced at the beginning of 2000.

Nelson Mandela – communal billing data

Location (defined by the macro-meter)	Households	Household consumption (Average monthly (m³))	Household bill (Average monthly (US$))	Share of bill (paid to date (%))
0758	556	6.4	1.06	26
0688	120	7.6	1.17	46
0890	194	7.4	1.17	21
01522	135	7.6	1.17	10
01516	1,188	2.1	0.33	25
0691	422	2.9	0.46	84
284490	444	8.4	1.20	42
106769	330	8.2	1.17	26
284039	170	9.5	1.35	50

Note: Calculations based on primary data supplied by AGUACAR (Feb/March–June 2000); US$1 = 2000 Colombian pesos

The increased financial burden that this causes to the majority of households who do pay may prove to be a source of conflict in the future. Finally, there is the danger that community leaders become viewed by residents as 'tax collectors' on behalf of AGUACAR and thereby lose their own legitimacy.

El Pozón, one of the 14 districts (*comunas*) within the municipality of Cartagena, has an estimated population of 38,000 and is the fastest growing area of the city. Within El Pozón there are an estimated 42 *barrios*, of which 27 are officially recognised by the municipality. All *barrios* within El Pozón are classed as Level 1 – the category with the highest level of unsatisfied basic needs in the system for determining tariffs for basic services. There is virtually no industry in the whole of El Pozón. The pipe network in El Pozón is inadequate, of narrow diameter and of poor quality. Many connections are illegal. As a result, the supply arrives intermittently (four days per week and 12 hours per day at the most).

Most residents of El Pozón still buy their water from private water vendors. These vendors are often residents who live on the tarred road where there is a connection to the pipe network. Although technically illegal, AGUACAR tolerates the resale of water. Vendors resell water in five-gallon (20-litre) plastic containers known as *canecas*. The cost varies from 50–250 pesos per *caneca*, depending on two factors: distance from the distribution point and the availability of alternative supply. There are two principal alternative sources of supply. First, there is an intermittent but unreliable supply of free water from tankers belonging to AGUACAR. Second, during the rainy season, residents store rainwater for domestic use. The fluctuation in the sale price of water is extremely sensitive to variations in these two alternative sources of supply. During the dry season, and when AGUACAR tankers do not appear for a long time, it is not uncommon for residents to queue from 4am in order to buy water from private vendors. Household expenditure on water is US$7.50 per month. According to provisional calculations by AGUACAR, residents in Level 1 *comunas* such as El Pozón can expect to pay 6000 pesos (US$3) per month for water when connected to the piped network, a potential monthly saving of around 60%.

As part of the World Bank loan, AGUACAR will undertake a major US$2.5 million investment programme to radically improve water supply to El Pozón. Prior to the design of the project, AGUACAR carried out a consultation with the citizens of El Pozón. First, meetings were held with members of the neighbourhood committees (Juntas de Acción Comunal, JACs). Second, there was a sample survey covering 1031 respondents, carried out by a local NGO. The over-riding conclusion of the consultation was to highlight the importance of devising appropriate mechanisms for payment of bills – mechanisms that would take into consideration the prevailing culture of daily management of the household budget.

Efforts are being made to reduce the financial burden of the connection charge and monthly payments in El Pozón. The standard household connection charge to the water network (including cost of the meter) is estimated at 213,000 pesos (US$106). The current plan is to spread the burden of payment as follows: a down-payment of US$15, followed by 36 monthly instalments of US$2.50 (at 1.2% interest). These payments would be added to the monthly water bill. However, it is feared that even this instalment system would be beyond the financial capacity of the poorest citizens in El Pozón and another possibility being mooted is a reduced connection charge of 150,000 pesos (US$75). To overcome the lack of a 'payment culture' in El Pozón, AGUACAR is also considering the replacement of the standard monthly billing system with a weekly billing system using mobile collection teams.

Sources: Nickson, 2001a; Foster, 1998

There is much debate over the effectiveness and sustainability of **subsidies** as a means to assist the poor (this debate is addressed in the financial options and arrangements discussion later in this chapter). The core issue is how, within the limits of political acceptability, to develop financial arrangements that support those who cannot afford a survival level of service without undermining the 'user pays' principle, without creating an unsustainable system and without providing unintended benefits to non-poor users. A second issue is that a subsidy for a particular service is only one component of municipal welfare expenditure. It is important for decision-makers to realise that there is an opportunity cost for subsidies in one sector, and it is likely that a subsidy in one sector will mean that another service or activity will not be funded. Who prioritises one subsidy over another? Such is the case with the subsidy applied in Stutterheim (see Box 7.17). Rather than effective tariff structuring, the municipality has allocated a national grant to subsidise the tariff – a grant that could otherwise be used for economic development activities with the unemployed.

Alternative methods of implementation can also assist in making services affordable. Labour-based approaches can reduce costs and provide opportunities for the poor to earn income or reduce costs (digging trenches, for instance). In relation to network services, this may relate to individual households, to enable them to obtain a household connection; or it may be organised at a neighbourhood or community level with larger groups, to facilitate works on secondary sewers, for instance. In El Alto (illustrated in Box 7.6), the operator facilitated community involvement at both levels in the construction of a simple condominial sewerage system.

☐ Alternative payment mechanisms

While it is obvious that access to services may be reduced because of the cost of the service, there may also be a range of other constraints relating to payment that are overlooked, or are confused with affordability. The access of poor households to services is frequently affected by the capacity each has to make payments in the form, at the time and at the place required by the service provider. Continued access can be threatened if there is no flexibility for poor households to take on an appropriate and feasible payment scheme.

This flexibility may be necessary to pay tariffs and consideration might be given to methods of:

* delaying/spreading payments during difficult times (e.g., taking account of the seasonality of incomes);
* adjusting monthly/quarterly payments to shorter timeframes, which are more applicable to the way the poor manage their money (e.g., weekly payments);
* ensuring greater predictability of costs (e.g., in some cases, pre-payment methods are requested by the poor (in others they have been rejected), low-cost communal meters); and
* reducing the constraints and costs of making payments (e.g., by introducing collectors, neighbourhood or area payment points, or community collectors).

Where connection costs are passed on to users, it may be necessary to improve the capacity of the poor to pay by arranging financing options. This might include, for instance, mechanisms for:

* delaying/spreading payments by paying in instalments at affordable rates and agreed intervals (e.g., 24 monthly payments to spread the capital cost of connections);
* establishing the possibility for householders to offset some costs by providing their own labour at the household or lane level (e.g., digging trenches for pipe work to be laid); and
* establishing or linking into existing micro-credit initiatives (e.g., working with poor householders to save and ultimately to obtain credit to fund connections).

As a part of the initial and detailed poverty assessments and willingness-to-pay studies, municipalities should explore the factors affecting payment and, where possible, design mechanisms to address constraints. Analysis should identify the reasons for low-cost recovery and the constraints affecting service provision and access. It is particularly important to identify those issues that characterise the way that poor households utilise a service – especially where solutions need to be adapted to respond to the circumstances in which the poor live. In the water and sanitation sector, the practice of communal or collective billing has developed as a response to the constraints and characteristics of consumption in poor areas. Yet, this needs to be signed in relation to the specific context. For instance:

- the practice of shared connections or neighbourhood resale in poor areas means that the consumption per meter may be very high. In such cases the application of a rising block tariff developed for individual use (and discussed later in this chapter) is inappropriate, penalising poor users through higher tariffs. In some areas of Cartagena, responding to shared connections and the different consumptive pattern of poor communities, the billing system is communal and the responsibility of a community leader (see Box 7.7).
- For some poor individual users consumption per meter may be very low, and call into question the need for the meters and the corresponding high connection costs.
- In complicated and unplanned settlements, the practice of block billing may be introduced, often by placing an intermediary in charge of household-level collection. This approach has been instigated successfully in limited areas of Buenos Aires. Such initiatives are useful for poor householders (as well as the private operators), who might otherwise have to pay for transport to a payment centre.

☐ Institutional support and community capacity building

Equity in service delivery is inevitably affected by the capacity of poor households themselves. The support they receive from other organisations (such as NGOs and donors) and the individual and group capacity building integrated into the partnership are thus vital elements of the framework and key aspects of promoting equity. (See discussion in Chapter 6.)

☐ Increasing choice

Options and alternatives are essential to the livelihood strategies of the poor, but are frequently missing from their lives. As a result they may attempt to make such options available by opting for an inadequate service during good times, because it allows them to go without during a crisis. Ensuring that the poor have access to choice is an empowering aspect of any development initiative. Yet often, choice is implicitly removed by not providing information or building awareness of the choices available. This book has presented some of the types of choices that can be pursued through partnership arrangements. These include, for instance:

- whether to have service improvements or not;
- which service improvements to have;
- what level of service to have;
- where the poor can make payments; and
- how and when they can make payments.

Gender Targeting of Service Delivery

Addressing equity is not only a matter of addressing the intra-urban service gap between the poor and non-poor households and communities; it is also necessary to consider the gap *within* households, and to consider in detail the unequal access experienced by women and other vulnerable members of the household and community. Services and infrastructure projects have, for decades, generated a vast number of lessons about differing gender roles and relations and provided information on the differentiated impacts of services. Yet it is noticeable that documentation on PPP arrangements fails to draw on this body of knowledge and PPPs rarely incorporate responses that might promote greater

7

Box **7.8** Gender Targeting

The impact of access on gender

	Water	Sanitation	Solid waste
Access to service	• Water collection consumes a major proportion of poor women's time	• Access to clean sanitation is a central component of women's personal safety	• The incidence of disease among women and children in areas without adequate waste collection is far higher than men
Level of service	• Improved levels of service reduce the incidence of ill-health, especially among women and children, because they spend more time at home	• In urban areas, access to in-house sanitation reduces both the risk and the fear of crimes such as rape	• As for water
Cost of service	• Because women tend to pay for domestic consumption, the proportion on of the household budget spent water is critical to determining the balance of resources for other items such as food and shelter. • Lower costs for water would improve nutrition rates etc.	• Improved public health and infant mortality and possibly reduced incidence of rape	• There are no necessary gendered gains from subsidising waste removal, as in the absence of an effective collection service poor households dump waste rather than incur costs of removal. But this may pose a public health threat

The impact of subsidy identification

	State identification process	Self-selection process	Registration process
Information distortions	• Because information is collected at the household level, the position of both men and women may be distorted. Distortion costs may be high	• Women often will not be able to make the effort to register because of a lack of transport or information about the subsidy. Lack of take-up of subsidy will reduce total costs but also under-mine the impact of the programme	• Household structure may be distorted to allow access to the subsidy • The cost will depend on the subsidy design
Incentive distortions	• Area-based targeting may trap the poor, especially women, in areas with no economic opportunities. • Unpredicted costs of exacerbated poverty may be very high	• Area-based targeting may trap the poor, especially women, in areas with no economic opportunities. Long-term costs of ongoing subsidies to unsustainable households are very high	• Gendered registration would not applyto the subsidy on water, waste, electricity and sanitation
Administrative and invasive losses	• Differentiating between the amounts allocated to women and men would not apply to the subsidies on water, waste, sanitation and electricity	• Gendered self-selection would not apply to the subsidies on water, waste, electricity and sanitation	• Gendered registration would not apply to the subsidy on water, waste, electricity and sanitation
Accuracy	• There is generally insufficient information that differentiates between the needs and position of women and men to make an informed selection	• Depends on the service design	• Gendered registration would not apply to the subsidy on water, waste, electricity and sanitation

Source: Parnell, 1998

gender equity through the partnership agenda. Moreover, the lack of emphasis on gender issues means that gender impacts are not currently monitored or evaluated.

The issues concerning gender in service partnerships involving the private sector are mostly similar to those found in existing service delivery arrangements, and it must be recognised of course that some municipalities have only limited experience themselves in addressing gender biases in service delivery. Yet evidence suggests that others have initiated a more gender aware and sensitive approach to development, particularly in some parts of South Asia where community development and participation processes have become established, often through women's organisations.

Any change to services and the manner in which they are delivered is likely to affect women first, and often to a significant degree (see Box 7.8). As women bear productive, domestic and reproductive roles, they are most affected by the access or lack of access that a household has to basic services. They are also likely to be disproportionately affected by the level of service and the cost of service. In most households, it is the women who collect water, organise household sanitation and determine whether any household money will be spent on the removal of waste.

A number of parameters underlie the development of a gender-aware service arrangement. These include the following.

- **Women prioritise services differently**   Gender disaggregated poverty assessments often expose the fact that women prioritise water supply improvements, while men prioritise electricity or income generation, for example. This seems linked to the fact that men do not work for their water; it is provided by female members of the family. Women pay for it, queue for it and carry it, and value its use for domestic, health and hygiene purposes more than men. Women are also likely to value sanitation services to a greater degree than men, as the lack of access to private and adequate facilities threatens their personal safety and hygiene. Women are likely to prioritise service improvements in relation to household needs; men will prioritise in terms of their individual needs.
- **Women tend to have responsibility for providing services to the household**   Women are generally responsible for collecting water, disposing of refuse and clearing flooded houses. Water collection can result in a loss of productive time and a loss of education for women and girls. Impacts of changes of location of standpipes and facilities will have beneficial and adverse impacts on them, and they are most aware of the constraints facing them, e.g., low water pressure, long waiting times, broken standpipes, inadequate household collection, inadequate lane-level waste collection etc.
- **Women tend to pay for household services**   Women are frequently burdened with the task of ensuring that payments for domestic consumption are made. They know what they can and can not afford at any time. Changes in the costs of services will affect what they can spend on other basic needs such as food and health care. Where there is a shortfall, it is often the women and girls who suffer by reducing their food intake or health care.
- **Women often undertake low-status activities to earn an income**   Many of the workers employed as unskilled labour or acting as informal providers of water and waste services, are women. Changes to the vehicles of delivery are most likely to affect women's incomes. In Biratnagar, over half the sweepers are women. In Dar-es-Salaam, illustrated in Box 7.9, over half those involved in micro-enterprise solid waste activities are women.

Recognising the importance of gender in decision-making is perhaps the first step, but how can gender be incorporated into the various aspects of service partnerships? It is not enough to simply cite gender equity as a goal of the partnership. It is necessary to define how it will be achieved. This means considering gender sensitive processes, the content of the arrangement and the financial arrangements that are established. Within the specific institutional and social context of a partnership arrangement it is necessary to examine the current role of women and identify the specific gender implications. These include, for instance, tariffs and fees, subsidies, procurement policies, payment options and facilities, performance management, job creation, actors, support systems, and the scope and nature of general and targeted activities.

7

Links to Boxes
7.15, 10.10

Box 7.9 | **Women in the Solid Waste Workforce**
Dar-es-Salaam, Tanzania

In Dar-es-Salaam, recent efforts to involve the private sector have helped to create more than 1500 jobs. Solid waste collection and street sweeping has been contracted out, since early 1999, to small-scale enterprises and CBOs. Coverage of waste collection increased from 5 to 40%, and these services now also reach the poor. The key recipe for better services and more jobs has been a comprehensive planning process involving relevant local actors. The inclusion of the local employment perspective in urban planning can be a primary motivation for shifting to a private sector approach in solid waste management. One of the most important contributions local governments can make is to create the right conditions to help the private sector to invest and generate jobs. The provision of services is a major opportunity to create employment directly. Services such as waste collection, water distribution and street and market maintenance can be delivered effectively by small-scale initiatives. This is also likely to improve and to expand coverage of previously unserviced segments of the population.

With support from an International Labour Organization (ILO) InFocus Programme under an inter-regional PPP programme, the Dar-es-Salaam municipality reorganised waste services in the city to facilitate a role for micro- and small-enterprise development in waste collection in the city. The contractors started operation in February 1999 and within two months had doubled the quantity of waste collected. A number of lessons are instructive for other municipalities, among them the issues of labour (discussed below) and fee collection (see Box 7.15).

At the time of starting operations in 1999, the contractors employed over 1900 people. To some extent, this number was needed to clear the waste that had accumulated in all areas. Many contractors, however, employed too many people due to their lack of experience. They were also under pressure from local leaders, who forced contractors to employ people of their preference in return for their support in the community. Not only did this contribute to over-employment, but many of these workers proved to be unreliable. Within two or three months, the contractors realised they could not collect enough fees to pay the wages of all their workers. They reduced their workforce to a total of about 1250 employees. This number included people who previously had been partially employed in other activities by the contractors. Some of the employment replaced the workers who had been retrenched earlier by the city commission, in particular street sweepers. It is estimated that the net increase in employment is about 900–1000 people.

Even before waste management was reorganised, women were prompted to engage in these activities because of the increasingly intolerable living conditions in some areas. Women's groups created their own work by starting waste collection services, for which they charged money.

> 'The Kisutu Women Development Trust Fund started as a group in 1995 with 5 members as a tailoring and embroidery group. Lack of a market for our products made us start informal catering service, also known as Mama Ntilies. This activity also did not bring us sufficient income. We became involved in solid waste collection and disposal as a result of not getting enough income from our other activities. The other reason is that we realized that the boys who were doing this job, were earning a living with this work. Moreover, solid waste was becoming a problem and many families were using children to dispose of their waste at cheap rates. One child was knocked down by a speeding car while doing this job. KIWODET started waste collection in June 1998 with 20 members, all women. Two years later, they were progressing well and had initiated more diversified activities in solid waste management. They had, as one of the first CBOs in the city, started composting activities after attending a course initiated by ILO in July 1999. They obtained extra income through recycling, by sorting out recyclable goods and selling them to industries.'

Women and previously unemployed youths have particularly benefited from the newly created job opportunities. Women constitute just over half of the total workforce of the waste contractors. They are, however, under-represented as owners and managers of the enterprises and CBOs, except in some CBOs, which are managed by women only. Almost all street sweepers are women, while the collection of waste from households and enterprises is done by men as well as women. Most contractors consider handcarts too heavy for women, and they also do not employ any women to work on trucks. On the other hand, women are preferred for the job of revenue collector; they are believed to be more honest and to approach the clients more efficiently. Male youths are contracted for the heavy jobs, such as pushing handcarts and loading trucks. They also constitute a considerable proportion of the waste collectors. Like women, they are under-represented in decision-making positions. None of the employees are younger than 18.

Not all jobs are full time. Many workers are paid only for the days on which they actually work, which varies between two and seven days per week. The more established contractors pay weekly or monthly salaries, as well as secondary benefits such as housing allowance. All workers are paid at least the minimum wage of US$1.50 per day.

Source: Adapted from Bakker et al, 2000

Integrating Service Delivery

To address the wellbeing of the poor and the most marginalised groups, the partnership framework should aim to address livelihood needs by integrating a range of poverty-related activities. Typically, this means that the partnership must build in processes and activities that lead towards a more holistic approach and a more targeted poverty response. The nature of the activities that address livelihood needs will be dependent on the assessments carried out at the outset (see discussion and illustrative boxes in Chapter 5). This will also help disaggregate the poor, drawing attention to the poorest and most marginalised groups, and provide important information on gender issues in relation to service delivery. As a key part of the partnership strategy, this analysis will lead to context-specific solutions for improving water, sanitation or waste services.

It is likely that actions to establish the needs of the poor and to respond to these needs (through the activities described below) will involve a number of civil society individuals or organisations, whose knowledge and experience in working with communities will enable better understanding of needs and solutions. The municipality will then need to assimilate this information and consider the range of activities that might be included in the formal partnership arrangement, or which may be linked to that arrangement to achieve an integrated holistic poverty response. Various actors within the partnership framework will need to be allocated responsibilities in accordance with their competencies. The aim is not to ask an unwilling or unskilled private sector actor to take on too much, but to carry out linked activities within a composite framework and ensure that maximum benefit is gained.

In addition to the specific activities targeting the physical environment in relation to water, sanitation and waste services, the partnership may facilitate other health, social capital, income generation and financial service initiatives.

☐ Health and hygiene activities

Increasingly, partnership arrangements are including health and hygiene promotion activities. Through the development of greater health awareness and understanding of the origins and risks of water- and faecal-borne disease, the BoTT in South Africa hopes to promote understanding of the importance of paying for water. Other initiatives, such as those established through the work of the operator in El Alto, have not promoted this link, but have focused on health and hygiene as a central part of their efforts to empower individuals, strengthen communities and raise awareness of some of the key dimensions of poverty. In order for benefits to be realised, the timing of health and hygiene promotion activities needs to match the programme for service improvements. Such activities may need to be linked into other important activities (such as mother and child care or financial services), and they should be delivered by agents that the communities trust.

☐ Social and community development activities

If a partnership arrangement is aimed at improving the wellbeing of the poor, it needs to reinforce opportunities for participation by the poor and prioritise participatory processes (see Chapter 6). Only with meaningful participation of poor householders and communities will services respond to their needs and build on their existing assets. However, communities cannot participate without having the skills to do so. The inclusion of participatory processes in a partnership arrangement must therefore be accompanied by the necessary training/capacity building. This not only requires the financial, human and organisational resources to be centrally placed within the framework, but it requires time. As such the programming of improvements will be affected by the initial capacity of the community and the execution of the capacity building process. Capacity building should acknowledge intra-community differences and target vulnerable groups within communities, not just dominant leaders. Women's groups may require confidence building and public speaking training, for instance, as well as team working and organisational formation skills training, as given to other groups within the community.

Apart from the community capacity building mentioned above, a pro-poor arrangement will consider the inclusion of other social and community development activities for poor groups. This is not without precedent; many water or solid waste sector projects delivered by government have realised the importance of developing social capital to increase the sustainability of project inputs. The past removal of such activities from infrastructure programmes involving the private sector (with notable exceptions) does not reflect the decades of learning about project delivery processes. Within infrastructure-related endeavours, social capital is essential to promote ownership, to encourage effective maintenance, and critically to ensure that the maximum benefit is being gleaned from the investment made. While the provision of physical improvements improves access, the development of social capital promotes the degree to which households are able to make use of the physical assets.

☐ Income generation activities

One of the critical concerns of householders signing up to the upgrade and formalisation of services will be their ability to make the required payments. Some alternatives for increasing the rate of cost recovery among poor consumers were presented earlier in this chapter. In addition, the arrangement might consider possibilities for economic development at the micro-level. Changes to the physical environment in poor areas – such as regular water supply or cleared open space (created by the removal of debris) – create opportunities that can supplement existing household assets that are available for income generation purposes. The time women spend collecting water could become a productive asset. Home-based income generation, for instance, may become possible where it was not before. Targeted vocational skills training activities, for instance, could be organised in association with physical improvements. Like the physical service provision, the activities must be demand-led and the partnership arrangement will need to identify appropriately skilled actors to facilitate these activities.

☐ Financial services

Access to financial services, such as savings and micro-credit, is another important aspect of a pro-poor arrangement, linking closely to opportunities for income generation, community development and the development of payment options for poor groups. Participatory needs assessments should have exposed the capacity of different households to save, their livelihood strategies and need for finances, patterns of debt, and the access poor groups have to existing financial services (such as exploitative money lenders). The facilitation of financial services (perhaps through civil society organisations) can play a central role in municipalities and poor communities achieving their objectives. In relation to the physical improvements it can enable otherwise excluded households to opt into a proposed delivery process, it can provide comfort and flexibility for those wishing to improve their services, and it can help to maximise the potential benefits of improved services.

Fair Treatment of Workers

A notable characteristic of municipal service delivery is that the workforce is predominately drawn from the poorer groups within the city. The provision of waste-related services – be they informal or municipal – is invariably carried out by the poorest groups. Their status and vulnerability and their marginalisation from society is closely linked to the low status of the jobs they perform. Many women take on street sweeping and rag-picking as a part of their livelihood strategy; and the poorest, lower castes in South Asia are invariably responsible for emptying and cleaning pit latrines. While it is common to see the partnership development process being concerned with the political sensitivities of municipal workers – and with concrete proposals for their re-employment in partnership arrangements – less attention has been paid to the impact of partnerships on informal sector workers, and it is vital that mechanisms are established to address their role in the future. The following section supplements the discussion on these actors provided in Chapter 6, and considers some of the key social issues concerning workers that should be addressed through the partnership framework.

Municipal workers

Meeting the needs of the municipality's existing workers – and hence of unions focused on members' needs – is often a primary objective and a critically important part of the transition from municipal service provision to one involving the private sector. Many (although not all) municipal utilities are overstaffed or inappropriately staffed for the immediate transfer of workers into private operations, and the partnership framework needs to address worker re-employment/transfer and redundancy. If this process brings with it too much political opposition, or if the price of addressing the needs of redundant workers outweighs the benefits of a partnership arrangement, the overall partnership approach may need to be reconsidered. Determining how, when and over what period of time the needs of potential opponents can be met is a critical issue facing partnership advocates.

Each municipality will have to find its own approach to the question of municipal worker employment in consultation with the unions, private sector and civil society partners. The aim is not the preservation of the status quo, but the empowerment of poor workers and the assurance that formal private sector involvement is not adversely affecting these poor groups without some mitigating initiative. The following options help to ensure that poor workers are empowered and not disempowered through the introduction of partnerships for municipal services.

- **Ensure job security of municipal employees**   Some operators have acknowledged the political sensitivity of worker re-employment and have offered guarantees to municipal decision-makers and trade unions to facilitate easier negotiations. While this may not be problematic with the employment of managers and skilled staff, the re-employment of labourers, mostly poor labourers, constitutes a major issue. A successful partnership arrangement will eventually employ many people and is likely to generate new (different) jobs in construction and management, but this can take time. Many tender documents specify the importance of the prospective operator developing an acceptable package for municipal workers that gives preference to existing employees. Despite the potential cost, others specify the re-employment of the municipal department labour force. Before private sector partners are selected, it is therefore common for proposals to detail the operator's offer in relation to termination of employment.
- **Offer existing employees retirement packages or transfers**   While this is sometimes very difficult if other departments are also overstaffed, some municipalities have exercised a moratorium on employment for some years prior to private sector involvement to allow natural downsizing. This creates opportunities for transferring staff into new jobs. Others have offered attractive severance/early retirement packages.
- **Promote improved worker conditions and rights**   In addition to job security, the partnership arrangement needs to address the terms and conditions of workers: their wages, hours of employment, and health and safety provisions. Municipalities should be ensuring that terms and conditions are better than those within the municipality itself. While this would appear to be the case in partnerships involving the international water companies, it is less likely in, for example, partnerships with national companies for solid waste management.
- **Offer training and career development opportunities**   One of the incentives for workers to move over to the private sector is the opportunity for career development and the promise of training, often including foreign travel. While this mostly applies to skilled staff, some operators fund staff HRD programmes, including job and literacy training. The more extensive the responsibilities of the partnership, the more extensive is the need to train staff in new ways of working with equipment, procedures with customers, etc.
- **Encouraging micro-enterprise development**   Some arrangements have provided the support necessary to assist existing municipal employees in their bids for small contracts (or parts of contracts) to provide services through independent micro-enterprises. While this requires motivation and confidence on the part of employees to become small-scale entrepreneurs, well-facilitated micro-enterprise development has proved to be a successful way of ensuring that workers have sustainable income opportunities. If a partnership includes significant capital investment, new construction projects will also generate new opportunities for local small businesses or residents of poor communities.
- **Distributing a percentage of the ownership shares to employees**   In highly unionised contexts, PPPs have been developed in such a way as to allocate shares to employees to create incentives and greater commitment to private sector involvement (see the case of Nelspruit described in Box 6.17).

| Box **7.10** | **The Aguateros Water Merchants**
Asuncion, Paraguay

In Paraguay (population 5 million), small private companies have been operating for several decades in the two largest cities (Asuncion and Ciudad del Este) alongside a highly inefficient state water company, CORPOSANA. Paraguay has one of the lowest water and sanitation coverages in Latin America: only 42% of the population have access to piped water, 11% have access to basic sanitation services, and there is no wastewater treatment. Some 22% are served with water by CORPOSANA and 13% by water cooperatives in small urban settlements that are coordinated by a state body, SENACSA. But a further 500,000 persons are supplied by small-scale water supply systems based on groundwater sources. These systems are operated by small entrepreneurs known as *aguateros* (water merchants). There are approximately 350–600 independent *aguaterias* currently operating. An estimated one-third of the connections made in the past 20 years in Asuncion and Ciudad del Este have been provided by these water merchants, representing some US$30 million total investment.

A typical system consists of a well and pumphouse, which supply a low-income neighbourhood of around 100 households through heavy-duty polythylene pipe. Water is pumped to household storage tanks for a limited number of hours each day. The customers plan their usage around this schedule, filling holding tanks with enough water for the day. The operation is completely private, and the infrastructure simple to install. The *aguateros* began operations with water truckers but due to the abundant presences of underground water moved on to create these small-scale water supply systems.

> 'The aguateros *selects an area where he calculates that his business can take root in a growing settlement, buys a lot, builds a well and pumphouse and begins by providing water to the first wave of settlers, however few. The* aguateros *has to move fast, before another stakes a claim in the area, because although aguateros can compete for customers who reside on the edge of one system or in between the two, once established, the pioneer* aguatero's *right to operate with a given area is generally respected.*
>
> *Even though the* aguateros *like to say they work in a an open and competitive market, it is clear that exclusivity must be respected to a limited degree; otherwise the battles for customers could make the business unsustainable. The existence of unclaimed areas on the edge of and between the* aguateros' *business zones where real competition goes on and the competition by comparison [benchmarking] on this reduced scale, assures that the* aguateros *do not take unfair advantage of their customers [elsewhere]. The existence of the Aguateros Association, at the same time, limits the possibilities of flare ups between them and tends to standardise service quality and prices.'* (Troyano, 1999)

Aguateros require capital to invest in the system. They outlay in full at the outset and assume all the risk. The customers pay a connection charge – the main way that the *aguatero* recoups the cost of his investment, which he attempts to do within three years, given the risky nature of the business, the phyiscially precarious nature of the infrastructure and the medium-term legal insecurity.

Unlike many large-scale water companies, it is in the *aguateros'* interest to support those households who cannot pay the connection charge and tariff. Most *aguateros* therefore operate a credit mechanism facilitating payment by instalment – like traditional moneylenders, at very high interest rates – recouping investment and ensuring the sustainability of his operations. This financing system is no doubt exploitative of the poorest households in that they pay over the odds for the same service, but like most services developed for the poor it provides opportunity and flexibility, based on local knowledge and close contacts with customers. The poor cannot provide collateral or obtain a loan elsewhere, and need some flexibility in payments during difficult times. While they pay dearly for the connection, the water charges are generally metered properly and are lower than the water companies'. Moreover, there is no incentive for the *aguateros* to cut them off as the different cost of supplying water is insignificant compared with the cost of disturbing the client base with bad will.

However, plans are now under way to privatise the state water utility, CORPOSANA. A new water law has been passed and a regulatory body is being created. But the Cámara Paraguaya de Aguateros (CAPA), the association of *aguateros*, is protesting vociferously against what it sees as an attempt to put an end to their activities. Under the present plans, private companies will bid for a 30-year concession to replace CORPOSANA. While the new law is unusual in not granting exclusive rights to the concession operator, the *aguateros* operating within the utility's jurisdiction will be granted operating permits for up to 10 years, and will become subject to tariff regulation. CAPA fears that the regulatory body will stifle competition and that the new concession operator will apply pressure for non-renewal of their licences, thereby leading to their demise.

The concerns expressed by CAPA have provoked a lively debate about the *aguateros*. Some observers see them as a shining example of the virtues of unfettered private competition, showing up the failings of the public sector in basic service provision. Their existence, it is argued, also challenges the conventional assumption that urban water supply is a natural monopoly based on economies of scale. The *aguateros* phenomenon, they argue, demonstrates that:

- private initiative can contribute to urban upgrading and improved access to services;
- private participation in the provision of services can ease financial pressures associated with extending coverage to new areas;
- large-scale state or private monopolies do not necessarily represent the only or best water supply option;
- small-scale operators are potentially able to serve the poorest because of the flexibility of their operations; and
- public limitations and/or inefficiencies can be overcome by allowing private sector participation in service delivery.

Notwithstanding the contribution of the *aguateros* in Asuncion and Ciudad del Este, there are a number of constraints that hinder replicability and issues that need to be addressed in any future arrangements:

- Physically, the approach is constrained by geology: they can only function where the water table is high enough to sink a well. While this means such an approach is only replicable in some places, it also highlights the importance of contextually specific solutions and building on the existing solutions and assets.
- The standard of service is variable and totally unregulated. Water supplied by *aguateros* is not treated and quality is sometimes poor. Supply is usually not continuous and subject to low pressure and interruptions. Once connected, customers are at the mercy of the *aguateros* and dependent on the *aguatero's* behaviour.
- In practice, each *aguatero* has exclusive rights over his area, which is respected by other CAPA members, and while there is an in-built price control mechanism (described above), at times competition is lacking.
- There is some question as to whether at present they cater for the poorest because they establish themselves and operate in neighbourhoods where potential customers can afford the US$250–350 connection fee. Although they provide a credit mechanism to the poorest in these areas, they have already selected the areas based on the ability of the majority to repay.
- Some are not cheaper than the public sector provision. Some monthly operating tariffs are 25–50% higher than those charged by CORPOSANA, although to some extent differences reflect subsidies received by public entities. In the main however they can offer a better price than any other service, except for community-managed systems.
- The *aguateros* phenomenon cannot be divorced from its social and political context. The provision of basic public services is woefully inadequate in Paraguay. As late as 1956, when CORPOSANA was created, Asuncion was the only capital city in Latin America without a water supply system. The very slow expansion of the piped network since then reflects the low priority attached to social concerns by a three-decades-old dictatorship, and the rampant level of corruption tolerated in CORPOSANA. The *aguateros* are thus an informal solution to this structural problem.

Perhaps the key issue is that *aguateros* do not currently provide sewerage services, and while this has been sustainable in the past through the use of individual septic tanks, conditions (leach lines, soil quality and lot size) may not always support this system. It is unlikely that the *aguateros* could operate conventional sewer systems and wastewater treatment plants due to their small scale and the need for substantial investment, but it has been argued that small-scale systems such as mini-plants, septic interceptors or ponds would fall within their investment and operational capacity.

While a large private operator might deliver water to the population of Asuncion more efficiently, in a more equitable manner and with a more effective coverage than *aguateros* could over the next 30 years, a crucial ingredient to ensure this outcome – an independent and competent water regulator – is very problematic in Paraguay. Corruption is endemic among the political elite and within the public administration. For this reason alone, there is a strong case for a tolerant posture towards the *aguateros* in water legislation that would allow them to continue to operate. There is also a case that greater promotion of their activities could lead to more extensive coverage in poor areas, and a wider service.

Sources: Adapted from Troyano, 1999, translated by Tovo Maria Solo; Andrew Nickson

☐   **Informal sector workers**

In practice, it may be the workers employed in the informal sector that are most affected by large-scale reform to policy and delivery systems. Yet the impact on these poor rag-pickers, manual conservancy workers or water vendors is rarely addressed, and the PPP can have significant impact on a large group of self-employed workers. As there are no regulatory provisions that protect the rights of informal workers, there is little incentive for municipalities and private sector operators to formulate a plan that addresses the social impact of the arrangement on the informal sector and the livelihoods of those affected. Yet a pro-poor partnership should do just that, and it is within the power of the municipal partner to ensure that the partnership strategy and the arrangement formed address informal sector activities.

Notwithstanding the inexperience of large-scale private operators in working with poor small-scale providers, potential approaches might include:

- identification of the roles of small-scale providers in the overall partnership framework;
- support for regularisation/registration or licensing as necessary to accommodate their inclusion in the partnership arrangement (see 6.8);
- support for the development of micro-enterprises to take on direct service contracts either with the municipality or with the formal operator (see 6.9);
- targeted retraining and skills development and income generation activities to reorient activities;
- negotiated arrangements where informal sector providers continue to provide the service for an interim period; and
- capacity building initiatives for formal private sector actors to sensitise them to the potential of small-scale providers.

One of the primary concerns for informal sector providers in some cities is that their investment is expropriated. The arrangement must ensure that existing facilities (no matter how informal) cannot simply be absorbed by a new operator without some form of discussion and compensation, especially for poor informal providers. In Paraguay, the *aguateros* water merchants, described in Box 7.10, provide a significant and recognised service, but the recent proposal for a long-term concession arrangement has not considered how these merchants and their assets will be incorporated into plans to broaden the very limited water network.

Financial and Economic Aspects of Partnership Arrangements

Inevitably, from the municipality's perspective, the primary partnership objective is to address financial constraints, and some of the key elements of the partnership framework will describe the financial requirements of the arrangement. The following discussion elaborates on some of the key issues in respect to:

- **private investment capital**   (risk management, sources of funding, municipal borrowing constraints, improved access to public investment capital, the costs of borrowing);
- **financial incentives**   (operator fees, operator profits, payment to NGOs); and
- **cost recovery**   (tariffs, subsidies, connections costs).

Private Investment Capital

A primary objective for many municipalities is to attract private investment capital into their efforts to improve urban services. But this intention is closely linked to the ability to ensure that there is a stream of revenue available for paying investors back. Policy on cost recovery and user willingness to pay is thus vital to any partnership framework.

Unfortunately, many governments vastly underestimate the time, energy and money they will have to invest in order to attract substantial amounts of private investment, particularly foreign investment. There are many different types of private investors: local and foreign, active providers of urban services and passive providers of money. They have different levels of comfort with different types of investments over different time periods. They also have alternatives. They make an investment when they conclude that it offers better opportunities for profit than their other alternatives. Finding the right balance between satisfying the needs of private investors and meeting the needs of the municipality and users is a time- and resource-intensive process. Depending on the size and complexity of the proposal, evidence suggests that the process (for network services) can take over two years and can incur significant (perhaps in the order of millions of dollars) transaction costs for the public sector.

Risk management

Why do private investors risk their capital by investing in any particular project? The key to this question lies in the risk/reward calculations carried out by the potential operator. They are concerned with risks of various kinds:

- **Project risks** are posed by the project itself – How much will it cost to provide the required services? How much will users pay for the services? How will government regulation affect the operations?
- **Country risks** are posed by the country in which the project is located – Does the government honour contracts? Will the currency be devalued? Are there mechanisms for resolving disputes? Can profits be taken out of the country?

Ultimately, however, the key question is whether the risks that a private investor takes on are likely to be rewarded by the profits they earn. Governments play a crucial role in determining the extent of these risks. How the partnership arrangement is structured and implemented is the key to project risks. How the country treats private investors is key to country risks. How the municipality protects the interests of users, communities and municipal workers affected by the partnership arrangement is key to political risks.

Many governments also assume that only foreign private investment is available. Increasingly, however, local sources of private investment are being tapped. In addition to local commercial banks, such sources may include pension funds, local stock markets and local firms – particularly those already providing urban services and seeking to expand their businesses. Country risks are often not as much of a concern for local investors, given that they operate in the country already. As such, in some cases they may actually offer more attractive financing terms than international investors.

Negotiations with the private partners will focus not only on how the company is to make money (such as the fees to be paid or the tariffs to be collected), but also on the question of who bears what risks. As to the level of fees, they should be high enough to cover the costs of providing the service, plus a reasonable profit. As much as possible (and as discussed above), they should also enhance the incentives for timely improvements in performance. As to who should bear which risks, an old saying usually applies: 'risks should be borne by the party best able to manage them'. If the private firm is installing equipment or treating water, it should bear the risk of the equipment or treatment failing to work. If the government is responsible for setting performance standards, it should bear the risk of additional costs if those standards are tightened over time.

Risks associated with customer demand are often major points of conflict in urban services: Who pays if the customers refuse to buy the offered service, or pay the authorised fees for it? Private firms will seek either to have the municipality bear such risks (by seeking to have the municipality pay fees directly for the services provided), or to allow for a higher level of profit (to offset the increased risks) in its bid.

Potential investors

Since the focus of any potential private partner is on the risk/reward calculation described above, the major new topic

Box 7.11

Links to Boxes
3.5, 5.5, 6.13, 7.2, 7.3, 7.18, 8.12, 9.8

Financing a Concession
Buenos Aires, Argentina

Financing for the Buenos Aires concession – including regular operations, as well as the US$4 billion capital investment programme – has come in a number of forms (primarily equity, user fees and debt), drawn from a range of private and public sources. On the equity side, the concessionaire – Aguas Argentinas (AA) – is owned by several different shareholders. The company's major owner is Suez Lyonnaise des Eaux (now Ondeo), a French water company. It holds 25% of concessionaire's equity. The other foreign companies holding shares are S.G. de Aguas de Barcelona (10.8%), Compagnie Generale de Eaux (now Vivendi) of France (7.6%), and Anglian Water of England (4.2%). Local shareholders include Sociedad Comercial del Plata S.A (19.6%), Meller S.A. (10.2%), and Banco de Galicia y Buenos Aires S.A. (7.6%). In addition, employees of AA own 10% of the company. Finally, after the concession was awarded, the International Finance Corporation (IFC) acquired 5% of the company's shares as part of a broader financing package (see below).

User fees have been collected by AA since it took over operations and have been a major source of operating capital. AA has been able to reduce its operating costs significantly – while still improving performance – and has also been able to increase tariff collections well beyond the levels achieved by its public predecessor (OSN). The result was a much higher level of income available for system operation and expansion. Though AA showed a US$23 million loss in net income for the first year of the concession (1993), by 1996 net income had risen to US$58 million.

Even with these infusions of equity and user fees, AA has needed to borrow large amounts of money to meet its expansion obligations (see Box 7.2). Prior to award of the concession, OSN's capital investment programme had averaged US$20 million per year. By contrast, AA will have to spend approximately USUS$130 million per year to meet its expansion requirements.

The first major borrowing was led by the IFC in 1994. In its role of using public money to catalyse private investment, the IFC: purchased a 5% equity stake in the company for US$7 million; lent over US$40 million of its own funds to the company; and found private, commercial banks willing to make funds available for a US$134.5 million syndicated loan (including BNP, Credit Suisse, SocGen, Banque Sudameris, La Caixa, Credit Lyonnais, BFCE, Banque Paribas, Deutsche Bank and Dresdner Bank). Other public sector lenders included the Inter-American Development Bank (IDB) and the European Investment Bank (EIB). A summary of AA's financing structure from July 1995 to June 1997 is provided in the following table:

Source of financing	Amount (US$million)
Equity (internal cash generation)	140
Debt	
• IFC 10-year loan	40
• IFC syndicated 12-year loan	173
• IDB 20-year loan	43
• EIB loan	90
• Short-term loans	54

Source: Haarmeyer and Mody

In 1999, Duff & Phelps Credit Rating gave a 'BBB' (triple-B) rating to the new US$120 million loan being arranged through the IDB. The transaction provides that the IDB will make a US$75 million loan from its own funds, with the remainder of the loan amount being contributed by private commercial banks.

Sources: Haarmeyer and Mody, 1997; PR Newswire, June 24, 1999

accompanying arrangements involving major infusions of private capital is the introduction of additional parties into the negotiating process: private and public investors. Potential investors fall into several different categories, each with their own expectations as to risk and return. These are discussed in turn below.

☐ Banks and other providers of debt finance

Banks and other providers of debt finance lend a specified amount of money (the principal), in exchange for a promise that the money will be repaid on a specified schedule (the term), plus payment of their profit (often in the form of up-front fees and interest over the term of the loan). Very large loans are often syndicated, a process in which one bank takes the lead in negotiating the loan, while many other banks also participate by contributing small portions of the total loan amount. To help ensure that they are repaid and make a profit, lenders also seek collateral or security by requiring that the borrower give them the right to take possession of borrower's assets should he or she fail to make the agreed payments. Deciding which assets of a partnership arrangement should be put up as collateral for loans can be a major topic of negotiation. For example, should a bank have the right to take over the operation – or even ownership – of system assets (pipes, treatment plants) if the partnership fails to pay on time?

☐ Equity investors

Equity investors purchase ownership shares in a private firm in the expectation of benefiting from the firm's profits over time. This can happen in a number of ways: annually (in the form of dividends, or distributions of annual profits); when they use their shares as collateral to borrow money; or when they sell their shares after the firm has increased in value (capital gain). Agreeing whether and how the ownership of firms involved in partnership arrangements can change over time will also often be a major topic of negotiation. For example, if an international operating company is the part-owner of a partnership company (and the primary source of technical and managerial expertise for the partnership), should it be allowed to sell some or all of its shares in the company and, if so, when?

☐ Guarantors and other insurers

Guarantors and other insurers agree to pay money to identified parties if a specified event (a claim) occurs, in exchange for payment of an up-front premium. Guarantees usually take the form of one party agreeing to step into another's shoes if it fails to fulfil its responsibilities. For example, if a municipal government agrees to buy all the water produced under a BoTT structure but fails to do so, its obligation may be guaranteed by the provincial or national governments, or even by a multilateral development bank. They would then have to pay for the water. Insurance is similar, but is usually based on the occurrence of specified risks such as war or expropriation of assets. Major areas for negotiation here include whether and/or on what basis guarantors or insurers will accept responsibility to cover specified risks. Increasingly, national governments are disinclined to provide guarantees for municipal financing, leaving it to lenders and municipalities to work out for themselves whether a borrower is creditworthy and a project viable.

☐ Grantors

Grantors give money away with no expectation of repayment, but with the requirement that it should be used to achieve specified goals. For example, technical assistance grants may be used to help design partnership arrangements or to build the capacity of regulatory agencies. Major areas of negotiation over grants include the extent to which the donor's or the municipality's objectives control the use of the grant, and the nature of the reporting required on how the grant is spent.

☐ Facilitating municipal borrowing

All of these different types of investment are offered by both private and public sources, on different terms reflecting their different risk/reward calculations. Each has its own methods for deciding whether or not to invest in any particular

7

Links to Boxes
7.7, 7.19, 8.2, 10.3, 10.6

Box **7.12**   **Private Sector Facilitates IFI Finance**
Cartagena, Colombia

In response to the enabling legislation introduced in 1994 (see Box 10.3), the municipality of Cartagena became a pioneer in Colombia with regard to the introduction of private sector participation in basic public service provision. It was also the first city to introduce a PPP for water and sanitation, with the creation of the joint venture company, AGUACAR. The prevailing poor economic performance of public service provision, itself linked to endemic clientelism and corruption, was a major factor in explaining citizen support in Cartagena for private sector participation in urban water supply. The short-term municipal objective was to rid itself of the fiscal burden of an inefficient in-house operation by delegating the management function, and to improve efficiency by attracting the necessary technical skills from the private sector. A longer-term objective was to secure access to soft loan finance from international financial institutions in order to upgrade and expand the system.

By the mid-1990s the municipal-owned Empresa de Servicios Públicos Distritales de Cartagena (EPD), responsible for public service provision including water and sanitation, was already in crisis. Water losses exceeded 50%. Current revenue did not even cover operating costs, producing a financial deficit that was a growing drain on municipal finances. There was not even money to pay for sufficient chemicals to treat water. The lack of an operating surplus meant that investment in maintenance and network extension had ground to a halt. Customer service was very poor, with constant interruptions in water supply and unacceptably low levels of water quality.

The negotiation of the joint venture between the public and private sectors was controversial, and powerful economic groups in the city opposed it. The tendering and bidding process for the contract was negotiated by the outgoing mayor Gabriel García (1992–94). Aguas de Barcelona (AGBAR) was the only bidder and the adjudication was completed on 30 December 1994, the day before he left office. The incoming mayor, Guillermo Paniza, had campaigned actively against the terms of the contract negotiated by his predecessor. These had envisaged a 50% shareholding by AGBAR, a 40% holding by private investors and only a 10% holding by the municipality. Paniza argued that the spirit of the pioneering legislation introducing private capital in basic services called for a minimum public sector participation of 50% in any joint venture. He also feared that the low value of the paid-up capital of the new joint venture company would put ownership of the 40% of the shares earmarked for private capital within the grasp of corrupt local politicians who had been involved in the negotiations carried out by his predecessor.

The original intention of Paniza was to annul the contract altogether and return to the previous arrangement under which water and sanitation in Cartagena was owned and delivered by a municipal company. However, during a four-hour discussion in Washington, the World Bank project manager made it clear to Paniza that PSP involvement was a precondition for future Bank funding for the water and sanitation sector in Cartagena. Paniza then dropped his objection to private sector participation and renegotiated the terms of the joint venture with AGBAR. In order to strengthen municipal involvement and to avoid the danger of political interference from a large local private share participation, the shareholding earmarked for the municipality of Cartagena was increased to 50%. The shareholdings of AGBAR and private local capital were reduced correspondingly to 46% and 4% respectively. Furthermore, the 50% municipal shareholding would be in the form of 'goodwill' and was not paid in cash. At the insistence of Paniza, the shareholding arrangement was also amended in order to incorporate an employee share ownership scheme within the 4% shareholding allocated to local private capital. In 1995 the municipality of Cartagena finally formed a joint venture with AGBAR to provide water and sanitation services in the city. The new company, known as Aguas de Cartagena (AGUACAR), signed a 26-year contract with the municipality to operate and maintain these services. In turn AGUACAR signed a management contract with AGBAR.

Under the terms of its 1995 contract with AGUACAR, AGBAR is only responsible for the management of and funding of the operation and maintenance of the system. Although it did not sign a concession contract, AGUACAR was entrusted with managing a major water and sanitation investment programme on behalf of the municipality. This investment programme is financed mainly by loans from the World Bank (US$85 million) and the Inter-American Development Bank (US$24 million).

It is significant that, in response to the history of corruption and mismanagement in the urban water supply and sanitation sector in Colombia, the World Bank insisted on private sector participation as a precondition for further lending to the municipality of Cartagena for water and sanitation. From the Bank viewpoint, the presence of a major international water utility (AGBAR) constitutes a guarantee that its lending resources will be subject to allocative efficiency (e.g., in the selection of investment priorities) and subject to productive efficiency (e.g., in avoiding over-invoicing in the awarding of contracts). From the municipal viewpoint, this insistence meant that a partnership with a major international player (AGBAR) has been instrumental in accessing foreign soft loan funding for its expansion plans; and from the viewpoint of AGBAR itself, the joint venture arrangement has the advantage of reducing the risk of foreign investment.

Sources: Adapted from Nickson, 2001a; Foster, 1998

project. Meeting all of the investors' needs, as well as those of the municipality, private operating firms, and users/communities, is what makes partnerships involving substantial private investment so time consuming and expensive to arrange.

The only way to navigate this maze is with good guides: the transaction advisors who help structure the partnership arrangement. If substantial amounts of private investment are sought, the municipality must have advisors who are the peers of those representing the potential investors. Only by negotiating on equal terms will a deal be struck that meets the needs of both the municipality and the investors over time. A primary concern will be the appointment of advisors (see discussion on the advisors in Manila, Box 7.14, and the role of advisors as discussed in Chapter 6, and illustrated by the recent consultancies undertaken in Johannesburg, Box 6.22).

Assuming there is a clear legal framework in place – one which provides the municipality with the authority to borrow and provides clarity over the conditions pertaining to debt, interest rates and foreign currency – a number of conditions relating to municipal capacity can determine the access a municipality has to credit:[7]

- their understanding of collateral – assets are often less than well documented in municipalities;
- their knowledge of lending and borrowing (do they have transaction advisors?);
- their banking capacity (do they have a credit rating?); and
- enforceability in the context of changing municipal governments.

Opportunities for increased public investment capital

Involving private firms in municipal efforts to improve urban services may also make the projects more attractive to the World Bank or other regional/national development banks. Private involvement is often seen as evidence that the municipality is serious about tackling problems such as inadequate services or ineffective tariff structures. This was certainly the case in Cartagena in relation to World Bank investment illustrated in Box 7.12. Accessing these public funds can be a benefit to the municipality – if it uses the funds to ensure that the partnership arrangement meets local objectives. Such 'soft' money is usually significantly less expensive than private investment. Some of it is grant money that can be used to reduce transaction costs. Some of it is debt, that must be repaid, but at lower interest rates or over longer periods of time than private loans.

At the same time, involving a public development bank in a project can make the project more attractive to potential private investors. Foreign private lenders often take comfort from the presence of international development banks in a deal. They calculate that local governments are more likely to honour their commitments if the World Bank is involved than if private investors only are present.

The costs of private investment

The framework for the partnership arrangement should reflect all the costs of delivering the service – costs that should be recovered through improved services and increased efficiency. The involvement of the private sector will comprise costs over and above the public sector cost of achieving the quality and efficiency of the service (e.g., bulk water, wages, chemicals, vehicles). These include:[8]

- the costs of finance (can be 10–12 per cent more than the public sector – higher for small firms that constitute a greater risk);
- government taxes and duties (customs duties, equipment insurance, vehicle and company registration, corporate income and property taxes);
- 'informal' costs associated with bureaucratic municipalities, and political manipulation;

Links to Box
7.14

Box **7.13** **Advisors in Water Privatisation**
Manila, The Philippines

In January 1997, the government of The Philippines awarded two long-term concession contracts to private consortia giving them the responsibility to operate and expand water and wastewater services in Greater Manila (previously operated by the Metropolitan Waterworks and Sewage System (MWSS)). Regarded as the largest water concession in the world, the service area had a combined population of 11 million and investment needs projected at US$7 billion over the contract period. The government tendered the contract competitively. Bids were invited from consortia that included at least two partners, a local company (owning a majority of the shares) and an international company with experience operating and managing such a large service.

Given the size of the project, seeing it through from the decision to privatise to the regulation of the private operations was an extremely challenging task, one with which none of the government officials involved had any experience. It was therefore decided to hire advisors who could help guide officials through the process. Doing so presented a unique challenge, however: never having undertaken such a project before, the officials concerned had no terms of reference with which to hire advisors, and in order to prepare such terms of reference, they needed another set of advisors for whom they also had no terms of reference. In addition, the advisors had to be selected in a transparent manner and had to be seen as impartial (especially not to be identified with any particular country or national government).

This resulted in a two-step process:

1. selecting advisors to prepare the terms of reference (ToR) for the advisors for the privatisation; and
2. based on those ToR, selecting the advisors for the ultimate privatisation.

Major questions arose over the size and sources of the fees to be paid to the advisors. None of the officials involved had any experience with such an enormous enterprise and therefore had no idea of what the fees should be. The government also had little money to pay the advisors. A decision was made to approach the French government for a grant. It was chosen because most of the companies that had the necessary skills to implement such a project (and that therefore would meet the pre-qualification requirements for the international partner) were French, giving the French government an interest in ensuring that the privatisation moved forward. The resulting US$1 million grant paid for a French engineering firm (with no formal associations with French water companies) to prepare the ToR for the privatisation advisors. The much larger costs of the government's privatisation advisors (many millions of dollars) were to be paid by the successful bidders, with the Philippine government providing a bridge loan to cover the costs as they were incurred.

Ultimately, the International Finance Corporation (IFC) was selected as the privatisation advisor. Unlike the Buenos Aires concession (which involved separate financial and technical advisors), the IFC acted as lead advisor, coordinating the activities of all the engineers, local lawyers, international lawyers, accountants, public relations specialists, economists and other expert advisors. It also bore the overall responsibility for the planning and implementation of the project, working directly with the government officials involved. This structure made it accountable to the government and the citizens affected.

Though it had hired a lead advisor, the Philippine government ensured that at all times it retained control over the process. This was important as the government was the IFC's client and retained ultimate responsibility for ensuring that the transaction met the needs of the public. This was critical, since, if there were any future investigations by the Philippine Congress, the courts or others, the advisors would no longer be involved and the project would need to be defended by the civil servants involved. The government therefore realised that it needed to strike a fine balance, retaining control without dictating everything and disregarding advice from its advisors. The transaction was therefore a partnership that required mutual respect between the government and the advisors.

Source: Dumol, 2000

- transaction costs (the costs of putting the partnership together, from tender through the negotiation of the partnership framework); and
- marketing costs (beyond those covered in transaction costs).

Financial Incentives

For potential private sector partners – large or small – the key incentives for opting into a PPP are financial. Such financial incentives are generally determined by three factors: compensation arrangements, the levels of competition and the levels of risk.

Compensation is one of the most important areas of negotiation between the municipality and its private partners. As much as possible, compensation structures should be designed to push the firm to achieve the municipality's most important goals, but ultimately, the result must be acceptable to both or the partnership will falter. Compensation structures for the private sector partner tend to fall into two major categories: those directly agreed by the government as part of the partnership arrangement (fees for services or profit from ongoing operations); and those pursued independently by the private partner as a result of the partnership arrangement (other contracts, capital gains from increasing share value). While the municipality should be aware of the latter and how they may affect the firm's interest and performance, the focus here is on the direct compensation agreed as part of the partnership arrangement.

☐ Fees for private operator services

Municipal officials will be aware that the basis of fee structures paid to private firms can vary significantly, as most will have experience of different types of payments on traditional construction contracts. The scope and nature of fee-type payments to operators is largely the same, with an added complexity when the large-scale private operator or small-scale enterprise brings some level of investment into the operations. Typically, payment types are based on:

■ Time and materials

The simplest form of fee structure is identical to the payments made to small contractors under some small maintenance contracts. Under this arrangement, municipalities agree to pay a private firm a specified fee for the performance of a specified service. For example, a firm might be paid for the time it spends repairing burst pipes and a unit rate for the installation of pipework. Municipalities tend to avoid this form of payment as it means they carry the risks of an elongated programme. Evidence suggests that many operators (or the people they employ) extend the job unnecessarily. However, many contracts will include a time-and-materials component for 'extras', and many urgent jobs are undertaken under this arrangement.

■ Fixed fee arrangement

The fixed fee arrangement is one in which the municipality specifies the task in terms of design and materials and the contractors bid for, or agree, a total amount to be paid. A fixed fee gives the municipality some certainty on price and gives the private firm incentives to be efficient. If the task is poorly defined or the sub-tasks unknown, many firms will be unable to estimate costs accurately and may not wish to enter into the arrangement; those with less capacity will enter into the arrangement and will make a loss or aim to restore profits through extras.

■ Fixed plus variable costs

In many operation and management arrangements a municipality pays the operator a fee comprising both a fixed and variable component. The operating fee may be calculated on a monthly basis, to cover the agreed fixed expenses of the

7

| Box **7.14** | **Operating Profits as the Basis for Compensation** | Links to Box 7.13 |

Manila, The Philippines

Prior to 1997, Manila's metropolitan waterworks and sewage system (MWSS) covered Manila and 14 adjoining cities and municipalities with a population of approximately 11 million people. When the privatisation of MWSS was conceptualised in 1994, it was supplying water to only two-thirds of its coverage population for an average of only 16 hours a day. Approximately 56% of the water it supplied was non-revenue water (or unaccounted-for water lost via leaks and theft). For sewerage, MWSS serviced only 8% of its coverage population.

Since positive public opinion is critical for any decision to privatise a water utility, the government officials involved decided that – following the model of the Buenos Aires water concession – the privatisation had to result in lower water tariffs. Therefore, the two concessions (one each for the 'East' and 'West' zones of the MWSS service area) were to be awarded to the bidders offering the greatest reductions in the water tariffs existing at the time of the bids – i.e., including a 38% increase in the water tariffs five months before the bids were to be submitted. Both concessionaires were required to use the tariff structure formerly applied by MWSS, an increasing block system that distinguishes between residential, commercial and industrial customers.

Since only private companies who believe they will make money on a contract will bid, the government took a number of steps to make the concession financially attractive. Most importantly, the concessionaires were allowed to keep the difference between the tariffs collected from users and the costs of running the system (both operating and capital costs). While the initial tariffs were set during the bidding process, procedures for regular and extraordinary tariff revisions were included (see below). The government also designed the water and sewerage expansion programmes so that the major capital expenditures started five years into the contract period. In addition, an automatic tariff adjustment was provided in the fifth year to cover funding for sewerage investments. Six-year income tax holidays were also granted to each of the concessionaires. Finally, in order to encourage capital investment towards the end of the concession period (when the concessionaires have less time to recoup substantial investments), the government agreed to pay the concessionaire the net present value of the remaining years' amortisation on such investments at the end of the contract period. All these measures helped the bidders propose large reductions in existing tariffs, while still enabling them to recoup their investments over time.

The same tariff escalation procedure was applied for both concessions. Government officials considered various approaches, including tying tariff escalation to changes in the retail price index, the consumer price index, or a composite index (based on a formula designed to account for expected efficiency gains and the cost of investing in wastewater treatment sufficient to meet European standards). The inflation-tied system was ultimately adopted as it was easy to explain and logical. In addition to annual adjustments for inflation, concessionaires were also permitted to renegotiate the tariffs under exceptional circumstances.

While government officials had hoped for a 10% reduction in tariffs, the bidders surprised organisers by proposing tariffs at much lower levels – ranging from 30% to over 70% reductions in existing tariffs. The final bids are given in the table below.

	Tariff bid (percentage of existing tariff)
West zone	
Ayala-International Water	28.63%
Benpres-Lyonnaise des Eaux (winning bid)	56.59%
Aboitez-Campaigne General des Eaux	56.88%
Metro Pacific-Anglian Water International	66.90%
East zone	
Ayala-International Water (winning bid)	26.39%
Aboitez-Campaigne General des Eaux	62.88%
Metro Pacific-Anglian Water International	64.51%
Benpres-Lyonnaise des Eaux	69.79%

Source: Dumol, 2000

operator plus a variable charge, e.g., for the volume of water supplied or sewage treated. This enables both parties to know, to some extent, that payment is directly related to the service provided – and some vary substantially due to seasonal variations. The nature and scope of the payment can be structured to provide a number of incentives for the operator to ensure the ongoing maintenance of the system. If the variable fee is based on the volume of water used at the meter, water leakage in the network is not paid for by the municipality but by the operator. Conversely, payment on the basis of sewage treated means that the municipality is responsible for greater payments in the wet season when volumes are higher. In Stutterheim, for instance, the variable fee is usually about one-third of the overall monthly fee.[9]

■ **Performance fees**

Performance fees can be used to supplement time-and-materials or fixed fee approaches by increasing the amounts paid to the firm if it exceeds specified performance targets. For example, while the municipality may agree a fixed fee for operations and management of a system, it may also pay a performance bonus if the firm reduces unaccounted-for water to a greater extent than that reduction specified in the contract. A performance fee thus gives incentive to the contractor to improve performance – including efficiencies – even though it does not make a direct profit; and it helps to create some confidence in the municipality that the operator is working towards its objectives.

All arrangements must address the need for price escalation. Municipalities must ensure that the agreements made include an escalation formula based on standard engineering practice (e.g., use of labour, material and energy price indices), that the calculations are based on national statistical data, and that the clauses also allow for decreases in pricing.

A number of issues characterise payment by fees (rather than profit):

- Payments are guaranteed to the extent that the private partner performs and the municipality is able to make the payments. While some private firms seek guarantees from higher levels of government to cover the possibility of the municipality being unable to meet its obligations, such practices detract from the authority of the municipality.
- The tariffs paid by the final consumers of the service are largely irrelevant to the compensation paid to the private partner. The municipality shoulders the risk of low-cost recovery for the service provided.
- Fee arrangements are generally not linked to improvements in cost recovery, as the private partner has little incentive to increase the rate of cost recovery through improved customer management practices.

☐ **Payments to private firms based on operating profits**

Where the responsibilities of the private firm go beyond narrow tasks to improving the overall level of service delivery, a compensation system based on operating profits from tariffs paid by consumers may be appropriate. The most extensive arrangements are those under which the municipality asks the private partner to provide the service as though it were a normal business, including responsibility for collecting user fees, paying operating costs and making capital investments, in exchange for keeping any remaining profits (see Box 7.14).

Despite the efforts that private firms make to increase their consumer base, they are fundamentally focused on the rates of return on their investment. For water and sanitation international operators, these are typically in the order of 20 per cent. The private partner has two clear aims in such arrangements: to minimise costs and maximise revenue. For the poor, this creates a relationship between the private sector operator and the consumer that is very different from that produced by fee-based remuneration. Private firms have considerable incentive to:

- increase tariffs;
- increase the rate of cost recovery (ensure effective billing and collection, ensure functioning of meters, establish targeted payment mechanisms);

Box 7.15   The Business of Waste Collection
Dar-es-Salaam, Tanzania

At seven in the morning the waste collectors of K.J. Enterprise report at the tiny office. They receive their handcart, forks and spades and set off in different directions. Each of the four teams of two men will collect the waste of about 70 houses. The collectors knock the gate to receive the waste, or find it already placed along the path. Most houses in their working area are big and the waste of four to five of these large households fills the handcart. The collectors push the cart to the main road and empty it at one of the temporary mini-dumps. In the course of the morning the company truck will pass to load the waste and transport it to the city dump. Meanwhile, the two fee collectors set out on foot to collect the waste collection charges, from households, shops, workshops, restaurants and small hotels. Most clients pay once a month, 1000 shillings (about US$1.25) per household, and there is a differentiated rate – according to size and type – for commercial establishments. Some of the street vendors pay daily: they cannot afford to pay a high amount at once and the fee collectors do not want to risk their disappeared before the bill is paid. The director of K.S. Enterprise is satisfied with the progress of his waste business. It is still difficult to ensure that enough clients pay, that he maintains a good relation with the local authorities and that he keeps his workers and equipment in good condition. But it is clear that people appreciate the service. Moreover, it provides him and his team with an income.

The shift to private sector involvement in waste management in Dar-es-Salaam (see also Box 7.9) has created a new business opportunity. A few had started with waste collection and already built up some experience, but most enterprises knew little if anything about waste management. In this light it is remarkable that out of the initial 62 contractors who started operation in 1999, 55 were still providing services a year later.

For the collection of refuse charges, each area of Dar-es-Salaam was designated by the City Commission as a high-, middle- or low-income area. The commission also determined the rates for refuse charges, after consulting the contractors about the expected operational costs and the willingness and ability of the public to pay these fees. Private households in high-income areas are required to pay approximately US$2.50 per month; in middle-income areas the rate per household is US$1.25 per month, and in low-income areas US$0.65 per month. Commercial establishments pay a fee according to the nature and size of the business, ranging between approximately US$6 and US$125 per month. The contractors, however, are allowed to negotiate the size of the fee with their customers.

The contractors collect the fees directly from the households and commercial establishments. They are free to decide on their fee collection system. Monthly collection is the most common system, although daily payment or payment per waste collection are also used. The financial relations between the contractors and the City Commission are limited. The contractors do not have to pay for their permit. After a grace period to allow them to start up the service, they would have to pay the City Commission dumping fees of about US$1.20 per tonne of waste. The City Commission also announced it would rent out its vehicles to the contractors. In practice, however, it provides a secondary transport of waste to the dumpsite to some of the CBOs, without charging them for this service. In this way the City Commission effectively subsidises the waste collection.

In the planning phase, it was assumed that it would be possible to cross-subsidise between high- and low-income areas – that revenue collected from high-income areas and business enterprises would compensate losses made in low-income areas, and this would be achieved by making one contractor responsible for high-income as well as low-income areas. Except for a few private companies, none of the contractors had the capacity to serve more than one area. In practice therefore, there are contractors who only work in low-income areas and whose earnings are barely enough for cost recovery. With the income earned from these low-income households, the costs for primary waste transport can be covered, but it is difficult to pay also for secondary transport of the waste to the dumpsite. The assistance of the city trucks is very important for these contractors.

To a certain extent, unintended cross-subsidisation is taking place, not between contractors or areas, but between clients. The fact that contractors are allowed to negotiate collection fees with clients has led to a better balance of paying clients and poorer clients within an area. Also, some contractors apply flexible payment schedules, so that clients can spread payments in smaller amounts. Others collect fees when picking up the waste, rather than making special trips. This entrepreneurial behaviour has been reinforced by management training courses. The more explicit involvement of ward leaders and committees has further contributed to increased fee payments, although lack of income remains the most important complaint of the contractors.

To finance their start-up costs, most contractors sought outside assistance in the form of handcarts, wheelbarrows, hand tools and protective gear; no substantial amounts of money were involved. Most start-up costs were covered by the contractors' own resources. But the contractors also pointed out the importance of their other income-generating activities, including street-sweeping contracts issued by the City Commission during the difficult start-up period. Some contractors also started to generate extra income through the sale of waste paper, plastic and tin cans for recycling, and voluntary labour.

Source: Reproduced from Bakker et al, 2000

- treat the consumer well to encourage payment;
- increase efficiency (e.g., reduce unaccounted-for water, remove illegal connections, improve ongoing maintenance and repair the system); and
- reduce the costs of production and disposal.

More limited arrangements include those in which the municipality continues to collect user fees, but pays a portion of any amounts above a specified level to the private partner. As with performance fees, payment systems based on operating profits give the firm strong incentives to control costs and provide high-quality services for which users are glad to pay adequate fees. If the services are provided in a competitive environment (such as recycling facilities), few complications arise beyond the normal ones of accounting for costs and revenues. If monopoly services (such as networked drinking water) are provided, however, extremely complicated regulatory issues arise, ranging from the levels of fees that may be charged to the levels of service to be provided (see discussions in this chapter on levels of service and tariffs).

A key concern arising in PPPs where compensation/remuneration is based on operating profit concerns the degree of transparency over profit margins. Obviously the private firm would prefer not to disclose profits, but this may cause some concern among other stakeholders and political pressure may be brought to bear. In the BoTT in South Africa, the private consortium operator includes an NGO that has an ideological objection to the lack of transparency in profit margins. When profit gets out of hand and is not thought to be in the interests of the poor, the municipality might explore whether or not this profit can be capped without creating disincentives that the private sector cannot bear. Obviously, the impact of any such actions on the willingness of the private firm to stay involved should be considered carefully, especially if the rules are changed after the partnership has been formed.

☐ Payment to non-governmental organisations

Notwithstanding the importance of how formal private sector firms are compensated for their efforts, it is also absolutely essential that the arrangement framework addresses the compensation for other partners providing services. These may include, for instance, NGOs, CBOs and independent service providers.

NGOs involved in service partnerships need to be paid for their time and costs. One of the primary areas of conflict in those poverty-focused partnerships that have relied heavily on NGOs to work with communities is that the basic framework arrangement has not adequately addressed the issue of payment for NGO services. As the driving force of the partnership arrangement, the municipality must not only ensure that payment mechanisms are established in the local context, but come to understand the implications of those mechanisms. This is discussed in terms of partnership arrangements in Chapter 8. However in relation to payments, municipalities should recognise that many NGOs will be concerned with the following:

- **The source of their funding**   Being paid by the private firm is generally to be avoided as it compromises the autonomy with which they can carry out their role, their standing with the communities with whom they are meant to work, and their reputation more generally in the NGO sector (see Chapter 8). Being paid by other agents (such as donors) can also be problematic, as the funding will normally be for a specific duration only.
- **The way NGOs are paid for their inputs**   The traditional assumption that NGOs should fund their own contributions may not be as marked in PPP development, but there is still some need for municipal and private sector capacity building to understand the need for appropriate payment to NGOs. This is a key source of conflict when they are clearly aiding the private sector to improve its customer base, and while they may see this as a means of improving services for the poor, they must also cover their own costs.
- **The duration of the arrangement**   NGOs often seek long-term rather than project-by-project agreements as they promote stability, allow NGOs to develop strategic plans, and promote capacity in the long term. These benefits need

7

Box **7.16** Elements of Cost Recovery

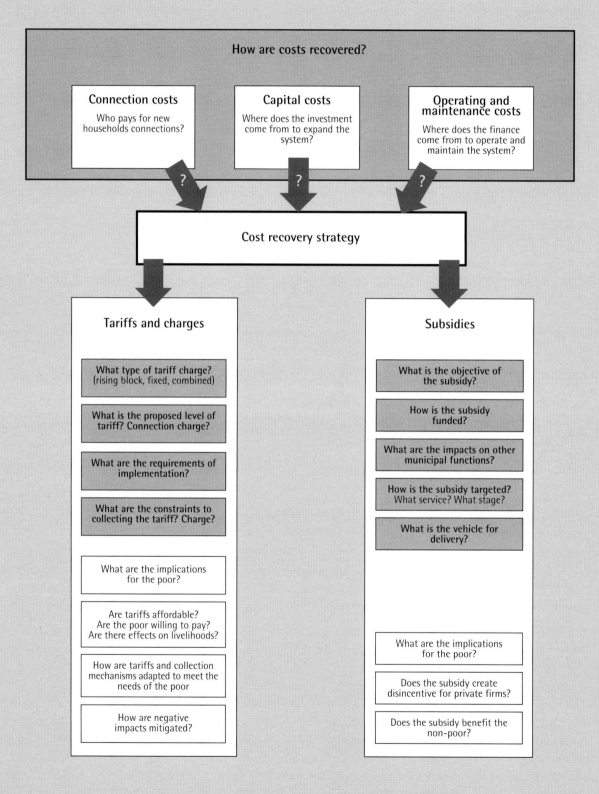

to be balanced against the exclusion of other NGOs from the partnership and the potential conflicts that may arise within their organisation.

- **The profit-making aspect of the partnership** NGOs may agree to be involved but an underlying concern with 'rich' private firms making profits from the poor will dominate their concern. For some NGOs, there is an inherent conflict in this situation: as NGOs they will aim to cover their own costs, but at the same time their own efforts (say, in promoting cost recovery) will lead to profit – sometimes substantial profit – for the private firm.

Cost Recovery

One of the primary objectives of many municipalities is to create economically sustainable service delivery, thereby removing the drain of service operation, maintenance, replacement and expansion on ever-dwindling budgets. As a result, many governments are changing their approach to the funding of urban services, whether or not they are considering private sector involvement. Efforts are under way to introduce cost recovery policies – to charge fees that cover operating costs, if not the costs of expanding the system as well. In some cases, subsidies are being used to phase those increases in over time, to help underwrite the capital costs of system replacement and expansion, and to help ensure access of the poor to system services.

Once a municipal utility has a stream of fee income that covers both operating and capital costs, it has options. It can stay under municipal ownership and management or it can seek private involvement in a variety of forms to meet local objectives. Most importantly, it will have the funds it requires to meet the needs of its users reliably over time. But if politicians have been elected for years promising the lowest fees for municipal services – often with the result of poor service – an extended period may be necessary to build public confidence that increased fees will lead to improved levels of service. Often, increases in user fees will be combined with efforts to restructure the municipal utility in an attempt to improve services.

The costs associated with service delivery – irrespective of the public or private nature of the delivery – are often disaggregated into three cost centres:

1. **Capital costs,** such as those associated with building infrastructure or purchasing trucks.
2. **Connection costs,** costs incurred by a household or community forming a new connection into a service.
3. **Operation and maintenance costs,** the costs of keeping the system functioning.

All three types of costs can be recovered from two sources: consumer tariffs/fees or subsidies (illustrated in Box 7.16). In relation to service delivery to the poor, these alternatives are inextricably intertwined, as discussed below.

☐   Tariffs

In order to recover costs from consumers, the operator responsible for cost recovery (be it public or private) has a number of options. For operating and maintenance costs in relation to water and sanitation, the supplier can impose a consumer tariff. This tariff can be structured in a number of different ways, such as:

- a (fixed) standing charge and a (variable) rate dependent on consumption;
- a unit rate for consumption;
- a fixed monthly charge – often the mechanism for communal standpipes; or
- a fixed rate per vessel – water vendors selling water by the bottle.

Box **7.17** **Regressive Tariff Structure**
Stutterheim, South Africa

Links to Boxes
6.1, 8.6, 9.6, 11.1, 12.1

Tariffs for water and sewerage services in Stutterheim are tightly controlled by the council; the operator, WSSA, plays no role whatsoever in setting or advising on tariffs. Given the elected council's explicit concern for improving basic services and the past conflict over non-payment and disconnection, it might be expected that a major revision of the tariff structure would have been undertaken. This is not the case. The current tariff structure has evolved since 1994 and is not one that has been structurally designed to meet the council's stated pro-poor objectives, nor does it respond to any affordability or willingness-to-pay surveys. In practice, the tariff structure is unfair and unfavourable for poor households. It is interesting to consider how this has happened, because it was not the intention of the council.

Domestic service tariffs

	Level of service	Monthly charge	Income group	Typical cost
Water	• Communal standpipe	Flat rate $3.79 per household (sharing a street standpipe)	Low income < $150	$0–$3.79 up to $7.60
	• Mlungisi household connection	Basic charge per stand $3.39 plus $0.38 per kilolitre consumed	Low income > $150	$3.79
	• Stutterheim town household connection	$2.73 basic charge + a minimum purchase of 11 kilolitres at $3.41, $0.38 per kilolitre thereafter	Low income — Middle–high income	$7.60 for 11 litres — $6.41 for 11 litres
Sewerage	• Tanker service	$4.98 per tanker service removal (2 per month)	Low income <$150	$9.96 for 2 removals
	• Mlungisi service connection	$5.20 basic charge	Low income > $150	$5.20
	• Stutterheim town service connection	$7.80 basic charge	Middle–high income	$7.80
Refuse removal	• Mlungisi	$4.42 basic charge	Low income < $150 Low income	$0–$4.41 $4.42
	• Stutterheim town	$4.42 basic charge	Middle–high income	$4.42

Note: Prices quoted in US$ (US$1 approximately equivalent to 7.2 rand)

Analysis shows that the tariff works to the benefit of middle-income rather than poorer groups. For any amount over seven litres, the poor are charged more for their water than their better-off neighbours. It is not uncommon in developing countries for the poor to pay more for their water than wealthier groups because they are procuring water informally. It is likely that this reflects a lack of capacity in the council to understand the implications of tariff structures. Moreover, the tariff structure does not differentiate between low-volume and high-volume users, i.e., the unit cost of water remains constant no matter what quantity of water is used. Far from being beneficial to the poor, this tariff structure penalises low-income households and, in a country verging on water scarcity, provides no incentive for conserving water.

Examination of sewerage service standards versus charges tells a similar story. The majority of people in the low-income areas of the town may well be charged more for sewerage services than middle-income households. While network sewerage charges in Mlungisi are US$5.20, the majority (70–80%) of households use septic tanks and request two removals a month. For this service they are charged US$9.96. This is 22% higher than the charge of US$7.80 for middle-income households connected to the sewerage network and receiving a higher level of service. In addition, these inequitable tariffs for water and sewerage are compounded by refuse removal charges, which are the same for low-income and middle-income households, despite the fact that there is marked evidence that low-income households generate significantly less waste. The inequity of the tariff structure for low-income households is countered by two factors:

A remission system for the poor on service payments. Approximately 30% of the households are subsidised through a remission system funded by a national government grant. This is calculated on a sliding scale in relation to their income. An income of R300 (US$42.00) per month draws the full rebate. The remission system means that approximately 10% of the population receive services free of charge or with payments of less than R6 (US$0.80) per month. However, this fund can be used for any purpose and there is an opportunity cost associated with its use to subsidise water and sewerage payments.

The pattern of non-payment for services among low-income groups. Cost recovery in the low-income areas is very low (28%) compared with the middle-income areas of the town. While, in practice, this results in a cross-subsidy for service delivery to those low-income households that are not paying, current efforts to install pre-paid meters will gradually remove this indirect subsidy and reinforce the impact of the biased tariff structure. This practice also only assists those obtaining a service and not those who are unserved.

Source: Plummer, 2000a

The tariff structure commonly adopted by utilities/municipalities aiming to introduce a socially equitable system is the rising block tariff. This form of tariff subdivides consumption levels into blocks (e.g., 0–20m^3, 20–50m^3, 50–80m^3, etc.) and then applies an increasing unit charge to each successive block. This seems to have the benefit of penalising high-consumption users with higher and higher tariff levels, thus promoting water conservation, and providing an affordable tariff to poorer households that consume only small amounts of water.

Despite the view that the rising block tariff is the most equitable tariff structure, evidence also indicates that the approach can have perverse outcomes because it assumes that usage patterns are the same for the poor and non-poor. As we have seen in the previous section on payment mechanisms, by assuming that one meter for one household is the norm, it overlooks the density of low-income areas and the livelihood strategies employed by the poor to gain access to services. For the poorest groups, services tend to be shared or sub-supplied, and multiple lettings lead to much greater consumption levels per meter.[10] The higher rates charged for higher consumption under the rising block tariff system mean that those vulnerable groups who share also pay some of the highest unit rates for water consumption.

In order to counter this limitation, in Cartagena (see Box 7.19) a rising block tariff structure is combined with a household strata resulting in a tariff that acknowledges different consumption patterns in increasingly poor areas. In Córdoba, a zone coefficient was introduced to factor in the relative income of the neighbourhood. Both aim to introduce a mechanism that acknowledges multiple use of meters.

In developing countries where network sewerage services may be limited and a range of different levels of non-network facilities are provided, the tariff structure for sanitation services may be more complex. It might include:

- a (fixed) monthly charge;
- a standing charge plus a charge per toilet;
- a flat charge (e.g., septic tanker service) and a variable charge (by weight and distance); or
- a charge per service (e.g., cleaning of septic tank).

Often, however, where the sewerage network is limited or non-existent, poor consumers will have no access to sanitation services. Yet there is often a tendency to combine water and sanitation tariffs, and poor households end up paying a charge for sanitation services whether or not they receive them. This combined tariff works against the poor (making the effective cost of their water supply exorbitant), and does little to create incentives for private operators to extend the sanitation service to these areas.

In situations relying on non-network sanitation services such as septic tanks, evidence suggests that the poor are also heavily penalised because they only have access to these service alternatives. Typically, for instance, annual costs of septic tank cleaning are higher than for piped sewerage systems. This discourages effective maintenance practices, often with dire public health consequences. Other participatory assessment work exposed corruption among vacuum tanker crews, who reprioritised municipal work schedules in poor areas in relation to informal financial incentives.[11]

For solid waste services, the approach to tariffs is more varied and more difficult, there being a much lower willingness to pay for collection. Some operators charge a flat rate fee for a collection service. Municipalities might add that fee to property tax, and thus those paying property tax are the only ones contributing to solid waste cost recovery. Under a franchise arrangement, operators collect a fee from consumers based on frequency of collection or the amount of waste collected. Further information is provided in solid waste guideline documents.[12]

In developing the tariff structure, municipalities and their advisors will need to consider the factors that will affect implementation. These may include, for instance:

7

Box **7.18**   Changing Tariffs and Fees
Buenos Aires, Argentina

It is widely believed that tariffs in Buenos Aires decreased significantly as a result of the shift to a PPP in 1993 (see Box 3.8). Yet the issue of consumer payment – of tariffs, tariff revision, connection fees and infrastructure fees – is both complex and controversial. Prior to the tender the government embarked upon a process of sectoral reform to counter inflationary pressure and prepare for the impending privatisation process.

- In 1991, the government announced a 25% tariff increase to account for inflation.
- In 1992, government imposed an 18% goods and services tax to be added to water bills (this was subsequently increased by another 8% in 1995).
- In 1993, the government announced a further 8% increase on the tariff.

Following the commencement of the concession in 1993, the operator Aguas Argentinas offered a reduction of 27%, the figure frequently quoted as being the reduction in tariff. Opposers might be forgiven for construing this government and private sector action as a strategy to curb any potential opposition to the concession.

Yet the story has developed further since then. The tariff level is determined by two primary factors: the price cap and the cost index. One of the primary financial requirements of the original contract was the inclusion of price caps in the first 10 years – a clause that effectively blocked price increases (from the price cap factor) for that period. However, this requirement was accompanied by the possibility of increasing prices through the company's composite price index (based on the costs of fuel, chemicals, electricity, labour, debt servicing etc.). If costs increase by more than 7%, the contract allows for the operator to apply for a tariff increase. However, when the operator applied for a 13.5% tariff in 1994, it was not due to an increase in the company's cost index, but due to what the operator saw as extra-contractual requirements for extension to poor areas and immediate upgrade in one particular municipality. That ETOSS (the regulator) granted this increase is a cause of concern for a number of reasons:

- The extension creates a fixed one-off cost, while the tariff increase generates revenue across the city for the remainder of the contract.
- This tariff increase sent a message that the contract was negotiable.
- It removed the incentive for private financing extension to expand the customer base.
- By 1998 it was known that the Buenos Aires concession was extremely profitable, with rates of return nearing 40%.

Equally problematic and contentious is the issue of the infrastructure charge in the original contract – a means of financing expansion plans that was applied as a surcharge to new network customers. Given the poverty profile of Buenos Aires, it is no surprise that the charges this implied (between US$43 and US$430 for water and over US$550 for sewerage plus a connection charge) were being imposed upon poor households that were unable to pay (with the possibility of a loan at 12% for two years). It is estimated that 30% of the population stopped paying.

By 1997, it is estimated that the operator was US$30 million in arrears, and key stakeholders ETOSS, Aguas Argentinas, the Public Works Secretariat and the Natural Resources and Human Development Secretariat began a renegotiation of the contract (in fact, the negotiation ultimately by-passed ETOSS). As a result the infrastructure charge was replaced by a universal service and environmental fee (SUMA), a surcharge of US$3 to fund environmental clean-up operations and network expansion. This system, which is currently in place, has resulted in a one-off connection cost to new users of US$120. Yet the implications of this renegotiation have been challenged and have raised a number of important issues for stakeholders elsewhere:

- Despite massive profit from the concession in the early years, the operator argued that its risk should be reduced and tariffs increased.
- The price cap system that has functioned effectively elsewhere was casually replaced by a system whereby the regulator had to respond to the operator's rate of return.
- Financial risk was further reduced by applying the charge in advance of any expansion works.
- Substantial charges might be accrued, requiring the operator to significantly reduce the level of private investment envisaged under the contract, to a level that the public utility could have achieved with the same tariff restructuring.

The controversy has led to some concern about the disrespect stakeholders show towards the contract, and particularly to the regulator's inability to impose penalties for failure to meet performance targets (instead providing an incentive for further stalling and price renegotiations). Unsurprisingly, later in 1998, Aguas Argentinas applied for a further 11.8% tariff increase and was granted 4.5% following another intervention by the national government; at the end of 2000, it was granted an additional 15%; and in January 2001, it successfully negotiated a clause that effectively released it from expansion targets.

Sources: Alcazar et al, 2000; Loftus and McDonald, 2001; Rivera, 1996; Artana et al, 1998

- the failure to link tariff regimes to productivity and thus ensure private sector incentives;
- the low metering levels in poor areas – thus undermining the 'user pays' principle;
- the distortions that pro-poor tariff structures produce in the market incentives for the private operator; and
- the lack of a clear mechanism for tariff setting and revision.[13]

The tariff regime selected must be designed in the knowledge that outcomes are complex and sometimes indirect. One of the primary problems for municipalities is that they have no experience in the intricacies of tariff design, the nature of outcomes and the implications of various approaches. Although tariffs have been a fact of life in municipalities for decades the objective has not always been cost recovery, and even today few have examined the impacts of their existing tariffs (see Box 7.17 on regressive tariffs in Stutterheim).

It is also possible to identify constraints to the effective collection of tariffs – not least because in many situations the tariffs have been set at levels that many of the poorest and most vulnerable groups cannot afford. While the concepts of affordability and willingness to pay are at the core of the debate over pro-poor tariffs, Chapter 5 has detailed the importance of understanding affordability in relation to livelihoods, and has stressed the need to understand the varying capacities of those who are called 'poor', and the opportunity cost of the payments they make.

A recent BPD study analysing tariffs in pilot areas[14] identified a number of 'strategies' for improving cost recovery. Apart from efforts to reduce the cost of provision and the tariff payable by the poor consumer, these strategies included rewards and punishments, payment options, customer education, community mobilisation and participation and communal billing; but they also highlighted the simple observation that one of the keys to increasing tariff collection is to ensure that it is associated with a better service.

☐ Connection fees

In addition to the cost of the service consumed, for services delivered by a network (drinking water, electricity) there is also the cost of connecting to the distribution system. Such connection fees are an important part of financing network expansion. The possibility of covering the costs of the connections and adding new paying customers gives private firms strong incentives to expand service coverage.

At the same time, the need to pay connection fees in order to receive services can shut poorer customers out of the network. While costs per unit may go down as customers move from informal to formal providers, the need to come up with significant amounts of money just to have access to the system can be a major barrier. It may well be an investment they cannot afford, or do not prioritise. Detailed understanding of how different poor households will behave – what they will do when faced with paying US$200 for a yard or house connection for potable water for instance – is an essential part of the decision-making process, which – like the affordability studies on tariffs – should be closely linked to poverty assessments that place these costs in a range of household expenditure profiles.

Formal service providers often envisage that the costs for poor households only involve those fees payable for the service. Yet households wishing to optimise the investment and obtain maximum health and hygiene benefits will also be concerned with the costs of the household appliances – taps, sinks, toilets and their upkeep.

The alternative payment mechanisms discussed earlier in this section might assist poor consumers where the full cost of connection is passed on to them, and financial services can assist them to cover the costs of any household appliances they may wish to purchase.

Box 7.19

Links to Boxes
7.7, 7.12, 8.2, 10.3, 10.6

Box 7.19   Tariff Structure and Cross-subsidies
Cartagena, Colombia

The national water tariff policy in Colombia is derived form the public services legislation passed in 1994 and inspired by the philosophy of social solidarity. This law states that the tariff structure of all basic services, including water and sanitation, must be based on the twin concepts of efficiency and equity. On the one hand, tariff levels must be sufficient to generate income that will cover the operating and investment costs of water utilities. On the other hand, the tariff structure must incorporate a pro-poor element by making provision for cross-subsidies in the form of a 'solidarity fund'. This national policy and legislation thus aimed to standardise and make transparent the approach to cross-subsidisation in all municipalities throughout the country.

In order to implement this pro-poor approach, municipalities were required to carry out sample surveys to categorise households in their jurisdiction into one of six levels (estratos). The criterion for classification is exclusively environmental, based on the nature of house construction (size, construction materials for walls and floor) and the environmental quality of the neighbourhood (services and amenities). The mayor is required to establish a Permanent Committee for Stratification (Comité Permanente de Estratificación) comprising the head of planning, the municipal ombudsman (personero), a representative from each of the basic service companies, and two citizens. This advisory committee has the task of monitoring the implementation of the stratification process, and responding, within two months, to complaints from householders who claim that their properties have been wrongly classified. In the event that the customer is still not satisfied, s/he may appeal to the national watchdog committee, the Superintendencia de Servicios Públicos (SSP).

Municipalities were required to rebalance tariffs over the five-year period 1994–99. The legislation requires that owners of properties classified in the medium level, Level 4, should be charged a tariff that covers the operating and capital costs of service delivery. Those classified as belonging to Levels 1, 2 or 3 should pay a subsidised tariff, while those householders placed in Levels 5 and 6 should bear the cost of this subsidy by paying a tariff in excess of the cost of delivery. Municipalities must ensure that the cross-subsidy element is identified on the bills in a transparent manner, and that the subsidy and surcharge ceilings applied to each strata are adhered to.

As shown below, the water tariff structure in Cartagena does have a strong pro-poor element. The standing charge for households in the highest (6th) strata is over 10 times greater than that for households in the lowest (1st) strata. For the lowest tariff block (0–20 cubic metres), households in the highest strata pay nearly four times more per cubic meter than households in the lowest strata. It should be noted, however, that the lack of universal meter coverage affects outcomes.

Domestic water tariff structure by household strata

Property classification	Number of households	% households	Standing charge	0–20m³	21–40m³	41+m³	Maximum subsidy element
Residential strata							
1	24,154	23%	$0.96	$0.12	$0.39	$0.39	50%
2	31,297	30%	$1.63	$0.15	$0.39	$0.39	40%
3	29,423	28%	$2.18	$0.26	$0.39	$0.39	15%
4	7755	7.3%	$3.14	$0.31	$0.39	$0.39	0%
5	6910	6.5%	$6.22	$0.47	$0.47	$0.47	Maximum surcharge 20%
6	5359	5.1%	$9.96	$0.47	$0.47	$0.47	

Note: Data supplied by AGUACAR: US$1 = 2280 Colombian pesos

On 31 December 1999, AGUACAR had over 112,000 water customers and over 90,000 sanitation customers. Over 53% of its residential customers belonged to the three poorest consumer categories (Levels 1, 2 and 3), which receive a tariff subsidy.

This approach does not result in a common national tariff for all water companies because the 'break-even' cost applied to Level 4 householders varies from municipality to municipality as a result of geographical factors (e.g., terrain and distance from water source) and the level of efficiency of the water utility. Cross-subsidies are not permitted between regions.

Source: Adapted from Nickson, 2001a

In partnerships focused on the poor there are also strong arguments for revising the approach to connection costs. Efforts by those promoting pro-poor service delivery in water and sanitation[15] challenge the inclusion of connection costs as a cost specifically to be attributed to new customers. It can be argued that connection costs, as a fixed asset, are capital costs and can be funded in just the same way as a treatment works; that there is little valid reason for demanding that new customers pay for connections any more than they should pay for the portion of the treatment works that they use. Given that connection charges limit new connections, ration demand and thus limit tariff increases to the rich households already connected, they are inherently marginalising the poor from the benefits of the service partnerships. The difficulties and controversies associated with connection fees are described in relation to the low-income areas of Buenos Aires in Box 7.18, where the operator was forced to reconsider the expensive connection fee and instead introduced an infrastructure fee applied to all tariffs to cover the costs of expansion and connection.

☐ Subsidies

Many municipalities continue to – implicitly or explicitly – rely on subsidies to ensure political acceptability of the costs of municipal service delivery. Subsidies are a tool that, arguably, can be justified because of their capacity to promote both equity and/or efficiency.[16] Improving access for the poor through lower costs for poor consumers can improve productivity and provide an inherent form of financial services to the poor. It also means that the service gap between poor and non-poor is reduced, by placing some of the financial benefits accrued through economies of scale in the hands of the poor. In simplified terms, subsidies are interventions used by government to affect the absolute or relative price level for consumers. They generally come in two forms.

1. **Direct subsidisation**   The financing mechanism used to cover the shortfall in supply costs by the injection of finance from outside the sector or industry. Examples of direct subsidies include the widespread financing of solid waste services, or donor support to governments undergoing sectoral reform (as seen in the proposal for the Kathmandu affermage contract where the World Bank proposed to assist in a five-year plan to subsidise the transition to full cost recovery).
2. **Cross-subsidisation**   A mechanism to cover costs by shifting the burden from one consumer group to another within that sector or industry. This may be illustrated in the cross-subsidy achieved when the tariff applied to rural or peri-urban consumers is the same as for urban consumers, but the costs of delivery are significantly higher in the more remote, less concentrated areas; or it may mean that high-consumption users pay a higher unit rate than low-consumption users.

Subsidies, however, do not operate in a vacuum: they are a part of a much broader decision-making and budgeting process (see Chapter 4). For the poor consumer in developing countries, they are, and should be, closely related to tariff levels and to livelihood strategies (demand, affordability, willingness to pay and income levels). In choosing to provide subsidies, municipalities must consider their other obligations. The primary step for a municipality considering subsidies is to determine what the fundamental objective of the subsidy is, and how that objective informs, supports or conflicts with the overall objectives for reforming the delivery mechanism through a partnership approach. This objective is important as it may help municipal decision-makers to determine how to structure the subsidy design such that greater equity in the allocation of resources, improved efficiencies or placated political sensitivities are achieved. It will also ensure that the objectives converge and that the subsidisation process is not creating a disincentive to which private partners may object.

In addition to this clarity on objectives, it is necessary for these same decision-makers to familiarise themselves with the nature and impact of subsidies applied to services in the past. This will provide some indication of the patterns of the local context. Accurate information on the costs of supplying a service (often not readily available in municipalities), and information on the patterns of service demand, are both critical to the decision-making process. With this information in hand, decision-makers then need to decide:

Box 7.20   Targeted Subsidies
Chile

Launched with the goal of ensuring that the poor do not pay more than 5% for water and sanitation services, the Chilean subsidy system is now well known as an illustration of a politically and financially viable subsidy and targeting system. As early as 1990, the national government of Chile introduced a direct subsidy system to assist with basic service provision throughout the country. Replacing the earlier cross-subsidy system, the Chilean government now applies a uniform tariff system to the water and sewerage sector with fixed (connection-related) and variable (consumption-related) charges. Utilising the municipalities as a conduit for payment, it then funds operators to subsidise selected low-income consumers. Unlike the former rising block tariff system, subsidies are captured only by the poorer households and are not enjoyed by the non-poor.

Criteria for assessing eligible households relate to supply characteristics as well as consumer characteristics, highlighting the different conditions found throughout the country. They include the average cost of water, the regional characteristics, the household income and family size. Eligibility assessments are undertaken every three years. Initially, the law allowed for a subsidy of 50–80% of the variable charge for connections with a consumption of 20m^3 or less, for the first 10m^3 of the bill, and the subsidy was restricted to households with both water and sewerage connections, and that were not in debt to the water company. In order to improve the effectiveness of reaching the poor, eligibility requirements were amended in 1991 and then again in 1994 to remove the requirements of sewerage connections and no debts. The amendment also increased eligibility by removing the upper consumption limit and raising the subsidised portion first to 15m^3 and then to 20m^3 per month. These amendments reflected the growing understanding of the ways in which the poor use water, and how the poorest households could be targeted by the subsidy. The lack of a sewerage connection, for instance, outstanding debts and the fact that many households shared connections all characterised household situations in low-income settlements, and yet were the very criteria excluding the poor from accessing the subsidy. Today, the scheme prioritises the poorest, and the subsidy covers 25–85% of the poor's water and sewerage bills.

The fine-tuning of this approach has taken some time, and a process of trial and error. Shifting the responsibility for identifying eligible households from the consumer (who had to declare him/herself to be needy) to the operator (which could seek out the households in need) was an important step in improving take-up and overall targeting. The operator (EMOS) took a leading role to bring the subsidy scheme to fruition. It argues that this was for social and commercial reasons. It had a social obligation to ensure that the subsidy ended up where it was supposed to. On the other hand, the failure to implement the scheme effectively would lead to extreme difficulties in collecting payments from poor customers. Not only did the company lobby for changes to the law – changes they could see were needed to ensure that the poor were targeted – but they also actively campaigned to improve awareness of the scheme, to assist in the application process, to verify technical eligibility and to facilitate the verification of poverty criteria. This increased their customer base by 10%.

The value of the subsidy in Santiago alone is about US$4 million, covering around 20% of consumers and 2.3% of the total billing. The success of the subsidy scheme is due a number of factors, some of which may be contextually specific and defy widespread replication. The water and sanitation sector was already well developed both in terms of physical coverage and institutional reform. Second, the considered and socially oriented planning on the part of the national government in instigating the scheme, the government's financial capacity to finance the subsidy (and thereby underpin water and sanitation services for the poor to a cost of US$25 million), and the strong capacity of local government to implement the policy, provided a supportive institutional framework. Despite this somewhat rare context, it is an illustration of a coherent and direct subsidy structure that seems to be reaching the intended recipients.

As a result of the tariff reforms (which actually led to a price rise of 80% in real terms), arrears diminished from 7.9% in 1990 to 2.9% in 1994. The key reasons cited for this success are better management, incentives for prompt payment and the government's agreement to allow disconnection for non-payment.

Sources: Komives and Stalker Propky, 2000; Rivera, 1996; Foster, 1998; Britan and Serra, 1998; Blokland et al, 1999

- what service they prioritise for subsidy;
- what element/stage/aspect of the service to subsidise;
- how the subsidy should be delivered; and
- who the recipients of the subsidy should be.

☐ **Who is the subsidy targeted towards?**

If the objective is to support the poorest groups and households, then municipalities need to design mechanisms for identifying who those recipients should be (for instance, through agreed poverty indicators) and for administering a carefully targeted programme. Increasingly, attempts are being made to target subsidies at the poor rather than depending on rising block tariffs that provide cheap water to all (including the non-poor) in the first block. The well-known example of the Chilean voucher system (see Box 7.20) is particularly informative for municipalities seeking to focus the subsidies on the poorest and to ensure others are not explicitly or implicitly capturing the benefits. In particular it illustrates the trial and error of improving targeting.

☐ **Which service/stage should be subsidised?**

In developing country urban centres of all sizes and capacities, services of all types tend to be deficient. Often, however, decision-making over subsidies accompanies sectoral reforms and may not reflect the same prioritisation that the poor themselves place on services. Typically this is found with sanitation and solid waste services, which are not always prioritised by poor households who lack food security. Yet it is perhaps important to reiterate that these priorities change as the capacity of communities improves. As with delivery systems, it is necessary to consider the flexibility needed to respond to changing demand.

For each service, it is also necessary to decide the focus of the subsidy. This will have a significant impact on all stakeholders – on the incentives for the private partner as much as for the poorest consumer. Is the connection cost to be subsidised, the fixed element of the tariff, or the variable element of the tariff? E.g., if the objective is to promote greater equity, is this best achieved through a rising block tariff structure, which creates a lifeline (or survival) tariff that reduces the unit rate for low-consumption users (but is also available to the non-poor), or by subsidising the costs of connection and infrastructure passed on to new poor consumers?

☐ **How is the subsidy delivered?**

In order to operationalise these aims, it is necessary to decide how these groups, stages and services should be targeted. These possibilities may be categorised in terms of delivering the subsidy, through:

- the tariff, to the consumer;
- subsidies to franchises or operators; or
- the regulatory framework.[17]

Each approach will result in different outcomes and different impacts on the poor. While it is clear that no solution is ideal – and any intervention that dabbles in redistribution will have unintended social consequences – some familiarity with the relative benefits of different systems is necessary to approach the outcomes required.

The degree to which subsidies can assist the poorest and most marginalised households and communities, however, is often misunderstood because the poor are often represented by those who have some (albeit limited) income, some capacity and some level of service. The very poor, however, may not reap any benefits from subsidies. They would need to be formal consumers. The benefits of cross-subsidies are therefore limited to existing consumers and exclude those marginalised from the service in the first place – normally the poorest households in the society.

7

At the same time, the tendency for the poorest households to occupy marginal unserviced land is also a key factor. In the rural context this might refer to inaccessible areas, but in the urban context it may refer to illegal settlements, low-lying swamplands, steep hillsides and/or peri-urban areas beyond the existing network. Efforts to provide direct subsidies that target these non-consumers (through, for instance, subsidies for infrastructure and connection fees) are thus an important aspect of a pro-poor approach to subsidies.

Criteria for evaluating the most appropriate delivery mechanism for subsidies have been devised for circumstances in transitional economies.[18] They include, effective targeting, predictability, minimisation of distortion, and associated costs. In the context of developing countries where the problem is not one of maintaining connections so much as expanding the number of customers with access to network or non-network services, these criteria need to be extended to reflect the specific objectives of different urban service networks, poverty and capacity. Central to this must be the extent to which the vehicle adopted is able to bring about sustainable change in the existing patterns of marginalisation. This will not just require consideration of the avenue for delivering the subsidy, but the capacity of the actors involved in the execution. Another criteria is the relative number of people who have an increased access to affordable service. While they may be second-best solutions from an economic perspective, subsidies often play an important role in reform processes, and it is generally necessary to look at how adverse impacts (e.g., long-term price distortion) can be minimised and how benefits can be maximised.

Despite the general understanding that subsidies are a key way of supporting the poor during reform (and that the injection of funds will support sectoral reform), in practice, one finds many municipalities that cross-subsidise other social and welfare functions. Despite service deficiencies, municipal funds often flow away from, not to, a revenue-earning sector. The widespread occurrence of this informal approach to balancing the books – even where separate accounts are required and the legislative framework guards against such practice – begs the question as to what will happen to other municipal services when these finances are ringfenced, and such cross-subsidisation can no longer occur. Informal practices such as these draw attention to the need for policy-makers to focus on the realities of implementation and include implementers in policy-making discussions.

Institutional Aspects of the Arrangement

The scope and content of the partnership framework must also address the institutional objectives established by municipal stakeholders. These may include objectives relating to:

- **skills development, technology development and improved management practices (including delegation);** and
- **organisational capacity building for the partnership itself.**

While these objectives may be met in part through the process of forming and implementing the partnership itself, it is also important for municipalities to specifically detail elements in the partnership framework through a capacity building strategy, allowing the function to be allocated to the most appropriate partner and the task to be costed. Yet the lack of skills may in itself prevent the municipality from articulating these objectives. In general, the institutional aspects of a partnership will concern municipal capacity building objectives in identified areas such as management, financial management and communication; and institutional strengthening to enhance the way the partnership itself functions.

Requirements must be defined clearly in the partnership framework. In particular:

- goals must be relevant and achievable within the overall scope of the contract;
- target stakeholders for skills development should be identified;

- target organisations should be identified along with their capacity requirements; and
- vehicles for delivery (including the partner responsible) should be agreed.

Ideally, a strategy should be developed within the partnership framework – one that is flexible and can be clarified in stages. Such flexibility, however, carries costs with the private sector, and the inputs of capacity building advisors at the outset may be a more cost effective approach.

☐ Skills transfer and technology transfer

The processes of skills transfer and technology transfer will also depend on the nature of the arrangement (and the contract) established, but the contract established should also depend on the institutional objectives. For example:

- The management contract is often used as a vehicle for skills transfer through the workplace. In this arrangement, public sector managers can work alongside those from the private sector, learning management and procedural tools and techniques.
- In Lesotho (see Box 8.4), the need for institutional strengthening was considered significant and advisors were unconvinced that a management contract would provide the level of skills transfer needed to take the Water and Sanitation Authority (WASA) forward to a stage at which it could launch a more ambitious PPP arrangement. Instead, a donor-funded technical assistance service contract will provide the foundation for future arrangements.

While it seems clear that some of the capacity building required to meet institutional objectives will require inputs from other actors such as consultants and NGOs, for the private sector partner, considering the municipality's institutional goals, the major questions are:

- How much will it cost to meet the municipality's institutional goals?
- How willing are they, and under what conditions are they able to initiate and then continue this investment?
- How they will be reimbursed for these activities?

☐ Organisational capacity building

One of the primary areas of institutional development in a partnership arrangement addressing the poor is the formation and capacity building of participatory vehicles – organisations – to carry the partnership forward. These vehicles will be required at a number of levels for the effective implementation of a complex partnership arrangement with ambitious expansion and improvement goals. For simpler arrangements (such as small-scale solid waste activities), delivery vehicles are still required but may be more modest in nature.

The partnership framework must account for the formation, definition and development of these organisations in terms of financial resources (how much it will cost), human resources (who will carry out the work), and time (what the effects of the programme will be). The transparency and accountability of these vehicles will determine the degree to which the partnership meets governance objectives. Examples of potential vehicles, their capacities and the organisational development required are as follows.

- **Steering committees**   The development of partnership committees at the strategic level is important for determining strategic directions and resolving structural differences. The partnership arrangement should propose mechanisms for establishing overseeing committees, and mechanisms should be put in place to ensure that steering committees do not become embroiled in practical matters that detract from their capacity to deliver on strategic matters. In the decision-making structure of the South African BoTT programme, described in Box 7.21, there is a steering committee

| Box **7.21** | **Vehicles for Decision-making** |
| | BoTT, South Africa |

Links to Boxes
6.11, 6.12, 6.26, 8.13

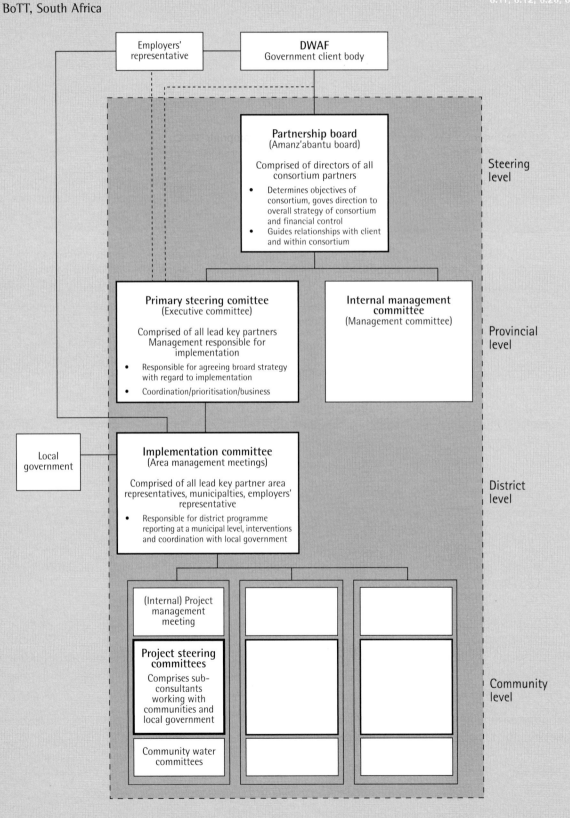

guiding the strategic direction of the consortium (the partnership board) and a steering committee working at a strategic level in relation to the entire BoTT implementation programme.

- **Implementation committees**   The partnership framework will also need to define the key vehicle for decision-making at the operational level. Evidence suggests that, like the steering committee, the efficacy of operational committees will often be facilitated by partner champions (or hindered by non-constructive individuals). The mandate and role of the operational committee must be clearly defined, and all key stakeholders must have a place at the partnership table. A partnership cannot be focused on the poor if decision-making processes do not include appropriate stakeholders and do not give them sufficient standing. The nature of the relationships required to form effective teams must then be reflected formally through appropriate contractual arrangements.

- **Community organisations**   The development of effective and sustainable participatory processes, and the extent of 'buy-in' from communities, will be dependent on the development of robust organisations at the community level. While some community organisations will already exist and may have been strengthened under previous development programmes, many others will be in their infancy. As discussed earlier in this chapter, skills (team-working, management, monitoring, accounting) may need to be developed and an organisational structure for community committees established. The roles to be played will determine the organisational capacity building required. Water committees, solid waste management committees etc., will need to build technical skills as well as more generic activities to perform agreed and defined roles.

The capacity building process for community organisations will need to be designed to suit the context – the objectives, the existing organisational framework, gender relations, and the capacity of both women and men to participate and be heard. In a poverty focused arrangement, following the discussion in Chapter 7, it is likely that that role will be taken on by an organisation skilled in this area of work, and not by a private sector partner whose competencies and goals are focused elsewhere. The broader urban governance agenda should provide a strategy for this process – one that is not purely related to a particular sector, but needs to be linked into other urban activities and mechanisms. The partnership framework needs to address these linkages, the organisational structure of delivery, the capacity needed to develop an effective structure, and the resources needed to build this capacity.

Chapter 8 **Key Questions**

- [ ] How are partnership agreements formalised?
- [ ] What are the key characteristics of existing contract models for service contracting, delegating management and granting concessions to the private sector?
- [ ] What are their strengths and weaknesses?
- [ ] What are organisational options for establishing partnerships?
- [ ] How are NGOs brought into bilateral public–private partnerships?

| Building on the assets of potential partners | Focusing the scope and content of partnership arrangements | Establishing appropriate organisational and contractual arrangements | Establishing sound partnership principles |

Liba Taylor/WaterAid

Establishing Appropriate Organisational and Contractual Arrangements | 8

Janelle Plummer and Brad Gentry

Chapter 7 has provided an overview of the primary elements making up a partnership framework focused on the poor. In practice, however, the development of the partnership framework is often determined not by a synthesis of elements appropriate to a particular context, but by the application of a predetermined contractual model. A primary concern with the existing approach to partnership development is this tendency to categorise the arrangement by contract type.[1] Commonly, a focus is placed on what contract should be employed, before considering what actors should be involved and/or what the network of arrangements should be. In the quest for establishing a partnership directly benefiting the poor, this has enormous ramifications. It hinders the development of an integrated approach to a partnership by prematurely drawing the boundaries, emphasising the contractual relationship with the main operator before first working through the strategy in its entirety.

While this book advocates a more inclusive and strategic approach that includes defining objectives and formulating a partnership framework prior to selecting a contract, it is nevertheless realistic to presume that municipalities will need information on the range of contract types currently on offer. They will need to know the typical characteristics of the contracts, their strengths and weaknesses and their implications for urban governance and poverty reduction. They will need to have an idea as to how different contracts can help or hinder them fulfil their objectives. They will need to familiarise themselves with the options that large operators will propose and to work through possibilities for other potential partners.

This chapter therefore presents the major types of contracts currently in use with the formal private sector: service contracts, management contracts, leases and affermage contracts, franchises, concessions, and BOT variants. In essence, these contracts can be distinguished by the role of the public and private organisations in ownership, investment, tariff collection and operation. Although there is a greater focus on water and sanitation, this chapter aims to cover contracts used in the water, sanitation and solid waste sectors. (The information provided is developed in far greater detail elsewhere.)[2] An even more complete list of structures for reforming municipal service delivery would include two other options: commercialisation (as in Botswana and Chile, where the governments have retained ownership of utilities, but corporatised the operations) and divestiture (best known in the context of England and Wales, where the government has sold its ownership interest in independent utilities to the public).[3]

In addition to the contractual relationships with the formal private sector, this chapter will consider the key organisational and contractual issues affecting the engagement of small-scale (sometimes informal) providers. We have seen in Chapter 6 that a small-scale provider may be the private partner in the partnership, (as seen in the case of the Lima water tankers illustrated in Box 6.8), may be one of a number of small operators, or may contribute to a partnership involving a larger operator. Finally, and in the light of the preceding discussion on the importance of NGOs in the formation of partnerships focused on the poor, the discussion will consider the organisational and contractual issues relating to the engagement of the NGOs within a partnership.

The first section, however, considers the organisational framework of municipal–private partnerships. In the light of an urban governance approach to public–private partnerships (PPPs) it is helpful to draw attention to these organisational options. They include joint ventures and independent corporatised utilities formed to manage (and perhaps finance) the service sector. The development of this organisational framework will form a primary part of the broader urban management objectives, and thus precedes a discussion on the delegation of service functions and the identification of contract types.

|Box 8.1 **Structuring Partnerships**
Operational Models

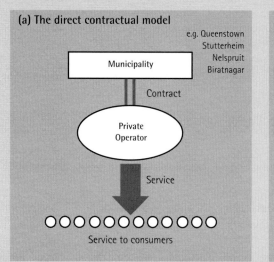

(a) The direct contractual model

e.g. Queenstown
Stutterheim
Nelspruit
Biratnagar

Municipality

Contract

Private Operator

Service

○○○○○○○○○○○○○
Service to consumers

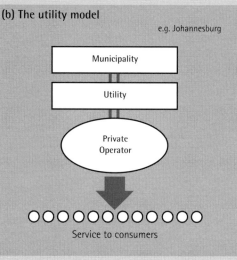

(b) The utility model

e.g. Johannesburg

Municipality

Utility

Private Operator

○○○○○○○○○○○○○
Service to consumers

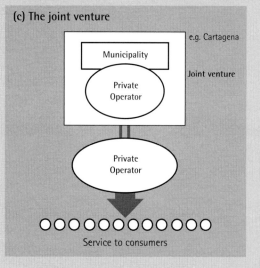

(c) The joint venture

e.g. Cartagena

Municipality

Private Operator

Joint venture

Private Operator

○○○○○○○○○○○○○
Service to consumers

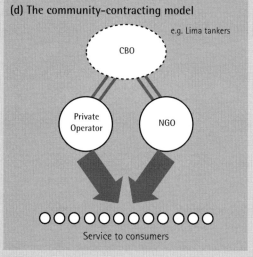

(d) The community-contracting model

e.g. Lima tankers

CBO

Private Operator   NGO

○○○○○○○○○○○○○
Service to consumers

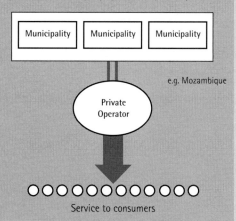

(e) Bundling
Organisation or service grouping contract a private operator

Municipality | Municipality | Municipality

e.g. Mozambique

Private Operator

○○○○○○○○○○○○○
Service to consumers

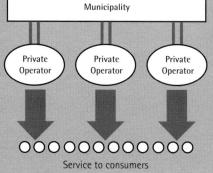

(f) Unbundling
Service or city is divided into parts to deliver service

e.g. Jakarta
Mexico City
Hyderabad

Municipality

Private Operator | Private Operator | Private Operator

○○○○○○○○○○○○○
Service to consumers

8

The Organisational Framework

☐ Defining organisational options

The most direct organisational arrangement for municipal service partnerships is that in which the private sector is contracted directly to the municipality. This creates a formal relationship between the municipality and the private operator, described in Box 8.1(a). It may be refined to include roles for higher levels of government or NGOs for instance, but the fundamental basis of the arrangement is a primary link between the municipality and the operator.

However, this is not the only organisational arrangement possible and municipalities are advised to explore other options.

- The municipality may wish to create an independent utility to separate responsibility for the service. In order to introduce private sector involvement, the municipality in Johannesburg first corporatised the delivery of water and sanitation through the formation of an independent utility. The municipality has an agreement with the utility and the utility has a management contract with a private operator (see Boxes 4.4 and 8.5). This organisational framework creates a series of contractual relationships at the higher level, supplemented by subsidiary (or secondary) contracts for delivery. This is represented by Box 8.1(b).
- In Cartagena, the municipality established a joint venture with the private sector for the delivery of water and sanitation services, and this public–private venture then established a lease contract with the (same) private operator (Box 8.1(c)).

In each of these cases the institutional relationship between the municipality and the formal private partner is more complex (and may even be a source of conflict), but the bilateral relationship at the operational level is maintained. These two models are discussed in more detail later in this section.

Other operational arrangements can be formulated when the existing constraints of a municipality – such as its the size and scope – hinder its ability to attract private partners. The concepts of bundling and unbundling the service-delivery package open up possibilities of multidimensional organisational arrangements that may be appropriate for smaller municipalities and for pro-poor partnership initiatives.

In order to establish an organisational framework, a municipality needs to consider what type of organisational framework will help it meet its objectives and respond to the specific opportunities and constraints of its situation. For instance:

- Who is the client? (Is the client body made up of more than one organisation? How is the client body organised?)
- Who is contracted? (Is one operator contracted on a single basis, or are there many operators? Are they large or small-scale, or both?)
- What function or segment of the service is being considered? (Will the municipal function be delegated in its entirety or in part?)

☐ Bundling

'Bundling' refers to the aggregation of components or functions to create a larger scope of work. For instance, a municipality may approach its neighbours to ascertain if there are significant benefits in them presenting their problems as a part of a consolidated package. This might include arrangements where municipalities group together to attract the private sector, to introduce economies of scale not possible in smaller municipalities, or to share high transaction costs.

In Nepal, in order to make a landfill proposal viable, Biratnagar Sub-municipal Corporation have proposed that in the future they work with two neighbouring cities to establish a joint operation. The Kathmandu water and sanitation

8

Box **8.2**   A Joint Venture
Cartagena, Colombia

In 1995, following an international tender and a period of controversy, the municipality of Cartagena entered into an agreement with the Spanish water operator Aguas de Barcelona (AGBAR) to form and jointly own a new joint venture company – AGUACAR. It was the first PPP for the delivery of basic services to be created in Colombia. The initial share capital of AGUACAR was US$8.8 million, of which 50% was owned by the Municipality of Cartagena (this was provided in the form of goodwill, it was not provided in cash); approximately 46% by AGBAR, and 4% by private Colombian investors, of whom a majority are company employees. In order to carry out its contract obligations, AGUACAR must issue a minimum share capital of US$4000 million and obtain the necessary loan finance as required. AGUACAR has the responsibility of determining the consumer tariff, subject to the requirements of national legislation.

In addition to its participation as a shareholder in AGUACAR, AGBAR also signed a separate, fee-based management contract with AGUACAR, as a private operator, for the day-to-day operations of the company. Thus AGUACAR has an independent affermage contract for the management of water and sanitation services in the city. The contract with AGBAR is for:

- the operation and maintenance of the existing water and sanitation system, including billing and collection; and
- a duration of 26 years.

Under the terms of the affermage contract with AGBAR, AGUACAR is only responsible for the management of the system, while AGBAR is responsible for capital investment. The capital investment component of the water and sanitation works in Cartagena had been under discussion with the World Bank well before the signing of the agreement, and in 1998, without a contract, AGUACAR was entrusted with the management of a major water and sanitation investment programme, the Plan Maestro de Acueducto y Alcantarillado. This investment programme is financed mainly by loans from the World Bank (US$85 million) and the Inter-American Development Bank (US$24 million). Consequently, under this complex arrangement, the private sector partner will carry out the functions normally found in a concession contract, but with protection from the capital investment risks inherent in such an arrangement.

As a result, AGBAR's remuneration comes in two forms:

- the declared profits/dividends of its 46% share in AGUACAR; and
- a management fee, which is calculated as a share of the gross income of AGUACAR.

In the first four years of operation, this management fee was fixed as a percentage of gross income, and increased gradually from 2.94% to 4.25%. In 1999, AGUACAR declared profits of US$1.96 million. In the same year, AGBAR received a total of around US$2.1 million from its involvement in the Cartagena joint venture – US$900,000 from its dividend share and US$1.2 million from its management fee.

The new and complex institutional arrangement for water and sanitation in the form of a joint venture, contracted out to a private partner also represented in the joint venture, poses two potential dangers to the sustainability of the PPP. First, the role of the municipality becomes blurred. This happens because, under the joint venture, the municipality is at both the service provider (as owner of the network assets) and service operator (as a major shareholder in AGUACAR). This overlap in the division of responsibilities blurs the lines of accountability and has a potentially damaging effect on the transparency of management decision-making. The lines of accountability are further complicated by the fact that the municipality has effectively relinquished its operational role to its private sector partner, through an affermage contract awarded to AGBAR.

Second, under this complex arrangement the private operator benefits from the advantages of the traditional affermage arrangement in terms of exercising day-to-day control of the management of the system, but with a much reduced financial risk in terms of working capital outlay and consequent higher effective rate of profit. This latter happens because, unlike the affermage arrangement under which the private operator is paid exclusively from a share of the gross revenue, AGBAR is paid both in the form of a management fee based on a fixed percentage of gross revenue and in the form of a share of the profits from the joint venture.

Source: Nickson, 2001a

affermage contract has been developed for three municipalities in the Kathmandu Valley, all under the jurisdiction of the national level of government.[4] In Mozambique, the Maputo contract is actually for seven cities in the country.

'Bundling' may also refer to the packaging of different cross-service sectors. For instance, electricity and water functions might be covered by the same partnership arrangement.[5] In Kavre, a rural area in Nepal, the district development committee initially proposed to pilot a PPP for the delivery of a wide range of local services including health, education, infrastructure and agricultural extension services. The bundled arrangement is illustrated by Box 8.1(e).

One question concerning private investors is how secure bundled arrangements are over time. If the mayor in one town is replaced, can that town pull out of a partnership – legally or practically? Does this suggest that higher levels of government (national or provincial) must be involved to attract private investors? On the other hand, does such an approach lead to a less competitive environment, with less possibility for benchmarking?

☐　Unbundling

'Unbundling' refers to the disaggregation of components within a service sector (see Box 8.1(f)). An 'unbundled' sector may enable a range of service delivery options to be adopted and may be politically helpful to introduce a private sector approach. Breaking a service sector down into a number of parts may enable municipalities to keep control of controversial functions, for instance, or it may allow them to involve a range of actors and build on existing local assets.

Vertical unbundling occurs when a service is disaggregated from the tertiary to the primary levels.[6] In India, for instance, it is not uncommon to find water and wastewater treatment plants or pumping stations effectively managed by the private sector, and water points managed by small-scale service providers. Horizontal unbundling occurs when a city is divided into zones and contracts are arranged for each area. At a large scale this was the approach taken in Jakarta and Mexico City, where the cities were divided into zones for establishing concessions for water and sanitation services. A key problem associated with this approach is that zonal divisions expose the inequalities in the city. If one zone is comprised primarily of the non-poor and another of the poor, the resulting partnerships can be very unequal, and opportunities for cross-subsidies can be lost or made very complex.

Unbundling does, however, allow for a degree of competition and benchmarking in situations tending towards monopoly. It is used at a small scale to franchise solid waste operations for different zones of the city, and is useful for establishing contracts with small firms for solid waste. This has been successfully adopted in Hyderabad in India for street cleaning, and solid waste collection and transfer.

Both horizontal and vertical unbundling can be achieved in sanitation by adopting the strategic sanitation approach to service delivery. As in water supply, vertical unbundling in sanitation occurs when the service is disaggregated from tertiary to primary levels. Different actors are responsible for different services at different levels – wastewater treatment for large flows generated by the city, and local operators for waste removal at household level. Horizontal unbundling occurs by dividing the city into zones for secondary services such as sewerage and drain maintenance. Wherever possible, the full cycle of health and hygiene and sanitation promotion, sanitation demand-generation, infrastructure provision (construction of facilities), operation and use, waste removal and waste disposal is carried out at as local a level as possible.

8

Box **8.3**   Contract Types

	Service Contracts	Management contracts	Affermage/ leases	BOT variants	Concessions
Asset ownership	Municipal	Municipal	Municipal	Private to municipal	Municipal
Capital investment finance	Municipal	Municipal	Municipal	Private	Private
Operating maintenance finance	Municipal	Municipal	Private	Private	Private
Tariff collection	Municipal	Muncipal (or private)	Private	Municipal	Private
System operation	Municipal/and private	Private	Private	Private	Private

- increasing investment by private sector
- increasing risk allocated to private sector
- increasing duration of contract
- tariff collection shifts to private sector
- operation and management tasks shift to private sector

The table above describes some of the roles commonly prescribed to private business and municipalities in relation to service, management, lease, concession and BOT contracts. Many 'northern' advocates of public–private partnerships specify particular requirements (or characteristics) for each contract type, but analysis of existing contracts and arrangements in developing countries suggests that these requirements are often relaxed in practice. Arrangements are often hybrids of more than one contract type and the definition of contract type seems to vary.

In the South, where flexibility is paramount, it is more common to find that the definitions are indisctinct and contract terminology varies, often within the same operating context. While hybrids may be the norm rather than the exception, there are trends in relation to ownership, investment, tariff collection and operation (such as that shown by the arrow above) that can help municipalities understand the opportunities offered by different contractual arrangements. Also, it may be that the standard northern form of contract acts as an incentive to private firms, and might increase the chance of doing a deal or reducing costs. Municipalities must weigh these advantages against the disadvantages if a particular model does not offer the components they require.

In the current PPP environment, an important question is whether or not predetermined contract forms are appropriate and whther the strong focus on the categories of contracts undermines the ability to craft partnership arrangements that meet local needs and constraints. The cases examined in South Africa illustrate the types of variations that are created in response to perceived requirements and contextual limitations:

- The Nelspruit Concession, as it was envisaged, intended to draw on capital investment from the private sector, but to date all finance has come from the Development Bank of Southern Africa.
- The Queenstown Concession does not include customer management. Tariff collection is still carried out by the municipality as a part of a composite service tariff. The private operator and the municipality still call it a 'concession', but is this really a performance-based management contract with a sizeable capital investment programme from a private firm?
- The Stutterheim Affermage – as it is called – also does not include tariff collection. The municipality sets and collects the tariff, but the operator funds all operation and maintenance costs. In this case the operator refers to the contract as an 'affermage' but is this really only a management contract?

The joint venture model

In joint ventures, public and private actors assume co-ownership of system assets and co-responsibility for the delivery of services. The public and private sector partners can either form a new company (as in the Cartagena example in Box 8.2), or share ownership of an existing company. Joint ventures create a new entity to implement various types of project structures. For example, the government may award the (jointly owned) firm a service, build–operate–transfer (BOT) or concession contract, depending on the service requirements.

Joint ventures provide a vehicle for governments, businesses and others to pool their resources and generate shared returns by solving local infrastructure issues. Under joint ventures, government remains the ultimate regulator but is also an active shareholder in the operating company. From this position, it may share in the operating company's profits and help ensure the wider political acceptability of its efforts. The private sector partner often has the primary responsibility for performing daily management operations.

Under the joint venture model, both the public and the private sector partners are responsible for investments. Joint ventures require that both parties accept the idea of shared risk and shared reward. Each must be willing to make quantifiable contributions throughout the project development and implementation process. Different approaches to financing can be used depending on the nature of the services to be performed – varying from contracts calling for limited technical services to those delegating broader responsibilities.

Among the strengths of joint ventures is their ability to combine the advantages of the private sector – dynamism, access to finance, knowledge of technologies, managerial efficiency and entrepreneurial sprit – with the social responsibility, public health/environmental awareness, local knowledge and job generation concerns of the public sector. Under a joint venture, both the public and private sector partners have invested in the company and therefore both have a strong interest in seeing the venture work. This can allow for better conflict management. Full responsibility for investments and operations gives the public and private sector partners a large incentive to make efficient investment decisions and to develop innovative technological solutions, since any gains in efficiency will directly increase their joint returns. Early participation by the public and private sector partners allows for greater innovation and flexibility in project planning; helps ensure that both the partners are able to optimise their goals; and can also help reduce the transaction costs associated with more traditional tendering processes.

The major weakness of joint ventures is that the government's continuing regulatory responsibilities may lead to a conflict of interest in both maintaining public accountability and maximising returns to the venture. This can increase the risk of political interference and reduce potential gains from private sector management. Private sector organisations also tend to focus on profit, governments on process. These differences (detailed in Chapter 6) are often manifested in the timetables each sector considers reasonable, and can create barriers during project development. Despite the advantages of working together towards partnerships, early dialogue between the public and private parties involved in some joint ventures may lead to alternative public tender procedures, such as direct negotiation. Improperly managed, this can raise concerns about transparency and corruption in the selection of partners, affect political acceptability and hinder additional private sector investment.

A community client arrangement

The arrangements described above all place the municipality in the client role, yet the municipality can also delegate this role to the community itself. In some situations, the municipality does not have a contractual relationship with the community, but through a structured programme of change, the community has established contractual relationships with the private sector. This is the case in Lima water tankers, illustrated in Box 6.8, where each community contracts an association of tanker drivers to supply its reservoir with water, and it establishes a lease form of contract with a private

8

Box **8.4**   **The Return of Technical Assistance**
Maseru, Lesotho

Since the landmark privatisations of state-owned utilities in the UK in the latter part of the 1980s, culminating in the privatisation of the water industry in 1989, it has become the accepted wisdom that the only way to improve the performance of such utilities is by some form of privatisation. However, the failure of some private sector management contracts in developing countries to deliver expected (and legally enforceable) improvement in standards has led to the questioning in some quarters of the previously unchallenged tenet, and the realisation that in some circumstances, technical assistance could be a better option than privatisation.

An interesting recent example is that of the Water and Sewerage Authority (WASA) of Lesotho. When it was established in 1992, the Government of Lesotho (GoL) declared a long-term objective of privatising WASA within a decade. GoL also recognised that this objective could not be achieved without improving WASA's performance to the point where some form of privatisation would be viable. The provision of long-term technical assistance for WASA was agreed between GoL and the UK's Overseas Develoment Administration (ODA and later DFID), and ran (through two phases and a number of interruptions due to political instability following Lesotho's return to democracy in 1993), for eight-and-a-half years from October 1991 to March 2000.

In October 2000, a project identification mission from the World Bank visited Lesotho as part of a proposed water sector reform project. Part of its ToR was to recommend options to improve the performance of WASA, and it was confidently expected that this would include some form of private sector participation. However, the report of this mission concluded that ...*it is unlikely that a long-term private sector contract would be feasible at this time, and that the core problems of WASA... cannot be remedied by the use of a management contract*. The report went on to recommend a performance agreement between WASA and GoL for a period of 3–4 years, supported by continued technical assistance (TA).

These conclusions/recommendations are all the more remarkable given the World Bank's insistence, in a previous mission to assess the water sector in Lesotho, on some form of privatisation as the only practical solution to the problems of WASA. A further reading of the report of the more recent Bank mission indicates an acceptance of the benefits and improvements that WASA has achieved through the provision of TA, and that its continuation is the most appropriate mechanism for maintaining the progress of WASA.

Behind this change of mind is an implicit admission of the limitations of the management contract concept, both financial and practical, to improve the performance of this category of public utility. The financial limitations of a management contract became clear once analysis by the World Bank team revealed that the improvements in WASA's performance, achieved through the provision of technical assistance, left insufficient scope for the additional cost savings upon which a management contract would rely in order to be viable. In other words, in this particular case, the cost of a management contract would be greater than the savings that would accrue from the greater efficiencies that such a contract would be expected to bring.

The practical limitations are exemplified in the second of the two conclusions reached by the World Bank mission: that, in this case, the core problems of WASA cannot be remedied by a management contract. These core problems are identified as staffing, tariffs, and the collection of government debts. The reason given is that these issues are outside the jurisdiction of a management contract, as they are primarily the result of policy decisions of the government. However, the World Bank mission felt that addressing them can be made a 'conditionality' by the Bank for a TA-supported performance agreement.

This project (now renamed the Lesotho Water Sector improvement Project) is still in the early stages of preparation, with the signing of the loan agreement not expected before the latter part of 2002. The performance agreement would require WASA to meet specific operational, financial and staffing level targets to be achieved over the duration of the agreement. In return, the government would agree to certain obligations which might include (i) a revision of the current tariff structure (including a mechanism for annual adjustments), (ii) to pay its water bills in a timely fashion, and (iii) to adopt a hands-off approach to the day-to-day running of WASA to enable the company to address its core problems on commercial principles. It is expected that the TA will provide support to WASA in the areas of engineering, finance, planning and human resources, which would be financed as part of the overall loan package.

The performance agreement concept has previously been successful in Swaziland, where the Water Services Corporation has a performance contract with government (in the form of the Public Enterprise Unit). This was a condition of a World Bank loan for the urban development project, and DFID supported the TA for the corporation. As long as the agreement is well drafted without areas of ambiguity, it provides the performance-based incentives normally associated with the private sector while leaving responsibility for achievement with the organisation's own staff. This is more likely to contribute to the overall objective of sustainable development than the handing over of responsibility to an international company.

Source: Wessex Water International

operator to operate and maintain the system and collect the revenue. While this model may be limited in size, the benefits of placing the community in the key role have been recognised in South Africa, and efforts are being made to increase the role of communities in mobilising contracts with small-scale providers. Significant community capacity building may be required to ensure this organisational framework is sustainable.

The organisational framework of the partnership is thus an important step in the decision-making process. The basic structure of the arrangement is not a fait accompli and municipalities are encouraged to compare different organisational arrangements to see how best to reach their objectives.

Contracting the Private Sector

This section provides a description of the various contract types that a municipality can adopt with the private sector for the delivery of services. While each has distinct characteristics, it is important to recognise that in practice, these model contracts are moulded to suit existing requirements. One rarely finds a contract that reflects all the aspects of the model (see Box 8.3). This is particularly marked in developing countries and is a key distinction between contracts developed and implemented in the North and South.

Service Contracts

☐   Key characteristics

The service contract, well known to some municipalities through the contracting-out of non-essential services, is established with a service provider to deliver an agreed service, within well-defined specifications, for a fixed period of time. Often concerning some form of technical service, the service contract may also be a supply contract, a civil works contract or a technical assistance contract, such as that being considered in Lesotho (see Box 8.4). It may involve sub-contracting or contracting a part of a municipal service.

In relation to water and sanitation, a municipality typically uses service contracts for:

- operation and maintenance of standpipes and kiosks;
- meter reading, billing and collection;
- sewer cleaning;
- pumping station operation;
- sanitation vehicles maintenance and repair; and
- tariff collection.

Service contracts are commonly found in cities without sewerage, when the upkeep of a fleet of special-purpose vehicles for septic tank cleaning is contracted on a fixed term to local entrepreneurs.

The service contract may be the key instrument used in municipal solid waste management after the operations are unbundled, enabling the municipality to let areas or parts of the service to small- and medium-sized enterprises. In relation to solid waste management, a service contract is often a preferred method of contracting an operator for collection services in middle-income areas.[7] Other potential uses include:

- collection of municipal waste;
- facility repairs, maintenance; and
- waste collection and maintenance and repair of transfer vehicles.

The service contract is not ambitious: it is often short in duration (1–3 years), and control is still firmly lodged with the municipality. Duration must be sufficient to allow contractors to fully write-off the cost of any equipment purchased (such as collection vehicles). Conversely, the duration will determine the level of investment (e.g., in collection vehicles) and therefore the standard of service provided.

The municipality retains ownership and control of all capital assets and property, and must finance fixed assets and working capital. The municipality establishes the performance criteria, evaluates the bids, selects and supervises the contractor and monitors the work to be carried out to ensure the contractor meets the performance specification. For the contracting of solid waste collection services (that do not always raise revenue), the municipality must ensure that it has sufficient revenue to pay the contractor. This must be calculated to include depreciation, interest on borrowing, salaries, consumables, insurance and profit.

Under the service contract, the contractor is normally responsible for managing personnel and services. To ensure the service contract results in greater efficiency, it should be awarded through competitive bidding, and this can be compared against the public sector costs through a benchmarking process. The selected contractor is obligated to carry out the service to the specification established in the agreement, and agrees to a fee for the service on a lump sum, unit cost or other basis. Unlike more complex forms of private sector participation (PSP), to the contractor, the municipality is still the client and the source of payments. The commercial risk for the private operator is that the municipality may default on payments.

☐ Strengths and weaknesses

For advocates of investment-linked partnerships, the service contract is considered a weak alternative, simply maintaining the status quo. This does not have to be the case. An innovative municipality could corporatise its own operations and, through the unbundling of different tasks, utilise the service contract as an opportunity to build the capacity of a range of small-scale local service providers. This may even involve contracting-out to previous employees who have established cooperatives or small enterprises.

The service contract is relatively simple to arrange, resembling the traditional construction contracts with which municipal engineering departments are familiar. The service contract does not bring with it the risk, and therefore does not need the complex regulatory environment critical to the concession. Municipalities are therefore able to embark on improvements much more quickly and not be concerned with the impact of the operating environment outside their control. The short duration means they can review the work done and make decisions easily, and the timeframe can adapt to electoral cycles.

The degree of competition achieved through the tendering process will vary considerably: it is dependent on the service, the historical development of providers and the performance requirements of the contract. The fundamental concern with the use of service contracts is directly linked to the short durations of the contract terms. Short terms provide little incentive to the private sector operator to make efficiency gains through its own investment (e.g., in better equipment or vehicles) or to build local capacity (in management or accounting skills). The individual or enterprise that takes on the service contract must guard against the risk that the contract will not be renewed. This often fails to meet a number of the economic objectives of private sector participation.

The capacity needed within the municipality is obviously very different for a service contract than more complex contracts. A skilled municipal official may well be able to successfully unbundle water and sanitation services and develop partnerships with a range of private and civil society actors. Most, however, will need training to broaden their perspective as to the opportunities available to them. Simple service contracts for specific improvement works or maintenance, for instance, can be administered by most engineering departments, and they are generally able to resolve most problems that arise.

The service contract thus offers enormous opportunities in relation to the development of small and medium micro-enterprises that deliver services to the poor, and it may also be one of the legal mechanisms used to engage NGOs to provide physical, social and institutional services. Yet the overall extent of reform taking place in conjunction with service contracts is limited, and thus their potential and impact is also limited. The key issues concerning the poor in relation to the three basic services of water, sanitation and solid waste are described below.

In less commercialised situations and those where large-scale inputs from the international private sector are not viable, the service contract can still assist a municipality in making small improvements in streamlining operations, promoting efficiency and developing a local competitive market of regularised entrepreneurs. In many situations where independent service providers supply poor-quality water or exploit poor consumers, municipalities can restructure provision by developing some regulatory instruments and utilising the service contract to structure service delivery more formally (see Box 6.15). Information on the existing methods of delivery is essential to the development of a strategy that utilises a service contracting approach to include independent providers.

Service contracts are also important stepping stones. Companies unwilling to invest or enter into lengthy contracts because of unstable political and economic situations may well be willing to enter into service (or management) contracts; or municipalities may wish to phase the work starting with a service contract to correct a deficiency (such as a lack of meters). In the Lesotho case illustrated in Box 8.4, due to the low capacity of the institutions, the World Bank recommended that a service contract for technical assistance be put in place as a precursor to any broader private sector participation.

Many of the water and sanitation projects funded by donors and delivered through NGOs or CBOs, for instance, have been carried out through service contracts. The lessons of these contracts are an important source of information for municipalities. The lack of sewerage networks in a vast number of cities means that the delivery of sanitation services may require quite different solutions than water supply. Existing independent providers currently provide a high proportion of the sanitation services available to the poor. Municipalities are often not a party to the arrangement. While some of these service providers are considered exploitative, others are not. Either way, it is clear that there is a need for the municipality to regulate their activities – for example, the dumping of sewage. The service contract may then become one legal instrument for bringing these important service providers into an integrated delivery system. Carefully planned and managed, this could result in improved reliability of service delivery and water quality, and less exploitation of poor households.

In solid waste, the service contract can bring enormous benefit to the city and to the poor, if municipalities are able to arrange effective agreements with contractors in sweeping and household waste collection. The service contract does not fundamentally change the informal system established with sweepers, waste-pickers, itinerant waste-buyers and resale agents.

Management Contracts

☐ Key characteristics

The management contract moves beyond the delegation of discrete service functions to the delegation of a range of delivery, operation and maintenance functions. The municipality retains ownership of assets and – like the service contract – is responsible for capital expenditures, working capital and the commercial risk associated with collecting service fees from users. Within the municipality, the engineering or health department normally monitors the management contractor to ensure that performance standards and other obligations are met. The contract emphasises outputs and a programme for achieving targets.

8

| Box **8.5** | **Selecting a Management Contract** |

Selecting a Management Contract
Johannesburg, South Africa

The process of transformation in Johannesburg (described in Box 4.4) included, inter alia, radical transformation of the city's infrastructure and services. The programme of reform to the utilities included a fundamental shift for the water and sanitation sector, the power sector and waste management. These three services accounted for approximately 9000 staff and approximately 50% of the annual operating budget. As they represent three basic urban services in need of significant capital expenditure and ongoing maintenance from dwindling resources, it was proposed that a fundamental change in approach should try to draw on new technologies, sophisticated customer management and revenue, and complex management skills.

The Igoli 2000 strategy thus proposed that each sector should be corporatised into an independent utility. These utilities are to operate under the terms of the Companies Act and should be professionally managed, while dividends, regulation and policy direction are kept under political control through the council. The creation of utilities addressed five key issues:

- access to capital;
- separation of regulator and operator;
- removing inefficiencies caused by the bureaucracy;
- attracting managerial and technical skills; and
- employment of existing workers on acceptable terms and conditions.

In the case of water and sanitation, it was necessary to consider how the utility would operate – once it became an independent entity – in order to achieve the objectives set down by the Igoli Plan. Various forms of contracts were matched against the agreed city objectives and the constraints of the operating context. The key challenges of the water and sanitation sector are to extend universal but individualised access to the 20% who do not have it and reduce unaccounted-for water (costing R176 million (US$25 million)) to more acceptable levels. The aim is to maintain the existing infrastructure, extend bulk infrastructure, improve the billing and revenue system, introduce a lifeline service, create more community delivery system partnerships, create interactive user forums and improve management systems in all respects.

A number of opportunities also guided the decision. By ringfencing and corporatising a new council-owned utility there was still a good potential for achieving efficiencies and improvements as a result of:

- greater autonomy from council;
- wider commercial and management freedoms;
- improved governance and greater accountability; and
- freedom to borrow funds commercially.

The option for establishing a concession contract was considered along with a full range of contracts, but given the strong ideological opposition to privatisation from the unions, the council judged that a concession contract would be highly contentious. Despite some of the benefits that would be brought to the city, the long-term concession option was not considered viable due to the local political context.

A decision was made to procure the services of a management contractor to help operate the utility and transfer skills to the local management over five years. The pre-existing water and sanitation services of the council employed a number of good technical specialists and managers. However, it employed very few staff with commercial and financial expertise. The purpose of the five-year management contract was to bring in experienced staff with the skills that were missing, and to accelerate the utility's progress to financial sustainability (i.e., give it a bump-start). It would also give the new utility exposure to world-class business systems, management etc. The criteria thus included technical and management ability, shared commitment to council objectives, skill transfer experience, maximum utilisation of South African managers, commitment and ability to correct historical imbalances, economic empowerment, price and willingness to take on risks. The objective of procuring a management contract was to ensure the quickest and most efficient achievement of the objectives and the transfer of skills and systems to the utility. The management contractor was chosen by competitive tender in early 2001 (see Box 9.1).

Sources: Gordhan, 1999; Chris Ricketson, Halcrow Group

In the management form of contract, a private operator manages the operations without committing substantial investment capital (beyond that necessary to win and perform the contract) or accepting the bulk of the commercial risks (unless its compensation is linked to the collection of user fees). In practice, management contracts vary substantially: from short-term contracts where the contractor manages specific tasks; to longer-term contracts where the contractor is responsible for all aspects of delivering the service, and has an obligation to introduce technical and management skills and to bring specific improvements to the service delivery process. Where the contract links compensation with improved system performance, it starts to resemble some of the more complex contract types described below.

The duration of the management contract is usually in the range of 3–8 years. The aim is to ensure that there is sufficient time for the operator to implement changes and be held accountable for results. Where the contract requires particular reform or efficiency gains, for instance, it is critical that the municipality does not micro-manage the process. The contractor must be given autonomy to implement commercial reforms. The contract must also contain effective incentives for good performance, including penalties for failure to meet agreed performance goals and/or bonuses for a job well done. Payment may therefore be based on an agreed fee plus a performance-based incentive (see discussion in Chapter 7).

Examples of the use of management contracts include:

- management of water and wastewater treatment plants and/or pumping stations;
- operation and management of distribution networks;
- training to operate and manage water and sanitation services;
- regional water supply management;
- waste collection; and
- solid waste treatment/disposal plant operation.

☐ Strengths and weaknesses

Like the service contract, the management contract is relatively easy to put in place and its short duration does not create the same level of concern as a long-term investment contract with the private sector. As a result, management contracts are sometimes seen as an attractive option when investment-linked long-term private sector participation is not appropriate (as seen in Johannesburg, illustrated in Box 8.5), or when private firms see the current risks as being too high. The management contract can address efficiency objectives, although not the structural problems associated with under-investment.

The contract might also be adopted where it is clear that the skills of the private sector would help establish a stronger information base about the infrastructure, the organisation and the market before further private sector participation options are considered. While this may have some benefits, this stepping stone approach also brings with it problems, and the municipality must weigh these against each other. If management contracts are seen as a precursor to longer contracts, the winning tender for a management contract secures a privileged position in the future tender for a longer-term contract. This can stifle the competitive process and give an advantage to one operator that may not be the best organisation for the tasks required in the later stage.

The lack of any input into or control over tariffs means that significant reform still lies in the hands of the municipality and the incentives associated with improved cost recovery are not in place. (Evidence suggests there is often a weak tariff discipline operating alongside an efficient management contractor.) As the management contract generally focuses on improved management, it does not facilitate a strategy for improving service coverage. Consequently, poor settlements that are currently unconnected to water supply and sewerage networks are unlikely to benefit from improved performance (unless the municipality or another agent funds a capital works programme). However, a management contractor may be

8

Box **8.6**   ## An Affermage Contract
Stutterheim, South Africa

When the partnership in Stutterheim was established, a primary goal of the council was to streamline municipal functions. The council aimed to redirect conventional forms of management to address the resource deficiencies of the council. To this end, they envisaged partnerships with actors outside the government and coordination with other municipal bodies. Among other issues, they sought to tackle the problems of small municipalities that cannot sustain sufficient technical capacity to run a properly skilled water and sanitation service. As the engineering department was going through a difficult stage (beset by uncertainty in contracting practices), service was deteriorating, and a partnership arrangement with the private sector for water and sanitation services solved particular and strategic problems. The objective of private sector participation was to buy-in the technical skills needed to improve the efficiency, management and delivery of water and sanitation services to the population of Stutterheim. However, the objective at that time did not include capital investment, and the pre-democratic council was only concerned with bulk supply to low-income areas. Decisions were set within the context of political change in South Africa.

In 1992, the council agreed to pursue private sector involvement in a range of municipal functions. In order to initiate the process the council agreed to test the market and advertised nationally for expressions of interest for the management of water and sanitation services in the town. In the early 1990s there was little direction for PPPs in South Africa; nor was there any significant assistance available internationally, and the process of preparation, tender and evaluation process was carried out with the methodology used for the construction of civil works.

The council was dominated by business acumen; the councillors were willing and able to identify gaps in council skills and were agreeable to the appointment of (and fees for) consultants to fill these gaps and manage the formulation of a contract. The proposal for the affermage contract was presented by WSSA in its tender. An investigation into alternative contract types was not pursued. The contract was considered appropriate because it met the council's key technical, managerial and efficiency objectives and did not include a significant investment component. (In some respects this decision has proven prudent: the Stutterheim Transitional Local Council has been very successful in obtaining reconstruction and development funds.) Despite its interest in private sector involvement in the delivery process, the council in power in the early 1990s was too cautious to enter into a 20- or 30-year commitment.

In that context, there was little concern for the mechanics of public consultation or the explicit involvement of stakeholders in the decision to enter into a partnership arrangement. The council had a mandate to manage the town and was not concerned with building a consultative approach or obtaining explicit approval for a decision on delegating management. The decisions made over the contract during its formulation were not specifically linked to poverty reduction initiatives in the adjacent areas, where the poorer communities lived. Effective town management was, however, a key issue, and the council envisaged a key role for the private sector in attaining this end.

The partnership arrangement in place in Stutterheim today is an affermage contract for 10 years. It contracts-out responsibility for providing management, operation and maintenance to the private sector. Unlike the management form of contract in the nearby town of Fort Beaufort in the Eastern Cape, the private operator must provide working capital, but capital investments remain the responsibility of the authority. Unlike the other nearby town of Queenstown, the Stutterheim contract does not provide for any capital investment.

The scope of the contract in Stutterheim includes the management, operation and maintenance of the water and sewerage system, replacement of pipework due to normal wear and tear, and record keeping. It also includes for customer management services as a future option. In addition, WSSA has an obligation for some rehabilitation works on the existing system: to replace a fixed amount of pipework annually, to replace all meters that are older than seven years by the fifth year of its contract, and to replace any malfunctioning electromechanical equipment. Thus, maintenance, replacement and ongoing repair are the responsibility of the operator, while upgrading and expansion are those of the council.

Eight years later, the actors and their roles and relationships have changed considerably. The council is oriented towards the achievement of social goals, and to some extent these goals are at odds with private sector involvement in service delivery. Perhaps the primary issue for the council is that the contract it inherited in 1995 does not meet its new objectives. The need for investment is significantly greater than it was under the previous regime. The desire to pass on additional risk to the private sector, the need to embrace the potential role of communities in demand-led decision-making and implementation, and the need to build institutional and community capacity, are all vital ingredients of a municipal service partnership designed to meet reconstruction and development objectives. The Stutterheim experience also illustrates the assertion made by the World Bank that the lease/affermage contract is politically demanding and complex to administrate.

Source: Plummer, 2000a

better placed to rethink the organisational structure of the water and sanitation network and service than a municipality. In cities with limited network coverage, this could result in the potential of a strategic approach to delivery, including the role of independent providers and NGOs and potentially larger-scale private firms.

Management contracts to date rarely provide incentives to improve delivery to the poor. Municipalities explicitly concerned with service delivery in poor areas must ensure that the contract clearly defines the responsibilities of the private sector in relation to poor households and low-income areas. One of the lessons of management contracts that encourage efficiency improvements but do not spell out any improvements for low-income areas is that the contractor will make efficiency improvements wherever possible to meet performance targets, without regard to the impact on the poor. If, for example, a primary inefficiency is unaccounted-for water and the management contractor identifies illegal connections as a key problem, then the contractor may remove these connections without concern or discussion as to alternatives for poor householders. If a primary inefficiency is revenue collection, management contractors will tenaciously pursue the inefficiencies of meter reading, billing and collection, but this improvement might not be associated with wider tariff reforms and could distort the tariff system further, as there may be implicit subsidies built into these inefficiencies. The performance target may be met, but at the expense of poor households' continued access to water for domestic and productive use. The implementation of the management contract in the situation described thus delivers adverse impacts on the poor.

It is therefore necessary to create management contracts that include efficiency improvements with targeted pro-poor actions, and it is necessary to ensure that the operator is obliged to implement these through contract provisions. Defining performance standards to ensure that efficiency is not gained at the expense of the poor is essential to the pro-poor management contract. This might include, for example, efforts to ensure that the poor have access to other affordable water sources when illegal connections are removed, or that options other than pre-paid meters are offered to facilitate improved payment rates.

Leases and Affermage Contracts

☐ Key characteristics

The lease contract aims to provide an arrangement through which a municipality (or utility) can lease infrastructure and facilities to a private firm, which then operates and maintains the service for a fixed period of time. There is no transfer of ownership of existing assets and the municipality is responsible for the capital investment required to upgrade existing assets or extend infrastructure to new areas. As such, the lessee is under no obligation to invest in new or major rectification of infrastructure. The only obligation on the lessee is for the operation and maintenance of the leased assets. This includes anticipated replacement and repair works, the standards and extent of which are specified in the contract. Obviously, distinguishing operation and maintenance expenses from capital investments is critical to the successful allocation and fulfilment of these responsibilities.

In exchange for the exclusive right to use the assets (infrastructure, facilities, vehicles etc.) to deliver services, the operator typically pays rent to the municipality and generates revenue by collecting fees from users for the services delivered. It profits from the lease if the user fees are higher than the rental payments and the other costs incurred in providing the service. The fact that the private operator bears the commercial risk of non-payment is often cited as the factor that distinguishes leases from management contracts. Improving service delivery and fee collection can take time. As a result, lease contracts are generally longer term, with a duration that falls between the management contract and the concession in the region of 8–15 years.

| Box 8.7 | **Issues Concerning Delivery to the Poor**
A Checklist for Concession Arrangements

- Are performance standards designed to ensure better-quality service for the poor? The very poor? Women?
- Is service expansion included in the arrangement?
- Has the arrangement included for alternative service delivery mechanisms?
- Has it included for alternative payment mechanisms for the poor?
- Does the arrangement allow the concessionaire to explore alternative technologies such as condominial systems?
- Does the arrangement promote temporary or intermediate arrangements to improve the services for the poor early in the contract?
- Are labour-based approaches explicitly defined in the contract for both operation and maintenance and new construction works?
- Has the arrangement addressed the problems of payment for connection costs (or emergency recurrent costs) through financial support services?
- What provision has been made for the adoption of participatory processes?
- How are the activities and the programme of the concessionaire being integrated with other municipal service activities?
- What provision is made in the contract to integrate and link physical activities with other poverty reduction responses? What tasks must be undertaken by municipalities to facilitate action in poor areas (e.g., land title)?
- What provision is made for hygiene promotion in relation to water use and solid waste activities?
- How are demand-led processes being incorporated into the activities? How does the contract make provision for the time and flexibility needed for community capacity building?
- How does the design of inputs in poor areas respond to the different needs of women and men?
- How have women and other marginalised groups been included in the process?
- How does the proposed tariff affect the poor? The very poor? Women?
- What are the indirect implications of the tariff and subsidy structure?
- What improvements will be made through the capital investment programme? Do they benefit the poor? Can they be targeted more closely towards benefit for the poor?
- Does the arrangement stipulate investment in poor areas? How is this selected and prioritised?
- What is the source of investment funds? Is cheaper capital available? Is this gain passed on in the tariff?
- What service options are available to poor households? Has the arrangement closed down or opened up options for them to adopt in their livelihood strategies?
- What incentives does the private operator have to deliver services to the poor? What are the disincentives? What are the programming incentives to ensure the poor are not left until last?
- What provision is made for the re-employment of municipal workers?
- What are the terms and conditions of their employment in the private sector?
- Is there an exclusivity clause restricting the role of informal service providers (ISPs)? What provision is made for those currently involved in service provision? What compensation will existing service providers receive if their assets are expropriated?
- How does the arrangement incorporate or build on these assets? What supporting tasks are needed from the municipality (e.g., promotion of registration and licenses)?
- What provision is made in the contract for improving awareness of service systems and institutions?
- What provision is made for community capacity building? Who will be responsible for working with communities? What provision is made for a skilled interface to be established with poor communities?
- What is the role of the NGOs in working with communities? How are they to be contracted? How will they be established as equal partners?
- How will efficiency gains be made (e.g., addressing leakages and illegal connections)? What provision is made to address impacts on the poor households affected by these changes? Are performance targets framed to ensure they do not provide incentives for the operator to reduce access to services by the poor?
- Is the tender evaluation weighted in favour of those operators that bring more immediate benefit to the poor (through tariff levels, coverage targets, proposed partners)?
- What provision is made for transfer of skills and technology?
- How does the management of risk impact upon the poor?

'Affermage', a term which originated in France and was brought into the market by the large French water operators, is similar to a lease, in that the operator bears the cost of running the business (or service network) and typically bears the commercial risk by having the responsibility for revenue collection. However, this is not always the case and municipalities should be aware that there are many situations where an operator is expected to provide investment but is not given the responsibility for the customer interface. While it can be argued that the two are inextricably linked, in practice municipalities often choose to separate them, much to the detriment of the arrangement. The important issue is not the name given to the contract but the implications of such decision-making. The experience in South Africa is that small municipalities have been reluctant to hand over the customer management function, and this has had significant impact on the operator's efficiency.

☐ Strengths and weaknesses

There are a number of strengths of a lease arrangement, suited particularly to contexts where there is no need to access private channels for capital investment. A key strength can be that the lease – unlike the management contract – forces the municipality to commit to a cost recovery tariff structure. The combined responsibility for tariff collection and effective operation provides the operator with powerful incentives to ensure that revenue is improved (i.e., metering and billing is improved and tariffs are collected) and operating costs are minimised (i.e., unaccounted-for water is reduced and efficiencies introduced).

The lease provides no incentives, however, for a revision to the tariff regime or for the reform of municipal management practice. The World Bank views the primary weakness of the lease/affermage contract as the split responsibility noted above – the responsibilities for operation and maintenance are conferred on one party, while responsibility for investments lies with the municipality. Yet these are often difficult to distinguish.[8] This leads to difficulties in coordinating investment decisions and operating needs, causing both the municipality and the lessee to blame each other for difficulties arising. Illustrations of the types of disputes arising are provided in Box 9.6.

Because the municipality retains responsibility for investment in capital works, budgetary constraints can lead to deterioration in the quality of the infrastructure, hindering the performance of the operator and, possibly, its ability to collect user fees. To guard against this situation, the lessee operator might seek a minimum revenue guarantee from the municipality. While such a guarantee reduces the incentives to perform efficiently, it exerts pressure on the authority to adopt adequate investment and tariff policies.

Franchises

☐ Key characteristics

Under franchise contracts, the municipality grants a private firm an exclusive right to provide a specific type of service within a specific area. Often used in solid waste, the franchise is similar to the lease but instead of leasing facilities and infrastructure, the operator is only given the right to deliver a service. This is often confined to a specified zone and constitutes a zonal monopoly for a fixed period of time.

As with a lease, the operator pays the municipality for the franchise. The revenues for making such payments are generated by collecting the fees from customers in the specified zone or by selling materials (such as solid waste by-products) removed from the zone. The operator thus bears the commercial risk of non-payment. Government still retains overall responsibility and accountability to the public under the franchise contract. The municipality is responsible for

8

Box 8.8   A Water Concession
Córdoba, Argentina

Links to Boxes
6.16, 10.7

In April 1997, the Provincial Government of Córdoba signed a 30-year concession contract with Aguas Cordobesas for the provision of water supply and sanitation services within the 24 square kilometre jurisdiction of the municipality of Córdoba. The contract came into force in May 1997. Aguas Cordobesas has a paid-up capital of US$30 million, and is owned by a consortium of Argentinian and foreign companies, in which the French utility multinational Suez-Lyonnaise des Eaux (now Ondeo) is the largest shareholder. In October 1998, Suez Lyonnaise des Eaux bought Sociedad Comercial del Plata's share in Aguas Cordobesas, thereby enabling it and its subsidiary, Aguas de Barcelona, to take a controlling interest in the company. In turn, Suez-Lyonnaise des Eaux is the technical operator of Aguas Cordobesas.

The concession contract stipulated that Aguas Cordobesas would operate and maintain the 2766km pipe network in the municipality, and that water coverage of 97% would be reached by the end of the concession (2026). In addition, the company would pay royalties to the provincial government for water abstraction (US$0.019/m^3) and for water transportation (US$0.077/m^3) as well as reduce the average tariff by 8.2% at the start of the concession. The contract also required that Aguas Cordobesas undertake an investment programme of US$150 million in the first two years

The total investment programme required in order to reach the coverage target has been estimated at around US$500 million. From 1997 to 1999, Aguas Cordobesas carried out investments worth US$84 million. A substantial part of this investment programme was financed by a US$40 million loan from the European Investment Bank (EIB). This was the first EIB loan to a private sector project in Argentina located outside Buenos Aires. The 10-year loan, inclusive of a three-year grace period, bears an EIB floating rate capped at LIBOR* plus 15 basic points. The loan represented 47% of the first five-year investment programme of Aguas Cordobesas.

The overall performance of the concessionaire to date is generally perceived as satisfactory by citizens and the provincial government. In the two years to March 1999, the number of inhabitants covered by the network increased from 1,000,000 to 1,140,000. In 1999 Aguas Cordobesas distributed 140m^3 of water. The number of connections rose from 208,526 in 1997 to 223,462 in 1999. By mid-2000 service coverage for water had reached 87%, compared with only 40% for sewerage. In addition, annual gross income in 1999 was US$65 million with net profit approximately 11% more than in 1998. Furthermore, Aguas Cordobesas had provided three direct benefits to consumers since the contract was signed in 1997: the 8% price reduction in average tariffs, an end to water cut-offs, and improved water quality leading to a sharp drop in sales of bottled water. There is a further indirect benefit in the form of the annual US$13 million royalty payment to the provincial government.

Despite this favourable performance to date, two issues could have a potentially negative effect in the future. First, there is the question of policy towards supply cut-offs. To date Aguas Cordobesas has not cut supply to customers who have defaulted on their water bills. However, in February 2000, the company began legal proceedings in order to obtain debts totalling US$2 million from 2500 customers, equivalent to 1.1% of the total number of customers, who have refused to pay their bills ever since the company was awarded the concession in 1997. There is little evidence that these debts are linked to problems of ability to pay among low-income residents. Rather they are the consequence of a long-standing and widespread practice of non-payment of utility bills across the social spectrum.

Second, there is the question of the sequencing of the investment programme. Under the terms of the contract, Aguas Cordobesas must achieve 97% coverage by 2026. The total investment required to meet this target has been estimated at between US$400 million and US$650 million. In contrast to the concession contract for Buenos Aires, the Córdoba contract does not specify five-yearly coverage targets within the framework of the total period of the overall concession. For this reason, there is the risk of 'backloading', whereby the concessionaire postpones major investment until the end of the concession period. In this eventuality, citizens of low-income neighbourhoods are likely to be the main stakeholders to suffer from delays in connection to the network.

* London Inter-Bank Offered Rate – a widely monitored international interest rate indicator

Source: Nickson, 2001b

setting performance standards, ensuring a competitive bidding process is established, letting the contracts and ensuring the performance of the firm through adequate monitoring of performance standards.

Although it does exist, the franchise arrangement is not common for primary collection in middle-high-income countries as it is too hard for an operator to collect solid waste fees and cover the costs to the municipality (In some variations, municipalities keen to facilitate collection services authorise an operator to undertake the collection with the understanding that they will not allow other firms to compete.) The franchise is sometimes the preferred method of privatising solid waste collection in low-income countries that have very constrained government revenues.[9]

Strengths and weaknesses

While it can be difficult for solid waste operators to collect user fees, in some countries where there is little confidence in government, there may be more confidence in paying the fee to the private sector than to the municipality, and residents may prefer the franchise method for collection services.[10] Franchisees have sufficient incentive to meet the requirements of their customers or they simply will not pay, hence evidence suggests that operators are usually responsive to demand. However, because a franchisee has a zonal monopoly, households have limited bargaining power with the franchisee and little influence over the quality of the service.

Concessions

Key characteristics

In a concession contract, the municipality turns over full responsibility for the delivery of services in a specified area to the partnership concessionaire, including all related construction, operation, maintenance, collection and management activities. The concessionaire is responsible for any capital investments required to build, upgrade or expand the system and for financing those investments. The public sector is responsible for establishing performance standards and ensuring that the concessionaire meets them. The additional responsibility to fund capital investments distinguishes it from a lease.

In a concession, the public sector must take on responsibility for the regulation of price and quantity. Such regulation is particularly critical in the water sector, given the argument that water has the qualities of a public good and piped delivery systems are natural monopolies. The fixed infrastructure assets are entrusted to the concessionaire for the duration of the contract but they remain government property. Concessions are usually awarded for time periods of over 25 years. The duration depends on the contract requirements and the time needed for the private concessionaire to recover its costs and profit.

Over the life of a concession contract, the private sector manager is responsible for all capital and operating costs, including infrastructure, energy, raw materials and repairs. In return, the private operator collects the tariff directly from the system users. The tariff level is typically established by the concession contract, which also includes provisions on how it may be changed over time. Tariffs may also be set under national, provincial or local legislation and regulation (see discussion in Chapter 10).

Structuring the tariff and the accompanying regulatory system is often the most complicated part of any concession arrangement. Tariffs need to be high enough to allow the operator to make a profit if it performs well, but not so high that the profits are excessive, causing a political backlash. The two most widely used approaches are the price cap and rate of return models. Under a price cap approach (the basis for the British regulatory structure), water prices are set for a number of years.[11] If the water operator achieves higher than expected efficiencies, and lower costs, it can keep the savings as profit until the next periodic price review. Under the rate of return approach (widely applied in the US), an

8

Box **8.9**   A Small Concession
Queenstown, South Africa

Queenstown in South Africa (population 200,000) first adopted a partnership arrangement for the delivery of water and sanitation services in 1992 prior to the democratic elections. In the apartheid context, the obligation of the Queenstown council at that time was limited to distribution functions in the 'white' town and bulk water supply in the outlying townships. A 25-year concession contract was established with a consortium (now WSSA – a consortium including Ondeo-Lyonnaise des Eaux and the South African national construction company Group 5). The operator services include water purification and distribution and sewerage services, but notably excluded consumer management.

After its election in 1995, the Queenstown Transitional Local Council was faced not only with a town split along ethnic lines, but also a public/private division in the delivery of water and sanitation services. The incoming council was not enamoured with the private arrangement it had inherited, but the duration of the contract, the perceived penalties for withdrawing, and the case made by the administrative officials and the operator, swayed the decision and, after a six-month interim agreement, and following a public consultation process, the council agreed to an amendment to the concession to extend coverage to include the three township areas.

A universal service standard was applied across the city. The contract obligations were changed both in terms of area and scope, to include:

- the operation and management of the bulk water and sewerage treatment facilities, water and sewerage distribution and collection from the pump stations to each house;
- the water and sewer network including connections and water meters;
- the repair and replacement of the system assets on a regular basis;
- funding and constructing an expanded sewage treatment plant;
- an accelerated programme of rehabilitation and upgrade of existing supply services to the underserviced areas; and
- a 24-hour standby emergency service and a 24-hour complaints line.

Meter reading, billing and revenue collection, however, remained the responsibility of the council. Under South African law in 1992, the billing and collection function was a municipal obligation and there was thus no provision for its delegation. While this legislation is no longer in place, the Queenstown council has stalled the transfer of this function for political and institutional reasons (and fears over its marginalisation from the service delivery process), and thus retains responsibility for customer management. Customers receive one amalgamated service bill covering water, sanitation and solid waste. WSSA has provided support to computerise the accounts.

The council is responsible for setting the tariff, which covers operating and capital costs, and is reviewed on an annual basis. The level of cost recovery is poor. Between 1997–99, R34 million (US$5 million) was accrued. The current estimated cost recovery in low-income areas is approximately 55%.

WSSA are paid a composite fee based on:

1. a fixed charge to cover the costs of the service (approximately 60%);
2. a performance-related fee measured against performance indicators;
3. a variable charge based on the water sold at the meter at R2.13/kl (US$0.30/kl); and
4. a supplementary charge for drawing water from a different source.

The compensation system provides WSSA with some incentives to reduce unaccounted-for water (which was 45%, and is now 21%). However, due to the fee arrangement, the municipality has also benefited substantially. Real costs have *declined* by approximately 20%.

Over the concession period it is expected that WSSA will invest R30 million (US$4.2 million). To date, capital investment has totalled R10 million (US$1.32 million). The capital investment is for the annual replacement of an agreed number of water meters and water-pipe networks, and routine replacement of electromechanical equipment. It also included the expansion of the wastewater treatment works at the commencement of the contract. All assets remain in the ownership of the municipality.

A number of reasons seem to explain the poor cost recovery. Due to the awkward agreement whereby the municipality carries out the customer management function – and does so inadequately – the increases in efficiency achieved by the operator are not being passed on to the consumer but are being accumulated by the municipality. The relatively high tariff in the province is a result of the poor cost recovery. The municipality must pay the operator fees from the tariffs collected from a minority of users. This is a vicious circle. High tariffs and poor customer management lead to higher tariffs and less cost recovery.

Sources: Plummer, 2000c; DBSA, 2000; information provided by WSSA

allowable level of profit (in the range of 6 to 12 per cent) is determined, and the operator is allowed to charge rates that result in that level of profit over its costs.[12]

In both approaches to setting tariffs, the key battles are over information. Does the regulator have enough information to make informed judgements as to the actual state of the concessionaire's finances during the concession period? Is the private operator meeting the performance standards and are the customers well served? Managing information flow among the concessionaire, the users and the regulators is one of the key challenges facing concession arrangements.

The financing for concession investments typically involves a combination of money from the private partners and international commercial banks (see Box 7.11 describing the financing arrangements for the Buenos Aires concession). Moving from guaranteed payments by governments to anticipated revenues from users increases the commercial risks to the private sector partner. This is particularly true for currency risks, as the revenues are in local currencies, while the debt payments for capital investments often need to be made in foreign currencies.

Like the application of the affermage/lease model, in practice municipalities can opt for, and operators accept, a range of variations on the basic elements of the concession. In particular, a municipality may wish to delegate the business, but may not wish to delegate the customer interface immediately, leading to a phased arrangement in which the municipality continues with the revenue collection function. Municipalities must understand the ramifications of these decisions, especially in terms of the changed incentive structure and overall efficiency that the operator can achieve.

☐ Strengths and weaknesses

Among the strengths of concessions is their ability to bring private money into the construction of new service systems or the substantial renovation of existing systems. Combining the responsibility for investment and operation gives the concessionaire strong incentives to make efficient investment decisions and to develop innovative technological solutions, since any gains in efficiency will usually increase profits. In some countries, concessions have been successful in improving water services and reducing water charges. Concession operations are also less prone to political interference than government-operated utility services, because the service stays under the same operator regardless of changes in governments.

Among their weaknesses is the fact that large-scale concessions can be politically controversial and difficult/expensive to organise. In particular, concessions often suffer from a failure to undertake sufficient dialogue and joint planning with affected parties (users, employees) prior to entering into long-term contractual commitments. Although concession contracts specify performance targets, price adjustment mechanisms and service standards, government oversight of the concessionaire's performance against those standards is critical. This often requires governments to significantly expand their regulatory capacity.

In addition, it is difficult to set fixed bidding and contractual frameworks for concessions that are to last for 25 years or more. No one can predict in advance – with the level of certainty applied in traditional public sector bid specifications – the most efficient and effective ways to provide the desired service over that period of time.[13] A number of methods for combining predictability and flexibility are being explored, such as having the bidders offer a total amount of investment that they are willing to make based upon a specified service fee – without specifying how the total investment will be allocated; or including contract terms that set the framework for agreeing revisions to capital investment programs and tariffs at specified intervals throughout the contract period.

Box 8.10   BOT Water-treatment Project
Izmit, Turkey

The 15-year, US$933 million build-operate-transfer (BOT) water project in Izmit, Turkey, was the country's first BOT water treatment project and one of the first BOT water projects in the world. The large size and long (36-month) construction period required multi-sourcing of finance to spread the risk. Export credit agencies (ECAs) participated in the transaction to help cover political and commercial risks. The municipal government was an equity holder in the project company.

Originally conceived in 1968 as a publicly financed, design-build 'turnkey' contract, the project faced many hurdles, including an absence of available public finance. The biggest obstacle to private investment in the project was the absence of a law that gave private operators the right to develop such BOT projects. This problem was finally remedied in 1995 when the Turkish Treasury developed a model financial structure to encourage private investment in infrastructure projects. The original design-build contract was awarded to a British company that was subsequently acquired by Thames Water in 1989. Chase Bank was appointed the government's financial advisor in 1990. Thames Water's ownership of the project was formalised in August 1995, when it signed an implementation agreement with the Turkish government for a 15-year operating contract covering Izmit's domestic and industrial water supply.

The primary components of the project were:

- completion of the Yuvacik dam (started in 1987);
- construction of a water-treatment plant with a capacity of 480,000m^3/day, two pumping stations and a 142km water pipeline to provide potable water to the city's domestic customers and untreated raw water to the city's industrial zone in the east;
- laying of a water distribution system in Izmit; and
- construction of more than 100km of trunk lines between Izmit and Istanbul that would supply 37 million gallons/day to Iski, the Istanbul water authority.

An implementation and water sales agreement governed the relationship between the project company and the municipality of Izmit by establishing the selling price and the payment conditions. Under the agreement, the contractor delivered water to the municipality on the basis of a take-or-pay agreement that obligated the city of Izmit to pay for a minimum of 300,000m^3/day (whether any water was taken or not) and a maximum of 480,000m^3/day. The agreement thereby set an annual price that guaranteed the coverage of costs such as debt service, operation and maintenance, taxes and a minimum return to investors. Repayments to the project company were in US dollars, thus mitigating the currency risk, while Turkey itself was the ultimate guarantor of the city's payment obligations.

To mitigate the construction risk, the project company was required to ensure that the construction contract was turnkey, lump sum, fixed price and without escalation, and that the liability of the construction contractor was joint and several. Thames Water had unlimited obligations to guarantee timely construction and thus faced significant penalties for not meeting the construction schedule. Undertakings by the municipality included securing rights of way, providing works and services, and arranging the subordinated loans to fund force majeure incidents, municipal default and increases in the project's costs as a result of changes in the scope of work or legal requirements. In order to secure the consortium's commitment to the project, shareholders could not sell their shares without the approval of the municipality.

Default or termination of the agreement could be activated by municipality payment default, force majeure or company default. In each instance, the municipality was required to buy out the shareholders' interest and assume all obligations to senior lenders. The buyout price allowed for the recovery of accumulated equity return (from the escrow, or bond, account in which the municipality deposited monthly revenues), legal reserves for dividends, and the nominal value of paid-in-equity minus any shareholder liabilities (such as unsatisfied claims, direct damages and deficits in working capital). The structure of the agreement thus allocates construction and operations risks to the parties that are in the best position to mitigate those risks.

The municipality's equity participation not only provided a clear signal of the city's commitment, but also provided it with the opportunity to share in the project's financial returns.

Source: Haarmeyer and Mody, 1997

Some also argue that the benefits of open competition are limited in the concession market since only a small number of large, international companies are usually able to meet the pre-qualification criteria for bidding to run a concession. In addition, concessions essentially create a monopoly, which then protects the concessionaire from most forms of competition during contract renegotiation. Comparing the performance of the concessionaire to service providers in other locations by collecting and publicising information on levels of service (see discussion in Chapter 7) is one way to address such issues.

Build–Operate–Transfer Contracts

☐ Key characteristics

Build–operate–transfer (BOT) contracts (and the variants such as DBOT, BoTT) are generally designed to bring private capital into the construction of new treatment plants or equipment. Typically, under a BOT, the private firm finances, builds and operates a new plant or network for a set period of time according to performance standards set by the government. The operations period is long enough to allow the private company to pay off the construction costs and realise a profit – typically 10 to 20 years. The government retains ownership of the infrastructure facilities and becomes both the customer and the regulator of the service.

Under BOTs, the private sector provides the capital to build the new facilities. In return, the government agrees to purchase a minimum level of output over time, regardless of the demand from the ultimate consumers. Having the government bear the commercial risk is what distinguishes BOTs from concessions. The purpose is to help ensure that the private operator can recover its costs over the contract period. This requires the government to estimate demand with some accuracy at the time the contract is set. Otherwise, it will have to pay for services that are not being used, even if demand is less than expected. The scale and timeframes associated with BOTs require the development of sophisticated and often complicated financing packages. Frequently, these involve substantial infusions of money directly from the private project developers (in the range of 10 to 30 per cent), combined with money from third parties, usually international commercial banks. The possibility of using bonds to tap the international capital markets is also attracting increasing interest.

BOTs tend to work well for new facilities that require substantial financing. Governments generally issue BOT contracts for the construction of specific infrastructure facilities, such as bulk supply reservoirs and drinking water or wastewater treatment plants (see, for instance, the water treatment project in Izmit, Turkey, described in Box 8.10). While BOTs typically involve the construction and operation of just one facility and not entire delivery systems, the variations among BOT type contracts are extensive and in South Africa the BoTT (build–operate–train–transfer) contract is the primary vehicle adopted by the government of South Africa to rapidly improve water and sanitation services in underserviced rural and peri-urban areas of the country. One of the operators (a subsidiary of Northumbrian-Lyonnaise), stresses that the consortium arrangement developed for the projects (serving 2.2 million people) is a promising entry strategy for Lyonnaise-Ondeo in an otherwise high-risk investment environment.

☐ Strengths and weaknesses

The strengths of BOTs include their ability to bring private money into the construction of new facilities or the substantial renovation of existing ones. BOT agreements also tend to reduce market and credit risks for the private investors because the government is the only customer, reducing the risks associated with insufficient demand and ability to pay. Private investors will avoid BOT arrangements where the government is unwilling to provide adequate assurances that the private sector investment will be paid back. As the BOT model has been used to build new power plants in many developing countries, potential financial partners and operators have less of a learning curve in structuring such transactions in the water and waste sectors.

Among the weaknesses of a typical BOT is the fact that it generally involves just one facility or a number of facilities, and thus restricts the partnership's ability to help optimise system-wide resources or efficiencies (notwithstanding the variations described above). BOTs can, however, provide a platform for increasing local capacity to operate infrastructure facilities by exposing local employees to international practices. BOTs provide some competitive incentives for efficiency, since private companies must compete on technical and financial terms to win the contracts. However, the duration and complexity of BOT arrangements make these contracts difficult to design, a fact that may eventually undermine the positive effects of the initial competition. For example, many BOTs have to be renegotiated to reflect changed circumstances once they are under way. These negotiations are then essentially conducted in the absence of competition.

Distinguishing between Operators and Investors

Whatever contractual type is used to introduce substantial private investment (concession, BOT, joint venture), it is critical to recognise that the technical and managerial skills needed to provide urban services are not found in the same firms that provide large amounts of investment capital, although many governments seek them as a package. For example, even the largest international water companies (such as Ondeo, Vivendi or Thames Water) have to go to international commercial banks and other financial institutions to fund their capital investment obligations under BOT or concession contracts.

This split between operating and financing skills has two major implications. First, it introduces yet another party into the partnership arrangement – one whose needs also have to be met. While urban services partnerships are usually negotiated first with the private operator, the lenders and other investors often require changes in the arrangement in exchange for their money. Second, if the municipality has the capacity to package the operating and financing skills itself, it may be able to arrange a more cost effective partnership by separating the two functions – for example, by pairing one or more local operators (including community groups) with a combination of local and international sources of investment capital (including public and not-for-profit sources).

Transaction Costs

The cost of procuring private sector participation projects in the water and sanitation sector is significant, especially if it entails international service providers or financiers. It is therefore necessary to identify (as far as possible) and effectively manage the so-called transaction costs – those costs incurred through planning and preparation of the project until financial and contractual closure.[14]

On the municipality's side, there are costs associated with professional advisors and with the time of its own officials. For a typical international concession, the consultancy costs alone will be upwards of US$1 million, and can reach many times that figure. The types of advisory services needed in any contract are substantial and those in a larger initiative can be overwhelming. Among the major costs are those incurred for:

- feasibility studies (financial models and options, appropriate levels of services and service options and consumer profiles);
- hiring of legal advisors (many complex issues can only be dealt with by specialised legal advisors);
- consultants to assist with procurement and contracting procedures and to support the municipality in its liaison with the private and other stakeholders.

Box 6.22 illustrates the scope of advisory services utilised for the preparation of the Johannesburg management contract. This included, for instance, the engagement of 16 separate specialist consultancy firms to provide legal, financial, engineering, communications and human resource and IT expertise. Part of the transaction cost can be recovered through a success fee, payable by the successful bidder upon closure of the contract, and in some cases, municipalities manage to get assistance from external agencies.

On the bidder's side, the cost of putting together a bid for a concession or lease will be a similar amount. Even bids for management contracts, such as the one used in Johannesburg, can cost upwards of US$400,000, with some bidders spending considerably more. With so much at stake it is imperative that the procurement process should meet the highest international standards.[15]

Municipalities can attempt to contain these costs by:

- reducing the bureaucracy of the process by simplifying decision-making and granting negotiators authority and clear lines of accountability;
- bundling activities together so that costs are shared;
- simplifying specification by stating expected outputs (quality and performance standards);
- ensuring that invitations to tender do not require too much additional (detailed or extraneous) information. (This can be done by making sure that information requirements are well thought out beforehand, and by providing a format that makes it easy to compare the information received from different bidders);
- inducing awareness of cost management among municipal staff;
- expediting access for new suppliers to staff and premises; and
- ensuring that contracts are flexible to reduce time spent on discussing contract variations.

The sheer cost of establishing a PPP is thus a key concern for municipalities, and finding the funding to facilitate this process should be an early task for a designated team or individual within the municipality. Keeping transaction costs down is often a determining parameter affecting the final outcome and long-term benefit of the arrangement.

Contract Enforcement

All private firms will seek fair enforcement mechanisms in the partnership arrangement. Foreign firms in particular will be concerned that they will not be treated fairly or in a timely fashion in local regulatory proceedings or court actions. As such, they will push to have any disputes heard by an international arbitrator. On the other hand, municipalities will seek to have local enforcement mechanisms apply. How the negotiations will proceed will vary, often with the level of capital investment the municipality is seeking from the private firm; the higher the amount of capital to be invested by foreign-owned private firms, the greater the likelihood of international arbitration.

Municipalities need to be willing to hold their partners to their obligations if the partnership arrangement is going to increase the efficiency and cost effectiveness of service delivery. For large-scale partnerships involving the international private sector, the arrangement will include a framework of legal and contractual requirements – for performance, for fees, for reporting. If the government is not willing to force the private firm to meet its commitments, its incentives to do so will be severely reduced, if not destroyed. The partners need to know that if they do not meet their obligations, effective enforcement will follow. Not surprisingly, negotiations over enforcement mechanisms will be particularly important to private partners, particularly those from other countries.

Typical enforcement arrangements include:

- information gathering, such as reporting by the private partner, complaints by users and inspections by the municipality;
- hearings, such as by regulatory bodies (increasingly including user representatives), courts or international arbitrators; and
- penalties, such as liquidated damages under the contract (amounts due if the contract requirements are not met), fines under local law or termination of the partnership arrangement.

Contracting Small-scale Providers and Micro-enterprises

The informality of many small-scale providers presents a significant concern for municipalities that decide to either work with these existing suppliers or to integrate their competencies into a new partnership arrangement. The nature and characteristics of small-scale independent providers (SSIPs) and informal service providers, and their potential roles in future service delivery partnerships, have been discussed in Chapter 6. Yet the complexities and constraints of engaging them in a partnership may seem insurmountable, even with a significant degree of attitudinal change.

In principle, SSIPs can be contracted through the same mechanisms as the formal private sector and many have service (or management) contracts and franchise contracts with municipalities. But in order for a micro- or small-scale provider to be paid by a municipality, it will be necessary for it to have a legal agreement or contract – and in order to enter into a legal agreement the municipality will need to know the contractors/operator has the correct legal status. This will normally require it to register as a business (see illustrative material in Boxes 6.8, 6.9 and 10.10).

Registration can be difficult, or it can be simplified by the development of supporting initiatives that encourage the process and assist individuals and small-scale entrepreneurs. Normally the bureaucracy can overwhelm and block entry for otherwise willing entrepreneurs. It is likely, for instance, that registration will require:

- a fee to be paid – this can act as a constraint unless credit mechanisms are established to facilitate payment;
- some form of legal assistance – the documentation itself may be overly daunting for an illiterate or semi-literate tanker driver; and
- some form of accounting/financial management assistance – to manage reporting and taxation matters.

While registration is probably required to ensure the municipality (or other contracting party) is acting legally, it also enables more effective monitoring and compliance with:

- environmental regulations (e.g., water quality, dumping, hazardous waste, pollution control);
- labour laws (e.g., work conditions, health and safety or child labour); and
- taxation (e.g., income tax, vehicle tax).

A number of studies in relation to water, sanitation and solid waste informal sector providers detail the problems, lessons and potential solutions of municipalities engaging with the informal and small-scale private sector.[16] Municipalities are encouraged to familiarise themselves with this information to the same degree as the information on formal private sector transactions.

Contracting NGOs

☐ Institutional arrangements with NGOs

Chapter 6 has provided a description of the nature and characteristics, and the potential roles of non-governmental/non-private stakeholders potentially involved in a partnership. Among other potential difficulties it has drawn attention to the manner in which relationships are formalised with NGOs, i.e. the organisational, contractual and financial mechanisms employed to engage them in a service delivery partnership.

It may seem obvious to some, but it should be reiterated that if a large-scale PPP envisages a central role for an NGO then the procurement process should be similar to the process of procuring the for-profit private sector partner. Tendering, compliance with bids and transparent evaluation and selection processes are essential. Like the private sector, the NGO sector is comprised of organisations with vastly different capacities. Many are bona fide, well staffed and competent in pursuing their mandate; others are not. Municipalities are likely to be aware of local NGOs but should always check their legal status and capacity to enter into contracts. In smaller ventures, perhaps at community level, smaller NGOs may be willing and appropriately skilled, and the procurement of their services through a contract may be less critical.

Evidence suggests that there are six potential organisational models for bringing NGOs into the partnership (illustrated in Box 8.11). These models can be combined to involve more than one function or organisation, and can be part of a fluid process where the nature of the organisational arrangement changes as the partnership goals and relationships mature. The appropriateness of these will depend on the service being discussed and the objectives of the partnership. While some are clearly not useful to large-scale water and sanitation improvements, they should not be discounted altogether from the delivery of less ambitious tertiary-level water supply, sanitation or solid waste collection. The key characteristics and strengths and weaknesses of these arrangements are discussed below.

☐ No contractual agreement

In the first model (see Box 8.11 (a)), the NGO acts as a provider of services to communities without any formal relationship being established between it and the municipality or private partner. In this type of situation, an NGO may have already, independently, become established in a community, and a municipal–private partnership may operate quite separately in the sector. The NGO activities would therefore function alongside the larger-scale city-wide activities of the PPPs. Relationships may be developed between the private sector (or the municipality) and the NGO, but they will be at the discretion of the various stakeholders. They are not obligatory. The NGO may not have any formal relationship with a community either, but if it is an established part of a support system, it may have established substantial commitment and an advocacy role. The community may ask, and expect, the NGO to represent their interests and advise them in a range of matters. This would typically include discussions with actors about service improvements and cost recovery.

The relationship may have no formal contractual status and involve no financial remuneration for the NGO. It is often of an indefinite duration, an ongoing commitment at the discretion of the NGO. There are no formal obligations on the private firm to listen to the advice of an NGO, and it can be easily by-passed. However, while the relationship may be informal, an important role is still performed and the NGO remains independent. It is able to act on its own and the community's behalf, and is not compromised or placed in conflicting roles.

8

Box **8.11**   **Contracting NGOs**
Organisational Models

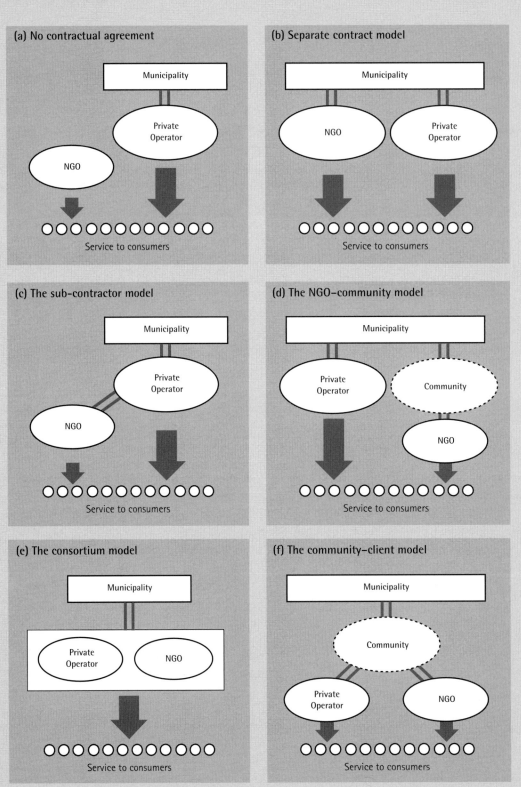

(a) No contractual agreement

(b) Separate contract model

(c) The sub-contractor model

(d) The NGO–community model

(e) The consortium model

(f) The community–client model

☐   A separate contract

A second model (see Box 8.11(b)) creates a contractual relationship between the NGO and the municipality but retains a separation between the private sector and the NGO. Like the private sector, the NGO provides a service for some agreed remuneration.

This model is advantageous for certain reasons:

- the NGO is presumably contracted for a payment;
- it has a formal contractual relationship with the municipality-client; and
- it is independent from the private sector, and its role in relationship to the community is not compromised or conflicting.

However, this arrangement can also create significant problems. The municipal–NGO contract arrangement may be significantly smaller than the municipal–private sector contract. The lack of any formal arrangement between the private firm and the NGO means that the NGO can be marginalised at the discretion of the other partners. The degree to which the private firm takes on board the NGO advice is dependent on the municipality, and in particular on the private operator's contractual obligations in relation to the NGO. The NGO is not a partner of the primary (lead) provider, and depending on the NGO role, the private firm can bring its own contractual provisions to bear (e.g., any exclusivity clauses) on the NGO's activities.

Depending on the responsibility a municipality wishes to delegate, the municipal–NGO contract is often a service or a management contract. In some instances it may be a franchise (as is seen with the franchising of toilet blocks in India, and water kiosks in various parts of Africa).

☐   A sub-contract agreement

A third model illustrated in Box 8.11(c) creates a contractual relationship between the private sector and the NGO, quite separately from the municipality. Probably the most straightforward to organise, the NGO acts as one of many sub-contractors (alongside material suppliers or works contractors) for the delivery of an agreed service, mobilising communities or promoting cost recovery to agreed performance targets, for instance.

The private operator pays for and defines the services required from the NGO. The municipality will have included a requirement in the tender for the engagement of an NGO to provide institutional and social development services. Ideally, the NGO has negotiated agreeable terms before agreeing to join the bid, but in practice this is rare, and the NGO often agrees to join without adequate reflection or knowledge of the implications; or the private operator discovers, through the course of its work, that it needs an agent to work with communities to assist them in meeting their obligations, and it approaches an NGO to perform this role.

Evidence suggests that under this model, especially in large-scale water and sanitation arrangements, NGOs often find themselves in an intolerable position. Their core values, mission and mandates to support poor communities are often incompatible with the motives of the actor employing them – the private operator applying pressure for results, the community organisations requiring more capacity building. At its worst, this leaves the community feeling aggrieved over payment and tariff issues and the NGO is seen as the agent of a private firm that is making profits from these payments.

This model does offer the advantage that the NGO is centrally involved in any discussions with the community and it cannot be marginalised or sidelined. This form of contract is typically adopted for an NGO to deliver particular (e.g. institutional and social development) services (see Box 8.12).

8

Links to Boxes
3.5, 5.5, 6.13, 7.2, 7.3, 7.11, 7.18, 9.8

Box **8.12** **Sub-contracted to an International Operator**
Buenos Aires, Argentina

In Buenos Aires, IIED-AL has worked with Aguas Argentinas since 1995. As an NGO committed to improving the urban environment for the poor, it sees the need to continue this collaboration in some form for as long as the poor have inadequate water and sanitation services. Yet despite this commitment, IIED-AL experienced a number of conflicts during the main part of its collaboration. Some of these expose the fundamental differences in the nature of the private sector and the NGO sector (see Box 6.13), and some arise through the nature of the arrangement in Buenos Aires and the particular relationship established between IIED and Aguas Argentinas.

IIED-AL has been engaged in the water and sanitation arrangement with Aguas Argentinas in two distinct ways. In the first instance, its activities in the field working with poor communities to improve the quality of their lives has led to an informal relationship with Aguas Argentinas in two *barrios*: San Jorge and Jorge Hardoy. In these contexts, IIED-AL has helped to facilitate the activities of the operator to increase formalised connections and cost recovery. This includes, for instance, the connection of the San Jorge mini-system to the city network.

In addition to this, IIED-AL has worked formally with Aguas Argentinas in a series of small service contracts in which it has provided social and institutional development expertise to supplement the skills of the operator. Some of the initiatives were relatively unambitious at the outset and developed as the problem became clearer. In each case, an agreement was established based on agreed terms of reference and an agreed lump sum contract. These included:

- **Staff training**   Over a six-month period, IIED was responsible for the training of regional managers on the characteristics, issues and processes involved in service delivery to low-income settlements. On a monthly basis, IIED-AL facilitated learning events such as workshops, site visits and community–leader meetings to familiarise AA staff in issues concerning the poor.
- **Social and environmental diagnosis of the concession area**   Given the lack of reliable data and qualitative understanding of the physical, social and organisational aspects of poor communities, AA contracted IIED-AL to undertake comprehensive social and environmental assessments throughout the shanty towns of Buenos Aires. These assessments provided the foundation for the operator to plan an approach to the prioritisation of water and sanitation upgrading in low-income areas (see Box 7.3), taking account of social and environmental indicators.
- **Environmental impact assessments**   IIED-AL was contracted to undertake environmental impact assessments for proposed facilities, such as the wastewater treatment plant, for government approval.

While the scope of this work generally fits within the competencies and mandate of IIED-AL, the nature of the arrangement whereby it were contracted directly to the private operator created a problematic environment for the effective work of an NGO. While a consultant is willing to prepare a report and leaves it to the client organisation to act on it as they see fit, an NGO working towards poverty reduction objectives has a vested interest in achieving the best outcome for the poor, and is concerned with how the information is ultimately used.

In other situations, an NGO with a dissemination objective needs to be able to disclose the information and knowledge collected; but most importantly, it needs to know that information is not going to be used in a way that brings disadvantage to poor groups or marginalises the poorest households from potential benefits.

IIED-AL has recognised that the lack of a comprehensive pro-poor framework accentuates these conflicts and makes the NGO effort somewhat random and expendable. Without a PPP framework – agreed at the outset – that establishes a non-negotiable foundation for working with the poor, NGOs will battle with the function they can best perform. The underlying conflict is that governments are trying to attract private investment and create incentives for the private sector, but this conflicts at its core with the difficulties, the time and the risk of working in low-income areas.

Source: Developed with IIED-AL

An NGO–community arrangement

The community model illustrated in Box 8.11(d) aims to strengthen the position of the NGO by reinforcing this connection through a contractual arrangement between the community and the NGO. Perhaps the most ideal of the five models, this creates an arrangement where civil society is seen as a single entity (comprising communities, NGOs and other civil society organisations). The key issues to be addressed include how the NGO is mobilised, and how the NGO is compensated for its inputs. Being paid by the private firm compromises and recreates the sub-contractor role; being funded by a donor is helpful and workable but may not be a replicable or sustainable model. Perhaps the only workable solution is that the municipality mobilises the funds and channels these through the community organisation. The CBO then contracts the NGO and acts as the NGO's client.

For the NGO this has the advantage that it can represent the community without external pressure. Its values are not compromised and there are no conflicts of interest. In practice, the weak capacity of community organisations is one of the key reasons for engaging the NGO, and the CBO may not have the capacity to perform this contracting role. In practice, municipalities do not have these funds, and in many cases will be reticent to ascribe this role to a CBO. The arrangement may also create a confrontational, adversarial relationship between the NGO and the private operator, rather than one in which they both striving for a common objective.

A consortium arrangement

The consortium model illustrated in Box 8.11(e) aims to create equal municipal–NGO and municipal–private contractual relationships. In theory, this approach empowers the NGO to have an equal say in the decision-making over the methods, programme and activities undertaken. The consortium approach may be a precondition of the tender, specifying the contractual relationship between the parties (and in all likelihood their roles). The contract type will be the same as that for the whole consortium (e.g., BOT, concession, lease, management or service contracts).

In practice, however, the NGO becomes part of a private entity. Although it has different goals and values, from the perspective of sceptical consumers or other civil society organisations, its contractual relationship implicates it in the goals of the larger entity and it can be associated with the profit orientation of that entity (see Box 8.13). Inevitably, being a smaller (non-funding) party in the consortium – and the one directly looking out for poor communities – its concerns can be ignored or overlooked by the larger group.

Yet there are distinct benefits. By having a place at the table, the NGO may be able to influence the process and decision-making. Like the separate contract model, the status of the NGO is dependent on the initial contractual requirements laid down by the municipal-client and contract; and the ongoing monitoring of these requirements ensure that the NGO is able to perform the role prescribed. In order to make such an arrangement sustainable, it is important for the partners to agree and establish the criteria on which the relationship is based – especially the areas which the NGO deems non-negotiable (e.g., community participation).

The community as client

This contractual model illustrated in Box 8.11(f) places the community at the centre of the process as primary stakeholder and client. However, like the NGO–community model, it requires a mobilised community organisation able to conduct its role in a transparent and accountable way. This type of arrangement is probably limited to a scale commensurate with individual communities, and is similar to that described in Box 8.11(d). The primary advantage of the model is that there is no conflict for the NGO, the contractual link to its client reinforces its primary objectives and does not result in any compromise on its objectives. As the private sector is also located in this relationship, the dominance of the private

8

Links to Boxes
6.11, 6.12, 6.26, 7.21

Box 8.13   Mvula Trust, a Member of a Consortium
South Africa

In 1997, the Mvula Trust, a South African NGO, entered into a private sector consortium for the delivery of sustainable water and sanitation services to the rural and peri-urban poor in the Eastern Cape province of South Africa. The national Department for Water and Affairs and Forestry (DWAF) designed and tendered a BoTT contract for this purpose.

The BoTT was envisaged as a one-stop shop arrangement. Consequently, one of the fundamental requirements of the bid was for the tenderer to provide skilled institutional and development services. The Amanz'abantu consortium, developed by the international operator Lyonnaise des Eaux (now Ondeo) and run through the WSSA office, approached Mvula Trust to provide these services in the consortium. Through the BoTT, the government aimed to establish new organisations as standing resources to implement a stream of projects. By only tendering once for multi-year engagements, the government cut down enormously on its traditional role and sped up the process while maintaining accountability and oversight. As well as increased speed, the BoTT strategy aims to reduce administrative costs for government and gain access to strong management resources.

The BOTTs in South Africa are intended as groups of organisations that collectively have the skills and resources to develop sustainable water systems. Under enormous time pressure and looking towards the fundamental objective of providing services to the poor in a rapid delivery process, the Mvula Trust agreed to join the consortium prior to the tender submission. As a well-established and respected NGO in the water and sanitation sector in South Africa (and given its previous links to DWAF), it can be argued that its presence was a key factor in the strength of the Amanz'abantu proposal. However, at this time Mvula was not in a position to see the potential drawbacks of the consortium or envisage the problems to come. It established its place at the partnership table, but did not negotiate any conditions of collaboration.

The Amanz'abantu consortium includes five original signatories: an international water operator, a construction company, design consultant and a national water resource consultant, plus the Mvula Trust. Three additional partners have joined since to provide various technical services.

There are four different levels of contracting partnerships with the private sector: the programme or provincial level (Amanz'abantu); the design level with technical consultants (Ninham Shand and FST); the construction levels with contractors (Group 5); and the operations and maintenance level (WSSA). All contract relationships follow the consortium model.

For the NGO, the clear advantage of the consortium approach to contracting the services of an NGO has been that:

- Mvula Trust has a place at the partnership table, and has been able to influence decision-making;
- Mvula has worked well with WSSA on the development of a sustainable operations and maintenance package;
- despite difficulties, the importance of the social and institutional development aspects of service delivery has become mainstreamed; and
- Mvula has been a party to far more information than it would have had access to if it had remained outside the entity.

However despite these benefits, the relationship has been fraught with difficulties. Mvula suggests that this could have been avoided by better planning and partnering at the outset, when relationships were being formed and precedents set. But in practice, the need to work quickly in the preparation of a bid led to partnerships being formed, and when the proposal was selected as the successful tender, commitments had to be met. For the NGO, some of the key problems arising from the consortium contracting model have been:

- the reputation of Mvula has been threatened by its closeness to the other private sector partners;
- the independence that the community expects of an NGO has been compromised by its contractual relationship; and
- Mvula has at times felt that it has been unable to represent the community effectively, and is unable to carry out its institutional and social development role effectively because of the pressure that can be exerted on it by the consortium.

Source: Interview with Jamie de Jager, Mvula Trust, March 2001

partner is kept in check by the community client. This could place the private partner at some risk in situations where the community organisation does not behave as per the agreement.

A final note on contracts

Establishing the organisational and contractual aspects of a partnership is crucial for implementation. Such aspects provide certainty and a structure for action, but as we have seen in earlier chapters, they do not result in the success of the partnership. The same emphasis needs to be placed on the process of partnering as on contract conditions if partnerships are to become an effective and sustainable means of targeting the poor.

Chapter 9 **Key Questions**

☐ **What are the fundamental principles of partnerships involving the private sector?**

☐ **What do the terms transparency, accountability, specificity, and contestability mean in a service partnership?**

☐ **How can these principles be achieved?**

Developing a Partnership Framework

| Building on the assets of potential partners | Focusing the scope and content of partnership arrangements | Establishing appropriate organisational and contractual arrangements | Establishing sound partnership principles |

Establishing Sound Partnership Principles

Chris Heymans

This chapter discusses the fundamental principles of partnerships involving the large-scale private sector. The discussion links with the preceding chapters that focused on the actors, scope and content, and on organisational and contractual aspects of a partnership framework focused on the poor. It focuses on the basic requirements for establishing sustainable public–private partnerships (PPPs), addressing the principles of transparency, accountability, specificity, legitimacy, flexibility, equity etc., as well as those specifically pertaining to PPPs for the poor.

The Fundamental Principles of Partnerships

A number of fundamental principles underlie the feasibility and sustainability of partnerships involving the private sector. It is particularly important that they are transparent, that the participants are appropriately accountable, that key stakeholders consider them legitimate, and that procurement is fair and competitive. At the same time, private sector participation (PSP) in service delivery must be adaptable and flexible. A major consideration in developing countries is that partnership outcomes are equitable – that poor people should benefit substantially from the shift in approach. Failure to adhere to these principles in the partnership framework is likely to result in a number of negative effects – discouraging investors, costing local governments too much to achieve their objectives, creating a volatile political context, and ultimately undermining the sustainable delivery of services.

The Principle of Transparency

Clear rules, fairness and transparency can ensure an attractive environment for private investors and other potential partners to work with local government in service delivery.[1] For the private sector, coupled with a secure legal environment, transparency ensures the sanctity of contracts and fair treatment for all parties, stimulating interest in partnerships, enhancing competition and reducing costs. For civil society, transparency is a vital aspect of more accountable, democratic and inclusive urban governance. It requires processes to keep stakeholders informed, to curtail corruption and to institutionalise openness and access to information. These facets are discussed below.

☐ Keeping stakeholders informed

Transparency is about inclusive processes that ensure all stakeholders – such as consumers, voters, labour organisations, bidders and the municipality – have proper information about potential impacts, policies, partnership objectives and procurement criteria and processes. It is concerned with awareness building. Quality information enables stakeholders to engage in informed debate about private sector participation options and decision-making, and then helps ensure fair procurement and pricing. This requires that services policies and priorities are well debated and publicised, and delivery options publicly explored. For example, the issue of differential levels of services to make services more affordable for poor people should be raised early and openly so that poor people have a role in decision-making and understand the implications of these partnership decisions. The reporting requirements for partnerships should be regular and appropriately detailed to ensure information sharing. Operating contexts with more democratic and participatory policy requirements have extensive requirements regarding information sharing (about bidders and financial flows) and the consultation of stakeholders. A local government should initiate such requirements in its own right to ensure that policy debates and procurement processes are as open as possible. In Gweru (see Box 9.4) the municipality created a particularly transparent process involving all urban stakeholders for the design of a water and sanitation concession.

9

Links to Boxes
4.4, 6.22, 8.5, 9.3

| Box **9.1** | **Transparent Procurement Processes**
Johannesburg, South Africa

In order to meet the highest international standards, the Greater Johannesburg Metropolitan Council chose a two-stage process for the procurement of the management contractor (operator). The first stage was a request for qualifications (RfQ), the purpose of which was to produce a shortlist of adequately qualified bidders. Applicants were invited to form consortia and submit a response to the RfQ that demonstrated that they met predetermined minimum criteria for financial strength and technical experience. The financial criteria related to turnover in the water and sanitation business, and consistent profitability. The minimum technical experience required revolved around operating water and wastewater systems for populations of over 1 million, and of managing a water-related meter-reading and collection operation serving at least 350,000 connections.

The optimal size for a PSP shortlist will depend on the circumstances of project, the level of appetite among bidders, and the anticipated cost of submitting a bid. A long shortlist can deter good bidders from bidding, while a too-short shortlist reduces competition and can result in bid failure if some of the shortlisted firms decline to bid. For the Johannesburg project, the RfQ criteria were developed with the objective of producing a shortlist in the range of five to seven firms. By setting clear minimum criteria for shortlisting, the RfQ evaluation became a simple and transparent pass/fail process. There was no need to undertake comparative scoring of applicants and little need for the evaluators to exercise subjective judgement. A total of seven applicants applied, met the minimum criteria requirements and were shortlisted.

The shortlist included a *Who's Who* of international water companies. Each shortlisted bidder was led by an international water company, and included one or more local South African partners. Experience has shown that the complexity of managing a large consortium can become a distraction to an operator, and for this reason the RfQ document limited the number of partners in any consortium to a maximum of three. The second stage in the process was the the request for proposals (RfP). RfP documents were issued in June 2000. Five bids were submitted.

The bid evaluation was based on a combined technical and financial score, with 60% of the score being allocated to the technical bid, and 40% to the financial bid. A two-envelope system was used. Technical bids (envelopes) were opened in public on the submission date. Financial bids were stored in a secure environment to be opened after the technical evaluation was complete, and bidders had been informed of their technical scores. The technical score was based on experience (25%), work plan (35%), staffing plans and the CVs of management staff (40%).

It was important to the council that the process was professionally done and demonstrably transparent. This was achieved in a number of ways including:

- Joint oversight of the evaluation by a specially convened Council Adjudication Panel (comprising members of the council) and the Water and Sanitation Advisory Board (comprising members who were mostly not members of the council).
- Using a professional evaluation led by external consultants. The council was concerned that there might be an external perception that its own officials could have a conflict of interest if they were directly involved in scoring the proposals. However, officials were involved extensively in a non-scoring capacity to challenge the findings of the scoring team, and to provide local knowledge.
- The appointment of an external probity auditor to monitor the evaluation at every stage and to report on issues of probity, process and fairness.
- Every stage of the technical evaluation was reviewed and challenged by a third party. Some parts of the bids, such as the CVs of key staff, were scored independently by two evaluators.

The RfP specified a minimum hurdle of 75% for the technical score. Three of the bidders scored more than 75%, and were thus defined as qualifying bidders and progressed to the next stage of the evaluation. Two bidders scored less than 75% and, in accordance with the rules of the RfP, their financial bids were returned to them unopened.

The opening of the three financial bids took place in public in October 2000. The combined scores were calculated in accordance with a formula specified in the RfP. A consortium comprising Northumbrian Water (UK), Lyonnaise des Eaux (France) and WSSA (South Africa) achieved the highest combined technical and financial score and became the preferred bidder. Following successful negotiations in November and December 2000, the consortium formed a local company under the name 'Jowam'. Jowam commenced services under the contract in April 2001. The procurement for the Johannesburg contract took only 15 months from the issuing of the RfQ documents to the signing of the contracts. The reasons for this include political commitment, strong leadership, a flexible and responsive consultancy structure (see Box 6.22), strong interest from local and international companies, and a demonstrably transparent and fair procurement process.

Source: Chris Ricketson, Halcrow Group, Consultants to the Greater Johannesburg Metropolitan Council

☐   Curtailing corruption

Transparency is also about preventing corruption in procurement. Corruption allocates contracts to undeserving bidders at the expense of other bidders and the public, and it obscures the basis of decision-making in the local government. Often it means that resources do not meet their planned targets: everyone suffers, and often the poor in particular.

In the current climate in developing countries, there are many incentives for private sector firms to engage in corruption. They may want to ensure that they are included in the list of bidders, whatever their merits; or they could attempt to influence the bidder specifications to favour them relative to other bidders; or simply attempt to be selected regardless of whether they are the best bidders. It is therefore important to create procedural disincentives for corruption.

☐   Ensuring transparency

Each municipality is encouraged to establish principles and techniques to enhance transparency, appropriate to the local context and trends. Some basic recommendations might include that:

- bidders have access to the same information about a project;
- proposals must comply with some minimum requirements;
- prospective operators are prohibited from soliciting support from anyone involved in awarding the contract;
- collusion with other bidders is prohibited;
- amendments after the award of the contract are prohibited (unless essential due to unforeseen changes in the operating environment); and
- public reporting of amendments, and general reporting throughout the project cycle, should be as open as possible.

In addition, the appointment of external consultants to work with the municipality on the evaluation of bids is often a helpful step because they create confidence in the quality and independence of the process. In Gweru, the involvement of a USAID-funded consultant at various stages, but particularly at tender evaluation, helped to enhance public certainty that the process was legitimate (see Box 9.4). NGOs offer a useful instrument to help monitoring of procurement, tariff-setting and implementation processes. Municipalities could make use of this capacity to assist them in ensuring the ongoing public scrutiny of partnerships.

Often, national legislation or local regulations provide for contractors guilty of corruption, or of tax infringements, to be barred, temporarily or permanently, from future private sector participation or other government contracts. For such an approach to work effectively and fairly, care must be taken to put in place appropriate institutional arrangements (i.e., a body with powers of debarring). It is further important to clearly define in principle what activities may result in debarment, to offer a range of debarment penalties appropriate for different degrees of contravention, and to allow for proper appeal procedures.[2]

The Principle of Competition

Competition among service providers helps to contain costs and ensure good service. It makes it possible for a municipality to test the market and get the best possible deal for its residents. Competition encourages those competing to set lower prices and offer good value for money. This serves as an incentive for the enterprise to become more efficient. As it achieves greater efficiency, the effects on price and quality of service benefits all consumers, including poor people.

Partnerships are only feasible where potential actors exist that are able to provide the required services at acceptable levels of quality and price. If capacity is lacking, or investors are averse to the risks involved, municipalities will fail to

Links to Boxes
5.3, 6.7, 12.5

Box 9.2   Unsolicited Bids
Biratnagar, Nepal

As it evolved, the PPP for solid waste management in Biratnagar, Nepal, has moved from an arrangement that pitted the municipality against an operator that overpowered it, beginning with an unsolicited bid, to an arrangement that favours the municipality excessively, imposing unsustainable costs on the private operator. The problems hold important lessons regarding governance, the management of unsolicited bids, and risk allocation in a partnership arrangement.

The contract for municipal solid waste management in the city was initiated at the instigation of a private company soliciting for the work. No prior attempts had been made to study the problems and needs with respect to solid waste in the city. Without the necessary expertise and without technical support, the Biratnagar Sub-municipal Corporation entered into a 10-year contractual agreement with a US-based company, Americorp Environmental Services, in 1997.

Municipal decision-makers were led to believe that a partnership with the private sector would not only improve the delivery of services within the city but would ultimately result in profits for the municipality itself. No institutional or financial appraisals or willingness-to-pay studies were carried out. No tendering, competition or other mechanisms were introduced to ensure transparency and accountability. There was no consultation process with civil society, the trade unions had little influence over the decision, and the contract was awarded without the inputs of independent technical advisors.

Based on the attractiveness of the proposal, the charisma of the company representative and the written support of the US Embassy, the municipality embarked upon a partnership. The proposal was accepted at face value. As a result little effort was made to confirm the viability of the company through financial checks and assessments of previous work. The municipality did not carry out any studies to test the viability of contract options, nor did it seriously question the validity or feasibility of the technical proposal. Similarly, no institutional or financial appraisals were carried out and no willingness-to-pay surveys were undertaken to test community reaction to the introduction of fees for rubbish collection.

Some progress was achieved in the initial stages, such as the purchase of a landfill site and some equipment, but soon the contractor borrowed widely from people and institutions locally and in Kathmandu. The municipality never knew about this. Then the investors began to realise that loans were not being honoured. In the final event, it was the local banks, through which the loans had been obtained, which exposed the financial incapacity of the company and refused the financing necessary for the project to move forward. The representative and instigator of Americorp fled the country.

A local engineering consultant, SILT, stepped in and assumed responsibility for Americorp (see Box 6.7). It managed to get municipal approval for another attempt at revitalising the partnership, following the high levels of embarrassment that followed the collapse of the previous arrangement.

Now, however, the allocation of risks has become a major problem and continues to threaten the sustainability of the partnership. The contract favours the municipality, and places an unfair risk on the private operator. In short, the risk arrangements are as follows:

- the private contractor assumes all the risk;
- the municipality is eligible for 10% of the profit, but no loss or investment;
- fee collection is the responsibility of the private contractor, the municipality has no liability for non-payment;
- the contractor is responsible for developing its own customer base for door-to-door collection, though the municipality plays some role in facilitating this process; and
- the private contractor undertakes to develop a landfill site and recycling facilities and to make this commercially viable without significant contribution from the municipality.

As a result, the partnership continues to flounder.

The experience of this partnership highlights at least two major contracting issues. The first is the risk of unsolicited procurement. The bidder clearly had an information advantage over the municipality, and by taking the proposal at face value, the municipality entered a contract with a dubious contractor, without any regard to the financial, technical and institutional feasibility of the arrangement.

Second, as far as the current arrangement is concerned, sustainable contracts are reasonable contracts. Contracts must be sensible and reasonable for both parties. Municipalities need to be aware that contracts that favour them, and transfer all risk to the private operator, have little long-term sustainability and are unlikely to lead to benefits to the poor. Municipalities may benefit in the short term, but ultimately – as an agency responsible for municipal service provision – the municipality cannot hope to secure workable arrangements while exploiting the private sector.

Source: Adapted from Plummer and Slater, 2001

procure the services they want from the private sector. Where the range of potential private operators is limited, it is crucial to ascertain whether they would in fact be able to meet the standards required. In the absence of effective competition, many of the presumed benefits of PPPs can become compromised.

There are many facets to creating a competitive environment. Most of these occur, however, at higher levels of government. At a policy and regulatory level, government can define rights and establish laws to make it possible for private parties to engage in PPPs at reasonable costs. Among the obviously important options in this regard are competition laws and enforcement mechanisms, dropping legal barriers to entry, and promoting an appropriate code of conduct for doing business. The latter could be made conducive to competition through ensuring fair and equal access to relevant information and perhaps specific programmes directed at building a market of potential service providers and technical experts. The environment for partnerships must unambiguously discourage and prevent suppliers from conspiring (e.g., through dividing markets or rigging bids). Furthermore, the public sector, at higher levels and within municipalities, should respect commercial freedom and avoid arbitrary intervention.

Where there is a need for regulation, the challenge is to balance controlling mechanisms with the promotion of market dynamics in the longer term. The ultimate aim is to ensure quality services at affordable prices for consumers. To this end, sound regulation entails the use of a variety of approaches and instruments, such as minimum contract requirements, sector-sensitive price or rate-of-return regulations, quality requirements and open entry. It is often necessary to specifically ensure that the interests of poor consumers are well represented in decision-making and monitoring processes, so as to create an incentive to the operator to develop service solutions that reduce prices and help expand service coverage at affordable levels.

The aim is to create opportunities for a wider range of competitors, but also to ensure that they are realistic bidders. Clear output specifications about the scope, duration, asset and service requirements, ownership and management conditions and standards and risk transfers provide important information that makes bidding processes more competitive. By being as up-front as possible about these project dimensions, municipalities can allow bidders to prepare themselves for specific criteria. Throughout, care must be taken to not restrict competition through unequal provision of information.[3]

☐ **Unsolicited bids**

Unsolicited bids can also spark an interest in partnerships. Such bids typically come from private entrepreneurs who offer the municipality some ideas about how services could be provided or expanded through their involvement. This can add useful ideas to the municipality's thinking, and help it to address problems to which it might not have had the answer. However, while unsolicited bids may introduce innovative solutions, they also pose complex questions of principle. The first issue is to ensure that a proposal actually addresses a priority of the council. Policy-makers are often concerned about ill-equipped municipalities being convinced of the desirability of projects by articulate entrepreneurs, without those projects really being important to the council's work. For this reason, any project proposal must ultimately be measured in terms of the normal criteria, and processed through the normal channels of planning and budgeting that apply to all municipal projects.

It is also important that municipalities manage such bids correctly to ensure that they do not compromise the council. The foremost dilemma is how to utilise the innovation and respect intellectual property appropriately, while retaining open, fair and competitive procurement. The design of processes to deal with unsolicited bids is therefore important. In some countries such bids are openly discouraged, but that does not have to be the case. A suitable compromise would be to accept such bids as useful ideas, but to then subject the proposal to the normal tendering process. This might mean that another bidder wins the contract, and it is therefore necessary to compensate the originator of the idea. For this

Box 9.3   **Participation and Public Awareness**
Johannesburg, South Africa

Links to Boxes
4.4, 6.22, 8.5, 9.1

Sparked by financial crisis in 1997, the Greater Johannesburg Metropolitan Council (GJMC) embarked on the Igoli 2002 initiative to undo the causes of the financial crisis, address infrastructure backlogs and essential maintenance needs, and eliminate duplication, inadequate coordination, lack of skills and the absence of a performance management system.

A primary challenge in an elaborate process (detailed in Box 4.4) of restructuring is whether the needs of all stakeholders can be met, and how to consider the right interests for the right reasons and the right services. This has been difficult, and the municipal management has been criticised at times for not sufficiently engaging with all relevant stakeholders. The leadership maintains, in turn, that it has to make certain trade-offs because it is not able to satisfy all the interests all the time. It has also decided to provide a broad strategic plan on the basis of its management assessment of key issues, and has pledged to deal with the specific stakeholders around specific issues as implementation of the plan unfolds.

Balancing these interests has indeed been an arduous task, not the least because of the diversity of interests. To provide structure to the process, the Office of the City Manager focused on principles, general problems and challenges, and the specific aspects of the Igoli 2002 plan. The consultation involved the various political and administrative parts of the metropolitan council, political parties, labour organisations, civic organisations and other community groups, business, national and provincial government departments, and other local governments.

Because of its concerns about employment conditions, the South African Municipal Workers Union (SAMWU) has throughout been considered as a major stakeholder. For this purpose, negotiations built on a national agreement between trade unions, government and local government . But it has also been necessary to discuss specific issues, and in particular to give labour, and individual staff, as much assurance as possible. A promise was made that no retrenchments would take place – a controversial aspect as many observers believed this would nullify the productivity effects of the plan. Relations with SAMWU remain tense, and there have been a number of militant protests. The unions, supported by their national leadership, continue to fight the plan, first because they in principle disapprove of private sector involvement, and second, because they fear that restructuring will threaten their interests and conditions of employment.

Consumers have been an important interest group and ongoing efforts are made to inform them of changes and to obtain their views. The foremost dilemma is that consumers vary so much – from the wealthy residents in the northern suburbs that fear excessive property tax and user-fee hikes in their areas as a means to cross-subsidise services in poorer areas, to poor people who have inadequate access to services and are unable to afford those services. In attempting to motivate consumers to pay for services, attention is focused on improved metering, more stringent credit control and continuous interaction to explain to consumers the benefits of paying for services. Politicians form an important interest; hence alliances were forged with the top leadership in the council while briefings of different parties were held. There has been some concern that the process was essentially driven by officials, but even top political leaders have argued that this was necessitated by the urgency of the reforms required and that the process would be more political as details unfold.

Financiers have been a major target audience. The city management wanted to reassure international and South African financiers that it is worth investing in, and that the municipality would be a creditworthy borrower. Interactions with financiers therefore informed many aspects of the strategy, and led to some major tenets, such as ringfenced revenue streams, assurances that political change will not compromise debt repayments, and a focus on effective management of assets.

Finally, national and provincial government have been major stakeholders. They were regularly briefed, asked for advice and support, and views were exchanged to ensure that the Johannesburg experience is captured in the development of policies at these other levels. In 2000, Johannesburg became the first recipient of a major national grant to assist in the transformation of big cities. The challenge has been to maintain the integrity of local decision-making, and as the city's finances improved and it greater independence was confirmed, this progressed.

The range of institutional options adopted shows that the council is seeking the most appropriate alternatives, instead of being driven by an ideological belief in private sector participation. This has enabled it to interact with the consumers on the basis of service concerns, rather than ideological positions. Such pragmatism is crucial when a council deals with such diverse interests and views, as it has to reconcile widely divergent perspectives while facilitating service delivery that meets specific needs.

Source: Govender and Aiello, 1999

reason, clear criteria for assessing the originality of proposals must be developed, and the municipality may choose to clearly compensate unsolicited bidders, once the proposal has reached the stage where it is actually put out to tender as a project. In Biratnagar (see Box 9.2), an unsolicited bid from a foreign solid waste management firm led to the council being deceived and many stakeholders defrauded. Had the municipality adhered to best practice established elsewhere and taken technical advice, the situation and embarrassment could have been avoided.

The Principle of Contestability

Where competition does not exist, contestable environments could be created to enhance the efficiency of contracted service providers.[4] This is done mainly through the municipality continuing to provide services in part of its jurisdiction, deliberately not contracting, out services across the whole area to a private partner. There are two obvious impacts of this approach. The first is that it provides a public sector benchmark against which to measure the private operator's performance. Second, it means that the municipality retains some capacity and instruments (such as collection vehicles for solid waste) that should enable it to step in if the private sector participation arrangement fails.

There are essentially four ways to strengthen the contestability effect of such arrangements:

1. reducing the period of the contractual agreement or providing for a periodic review of performance, in consultation with the affected consumers;
2. introducing performance targets related to the quality of the service, the range of services, the prices charged for the services and overall market share, linked to penalties, or provisions that may lead to early termination of the agreement;
3. requiring comparable performance, relative to other providers (including the municipality) in similar circumstances, or in terms of international benchmarks; and
4. choosing a form of price control that explicitly requires the operator to make efficiency gains.

Clearly, these methods all require the development of effective and credible criteria and processes that must also be acceptable to the partner. If the regulation introduced in this manner increases uncertainty and risk to excessively high limits, the municipality may find it difficult to find willing partners. It should also make sure that the costs of such regulation do not exceed the efficiency gains obtained from contestability.

The Principle of Accountability

Private sector participation raises accountability questions because partnerships place certain responsibilities, normally carried by the public sector, in the ambit of private operators.[5] This has raised fears that the democratic control of local electorates may be compromised. There are also concerns that if privately provided services are disrupted, the public's hold on the service providers may be weakened.

As we have seen in Chapter 6, it is critical to define responsibilities very clearly and establish mechanisms for ensuring clarity even as roles develop, so that partners can be held accountable for their performance. Chapter 6 develops the discussion on the potential roles of the private sector, civil society and municipalities, and Chapter 7 stresses that the goals of a partnership and the expected outputs must be articulated clearly if such accountability is to be established. It is also essential for the municipality to put in place effective ways to monitor the achievement of goals over the duration of the project. Effective partnership contracts with the private sector thus tend to address standards and quality, continuity, termination, regulation, cost recovery, assets, maintenance and expansion of infrastructure, compensation for public sector failure, new connections, and monitoring mechanisms (see Chapter 8).

Links to Boxes
4.5, 9.5, 10.4, 11.3, 11.4, 12.7

Box **9.4**   **Building Transparency and Accountability through Consultation**
Gweru, Zimbabwe

Complete transparency throughout the process of establishing and implementing a partnership builds public confidence and counters concern that the partnership will lead to corruption. The experience of Gweru City Council in Zimbabwe shows that effective consultation with interest groups creates a supportive environment for PSP.

Once the council had agreed with the general principle of private sector participation in water and sanitation services, the municipality went about establishing the partnership in as transparent and accountable a manner as possible. This meant ensuring that the choice of a private sector partner was made with the people, for their benefit. This was not only desirable but essential in the context of Zimbabwe, where a relatively active civil society exists, consisting of ratepayers' associations, trade unions, cooperatives etc. It is common to seek a consensus between the municipality and civil society through discussions (particularly at ward level), consultation and public debates. The role of the councillor is critical to this end, consulting with different organisations in policy development and listening to the grievances and aspirations of the people. This process has helped to ensure that local government is responsive to public demand.

Both the political and administrative arms of the GCC have therefore fostered a series of relationships with key individuals and groups within the community. It is argued that the fear and scepticism that characterised the attitudes at the outset have gradually been replaced with the support of most stakeholders. This high level of transparency has created confidence and ultimately shielded the municipality from criticism.

The relationship with the trade union, has been treated as important throughout the process. A number of lessons have been learnt in relation to dealing with trade unions, and many of the hardest lessons were learnt on other privatisation initiatives within the municipality. To some extent, the municipality and the unions had undergone a massive learning curve by cutting their teeth on the contracting-out of the theatre and security services, and commercialising the distillery. As a result, the Municipal Workers' Union has been involved in all parts of the process, and the municipality has nurtured that involvement and respected the concerns of the employees. The preferred contractor, SAUR UK, has also played an important role in building confidence and providing guarantees from the private sector perspective. The trade union has been present at negotiations with the private sector and at the tender presentations. It has met separately with SAUR UK and has heard from all parties that:

- all staff will be given jobs within the operating company – there will be absolutely no job losses;
- the terms and conditions of employees at all levels will improve; and
- management staff will be offered incentives (overseas travel and work opportunities) that are unlikely in the public sector.

The relationship with the chamber of commerce was also treated with great importance. Little work needed to be done to encourage Gweru business, however, and support from the chamber of commerce has been unanimous from the outset.

While it is reported that community leaders have participated in discussions and presentations, there is little clarity provided on the community consultation process. The community representatives are community leaders or those known to be influential; there is no indication of any grassroots participatory process. This may be something to be taken up with other pro-poor initiatives in the future. The municipality stresses that a key lesson was that community support can be easily achieved if leaders are involved from the start.

A number of officials highlighted the importance of NGOs (mostly church groups) in the process through their public support. Apart from this 'spiritual' support, there is no defined role for NGOs in the forthcoming partnership. In the cultural context of Gweru, the support of the churches was important to underpinning community support for the process.

The actors selected by the GCC to describe their consultative process include a range of governmental (central level), business and NGO stakeholders. The GCC has always stressed the importance of involving central government representatives at key steps in the process. This has had the added benefit of linking the local process in Gweru with policy-making on partnerships at central level, and a process of lesson learning that stretched beyond Gweru itself.

Sources: Adapted from Plummer and Nhemachena, 2001; see also Masuko, 1996

Accountability is closely linked to creating incentives for the different parties. Elected councils have the incentive of meeting voter demands. Municipal officials may be encouraged through performance measurement that is linked directly to successful delivery through the partnership. The private partner has the incentives of maintaining a sustainable business and winning future contracts. Such incentives should be carefully considered during the negotiation of a partnership contract. Often, accountability is reinforced though penalty clauses applied if contractors fail to meet the expectations set out in the contract.

Mechanisms that allow rapid response to customer needs also facilitate accountability. Customer complaint handling systems is one important element, and the introduction of the necessary support systems should enable service providers to function with sufficient accountability. Such systems enable end-users to make known what they require from the service industry, and help service providers to respond to those requirements. Throughout, it remains important for a local council to make the best use of its links to the community that elected it, as a primary channel to gather information and to continuously convey customer views on the quality of services.

The Principles of Legitimacy and Legality

To be credible, partnerships with the international and large-scale private sector need support from key stakeholders and a firm legal basis. This creates a safe environment for investors, and a sound basis upon which the delivery of services can take place. However, as we have discussed in Chapter 3, partnerships involving the private sector frequently face political, ideological and historical objections, and some stakeholders will want basic service delivery to remain a public sector function. Employees within the municipality may feel threatened by private sector participation, believing that their jobs are at stake. Consumers too may fear that private control over services will lead to tariff hikes, and reduce their access to decisions about services. The poor are particularly vulnerable, because private operators often receive better returns on services that have a safe revenue stream and higher profit margins.

Furthermore, if the process of awarding contracts is in question, losing bidders may oppose the procurement of the winning bidder's services, and this could engage the municipality in protracted and expensive legal battles. If the legal basis of a partnership is in question, the accountability of the parties will be tenuous, compromising certainty that the contract obligations will be met.

The key to addressing these challenges lies in effective process management and due legal process. First, stakeholder participation is essential, as it enables the different parties to air their views, raise their concerns and feel that they are part of the process. Special arrangements may be necessary to ensure that poor communities are well informed, and are able to influence decisions about various aspects of the partnership, such as service levels or tariff levels. Second, the municipality should be clear about what it wants to achieve through private sector participation, as this would enable it to engage with stakeholders, either to convince them or at least to ensure a working arrangement that would avoid any stakeholders fundamentally opposing the partnership in ways that make it unworkable. Third, it pays to be as open as possible. Policy frameworks should be clearly articulated, information made accessible to all, and procedures for procurement should be open, fair and credible. Finally, the legal basis of the contract must be beyond doubt. This means that the municipality must be duly empowered to enter into such a contract, the statutory framework must provide for such municipal contracts, the rights and obligations of the participating partners and any regulators must be clear, and the legal basis must provide certainty for the partnership.

The more transparent the process, the more accountable the council, the more extensive the inputs and open the debates, and the firmer the legal basis, the better the prospects that private sector participation will become a legitimate option. All the stakeholders may not be equally enthusiastic, and some may continue to believe that direct municipal service

9

Box 9.5   Stakeholder Consultation
Gweru, Zimbabwe

Links to Boxes
4.5, 9.4, 10.4, 11.3, 11.4, 12.7

The process of consultation in Gweru discussed in Box 9.4 was initiated at an early stage, and involved all stakeholders in the city. The council aimed to address the concerns of each stakeholder group throughout the preparation stage to build ownership for the shift to private sector delivery. The following table provides a summary of the diversity of concerns and the GCC response.

	Concerns/interests	Response
Consumer council	• To protect consumer rights	• Control of tariff remains with GCC • Performance standards ensure quality of service
CBOs	• To ensure transparency in the PPP process • To protect consumer interests and reliable and affordable service	• Public tender and public meetings over council retaining control of tariffs
Churches	• To protect poorer groups from any negative impacts of PSP	• Control of tariff remains with GCC • Performance standards ensure quality of service
Chamber of Commerce and Chamber of Industry	• To ensure reliability and efficiency of service • To ensure commercial tariffs are kept to a minimum	• No GCC response required, commerce positive towards PPP
Zimbabwe Congress of Trade Unions	• Employees would not lose jobs • Conditions same or better than existing	• Ensure handover of all staff to operator • Terms and conditions the same as or better than existing conditions • Future conditions pegged against council terms and conditions • Skills development (local and international) would be provided by operator to meet requirements
Municipal Workers' Union	• As above • Pension scheme carried over to new jobs	• Assurance that current scheme would be maintained – the operator pays into LAPF • Seeking an amendment to local authorities pensions act to enable transferred employees to retain fund membership
Zimbabwe Electricity Supply Authority	• To ensure that the PPP does not disrupt existing operations	• Ensure notification of all stakeholder meetings and decision-making forum • Enable operator access to ZESA in preliminary survey
Ministry of Local Government and National Housing	• To monitor process to ensure government policy on PPP is met • To promote the first water and sanitation • PPP in Zimbabwe • Disseminate experience to other local authorities	• Ensure notification of all stakeholder meetings and decision-making forum • Provided access to the development of all documentation
National Economic Planning Commission	• To understand and promote their role in capital financing	• Ensure notification of all stakeholder meetings and decision-making forum
Ministry of Water Resources and Development (Provincial Water Engineer)	• To continue to supply bulk water to Gweru • To ensure that existing bulk water charges are met the private operator	• Ensure notification of all stakeholder meetings and decision-making forum • Enable operator access to Ministry

Source: Adapted from Plummer and Nhemachena, 2001

provision would have been preferable. But if they know that the processes of debate were open, the negotiations and procurements fair, and the contracts credible, they are more likely to accept the actions taken.[6]

The Principle of Stakeholder Participation

A range of stakeholders have an interest in the increasing involvement of the private sector in service delivery. It is important to ensure the involvement of such stakeholders and the ongoing flow of information to them. Stakeholder participation is vital in enhancing ownership and sustainability. This would enhance the overall legitimacy of the project, and also help to ensure that the service providers act accountably and with sensitivity to the needs of consumers.

Participatory decision-making ensures a better fit between public investment decisions and community realities and preferences. Even where elected local governments exist, their representative capacity and reach into society is often too limited to enable them to speak on behalf of those directly affected by change, whose cooperation is required for successful development projects. In particular, poor communities and individuals are often not able to make their voices heard, and special effort is necessary to ensure that low-income households and marginalised groups (such as women and young people) make effective inputs. For these reasons, as we have discussed in Chapters 6 and 7, successful private sector participation requires systematic efforts to involve key interest groups in the policy, planning, implementation and monitoring process for a partnership. A central tenet of stakeholder participation is to engage with stakeholders from an early stage when the partnership is being conceptualised, and to ensure ongoing meaningful participation throughout. Many PPPs have merely tried to co-opt stakeholders once the deal is done.

Municipalities sometimes appoint full-time community liaison officers or units to ensure such inputs, or they may create special forums to facilitate debate and exchange about the private sector participation projects. It remains important, however, that the inputs received are treated seriously by the leadership within a local government, and that the links between the community officers and line management be consciously strengthened. Unless this is done, the participatory process can easily become nominal, with little real effect on planning and decision-making in the council as a whole and in project management. Any initiative will flounder if stakeholder involvement is superficially consultative, with the stakeholders feeling that they have no real impact on outcomes. All stakeholders should be consulted with due sensitivity to their particular interests. Important groups are:

- consumers, who will have to pay for the services, and who have an interest in the standards and costs involved;
- residents directly affected by the construction of a new facility, such as people living next to a new reservoir or landfill site;
- poor households and communities, who often lack the means to participate effectively in public policy and project processes. Their involvement is critical to partnership design, implementation and monitoring because it helps to incorporate the perspectives of people who experience delivery problems first hand;
- municipal employees, who often fear the implications of private sector participation for their employment conditions, if not for their jobs. It is critical to engage with them from the outset, to ensure that they understand the need for transformation, and that they are able to make an impact on the decisions that are eventually made about partnerships; and
- existing informal service providers, who stand to lose their source of income if their interests are ignored.

While it is advisable to always keep all interested parties informed, the levels of engagement may vary according to the specific issues at stake. For example, while trade unions are very important stakeholders when labour and employment issues are being discussed, they may not be a primary actor when the original principle decision to engage in a partnership is decided, or when levels of services are being determined.

9

Box 9.6 **A Partnership Lacking Clarity**
Stutterheim, South Africa

Perhaps the primary problem of the affermage contract is that the responsibilities for operation and maintenance, on the one hand, and for investments, on the other, are conferred upon different parties, yet are often difficult to distinguish. For an affermage contract to succeed it is commonly agreed that it must *clearly* define which items constitute operation and maintenance (and are therefore the responsibility of the operator), and which items are long term and strategic (and are therefore the responsibility of the authority). In Stutterheim, however, a number of problems have arisen due to the lack of agreement over the definitions and scope of maintenance versus capital improvement. A primary question in such a contract is *who* will distinguish between routine maintenance and capital expenditure, and this is not resolved in Stutterheim or in South Africa because of the lack of a regulating body (see Box 8.6). The lack of clarity and the ambiguity in the contract has been at the core of many disagreements and much discontent. It is informative to consider what types of problems are embodied in this lack of clarity over operation and maintenance a versus capital works. The specifics of four disputes are described below:

1. During severe floods in Southern Africa, a length of trunk-main on a steep hill was badly damaged by the heavy rainfall and flooding in the vicinity. The pipework had been designed and constructed by the council as a part of a capital improvements programme. The council is now in a dispute with the private operator over the responsibility for the cost of rectification of this pipework. WSSA has argued that the pipework foundation was not properly compacted and failed due to poor preparation and workmanship during construction. It sent the council a letter to this effect some months before the damage occurred, and argues that rectification costs are not therefore a matter of maintenance. The council, however, interprets the operator's obligation under the contract to ensure joint supervision and assistance to optimise operations differently. It argues that WSSA should bear some responsibility for the failure of the design under unusual flooding conditions. While WSSA have reduced the cost to the council to some extent, this difference of opinion has not been resolved.

2. A failure at the boreholes meant that WSSA undertook large-scale replacement and rectification works. It argues that the boreholes constructed by the council before the contract were not properly lined, and that the specification of the pump size was too great for the mechanism. As a result, unexpected vibration led to the collapse of the lining. The council argues that the boreholes have been functioning adequately since 1990 and that the problem is one of operation and maintenance.

3. A disagreement also arose when a pit latrine vacuum tanker, specially designed to enter narrow streets, broke down and needed replacing. Under the contract such capital equipment must be provided by the municipality. The process of approving the expenditure on a new vehicle was slow. To cover the period of four months, WSSA brought in another vehicle from a nearby town which could operate but required maintenance and upgrades to carry out the task. WSSA has since billed the council for the maintenance carried out on the tanker and disagreement has ensued over responsibility for the costs of upgrading a tanker not owned by and no longer benefiting the council.

4. When the wastewater treatment works was extended in 1994–95, WSSA noted that ungraded river sand was being provided as the media for the sludge drying beds. At this time WSSA expressed concern to the council that this cheap, ungraded river sand was specified by the consulting engineer, instead of graded sand in accordance with standard engineering practice. The council did not accept WSSA's concerns but chose to go ahead with the sand specified by the local consulting engineer. Following an exchange of correspondence, an independent investigation was carried out, and the final report stated that ungraded river sand has reduced filtration capacity, restricted the drying tempo of the sludge and resulted in a higher rate of sand loss. This is of particular concern during extended wet periods when sludge drying capacity becomes critical. WSSA has therefore stated that it cannot be held responsible for the early replacement of the sand due to inadequate specifications on capital works.

Apart from the lack of clarity in the contract and the lack of a regulator to resolve differences, the lack of effective communication between the partners has added to their disagreements. While it is clear that STLC prefers not to negotiate at a strategic or practical level, WSSA has not communicated as well as it could have. The affermage contract requires trust between the client and the operator and particularly some mutual understanding over investment. At its worst, the contract falters if a client does not invest in the infrastructure necessary for the operator to provide an acceptable level of service. While this is certainly not the case in Stutterheim (where the council has invested appropriately), there is nevertheless a lack of mutual agreement on the manner and spirit in which capital works are carried out. On the one hand, the council believes that WSSA does not provide the joint supervision described in the contract, and does not always show the interest it should. On the other hand, WSSA argues that its voice is not heard, that the council does not accept that the technical resources of an international water operator exceed the generalist skills of a local engineering consultant, and that the council has acted naively towards investment at times. Capital works in an affermage contract become a three-way partnership including the client, operator and engineering consultant. This relationship has not been an easy one in Stutterheim.

Source: Plummer, 2000a

Sometimes, interest groups might be opposed in principle to partnerships, and the municipality will then have to carefully assess the costs and benefits of being in opposition to those policy stances. It is rarely possible to satisfy all interests, but all effort should be made to ensure that all inputs are heard, mediated and taken seriously through the processes of participation.

The Principle of Equity

While service partnership objectives will vary (see Chapter 3), one of the primary principles of partnerships aiming to deliver benefits to the poor, must be equity. Yet, service partnerships aimed at physical objectives (such as improving the quality of services) and economic objectives (through greater management efficiency) can result in higher costs, at least in the short term. Without careful attention, this can exacerbate existing patterns of exclusion. Partnership champions need to develop the capacity to create partnerships that are effective as instruments for service delivery to the poor, and to utilise them to attain derived benefits – like job creation – for poor people. At the same time, they need to understand where adverse effects might arise and how to mitigate them.

Without explicit provision in the partnership framework (and in the contract), large-scale operators often do not have much incentive to cater for the needs of poorer consumers, as they are mostly able to achieve higher profit margins with less risk in non-poor communities. The scope and content of the partnership arrangement, and the inclusion of pro-poor actors, will begin to change the traditional form of PPP. The key mechanisms to ensure equitability have been addressed in Chapters 6 and 7. They include:

- differentiated service levels that make it possible for the poor to afford the services;
- alliances or partnerships with community-based service organisations, as these often specialise in delivering low-cost service;
- flexible payment options, such as phasing in payment for new connections or pre-paid meters; and
- appointing NGOs as advocates for the poor in the partnership arrangement.

The Principle of Clarity and Predictability

The partnership framework (and the contract that results) must be as clear as possible to create a stable context for the activities related to the partnership. A lack of clarity discourages investors, and even if they do enter an agreement with a municipality, the lack of clarity leaves the whole arrangement vulnerable to inadequate performance, legal and technical disputes, and uncertainty. It also makes it more difficult to accurately monitor and evaluate the partnership, and thus to take action if service providers do not perform to the standards expected. Chapter 8 has provided a list of what the contract should cover (see Box 8.3). Ensuring contractual clarity and completeness helps a municipality create an effective working environment.

On the other hand, partnerships are vulnerable when there is uncertainty. Predictability can be developed through the actions of key actors and the regulatory arrangements. For example, investors want to know that a change in political leadership would not jeopardise the municipality's commitment to the partnership. The clearer and firmer the rules about tariff-setting, determination of levels of service, and decision-making processes in general, the more attractive a partnership becomes to private and community partners. Inevitably, arrangements need to evolve to suit changing capacities and circumstances, and a certain level of flexibility is mostly required to keep the partnership attuned to the demands of this environment. But it is essential that clarity and predictability are re-established following review and revision. Arbitrary decision-making and unexpected changes in policy and regulatory stances discourage parties outside the municipality to engage in a partnership, and undermine the efforts of those within the partnership.

Box 9.7   Managing Risk through Partnership Contracts

	Typical arrangement
Political risk	The municipality takes on this risk in the local environment and therefore has a key role in working with other levels of government, community groups and all stakeholders to ensure the highest possible level of stability. It is often difficult to provide a clear projection at the outset, especially in the case of long-term contracts.
Design risk	Typically this risk is transferred to the private operator. It means the risk linked to design of goods and services, and the operator could be penalised if the required standards are not met. The municipality should ensure that the standards are very clearly specified.
Construction risk	There should be clear specifications and time schedules for construction, agreed between the municipality and the private contractor. The latter then assumes the risk of meeting those criteria, and the contract should provide for appropriate penalties if these criteria are not met. It must also be clear who carries the risk of cost over-runs (probably the private partner). The municipality should put in place effective monitoring mechanisms to ensure compliance with agreed-upon standards.
Operating and maintenance risk	The private party is normally made responsible for all operating risks, and is expected to manage all operating costs, including staff costs. For this reason it is important to clearly distinguish between capital and maintenance expenditures and to indicate who will be responsible for which aspects. Any restrictive conditions or incentives should be clearly defined up-front, in order to allow the contractor to incorporate them in preparing a cost estimate at the bidding and contracting stages. The municipality should put in place effective monitoring mechanisms to ensure compliance with agreed-upon standards.
Demand risk	Contractually, the private operator is mostly expected to identify the demand for the service and users' willingness to pay. The operator's risk assessment will affect the pricing projected in its bid. The municipality should attempt to provide bidders with as much information as possible to facilitate accurate projections and pricing.
Tariff risk	Risk is normally managed through an agreed formula and procedure outline that sets the framework for future increases. It is important not to grant the private operator free reign to adjust tariffs, but it would also probably find the risk unacceptably high if government wants to retain this power for itself. It is in all parties' interests to ensure a fair and mutually acceptable formula and procedure.
Tariff collection risk	Ideally, this risk should be placed on the private partner as it relates directly to demand and operational risk, and the operator has the incentives to achieve targets.
Credit risk	The private party should carry its own credit risk, but the municipality should ensure that clarity exists as to what will happen if the private party becomes incapable to deliver the services, especially through insolvency. Contracts must ensure uninterrupted service.

Source: RoSA, 2000; World Bank, 1997c

The Principle of Risk Management

Long-term contractual arrangements always involve risks, and the essence of a successful partnership is the clear allocation of risk between a municipality and its partners. When risk is transferred to a private operator, the management discipline of the operator is brought into the delivery of a service. It gives the partner a real stake in the success of the venture. This does not mean that the municipality can avoid all risk. While the efficiency gains obtainable from private sector involvement are based on private entrepreneurs' willingness to venture into risks, private investors do have risk ceilings. They are not likely to be interested in partnerships if borrowed capital cannot be paid back in a timely fashion or if inflexible government or municipality attitudes create pricing delays or obstruct projects.

In general, the deal should be structured so that each risk lies with the partner that is best able to manage it. In this way, value for money is obtained because appropriate allocation minimises the price of the risk. Where the private party has better systems and knowledge to manage risk efficiently, the PPP will achieve value for money. The municipality must, however, avoid placing arbitrary or onerous burdens on private partners. PPPs should not be adversarial relationships; government must always be fair and reasonable in taking its negotiating positions with respect to risk-sharing. It is also important that the municipality deals with those risks it has control over. For example, government is normally in a better position to manage legislative risk and would obtain little, if any, value for money by transferring that risk to private partners.

On the whole, risk management aims to minimise risks, either by eliminating them, reducing the costs of controlling them, or reducing the financial consequences of the risks that materialise. This requires the systematic identification and quantification of the risks associated with a project, including each possible event that could result in failure to achieve project objectives. Risk management therefore entails clear identification of the controllable elements of each risk and the assignment of responsibility for controlling that element. For example, completion risk may be considered the risk of the construction contractor, but in reality it has many sub-components, including environmental clearances and the securing of the appropriate building and operating permits from local authorities. To the extent that government and municipalities can facilitate clarity in the project implementation process and reduce the levels of uncertainty regarding their own roles in a partnership, perceived risks and costs may be reduced.

The Principle of Economic and Financial Sustainability

A PPP is only feasible (for the public sector and private operator) if it is economically and financially sustainable. Financial sustainability depends first on whether there is sufficient demand for the contracted service to sustain consumer willingness to pay, or a governmental acknowledgement that it needs to support the service through subsidisation because people who cannot pay need the service (for this reason, accurate tariff-setting that reflects demand is essential).

Economic sustainability can be affected by the economic activity the partnership generates. For example, if it uses local labour, stimulates new entrepreneurial activity, and creates new opportunities in the informal sector, the partnership is likely to attract community support. This would also have the effect of creating more demand. In this manner a project could have many spin-offs, which in turn become factors that sustain or even accelerate its momentum.

The Principle of Specificity

To be successful, the partnership framework and the options for private sector participation must be targeted to the specific objectives of the municipality and the service needs under consideration. National policy guidelines, and the lessons of experience from other countries or from other local governments, are obviously useful and can assist

9

Links to Boxes
3.5, 5.4, 6.13, 7.2, 7.3, 7.11, 7.18, 8.12

| Box **9.8** | **Private Sector–Community Cooperation**
Buenos Aires, Argentina

The experience in Buenos Aires provides numerous insights into the opportunities and obstacles to harnessing the private sector to better service provision for the poor. Local governments, the private utility (Aguas Argentinas) and civil society organisations (CBOs and an NGO, IIED-AL) collaborated to improve the provision of water and sanitation in four *barrios* within the Buenos Aires concession.

However, the original concession agreement was negotiated without representation from the local government or civil society groups. These provisions effectively placed a large share of the urban poor outside of the area to be served, and burdened those living in newly serviced areas with a debt they could ill afford. Without pressure from civil society organisations and support from local government, the projects would not have come to be. Aguas Argentinas, who had no experience working in *barrios*, nevertheless began to collaborate in 1995 on improving the provision of water and sanitation in a small number of low-income settlements with insecure tenure.

The collaboration took a similar form in each of the *barrios*, including:

- **residents** providing labour and some financial contributions;
- **local government** sanctioning the project (despite unresolved land issues) and in several cases providing materials and more active support;
- **civil society groups** firstly negotiating for the project and then acting as a mediator between the residents and the other parties, as well as organising the residents' contributions; and
- **Aguas Argentinas** connecting the local networks to their systems and taking various degrees of responsibility for the construction of the local networks.

The results indicate considerable potential for engaging private utilities in improvement efforts, but also demonstrate that switching to a private utility does not in itself solve the problem of improving water and sanitation in low-income areas. Although the experiences proved to be quite different, in general the results of the experiences of these four *barrios* with tri-sector collaboration went against the conventional wisdom in the water and sanitation sector. Thus, for example:

- Piped water and sanitation provision contributed to (rather than followed) housing security, in the cases where the community organisations achieved local government authorisation to connect networks despite unresolved land issues.
- Civil society organisations play a key role in making PPPs work for the poor.
- Pro-poor negotiations are important before and after the concession agreement has been signed, i.e. the utility, the local government and the communities may all have reasons for negotiating after the agreement.
- The need for multi-party collaboration continues after water and sanitation connections are installed, in order to ensure a sustainable supply of water to low-income residents.
- Privatisation does not, in itself, prevent electioneering and political clientelism in service provision.

In most respects, the experiences of these communities are very encouraging for multisectoral collaboration. Through such collaboration, residents and community leaders acknowledged that each of the major parties achieved important goals. Residents received reliable and convenient water supplies. The utility expanded its system at a low cost. The local government enhanced its authority and gained local support. The civil society organisations served the local communities and gained credibility.

This was accomplished in the face of the low-income residents' considerable mistrust of politicians and offers of assistance; the utility's profit-orientation and lack of experience in low-income areas; the local governments' persistent clientelism and lack of local accountability; and the civil society organisations' own accountability problems and lack of experience with water and sanitation projects.

On the other hand, there are visible limitations to the approaches taken in all four *barrios*. While the water and most of the sanitation systems are in place and functioning, the procedures for maintenance, billing and collecting payments have not been adequately developed. Non-payment is a particular problem, despite Aguas Argentinas' low incentive to disconnect residents, given how that would harm public relations and incur legal costs. However, in order to ensure the long-term viability of the water and sanitation provision, and moreover to provide the basis for replication in other low-income *barrios*, collaboration should be extended, continuing for a period after the beginning of service operation.

Source: IIED-AL

municipalities to develop an approach to private sector participation. Ultimately, however, any partnership needs to be designed according to the specific problems and circumstances it is supposed to address. This section on establishing a partnership framework provides the structure to enable such specificity to be developed.

The principle of specificity (i.e., creating a specific partnership appropriate to the context) is closely tied to the process of establishing particular objectives and analysing the local conditions. Has the municipality agreed to improve operational efficiency, broaden service coverage, improve quality, and target poor communities, or achieve a combination of these objectives? It needs to consider the potential range of partners in a given context. It needs to consider the range of tariffs different types of consumers can pay, and are willing to pay, and it must address the concerns of different stakeholders. It also should deal with specific development needs in the community, and utilise and develop local resources as far as possible.

For this reason, partnership arrangements must be framed to encourage the use of local labour, arrangements with small enterprises, the use of local materials, and other locally relevant development interventions (and this will then need to be specified in the contract). Considering all these factors, and the concerns of potential partners about the local environment, a good partnership arrangement is one that builds on the assets of local conditions, and that is planned and implemented in a thorough and credible manner to address the specific issues within that local context.

The Principle of Empowerment

Empowering the poor is a central principle in partnerships focused on bringing benefits to poor communities. The success of such a partnership is not only measured in terms of the services covered by the partnership contract: the test is also whether the partnership leaves a sustainable legacy in the community. Has it contributed to the development of social capital, skills, or new businesses, or created new opportunities for people in the community?

Stakeholder participation and the mechanisms established for creating meaningful and appropriate participation of the poor are at the core of an empowerment approach. The extent to which poor stakeholders themselves have a role in decision-making over their own development is an important indicator, and the ownership, management and operation of services are all important to empowerment. In some contexts, procurement criteria can be structured to create opportunities for small-scale providers, the unemployed and other vulnerable groups.

Inevitably, the benefits of involving the poor in the delivery process need to be balanced with the need to deliver the service efficiently and sustainably. Different private sector operators respond very differently to the involvement of communities and poor groups in construction and management. Municipalities can seek views during early discussions to see how a particular operator thinks on this issue. Selecting a sympathetic and knowledgeable operator can make a significant difference and largely determine the extent to which the partnership focuses on pro-poor ends.

Partnerships can become more focused on empowerment through the development of appropriate procurement procedures for formal private sector arrangements. For example:

- ensuring participation in all appropriate phases and activities (design, building and operation), and providing the individual and organisational capacity building necessary to do so;
- ensuring that community representatives play a role in decision-making bodies;
- promoting the participation of vulnerable groups in construction by building capacity (skills development, etc.);
- creating supportive institutional mechanisms to make it possible for them to enter into formal contracts, etc.;
- shaping employment practices to build local capacity;

- supporting the rights, conditions and compensations of employees by improving skills, training and benefits; and
- ensuring that informal service providers are empowered to take on greater roles and that they are not disempowered through expropriation of infrastructure (or put out of business through monopoly clauses).

The test for a poverty-focused partnership thus lies not only in the service it delivers, but also in whether it leaves the local communities empowered.

Part 3
Enhancing Capacity to Implement Partnerships

Understanding the operating context of municipal partnerships	Enhancing human resources	Supporting organisational development
Chapter 10	*Chapter 11*	*Chapter 12*

Chapter 10 **Key Questions**

☐ Which external factors influence the capacity of municipalities to create and focus partnerships?

☐ What do municipalities need to know about the issues outside their control?

☐ Which steps can be taken to mitigate adverse effects of the operating context?

Enhancing Capacity to Implement Partnerships

| Understanding the operating context of municipal partnerships | Enhancing human resources | Supporting organisational development |

GHK

Understanding the Operating Context of Municipal Partnerships

10

Chris Heymans and Janelle Plummer

The capacity of a municipality to develop an effective, focused partnership is often strongly shaped by a sound external operating context. Municipalities do not operate in a vacuum. In most situations a number of the factors determining this context will be outside municipal control, and as with other municipal actions decision-makers must adapt their approach to respond to the opportunities and constraints of the broader context. Politics, economic realities, policy and regulatory frameworks, and the political and administrative relationships between local government and other levels of government all play important roles.

It is not possible to describe a perfect operating environment. The factors making up the environment and influencing the development of a service partnership in developing countries are mostly in a state of flux. Even where effective institutions and instruments are developed, the social, economic and political realities are changing. However, experiences in diverse contexts have highlighted a range of issues affecting the operating environments of local governments – issues that may severely affect their capacity to develop a partnership, and will help to determine the approach they adopt.

The general political and economic conditions normally set the scene for private sector participation (PSP), and can make or break it at the outset. It becomes difficult, for instance, to establish partnerships if public sector decision-makers are sceptical of the private sector, or if resistant trade unions have a strong influence on political decision-making. In a weak investment environment, the private capital or operational skills to engage in partnerships may simply be lacking. Coherent private sector participation policy fosters general public sector commitment to partnerships, and helps ensure that the general thrust of legislation and regulation works to streamline partnerships.

Regulation and legislation shape standards, incentives and processes for private sector participation and thus affect the form it might take. Procedures and pricing frameworks influence private sector interest, and the local government's power of decision-making is often an important factor, because potential partners may be reluctant to enter into contracts with an entity that can be over-ruled by higher authority. On the other hand, some investors want guarantees from higher-level authorities, to provide them with more security about their contracts with municipalities. This chapter discusses how these factors – factors over which the municipality may have no control – obstruct, encourage or generally influence partnerships. All factors fundamentally influence the capacity of a municipality to enter into a partnership and to target its efforts to the benefit of the poor.

Political Context

☐ Political stability

A primary external factor affecting the development of public–private partnerships (PPPs) will be the political stability of the country. As with economic stability, investors look for certainty. An unstable political regime – as in Zimbabwe (Box 10.4) – can undermine confidence enough to stall the finalisation of agreements. Political instability brings with it economic uncertainty and financial risk.

It is also true, however, that established PPPs have survived political instability and widespread corruption. In Colombia, despite civil unrest at least eight cities have launched concessions/joint ventures with major French water companies.[1] In this case, the existence of a regulatory body in the water sector, and a watchdog for the delivery of basic services, promoted the certainty required, and precedent provided enough comfort to ensure that the citizens themselves were willing to give the private sector the support it needed to ensure reliability and quality of service.

| Box **10.1** | Political Will Sets the Context for Partnerships |

	Expressions of political will
Argentina	Both the Argentinian national government and the provincial government in Córdoba greatly supported municipal PSP. The central government committed itself to PSP generally through a range of supportive policies and reforms. Prioritising economic growth and deficit reduction, in 1989 a new government initiated a series of reforms that included widescale privatisation of state entities. The government anticipated major revenue gains as a result of the sales of assets, and believed that service quality would improve through private sector involvement.

While the focus was not on local government, government encouraged municipalities to follow similar pro-PSP policies at local level. Some provincial-level governments then reformed local government legislation to allow for greater decentralisation. In Córdoba, the provincial government gave the municipalities greater discretionary powers, including a capacity to engage with private and non-governmental partners in service delivery. The provincial government also established a private concession for the delivery of water in the municipality of Córdoba, mainly to raise additional revenue through payment of royalties. This support for PSP gave a positive signal about PSP to both private investors and municipalities. |
| **Colombia** | PSP formed an integral element of wider state reform in Colombia, and state support therefore added considerable impetus to an enhanced role for the private sector in municipalities. In the midst of extensive state reform and decentralisation in the early 1990s, and pressurised by international financial institutions to adopt market-orientated policies, the Colombian government passed legislation in 1994 that explicitly provided for the involvement of the private sector in public service provision. Furthermore, a national water and sanitation plan was created in 1995 to increase the coverage of water supply and network sewerage by 2010. The achievement of these ambitious targets required institutional reform of the water sector. New legislation in 1994 laid down explicit criteria for efficiency in planning, regulation and supervision.

This marked a radically positive attitude towards the private sector. Opting for a market approach, the government acknowledged that the country could not afford the level of public spending needed for building and improving infrastructure. It made clear its belief that private resources were needed to fill the gap. Both private capital and technology were seen as crucial to the institutional reform process, thereby finally opening the door to PSP in public service provision in Colombia. |
| **South Africa** | Since 1996, in line with a macro-economic policy to promote growth, investment and employment creation, the South African government has actively encouraged PSP. The Local Government White Paper of 1998 names PSP – along with profit and community organisations – as a distinct service delivery option. Subsequently, new local government legislation and a published policy framework provided a firm commitment and spelt out government's approach. A dedicated unit was also established to advise municipalities on partnership deals, and to promote the PSP concept.

The strong commitment to PSP is also embodied in a strategic framework for partnerships at national and provincial levels, with related treasury regulations and another dedicated capacity. There have also been a number of explicit statements in support of partnerships. Extensive consultation took place with stakeholders at policy level, and around projects, with government departments, provincial governments, organised local government, trade unions and consumer groups. Trade union resistance continues to test the government's commitment to PSP. |

Source: Nickson, 2001a, 2001b; Goldin and Heymans, 1999

Political will

There is little question, however, that formal private sector participation hinges on political commitment. Strong, committed leadership helps to drive a process of change in pursuit of objectives, to establish and maintain a focus and to motivate participants to overcome problems. It gives direction to public officials, departments and sub-national governments, and provides assurance to potential investors. Investors normally want to know the degree to which government is committed to private sector involvement, whether it will sustain that commitment throughout the life of transactions, and whether politically sensitive issues have been dealt with effectively. Such commitment is needed at both local and higher levels of government. While this chapter focuses on the impact of political will outside local government, the importance of local leaders and champions of private sector participation should not be underestimated and is discussed in detail in Chapter 12.

In most countries, despite decentralisation policies and autonomy rhetoric, the links between higher and lower levels of government are still extremely strong, and the commitment and understanding at national (and perhaps provincial/state) levels is therefore critical. Municipalities must consider how private sector participation can become politically desirable, how support for it can be mobilised, and how political commitment can be translated into action conducive to engaging the private sector. Box 10.1 describes the political will and driving force for change found in diverse political contexts.

Political desirability

PPPs generally seem to become a political priority under three conditions, which are sometimes related to each other. First, a government may voluntarily decide to explore the engagement of the formal private sector for ideological reasons, or to reform a public service. Such a shift of direction typically, albeit not only, occurs when there is a change of government. Second, an economic crisis may encourage a government to explore new ways of managing public assets and services, including partnership approaches. Finally, amid such crises, donor or lender structural adjustment programmes may require governments in developing countries to introduce private sector participation.

Municipal capacity to work in partnerships involving the international private sector may be promoted by any one of these conditions, but action is often initiated at the local level as well. In Zimbabwe, for instance, the national initiative for corporatisation and privatisation was promoted by the World Bank Economic Structural Adjustment Programme. At the local level the change in government and political mismanagement of municipal finances also created the inclination among administrators to pursue PPPs in earnest. Despite the unrest in Colombia, certain other factors created a politically supportive context in which to launch a partnership initiative. These included a protracted economic recession, institutional reforms to the water sector that promoted a market approach, an ambitious national-level water and sanitation plan, a deepening fiscal crisis in local government, and rapid urbanisation.

Building political support

Political support for private sector participation is not, however, driven only by externalities. In many countries the impetus in favour of private sector involvement is driven by high-ranking political champions who spearhead the process of policy and legislative reform. In many countries it is possible to identify the individual(s) who championed the process at the outset and who worked with sectoral departments or local government to put policy in place. It is also vital that policy-level leaders bring about a convergence of departmental attitudes and objectives and build support in relevant administrative departments. Cross-sectoral capacity building programmes at the national level are often significant turning points, enabling change at lower levels of government.

This may not always be the case, however, and irrespective of the policy environment, political resistance can thwart efforts at the lower levels of government. In those situations in which policy on PPPs is relatively quiet, not actively

10

Links to Boxes
4.3, 10.5, 10.8, 12.4

Box **10.2**   **National Support Structures**
South Africa

Since 1994, the South African government has placed considerable emphasis on the elimination of service backlogs from the apartheid era. The Municipal Infrastructure Investment Framework, published in 1995, was the first attempt to quantify the investments needed. It demonstrated that this challenge could not be met by the public sector alone: it needed partnerships with private investors and operators. Thus, subsequent government policies on urban development and local government have recognised the need for partnerships. Some municipalities began to explore options involving the private sector, adding to the pressure for clearer government guidance on approaching partnerships. In 1997 the then Department of Constitutional Development published a first set of guidelines for PPPs at the municipal level. Government departments and the Development Bank of Southern Africa (DBSA) introduced municipalities to the partnership concept, but soon the need for a more consolidated initiative became apparent.

In 1997 the Departments of Finance and Constitutional Development and the DBSA joined forces to establish a support unit to act as a catalyst for PPPs. The Municipal Infrastructure Investment Unit (MIIU) has the explicit objectives of encouraging private sector investment in municipal services, and building sustainable capacity in the municipal, private and consultancy sectors. Located at the DBSA, the MIIU was conceived as a five-year project. Staff are either seconded from the DBSA or are international experts supported with funding from USAID.

In practical terms, the MIIU provides technical assistance to municipalities that are preparing service projects for private sector investment. It provides funding support, on a cost-sharing basis, for municipalities to appoint the specialist consultants who are needed for project preparation, and also provides direct technical assistance to municipalities regarding the process of structuring PPPs. Typically, this includes guidance on the conceptualisation and design of PPP initiatives; the selection, supervision and evaluation of local consultants charged with preparing feasibility studies and bid document packages; the negotiation of PPP contracts; and appropriate means and methods for interacting with national-level stakeholders such as labour unions and relevant ministries (Hlahla, 1999). It then provides limited support for municipalities when they move forwards into the initial stages of implementation.

The MIIU is currently addressing approximately 40 municipal projects in water, electricity and solid waste as well as other non-basic municipal services. The unit has received over 40 applications from other interested municipalities. Deals concluded to date include the two most prominent water concessions in the country, in Nelspruit and Dolphin Coast. Its support is demand-led. Municipalities must request assistance and meet rigorous procedures to qualify for technical and financial assistance. Given the aim of creating PPP 'success stories' within the country, it is therefore likely that those municipalities receiving support from the MIIU and launching PPP initiatives already have a significant degree of financial capacity and technical skill. Basic municipal management skills are being developed through broader initiatives, led by the Department of Provincial and Local Government, the DBSA and donors.

The process adopted by the MIIU in the development of PPPs also aims to build a national consultancy sector with the ability to underpin municipal initiatives in the future. This is envisaged as a key tool in the creation of a sustainable market for PPPs in South Africa. To this end, local consultants have worked beside international consultants on the projects, building skills as core team members but accompanied by expertise and experience. The unit places a high degree of importance on learning from international experience and the inputs of the World Bank and bilateral donors.

In the light of its experience with municipal PPPs, the MIIU has been able to contribute significantly to the government's development of policy and legislation. South African government policy on partnerships was contained in a Draft White Paper on Municipal Service Partnerships published in April 2000. Partnerships are also specifically described, and their procurement regulated, in the Municipal Systems Act of 2000.

Sources: Hlahla, 1999; Barry Jackson, MIIU

promoted, ambiguous or in its infancy, municipalities may need to build political support at higher levels of government for specific initiatives. In Nepal, high-ranking national politicians refused to grant permission to Kathmandu Metropolitan City to introduce a concession for a bus terminal, and the initiative was abandoned after the papers were signed.

Municipal officials will also be interested in the political position of key stakeholders such as trade unions and consumer groups. Key national-level stakeholders involved in private sector participation will include national federations of unions, and national unions representing local government workers. Many are ideologically opposed to the process; others may be concerned merely about the interests (particularly job losses) of their members; others may object because they have not been adequately consulted. Evidence from various countries highlights the difficulties created at local level when national trade unions elect to oppose private sector involvement. In Nelspruit, South Africa, for example, the national trade unions resisted private sector participation in the water sector even though the local unions had agreed and worker terms and conditions had been addressed.

The role of national-level consumer groups may also be critical, and municipalities will have to familiarise themselves with the potential roles of such groups. In some countries consumer organisations have taken a strong interest in private sector participation. In Indonesia, the consumer organisation has a good relationship with the water companies and a strong voice in the media, advocating sensible tariff levels to ensure sustainability while also promoting consumer rights.

Municipal efforts will also be affected by the political credibility that the national government establishes with potential partners. Consistency, authority, and commitment to appropriate policies, laws and institutions will reduce risk, while failure to enforce, slowness in decision-making, and uncertainty will deter investors and increase costs for the municipality and the consumers. Municipal officials can bring some pressure to bear by joining task forces and representing local-level interests clearly and persistently.

☐ Expressing political commitment

Clear expressions of political commitment supported by action from higher levels of government will enable municipal champions to bring about change more rapidly and ease the process. This expression may be in the form of:

- policy statements, verbal and written commitments;
- development of private sector participation strategy;
- creation of task forces and vehicles to promote discussion and knowledge;
- establishing policy and enabling regulatory frameworks and institutional conditions that remove obstacles; and/or
- publication of rules and guidelines.

Some governments have created dedicated capacities to support private sector participation: The Philippine's BOT centre and South Africa's Municipal Infrastructure Investment Unit (MIIU) (described in Box 10.2) include private sector participation experts that advise participants and promote private sector participation. Such capacities help to highlight technical issues, raise awareness of private sector participation as an option, and cut across departmental and other divides. Such experts can advise local governments or enforce policy conditions, such as treasury requirements. Their ability to enforce such conditions is, however, restricted because their role is advisory and they have no fiscal hold over municipalities.

☐ Coping with changing politics

It is also not uncommon for municipalities to find that a change in government (and to a lesser extent a change in political leadership) is accompanied by revision to the policy framework concerning private sector involvement in services.

| Box 10.3 | **Policy and Legislation for PSP**
Colombia

In the early 1990s the Colombian government decided to prioritise the nation's needs for water and sanitation. This decision followed decades of decline in the public water service, as well as the decentralisation process that was taking place in Colombia (see Box 10.6). In 1995, the national Water and Sanitation Plan was ratified by the national economic and social policy council, addressing the coverage, efficiency and quality of water and sanitation provision throughout the country. The primary goal was to increase water supply by connecting nearly 7 million people, to reach an average connection rate of 90%. In sanitation, the goal was to reach 77% of the population with mains sewerage by 2010. The estimated capital cost for achieving these two targets was US$1400 million. The plan also aimed to improve drinking water quality and reduce leakage rates, and it included environmental conservation measures.

In order to achieve these ambitious targets, significant institutional reform of the water sector was necessary. The 1991 Constitution emphasised the importance of efficient public services, and in 1994 a major change in national government policy re-emphasised basic service provision. New legislation (Law 142) laid down explicit criteria for efficiency in terms of planning, regulation and supervision, and marked a radical shift towards a more positive attitude to the private sector. As in other sectors, the government promoted a market approach that assigned a key role to private capital and technology in the institutional reform process. There were three reasons for this major policy shift:

1. a recognition that the country could not afford the level of public spending needed for infrastructure, and that private resources were needed to fill the gap, leaving public funds for social programmes;
2. a response to the fear in central government that the devolution process could lead to a re-emergence of inefficiency in the provision of services under direct municipal control; and
3. the growing pressure on central government from international financial institutions to open up basic service provision to PSP.

The legislation introduced in 1994 made explicit provision for the regulation of PSP. Article 69 created separate regulatory bodies for water and sanitation, electricity and gas, and telecommunications. A regulatory body for water and sanitation, the Comison de Regulacion de Agua Potable y Saneamiento Basico (CRA) was set up as a semi-autonomous body under the Ministry of Economic Development. Its aim is 'to promote competition, encourage investment and prevent abuse of monopoly power, in order to ensure reasonable tariffs, high quality and ample coverage in service delivery'. One of the most important tasks of the CRA has been to authorise a new tariff structure that reflects the true cost of delivering water and sanitation and establishes transparent rules for cross-subsidies in favour of disadvantaged groups.

The same law specified that a public services watchdog, the Superintendencia de Servicios Publicos Domiciliarios (SSP), should monitor the day-to-day operation of the companies entrusted with the delivery of basic public services. The SSP has separate departments for water and sanitation, electricity and gas, and telecommunications, and is supported by a network of branches at the departmental level that liaise with municipal authorities. In the case of water and sanitation, its key tasks are to ensure that the regulatory decisions of the CRA are applied, in particular with regard to cross-subsidies, complaints from customers, and the examination of corporate financial management. The SSP has the power to fine water companies for the violation of agreed norms.

The joint venture (*empresa mixta*) emerged as the institutional arrangement preferred by central government to fulfil the twin policy objectives of strengthening local government and encouraging PSP. The arguments put forward in favour of the joint venture were economic and political. The economic argument emphasised that the municipality retained ownership of the assets, as under the more conventional concession contract arrangement, but with the added advantage that, as a major shareholder in the joint venture, the municipality had a financial interest in promoting efficiency in service delivery. The political argument emphasised that, as a major shareholder, the municipality was better positioned to monitor and control the activities of its private sector partner. This was contrasted with the conventional concession contract, under which the public sector effectively handed over control of the day-to-day operations to the concessionaire. Consequently (and despite the resultant conflict of interest) the traditional criticism from public sector unions that the municipality had 'sold out' to the private sector was muted by the joint venture arrangement. |

Sources: Nickson, 2001a; www.suderservicios.aov.co; CRA website, www.cra.gov.co

This can happen at the local level as well, as seen in Cartagena or The Philippines, where the newly elected mayor of the city of Cebu threatened that his city would not honour a debt incurred by his predecessor. The impact in this instance was absorbed by other municipalities, which became unable to raise finance on capital markets due to the loss of confidence in municipal administration and its capacity to act as a reliable partner. While it is necessary for municipal officials to look out for the impacts of changing political landscapes, increasingly, partnerships with the formal private sector, bound by legal agreement, will need to be formally renegotiated. They cannot be simply overturned without widespread ramifications.

Economic Context

Municipalities have relatively little control over the economic context within which they operate, yet it severely affects their ability to implement PPP approaches to service delivery. Even amid the greatest political commitment, and the soundest policy and regulatory frameworks, negative economic conditions constrain private sector involvement. Conversely, in buoyant economies, the opportunities and incentives for private sector participation increase.

Various aspects of the economic environment shape the scope for, and affect the capacity of, a municipality in a developing country to establish private sector participation. They are: the changing global economy, the pressure to balance growth strategies with effective interventions to alleviate poverty, and national macro-economic trends and policies.[2] While they are outside the scope of the municipality, these factors will determine private sector incentives and the attractiveness and risk of the proposition. Municipalities must familiarise themselves with the impacts.

☐ The changing global economy

The last two decades of the 20th century saw a dramatic surge in the levels of economic integration across national boundaries. This has been due, first, to the revolution in information technology, which made telecommunications more accessible, international transport more streamlined, and investors more mobile. Second, in the aftermath of the Cold War international relations have shifted, both politically and economically, to a greater emphasis on market forces. The outcome of policies being shaped by this range of interests has been a market-led approach to economic management, a reduction of state involvement in the economy, privatisation of service delivery and deregulation of the economy, including the removal of trade barriers.

With exposure to global trends, the need to be competitive has increased, and the ability of the state to control its economic and political environment has diminished. States remain vital parts of the global system, but their roles are increasingly defined in relation to other players. Municipalities need to understand the enhanced role of multinationals and the role of multilateral organisations. In relation to infrastructure, this includes the World Bank, the International Monetary Fund and regional bodies. Municipalities must also become familiar with, and understand the influence of, the new mobility of participants in the global economy and the factors that affect their decision-making. Because investors choose investment locations on the basis of factors like the quality of infrastructure, tax regimes and planning flexibility, city management is proving increasingly critical in their ability to attract international investors.

As deficit reduction and public sector reform have become major indicators of the quality of economic management, the fiscal restraint required in this international context means that governments face the challenge of balancing this with the other financial pressures. In particular, while attracting foreign direct investment and increasing employment opportunities by fostering economic growth and development, government has also to confront poverty and work directly towards poverty reduction. This is one of the major policy tensions that affect economic policy generally, and the involvement of the private sector in service delivery specifically.

Links to Boxes
4.5, 9.4, 9.5, 11.3, 11.4, 12.7

Box **10.4** **How Political Economy Impedes Municipal-level PSP**
Zimbabwe

In 1997, Gweru City Council in Zimbabwe agreed to launch a PPP in water and sanitation services in the city. The preparation process entailed many of the actions and approaches associated with PSP best practice. There was also significant national support, and a national task force assisted Gweru and other councils that were willing to explore private sector involvement at the local level. Yet, by mid-2001, Gweru City had still not signed a final agreement. Mounting political unrest and macro-economic turmoil led to growing caution on the part of the private operator.

The experience of Gweru City Council demonstrates powerfully how the macro-economic environment, and the political developments that shape that environment, determine the scope for PSP. Despite a cautious preparation process involving a range of stakeholders, including the Zimbabwean government, the political and economic instability of the country has to date prevented a water concession agreement being finalised.

The political and economic instability in Zimbabwe is now a matter of widespread international concern. In 1980, at Independence from the UK, the average income per person was US$950, and a Zimbabwean dollar was worth more than a US dollar. The government actively pursued policies to promote a more equitable life for the citizens, and focused particularly on improving health and education services for those who had been disadvantaged under the colonial regime. However, during the 1980s the country developed large budgetary deficits. By early 1991, the rising unemployment led the government to accept a stringent economic structural adjustment programme (ESAP). As a result, policies of liberalisation, deregulation and macro-economic stabilisation were adopted, mainly to improve the balance of payments and increase foreign investment to stimulate growth and employment.

By the mid-1990s, unemployment was estimated to be running at 25–30%, the budget deficit rose, and public borrowing amounted to 10% of GDP. International agencies like the IMF, the World Bank and the EU withheld financial assistance and development support. By the late 1990s, some government policies invited further international disapproval, and undermined international confidence. Prominent among these were a decision to pay out (unbudgeted) pensions to war veterans and political detainees, and a threat to expropriate land belonging to white commercial farmers. In 1998–99, the government spent approximately one-third of its annual budget on the Congolese war and failed to repay IMF loans. By 2000, the land issue had become a major source of tension between Zimbabwe and some of its major trading partners, including the UK. This situation has since escalated amid concerns about government curbs imposed on opposition parties and the press.

By 2000, the country was hampered by a scarcity of fuel and sporadic power cuts. Unemployment had reached 50%. The central government also gave pay rises of 60–90% to civil servants. The net result has been an even greater shortage of international currency and a failure to meet balance-of-payment obligations. Inflation averaged about 50% for the financial year 1999–2000, and international confidence is at its lowest point since Independence. Investment has therefore been seriously curtailed. During the period in which the Gweru Concession was being formulated, the Zimbabwean currency suffered from massive devaluation. When the tender for Gweru was advertised in November 1997, ZD 18 was equal to US$1; this was followed by a plunge to ZD 40 in late 1998. With inflation peaking at 70% in October 1999, confidence declined further. By December 2001 the value was around ZD 80 to US$1, with an average inflation rate of well over 50%.

As an agricultural centre with a limited industrial base, the problems of the country are directly reflected in Gweru, and the well-run council has been badly affected by national government actions. Yet Gweru City Council's initiative was nonetheless a bold one, testing new options and preparing an ambitious concession contract that attracted great admiration from consultants and the private sector. With economic confidence at particularly low ebb, however, the concession seems unlikely to be signed soon, if ever. With a Memorandum of Understanding in place, the city council and the private contractor entered a renewed round of talks to resolve a revised business plan. The contractor argued that the main issue was tariff policies; but having resolved this, the city council is in little doubt that the increasingly unstable economic and political environment is the biggest impediment.

The future of the whole initiative, which was in preparation for more than four years, remains uncertain.

Source: Plummer and Nhemachena, 2001

Macro-economic trends

Typical macro-economic trends and policies that affect private sector interest and confidence are:

- size of budgetary deficits;
- levels of inflation;
- value of the local currency;
- employment trends; and
- state of a country's key economic and service delivery sectors.

The perception of economic instability severely undermines the confidence of investors, because it increases the risk around market demand, prices, costs, political stability and other such factors. This loss of confidence often starts a vicious cycle. It breeds greater loss of confidence, lower investment levels, and hence a worsening in many of the indicators. It is possible for countries to turn this around, as a number of developing countries have shown, but it takes time to rebuild confidence and thus to attract private investors. Overall confidence in the economy, and the vibrancy of the economic climate, thus shape investor perceptions and their propensity to invest in public services. Box 10.4 illustrates how the macro-economic environment in recent years affected Zimbabwe's ability to engage the private sector in service delivery. The challenges that face Zimbabwe often face other developing countries.

It is essential for municipalities to understand, in a timely manner, the implications of economic instability on the potential involvement of the private sector. A great deal of time and money is wasted by both the public and private sectors if municipalities pursue a partnership arrangement that is not viable. International economic advisors and multilaterals such as the World Bank are well placed to provide municipalities with assistance to ensure that partnerships are compatible with economic conditions, and that the management of economic risk is placed centrally in the decision-making framework from an early stage. But this is not to say all PPPs are doomed in unstable economic contexts. Many of the partnerships described in this book are still relevant. One option is to establish private sector arrangements that promote skills and management inputs but not investment. Another is to make arrangements with national private firms that are less concerned about repatriating profits and less cautious about the economic environment. Municipalities could also involve the local small-scale private sector.

Policy Framework

Public policy reflects the critical choices a government makes about its general direction and the various activities required to support that direction. Policy provides a rationale, sets the framework for the allocation of budget resources, and creates the programmes and projects to be implemented with the resources available. Through policy (as seen in Box 10.5) government can translate its political commitment to private sector participation into specific guidance for municipalities (and government at all levels), private participants and other actors.

In some contexts, by refraining from PPP policy formulation policy-makers are also making a statement – sending signals to lower levels of government, private sector operators and financiers that the government is ambiguous about or hostile towards an increase in private sector involvement. Even though many municipalities may launch partnerships while remaining silent on private sector participation policy, it is important for municipal leaders to acknowledge the messages that large private investors are receiving, and the financial consequences of the risks they perceive. Private firms will balance this risk in relation to other externalities and the reward they have calculated they will receive from the arrangement.

10

Box 10.5   The Policy and Legislative Framework of PSP
South Africa

Since South Africa's first democratic government came to power in 1994, the country has been developing numerous new policies to facilitate the reconstruction and development of the nation, and in particular to redress the highly prevalent disparity in access to services and infrastructure. This has included new approaches to economic management, infrastructure and service provision, and local government. The sum of these policies supports PSP both directly and indirectly.

The developmental cornerstone of the new policies is the Reconstruction and Development Plan (RDP), a multi-sector strategy aimed at establishing new paradigms of economic growth, redistribution, public sector reform, participatory development and new modes of service delivery. For macro-economic policy, the growth, employment and redistribution strategy (GEAR) was put in place, focusing on debt management, attracting investment, liberalising trade and creating employment. Both strategies emphasise that government cannot achieve its growth and development objectives without partners. On this basis, a range of other policy frameworks were added to the policy environment that allows for PSP. A strategic framework for PPPs, published in 2000, confirmed the national commitment to PSP, and provided the basis for regulatory and institutional measures specifically targeted at assisting national departments and provincial governments that are negotiating partnership contracts.

In relative terms, local government in South Africa has a more autonomous fiscal relationship with the national treasury, and PSP in the municipal sphere required a specific set of policies. The baseline paper in this regard is the White Paper on Local Government published in 1998. It proposed a more developmental role for municipalities, and among other things emphasised the importance of municipal borrowing on private capital markets, and of service delivery partnerships with private sector, other public agencies and civil society organisations. This policy paper coined the term 'municipal service partnerships' (MSPs) to move away from the implication that only the public and private sectors could be involved in a partnership approach. A White Paper on Municipal Service Partnerships produced thereafter provides local government with the policies and guidelines for action at the local level. It spells out the philosophy behind partnerships and highlights the need for strategic assessment of challenges and issues, stakeholder consultation, and firm institutional and legal measures to firm up the policies.

This policy framework confirms the South African government's commitment to municipal-level PSP and provides directives to municipalities as to how they can implement this partnership vision. Informed by South Africa's experience in consulting trade unions and other stakeholders, the policy framework emphasises the importance of stakeholder involvement in the implementation of PSP.

More specific infrastructure policy is articulated in the Municipal Infrastructure Investment Framework (MIIF) (see Box 10.8), and further policy development is taking place to establish a framework for the provision of free basic services to people who cannot afford them. These policy statements have informed various legislative initiatives to direct municipal services partnerships. The Municipal Systems Act deals with most aspects of municipal administration, and includes specific provisions regarding partnerships. At the time of writing, a Municipal Finance Management Bill was in progress, aiming to improve the quality of municipal financial management, and to enhance the creditworthiness of municipalities. It contains proposals specific for a borrowing framework that would improve the quality of information available to the markets, and enhance certainty in the municipal system.

Inter-governmental transfers from the national to local levels add momentum to these policies. Some grants are specifically aimed at restructuring and reforming municipalities, so as to streamline their activities and make them more efficient. Others target service delivery and infrastructure development, with incentives to leverage PSP.

The policy framework for municipal PSP in South Africa fits into one of the most extensive enabling policy environments in the world, supported by this array of macro-economic, fiscal and development policies, laws and financial support measures. Critics argue that the policy frameworks are too intellectual, that they are lacking in practical application and have not been accompanied by a commensurate level of capacity building for local government. Progress with municipal-level PSP suggests, however, that the policies do have some practical relevance, although some problems have been encountered (notably with regard to tariff-setting procedures), and implementation is still in its infancy. The broad and specific policy framework in South Africa provides a detailed example of the wide-ranging issues at stake, and the value of systematically addressing those issues in a strategic manner.

Sources: DBSA, 1998;RoSA, 2000

A municipality might find that the policy environment, especially for PPPs, is mostly grounded in macro policies aimed at liberalisation, reducing fiscal deficits, promoting economic growth, and institutional reform. The basis for action at the local level is a broad political commitment to private sector participation, and outlines of the priority areas and issues regarded as pivotal to making PPPs work. The government may or may not have proposed institutional, regulatory and legislative steps to implement the policy position. Of course policy is not just about the international formal sector or the role of national firms in partnership consortiums. Policy (and regulations) on the role of the informal sector will also determine the latitude that a municipality has to engage in a targeted partnership benefiting the poor.

☐ Policy content

When municipal officials are investigating the existing policy context in relation to formal private sector participation, they need to consider where national government stands on a wide range of issues. These might include:

- whether private sector participation is considered a legitimate or desirable option (e.g., is a municipality required to prioritise the private sector option, or is it the least preferred option?);
- whether particular stakeholders are preferred (e.g., profit, non-profit businesses, micro-enterprises, etc.);
- whether a policy in relation to the poor has been established, and what this policy is;
- whether the government has a policy on competition;
- who sets the price and controls the tariff structure;
- how it intends to regulate the relevant sectors to achieve goals;
- which sectors are to be prioritised (e.g., water, electricity, solid waste management);
- which areas and functions are to be prioritised (e.g., bulk supply, reticulation);
- which organisational arrangements are favoured (e.g., bundling or unbundling);
- whether and how government sees linkages between private sector participation and other policy considerations (e.g., alleviating poverty, job creation);
- how private sector participation will operate within the institutional framework;
- what the opportunities are for piloting innovative approaches as yet untested by the government;
- which institutional reforms ensure policy development, regulation, implementation, monitoring and evaluation; and
- the resources that government is willing to allocate to implement its private sector participation policies.

☐ Policy process

Apart from these issues of content, a municipality should be concerned with understanding the government policy on the process and sequencing of reform that enables private sector participation. Are different interests mobilised in support of policy? Is there a coherent view among sector departments, agencies and levels towards private sector participation? How is government planning to address the vast range of issues concerning private sector participation? Will it resolve all the issues together, or proceed pragmatically with private sector participation and address barriers on the basis of need?

Clearly, the involvement of the large-scale private sector in municipal service provision benefits if there is cross-governmental policy coherence and consistency. However, in the context of resource-deficient government, when policy is developed at the insistence of donors, the capacity needed to facilitate such coherence is often lacking. Furthermore, incoherence often reflects a broader debate concerning the role of government in the provision of public services.

To support partnerships and promote key public policy objectives, the policy framework must be linked to sound regulatory practices such as curbing monopoly practices, alleviating poverty, promoting universal service access and fostering empowerment. This often requires dedicated institutional capacity to drive and coordinate policy and regulatory reform. If this leads to greater coherence, the foundation is in place for municipalities to embark on partnerships with private service providers. The following section considers the critical issue of this regulatory framework.

Box **10.6**   **The Impacts of Decentralisation Policy**
Colombia

Links to Boxes
7.7, 7.12, 7.19, 8.2, 10.3

As part of a wider state reform process, Colombia underwent one of the most far-reaching processes of decentralisation in Latin America. Moving from a system of centralised departmental government, responsibility for major functions has been gradually devolved back to local government since 1987. This includes responsibility for water supply and sanitation, environmental health, construction and maintenance of schools, health clinics and roads, low-cost housing, agricultural extension, urban transportation and cadastral surveying (surveys that show the extent, value and ownership of land for taxation purposes). This decision to decentralise led to the closure of a number of ministerial departments and autonomous agencies of central government, such as the municipal development institute, which had previously held overall responsibility for water supply, school construction and environmental health. The implementation of this reform was not always properly planned and sequenced, however. For example, the hasty closure of the state water corporation led to considerable disruption in water supplies because many municipalities were not prepared for assuming this new responsibility.

Following a public campaign spearheaded by university students, a new Constitution was promulgated in 1991. Its over-riding concern was to build a participatory democracy by opening up the political system, by including former guerrilla groups, decentralising political power, reducing bureaucratic controls and giving the executive more direct control over the administrative structure. The new Constitution defined the Colombian nation as 'decentralised', and several articles granted a new degree of political and financial autonomy to local government. The term of municipal office was lengthened, and the discretionary system of central government transfers to local government was replaced by one based on a constitutional guarantee.

In 1993, legislation (Law 60) enabled the radical re-allocation of responsibilities between different layers of government that had been envisaged in the 1991 Constitution. This further deepened the process of fiscal decentralisation. Municipalities began to receive a new central government transfer, the *situado fiscal*, which arose from the devolution of responsibilities for health care and education. The VAT transfer was replaced by a general revenue-sharing agreement, the *transferencia*, under which the share of national fiscal revenue transferred to municipalities was envisaged to rise gradually from 14% in 1993 to 22% by 2001. The *transferencia* was earmarked for social investment. A minimum of 80% of the total received by each municipality must be spent on basic public services: education (30%), health (25%), water supply (20%) and recreation and culture (5%). By 2002, according to current constitutional requirements, the combined transfer to municipalities from the two main central government grants (*situado fiscal* and *transferencia*) is likely to surpass 30% of national fiscal revenue, the highest share in Latin America.

The reform of the public water service (described in Box 10.3) in the early 1990s placed strong emphasis on efficient public services and promoted a market-oriented approach. Decentralisation created the scope within the state machinery to allow for localised services management and innovation, and PSP became a strongly supported way of assisting local governments in doing this efficiently. Municipal PSP is greatly facilitated by local government being able to effectively negotiate with potential private sector and community partners. The more municipalities have to get approval from higher strata, the less effectively they engage with other parties and the less confidence private partners have in them. This was avoided in Colombia through effective decentralisation policy and implementation.

Often cited as a good example of decentralisation, the Colombian approach has placed municipalities in a position where policies can be developed that are appropriate to the local context, ultimately allowing partnerships to explore innovative alternatives and a range of service delivery options. Decentralisation helped to create a favourable environment for PSP in the 1990s, and together with a new pro-PSP stance, decentralisation policy and legislation opened opportunities for an enhanced private sector role in the provision of what were traditionally thought of as public services.

Source: Nickson, 2001a

10

The Legislative/Regulatory Framework

Decentralisation

At its broadest level, the legislative framework for municipal action is provided through decentralisation legislation. It is likely that municipalities will be very familiar with its content, and will know the extent to which it limits or permits any action they may wish to take with the private sector (both large and small scale) in service delivery.

There are basically three dimensions to effective decentralisation:

1. functions are constitutionally or legally decentralised to the municipal level;
2. municipalities have appropriate capacity to perform their functions; and
3. municipalities have access to the financial resources required to perform their functions.

In many so-called decentralised contexts, however, local governments do not have the power and responsibility to represent their citizens and deliver services; nor do they have staff who are appropriately trained and experienced, or access to their own revenue. They often depend greatly on external sources of finance and the conditions applied to it.

In the context of clear and realistic policy direction from higher levels, if local government has adequate capacity and funding, they should be able to identify and pursue a range of appropriate options for service delivery. This includes partnerships with the formal large-scale private sector (see, for instance, the process in Colombia described in Box 10.6). Where they lack that capacity, power and funding, municipalities cannot negotiate contracts with authority. Under a decentralised governmental structure that brings government closer to the people, municipalities will also have more capacity to consider opportunities for local solutions and the involvement of local stakeholders (such as NGOs and small-scale local service providers).

The Regulatory Framework for Private Sector Participation

Perhaps the most critical aspect of the external operating context for the success of PPPs is the regulatory framework. Understanding this framework is essential. It fundamentally affects the 'what', 'who' and 'how' of service partnerships, and determines, to a significant degree, the capacity of a municipality to structure benefits for the poor. The nature of the regulatory framework will fundamentally affect the capacity of a municipality to attract private investors and to create effective sustainable arrangements. From the private sector perspective it creates incentives, outlines roles and responsibilities, and perhaps standards, and should produce a predictable investment environment. Municipal officials must have a grasp of what it all means.

In some countries government will have created a legislative framework that explicitly allows for private sector participation, describes the limits of private sector involvement in municipal services, and enforces certain types of behaviour. The regulatory framework may be comprised of instruments regulating investors and non-state operators in the private and voluntary sectors, the users of services, government decision-makers at different levels, and consumers. In many other countries, such a regulatory framework does not exist and municipalities must depend on the contract as the primary regulatory instrument. In this unregulated context, key aspects of the regulatory environment are no longer external to the municipality but will form a key part of how they set up the partnership.

Partnerships will also be determined by other laws (e.g., employment and labour practice). These laws must be coordinated and form a coherent whole to avoid any disputes. It is therefore often necessary for municipalities to utilise and coordinate the range of instruments that regulate private sector participation and the sector.

Box 10.7   The Quest for Better Regulation of PSP
            Córdoba, Argentina

Links to Boxes
6.16, 8.8

Following the introduction of pioneering legislation in 1989, and in the context of widespread state reform, PSP has proliferated in the provision of a wide range of basic services throughout Argentina. In the case of water supply and sanitation, contracts have been signed with the private sector in the capital city, Buenos Aires, as well as other major cities including Córdoba, Formosa, Corrientes, Santa Fe, Mendoza and Tucumán. Growing dissatisfaction in Argentina at the weak regulation of the private sector in service delivery has, however, characterised initiatives since the early 1990s. By the end of the millennium there was widespread concern in Argentina at the laxity of regulation during the previous decade. In several cases, regulatory bodies were established after the key privatisation decisions had been taken, but high price rises and poor service quality were major sources of complaint. This criticism reached a high point during the power failure that blacked out large parts of Buenos Aires for 10 days in February 1999. At that time regulatory agencies in general were strongly criticised in the media for their weakness.

At the federal level, in 2000 the incoming government sought to encourage greater competition among privatised utilities by clamping down on what were seen as abuses of privilege by private companies that had benefited from monopoly conditions under weak regulation for nearly a decade. This tighter regulatory stance by the federal government was mirrored by the incoming provincial government of Córdoba in May 2000. The regulatory framework for public utilities, including urban water supply, was radically altered by the creation of a new Secretariat for the Control and Management of Contracts, Secretariado de Control y Gestión de Contratos. Hitherto, water regulation in the province had been the responsibility of the Water and Sanitation Department (Departamento de Aguas y Saneamiento, DAS) of the provincial government.

In addition, the new provincial government created a novel multisectoral regulatory agency, known as the Ente Regulador de Servicios Publicos (ERSEP), which will regulate a diverse range of privatised public services. At present there are only two privatised utilities that come under its remit: Aguas Cordobesas and the privatised road company, Red de Accesos a Córdoba. The latter maintains and improves the five major access roads to the city of Córdoba under a 25-year concession signed in September 1997. However, four more activities will soon be added to ERSEP's remit as a result of privatisation plans in progress.

The mixed bag of responsibilities of the new agency reflects the complex mosaic of public sector ownership under Argentina's federal system of government. For example, although Aguas Cordobesas supplies water only within the jurisdiction of the Municipality of Córdoba, the assets belong to the provincial government and not to the municipal government. In contrast, the regulation of the company that operates Córdoba's international airport, Aeropuertos Argentina 2000, will not become part of the ERSEP remit because this 30-year contract was awarded in February 1998 by the federal government, which owns the assets of this and 35 other airports included in the concession.

The new regulatory agency is collegiate in nature. The six-member board comprises three members appointed by the governing party in the provincial assembly, two members from the opposition parties and one member representing consumers. This direct representation of consumer interests on a regulatory body is unique, reflecting the widespread dissatisfaction among consumers over the Argentine privatisation programme. But the direct inclusion of consumer interests in ERSEP has also come in for criticism because of the danger of them being overwhelmed by the other political interests represented on the board. ERSEP will be financed through a 1.5% levy on the tariffs of the privatised utilities, as well as any fines that it imposes.

In the particular case of urban water supply for the city of Córdoba, ERSEP contracts out responsibility for monitoring water quality to a state-owned laboratory that examines 600 samples per month. ERSEP also monitors implementation of the investment programme of the concessionaire, Aguas Cordobesas. The company carries out repairs worth US$20,000 per month and submits a monthly report to ERSEP. It is still unclear whether the newly established ERSEP will play the role of a regulatory body, *ente regulador*, balancing the interests of consumers and of the private concessionaire, or whether it will play the role of contract enforcer, *orgáno de control*, on behalf of the provincial government. The confusion is enhanced by the fact that ERSEP is not an autonomous body, nor does it report directly to the provincial governor. Instead, it comes under the remit of the provincial government's Ministry of Public Works. In practice it seems that ERSEP is likely to carry out both functions – contract compliance and wider regulation.

In summary, the new regulatory agency established in Córdoba is highly novel but also controversial. Its collegiate members are overtly political, its multisectoral remit endows it with a range of complex responsibilities, and the inclusion of consumer interests on its board (rather than in an independent body), while promoting transparency within the regulator, runs the risk of their domination by political interests.

Source: Nickson, 2001b

A regulatory framework needs to balance sometimes-conflicting interests and concerns. Both financiers and operators want to know that they can run effective businesses, and so incentives for private partners mostly aim to create certainty about the operating environment and their ability to recover costs (see, for instance, the regulatory framework in Córdoba described in Box 10.7). A municipality will need to explore whether or not the national regulatory context provides this certainty and, if it does not, develop ways of promoting the development of such a framework and creating it through the contract. In cities with a high proportion of low-income households, municipalities need to ensure that the nature and scope of the regulatory context also implicitly addresses the needs of the poor. Recent World Bank activity in this area[3] provides a substantial base for understanding the form this regulatory environment might take, although experience of implementation is still limited.

Why regulate?

The purpose of regulation is to control private sector activity to limit the likelihood of market failure. There is much debate over the validity of such intervention,[4] but the potential sources of market failure in relation to infrastructure include: the monopolistic tendencies of some service sectors, externalities causing the unintended capture of benefits, and the lack of information.[5] The increasing role of the private sector in infrastructure and service-related activities now means governments are withdrawing from the role of provider but stepping up their role as a regulator.

What are the objectives of regulation?

There is much debate about the benefits and drawbacks of government intervention in market mechanisms. The objectives of regulation occur at various levels and may cover a range of national policy and municipal goals including efficiency and economic growth. Putting poor people at the centre of the question, however, the objective of regulation is to ensure that the delivery process and the outcomes achieved address the basic health, environmental, access and equity concerns of the municipality and the society. Municipalities may need advice to determine whether their own objectives are best met through regulation or market forces, the degree of regulation and the nature of the regulatory mechanism.

What is regulated?

In order to achieve municipal objectives for service delivery it is necessary for municipal decision-makers to consider the regulation of the price of the service, the quality of the service, and the entry of providers into the service market.

■ Price

The need for price regulation is linked to the existence of a monopolistic environment. If there is adequate competition, the price may be determined by the market. In some network services such as telecommunications and electricity and to some extent water and sewerage, many providers have market power, suggesting the need for price regulation. This is likely to include the level and structure of the price (tariff) and the mechanisms for adjusting the price (Who? When? Which calculation?).

Experience suggests that the most positive outcomes from private sector behaviour come about through incentive- or performance-based forms of price regulation. Disincentives may be created by overly prescriptive control mechanisms that threaten the viability of business, and give operators no mechanism to influence price in relation to cost.

Service delivery to the poor will be affected by price regulation. On the one hand, it is important to recognise that price regulation may be hindering improvements.

10

Links to Boxes
4.3, 10.2, 10.5, 12.4

Box 10.8   Policy for Affordable Services
South Africa

At the national level, South Africa has developed a Municipal Infrastructure Investment Framework (MIIF) to deal with the challenge of improving basic services for the poor. As in many middle- and low-income countries, a large proportion of the South African poor lack the income to pay for services at rates that would make service provision viable for private operators, and poverty tends to create a disincentive to potential private investment. Recognising the implications of this, and with a clear mandate to improve basic services as part of the post-apartheid Reconstruction and Development Programme, the government introduced a differentiated service plan that matches affordability.

The MIIF policy statement, established in 1995, now provides guidance for (mostly municipal) service delivery, dealing with national and municipal priorities and the challenges of realistically addressing backlogs. The aim is to facilitate PSP by providing municipalities, service providers and communities with a framework within which they can negotiate service levels and costs.

The Municipal Infrastructure Investment Framework:

- estimates services backlogs for local governments throughout South Africa;
- proposes affordable service levels;
- suggests how the backlogs can be addressed in an affordable manner; and
- suggests institutional and financial approaches to the challenges of providing services.

As such, it forms the basis for a Consolidated Municipal Infrastructure Programme (CMIP), established in 1997, to ensure:

- at least a basic level of services for all South Africans within 10 years;
- long-term financial sustainability;
- strengthened institutional capacity of municipalities;
- a single coherent funding process for municipal infrastructure;
- rapid improvement of delivery;
- synchronised housing and infrastructure delivery; and
- integration of rural and urban service delivery.

As a guideline to stakeholders and municipalities, the MIIF defines different levels of services. This is intended to allow for the installation of services in combinations, and in sequences, that consumers choose and can afford. The proposed levels are depicted below.

	Basic services	Intermediate services	Full services: low-income households	Full services: high-income households
Water	Communal standpipes	Yard taps	In house	In house
Sanitation	Ventilated improved pit latrines	Full waterborne	Full waterborne	Full waterborne
Electricity	5/8-amp supply	20/30-amp supply (pre-paid)	60-amp supply	60-amp supply
Roads	Graded	Gravel	Paved	Paved
Stormwater drainage	Earth-lined open channel	Open channel, other linings	Piped systems	Piped systems
Refuse removal	Communal	Kerbside removal	Kerbside removal	Kerbside removal

While these levels are merely indicative, they provide a basis for differentiated levels, structured around what municipalities and customers can afford. The South African government has made a commitment to ensuring the delivery of at least a basic level of municipal services to all households, and free basic services for poor citizens who cannot pay. The gradation of service standards in the MIIF establishes a stepping stone towards that end.

Sources: RoSA, 1997a; DBSA, 1998

- Lower tariffs for services to the poor only help those who already obtain a service from a regulated provider. Many of the most vulnerable groups will obtain their water and sanitation services informally, and many will not obtain any solid waste service at all.
- Regulated tariffs that do not reflect real costs often work to the benefit of those in remote locations (where the cost of supply is more expensive) – this will include the poor and the non-poor. But it will deter private providers from extending networks to remote areas, and thus exclude further the unsupplied vulnerable groups.

On the other hand, the suppliers of many poor communities have been unregulated for decades, and in those instances where the market has failed to produce reasonable prices, the poor may be paralysed by exorbitant rates. The regulation of the informal sector (such as provider associations) needs careful consideration, and municipalities should be aware that this is likely to be most effective at the local level, closer to the consumer and the suppliers. That is not to say that it becomes a municipal role, but that municipalities may need to facilitate at an early stage options that address the reality of service delivery to the poor. Municipal action towards such regulation is described in Box 10.10.

Price regulation is complex and it needs to address the range of suppliers and balance the key issue of improving access for the poor, which is linked to affordability, against political pressures and pressures from the private sector. In practice, price regulation is difficult to resolve and, in any case, used for political gain. Removing it from the political domain is the only way to ensure that mechanisms are structured to meet predetermined and agreed transparent objectives. This issue concerns the process of regulation.

■ Quality

Closely linked to the regulation of the price of the service is the quality (level) of service provided for that price, as described in Chapter 7. While it is possible that competition may reduce the need for regulation of quality, a number of guidelines are suggested to ensure that municipal objectives are met through the existing regulatory framework. These include:

- The use of outcome-based or possibly output-based performance measures rather than input- or process-based rules. This means measuring results (e.g., reduced mortality and morbidity, or the number of households serviced) rather than monitoring materials and construction methods.
- Ensuring that the regulatory environment enables graduated improvement rather than unachievable high levels of service. As we have seen earlier, regulatory environments that establish ambitious universal coverage rules can be inappropriate. South Africa's Municipal Infrastructure Investment Framework, illustrated in Box 10.8, is an example of a national policy framework that specifies in principle what levels of service government regards as acceptable.
- The regulatory framework for graduated service provision should provide incentives for change over time: for the consumers to improve the service they receive, and for service providers to improve the service they provide. This approach tends to encourage immediate (perhaps temporary) improvements rather than lengthy delays before the poorest groups see any change to the quality of service provided.

■ Entry

The degree of regulation necessary for price and quality has been determined to a large extent by whether or not a competitive marketplace can be established. The days of infrastructure and service delivery being natural monopolies have passed (and perhaps never really existed in relation to service delivery to poor areas). Services such as solid waste can be unbundled (see Chapter 8) and effective levels of competition established for collection, for transfer etc. Tendering processes can be established to ensure that disposal and recycling activities operate in a competitive environment. Given low levels of network coverage, sanitation services exist in a market that is far from monopolistic. In practice, a wide range of (unregulated, informal and/or illegal) small-scale service providers has filled sometimes massive gaps in the sewerage

| Box 10.9   What Is Regulatory Capture?

The independence of regulators is sometimes compromised. This is often referred to as 'regulatory capture'. It means, in short, that regulators advocate the interests of the producers they are intended to regulate. This happens either because they are under control of those interests or unable to stand up to them. This problem can take different forms:

- A regulatory agency might further the industry's interests at the expense of consumers, be more responsive to the industry pressures, or become too closely identified with the industry.
- Some regulators become overly protective of the regulated firms.
- Others identify too much with regulated firms' decisions or objectives.

Regulatory capture mostly reflects power imbalances.

- The ability of regulators to maintain their independence is, for example, often compromised because the regulator and the regulated industry both draw experts from the same limited pool. Regulatory agencies mostly require the services of individuals who are experts in the industries to be regulated. The regulated industry is therefore often an important source of future employment opportunities for the regulatory agencies' staff. This problem is more likely to occur in developing countries, where utilities are strong and the pool of experts limited.
- Sometimes, the officials in the regulatory agency are of a lesser professional standing and expertise than those within the industry. Often, regulatory agencies cannot offer remuneration that competes with that offered by industry participants, so the former's staff are less experienced or are not industry pacesetters. This weakens a regulator's capacity to exert effective control, especially if it deals with well-staffed and highly skilled firms and utilities.
- Personal relationships provide incentives for regulatory officials to soften their stance towards regulated firms. As part of the industry, such experts are likely to be sympathetic to the industry's interests, and are often likely to have had ties with those they are supposed to regulate.
- Regulators are sometimes also not as well organised as interest groups. The latter tend to have a more direct interest in the sector than broad groups of consumers with only an indirect or distant stake. Industry interest groups therefore exercise political pressure on regulators and legislators. Such pressure is not always actively exerted: for example, industry participants may simply exhaust the agency's capacity by engaging it in endless, costly and even trivial appeals.
- A related cause of regulatory capture is asymmetrical information. The firms and utilities in a particular industry often have more and better industry information at their disposal than regulators and governments. In fact, the main source of information is often the regulated firm; it has the incentive to acquire and hold good information because of its sizeable investments. They stand to lose if they lack such information. Industries are therefore often ahead on information, and regulators behind; hence, the former are often in a position to bias regulators through the manipulation of information. They control information that is vital to regulators and they know how to use it to their own ends. This is a powerful weapon, because the ability of a regulator is closely linked to its access to information, which forms the basis for its decision-making capacity.

It is always important to keep an eye on the regulatory environment, and to ensure that the risks of regulatory capture are countered. The starting point is to institutionalise regulators' autonomy. This could be achieved, mainly, by legislating for their status, and continuously monitoring the laws to ensure that they remain effective. One particularly important area is to regulate the composition of boards, and to provide for inquiry and review teams. Such teams should include appropriate professionals and representatives from civil society. It is also a good idea to actively seek membership renewal legislation for the boards, to prevent one particular group of people developing too tight a hold over the structure.

It is also important for regulators to actively try to attract and keep quality staff. The obvious option is to offer competitive compensation packages, but this is often difficult for government agencies, especially in developing countries. Other methods could also be used, such as giving regulatory agencies some form of a reward for every case or appeal resolved in favour of the general interest. The agency must then put in place internal processes to ensure that these benefits filter through to staff. It is difficult to overcome the information problem, but not impossible. Through widespread linkages throughout the sector, a regulator could gain good access to quality information. It is also advisable for central statistical services to attempt to develop some data that could assist regulators.

Sources: Lafont and Tirole, 1990; Ogus, 1994; Villasenor, 2000

network. While the water sector shows a tendency for economies of scale and greater network coverage, various factors could create a competitive environment. These include new technologies, competitive tendering and benchmarking, as well as the increased role of small-scale providers able (and willing) to service the poor in marginal areas.

Existing barriers to entry currently include legal monopolies, exclusivity rights, zoning restrictions, technical standards and import tariffs or taxes. However, it is essential that municipalities look at whether the regulatory framework excludes those who currently serve the poor, and whether it effectively provides monopolies (and little incentive to expand) to those that do not. Municipalities should consider their own contexts, the existing coverage and the profiles of unsupplied households, and think about how markets can be opened up, and the existing small-scale independent providers legitimised and regulated. Large-scale operators have indicated they are less threatened by the role of small-scale providers than originally presumed and addressed through exclusivity agreements. The context will determine whether this could be done across the municipality or in specifically targeted areas.

How will the entry, price and quality of the various types of suppliers be addressed? There is no single answer and little experience to show what works and what does not. In fact it is 'possible to envisage a multi-tiered regulatory structure, with the smallest providers subject to minimal regulatory scrutiny at entry, larger firms subject to closer scrutiny, and the traditional utility subject to a more conventional licensing regime'.[6]

Private operators want to know that the procurement process is fair and competitive. It also provides comfort to government and end-users if service providers know that they are in competition with others, and that the quality of service they provide will affect their ability to attract more business. International experience shows clearly that where private sector participation benefits have failed to materialise, the problems can often be traced back to the absence of rival suppliers. Monopolies tend to weaken users in their efforts to exert pressure for better service.

The regulatory framework could shape levels of competition in different ways. One way is to separate bulk generation and supply of a service from distribution and reticulation. Bulk provision often requires economies of scale that could not be met by private suppliers, whereas reticulation lends itself more to smaller service providers. By separating bulk supply and reticulation, governments could therefore open opportunities for competition between distributors. Another way to enhance competition is to require tenders before contracts are awarded. Governments may also force competition between public utilities, or allow private companies to compete with those utilities. Even with these arrangements, however, some parts of a sector may tend to be monopolistic. In such cases, government's regulatory challenge is to set rules that will prevent abuse of power, encourage private sector participation and monitor performance. Once reform towards private sector participation is chosen, it becomes particularly important to ensure that government businesses do not enjoy any competitive advantage or disadvantage as a result of their public ownership. Public monopoly reform also involves the separation of the regulatory functions of a monopoly from commercial activities that can be subject to competition.

Who is regulated?

Through a range of instruments, a regulatory framework regulates investors, non-state operators in the private and voluntary sectors, government decision-makers and consumers.

From a people's perspective, a regulatory framework is there to protect the consumer. It does this directly or indirectly by requiring quality of service at a reasonable price and by encouraging choice through a competitive environment, creating incentives for the private enterprise to perform, value for money etc. Municipalities should seek to understand the implications of the regulatory framework on consumers (particularly poor consumers) and facilitate vehicles for consumers to effectively articulate their interests.

Box 10.10 Regulating Small-scale Providers
Dar-es-Salaam, Tanzania

Environmental conditions in many of the informal settlements in Dar-es-Salaam are poor. Large areas are either waterlogged or have a high water table, and more than 85% of the city's residents depend on on-site sanitation facilities. Most households use latrines, including traditional unlined latrines. As a result of poor environmental conditions, many latrines fill up with water and require more frequent emptying.

Until 1996 the Dar-es-Salaam Sewerage and Sanitation Department (DSSD) operated a fleet of four pit-emptying tankers for sewer maintenance, through which it also provided pit-emptying services. These tankers served a small portion of the 85% of households relying on on-site sanitation services. As demand from the fast-growing Dar-es-Salaam population increased, the Dar-es-Salaam City Commission's (DCC's) capacity to respond to the long waiting list of customers who had paid up-front for tanker services declined.

The advent of the El Niño floods of 1996, and a subsequent cholera outbreak in various areas of the city on a scale that was unprecedented, forced DCC to look for alternative means for improving access to cess-pit-emptying services by allowing private cess-pit-emptying service providers.

Through the Habitat-funded Sustainable Dar Project, the DCC started exploring the possibility of enabling private provision of cess-pit-emptying services. A study was therefore conducted in the Sinza suburb of Ilala District to determine the true cost of operating a pit-emptying service within the city of Dar-es-Salaam. The study concluded that the minimum operational cost was in the region of 22,000 Tanzanian shillings (TShs), the equivalent of US$25 per trip.

DCC thereafter organised a meeting with potential operators of private pit-emptying services in 1995, to discuss the findings of the study and agree a way forward. During this meeting it was agreed that private pit-emptying services would be licensed to operate provided that they complied with a set of rules and regulations intended to ensure fair pricing and the proper handling of waste by all actors.

Based on the goodwill generated by the consultation meeting, several private pit-emptiers immediately sought to obtain licences (at a cost of US$2) and initiate operations while the DSSD was working out arrangements for issuing dumping permits. Eventually all operators received dumping permits, and all are now complying with the terms agreed at the initial meeting. To ensure access for low-income households, tankers are expected to maintain a minimum charge of TShs 17,000 (US$21.25). Any operator who is reported to have contravened this requirement will have his/her permit revoked.

The terms for obtaining a dumping permit include that:

- waste dumped at sludge-dumping facilities should be organic waste only (attendants visually inspect discharge);
- operators must discharge waste at the specific treatment plants defined on their individual permits; and
- a dumping fee of TShs 3000 (US$3.75) per trip must be paid to the DSSD.

To reduce the likelihood of collusion between drivers and dumping-site attendants, the dumping fee is charged monthly in advance of operations, based on an average number of five trips per day. The number of actual trips carried out is verified at the end of the month, against receipts collected from the attendant at the dumping point.

Cess-pit-emptying services are supervised by the head of Waste Management Department of the DCC. He is assisted at the waste treatment sites by attendants who record cesspit-emptying tanker arrivals, confirm the quality of the sludge being dumped, and collect and record the number of trips made per tanker. At the operational level, service providers negotiate service charges with customers on a case-by-case basis. The main parameters considered are: seasonal service demand (the rainy season generates higher demand, which results in higher prices); the distance from the site to the disposal facility; the socio-economic circumstances of the customer (the rich pay more); and the type of facility to be emptied. Pit latrines sometimes attract higher fees than septic tanks due to the risk of damage to the equipment.

To date, legislation formalising these arrangements has not been put in place. However, it is anticipated that this will be done to ensure that ongoing operations are in line with the legislation transferring management responsibility for sewerage facilities to a private operator. Despite the semi-formal nature of these arrangements, the number of pit-emptying operators has increased and the price of services has dropped.

Source: extract from Kariuki and Wandera, 2000

The regulatory framework is also one of the key instruments that determine the performance and behaviour of the private sector. In terms of private operators and investors, a sound regulatory framework will aim to create certainty about the operating environment and the ability to recover costs. Both financiers and operators want to know that they can run effective businesses and that the service context is free from arbitrary state interventions. This will be achieved through the price and market control mechanisms described above. A municipality will need to explore whether or not the national regulatory context provides this certainty and, if it does not, explore ways of promoting the development of such a framework and creating it through the contract.

But the framework is also there to support and define the role, behaviour and performance of government. A regulatory framework is effective when it gives municipal decision-makers incentives to engage private operators and guide them as to how they could do so in the best interest of effective service delivery. This includes, for instance: the legal provision for private sector engagement, the definition of the regulatory role of public sector organisations (including the regulating body discussed later), the requirement for proper budgeting, planning and financial acumen, and incentives for individuals to change (such as the inclusion of performance indicators). Municipalities need to explore the regulatory framework that determines these areas and, if incomplete, take local-level steps to create or enhance it.

In practice, service delivery to poor households comprises an array of other small-scale providers (such as water tankers, septic tank vacuum trucks, cooperatives of solid waste workers – see Chapter 7). In the past, the lack of regulation at the small-scale and neighbourhood level, particularly among informal enterprises, has resulted in an unpredictable environment (sometimes competitive, sometimes exploitative), and frequently, poor-quality service. A regulatory framework in support of poverty-focused service delivery will need to address small-scale providers as well as the large national or international firms.

☐ Who regulates?

One of the primary features determining the operating context for private sector participation, and the regulatory framework particularly, is whether or not a regulatory body exists. The role of the municipality and the overall regulatory climate will be fundamentally affected by the presence of such a regulator. Experience has suggested that there are some key parameters guiding decision-making over regulators and municipalities should develop an understanding of the sort of regulatory body most suited to their contexts.

In the context of large-scale complex partnerships with the international private sector, current guidelines propose the need for a regulatory body that administers pricing, monitors compliance and enforces obligations. It is essential that this body is independent – and that means that the municipality cannot be both regulator and monitor/manager of private sector operations. Ideally, policy formulation should be handled by an agency different from the one that regulates, and so too with implementation. This helps avoid conflicts of interests, and therefore enhances the overall integrity and credibility of the regulator. Those arrangements that do not include an independent regulator but are based on a municipality playing conflicting roles undermine confidence and threaten the legitimacy of arrangements.[7] It may also be essential that the regulator is independent from political interference. If the regulator assumes responsibility for pricing, it will be important for investors to see the regulator as being as independent as is possible in a given context. The problems of regulatory capture are described in Box 10.9.

The efficacy of regulatory bodies in developing countries can be largely dependent on the financial and human resources available to them, and by extension on the competencies of the staff, and the definition of their roles. The broad range of skills required, along with independence and diplomacy, are not always found with ease. However, the regulator's ability to enforce is critical to its credibility, as illustrated by the case of Buenos Aires in Box 7.18.

10

Box 10.11 The Role of Water and Sanitation Regulators
Latin America

	Who regulates?	Key functions/characteristics
Argentina	Provincial regulator in Buenos Aires Province ETOSS – an independent regulatory agency responsible for water and sanitation in Buenos Aires, created May 1993, financed by 0.67% user fee levied on consumers	• Enforce compliance • Monitor and approve five-year investment plans and proposed maintenance • Determine tariff provisions • Ensure quality of service • Investigate customer complaints and oversee consumer affairs
	Provincial regulator in Córdoba province A secretariat for the control and management of contracts ERSEP – a multisectoral regulating agency responsible for a diverse range of PSPs in public services, financed by 1.5% user fee levied on consumers	• Monitor water quality (contracts-out to a state-owned laboratory) • Monitor implementation of the investment programme of the concessionaire • It is unclear whether ERSEP will balance the interests of consumers, or if it will play the role of contract enforcer
Bolivia	National level Superintendency de Aguas established in 1994, specific powers and responsibilities established in 1997	• Grant concessions – control over who provides service and what type of service the providers offer • Approve contracts • Regulate and supervise contracts • Approve tariffs
Colombia	National level CRA – regulatory body for water and sanitation, semi-autonomous body located in the Ministry of Economic Development	• Promote anti-corruption measures, encourage investment and prevent abuse of monopoly power • Ensure reasonable tariffs, high quality and ample coverage in service delivery • Authorise tariff and subsidy structure
	SSP – public services watchdog oversees water and sanitation, electricity and gas, and telecommunications	• Monitor adherence to national policy and standards to ensure that the regulatory decisions are applied (e.g., cross-subsidies) • Monitor contractual arrangement between municipality and operator • Hear and decide on customer complaints • Examine corporate financial management • Fine companies for violation of agreed norms
Chile	National level SWSS – Superintendency of Water and Sanitation Services established in 1989	• Regulate service quality • Set prices

Municipalities need to build an understanding of the nature and scope of the regulator, and if a regulatory body is being formed, seek to influence the capacity of the organisation. All such efforts bring reduced risk – and lower costs. It is also necessary to understand the degree to which the regulator is able to embrace appropriate technologies and service standards, small-scale suppliers and service providers, and other strategies for delivering to the poor. This opens up a much broader set of skill requirements including: barriers to market entry, anti-competitive conduct, and public awareness. It is not necessarily desirable for a regulatory body to perform all functions itself. It should, however, ensure that these functions are carried out in a transparent manner, and that there are adequate and ongoing capacity building programmes set up to enhance its capacity to perform its role.

The location of the regulator is also a key issue. Municipalities must understand the implications of placing regulators at national, provincial or regional/local levels. National regulators may well provide the best solution for the regulation of partnerships involving the international private sector (offering distance, better skills and reduced susceptibility to capture) and thus be a more appropriate location for appeals and arbitration. However, it is unlikely to be a practical or desirable location for the regulation of small-scale service providers. Municipalities may need to explore where such regulation is best placed at a local level.

The overall role, competency and perceived legitimacy of the regulator are very important to municipalities. This must be known by all parties at the outset, such that supplementary measures are taken in the formulation of the contract. Examples of different forms of regulatory bodies in Latin America are provided in Box 10.11.

☐ How is it regulated?

A number of process-related factors will determine a regulator's general effectiveness and are particularly critical in establishing a pro-poor focus. These include:

- degree of transparency and objectivity of the procedures adopted (for instance, transparent and consultative processes over key issues such as tariffs and service standards, fair and competitive procurement procedures);
- clarity of criteria determining the regulatory framework;
- predictability of processes;
- engagement with stakeholders, and thus the formulation of strategies to enable them to reach stakeholders (such as consultation processes with NGOs, community and consumer organisations, and different types of private sector organisations involved in the delivery process (see Chapter 6));
- introduction of mechanisms enabling the poorest to be heard; and
- means to access information on an ongoing basis and the feedback of this information into the regulatory framework (regulatory impact assessments).

Regulation is complex. It is often the most difficult issue to resolve. There are no clear answers, but in the context of weak national regulatory environments the solution normally lies in specific clauses in the contract.

Administrative Context

The relationship between local government and other levels of government determines how much scope there is for municipalities to develop their own policy frameworks, and to engage in contracting with private service providers. Even where decentralisation policy and legislation have provided municipalities with greater autonomy, the reality in developing countries is that there is a high degree of dependence, control and interference determining municipal capacity.

10

Box 10.12   Effects of the Operating Environment

	Key elements	With supporting context	Without supporting context
Political and economic stability	• Macro-economic policies • Political stability • Economic trends	• Creates confidence • Investors willing to invest	• Undermines confidence • Investors not willing to invest, unwilling to commit to long-term contracts • Counters positives like political will, policies, regulatory frameworks
Political will	• Champions of PSP approaches • Specialised vehicles (e.g., BOT centre in Philippines and MIIU in South Africa) • Policy commitment	• PSP can move forward at municipal level • Support mustered within municipality and community • Options for change gain legitimacy	• Difficult to create interest from investors • Officials could frustrate PSP and community obstruct it • Change blocked
Regulatory framework	• Specifies roles of public and private sectors • Controls or directs price, quality and entry • Specifies rights of consumers • Facilitates competition • Determines levels of decentralisation	• Increases certainty • Clarifies who does what and how, and creates incentives for different actors • Boosts confidence of potential investors • Reduces risk and cost • Protects consumers • Guides fair procurement and facilitates entry of market participants	• Contracts can cover some aspects required by investors but with less confidence • Municipalities often move forward in a vacuum • Delays in procurement • Quality and price become unpredictable
Policy framework	• Specifies overall objectives and priorities (e.g., infrastructure development, pro-poor development, environmental protection) • Outlines institutional approaches	• Legitimises partnership approach • Municipalities more confident to act • Clarifies priorities and government resource commitments • Highlights special objectives, such as pro-poor approach	• Municipalities can drive change • Municipalities can interpret policy to suit their objectives • Municipal objectives hindered by conflicting policy environment
Administrative framework	• Shapes autonomy of municipalities • Can establish guarantees • Affects skills levels in municipality • Can underpin municipal efforts	• Facilitates change • Removes possible barriers to effective implementation	• Can obstruct change (delay processes) • Municipal leaders may sidestep barriers • Well-connected municipal leaders will be able to facilitate change

In addition, municipalities frequently have low status in the overall government framework. This will severely affect their capacity to establish relationships with international private operators, or in some cases to bring about a shift in the manner in which they plan, manage and operate municipal services. To a large extent, especially in those systems where staff allocation is the responsibility of higher levels of government, the problem has been one of status, capacity and perceived capacity. This is exacerbated when state or provincial levels of government exert the control they have over staffing in ways that undermine municipal efforts and destroy continuity. However, the traditional pattern in which municipalities have the weakest government staff is changing, even in these contexts. The process of decentralisation is slowly drawing attention to the need for more skilled managers, and in some large cities it is now possible to see very skilled managers involved in city management.

Nevertheless, resource-poor municipalities can be made poorer when higher levels of administration hold the strings. This is particularly marked where power plays still exist – often where provincial/state government is not yet comfortable with decentralisation processes, and where politics creates rifts between different levels of government. It is also a problem where municipalities are still wholly reliant on inter-governmental transfers as their main source of revenue. Municipalities can have a great deal of autonomy (even in bureaucratic contexts such as India) if they have established their own revenue streams.

Of the external factors affecting municipalities in efforts to establish partnerships, it is perhaps the administrative factors that present the most perverse actions. While it may be expected that higher levels of government will create an enabling environment and be the facilitators of change, in practice, this is not always the case. State and national governments can hinder municipal efforts through staff policies and practice that downgrade the importance of municipal matters, and through administrative procedures that create barriers to municipal action. For example, tedious procurement policies and procedures often create such barriers. The issues of staffing and procedural change are taken up in detail in the following chapters.

In addition to this, municipalities will be affected by administrative procedures such as government guarantees (discussed in Chapter 7). These undermine municipal authority and accountability even if they do facilitate partnerships, and increasingly governments across the world are moving away from such guarantees. This means that the financial and operational soundness of the deal itself becomes more important, shifting the focus to the municipality's own capacity to engage in binding and enforceable contracts. Other examples of higher levels of government determining municipal outcomes are the control over tariff-setting seen in Zimbabwe, and the bulk water pricing seen in South Africa. The more control higher levels exert, the more municipal accountability becomes compromised. It also often discourages private investors, as it subjects aspects like tariffs to considerations beyond the immediate regulation of a private sector participation arrangement.

| Understanding the operating context of municipal partnerships | **Enhancing human resources** | Supporting organisational development |

Chapter 11 **Key Questions**

☐ **Which skills does a municipality need to formulate and implement partnerships?**

☐ **Which skills are needed to focus the partnership on the poor?**

☐ **How can these skills be acquired?**

☐ **How can these skills be sustained?**

Guy Stubbs

Enhancing **Human Resources**

Janelle Plummer and Richard Slater

Municipal efforts to encourage partnership initiatives will be affected by the human resource capacity of the municipality. Unsurprisingly, evidence from case studies in various parts of the world strongly suggests that the greater the capacity, the more likely a municipality is to succeed in developing and sustaining effective partnerships. The paradox is that those without capacity – those most in need of support from the private sector – are likely to find partnerships furthest from their reach.

Many of the issues discussed throughout this book have drawn attention to the capacity constraints of municipalities, and in particular the basic lack of skills required to meet the new challenges of government. At the same time, the book describes the wide spectrum of issues that municipalities must absorb if they are to develop and sustain partnerships with the private sector. The sheer extent of this information requires the municipality to become a learning organisation. This chapter presents a framework of the skills a municipality requires to enter into and sustain effective service partnerships for the poor. Two case studies are used to illustrate the key issues: Stutterheim, South Africa, and Gweru, Zimbabwe.

The human resource pattern in municipalities will vary quite considerably from one case to another, yet as we have seen in Chapter 6, municipalities display some basic similarities that characterise their core competencies, and the functioning of the organisation, staff and management. Most municipalities are based on a separation of the political and administrative functions. A typical municipality will be structured in relation to the primary functional areas, resulting in engineering (including water supply), public health (including solid waste and perhaps non-network sanitation services), finance, administration, and planning divisions or departments. This structure (discussed in Chapter 12) is a key factor influencing human resource capacity. The skills deficiencies of municipalities are well known and are not repeated here. The discussion below focuses on the skill sets required and mechanisms municipalities must employ to sustain those skill sets. Box 11.2 provides a summary table of this skills framework.

What Skills Do Municipalities Require for Partnerships?

In this context of mixed capacity and diverse operating environments, it is necessary for municipalities to improve their awareness of which skills they have and which skills are needed for the development of service partnerships. This section sets out the core competencies required in relation to the partnership framework established in Part 2. It describes specific skills sets[1] in terms of the following areas:

- strategic and practical understanding of the problem context;
- strategic understanding of solutions;
- capacity to analyse needs and develop a strategic response;
- capacity to implement the strategy and establish a transaction;
- capacity to maintain effective partnerships;
- capacity to engage with stakeholders; and
- understanding of capacity building needs, and ability to improve capacity.

11

Links to Boxes
6.1, 7.17, 8.6, 9.6, 12.1

Box 11.1 **Capacity Constraints and Capacity Building**
Stutterheim, South Africa

Perhaps the most critical issue in the Stutterheim partnership arrangement is the marked imbalance in the capacity of the private and municipal partners (see Boxes 6.1 and 8.6). The council recognises this imbalance, and suggests that it is severely hampered in the partnership because it lacks the knowledge and skills needed to create a level playing field. While capacity deficiencies affect ongoing partnership arrangements, the lack of confidence to bring about structural change in the partnership to embrace the council's pro-poor alternatives is the key issue that concerns the municipality itself. In order to understand the lack of municipal capacity it is necessary to understand what this involves, and to distinguish between those capacity issues that are just matters of perception and those that are likely to affect the partnership in practice. The following discussion considers skills sets in the context of Stutterheim council and its administrative officials.

Understanding the external operating context of municipal service partnerships
During 2000, knowledge about the political and policy context of partnerships in South Africa grew significantly among the councillors, especially those who had become familiar with national government policy and trade union agreements. However, the schism between the national level and the implementation level in remote areas warrants attention from national-level supporting organisations. Administrative staff and councillors would benefit from capacity building to enhance their understanding of the opportunities and constraints created by the national policy context, including the policy on municipal service partnerships, integrated development planning, and service delivery to the poor. The ability of councils to provide feedback about implementation problems to national-level policy-makers should also be strengthened.

Strategic understanding of PPPs
The most significant capacity constraint in the municipality concerns the strategic understanding of PPPs. While a detailed skills assessment has not been carried out, gaps are evident in the capacity of both political and administrative officials. In particular, there is a fundamental lack of understanding of risk, and of the links between risk and contract duration. There is only limited knowledge of contract types, the role of service partnerships in urban management, and the strategic role of the private sector. In particular, there is little understanding of partnerships in the context of poverty-reduction activities, and the potential roles and benefits associated with private sector involvement in low-income areas.

Strategic management of the contract
One of the primary constraints on the development of a pro-poor contract is the capacity of the recently elected Stutterheim Council to bring about strategic change. In Stutterheim, the municipal management of the partnership has been limited to day-to-day operations. Decision-makers have lacked the confidence to reorient the contract so that it meets the redefined objectives of the municipality. Yet the council does have a strategic vision, which seems to be compatible with the institutional and social development objectives of contracts elsewhere. It has been hampered by its understanding of private sector opportunities, an imbalance in negotiating skills and a lack of understanding of the potential of the contract.

Financial analysis and planning
Another fundamental constraint on the effective implementation of the contract is a lack of financial analysis and planning, specifically in relation to water and sanitation services. Yet the council has a strong record in financial management and, properly motivated, should be more than able to lead a meaningful cost–benefit analysis of the PPP. The lack of this analysis to date stems from a narrow understanding of the contract – resulting in the belief that it is inflexible – and a strong feeling in the financial team that such an exercise would be pointless. There has been no attempt to compare the PPP with international benchmarks. This is an attitudinal constraint rather than a skills constraint. An improved understanding of the customer base and the implications of tariff structures is essential. The formulation of a tariff structure that benefits the poor over the non-poor and promotes water conservation and cost recovery is urgently needed. Exposure to alternatives developed elsewhere would broaden the understanding of the options available.

Ability to maximise the benefits for the poor

The municipality needs support in developing links between private sector activities in water and sanitation and low-income groups. The council's strategic goal contrasts with the existing implementation arrangements, in which the municipality itself carries out extension work to low-income areas and is responsible for the tertiary level of service. The council does not carry out hygiene promotion or community development activities in relation to water and sanitation service delivery.

In addition to the issue of tariffs mentioned above, the Council does not have the in-house knowledge to understand the role of willingness-to-pay and affordability studies (e.g., pre-paid meters are being introduced without proper analysis), and – critically – the concept of service gradation for the poor is not understood. Significant capacity building in pro-poor water and sanitation services and pro-poor partnerships would benefit the decision-making process.

Ability to develop a consultative and inclusive process

Most Stutterheim councillors are confident and skilled in their relations with civic organisations such as CBOs and trade unions. The structures for consultation are well established and effective. If and when the contract is renegotiated, the council is committed to conducting a consultative process, and to establishing a contract that includes community involvement. The council has less experience in working with NGOs, but key councillors appreciate the importance of filling gaps with NGO expertise.

Understanding of legal and contractual aspects of partnerships

With the notable exception of the town treasurer, there is only limited understanding of the legal and contractual aspects of the contract. The legal jargon has proved to be a major hurdle to the understanding of key contract provisions, and the lack of ownership can be attributed at least in part to the lack of involvement of the existing council in formulating the contract. Although some staff members were in place at the time, the contract is not 'owned' by anyone.

There is of course some debate as to the extent of legal and contractual knowledge that is required. A number of factors currently make it necessary to improve capacity in-house: the complexity of administrating this particular contract, the marked disillusionment with the consultancy sector, and the reliance on municipal staff to undertake all tasks.

Ability to initiate and conduct contract negotiations

The council has a clear lack of confidence and ability to initiate contract negotiations. To date, the prevailing attitude has been to leave the contract alone. The nine contract amendments that have been made were initiated by WSSA. Yet the council has been discontent with the arrangement for some time. This inaction can be attributed to the lack of detailed provision for renegotiation in the contract, the imbalance in perceived negotiating skills, the lack of access to 'objective' support, and fear about the implications of decisions. Capacity building in negotiation is essential if the council is not willing to accept the support of skilled specialists.

Understanding of the management of water and sanitation services

Given the council's commitment to ongoing investment in infrastructure, it is essential that the administrative arm of the municipality is able to translate technical issues for the council. Other the last seven years, technical understanding has varied and capacity to advise the council has been mixed. Most importantly, there is a general lack of appreciation of the complexities involved in managing water resources, and of the social, health, economic and urban management issues surrounding water and sanitation services. The capacity that is required to promote innovative mechanisms to meet service needs is not apparent. Skills gaps in these areas need to be addressed through training or external support if council is to be properly advised in the future.

Source: Plummer, 2000a

11

Strategic and Practical Understanding of the Problem and Context

☐ Basic understanding of the operating context for service partnerships

The municipal officials and political representatives leading the drive towards more effective forms of service delivery need to develop an overview of the national operating context. An understanding of the external operating context described in the preceding chapter requires the ability to understand the constraints and implications of the macro-economic and political context, the policy context, the legislative framework and the administrative context within the broader national and provincial government framework.

In those situations where the operating context is unfavourable, successful municipal representatives will have developed the ability to initiate change from below in order that they can formally pursue their partnership strategy. Alternatively, municipal officials may need to work within an unfavourable context by driving change locally and interpreting legislation to suit their own ends. In either case, municipal managers need a general overview of the context that affects their actions. This is not to say they need to have absorbed all the details of the operating context set out in Chapter 10, but there needs to be an awareness of the potential importance of the operating context, they need to understand the key determining factors, and must have access to detailed knowledge should they wish to explore new avenues. Within the organisation, there needs to be an understanding of what the barriers and opportunities are, what is possible, what is not possible and what can be facilitated.

☐ Understanding of poverty and the perceptions of the poor

The capacity of the municipality to develop a partnership focused on delivering benefits to the poor will also be influenced by the more general understanding of the poverty context and services in relation to the livelihoods of the poor. Increasingly in South and South-East Asia, municipalities have dedicated community development staff and extension workers, who have developed extensive first-hand knowledge of poor communities. The problem is often that this knowledge is not effectively absorbed at decision-making levels. Yet in the context of long-term changes in basic service delivery, it is critical that decision-makers are informed about poverty and its implications in their city.

In Cartagena, Colombia, for instance, the process of establishing the joint venture for water and sanitation services paid only minimal attention to the water and sanitation needs of the urban poor, and in more recent years it has been necessary to initiate efforts outside that arrangement.[2] Partnerships developed without this understanding of poverty are unlikely to be targeted effectively. In the city of Gaborone in Botswana, the shift to household water connections for all brought with it a policy for removing communal standpipes.[3] The authority's lack of understanding of the poor's livelihoods, and their willingness and ability to pay for this level of service, meant that many households were left without access to water. Authorities thought that by removing the standpipes, households would be forced to connect, but they did not. This ultimately led to the reinstatement of the communal standpipe, with significant consequences for cost recovery. Those who could afford it and had household connections still used the communal standpipe for some of their (mostly bulk) water needs as this kept their water bills low. Better understanding of the poor and their perceptions would surely have led to a more informed solution.

☐ Understanding the limitations of existing service delivery mechanisms

Quite irrespective of the external operating context, a primary problem facing municipal government in many parts of the world is that it does not acknowledge the causes of urban service problems. Many municipal officials may not have had exposure to more effective service delivery and have limited grounds for comparison. They may not have had significant exposure to alternative forms of service delivery, and they may not be willing or able to recognise institutional blockages.

Acknowledging the problems and understanding the limitations is a key basic skill that enables municipalities to bring about change.

☐ Understanding the limitations of the regulatory framework

Municipal officials will have some knowledge of the legislative context of the municipality – its legislative functions and limitations, and where the ambiguities lie. It will also be necessary for nominated officials to develop a broad understanding of the regulatory framework for public–private partnerships (PPPs), particularly the specific regulations and legislations, and those that affect municipal action towards PPPs (described in Chapter 10). It is necessary for municipalities to understand, and obtain advice about, the aspects of the regulatory framework that affect incentives for the formal private sector (e.g., price controls), or the involvement of small-scale providers. They need to be aware of contractual and institutional options for countering regulatory deficiencies.

Strategic Understanding of Solutions

☐ Strategic understanding of partnerships in urban governance

Perhaps the primary skill lacking in the 'traditional' municipal organisation is a strategic understanding of partnerships, their benefits and the opportunities they create. That is not to say there is not an awareness of the issues, but evidence does suggest that misinformation and preconception play key roles in forming councillors' and administrators' views, and attitudinal change is necessary to remove scepticism where it is not warranted. Conversely, there are some municipal managers who see partnerships with the private sector as the panacea to all municipal illnesses, and are unable to critically evaluate the pros and cons of private sector involvement in a particular context. There is little doubt that training in PPPs assists municipal officials to make informed decisions that are more consistent with broader urban management goals. This will include, for example, the ability to select options – to identify appropriate alternative options for a diverse range of municipal functions, evaluate private sector participation (PSP) options and compare them against other forms of delivery.

In the pursuit of more poverty-focused partnership arrangements, it is necessary for municipalities to be able to consider private sector participation in the context of local or national poverty-reduction strategies. This issue has been addressed in detail in Chapter 5, where the discussion focused on the importance of understanding the lessons of poverty reduction, and the processes through which a formal private sector arrangement will add value to, and not undermine, poverty reduction efforts. Still more ambitious is the understanding of how private sector participation in basic services can be developed to converge with poverty-reduction activities. As we have seen, this involves a strategic insight and a practical capacity to create a coherent coalition of stakeholders and activities. In terms of process, it involves community participation and demand-responsive decision-making, as well as the involvement of NGOs and ISPs. Municipalities need the vision and skill to bring these functions and actions together and it is most likely that skills development is required to this end.

☐ Basic knowledge of financial arrangements

A primary part of any partnership solution will concern financial arrangements that are incorporated to meet financial (and other identified) objectives (see discussion in Chapters 3 and 7). In order to ensure that basic objectives are met and goals are viable and sustainable, a moderate level of knowledge is necessary among those municipal individuals leading partnership development and negotiations. It is necessary for a municipal decision-making team to have some grasp of *why* the private sector acts in the way it does. Knowledge of rates of return, financial viability (especially in relation to tariffs and subsidies), debt servicing and the financial conditions needed for investment will be important in understanding basic incentives, and understanding the financial, political, social and environmental implications of tariffs is essential to achieving objectives. While many of the skills needed to analyse the existing conditions (to prepare a PPP) may be bought from specialist advisors, it is essential that advisors are given a full picture of the operating context, and thus it is necessary to have sufficient in-house skills to brief advisors and understand the advice being given.

The set of issues that need to be addressed in relation to financing include:[4]

- benchmarking (in relation to assets, efficiency, cost effectiveness of service delivery);
- project finance (principles of net present value, rates of return);
- local and international finance markets (how local financial markets affect international investors and the implications of international financing on the service being delivered);
- guarantees and lenders' rights (security etc.);
- currency exchange and interest rate risk (what do exchange rates imply for rates of return);
- credit enhancement (additional investment by government if necessary);
- risk (how risks affect financial viability and how they are factored into cost recovery);
- tariff structuring and subsidy design (their implications on equity, affordability and revenue flows) as well as tariff adjustment mechanisms; and
- credit control (risks of bad debt, assurance of government revenue, insurance and guarantees).

Strategic understanding of risk management

A key capacity that will need to be developed among municipal leaders is the understanding of and ability to effectively allocate risk. Inexperienced municipal actors fail to recognise that all partnerships involve some risk, especially long-term partnerships, and that these risks need to be allocated fairly if partnerships are to remain viable. The key rule reiterated by specialists is that risk should be allocated as far as possible to the party best able to handle it.

Chapter 7 has detailed some of the primary factors in relation to construction, operation and maintenance, political, revenue and regulatory risks. In order to achieve an appropriate level of capacity in relation to risk management it is necessary to ensure that the principles are understood, that the municipality understands the key risks affecting the performance and decisions of all actors involved in the partnership, and that the very different risks of different forms of contract have been recognised.

Understanding the nature, capacity and potential roles of all actors

Developing a partnership strategy also requires the capacity to envisage the roles, responsibilities and relationships of the wide range of actors potentially involved in a service partnership. The easiest solution for municipalities is to create a bilateral partnership with a private sector operator (or NGO or CBO). Yet the complex nature of developing cities and the diversity of inhabitants establishes a context that requires multi-faceted solutions, and the municipality is ultimately the actor responsible for the vision, and for applying this vision to a working partnership. The challenge is to weave a coherent tapestry of functions, actors and roles.

In those situations where partnership visions are broad and inclusive, the understanding and coordination of actors may well be an implicit part of developing the partnership. Building a comprehensive strategy requires clarity – a good understanding of the problem, the existing assets and untapped capacities. Yet in many municipalities, engineers educated in the 'old school' approach will lead service partnerships, and their knowledge of NGOs (for instance) may be limited or coloured by biased judgements about their capacity and purpose. The same engineer may still be driven by the 'provider' role and may not have taken on board the importance of consultation with trade unions, community organisations and other interested consumer groups. The question then arises as to where the responsibility for an inclusive process lies.

Stutterheim, the example described in Box 11.1, is an interesting case in this respect. It illustrates how the incapacity to perceive roles for all actors can constrain the potential of partnership arrangements. Stutterheim is a town with both a PPP (in water and sanitation) and an effective and well-established community forum, yet the operations of the two initiatives are divergent. No attempt has been made to capitalise on the opportunities of both private sector and community initiatives, to bring these together into an arrangement that brings broader benefits to the town. The potential roles of stakeholders have not been identified or applied to the service delivery process.

Chapter 6 provides a detailed discussion of the various stakeholders, their potential roles and strengths and weaknesses. Building the capacity of the municipality to formulate and execute effective partnerships requires both an understanding of human and organisational resources and an ability to apply these resources within the partnership strategy.

Capacity to Analyse Needs and Develop a Strategic Response

☐ Ability to understand the context and define appropriate objectives

This book has emphasised that the development of a partnership strategy will depend on the extent to which the problem is accurately perceived. An understanding of the potential causes of service deficiency, be they political, economic, social, environmental and/or institutional, is required. Training may be necessary for those municipalities that do not have the capacity to analyse the problem context. Alternatively, external specialists can be brought in to assist in the analysis, but it would then be crucial that the process was 'owned' by the municipality and that, ultimately, the findings could be understood and taken on board.

The capacity of the municipality to define the partnership objectives will fundamentally depend on the political will of key leaders to acknowledge that the diversity of their cities and the range of urban stakeholders will bring with them a range of objectives, some of which will conflict with one another. Once this political will is in place, it is necessary to consider the skills that are needed to coordinate and structure objectives into a form that can be used for decision-making purposes. Municipal actors must have the skills needed to recognise where objectives converge, even if they have originated from different perspectives.

Yet the very process of capacity building and the focus on services (that may develop as a result of the partnership development process) will bring with it (either directly or indirectly) a greater ability to recognise what the real (rather than perceived) objectives are. This will then result in revised objectives and the need to negotiate and coordinate approaches that respond to these redefined needs.

☐ Understanding of and ability to plan strategically

In order to create pro-poor partnerships integrated with other poverty responses, and to create new strategic approaches to the development of partnerships within the urban management framework, it is vital that municipal leaders should grasp the importance of planning strategically. While the capacity to compose an effective strategic response depends on the thorough identification of problems and the formulation of objectives, it is also relies on a degree of skill in understanding the problem in its entirety, the broad implications of options, and recognising that a strategy has short-, medium- and long-term requirements and implications. At the core of this are the conflicts that may arise between the timing of delivering affordable services for the poor and the financial viability of any arrangement. A key aspect of this competency will be the understanding of whether or not a partnership arrangement is the best approach, and if so, what type of partnership is appropriate, which roles need to be filled and when such an approach would best be launched.

Capacity to Implement the Strategy[5]

☐ Ability to collaborate

One of the most overlooked aspects of partnerships is the ability of all partners to behave as partners, and carry out their tasks in a collaborative manner. While clarity of function and contract is important, the process of partnering (described in Chapter 6) is ultimately more critical. Municipalities often lack key skills such as listening and learning. Managers are accustomed to having to always know the answers, and have created dictatorial rather than flexible learning organisations. Implementing a partnership strategy that unifies a range of actors requires the municipality to facilitate a collaborative spirit. This is of paramount importance to the sustainability of the partnership, irrespective of what the contract says.

☐ Ability to implement transparent tendering and evaluation procedures

In the past, much of the focus of PPPs has been on procurement rather than on preparation and strategic planning, and there is a wealth of literature on tendering processes and procedures.[6] Once strategic decisions have been made, it is vital that the municipality has the knowledge and ability necessary to tender, evaluate and procure the contract. The quality of preparation for tendering sets the scene for the quality of the tenders. The tendering process not only formally sets out the objectives, parameters and scope of the partnership, but also sets the agenda for the process. A corrupt or unprofessional tendering process is unlikely to result in a transparent and accountable partnership.

Skills for tendering are not new in municipalities accustomed to the construction of large-scale urban infrastructure. Yet in many situations, cost-effective procurement has been thwarted by well-established informal practices that largely determine the price and the winner. Replacing corrupt practices with transparent and accountable procedures is an extraordinary challenge. Champions of change often run into resistance over the partnership approach, not because of the private sector involvement but because it threatens pre-established systems of informal payments.

Of course, where long-term partnerships are envisaged, most municipalities recognise that they do not have the skills to carry out all the parts of the procurement process. But it is necessary for someone in-house to be able to supervise the tendering process (be it the chief engineer, another operational manager, the town clerk or a second-in-command). In Gweru, for instance, the municipality had the support of a PPP specialist who advised them on issues such as transparency and evaluation (see Box 11.3). The key to absorbing such specialist expertise lies in understanding that there is a skill gap within the municipality, and in funding, selecting and effectively briefing the advisor.

Important skills sets relating to the knowledge of the process and clarity in bidding documents include the ability to:

- identify what information is required and to undertake feasibility studies;
- carry out or identify gaps in expertise within the municipality in relation to the tender procedures; and
- ensure that some of the traditional norms of procurement do not creep into the tendering, evaluation and procurement process.

☐ Understanding of legal and contractual aspects of PPPs

The legal framework for the partnership arrangement will involve the basic legal framework pertaining to municipalities and municipal service provision, as well as the specific framework pertaining to PPP arrangements. While municipalities are typically familiar with the legal framework under which they have the authority to act (e.g., through decentralisation or local government acts), there is less familiarity with the PPP legal framework, and indeed this specific legal and policy framework is either new, lacks clarity (through a number of separate and often conflicting acts), or is constantly undergoing change.

Municipal decision-makers will need to ensure that they have identified the individual or legal team responsible for legal advice. This may be the legal department and/or a specialist brought in to provide this advice. It is essential that the skills exist in-house to some degree to ensure a basic understanding of legal requirements.

☐ Ability to conduct contract negotiations

Perhaps one of the greatest skills gaps in municipalities, and one which has been seen to cause great concern to municipalities, is their inability to negotiate contracts and contract amendments with their partners. In those cases in which the partner is an international operator skilled in this process, municipalities often feel exposed and fear an uneven playing field. This inability is particularly noticeable when juxtaposed with skilled negotiators in the private sector.

For this reason, municipalities must heed the advice of PPP advocates, who strongly recommend that the municipal negotiating team should include someone skilled in contract negotiation. As with the appointment of specialists discussed above, municipalities need to have developed knowledge of how to fund, appoint and manage such a specialist technical advisor, and how to formulate and manage a team of officials to implement the process. In taking this step, municipalities must be prepared to listen to the advice given, and must be in a position to judge whether the proposals meet their own objectives. The Gweru case (Box 11.3) provides an account of this process.

Capacity to Maintain Effective Partnerships

☐ Understanding of technical scope and ability to engage with the private operator about technical problems and solutions

Many municipalities assume that by delegating service delivery operations and management, they no longer need the technical expertise required for delivering that water or waste service, but experience suggests that more skilled municipal coordinators lead to more effective partnerships. Indeed, the more technical understanding a municipal manager/coordinator has, the better the partnership relations, and the more able the manager is to relay key problems and issues effectively to council decision-makers. Evidence also suggests that one of the primary skills to be acquired by technical staff is knowing when to leave well alone – to avoid micro-managing, drop their old-guard role of engineering design, and allow the private operator to do its job.

☐ Contract management and supervision

When the contract is in place, it is necessary for municipal leaders to manage the contract, and both strategic and practical skills are necessary to perform this role. It is essential to ensure that the contract continues to meet the municipality's needs, and to ensure effective management and supervision of day-to-day matters. Interaction between these levels is critical to the success of effective decision-making.

- The greater the involvement of councillors, and the greater their knowledge of the details of the contract and its problems, the more effective the municipality is as a partner.
- The more comprehensive the understanding of contract options, scope and the potential of private sector involvement, the greater the ability to make strategic decisions.

☐ Capacity to develop monitoring, evaluation and feedback mechanisms

Most partnership arrangements lack effective monitoring and evaluation. Municipal leaders need to understand the importance of monitoring performance and outcomes on an ongoing basis, the need for strategic evaluation, and the even greater importance of how these results will feed back into the process and result in redefined arrangements. The leadership will need to define how this is to be achieved, by whom, and at what intervals. This might be internally driven or contracted-out to NGOs, whose focus on equity, for instance, may contribute important information about targeting. Political will is an important parameter underpinning effective monitoring and evaluation.

☐ Renegotiations

Medium- to long-term contracts will inevitably encompass a number of electoral terms, and new, often inexperienced councillors may find they are responsible for a contract that does not meet the policy of a newly elected council. Frequently, councillors and inexperienced administrative officials do not have the capacity to launch into contract renegotiation. Often this is fuelled by insufficient information about cost–benefits, and old-guard administrators who prefer to maintain the status quo and lack knowledge about their options. The Stutterheim case (Box 11.1) exposes the kind of municipal inaction that can be the result when leaders feel unable to conduct renegotiations. This is not an atypical case.

As with the initial negotiations, in order to enter into renegotiation, municipal teams must have:

- confidence to sit at the table with private operators (perhaps with the support of specialist advisors);
- knowledge of service standards, and the efficiency and cost effectiveness of service delivery (perhaps with benchmarking or cost–benefit information); and
- comparative information and access to advice about options.

☐ Financial management and planning

If a municipality is to engage in partnerships with the private sector it is important that it develops a sound financial base, especially if such partnerships are to be sustained through a revenue stream from the municipality in return for services rendered. Staff must have skills in revenue mobilisation, accounting and administration (see also Chapter 12).

The bulk of tax receipts in most municipalities derive from property taxes that are commonly based on annual rental values, but many properties remain unassessed and therefore outside the tax base. There is a distinct capacity requirement for municipalities to ensure that all properties are assessed and any exemptions are clearly listed. It may be necessary temporarily to add to revenue staff to enable them to undertake this task, preferably on a routine basis or at least as part of a periodic revenue drive.

In a similar manner, other revenue could be significantly improved in areas such as water charges by ensuring that all water connections and standposts are properly listed and assessed. Water rates and charges need to be set at a rate that will recover the cost of operations and maintenance.

Accounts staff may need to strengthen their capacity to operate accounting systems that improve the overall management of income and expenditure. Accounts staff should be able to highlight deficits in the capital account, revenue surpluses that can be used to meet such deficits; they should be able to operate accrual-based accounting systems to present a complete picture of assets and liabilities. Manual book-keeping methods persist, and staff may not have access to the computer-based accounting systems that would structure and maintain their accounts in a more efficient manner. In the absence of such systems and without adequate training, accounts staff may not be able to provide an adequate picture of cash flow or undertake bank reconciliation on a routine basis.

Capacity to Engage with Stakeholders

☐ Ability to plan and carry out effective stakeholder consultations

The earliest PPPs were developed behind closed doors. More recently, the public sector in many countries has recognised that efforts to create sustainable partnership arrangements fundamentally rely on widespread support. In municipal partnerships, evidence suggests that leaders must have the skills and capacity to plan and facilitate a process of stakeholder consultation that leads to transparent, inclusive decision-making. Diverse skills sets are required to carry out consultations with communities, NGOs, trade unions and the business community. A coherent council, committed to the partnership process, will facilitate this, but in those cases in which there is split in the council between those for and against partnership approaches, the process of broader consultation will be more difficult. To ensure that consultation is effective, the process needs to be planned and its implementation monitored.

☐ Understanding of and ability to engage with the private operator

Irrespective of the quality of preparation and the contractual arrangements, the ultimate outcome of a partnership is determined by the interaction between the client (the municipality) and the contractor (the private operator). Given the changes that municipalities have had to deal with, it should be no surprise that many find interactions with the private sector difficult and fraught. The disparity in capacity, mutual mistrust and different work practices do not provide ideal starting points, and are fundamental barriers to effective communication. Municipal actors and private operators must build the capacity to understand and accommodate one another.

Partnerships that have seen years of miscommunication inevitably provoke constant confrontation. While this problem arises from both parties, evidence from case studies in South Africa suggests that municipal actors need to learn how to be partners. If partnerships have not been established with widespread support, and there is little recognition of the benefits of private sector participation, then there will be a weak basis for communication. If municipal managers are not versed in the key aspects of private sector operations, they will lack understanding of their partners' motivations and will not be able to appreciate their reasons for certain actions. The greater the knowledge of the goals, methods and concerns of the private operator, the more attuned the municipality will be, and the more skilled it will become in its interactions.

It must be remembered, however, that the interface between the private and public sectors often occurs on a day-to-day basis between project managers and engineering departments or public health departments. The municipal officials at the interface have generally been trained to perform the function themselves rather than managing or monitoring others. Not only do they find themselves in a role for which they are not trained, but many oppose, and have not been adequately consulted over, the whole privatisation process. The capacity of the municipality to engage effectively with private sector partners is thus constrained by the attitudes of the officials at the interface, and careful attention should be paid to ensuring that they feel supported and able to manage their role.

☐ Understanding of independent service providers and ability to engage with them

At the other end of the spectrum, small-scale service providers (SSIPs) are a much-maligned element of the private sector. Often owing to their informality, it is easy for municipalities to ignore and marginalise them in service delivery reforms. Yet many municipalities will find that some of their extension staff understand and have the skill to engage with rag-pickers, poor teenagers selling water by the bucket, or handcart vendors, while some of the engineering staff may be able and willing to engage with water tanker drivers or vacuum tanker drivers. Whether or not these skills are present, it is necessary for municipalities to consider how they will engage with formal and informal SSIPs. Knowledge about informal activities should be fed back and absorbed by decision-makers.

Unlike large-scale formal private sector operators, small-scale service providers have only limited capacity and they may need to receive capacity building training before they are able to participate meaningfully in partnership arrangements. Municipal understanding of this skills gap will enable more effective engagement with this sector, and thus an opportunity to build on the activities and services that SSIPs provide.

☐ Understanding of and ability to engage with NGOs to promote their involvement

While some municipalities have extensive and positive experience in working with NGOs, others do not, and the two sectors have often failed to produce collaborative arrangements. The cities of Ahmedabad and Kolkata (Calcutta) in India provide a useful comparison. In Ahmedabad there is an established NGO sector able and willing to work with the Ahmedabad Municipal Corporation (AMC) – the AMC recognises the important role played by NGOs in the town and promotes it. In Kolkata, the idea that working collaborations might be developed between NGOs and local government is ambitious: the two have acted independently and maintained mistrust for decades. While political factors have affected this relationship, a lack of skills and organisational capacity has also led to blockages between local government and NGOs.

Broader partnership initiatives that include the civic sectors require a fundamental understanding of all the actors who represent community interests. Even if this understanding is established, organisational factors will also influence the relationship. NGOs need to be treated as equal partners, and they must be given the same access to municipal managers as the private sector. These managers must know about the opportunities and constraints of the NGO sector, must be able to communicate with it effectively and identify potential roles for it within the partnership.

☐ Understanding of and ability to engage with consumers, particularly poor consumers

Historically, municipalities have played the traditional role of service provider, and services have often been free of charge, or heavily subsidised. As such, not much time and energy has been devoted to thinking of the end-user as a client, often a paying client, with specific service demands and rights. Training, time and fundamental shifts in attitude will frequently be required to introduce municipal officials to this concept. It is often difficult for municipal officials to take on board the idea that poor consumers should be given a voice. Except in certain innovative schemes in which poor communities have established direct communication with municipal governments, it is important for municipalities to seek the assistance of NGOs to help them understand and engage with poor consumers.

☐ Understanding of and ability to undertake consultation with trade unions

In many countries with active trade unions, a primary concern for a municipality considering reforms that promote private sector involvement will be the negotiations and discussions with trade unions. While this may have been addressed at a national policy-making level, with national-level associations (such as SALGA in South Africa), the process of change requires extensive consultation at the local level, and municipalities need the skills and organisational capacity to listen, present and negotiate with trade unions over the process of introducing the private sector into traditional public sector functions.

Trade unions generally have valid concerns about job security and the profit element of private sector operations. It is necessary for municipalities to have the ability to:

- engage with trade unions over key labour issues, to understand their concerns and ensure that these are addressed in the partnership arrangement;
- present the benefits of private sector participation to trade union forums, particularly in relation to the poor sections of society;

- prepare and operationalise ongoing and meaningful consultation processes with unions;
- build consensus around a project; and
- manage conflicts of interest, should they arise.

Capacity Building

☐ Understanding of and ability to develop and implement a capacity building strategy

In order to build capacity it is necessary for a municipality to develop and implement an effective capacity building strategy, and a key to this is for a municipality to come to an understanding of the gaps in their capacity. Recognising skills gaps, or being able to carry out assessments that provide details of the nature of skills gaps, are important skills in themselves. Once this is in hand (perhaps through human resource staff or heads of departments, or through a structured assessment), municipal leaders need to determine a capacity building strategy in relation to municipal objectives. This must consider all the municipal actors, and their potential roles, in a framework that addresses both the short and the long term – and the ongoing requirements of capacity building throughout the contract.

A key aspect of the capacity building strategy will concern the provision of skills training. Who provides the training? How is capacity building achieved – short- or long-term courses, study visits, learning-by-doing or exchange programmes...?

☐ Understanding the potential roles of specialists

A number of the issues described above have drawn attention to the role of skilled specialists in the development of partnerships. A particularly notable aspect of the PPP procurement process is the need for expertise in a number of areas. Given the long-term nature of some forms of contracts, it is not always necessary for municipal officials to acquire skills, as they might never use them again in the course of a 30-year career. But it is essential that municipal leaders have the knowledge and capacity to brief specialists, and to manage and maximise their inputs. In many cases it is necessary to promote the idea of bringing in such expertise before consultants are appointed, to ensure that key decision-makers are willing to listen to and work with outsiders. It is also necessary to know how the funding for this technical assistance can be obtained. In most cases it is funded by donors, but the sustainability of this mechanism must be called into question as the partnership approach spreads.

How Are these Human Resources Developed and Sustained?

Developing a Capacity Building Strategy

A capacity building strategy will describe:

- *what capacity* (through training-needs assessments and the identification of skills gaps);
- *whose capacity* (by building on assets in relation to the implementation strategy);
- *how capacity is to be built* (what methods are to be adopted);
- *when initiatives will be undertaken* (the programme in relation to partnership processes); and
- *who will pay* (where the funds will come from for this purpose).

The preceding section has established a framework describing the types of skill sets needed for planning, developing and implementing partnerships. Municipal managers must then identify skill gaps, assess training needs, agree who should be targeted for skills development, decide how and when skills development should be undertaken.

| Box **11.2** | Skills Framework

	Core competencies	Poverty-related competencies
Strategic and practical understanding of the problem and context	• Ability to understand existing operating context macro-economic, political, policy, administrative) • Ability to understand the limitations and implications of the regulatory framework and the limitations of existing delivery mechanisms	• Ability to understand poverty context and the perceptions of the poor • Ability to understand service partnerships in relation to the livelihoods of the poor • Ability to disaggregate the low-income group and identify different intra-community and intra-household needs

Strategic understanding of solutions	• Strategic understanding of opportunities and constraints of PPPs in urban governance and municipal management
	 • Capacity to exercise informed decision-making on PPPs in service delivery in relation to urban management goals
	  – to evaluate PPP options against other forms of delivery
	  – to promote PPPs in appropriate municipal functions
	  – to identify misinformation and develop an objective understanding of PPPs
		• Ability to consider PPPs in the context of poverty reduction strategies

	• Ability to define the situation and objectives to engage with partnership concepts in a competent manner
	  – to understand the municipality's objectives and define the requirements of a partnership arrangement
	  – to understand PPP options and implications
	  – to initiate and prepare projects
		• Ability to understand direct and indirect implications of PPPs for the poor, including financing aspects, arrangements, processes and actors
		 • Ability to develop and institutionalise the role of the poor in the contractual arrangement from the outset
		 • Ability to mediate between private sector and community, and facilitate three-way partnership arrangements
		 • Ability to recognise and mitigate potential secondary impacts

	• Basic knowledge of financing arrangements:
	  – understanding of tariff structures, implications,
	  – connection costs, subsidies
	  – understanding of investment plans and implications
	  – ability to balance tariff requirements with other political and social requirements
	  – understanding fee structures/implications
		• Ability to develop a tariff in the light of affordability and willingness to pay balanced against cost recovery for service and service expansion
		 • Ability to promote and establish flexibility in payment arrangements for poor households
		 • Ability to promote better understanding of tariffs in relation to livelihoods

	• Strategic understanding of potential risks likely to affect performance under a contract • Knowledge and understanding of risk allocation	• Understanding of risks of extending coverage and quality of service to low-income areas, and incentives for private sector operation in low-income areas • Ability to develop mechanisms to reduce risks and promote improved services for the poor
	• Understanding of the nature and potential of all actors	• Specific understanding of local and potential actors able to partner in service delivery to the poor (NGOs, small-scale independent providers, CBOs)

	Core competencies	Poverty-related competencies
Capacity to analyse needs and develop a strategic response	• Understanding of information requirements, knowledge of information available – to ensure thorough identification of problems, and – to undertake or facilitate a feasibility study • Capacity to formulate municipal objectives with all stakeholders through participatory processes	• Ability to balance urban management with poverty-reduction objectives
	• Ability to plan strategically to fulfil objectives – to recognise whether partnerships are viable or not in the local context – to create a partnership strategy workable in long/medium/short term	• Ability to plan for interim improvements to match affordability, programme and funding, as well as long term improvements
Capacity to implement the strategy	• Ability to implement transparent tendering and evaluation procedures – basic knowledge of invitation and tender process – ability to clearly outline requirements of potential projects for bidders and to represent departmental objectives and interests – ability to develop criteria for selecting private sector partners	
	• Understanding of legal and contractual aspects of PPPs – detailed knowledge of opportunities and constraints – ability to preserve departments' interests in contract negotiation and administration – ability to understand performance requirements and the implications of definitions	• Ability to ensure that performance standards (including expansion mandates and service options) are beneficial to poor and do not create unintended impacts of legal frameworks governing PPPs
	• Ability to conduct contract negotiations – to oversee contract development process – to recognise what preparatory work needs to precede tendering to minimise delays in contract negotiations over specific provisions – to understand/pursue/defend departmental interests and objectives in contract negotiations	
Capacity to maintain effective partnerships	• Understanding of technical scope, and ability to engage with private operator over technical problems and solutions – to understand problems with existing systems and processes – to understand technical proposals for reorganisation (solid waste management), rehabilitation, extension and upgrade (urban water supply) – to engage with the private operator in the management of the contract	• Ability to understand or initiate a range of technological options • Ability to understand or initiate the role of poor households in construction and upgrading works (e.g., labour-based construction options)

	Core competencies	Poverty-related competencies
	• Ability to perform contract management and supervisory role – to structure departments to optimise use and oversight of PPPs – to provide effective supervision (avoiding micro-management) – to evaluate whether a service is being delivered efficiently and effectively – to manage contract problems such as non-compliance	
	• Capacity to develop monitoring, evaluation and feedback mechanisms – to establish effective monitoring procedures – to implement monitoring and evaluation, and ensure meaningful feedback is achieved and brings about change	• Ability to establish effective baseline studies and impact assessments of service delivery on poor households • Ability to establish participatory monitoring processes
	• Strategic management of contract – ability and confidence to respond to impact assessment and revise arrangements within or at the completion of contract period	
Capacity to engage with stakeholders	• Understanding of and ability to engage with civil society – to engage with communities and community representatives (NGOs) – to prepare and operationalise a stakeholder analysis	• Ability to conceive and implement meaningful participatory processes with the poor • Ability to ensure participation of women and other vulnerable groups • Ability to perceive a range of actions and involvement by poor communities and NGOs in the partnership • Ability to initiate practical and strategic changes to contract proposals to maximise benefits for the poor
	• Understanding of and ability to undertake consultation with trade unions – to prepare and operationalise ongoing and meaningful consultation processes with labour unions – to build consensus around project – to manage conflicts of interest should they arise	
Understanding of capacity building needs and ability to improve capacity	• Ability to undertake training-needs assessments, identify skills required and gaps in municipal skills – to initiate and facilitate sustainable capacity building to underpin PPP initiatives – to ensure skills transfer throughout PPP – to recognise the need for specialist advisors and brief them adequately – to identify funding sources for specialists	• Ability to work with and develop community capacity to perform agreed role, including the role of women and other vulnerable groups

PPP capacity should ideally be developed in situ. The conventional approach will be through training exercises and manuals. However, experience shows that formal training may have only limited success. Evidence suggests that the most effective way to build skills and expertise is not through simple knowledge transfer (which tends to underpin training courses and manuals) but through a participative experiential learning process. This process can build on existing knowledge to provide solutions that are relevant and 'owned' by the learners themselves. This process requires an on-the-job learning programme involving a careful blend of technical assistance and training.

The main personnel to be targeted for PPP capacity building are likely to be those involved in decision-making and those working at the interface of the partnership (see discussion on task forces in Chapter 12):

- political leadership;
- chief executive officers;
- line heads of service departments (e.g., water and sanitation);
- senior departmental staff;
- senior financial managers; and
- legal/administrative officers.

The capacity building strategy needs to be designed and implemented well in advance of the specified dates for launching any PPP initiative. Timing will depend upon the availability and dates of training courses and/or external facilitation. Capacity building activities should be programmed into the overall PPP programme and should not be rushed into as a last-minute remedial measure, especially in cases in which the municipality has little or no previous experience of PPPs.

Finally a municipality will have to give careful thought to how it will finance any capacity building strategy. There are a number of options available:

- Obtain council approval to allocate funds for training. Some municipalities have made it mandatory to ensure that there is annual budgetary provision for training.
- Obtain funding from a higher tier of government, such as the province or state, which may have responsibility for training all public servants. Here, municipalities should improve their networking skills with trainers and training institutions at a regional level.
- Seek support from a donor agency funding technical assistance for decentralisation, local government and private sector participation initiatives. Many agencies, including the World Bank, ADB, EU, UNDP, DFID and USAID, now actively support capacity building at the local level of government.

Developing Skills

There are a number of approaches that can be taken to develop municipal skills.

■ Training

Training becomes a support function of the overall capacity building programme, which is grounded in experiential learning. A training programme should be developed by a specialist trainer/training advisor and based on a training-needs assessment exercise designed to highlight the main skills gaps and deficiencies discussed above, in relation to the training objectives associated with the design and management of municipal PPPs. The training programme will need to address the knowledge requirements associated with PPPs as well as the specific skills required for design and implementation, and the kinds of attitudes that will best foster such initiatives. Knowledge deficiencies are best addressed through straightforward technical training, while skill and attitudinal deficiencies may be addressed through experiential training methods such as simulations, case studies, role plays, brainstorming etc.

Links to Boxes
4.5, 9.4, 9.5, 10.4, 11.4, 12.7

Box **11.3** **Supplementing Municipal Skills**
Gweru, Zimbabwe

The Gweru case also provides an illustration of the support provided by a specialist PPP consultant. Following presentations from the private operators, the GCC management team evaluated qualifications and produced an evaluation report shortlisting three tenderers. At this point some concern developed within the management team. While it had successfully reached this point of the process without support, concerns were raised about the imbalance in skills that now existed between specialist international operators (familiar with the process) and a management team embarking on this process for the first time. This concern was accentuated by an increasing shift towards a longer-term, investment-linked contract. As the tenderers had each proposed different arrangement and options (including affermage, concession and joint venture arrangements), the GCC was tasked not only with evaluating proposals, but making judgements as to which was the most appropriate contract option. It therefore decided to seek the advice of international specialists in the completion of the evaluation stage, and in June 1998 the GCC approached USAID for technical assistance.

To secure these consultancy services, the management team drew up terms of reference for them. In essence, the GCC proposed that an international multi-disciplinary consultant should assist in the evaluation, advise on the way forward for the GCC and advise on the appointment of the private operator. The consultant was to have a range of skills, including financial, managerial, legal and technical expertise. An internal task force was convened to work with, assist and learn from the consultant.

In the first instance, the consultant proposed that an addendum be issued to each tenderer, in order to clarify the GCC position, to obtain more information on the capacity of the private companies and to understand in more detail the approach proposed. This addendum asked each consortium to provide responses to issues relevant to the changing concerns of the council. These included, in particular:

- *tariff increases:* a proposal describing how the proposal would deal with tariffs in the context of inflationary pressures;
- *capital improvements:* a proposal indicating the willingness and ability to fund capital improvements (replacements, major rehabilitation, new plant and network), indicated a major shift in thinking, from a management contract to a concession agreement;
- *interim period/data gathering/contract negotiations:* a proposal for how the operator would proceed in the period between selection and contract signature (including management assistance during the data-gathering/negotiation period); and
- *identification of a sole responsible party:* naming the party responsible for all aspects of the contract, and the individuals who would staff the project.

This addendum enabled the council to clarify its own requirements and to state them as specific actions or conditions. It covered the key concerns of company viability, re-employment of council workers, and capital investment. In order that a plan of action could be clearly established once the responses were received, the council was taken through the benefits and drawbacks of the options open to it. These included one of the following:

- proceed with the concession, with data gathering and management services provided at a fee;
- proceed with the concession, without data gathering and management services; or
- hire the preferred firm to manage water and sanitation services for one or two years, and to generate data and plan ahead.

In addition to these tasks, the consultant also carried out a significant amount of capacity building, through formal sessions (such as working with the middle-management task force) and informal information sharing with the management team and the council. The consultant was also tasked with the responsibility for developing the methodology for selecting the operator. Accordingly, a matrix system for evaluating proposals was defined, which identified the criteria to be considered and their relative importance. This evaluation method, which aimed to promote and ensure transparency in the decision-making process, included eight criteria including business experience, financial capacity, management skills, technology transfer, specific project personnel, reemployment of GCC staff and tariff levels.

The consultant and the internal task force reviewed the three responses and prepared a report for consideration by the town clerk. The consultant then presented the findings to the full council, recommending the appointment of the tenderer with the highest score at evaluation. As a result of this process, in September 1998, SAUR UK was notified that it had been selected. In the following month, the council and SAUR UK began negotiations to define and agree the necessary steps for implementation (see Box 10.4).

Source: Plummer and Nhemachena, 2001

■ Technical assistance

External facilitation can act as a catalyst to maximise the learning opportunities associated with PPP design and implementation. External facilitators skilled in PPP operation might usefully work with the municipality to help diagnose problems, weaknesses and skills gaps in relation to partnerships, and create learning opportunities so that these can be addressed in the workplace through on-the-job training in PPP systems and procedures.

■ Improving staff quality through recruitment

Many municipalities face capacity constraints; their key staff are not able to manage the whole partnership process in terms of commercial planning, monitoring and technical support. Such municipalities may find it necessary to increase the capacity of certain staff to ensure sufficient capability to oversee the partnership. At the same time, it may be important to find mechanisms to fill vacancies in key areas that concern the formulation, negotiation, management and monitoring of partnerships. While this may not be possible in all municipalities, it is important to recognise that it is necessary to create an even playing field between the municipal and private sector partners, and ultimately this can lead to more strategic appointments.

■ Supplementing internal capacity with external specialists

A recurring theme throughout this book is the need to supplement internal staff with external specialists. Specialists must be able to work with key staff in the municipality to devise appropriate systems and procedures for the design and management of partnerships with the private sector. This may require helping staff to interpret, understand and/or modify technical manuals, as well as devising new systems and formats to assist the introduction of new procedures and/or responsibilities.

■ Developing political capacity

Another area of capacity building that is often overlooked by HRD specialists is the building of decision-making skills in the elected body. Here, it may be necessary, for example, to devise ways and means of helping councillors to improve their decision-making skills, so that they will be in a position to assume greater responsibility for initiating and overseeing new service delivery arrangements.

■ Transfers and secondments

A common approach to capacity building in local government is to transfer or 'second' skilled workers to the local level. This approach is not an ideal way of strengthening local democratic institutions, as it encourages them to become dependent on personnel from other agencies. However, short-term transfers and secondments can be a useful means of injecting PPP expertise into a municipality for a limited period to assist with specific tasks. Seconding municipal staff to other organisations involved in PPPs enables staff to gain (and bring back) first hand experience.

■ Monitoring of and feedback into capacity building strategy

The capacity building strategy for PPP will include the monitoring of new systems, procedures and arrangements in relation to outputs and outcomes. This should be developed as a learning tool for adjusting and modifying the content of capacity development as well as learning methodologies. Training programmes should be monitored to assess the degree of effectiveness of information transfer, while technical support and on-the-job learning will need to be assessed in terms of its success in imparting appropriate PPP knowledge and skills. On-the-job capacity building methods will require constant monitoring and feedback to ensure that systems and procedures conform to desired outcomes.

11

Box 11.5   Skills Development in PPPs
Gweru, Zimbabwe

Links to Boxes
4.5, 9.4, 9.5, 10.4, 11.3, 12.7

	Training	Participants	Appreciation	Impact for GCC
1996	• Privatisation and commercialisation of public services (ZIPAM) (UK Civil Service College) • Commercialisation of local authority services (Price Waterhouse) • PSP in water and sanitation services (World Bank workshop)	• Executive mayor; • Town clerk; • City treasurer • Executive mayor; • Town clerk; • City treasurer • Director of engineering services	• An appreciation of the scope and nature of PPPs • Orientation to the potential of PPPs in the context of local authorities in Zimbabwe • Sector-specific orientation for municipal engineers in water and sanitation PPP	• Acceptance of PPP concept • Awareness of the range of options (commercialisation, full privatisation, PPP) • Identification of services to be commercialised • Confidence to propose water and sanitation PPP • Ability to prepare, pre-qualify and evaluate tenders
1998	• Best practice in local government administration (regional conference) • In-house workshop for senior management • Three in-house workshops for middle management provided by USAID • Municipal cooperation (SADC Local Government Conference, Johannesburg)	• Town clerk; • City treasurer • Town clerk; City treasurer; • Director of housing; • Director of medical services; • Chamber secretary; • Director of engineering services; • Chairs of standing committees • Inter-departmental task force; • All council departments; Union representatives; Councillors • Town clerk	• Dissemination of best practice including PPPs • Familiarisation with the concession contract and the negotiation process • Familiarisation with the process of developing the PSP for water and sanitation services • Understanding of proposals and amendments, city options, PPP models, methodology for evaluation, model concession agreement • Promoting municipal cooperation and PPP for development	• Determination to develop PPP approach • Enhanced capacity to manage PPP process • Enhanced capacity for all activities in pre-concession period, including the • Memorandum of Understanding • Better capacity to evaluate tenders • Improved dissemination of objectives • More champions of PSP in GCC • Supplementary capacity buildng for PPPs
1999	• USAID-sponsored study tour of South Africa: Municipal finance and management • Integrated water management	• City treasurer • Director of engineering services	• Familiarisation with private sector financing of urban infrastructure (Nelspruit) • Importance of involving all stakeholders including private sector in water management	• Better understanding of financing arrangements of the proposed concession • Enhanced commitment to stakeholder involvement in the management of water and sanitation services
2000	• Municipal capital markets (World Bank, New York) • Infrastructure for development: private solutions and the poor (World Bank, London)	• Town clerk • Town clerk	• Role of private capital in urban development • Reaching the poor through private sector involvement in infrastructure	• Enhanced capacity to deal with concession agreement • Commitment to investment- linked partnerships • Commitment to including pro-poor objectives in concession contract

Source: Plummer and Nhemachena, 2001

Retaining Skills through Staffing Policy and Practice

An important part of PPP capacity building strategy is maintaining the new capacities that have been developed so that they will make a sustainable contribution to the organisation. It is important for the municipality to consider different options for retaining skilled and trained staff who are capable of managing effective PPPs.

■ **Incentive systems**

Municipalities rarely have incentives systems to reward staff performance. Most personnel systems have rigidly defined scales of pay, and remuneration packages that are often on parity with those of other public servants. Pay, however, is reinforced by a range of allowances over and above those covering inflation. In some local government systems these allowances have been used to compensate for deteriorating pay scales. It may be highly desirable for a municipality to sustain its capacity building efforts through the introduction of incentives designed to reward the effective management of successful PPP arrangements.

■ **Appropriateness of roles and responsibilities**

The introduction of PPPs in a municipality will tend to alter the balance of staff and their respective roles and responsibilities. When departmental managers who were previously responsible for overseeing the direct delivery of services become responsible for monitoring, regulating and managing contracts, it is imperative that roles and responsibilities match the tasks assigned. It can be useful for a municipality to undertake a management audit to focus on the following issues, all of which will need to be reviewed in the light of the introduction of PPPs: appropriateness of reporting lines, overlapping responsibilities, spans of control, new job descriptions, work plans, and specifications of work standards.

■ **Promoting more autonomy to match decentralised decision-making**

In order to enhance municipal capacity to undertake PPPs in an effective manner, it is useful for higher government authorities to relax their control over staff recruitment. This is especially important if the recruitment of new staff is directly related to PPP initiatives designed to reduce costs and/or improve service levels in a tangible manner.

■ **Employee relations**

An important aspect of personnel management concerns the manner in which relationships between management and staff are conducted, and how changes in work conditions or employment terms are negotiated and agreed with staff at all levels. The level of unionisation within the municipality is a major issue that will determine how the dialogue is conducted both during and after the introduction of PPPs. An important strategy in maintaining skilled staff is to ensure that the municipality has an effective employee-relations system in place, although the focus of such a system after the introduction of a PPP might be on senior and professional staff rather than junior labourers and field staff.

Enhancing Capacity to Implement Partnerships

Chapter 12 **Key Questions**

☐ **What is the management capacity required for partnerships?**

☐ **What are the procedural constraints and requirements for PPPs?**

☐ **How do municipal structures constrain partnerships? Which structural vehicles can be used to take partnerships forward?**

☐ **What are the financial constraints and requirements for PPPs?**

☐ **How can attitudes be changed to enhance municipal capacity for partnerships?**

| Understanding the operating context of municipal partnerships | Enhancing human resources | Supporting organisational development |

Guy Stubbs

Supporting Organisational Development | 12

Janelle Plummer, Richard Slater and Chris Heymans

Any municipality embarking upon public–private partnerships (PPPs) will be forced to undergo some form of organisational change. These changes may be necessary to attract the large-scale private sector and its investment, to adapt to the changing role of the municipality in service provision, or to ensure that the partnership is focused and sustainable. The nature of these changes will depend on the characteristics and capacity of the municipality at the outset and the extent of the reform that the municipal government has embarked upon.

Chapter 4 has highlighted the important premise that the PPP itself may prompt or accompany reform, but good governance brings about a range of changes, one of which may be the development of PPPs. This discussion – supporting organisational development for PPPs – must therefore be seen as a part of this larger process.

In order to establish PPPs, and particularly partnerships focused on bringing benefit to the poor, it is necessary for municipalities to develop and implement an organisational development strategy: first by identifying the organisational factors constraining effective partnering and partnerships, and then by identifying the most appropriate mechanisms for bringing about that change. The following discussion outlines the key aspects for consideration. It emphasises the importance of champions and creating effective management; of establishing targeted procedures and processes to facilitate transparent partnerships; of addressing sometimes significant structural change; of establishing a sound financial base; and of reforming municipal attitudes. Accordingly, this chapter is structured in terms of:

- Municipal leadership and management
- Municipal procedures and systems
- Municipal structures
- Municipal finances
- Municipal attitudes

Municipal Leadership and Management

Leadership and Management Challenges

One of the most critical issues in capacity development for partnerships is municipal leadership and management. Probable key figures include the mayor, the chief executive (town clerk/municipal commissioner etc.), the chief engineer, the public health engineer, the city/town treasurer, or perhaps a senior councillor or head of department in a particular sector, like water. If a partnership arrangement is to succeed, it will require sound management on the part of the municipality (as well as the private sector operator) and thus the nature and characteristics of management within the municipality will strongly influence the partnership formation, implementation and sustainability. A key ingredient of sustainable partnerships is political leadership with the capacity, authority, vision and commitment to change. Political leadership needs to be supported by effective administrative leadership that has the power and status to supervise other senior management and work without political interference.[1]

☐ Political leadership

The growing role of democratically elected representatives in municipal administration has had a significant impact on the composition of councils and on the manner in which municipal functions are managed. For decades, municipalities

Box **12.1**   **Management Constraints**
Stutterheim, South Africa

Links to Boxes
6.1, 7.17, 8.6, 9.6, 11.1

Perhaps the primary constraints to the development of a partnership that effectively addresses the needs of the poorer groups in Stutterheim are unequivocal political support and management capacity for targeted partnerships. After the 1995 democratic elections, politicians in Stutterheim belonged to the school that ideologically opposed PSP in basic service delivery. More recently though, councillors have softened this stance as their understanding of governance and appreciation of finance constraints has developed, and as the national- and provincial-level political structures have formed agreements, the political wing has recognised the importance of tapping into external investment and management skills. It is therefore likely that, given the choice and with extensive public consultation, they would themselves enter into a partnership with the private sector in the future. Nevertheless, they are cautious and sceptical and have many grievances towards the arrangement they have inherited. Their understanding of and decision-making over issues concerning the role of the private sector is based on ambiguous messages, a weak contractual position, unclear financial information and an unequal playing field.

As in many municipalities in South Africa, human resources in Stutterheim are characterised by an old-style administration working with newly elected, mostly African National Congress councillors. In general, the relationship between the two wings in Stutterheim is smooth. Unlike some neighbouring towns that replaced existing administrative staff, the Stutterheim council chose to keep the senior administrators in post before the local democratic election in 1995. Other posts, such as treasurer, have changed since that time. It is important to understand this split and to consider its implications for capacity.

The councillors are politically agile but for historical reasons have not yet had significant exposure to management practices or governance. Since the election in 1995, council members have been trained and 'workshopped' in a wide range of skills necessary for them to perform their leadership and representative roles. The changing policy environment, the development of skills and understanding of governance has resulted in an acknowledgement that private sector resources are needed to meet reconstruction and development targets.

The issue of administrative capacity, however, is somewhat contentious in Stutterheim. The administrators are able managers but there is no doubt that they would benefit from specific training in PPPs. Since this private sector approach to service delivery was introduced, no training has been undertaken by any official. Their lack of exposure to contract options has been limited, and attitudes have developed solely in relation to the one limited contract with which they are involved. Compared with other municipalities, administrative managers in Stutterheim lack the skill of recognising skills deficiencies. This has proven to be particularly problematic, as they are the main advisors to the council.

Perhaps the primary areas in which the lack of skills has come to the fore are the financial side of water and sanitation delivery, and the understanding of partnership costs. The council has a mandate to provide services of the highest quality at the lowest cost. In Stutterheim it is currently assumed that the council can deliver the same standard of service at a lower cost, and as a result it has pursued a dual system of municipal and private sector delivery. It is not immediately clear what underlies this assumption: there is no evidence available to prove that this is the case. A number of councillors suggested that any private sector involvement implies a 'profit' element, and it is therefore necessarily more expensive than the cost of public sector operations. Unfortunately, this argument ignores the efficiencies and savings that can be made in the private sector. It is not supported by cost comparisons in the region or evidence from other parts of the world.

There is also no doubt that management and leadership in Stutterheim would be improved by a cost–benefit analysis that itemises all the costs and benefits and enables a proper comparative assessment of alternative delivery approaches. Such a study would compare operator performance with international benchmarks. Accurate cost information will strengthen the municipal position whatever the findings. If private sector costs are indeed found to be high, the council will be in a strong position to negotiate. If they are found to be low, this knowledge will create a more receptive and conducive operating environment in which a more appropriate contract could be developed. At this stage, the reluctance of the administrative management to pursue such a comprehensive analysis is intriguing; councillors do not have the capacity or the time to prioritise it.

A second common assumption in Stutterheim is that the water and sanitation contract with WSSA cannot be changed because the council cannot afford it. This assumption is based on the understanding that costs would be higher with additional private sector involvement, but revenue would remain the same. The council has not seriously examined the revenue benefits that the private operator could bring if an effective contract extension was negotiated, including customer management and payment awareness campaigns. Conversely, the private operator has not explored willingness to pay, nor has it effectively framed or communicated the opportunities for linking increased cost recovery, capacity building and community development with improved levels of service for the poorer communities.

Source: Plummer, 2000

have been run by civil servants keen to maintain the status quo. While this is often still the case, in many parts of the world democratically elected representatives are beginning to lead the transformation of municipal management, and there is an increasing recognition of the importance of training councillors to perform their role effectively. Strong leadership does not guarantee progress towards PPPs, but the political mandate does place the mayor in a stronger position to negotiate the various demands and come up with integrated solutions. This is often needed in contentious matters such as service delivery, planning, tariff-setting. It may not be appropriate for political leaders to assume actual management roles, but they do have an important oversight function to align municipal management to the council's political mandate and priorities.

However, the capacity of councillors to launch new approaches to service delivery or to oversee existing contracts varies significantly. Even where a clear policy framework exists, the success of policy relating to basic services lies in the implementation at local level, and this is very much determined by the human resource capacity of municipal decision-makers. The ideological bias of the council members, their level of education, their ability to conceive of a collaborative effort, and their understanding of their overall role as custodians of municipal finance, all contribute to their capacity to conceive of new arrangements and make these plans happen.[2]

Much depends upon the new leaders' perceptions of voter interests, and these perceptions are commonly framed as part of a short-term perspective that may not reflect the long-term advantages arising from partnerships. Some councillors see the role of the council as critical in promoting sectoral reform, cost recovery and partnership approaches, and they may play a vital role in disseminating an understanding of the scope and nature of private sector participation (PSP) and partnership approaches to service delivery. Indeed, as councillors are so often engaged in the private sector themselves they can be important advocates for promoting partnership, and may also be very skilled at working with stakeholders.

As most councils will have some form of committee system that will enhance councillor involvement in municipal management, it is likely that a number of councillors as well as the mayor and deputy mayor will be directly involved in the strategic and practical management of service delivery. The public health and engineering committee chairpersons will probably be responsible for waste and water respectively. Once again, the degree of influence they have over these committees will depend on a number of factors including municipal precedent, interest and skill. It is possible to see too that partnerships that appear to be failing often have lacked the direct contact (or understanding) of a councillor familiar with the nature, scope and problems of partnerships.

As councillors are usually elected for a relatively short period (three to five years), a primary issue for long-term partnership arrangements is the capacity and frequent turnover of municipal decision-makers.[3] When newly elected councils are thrown into partnerships for basic service delivery, they must undergo a steep learning curve to come to terms with PPPs. Evidence suggests that there is little institutional learning, and the learning curve starts again after each election. This will vary as each council will have a different balance of business, social and political skills and interests. In South Africa, for instance, newly elected representatives have struggled with the concept of private sector participation in Stutterheim for years. While they were ideologically opposed to the partnership at the outset, as experience with municipal management increased they began to see the benefits of the partnership. Yet the real problem is that the former council which put the partnership in place was managed by businessmen, and the newly elected democratic council is more socially oriented. Its perceived lack of skill in negotiating change has fundamentally undermined the efficacy of the partnership (see Boxes 11.1 and 12.1).

Administrative leadership

While the driving force of a partnership arrangement may lie with the mayor or the chief executive officer (CEO), the process of making it happen will normally rest with the administrative leader and the senior management of the

Box **12.2**   **Local Champions Drive Partnerships**
Nelspruit, South Africa

Links to Boxes
6.17, 6.18

While national political will is mostly critical to successful PSP implementation at the municipal level, local champions add considerable momentum to PSP in municipal service delivery. The experience in Nelspruit, the capital of Mpumalanga province in South Africa, demonstrates the role of such PSP champions.

In 1994-95, after the democratisation of government at all levels in South Africa, the newly demarcated Nelspruit municipality faced significant service delivery challenges. The capacity of the municipality, previously used mainly to serve the relatively well-off white population of 24,000 people, now had to support delivery to the whole area, with more than 240,000 residents, many of whom are poor. By 1997, the council began exploring private sector involvement. Once the PPP option was chosen, the commitment of key officials and councillors in Nelspruit helped steer the PPP through various critical phases. The continuous drive and commitment of the mayor played a major part in mobilising councillors, including the chairperson and the members of the executive committee that was behind the PPP. This political core was strengthened by the fact that one councillor, an engineer, added technical understanding about the water and sanitation aspects of the project.

The commitment among the political leadership was bolstered by the active role of key officials. The town manager, in particular, with the top financial and engineering officials, realised at an early stage that the municipality would not be able to extend its coverage of water and sanitation supply on its own. Its operations were geared to the needs of the former apartheid-defined 'white' area of Nelspruit, and low-income areas newly incorporated into the municipality were without adequate infrastructure to support effective service delivery. They approached the Development Bank of Southern Africa (DBSA) for advice, and were told of the PPP option.

In the debates about the project, and preparation for its implementation, inputs from experts within South Africa and abroad played a major role. This enabled the municipality to apply lessons from elsewhere in the world and to ensure the PPP alternative made technical and financial sense. This also bolstered their ability to engage with stakeholders to ensure the project gained greater political acceptance.

Their commitment was severely tested by very poor infrastructure, vast service backlogs and strong trade union resistance. Initially, the local branch of the municipal workers' trade union accepted the PPP option, but the national leadership opposed the participation of the private sector in local service delivery. Negotiations dragged on, and conflicts arose.

The top officials remained committed to the PPP option, convinced that it would be the only way to extend water supplies to previously disadvantaged areas. Specific care was taken to ensure that projected prices reflect an allowance for substantial capital investments over 30 years. In general, the tariffs will be lower that would have been the case if the municipality had made the improvements itself. Mobilising the best technical expertise from within and outside South Africa, they also ensured that the national and provincial governments remained well briefed. They actually received significant support from these levels, especially from the national department responsible for local government.

Finally, the concession was concluded in 2000, and the project is one of the first major water projects in a post-apartheid municipality to involve a private operator at such a large scale. But it retains a critical regulatory and oversight role for the municipality. The council will approve the tariffs levied for water and sanitation services. They will also monitor the way in which these services are provided. If the contractor stops the supply of these services to any residents, the municipality will have the right to investigate the situation and engage with the service provider to facilitate a resolution of the issues. The councils will also monitor the environmental impact of the services on the environment. It has informed the development of policy on PSP in South Africa. Problems remain concerning regulatory issues that have thus far influenced private financiers not to finance the project. But the DBSA, a public loan financier independent from government, has shown considerable faith in the project and granted a loan. Efforts to attract other investors continue, driven in spirited fashion by the political and administrative leadership in the council.

Sources: National Business Initiative, 2000b; Kotzé, Ferguson and Leigland, 1999;
National Business Initiative and Municipal Infrastructure Investment Unit, 1999

municipality. The capacity of the CEO (town clerk or secretary) to work towards the defined municipal objectives, and instigate and manage the strategic planning, consultation, transaction and ongoing monitoring processes, will determine the sustainability of the partnership arrangement and the benefit it brings to the urban poor.

Forms and styles of municipal management vary considerably throughout the world. At one extreme is the innovative manager, highly trained and flexible, able to manage coherent teams, coordinate effectively with the elected members, and understand the municipality as a tapestry of interwoven functions. This manager is often thwarted by rigid procedures, limited finances, the poor skills base of the municipality and externalities impacting on effective management. At the other extreme is the inflexible manager, unable to manage personnel effectively, maintaining authority through a strict departmental division of functions, diametrically opposed to the notion of delegating to the private sector or involving communities as active participants in municipal affairs. Yet in many municipalities, this person is the primary means of implementation and can strongly affect the efforts of innovative political leaders.

In some cases the development of skilled managers has been addressed through a process of professionalisation of local government. In The Philippines, for instance, in the wake of an era when local government acted as a pool for unqualified local personnel, the Local Government Code now details specific requirements in terms of qualification and experience for a range of senior positions. This approach does seem to have had some success in the appointment of skilled professionals, but local government staffing is typically constrained by the low salaries offered to administrative and technical staff, and such staff may still face procedural constraints and obstacles that inhibit the process of change.

Creating Management Capacity for Partnerships

The management capacity needed to fulfil municipal objectives can be understood through the basic stages of the capacity building strategy presented in this book. Municipal management must, through organisational capacity building and skills development, be capable of working through the strategic planning, partnership development and partnership implementation stages. Most managers will have strengths and weaknesses. The key to ensuring capacity lies in skills development and identifying where existing capacity should be supplemented.

☐ The driving forces of change

Notwithstanding the importance of political commitment at higher levels of government (discussed in Chapter 10), experience suggests that partnerships flourish if there is marked commitment within a municipality and its immediate local environment. Strong, committed leadership helps to maintain focus and motivate those involved to overcome problems and find solutions. A general level of competence and vision on the part of managers and leaders is essential if the opportunities of partnership approaches to service delivery are to become understood. Yet the very nature of this championing process means that partnerships can become tied to individuals, and that creates ownership problems when those individuals are transferred.

- **Lead champions**   The commitment of top political leaders or officials is particularly vital for the development of alternative forms of municipal service delivery. Such local champions help raise awareness of private sector participation as an option, manage their councillors or officials through difficult times, technical complexities or political resistance, mobilise communities, and generally ensure that the vision of private sector participation remains intact. They act as champions for efforts at organisational improvement that normally attract little support. It is they who ensure that councillors and officials, as well as the community, receive sound information about the private sector participation option, and that informed debate occurs. In this way, fertile ground is developed for conceptualising, developing and implementing private sector participation. The absence or frailty of such champions often curtails partnerships – if not completely, then at least in terms of their scope and momentum.

- **Support networks**   In municipalities promoting change, champions often develop a network of support for private sector participation at different levels and sections of the municipality. If the capacity exists, senior managers appoint middle management to undertake changes in day-to-day operations, and apply new processes and learning to specific municipal functions. They can mobilise managers and staff to push for change, articulate some of the guiding ideas and encourage those within the organisation and outside who are trying new things. Inspired by lead champions, internal supporting networks at other levels play an important role in putting policies and new approaches into practice.

- **Clear mandates**   It is often easier to establish partnerships if the leadership has a clear mandate with firm control. Local coalitions may ultimately help to achieve broad-based commitment, but in coalitions, political differences often get resolved through compromise and delays in decision-making. This weakens the focus on the vision, and more powerful mobilisation of key parties is needed to bolster the partnership and its management.

- **Continuity**   Political changes will also affect the focus of partnerships. For example, one council may enter into partnerships for a particular reason, with specific political objectives in mind. If the leadership is replaced, the successor council might have different priorities, or even be differently disposed towards private sector participation. This is why the commitment of top officials must be decisive, because they deal with councils across political changes. If the leading officials are committed to partnership approaches and understand the intent, they can ensure that councils are well informed and understand the basis for and nature of partnerships. The joint commitment of key officials and top politicians helps to ensure that partnerships stay on course despite considerable opposition and scepticism. The levels of ideological cleavage and political trust between different political regimes have significant effects on private sector partnerships. In countries where the entire basis of a previous local government is in question, its successors may not be keen to uphold or further develop partnerships. From the point of view of potential partners, it is important to provide certainty that the municipality will respect the integrity of contracts. A perception that a change in political leadership will put contract compliance at risk jeopardises levels of interest in partnerships among potential partners.

Ultimately, to instigate sustainable partnerships municipal managers must build momentum and commitment towards partnerships among their staff. They will need to champion the approach and establish team-building mechanisms able to take the partnership approach forwards. In the words of a town clerk who instigated a water concession, 'it is necessary to build a change-friendly environment and to remove any bureaucratic inertia that hinders us from solving the problems of the municipality through whatever means we have'.

☐   Managing the strategic planning and partnership development stages

Many municipalities lack the strategic management capacity to develop PPPs that are integrated with broader municipal functions (see discussion in Chapter 11). The lack of any clear definition of service objectives, definitions and desired service standards tends to hinder the whole process of strategic planning. Management is often unfamiliar with or unable to assess realistically the potential value and commercial viability of a partnership. Partnerships are often conceived and developed without sufficient clarity on a range of strategic issues, such as: the current and future demand for services; and the current and desired supply of services in relation to coverage, distribution, equity, efficiency and quality. At the same time, municipalities must assess and understand a variety of key issues of concern to rate payers in general and the poor in particular, such as affordability and willingness to pay. Senior officers tend to get absorbed in day-to-day management matters, meaning that strategic decisions are dependent on the outcome of ad hoc meetings and informal discussions.

In the strategic planning and partnership development phases, managers must ensure the effective management of information, preparation and planning processes. Municipalities rarely integrate participatory, qualitative processes with quantitative information, and are thus unable to assess demand and provision options. It is important that a practical approach to information collection and synthesis is established at the outset by the management team, and that departmental managers are tasked with the processes that yield the information required.

Another key area of management in the initial stages of partnership formulation and development is stakeholder consultation. This process is often at odds with a more traditional bureaucratic management culture that is used to operating in a remote hierarchical manner. Building consultative capacity requires changing the organisational culture to promote openness and accountability, by institutionalising consultative processes in key planning and decision-making processes. Useful lessons can be gained from Gweru, where transparent and predictable procedures were adopted in the planning stages of privatisation in a range of services (see Box 9.4).

In order to create a viable partnership framework it is necessary for managers to have created a change-friendly, transparent process through which the municipality can be seen to be a credible partner. Managers should ensure that appropriate skills are available or acquired, and that the general level of awareness of partnerships within the municipality is raised. The partnership development phase thus requires management skills for building consensus, planning, analysis and strategising, as well as the ability to synthesise the objectives and constraining factors into a partnership framework. The development of skills has been considered in Chapter 11, but it should be noted that managers will probably need to initiate changes in procedures, structures, finances and attitudes in order for the partnership to be developed in line with objectives.

Managing implementation

The overall concern of managers involved in partnership implementation should be the promotion of key principles such as accountability, competition and transparency that underlie the partnership. Trust and transparency are crucial if the parties are going to work effectively as partners on a sustainable basis. All stakeholders should be aware of what is being done, how it is being done and why.

Trust and transparency can only be fostered if procedures and systems for awarding and operating partnerships are acknowledged to be fair and clear, and it is the municipal manager's responsibility to put such procedures in place. Central among these is the process of choosing a partner. Municipal managers must be able to create trust with all potential partners (tendering operators, NGOs, CBOs) as well as public stakeholders. This kind of trust does not appear overnight. It requires forethought, honesty and openness among those who lead the process. It requires openness of information and constant dialogue.

Municipal management will also take the lead in the appointment and supervision of external consultants. The actions of a municipal manager who has taken the initiative to hire external advisors will largely shape how others work with that external agent. A municipal manager who has instigated the process of finding and funding a strategy or transaction advisor is likely to be a good listener, able to act on advice and contribute to the development of effective solutions. This sends a strong message to other municipal staff that cooperation is essential, and that the advice is respected and wanted.

The role of councillors in forums established for managing municipal partnerships cannot be overemphasised. It is not enough to have councillors who sit on decision-making boards but do not understand the principles, mechanics and key issues of the partnerships. Councillors should play a primary role in determining the objectives and character of the partnerships being established. Best practice suggests that councillors are most effective when they understand the detail of the partnership, although not all will wish to do so (see discussion in Chapter 11). Consistency (a low turnover) in the

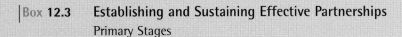

Box 12.3   Establishing and Sustaining Effective Partnerships
Primary Stages

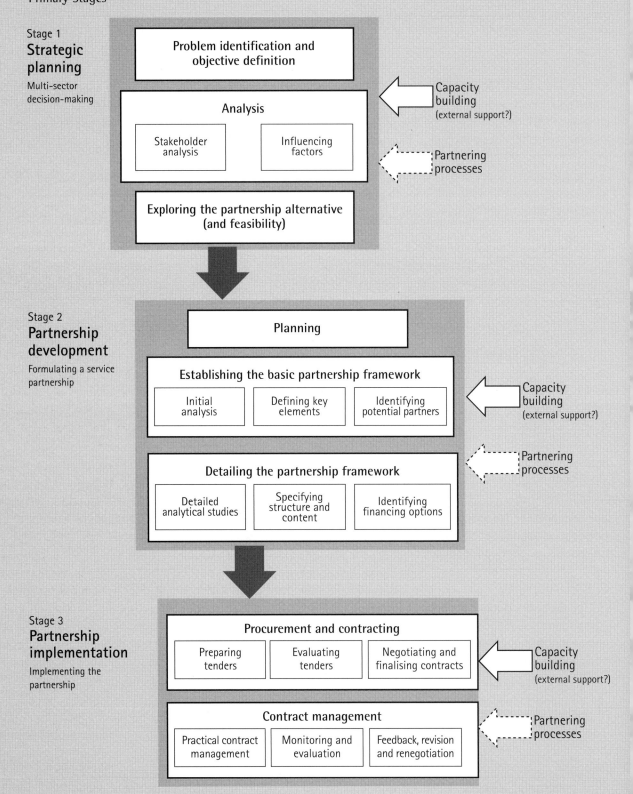

post of the chairperson for public works, capacity building more generally across the councillors in the partnership (especially for new councillors), and effective channels of communication to the partners and the council decision-makers are all essential in bringing about effective political leadership.

As partnerships proceed and evolve, a common problem in municipalities is that management is unable to assess realistically the potential value and commercial viability of the partnership. Most managers have only a limited familiarity with service measurement and performance assessment. Poor contract supervision often arises because the correct procedures and performance indicators were not established at the outset. This results in a lack of contract monitoring in relation to key objectives and corporate strategy and, in turn, leads to an inability to address issues of non-compliance and revise contract arrangements. Managers must take care to ensure that they are aware of staff performance, and especially that staff are appropriately skilled to perform the role of technical liaison with the private operator.

Municipal Systems and Procedures

The Constraints of Existing Municipal Systems and Procedures

Typically, municipalities are accustomed to working within the limits of well-established in-house or governmental procedures for the delivery of services. Bringing about change to these procedures may require formal waivers or legislative amendments (for legal procedures), or it may simply require the attitudinal change of those responsible for executing the process (to promote collaboration). In most cases, municipalities can facilitate change if they want to.

Municipal systems and procedures regulate the way in which tasks are carried out. Their formality may vary from rigid financial management or procurement procedures to more ad hoc procedures for community liaison. For service-related projects, standard procedures will cover the planning, design specification, contract tendering, evaluation, mobilisation and supervision stages of the works (or the implementation undertaken by a works department). Most systems will affect private sector participation in some way at some time, and many new processes and procedures will need to be adopted. It is rare for a municipality to feel immediately comfortable with the processes required to formulate, design and implement a service partnership, and few will be familiar with the key procedures that take a partnership forwards.

As we have discussed above, the procedural challenge involved in PPPs is also often set within the context of wider municipal reform. Changes to financial management may already be under way and professionalisation, delegation and consultation processes may be being pursued. In some cases the very idea of PPP will have arisen because of this reform. Yet, with the exception of a few rare cases, evidence suggests that municipalities are slow to change. Some will have only limited capacity to make changes and the processes, systems and procedures necessary to address the broad range of partnership issues discussed in this book may seem insurmountable.

Supporting Procedural Change

The strategic framework presented in this book has recommended that municipalities take up the three-stage process illustrated in Box 12.3. Procedural change is necessary for each of these stages.

☐ **Strategic planning**

The importance of locating a partnership in the context of urban management objectives and processes has been discussed in Chapter 5. Ensuring that the partnership emerges from a strategic planning process is obvious and natural in some contexts, but not all. In some municipalities, strategic planning is neglected in the heat of the moment. Municipal decision-makers may be so keen to solve the problems of one service that they fail to consider the demand, service priorities, impacts and implications of their choices for the city as a whole. In other municipalities the capacity to initiate a strategic, planned approach does not exist.

Strategic planning for municipal partnerships essentially involves a comprehensive approach to the development of solutions. It entails a process of long-term planning based on sound information and stakeholder participation. It is an essential step in the preparation for PPPs to ensure that municipalities know:

- what the objectives of the partnership are;
- how the partnership fits within their overall goals;
- whether a partnership is actually the best solution;
- how it relates to other municipal functions and objectives; and
- how it contributes to poverty reduction.

The process of developing a strategy creates a platform for decision-making linked into broader municipal management, service delivery and poverty-reduction goals. This will mean, for instance, that the proposed strategy for water and sanitation services might be developed alongside a strategy for solid waste management or energy. The aim is to ensure that a coherent pattern of infrastructure development occurs – one that recognises opportunities, constraints and livelihood implications as well as community and municipal capacities.

In particular, the strategy will need to address how proposed service improvements will be undertaken in relation to the poor. It will address key issues such as service prioritisation and linkages; the poverty and gender focus of the approach; the approach to labour deployment; and the approach to independent service providers.

Municipalities must be inclusive in this process, drawing in key stakeholders to work and collaborate with them in the development of the framework. The early involvement of stakeholders of all kinds creates greater ownership. Involving primary stakeholders (communities, employees) is essential in building the commitment needed for sustainability; despite the thorny issue of procurement, efforts to include the private sector can be beneficial as this establishes a partnering ethos at the outset.

The strategic planning process requires basic information about the demand for and existing supply of services – information that will underpin the decision-making process and form the basis for further information collection in the partnership development stage.

Strategic planning also provides the opportunity for stakeholder capacity building in partnership alternatives. This will enable more focused decision-making in the next stages, and provides sufficient information to address preconceptions and facilitate policy and operational choices. Ensuring that potential partners are able to participate meaningfully is a recurring theme in this book, and the processes a municipality develops will strongly shape how this capacity building is achieved.

☐   Developing a partnership framework

Once the municipality (with key stakeholders) has agreed a broad strategy for services and has decided on the partnership approach to the delivery of a specific service (such as water, sanitation or solid waste), a process of developing a partnership framework should be undertaken. This book has proposed key elements determining the nature of a sustainable partnership framework focused on the poor: potential actors, content, scope, fundamental principles, linkages to poverty reduction and urban governance, and the importance of capacity building. Yet putting all the pieces in place is not necessarily straightforward.

The first stage of developing the partnership is preparatory. This requires a municipality to plan its way through the process, and will determine the overall spirit of the partnership development process. In the first instance, it is necessary to establish a dedicated management team or task force (see the discussion on municipal structures later in this chapter), to agree the timeframe and methodology of developing the partnership. Most importantly, the municipality must decide how it will approach consultation and participation with potential partners and public stakeholders. It is also necessary to identify what support will be needed for this process. The strategy for collaboration should then be carried forwards in the following steps. For the more ambitious PPPs with the international private sector, this will involve appointing transaction advisors and formulating the way they will be managed.

A second key stage – and the most time-consuming – in the preparation of a partnership (especially one involving the formal private sector) is the collection of information. Information creates a more predictable and secure environment in which PPPs can develop, and reduces the risk of them being called off when unknown factors come to light. However, the level of detail that a municipality aims to achieve will vary. Some arrangements are prepared in great detail, often produced with the support of external agencies; but smaller municipalities may not have the resources needed to engage the recommended consultants. Sometimes it is inevitable that they proceed with less information. It is nonetheless essential that a strategy should define who will be responsible for collecting this information and when. Various guidelines recommend that the feasibility process should be conducted in two stages: an initial analysis that creates a stepping stone and provides enough information to establish the feasibility and structural parameters of a partnership; and a more detailed, focused stage of problem analysis that leads to detailed solutions in the procurement process.

In consultation with a broad range of stakeholders (and utilising a range of participatory tools and techniques), the key elements of the partnership should be defined, discussed and agreed. As discussed in Part 2, this will include:

- clarifying realistic objectives;
- defining the basic principles of the partnership;
- establishing the programme of change;
- defining the scope and functions of the arrangement;
- identifying the key partners, their roles and relationships;
- defining the levels of service, and how the poor will be targeted;
- identifying the potential financing mechanisms;
- establishing the legal and regulatory framework; and
- identifying the major risks.

This outline framework will then have to be detailed to varying degrees, dependent on the nature of the arrangement envisaged. For complex investment-linked partnerships, this stage will involve detailed analytical studies and proposals carried out by skilled experts. Ideally, in such a contract the municipality will have enough financial backing to make sound preparations.[4]

Detailed schedules of the analytical stages in the preparation of PPPs for water and sanitation and solid waste management have been produced in toolkits produced by the World Bank and others.[5] They are very helpful sources of information for municipal officials. Typically this will include:

- technical assessments;
- financial studies and financing options;

Box **12.4** Lessons of Tender Assessment and Negotiation
South Africa

A number of parameters underlie procurement procedures.

- All bidders should receive the same information and they should be made aware of direct and derived project goals. The clearer this information, the more clearly bidders can respond to the municipality's requirements. This makes evaluation of the bids more focused.
- Unsolicited bids should not be encouraged as they stifle competition and also because many municipalities are not able to assess them properly. However, where such unsolicited bids are received, a proper process for evaluation should be established and it should be made as competitive as possible.
- The rules regarding sub-contracting should be clearly outlined, and the bidders should make firm commitments that sub-contracting would not compromise the standards and quality of services or facilities managed through a partnership.
- The rules of the process should also be very clear and strictly enforced. Late submissions should not be accepted at all. To promote a transparent process, tenders should all be opened in public, and the evaluation should be based strictly on the contents of the bids and not on circumstantial information.
- The evaluation committee should include technical experts and community members to ensure that the full range of factors is considered. It may also be advisable to use independent experts from outside the municipality. Not only does this strengthen the quality of assessment and decision-making, but it also helps to create confidence in the procurement process.
- Specifications should also focus on outcomes and outputs, and not on inputs. This opens up opportunities for the private bidders to use their innovation to ensure the most effective and creative use of resources to achieve the objectives of the partnership.

Contract negotiations with private firms are often complex, especially in the case of long-term contracts. If negotiation teams are not highly skilled and experienced, negotiations can drag on, or crucial clauses can be omitted that eventually affect the focus and outcomes of the arrangement. Moreover, international private sector partners often have vast experience, while PSP is still a new approach for many municipalities. It is therefore important that the municipality establishes a competent team to negotiate on its behalf. This relative incapacity of municipalities is particularly marked in smaller cities, and such councils would be well advised to appoint advisors.

The first important choice is that of a team leader. While teamwork will prove essential, this person's authority must be firmly established, and he or she must be empowered to take responsibility and accountability for the process and results. Once selected, the team leader and relevant managers must select a team that covers all aspects of the negotiation process: providing specialised advice, interpreting documents, interacting with peers, communities and other stakeholders, providing administrative support, and taking notes. The team would thus include technical experts with knowledge of the service at stake, legal and financial experts, poverty specialists, and administrative and logistical staff.

Both internal and external experts are necessary to ensure that the contract accurately reflects the municipality's interests, as well as those of the public. Good specialist advisors are worth the expense because they help the municipality to master the process, and define and achieve objectives. Careful selection of the internal members of the negotiation team also helps to mould a team spirit and internal commitment to the process, and helps to ensure that the process is moving towards the conclusion of the deal.

The negotiating team's preparations entail setting objectives, planning strategically and preparing to deal with project factors and the private partner. This means a focus on the long term and the flexibility to deal with the unexpected. Successful negotiations are shaped through good preparation. When strategic objectives are well defined, a confident and well-prepared team can negotiate a deal that meets objectives, but simultaneously allows flexibility. The team must be well versed in the technical aspects of the proposed partnership and the history of the process up to the negotiation stage. The team members should know clearly what is negotiable and what is not. Information about the partners is important. The aim is not to 'win', but ultimately to collaborate, and negotiate a deal that serves the public interest well and protects the local government.

Source: Sinclair, 1999

- legal and regulatory framework analyses and recommendations;
- institutional analysis; and
- poverty analysis and social assessments.

The results of these studies will determine the detailed structure and content of the partnership arrangement. They will lead to the articulation of the key components of the partnership framework and guide the identification of potential partners. Based on the understanding of the fundamental nature and characteristics of the organisational sectors (discussed in Chapter 6), the roles and relationships between key actors such as the large-scale private sector, the small-scale private sector, NGOs and the municipality will need to be defined, although it is clear from experience that such roles and relationships change, and partners should work together to formulate their agreed method of implementation. To this end the procedures undertaken in the development of the partnership framework must be flexible.

In most cases, the framework will then define the contractual aspects of the arrangement with all parties. In the case of the main commercial operator, this may be based on a pre-existing model, or it may be an arrangement developed by the contractual parties to suit the context and required outputs. In the cases of NGOs and small-scale providers, municipalities may have to develop new innovative mechanisms for drawing these key parties into the partnership (see Chapter 8). Experience of contracting NGOs and multisector partnerships within municipalities will be limited and it will be critical to test the arrangements and/or seek specialist advice where lengthy arrangements are envisaged.

This stage will take a municipality through the process of translating its objectives into a defined arrangement whereby partners can be procured.

☐ Partnership implementation

■ Collaborating

While the emphasis of implementing PPPs is often placed on the legal mechanisms described below, increasingly the focus of sustainable partnerships lies in the development of a collaborative process – a process with which municipalities will be unfamiliar and for which they will have few established or appropriate procedures to draw upon. Procedures for this collaboration will have been developed in the earlier stages and need to be upheld throughout the implementation stage. Keeping the doors of the partnership open, ensuring flexibility and dialogue through joint capacity building sessions, regular reviews and reconsideration are all essential mechanisms for ensuring partnership sustainability. Unlike the legal work involved in the partnership, collaboration requires experimentation and flexibility, a piloting and testing approach within the bounds of a loose legal framework (such as a memorandum of understanding). This collaboration builds on that established in earlier stages of the partnership development, and forms a key part of the procedures described below.

■ Procurement and contracting

While legal processes are undoubtedly important in ensuring clarity, predictability and certainty, municipalities should be aware that different approaches to the procurement process can be adopted, and are relevant to different arrangements. Some are much more relaxed than others. The differences mostly reflect the scale of the proposal, the extent to which the municipality can define its requirements, and how well it knows the prospective bidders. The less complex and the shorter the planned partnership, the greater the scope for some pre-selection; the more complex and the longer the planned arrangement, the more likely it is that the municipality will issue a wider and more open invitation to bidders and embark on a more formal process. There are, however, drawbacks to over-formality and over-specificity: the South African BoTT has cost far more than it should have because it was over-specified. The more a municipality can work with the partners to create a truly collaborative arrangement, the more sustainable partnerships will be.

Whichever method is selected, the procurement process underpins the selection of service providers who are appropriate for the project, and the process lies at the heart of how some key aspects of good governance are reflected in a partnership. A fair process prevents corruption and makes it possible to select the best contractor for the job. Unfair procurement skews decisions away from the most efficient options – decisions that cost the municipality and consumers in the end, and can place the delivery of the relevant service at risk.

In the traditional approach to large-scale PPPs, an early 'request for proposals' stage enables municipalities to gain a better understanding of interested actors, and may even be used to select the partner. This is usually the case if the partnership term is relatively short (e.g., a year) or the monetary value low (exemplified by a service contract for solid waste collection services). Such a process could also be adopted if the goals of the partnership are well defined and simple, if the local government is able to identify potential partners of its own accord, and if the risks of the partnership are relatively small. As a result, the process and the required documentation are generally simple.

Where the duration and monetary value of the partnership is more extensive and large-scale operators are involved, then a more elaborate procurement procedure can be adopted. This will probably entail an initial stage that screens potential partners through a 'request for expressions of interest' or a 'request for qualifications'. This screening enables a municipality to consider a wide range of providers before narrowing the field down to the best qualified, and identifying its objectives more comprehensively. This qualifications stage is used when the local government and the project team have a more defined project but do not know if there are any private sector partners with the resources, experience or interest to meet their requirements.

Competitive tendering is necessary in the case of expensive and long-term partnerships. It helps if the municipality knows exactly what it wants to achieve, as that enables it to weigh the different bids against each other. Such clarity reduces the cost involved in developing a PPP, both for the municipality and the potential partners. But this is rare in weak municipalities. Before requesting proposals, a schedule of the local government's timeframe for completion of the project or initiation of a service should be developed. It may spell out the process and timeframe for evaluating proposals, including the time set aside for public consultation, the activities and timeframes for contract negotiations and appeals, and the outline of project implementation and completion. For large-scale operators it is also important to state related objectives, such as empowerment, environmental sustainability, stakeholder involvement, and the involvement of other actors like NGOs, CBOs and small-scale providers.

The tendering procedure often requires two bidding envelopes: one dealing with the technical aspects of the partnership, and another with the financial aspects. While the bidding documents must provide in-depth information, and the process must ensure the greatest levels of fairness, care should be taken not to overcomplicate either. This is necessary to make the bids accessible to the evaluators, and to ensure that they address the core issues the municipality wants to be dealt with. Furthermore, highly complex processes and documents tend to work against small enterprises and NGOs.

■ Negotiating

Few municipalities have been trained in negotiation skills and techniques. Many municipalities are not well prepared for negotiations with the private sector and hence may have agreed to contract provisions and amendments that were inappropriate to the task. Building municipal capacity for improved negotiation requires an emphasis on the need for attentive listening as opposed to lecturing, careful analysis and measured reflection as opposed to instant responses, an ability not to accept facts and figures at face value but to analyse them at length, and careful consideration of the extent to which any proposal addresses the required needs and objectives, especially those regarding the poor. These skills are best learnt by watching others apply them in practice. This means that it is advisable for any municipality to enlist the support of an expert negotiator in the first instance, and thereafter to attempt to negotiate one or two smaller contracts as part of the learning process.

Municipalities can enter into a legal agreement called a Memorandum of Understanding, which enables them to pursue a negotiated form of contract. This stage is helpful for a wide range of reasons. For the private operator it provides an opportunity to collect the information it needs to clarify on price. For other actors such as NGOs and small-scale providers, it provides an opportunity to increase familiarity, and for the municipality it provides an opportunity to develop a collaborative partnership and establish the participatory ground rules of the partnership. It allows the partners to explore each other's objectives and competencies and to try to create an appropriate partnership that fits the skills of each partner. It enables the partners to identify skills gaps and develop pilot schemes and other mechanisms for working with the poor.

This final stage leads to the development of contracts that spell out the key aspects of the arrangement and establish the legal framework for the service delivery.

■ Contract management

A key aspect of the contract management process will be the identification of a dedicated contract manager within the municipality, appointed to supervise implementation on behalf of the municipality. Ensuring that this individual has been involved throughout the process helps to ensure the ownership and understanding of partnership objectives and the required form of contract management. While it is important that the municipality works towards being a partner, it is important for contract managers to ensure that they do not micro-manage. The municipal team's role in contract management is one of monitoring the progress and performance specifications agreed at the outset. Procedures should be established to ensure that the municipal team does not interfere in details: it can undermine performance goals and create confusion about accountability.

Disputes are inevitable, but can be alleviated more easily if a collaborative approach, and procedures for addressing disputes, are agreed at the outset. In the event of a breakdown in partnering, the contract should provide for mechanisms to avoid disputes, methods (such as conciliation, mediation and arbitration) aimed at minimising litigation, and procedures to be followed which ensure that services are not disrupted.

■ Monitoring and evaluation

Successful implementation requires monitoring through regular checks and accurate record-keeping to ensure that the intended target groups are being reached, and that the changes are not adversely affecting those least able to bear them – the poorest and most vulnerable households in the community. In many cases municipalities will play the primary monitoring role. The definition of performance standards in the contract is critical for effective monitoring. It will affect how the monitoring is done and by whom. The discussion of performance standards in Chapter 7 highlighted the importance of defining performance standards in terms of outcomes and outputs rather than specified inputs, as this gives the private sector an incentive to innovate and does not hinder the quest for efficiency. It is necessary for the municipality to build capacity for this function and to locate it within the organisation, ensuring that the process is inclusive, transparent and accountable.[6]

The techniques for monitoring should also be injected with the participatory spirit defined during the earlier stages of developing and implementing the arrangement. In partnerships, it is essential to ensure that all stakeholders play a role in monitoring.

- The private sector and NGOs should have responsibility for evaluating their performances in a transparent way.
- Non-poor and poor consumers will be able to express their satisfaction or dissatisfaction clearly by paying or not paying, or opting out of the scheme if other choices exist.
- Consumers should be given opportunity to feed back their concerns through complaints procedures established by the operator, the municipality or with consumer watchdogs.

Links to Boxes
5.3, 6.7, 9.2

Box **12.5**   ## Management and Monitoring
Biratnagar, Nepal

A solid waste management partnership with a local private operator has been functioning in Biratnagar in Nepal since 1998. The partnership is a complex set of contracts of various scopes and contents, including a service contract, a franchise and various other ad hoc arrangements.

On the municipal side, the three primary actors in the partnership are the mayor, the deputy mayor and the supervising engineer. Strategic aspects of the partnership are managed by the mayor, with contributions from the deputy mayor and the board. Although the original contract was signed and agreed by the former mayor, the present mayor is thoroughly committed to the concept of a partnership for solid waste management and to an increased role for the private sector to achieve effective and sustainable municipal services. Notwithstanding this commitment, management to date has not been informed by experience elsewhere and has not ultimately brought about a sustainable arrangement. To this extent, the partnership lacks strategic management and planning. The coalition nature of the council has also meant that, on occasion, disagreement and debate on policy matters has resulted in compromise and delays in decision-making. The municipal board members are supportive of the partnership arrangement and any disagreements are over minor issues. Despite the fact that the majority of council members are in favour of the partnership, there is still a need to mobilise further support among ward commissioners and members to improve capacity for decision-making.

The private operator has been pursuing a contract amendment for some time. The changes proposed address some, but not all, of the inadequacies of the initial contract and begin to address some of the issues threatening sustainability. It is not altogether clear why there have been management delays in finalising this contract amendment. Operational aspects of the partnership are managed by the deputy mayor and supervising engineer. The Monitoring and Evaluation Committee defined in the contract is headed by the deputy mayor and includes the engineer responsible for waste and the general manager of Americorp. Meetings are held monthly to discuss problems and progress, and this has been a helpful and effective vehicle for addressing a number of the routine obstacles facing the partnership. All parties generally agree on the basic parameters and goals.

The deputy mayor plays an active role in the day-to-day supervision of the partnership, and stresses that, despite the problems to date, the partnership has introduced and proved the effectiveness of private sector management practices in municipal operations. The municipal engineer in charge of waste is the main liaison point. He believes that the partnership arrangement has had a positive impact on waste operations, although he is aware that his own lack of specialist knowledge in solid waste has limited his ability to understand the technical alternatives and to monitor the contract more effectively.

There is, however, very little monitoring as such. In the absence of any performance standards or understanding of the components of systematic monitoring, monitoring is informal and ad hoc. At this stage the only way the municipality judges the performance of the operator is by public complaints, which they receive and pass on to Americorp with the expectation that the problem will be immediately rectified. This is normally carried out satisfactorily: the operator is generally quick and cooperative in solving problems. Most complaints to date have concerned the collection (rather than transfer or disposal) of solid waste, indicating that there has been no visible deterioration of the upstream aspects of the service (transfer and disposal) since the private operator became involved.

When this monitoring arrangement is queried, municipal officials point out that the level of performance is not perceived as a problem, and the quality of the service provided is deemed to meet expectations. Indeed, the mayor and deputy mayor both pointed out that prior to the partnership, there had been many complaints from members of the public concerning poor collection and cleaning services in the city, and that the number of these complaints has drastically reduced.

One of the key characteristics of the arrangement, and one that differs from the norm, is that the private sector role in municipal solid waste management has not led to a convincing commercialisation of the service. Typically, PSP is associated with improved commercial practices that include long-term planning and the updating of municipal accounting systems that do not capture costs or present grants and transfers in a transparent manner. However, the partnership approach in Biratnagar has not led to strategic planning and budgeting for solid waste services in the municipality; the sector has not been ringfenced, which would isolate the costs to the municipality of providing solid waste services (including direct and indirect staff salaries, vehicles, repair, leases, interest on loans etc); and it has not led to an informed examination of the potential sources of revenue needed to support this improved level of service.

Source: Plummer and Slater, 2001

The participation of the poor in the monitoring process is less well established in PPPs, but participatory monitoring is critical to a focused partnership. It allows the poor to define in their own terms their concerns about, and the impacts of, the service. Effective participatory monitoring is characterised by:

- a simple, open evaluation methodology;
- a process that is appropriately tailored to a local context;
- the development of contextually relevant indicators, defined by the communities and reflecting their livelihood needs;
- being established well ahead of evaluation with appropriate capacity building; and
- the flexibility to accommodate and facilitate change as community inputs provide direction during the partnership.[7]

Municipalities that are focused on broader poverty reduction objectives will also be interested in conducting impact assessments. Such assessments should measure, for example, the impacts of improved water, sanitation or solid waste services on poor communities (e.g., the higher attendance of girls in school due to less queuing or reduced distances from water supply, increased home-based economic activity etc.). This will require sound, carefully prepared baselines.

It is also useful to monitor the partnering process so that all the partners can improve the way in which they interact and contribute. This is a less concrete area, but a number of basic questions can help to define the key issues. Is there added value in the partnership? Could these results have been achieved through a restructured and commercialised government provider? Can the impacts of working in partnerships be measured? Is it necessary/possible to measure or evaluate the relationship?

■ Feedback and revision, renegotiation and change

The final step is the feedback of the lessons learnt into the design of the arrangement. Lessons may relate to the partnership objectives, content, the process or its implementation. The process of implementation will reveal whether the objectives were clearly defined, overly ambitious or not ambitious enough, or whether the partners are simply under-performing. Another type of lesson will concern the contract itself, and will vary significantly with contract type. Implementation will reveal that there are critical gaps, that some clauses are too loose and others too constraining. Some activities will be found difficult to implement simply because the right structures or skills are not present.

Without an established mechanism to facilitate change on the basis of observed trends, the motivation for monitoring diminishes. If monitoring and evaluation conclude that target groups are not benefiting, for instance, there must be a means to revise the arrangement framework. Regular reviews, structured revision processes and contractual flexibility are thus key ingredients of the procedures established for feedback and revision.

Once the partnership strategy is reconsidered on the basis of the lessons learnt, it may be necessary to instigate a renegotiation of the arrangements that formalise the partnership. It is in all the parties' interests to be able to renegotiate the contract, and the procedure for doing so will need to be defined in the contract at the outset. The provisions for contract renegotiation and amendment must identify processes and timeframes for different types of changes. For example, the contract should stipulate the timeframe and approach to the renegotiation of financial aspects (e.g., tariff structures, connection fees and investment programmes). Municipalities should be aware of the implications of allowing the private sector to shift the goal posts too far or too frequently (see the experience in Buenos Aires in Box 7.18).

12

Box 12.6   Building Structural Capacity for Partnerships
Ankara, Turkey

As is commonly found elsewhere, municipalities in Turkey are based on a rigid hierarchical organisational structure with limited control over their finances and restrictive rules governing staff. In the early 1990s, Ankara municipality – with a population of 3.67 million – embarked on an ambitious US$3 billion development programme for improving urban transport, water supply and urban renewal under Murat Karayalcin's administration.

This programme required the establishment of new support structures within the municipality, as a means of coordinating and managing new working relationships between the municipality and private sector partners that were involved in the construction and management of new facilities and the operation of services established under the programme. Ankara thus provides an interesting example of a municipality that has adapted and modified its organisational structure in order to improve municipal programme planning and management in partnership with the private sector. This has taken place at two levels: external (to enhance inter-agency coordination) and internal (to establish more effective and coordinated support within the municipality).

External Structural Arrangements
A variety of formal structures have been either strengthened or established to assist with this task. The main focus has been on establishing coordination units designed to enhance inter-agency and intra-agency activity:

- an Infrastructure Coordination Centre for improved coordination of all infrastructure-related activities and projects of the municipality with other related public bodies;
- a Transportation Coordination Centre responsible for all transport management;
- a Development Plan Coordination Centre comprising eight sub-provincial mayors and heads of planning to coordinate all planning activities; and
- an Advisory Board to provide the city with vision and strategy.

Internal Structural Modifications
In addition to these external structural arrangements, Ankara has undertaken further structural innovation to overcome the obstacles of fragmented and inefficient administration associated with the traditional Turkish municipal system (which has in the past been a powerful disincentive to the entry of private sector partners). In order to address this problem, the municipality has attempted to substitute and by-pass the formal organisational structures with a number of informal initiatives designed to facilitate effective project management and partnerships. Such partnerships are thought to be necessary to supplement existing financial resources with new internal and external sources, and to encourage public participation in project design and implementation.

The main structural changes that have been introduced include:

- Reorganising existing departments of the municipality to introduce a greater corporate orientation, and to address the issue of the reallocation of responsibilities and redeployment of staff in response to changing departmental functions and priorities.
- Setting up new work units within departments, mostly on an informal basis to avoid lengthy delays. Such units have been entrusted with specific responsibilities in relation to managing partnership relations and overseeing and monitoring work contracts.
- Staffing new units with expert personnel from within the organisation to ensure that such units and departments have access to the necessary range of skills and expertise at all times.
- Recruiting new expert staff through municipal firms to allow for more flexible employment terms and conditions. This has proved to be an important way of injecting the right calibre of staff into the municipal structure without having to work through the formal bureaucratic channels.
- Retraining and equipping personnel with specific skills needed for project design, bidding and tendering, contract management, monitoring and auditing.
- Creation of a special Executive Committee to meet monthly to monitor project activity.
- Establishment of a Mayor's Bureau to undertake all central support work related to new projects and partnerships.
- Constitution of an annual convention to inform citizens of project activities and progress.
- Setting up of consultative project-decision boards to mediate discussions with all stakeholders.
- Regular interaction with neighbourhood committees.

Source: Goymen, 2000

Municipal Structures

The Constraints of Existing Municipal Structures on Partnerships

In most municipalities, the administrative function is structured into separate functional departments. In relation to service delivery, engineering departments may be responsible for network services (although this may be further sub-divided into a construction arm and an operation and maintenance arm). Public health departments are typically responsible for solid waste management and also frequently for on-site sanitation services. Social welfare or community development departments are responsible for a range of poverty reduction activities; planning departments are responsible for planning and enforcing regulations; revenue departments are responsible for billing and collection.

This compartmentalisation has resulted in (and is also reinforced by) the tendency for municipalities to create a hierarchy of departments which behave as independent entities without due concern for integration. They compete for status and power, and often lack a cooperative spirit for common development. At the same time, the hierarchical nature of the departmental structure results in limited managerial devolution or slow decision-making: all key decisions are referred upwards. Engineering departments are often at the top of this hierarchy. The largest municipalities may have very senior town engineers – sometimes more senior, in administrative terms, than the town clerk/commissioner. The department obtains its power through this seniority, its relative size and the allocation of financial resources. It manages large capital budgets for infrastructure development, significant operation and maintenance budgets, and a large unskilled workforce.

When partnerships of any kind are introduced – be they with large-scale service operators or with communities – the impacts and characteristics of separated functions are accentuated. The barriers created by compartmentalisation will need to be removed if partnership arrangements are to become sustainable. For instance:

- The lack of integration has a marked impact on poverty reduction initiatives, and efforts must be made to work towards common goals if a partnership is to achieve a poverty focus.
- The low level of collaboration between departments means that communication channels have often not been established, and officials are unfamiliar with team-working even within the municipality. This is a critical issue in partnerships focused on the poor, as many design and process management functions require a combination of skills and expertise found in different professions and organisations.
- The limited spans of authority and low levels of decentralised decision-making mean that frequently, technical officers with responsibility for managing service delivery do not have sufficient authority to execute their responsibilities. In a partnership arrangement, senior technical officers may be unable to take initiatives without gaining approval from the municipal administration. This also results in many routine management decisions concerning operation being delayed as decisions are referred upwards. This problem was experienced in Biratnagar in Nepal, where all key decisions relating to the solid waste partnership are made by the mayor or deputy mayor (see Box 7.7).

Moreover, the typical departmental structure of municipalities in terms of technical competencies and functions has meant that, in terms of staff allocation, the engineering and public health departments tend to employ by far the greatest number of staff. These are precisely the areas that are most susceptible to change resulting from a new partnership arrangement. The nature of the work undertaken in these departments means that significant numbers of labourers work within each of these sections or departments. In a larger municipality serving a population of 1 million or so, one might expect to see up to 500 labourers involved in water and waste services. Changing service delivery approaches has a considerable structural impact on these departments and the workforce within them. Human resource policies will need to be formulated to address the specific labour issues in these departments.

Introducing Partnerships and Adapting Municipal Structures

☐ Identifying potential impacts

In any municipality, it is necessary to identify the potential impacts of PPPs on the municipal structure and vice versa, and take steps to consider, over an agreed timeframe, structural changes within the municipality that promote partnerships. The factors affecting structure will include:

- municipal objectives, and the proposed scope and content of the partnership;
- the roles envisaged for the municipality and their impacts (Is the municipality regulating the contract? Is the municipality separating the function into a utility? What is the impact of shifting functions and power?);
- potential roles and relationships of all actors;
- the level of senior management involvement and their commitment to coordinating changes in management, procedures, finances and other organisational factors; and
- capacity gaps between the municipality and the private operator and the need for capacity building.

In order to focus the partnership on the poor, other factors will determine the most appropriate structures and vehicles. These include:

- the potential role of the community, the capacity building needed for the community and the importance of improving access for communities to decision-making and dispute resolution;
- attempts to integrate partnership activities with other poverty-reduction responses wherever possible; and
- any alternative mechanisms for delivery, and the payment options envisaged (where municipalities still play a role in cost recovery).

The development of partnerships will often require a municipality to reconsider the location of functions, and may lead to task convergence or departmental mergers. In water and sanitation arrangements, consideration will have to be given to the management of each function (if they have been placed in separate departments in the past); for solid waste partnerships, more departmental separation may be required (solid waste is often located within the health department); and in partnerships that exclude customer management, consideration needs to be given to the capacity and role of the revenue department to coordinate this function.

☐ Establishing new structures for improved coordination

One of the key steps to be taken by municipal managers is to establish a vehicle for investigation, decision-making and implementation within partnerships. To this end, municipalities frequently establish a special committee, task force or unit tasked with defining and carrying out the steps necessary to bring about a service partnership. Ideally, an integrated team of senior or middle managers will be formed and exposed to alternative options for service delivery, and this team will have some basic training or experience in PPPs. It should also have some training in working together to optimise its outputs.

Typically, this task force will be comprised of skilled representatives able to provide expertise in planning, consultation, tendering, contract design and negotiation, and contract management and monitoring. They should be particularly committed to, and develop skills in, the very process of partnering. A unit similar to this was established in Gweru and in Ankara (see Box 12.6), and has proved to be a useful structural mechanism for establishing PPPs in a municipality. In Ankara, a separate bureau has been established to coordinate new policy initiatives such as partnerships. Staff assigned to this bureau have been trained in private sector participation design, and the bureau has been assigned special powers to work closely with the senior management team in order to avoid lengthy delays in processing documents and approvals that will impact negatively on any private sector operator.

The task force may change in nature and capacity as the process develops. The skills sets needed to undertake the strategic planning and partnership development stages may be very different from those required for the third stage of partnership implementation (see Box 12.3). In focused partnerships, the role of social/community development workers, for instance, will be crucial. In the case of large-scale partnerships, a task force should be underpinned by the expertise of an experienced external advisor.

Inter-departmental coordination for private sector participation design and implementation can be enhanced by working parties to assess alternative private sector participation options and contract types, and technical meetings to assist with planning specifications, documentation etc. These structural mechanisms provide crucial ways of enhancing the task force and the municipal capacity to identify, plan and manage the private sector participation process. They bring together different skills and expertise within the organisation to consider a range of issues such as technical and commercial viability, service performance and quality, pricing and tariff adjustments, employee relations etc. A number of these coordination mechanisms have been successfully introduced into Ankara to enhance private sector participation operations (see also Box 12.6).

Whichever vehicles are adopted, municipalities should seek to achieve consistency and continuity in the PPP management team. They should delegate authority to conduct tasks, establish regular, direct and efficient communication lines to decision-making forums (particularly to elected councils), and ensure the integration of a range of skills at all stages. The process itself will build capacity among the members of the team, creating a more skilled base for future partnership initiatives.

☐ Managing downsizing

Where arrangements envisage the delegation of management and operation to a private sector operator, an obvious outcome of the municipal service partnership will be a reduction in the size of a particular department or sub-department in the municipality. This downsizing raises a number of important questions for municipalities – not just about the re-employment of workers (discussed in Chapter 6) but also about the organisational implications for the municipality. E.g.,

- Does downsizing result in a loss of departmental status and power?
- Does downsizing result in significant changes in managerial power? If so, how do municipal managers absorb these changes? Which steps should be taken to ensure that skilled, committed staff have incentives to work in new, challenging situations?
- Does delegation reduce the power and status of elected committees that were previously responsible for large capital and recurrent budgets?

The creation of an effective municipal structure to take PPPs forward is not an easy process. It is necessary to merge structural reform with procedural reform, attitudinal change and skills development to ensure that the municipality, in all its parts, takes on board the revised structural framework. The organisational development strategy – which has emerged from the organisational change required to fulfil the larger municipal agenda, and is dependent on the skills and experience of the human resources in that structure – will be essential to this end.

Municipal Finance

In order to achieve the municipal objectives of PPPs – financial and economic objectives particularly – many municipalities recognise that it is essential to establish a sound financial base if they are to attract private sector partners and be seen as potentially reliable partners themselves. No external investor, whether a donor or a private sector organisation, is likely to choose to risk funds in an organisation that is unable or unwilling to improve its financial position.

Detailed literature on urban government finances and financial reform is readily available.[8] This section aims only to reinforce the content of previous chapters by outlining the key constraints and areas of change required for PPPs. While healthy finances are important for all partnership ventures irrespective of size and capacity, partnerships with the formal private sector may require more significant and targeted improvements.

☐ **General finances**

The efforts of many municipalities in providing services are undermined by ever-increasing deficits: diminishing grants, inadequate revenue, poor revenue mobilisation and collection, unrealistic budgeting and inadequate financial management practices.

The delegation of tasks to the municipal-government level has not always been accompanied by the funds necessary for delivering basic functions. Inter-governmental transfers are discretionary, their amounts are decreasing and they are unpredictable. Municipalities must identify new ways of obtaining revenue for capital and recurrent expenditure. However, in most developing cities the structures needed to improve the primary independent sources of revenue – local taxes and charging – are often missing, and collection systems are non-existent. While sources of revenue for urban government may vary considerably across developing countries, most municipalities suffer from unpredictable and low revenue streams.

Revenue constraints are, typically, worsened by weak financial management practices. Municipalities rarely have the luxury of aiming to maximise efficiency: they struggle to maintain the status quo while trying to meet the new demands of a vast range of stakeholders. High administrative overheads, unrealistic budgeting, accounting arrears and inadequate monitoring all lead to uncontrolled expenditure, matched with inflated annual revenue reporting. Burdensome procedures and simple gaps in skills are manifest in:

- time delays in processing payments due to the hierarchy of accountability structures;
- lack of expertise in cost accounting, which allows trends in unit costs (or comparisons with alternatives) to be tracked;
- lack of accounting methods that match revenue and expenditure at the service level;
- lack of information on assets and liabilities and no procedures for accrual accounting;
- low ability to manage risk and to make service managers accountable for risk; and
- a lack of understanding of the idea of profitability.

Private operators will be keen to form partnerships with municipalities that have improved their financial position and knowledge through reform processes. They, like donors, will be looking for more stable and buoyant revenue streams, sensible budgeting and efforts towards sound financial management. While they are interested in the general state of finance, they will be keen to ensure that particular concerns are put right to minimise their own risks, and these may become conditions of the partnership contract.

Best practice in various parts of the world provides an indication of the types of efforts that can improve the general state of urban government finances. These include:

- strategic planning and budgeting (see discussion in Chapter 4) as an essential part of a reformed financial management system;
- establishing sensible procedures that speed up financial monitoring and reporting, and enable financial management practices to be effectively adopted;
- building sufficient capacity by improving the skills and experience in the accountancy department. This might include, for instance, the introduction of accounting technicians, training in financial awareness for senior managers and

simpler sessions for lower-grade staff (clerical/executive), drawing on the expertise of construction contract management, allowing greater movements of staff between service and finance departments, and providing business orientation training and promoting secondments to the private sector;

- building revenue mobilisation capacity through professionalisation, credit ratings and municipal bonds; and
- strengthening property tax and tax collection, increasing the frequency and thoroughness of reassessments, simplifying procedures through the introduction of composite area-based assessment (or moving to self-assessment) to reduce the scope for anomalies and corruption.

☐   **Infrastructure-related finances**

The finances relating to infrastructure and service delivery often form a significant portion of the overall municipal budget, and financial management practices and systems for the entire municipality are reflected in the micro-management of service finances. Yet there are a number of specific practices relating to services that are worth highlighting, and a number of typical practices have particular effects on service management.

Poor financial management capacity will inhibit the proper functioning of any service delivery system, but PPPs, particularly those involving the large-scale private sector, impose a much greater need to understand commercial practices. Some of the more general management deficiencies are made clear by considering the day-to-day management of service finances. It is not uncommon to see, for instance, the following:

- A lack of clarity as to what a service costs to provide and a lack of information in the right form. This may be accompanied by a lack of interest in investigating and carrying out cost–benefit analysis and benchmarking to spell out cost and tariff implications.
- A lack of separation (or ringfencing) of finances for individual services. Even those municipalities that run separate accounts for water or for solid waste do not always include all the recurrent costs under that sub-head (e.g., staff costs and vehicle maintenance are often included in general overheads).
- A lack of structured decision-making over the allocation of subsidies, and a lack of transparency in relation to the cross-subsidisation of welfare services by revenue-earning services.
- A lack of good financial expertise within a line department. Service departments do not have book-keepers, accounting technicians or accountants; senior service managers that have little financial awareness. Service managers are more used to payroll accounts than to monitoring contract payments.
- A lack of knowledge of the business of the service in the central finance department; revenue staff, especially counter staff, are rarely customer oriented; a lack of responsibility for promoting new parallel business opportunities.

The impact of service financing (and thus the changes needed) will vary between sectors and with the differing scope and content of the partnership arrangement. The impacts of municipal finances on solid waste management, for instance, are very direct, as a large number of solid waste operators working under service or management contracts are paid directly by the municipality. They take on the risk of providing a service for a given period of time on the assumption that the municipality has the finances to pay them. While this is also the case with water supply and sanitation service and management contracts, the more ambitious forms of contracts in this service sector depend on the customer for payment. They also, however, depend on sound financial policy within the municipality in relation to tariff setting and subsidies.

In addition to the improvements in the general financial management and health of the municipality, effective financial management of service partnerships specifically includes:

- **Cost recovery**   The introduction and implementation of cost recovery principles are central to the creation of sustainable service delivery. To ensure that they will be compensated for the service they provide, private operators will want to see that cost recovery has been addressed before they enter into partnerships.

- **Clarity and information**   Many of the municipal objectives of partnerships will not be fulfilled unless there is more information on which to base decisions. Service costs must be ringfenced in financial reporting and must include all known costs.
- **Transparency**   To improve accountability, cost reporting must be made transparent. All stakeholders become nervous when financial reporting is not open.

Municipal Attitudes

Staff attitudes to municipal reforms generally, and PPPs specifically, will fundamentally affect the way that new arrangements and systems are conceived, designed and implemented. One of the main problems concerning attitudes within a bureaucracy such as a municipality is a natural resistance to change in the status quo. As we have seen in Chapter 3, this resistance springs from a range of ideological, political, economic and financial reasons. In the context of partnerships focused on the poor, attitudinal change may be required to work with small-scale providers, and to include NGOs and the poor themselves.[9] Thus the issue of attitudinal change becomes significantly more complex.

It is important to recognise that municipal attitudes are not uniform. Attitudes vary among stakeholders at the outset, ranging from the very supportive to the very cautious or resistant. They may also undergo significant change. Particular attitudes towards partnerships may be formed by groups or by individuals, and may be due to a number of factors, including:

- a lack of understanding about the nature, form and objective of partnerships;
- concern about loss of individual or departmental power and status;
- concern with losing control over resources; and
- concern for job loss or loss of existing employment terms and conditions.

☐   Structuring a process of attitudinal change

A key step in enhancing the organisational capacity of the municipality will be changing attitudes, and champions of partnerships will inevitably take on this role to enable the process to move forward. One of the keys to attitudinal change is understanding different viewpoints. It is necessary to:

- identify the scope and nature of the concerns of each municipal stakeholder. (E.g., is their primary concern profit, the size of an international organisation, the need to interact with the poor, or loss of employment?);
- recognise and validate these concerns (whether group or individual) and the nature of the blockages created;
- identify the specific benefits of partnerships, or areas of potential mitigation relating to sub-groups;
- present holistic responses, tailored to particular concerns;
- outline benefits, adverse effects and mitigating approaches (on an individual basis); and
- ensure concerns are included in the partnership framework.

☐   Responding to the key concerns of stakeholder groups

Frequently, but not always, concerns can be grouped around professional or job interests. The following discussion raises some of the key issues in relation to municipal stakeholder interest groups (see also discussion above concerning municipal leadership and management). An illustration of the range of municipal stakeholder interests (and the responses generated) is provided in Box 12.7.

Administrative staff will be concerned to see that existing procedures and systems are followed correctly and that change and disruption within the organisation is minimised. It is likely that administrative staff have enjoyed a degree of authority over municipal resource deployment. From their perspective, a partnership arrangement might undermine the degree of direct power and influence they hold. Most municipalities suffer from the problem that even minor decisions are referred upwards to senior administrative staff who regard it as their right to direct and supervise almost all routine decision-making. A partnership arrangement with a private sector operator would change the nature of administrative authority; rather than directly controlling all decisions at all times, it will have a monitoring and/or regulating role. This role change not only requires different attitudes towards administrative supervision (a change from direction to enabling), but also a greater measure of objectivity in management. It requires different, transparent behaviour patterns. Administrative staff may well find that they are under pressure to raise the level of efficiency of many internal operating systems to match the new standards of the private operator.

Elected representatives are typically concerned about the loss of direct control over service delivery, particularly if their voter base is dependent on them being seen as the provider. In many municipalities, elected members at council and ward level have a tradition of getting involved in service delivery rather than policy-making. They are commonly identified with new infrastructure or infrastructure improvements or specific services that they have personally backed. A partnership arrangement may curtail their influence over contracts, jobs and resources as well as service planning. They may be concerned that they will be held responsible, or that success will reveal past inefficiencies. Success, however, is normally the key to changing political members' attitudes, and examples abound of politicians wishing to be associated with successful projects in the public domain.

Political members will also be concerned about the impact on voters: Will the partnership approach have an adverse impact on particular groups of voters? A key concern will be the tariff. Few politicians are keen to be associated with the introduction of a higher tariff for basic services, irrespective of the baseline situation. The short tenure of councils and mayors means that they may not be associated with the medium-term benefit. Many are concerned only with the results achievable in the immediate future.

In order to develop a group of elected members who are supportive of the idea of partnerships, champions will need to highlight the immediate benefits that are achievable and create partnership frameworks that maximise them; it may be necessary to devise strategies for implementing tariff increases. Capacity building is essential: exposure to successes elsewhere helps to remove some attitudes based on assumptions. Exposure to their own success offers the greatest attraction, and it is clear that politicians do change their attitudes as they see successful municipal partnerships developing. Most critical, however, is the support of the voters, and the development of a transparent process through which politicians can 'see' voter opinion is probably the key to creating attitudinal change among elected members.

Technical staff, particularly those directly associated with the service provision, will not only be concerned for their jobs; they will have entered into their profession with a certain expectation of their career. A PPP may completely reverse that expectation, and create opportunities in other areas with which they are not familiar. For instance:

- Partnerships may be a direct threat to their professional credibility. Many fear that a partnership approach sends a message that senior line managers (or a department) have failed, and ultimately new levels of performance may reveal pre-existing inefficiencies and incompetencies.
- New financial systems may remove opportunities for traditional forms of rent-seeking.
- Some technical staff will experience a loss of power and authority over the control of line staff and day-to-day responsibility for all forms of expenditure. These are important issues in an organisation in which salary and status may be judged on the size of departmental budgets and resources.

Box 12.7   Responding to Stakeholder Interests
            Gweru, Zimbabwe

Links to Boxes
4.5, 9.4, 9.5, 10.4, 11.3, 11.4

	Concerns/interests	Response
Town clerk	• More effective and sustainable urban management practice • Better service provision • To introduce capital and technology not available in the city • To enlist the support of the community • To ensure that the PPP succeeds in meeting council objectives • To ensure government support	• Careful selection of an experienced private sector service provider • Competitive tendering of water and sewerage works • Request for Proposals (RfP) had specification for capital and technology transfer to Gweru • Invited stakeholders to consultative meetings with bidders • Enlisted the support of government, development agencies, consultant and community for successful implementation of proposal • Conferred with government throughout the process
Treasurer	• To alleviate the drain on capital resources within the municipality	• RfP included capital investment
Health department	• To remove the septic tank service from departmental functions • To bring about improved access to basic services affecting public health	• RfP included septic tank services • Partnership requirements ensure maintenance of public health standards and safety
Engineering department	• To provide more effective services • To introduce new technology • To introduce new plant and equipment • To ensure job security for staff	• Assessed service provider's capacity in financial resource mobilisation and credentials of strategic staff to run the service • Technology transfer requirements included in proposal • Rehabilitation of plant and equipment is part of the contract • Proposal ensures some job security
Water and sanitation staff (maintenance staff operators professionals meter readers)	• Job security • Terms and conditions of employment	• Ensure handover of staff to operator • Terms and conditions the same as or better than existing conditions • Future conditions pegged against council terms and conditions • Skills development (local and international) provided by operator
Political representatives (mayor committee chairs councillors ward development committees)	• Not to lose votes and popularity • Seen to handle PPP transparently • To provide better affordable services to all residents	• Ensuring transparent tender procedures • Retain control of tariffs • Ensure performance standards
Ward development committees (WDCs)	• To ensure reliable affordable service • To ensure they are involved and adequately consulted	• Municipality invited WDCs and all stakeholders to become a part of the process of formulating the PPP

Source: Plummer and Nhemachena, 2001

- Partnerships may also change the career paths of professional staff. In a large city corporation, the position of chief engineer brings enormous status and power, ostensibly because of the large budgets and capacity to take decisions on capital works. The municipal delegation of responsibility for the water and sewerage network may radically change the nature of the position in the eyes of middle managers.

It is also common for junior staff to display the same attitudes as their line managers. Changing attitudes from the top–down is therefore probably most effective. One of the reasons for hesitation among senior members of staff is their lack of familiarity with partnership arrangements, and they tend to pass on assumptions to more junior members of staff. Junior staff, on the other hand, may have more to lose. They have embarked on a municipal career with a certain expectation as to how a municipality is managed and, despite low pay, they are familiar with the status and power associated with their specific line of work. The impact of partnership approaches and other areas of reform that undermine these expectations should not be underestimated.

Changing the attitudes of technical staff requires an understanding of deeply ingrained professional concerns. These arise from education and from the position adopted by their professional associations. They are reinforced by the operating hierarchy of line departments and the low level of skills in partnerships among senior technical managers. Changing attitudes may also mean creating new opportunities. Many municipal engineers who are interested in the design and construction side of their profession may see that the best long-term solution is for them to join the private sector. Others may be interested in developing capacity to prepare partnerships and to fine-tune the monitoring role. Still others may see their position in terms of regulation, and wish to move into an agency that plays a regulatory role.

Where partnerships have not been preceded by adequate consultation, perhaps the greatest immediate resistance to new partnership arrangements will come from those **manual staff** currently employed in the service area (see Chapter 6). They will be concerned about job security, opportunity, pay and conditions. Many may wish to remain employed by the public sector (often preferring the known to the unknown, secure in the knowledge of a predictable pension etc.). However, sometimes consultative processes can bring about attitudinal change among local workers that is not reflected in union representation. At an individual level, assurances that jobs are safe and that current terms and conditions – including pensions – will remain at the same level or improve, is often enough to convince unskilled workers of the benefits of moving to the private sector.

There are a number of ways of attempting to overcome resistance to change. The most important factor is to recognise, validate and address the different viewpoints of the actors involved. Another important step is to create a transparent process that removes scepticism and fear of corruption. The involvement of stakeholders in Gweru (see Box 12.7) was successful in changing public opinion for both these reasons: a conscious attempt was made to involve all stakeholders in the discussions about proposed PPPs, and to educate staff in the concept of partnership. A consensus was sought among ratepayers' associations, trade unions, cooperatives and the council. Both the political and administrative arms of the council fostered a series of relationships with key individuals and groups in the community. The fear and scepticism that characterised attitudes at the initial stages were gradually replaced by the support of most stakeholders.

Finally, visible success and sustained capacity building often bring about the attitudinal change required.

Guy Stubbs

A **Framework** for Action

This brief chapter attempts to summarise the various elements of municipal capacity building for public–private partnerships (PPPs) discussed in the preceding chapters and place them in a broad framework for action.

The complex arena of PPPs makes such an outline a matter of debate. This particular framework stresses urban management, poverty reduction and a broad perspective of PPPs. It aims to provide a structured way of considering PPPs in their municipal context and supplements programmes and technical toolkits presented elsewhere. This complexity is accentuated further by integrating poverty responses into the PPP and not separating them as optional extras.

Central to this complexity is the untidy way in which vastly different organisations are simultaneously referred to as 'private sector'. Yet this complication reflects the real nature of service delivery in developing cities. The private sector participation (PSP) process is not a matter of shifting from purely public operation to purely large-scale private operation. It is a matter of shifting from a mixed composition of providers to a hopefully more integrated structure. This framework for action is therefore more focused on outlining the key elements and processes in this bigger picture than it is on the detail of large-scale private sector procurement. The reader is strongly advised to obtain detailed source material on these topics (see Appendix A).

Like any such framework, this is only a guide and must be adapted to suit the context, and the highly specific and general aspirations of the municipality. Local conditions will spell out what is possible and what is not. They will provide key areas of concern, whether political or regulatory. While action at the policy level is largely outside the scope of this book, it is a vital aspect of the potential of municipal capacity. Existing stakeholders and their respective capacities will further affect the key areas of action. The existence of a fleet of water tankers and reservoirs provides an asset for water delivery that cannot be overlooked in more ambitious network planning. Competent NGOs working with the poor in sanitation and hygiene promotion play a key role in linking the benefits of services to poverty reduction. The willingness of the international private sector will also clearly influence a municipality's approach to achieving its objectives. The balance of these is particular to each context.

What is unambiguous and straightforward is the need for greater support, at the municipal level, to focus PPPs and to integrate them into urban governance strategies. This framework aims to point municipalities towards the key areas of action in which more sector-specific action plans can be developed – hopefully with the assistance of external experts skilled in partnering and the planning, design and negotiation of contracts. This framework is thus just a structure for municipalities to use in creating the skeleton of a partnership focused on achieving urban and poverty objectives.

13

Focusing Partnership Goals

Meeting municipal objectives through partnerships	Identify municipal objectives for service partnerships • social • economic • financial • physical • political • institutional

Locating and linking partnerships in urban governance and management	**Establish approach to partnership development that contributes to governance objectives** • participation and consultation • integrated planning at the strategic level • financially sound management • accountable and transparent actions • collaborative and innovative management **Link partnership activities into other poverty-related activities,** e.g. • community mobilisation, empowerment and organisation • demand-led initiatives • service gradation • land tenure resolution **Develop partnerships in relation to broader municipal obligations and functions** • create a strategic approach • agree priorities through public consultation • create confidence through effective sequencing of service reforms • build on the lessons of each partnership

Contributing to poverty reduction	**Identify the needs and objectives of the poor** • carry out participatory poverty/livelihood assessments • identify areas of institutional and political marginalisation • clarify objectives of diverse groups **Incorporate the lessons of poverty reduction,** e.g. • facilitate demand-led service delivery • enhance community capacity to participate • integrate solutions at the micro-level • respond to variability and diversity within poor communities • address gender bias and marginalisation **Identify and respond to key concerns of the poor,** e.g. • lack of choice • affordability • accessibility • exploitation • security of tenure • employment opportunities **Identify existing actors, assets and mechanisms involved in service delivery to the poor,** e.g. • municipal actors • private operators • informal service providers • NGO support • other poor households

Developing a Partnership Framework

Building on the assets of potential partners	**Explore the attributes and roles of actors in the partnership** • the municipality • international private sector • national private sector • small-scale providers • NGOs • CBOs **Identify potential roles and contribution of external actors** • donors and international funding agencies • specialist consultants **Develop appreciation of the different characteristics that partners bring to the partnership** • complementary skills and competencies • conflicting attitudes and approaches **Design mechanisms for partnering, i.e. for promoting effective interaction**, e.g. • creating a learning approach • ensuring adequate preparation • establishing clarity of and commitment to roles • reviewing and monitoring partner performance • building on assets and differences
Focusing the scope and content of partnership arrangements	**Consider the scope and content of the partnership framework in terms of municipal objectives** • identify key components that respond to objectives • include these aspects in the partnership framework **Address physical objectives**, e.g. • service coverage • service options • service quality **Address social and political objectives**, e.g. • equity and access to improved services • integrating service delivery • gender targeting of services • fair treatment of workers (municipal workers and informal serrvice providers) • community participation and capacity building **Address financial and economic objectives**, e.g. • attracting private capital • ensuring effective risk management • establishing financial incentives • establishing appropriate cost recovery policy and implementation **Address institutional objectives**, e.g. • skills transfer • technology transfer • capacity building • decision-making structure

13

Establishing appropriate organisational and contractual arrangements	**Consider factors affecting the way the partnership should be structured** • the degree of influence required by the municipality • the relationships between actors • the bundling and unbundling of service functions **Identify the key factors affecting the procurement of large-scale operators, e.g.** • transaction costs • capacity • information **Develop knowledge of the various models of contracting the large-scale private sector partner, and their limitations and oportunities in relation to agreed objectives** • service contracts • management contracts • leases and affermage contracts • franchises • concessions • BOT contracts **Develop understanding of the key issues involved in working with small-scale providers** • constraints to meaningful involvement • mechanisms to overcome barriers **Develop understanding of the key parameters concerning the role and position of NGOs** • separate contracts • sub-contracts • contracts with community • consortium arrangements
Establishing sound partnership principles	**Agree and work towards the key principles of partnerships** • transparency and accountability • competition and contestability • legitimacy and legality • specificity • stakeholder participation • equity • clarity and predictability • risk management • economic, financial and environmental sustainability

Enhancing Capacity to Implement Partnerships

Understanding the operating context of municipal partnerships	**Develop understanding of the operating context of the municipality and its impacts on PPPs** • political context and political will for partnerships • economic context • legislative framework • policy context and leaders • administrative context **Develop understanding of the regulatory environment for PPPs** • who is the regulator? • what is being regulated (price, entry, quality)? • who is being regulated? • how is it regulated?

Enhancing human resources	**Develop appropriate skills for developing, implementing and sustaining PPPs,** e.g. • capacity to analyse needs • capacity to develop a strategic response • capacity to implement agreed strategy • capacity to maintain effective partnerships • capacity to engage with stakeholders • ability to act as an effective partner • ability to understand capacity deficiencies **Develop and implement a skills development strategy** • identify key skill gaps • identify how to fill these gaps internally or without external technical support • carry out programme of skills development • ensure ongoing capacity of decision-makers • develop mechanisms to ensure skills are sustained
Supporting organisational development	**Develop an organisational development strategy to respond to partnership strategies** • identify key organisational factors constraining effective partnering • identify mechanisms for change **Address management capacities** • lead participatory process • champion process, create environment for change, remove bureaucratic inertia • ensure depth of skills and partnership awareness • determine strategy and mechanisms for implementation • establish the municipality as a credible partner **Address procedural constraints** • strategic planning • partnership development • partnership implementation including procurement, contracting etc. **Address impacts of and on municipal structures** • effective internal coordination • impacts of downsizing engineering departments • separation of water and sanitation • location of solid waste function, revenue functions, low-income settlement upgrading initiatives • capacity to facilitate multi-sectoral responses **Address financial capacities to ensure strong financial base and reliable partner** • general municipal finances • management, improved revenue base) • finances for services • cost benefit analyses, monitoring and benchmarking **Address municipal attitudes** • identify key attitudinal blockages • recognise differences between viewpoints and impacts • identify motivation for change • address and alleviate issues where possible through direct action • establish open information policy • invest in capacity building

GHK

Appendix A
Useful Contacts

☐ Water and Sanitation Program (WSP)

The Water and Sanitation Program (WSP) is an international partnership to help the poor gain access to improved water supply and sanitation services. WSP has carried out a large number of studies on independent service providers and large-scale providers, focusing on the impacts of different types of service provision on the poor. They are currently producing guidelines for pro-poor transactions. The website contains a large number of publications available online or on request. WSP can be contacted through the headquarters or regional offices.

Water and Sanitation Program Headquarters

Water Supply and Sanitation Division
The World Bank Group
1818 H Street, NW
Washington, DC 20433
USA
tel: +1 202 473 9785
fax: +1 202 522 3313
email: info@wsp.org
website: www.wsp.org

☐ Public–Private Partnerships for the Urban Environment (PPPUE)

UNDP's Public–Private Partnerships for the Urban Environment (PPPUE) facility supports the development of innovative partnerships at the local level. Focusing on assisting small- and medium-sized cities, PPPUE works with all potential stakeholders. PPPUE has three inter-related components to support developing countries. The National Programmes oversee policy development, capacity building, and pilot projects at the country level; the PPPUE Flexible Response Facility, which provides PPP expertise and support for ongoing projects that require short-term interventions; and PPPUE Global Learning Network, which utilises the powerful networking capacities of the internet to research PPP policy tools, exchange best practices and case studies on global and regional levels, and provide PPP training.

UNDP/BDP/PPPUE

Cnr. Visagie & Prinsloo Streets
Petoria 0001
South Africa
tel: +27 (0) 12 320 3820
fax: +27 (0) 12 320 2413/4/5
email: pppue@undp.org
website: www.undp.org/pppue

Postal address:
UNDP/BDP/PPPUE
UN House
351 Schoeman Street
PO Box 6541
Pretoria 0001
South Africa

☐ Public–Private Infrastructure Advisory Facility (PPIAF)

PPIAF is a technical assistance facility aimed at helping developing countries improve the quality of their infrastructure through private sector involvement. It disseminates best practice, and is able to channel technical assistance to governments on strategies and measures for private sector involvement. It can finance a range of country and multi-country advisory and related activities in most municipal services. Applications for support can be made through the PPIAF website.

PPIAF

Program Management Unit
c/o World Bank
Room 19-061
1818 H Street NW
Washington, DC 20433
USA
tel: +1 202 458 5588
fax: +1 202 522 3481
email: info@ppiaf.org
website: www.ppiaf.org

☐ International Labour Organization (ILO)

The International Labour Organization is the UN specialized agency that seeks the promotion of social justice and internationally recognized human and labour rights. It provides technical assistance primarily in the fields of vocational training and vocational rehabilitation; employment policy; labour administration; labour law and industrial relations; working conditions; management development; cooperatives; social security; labour statistics and occupational safety and health. It promotes the development of independent employers' and workers' organisations and provides training and advisory services to those organisations.

International Labour Organization

4 route des Morillons
CH-1211 Geneva 22
Switzerland
tel: +41 (0)22 799 6111
fax: +41 (0)22 798 8685
email: ilo@ilo.org
website: www.ilo.org

☐ Municipal Infrastructure Investment Unit (MIIU)

The MIIU was established by the government of South Africa to help municipalities to find innovative solutions to critical problems in the financing and management of essential municipal services such as water supply, sanitation, waste, energy and transport. These solutions include the involvement of new parties in service delivery in various forms of PPP arrangements. The MIIU provides assistance within South Africa.

Municipal Infrastructure Investment Unit

Development Bank of Southern Africa
1258 Lever Road
Headway Hill
Midrand
PO Box 8151, Midrand 1685
South Africa
tel: +27 (0)11 313 3413
fax: +27 (0)11 313 3358
email: info@miiu.org.za
website: www.miiu.org.za

☐ Business Partners for Development (BPD)

Business Partners for Development is an informal network of partners who seek to demonstrate that partnerships between three sectors – public, private and civil society – can achieve more at the local level than any of the groups acting individually. The Water and Sanitation Cluster of BPD aims – through focus projects, study and sharing lessons learnt – to improve access to safe water and effective sanitation for the growing number of urban poor in developing countries. Through focus projects, the cluster seeks to illustrate that by pooling their unique assets and expertise, tri-sector partnerships can truly provide mutual gains for all. The cluster disseminates findings through newsletters, their website and other key publications to share best practice widely.

BPD Water and Sanitation Cluster

c/o WaterAid
Prince Consort House
27–29 Albert Embankment
London SE1 7UB
UK
tel: +44 (0)20 7793 4557
email: info@bpd-waterandsanitation.org
website: www.bpd-waterandsanitation.org

Notes

Chapter 1

1   See, for example, the early Slum Improvement Project work in Hyderabad, India, funded by the-then Overseas Development Adminstration (ODA, now DFID) of the UK.
2   The Building Municipal Capacity Series is a series of sourcebooks for local government capacity building funded by the DFID Knowledge and Research programme, and published by Earthscan.
3   Plummer, 2000.
4   Case studies are available at www.ghkint.com/publications and www.undp.org/pppue.
5   See the work of the Water and Sanitation Program; and the World Bank Private Sector Development Notes.
6   Previous publications have focused on the importance of partnerships between civil society and municipalities. There is no doubt that more municipal capacity building could be undertaken in this area, and a subsequent volume of this series is intended to develop municipal capacity in relation to civil society.

Chapter 2

1   For more detail on leases and affermage contracts, see Chapter 8, p192.

Chapter 3

1   See Estache et al, 2000. See also references to the recent work of the Water and Sanitation Program.
2   Frequently, the 'vicious cycle of municipal infrastructure management' is stressed – that operating inefficiency causes poor service delivery, which results in low-cost recovery and then inadequate maintenance, deteriorating facilities, poor service delivery and operating inefficiency, etc. This theory does not draw attention to the role of externalities or to capacity deficiencies, focusing only on the financial causes of service deterioration.
3   See, for instance, Shafik, 2001.
4   To date, little of this private capital has gone to the poorest countries and an insignificant amount to the municipal level of government.
5   There are examples of well-managed water utilities, for example, in Chile and Botswana – achieved through the corporatisation of public utilities. In Zimbabwe, where network coverage is high, the Bulawayo City Council has itself established efficient management of water and sanitation services in the town.
6   Jackson, 2000.
7   The components of sector reform have been explained in terms of industry restructuring, regulation, cost-reflective pricing and PSP. Each of these components brings with it potential impacts and benefits – often confused with PSP. See Alexander and Estache, 1999.

Chapter 4

1   Adapted from Batley, 1997, quoting Stoker, 1996, pp10–11.
2   These include holism, flexibility, subsidiarity, particularity, fiscal transparency and control, coherence, participation and competitiveness. This section draws heavily on the work of Batley, 1997 and Neilson, 2000.
3   There is, however, a tendency to group network services such as telecommunications and electricity. As these are not all municipal functions (with the exception of water supply), there is only limited opportunity for municipal officials to gain a more comprehensive picture or understanding of the complexities of urban management.

Chapter 5

1   Business Partners for Development is funded by the World Bank, DFID and private company contributions.
2   The Water and Sanitation Program is funded by bilateral donors through the World Bank.
3   Such as those typically used by economists in discussions about demand, affordability and willingness to pay.
4   While this book aims to stress the importance of community participation, mechanisms and capacity building to this end are not its primary purpose, and the benefits and processes of participation are documented in detail elsewhere. Participation can take various forms and no one particular form is ideal or static throughout the delivery process. Communities, like delivery agents, are likely to develop capacity to participate and to create their own evolving processes. Participation will also be affected by a range of social,

political, cultural, economic and physical factors, and will vary according to the service type (whether solid waste, water supply or sanitation), the stage of delivery (design, implementation, operation or maintenance), and the level of service. The keys to participation are appropriateness, ensuring that roles are understood and objectives agreed, and facilitating capacity building for all partners.

The lessons of participatory poverty reduction initiatives provide a wealth of examples of the benefits of targeted activities, which the poor themselves identified and formulated; they illustrate the increased ownership, status and empowerment that have resulted from the process. Yet participation can be difficult to achieve. One of the corollaries of the involvement of a wide range of stakeholders is the need for time and flexibility. Driven by expenditure goals, few projects have enough time available, and fewer have the flexibility to accommodate the change, feedback and revision processes that make participation meaningful.

These concepts are developed in Municipalities and Community Participation; Plummer, 2000.

5   Amis, 2000.

6   See Plummer, 2000b, describing a participatory assessment of urban poverty in Vientiane.

7   As in society at large, women's groups are also dominated by more powerful (and probably wealthier) women, and their needs are unlikely to reflect the needs of the more vulnerable.

8   DFID definition, available on the DFID sustainable livelihoods website www.livelihoods.org.

9   The SL approach is now mainstreamed by a number of agencies, including the UNDP and DFID. The UNDP has included SL as one of its five corporate mandates.

10   In order to keep to an established framework, the following section draws heavily on the descriptions and structure of DFID literature on SL, predominately the DFID SL guidelines (DFID, 1999).

11   DFID, 1999, 2.4.1.

12   DFID, 1999, 2.4.2.

13   The municipality can choose to elect another actor, such as an NGO, rather than place itself in the coordinator role.

Chapter 6

1   See also the comparative table in Box 6.23.

2   Elections also play an important and valuable accountability function, and their role must be categorically factored into a partnership, because they have significant and potentially harmful effects. See the discussion on political will and change in Chapter 10.

3   Political turnover can also be the very reason why partnerships are established. However, in these situations, when decision-making is taken out of a council's hands, the council may well lose interest in the partnership and pursue functions over which it has more influence.

4   These cases also expose the dangers of unregulated partnerships.

5   Mission statements are generally made available on operator websites.

6   Bartone, 1999, p10.

7   Unpublished GHK International research from India.

8   The participation of national businesses may be seen as a temporary convenience for the international company, enabling it to ensure that a bid complies with the regulations, or making it seem that a consortium has local knowledge.

9   Extensive work has been undertaken on the existing pattern of informal service provision and the potential roles of these providers in the delivery of services to poor communities. Of particular interest is the work carried out by the Water and Sanitation Program in East Africa, which has provided greater understanding of the types of service providers and their scale of operations, the benefits for poor users, the effects of institutional and legal contexts, and the development constraints and opportunities for these activities. This section draws heavily on this work. It is an extremely useful and highly recommended source for municipalities all over the world, not only to improve understanding of the benefits of informal service provision, but also to understand how formal PSP affects such providers (see Collignon and Vézina, 2000). In the solid waste sector, useful studies have been undertaken by WEDC (see Ali and Cotton, 2001).

10   Collignon and Vézina, 2000, p2.

11   Ibid.

12   It would not be correct to say that the primary interest of all NGOs is social, as it varies according to their mandate – they may be environmental, legal and so on.

13   Very often, international NGOs have national and regional offices, and have partnership relationships with other levels of local NGOs. National NGOs are sometimes federations of local NGOs, or they may have branches in local communities. Like other sectors, there are tensions between these levels in terms of resource allocation and roles. However, the parties are often quite independent, so a key challenge for them is to learn how to work together and develop trusting relationships. Over the past few years, with the increasing capacity of local and national NGOs, international NGOs' roles are being redefined.

14   Plummer, 2000, pp74ff.

15   The concept of 'interface' is discussed in detail in Plummer, 2000, pp61ff.

16   It is important to understand that community-based organisations (CBOs) are different from NGOs. The latter's membership is usually open to anyone interested in the purposes of the organisation. They are, therefore, accountable to their memberships who are not just people receiving services (residents), but are people who are committed to taking an active role in their development. A CBO might have quite a general purpose to raise the quality of life of its membership community. Or, it might have a quite specific purpose to address a specific issue such as water services (this might also be a focus of a general-purpose CBO committee). CBOs are discussed as consumer organisations.

17   The development of effective community organisations is also addressed in the first book in this series (Plummer, 2000). This section also addresses the sustainability problems associated with newly formed project-oriented CBOs.

18   World Bank, 1997; Cointreau-Levine, 2000.

19   See for instance the papers from the Private Infrastructure Solutions and the Poor Conference. PPIAF, 2000.

20   With the exception of the important matter of social issues, this information is compiled using the water and sanitation toolkits produced by the World Bank. See World Bank, 1997, p13.

21   Some municipalities have pointed out that the lack of country experience is also a major problem. However, in those municipalities that are paving the way in their national context, it may not be possible to combine PPP expertise with country expertise. In such cases, municipalities should look at the overall team, and ensure that local knowledge is represented as well.

22   World Bank, 1997.

23   The state (government), the market (business) and civil society (civil society organisations including consumers, NGOs, unions).

24   This discussion focuses upon *comparative* competencies between the three organisational types. Of course, some businesses are better at producing profits than others – but in general, the organisations in the private sector are far better at profit-making than those in any other sector. The same goes for government's rule-making competency and civil society's competency in addressing equity and justice.

25   The corporatisation process is, of course, a possible option. A small number of utilities (e.g., those in Chile, Botswana and Durban, South Africa) have proved that the public sector can, through a process of corporatisation, achieve economic objectives.

Chapter 7

1   By the contribution of labour and/or by introducing community-based distribution systems.

2   For instance, in most sub-Saharan African cities there is a very limited sewerage network.

3   The illegal dumping of rubbish by the poor and the non-poor is much more difficult to resolve, and municipalities frequently bear the cost of such dumping through their municipal sweeping/street cleaning functions.

4   See, for instance, the land-sharing initiatives of the municipality in Hyderabad in India in the early 1990s.

5   De facto tenure security can arise when inhabitants of irregular settlements do not feel under the threat of eviction. They do not have the paperwork confirming ownership, but they do not act as though they live at risk. This may be due, for instance, to legislation effectively making their occupation legal after a statutory period, or it may be because the municipality has installed services.

6   See, for instance, Suez Lyonnaise des Eaux, 1998; PDG, 2000b.

7   Heymans, 2000.

8   Cointreau-Levine, 2000, pp12–13.

9   Plummer, 2000, p21.

10   Foster, 1998; Plummer and Jones, 1999.

11   See for instance Plummer and Jones, 1999.

12   Cointreau-Levine, 2000.

13   Rivera, 1996, pp30–34.

14   Komives and Stalker Propky, 2000.

15   See, for instance, the work of Richard Franceys at IHE on connection costs.

16   The economic debate on subsidies is documented elsewhere. See Waddams Price, 2000, for a discussion on how subsidies can improve efficiency.

17   Waddams Price, 2000.

18   Ibid, referring to the work of Lovei et al, 2000,.

Chapter 8

1   These contract models have been developed for a particular application and have proved to be useful legal mechanisms in specific sectors.
2   World Bank, 1997; Cointreau-Levine, 2000.
3   As neither of these results in a partnership involving more then one sector, they are not included in this discussion.
4   While the physical water problem clearly lends itself to this bundled approach, the municipalities are not centrally involved, and they are unable to work towards an integrated approach for service delivery when this important service is excluded from their responsibility.
5   This approach was adopted in Chile and led to significant problems. Legislation was consequently introduced to ensure that electricity and water were not in the hands of the same company.
6   Primary, secondary and tertiary refers to the municipal, ward (sub-municipal) and neighbourhood levels of service, respectively. See Plummer, 2000, p38.
7   Cointreau-Levine, 2000.
8   World Bank, 1997, republished in RoSA (no date).
9   Cointreau-Levine, 2000, p19.
10 Ibid.
11 Usually five years.
12 Klein, 1996.
13 Bennett, 1998a.
14 We are grateful to Chris Heymans and Chris Ricketson for their contributions on transaction costs.
15 Text provided by Chris Ricketson, Halcrows.
16 WSP field notes and publications available on www.wsp.org; Coad, 1997; Ali and Cotton, 2001.

Chapter 9

1   Cointreau-Levine S, 2000, p9.
2   Sinclair, 1999, p602; RoSA, 2000a.
3   Cointreau-Levine, 2000, pp23, 28; World Bank, 1997, pp30–32.
4   Cointreau-Levine, 2000, p15.
5   Vaillancourt Rosenau, 2000, pp226–228.
6   DBSA, 2000, pp128, 130; World Bank, 1997, pp22–23.

Chapter 10

1   Nickson, 2001a.
2   DBSA, 1998; DBSA, 2000.
3   World Bank, 1997; Cointreau-Levine, 2000.
4   See, for instance, Smith, 2000.
5   Smith, 2000, p1.
6   Ibid., p8.
7   In situations where the contract is the instrument of regulation, the key question is whom the contracting parties go to in a dispute.

Chapter 11

1   This section develops work carried out by the University of Witwatersrand, South Africa, on capacity building for PPPs.
2   Nickson, 2001a, p29.
3   GHK International, 1999.
4   This section draws on an unpublished document produced by a task force including the University of Witwatersrand for the National Treasury in South Africa; see RoSA 1999a, p40.
5   RoSA 1999a.
6   World Bank, 1997; Cointreau-Levine, 2000; RoSA, 2001.

Chapter 12

1   Davey, 1993.
2   In certain parts of the world, such as South Asia, laws that ensure that councils are more representative of their constituency may determine the composition of the elected body. In India, the reservation of seats for women and marginalised groups has fundamentally changed the nature of local council representation. It is not uncommon for relatively poor and uneducated but highly motivated women to be elected to council. While they may lack formal education and technical or business competence, such councillors often bring a social awareness previously lacking in the male-dominated elite.
3   Evidence also suggests that in some (but not all) cases, the capacity of smaller municipalities is affected by their distance from national-level policy-makers.
4   See Chapter 7 on the role of donors in partnerships.
5   World Bank, 1997; Cointreau-Levine, 2000.
6   In a partnership involving the formal private sector, it is likely that monitoring and evaluation will be undertaken at various levels. It is likely that large-scale service providers will carry out an internal process of self-monitoring. In South Africa, for instance, WSSA has adopted its own technical performance standards. Each project is monitored internally and collated every reporting period. In the absence of any regular monitoring by the council, this self-monitoring is a critical means of ensuring that performance standards are met.
7   Plummer, 2000, p51.
8   See, for instance, Schaeffer, 2000. This urban and local government World Bank toolkit provides a straightforward and very useful outline of municipal finance.
9   See discussion on municipal attitudes and 'the poverty layer' in Plummer, 2000, p113.

References

Alcazar, L, Abdala, M A and Shirley, M (2000) **The Buenos Aires Water Concession** World Bank, Washington, DC

Alexander, I and Estache, A (1999) **Infrastructure Restructuring and Regulation: Building a base for sustainable growth** background notes prepared for an IDRC/TIPS conference 'The Role of Regulatory Reform and Growth, Lessons for Latin America ',19–22 September

Ali, M and Cotton, A (2001) **The Sweeping Business: Developing Entrepreneurial Skills for the Collection of Solid Waste** WEDC, Loughborough, UK

Ali, M and Snel, M (1999) **Lessons from Community-based Initiatives in Solid Waste** Task No 99, WELL Study, London

Ali, M, Cotton, A and Westlake, K (1999) **Down to Earth: Solid Waste Disposal for Low-Income Countries** WEDC, Loughborough, UK

Amis, P (2000) **Final Report on Impact Assessment Study of Slum Improvement Projects** DFID, New Delhi

Amis, P (2001) 'Municipal Government, Urban Economic Growth and Poverty Reduction: Identifying the Transmission Mechanisms between Growth and Poverty' in C Rakodi with T Lloyd-Jones (eds) **Urban Livelihoods: A People-centred Approach to Reducing Poverty** Earthscan, London

Amis, P (no date) **The Role of Government in Adjusting Economies – Urban Water Supply: Ghana Water and Sewerage Corporation** Paper 21, University of Birmingham, UK

Artana, D, Navajas, F and Urbiztondo, S (1998) **Regulation and Contractual Adaptation in Public Utilities: The Case of Argentina** IADB, Washington, DC

Asley, C and Carney, D **Sustainable Livelihoods: Lessons from Early Experience** DFID, London

Bakker, S, Kirango, J and van der Rees, K (2000) **Both Sides of the Bridge: Public-private partnerships for sustainable employment in waste management, Dar-es-Salaam** paper submitted for ILO workshop, Manila, 18-21 September

Bartone, C R, Leite, L, Triche, T and Schertenleib, R (1991) **Private Sector Participation in Municipal Solid Waste Service: Experiences in Latin America** vol 9, Urban Development Division, World Bank, Washington, DC

Bartone, C R (1999) **Private Sector Participation in Municipal Solid Waste Management: Lessons from LAC Solid Waste Management** roadshow, India, 11–19 November

Batley, R (1997) **A Research Framework for Analysing Capacity to Undertake the 'New Roles' of Government** DAG, University of Birmingham, UK

Batley, R (1998) **The Role of Government in Adjusting Economies – Urban Water in Zimbabwe: Performance and Capacity Analysis** Paper 33, University of Birmingham and DFID, Birmingham, UK

Bavon, A (1998) 'Does Ownership Matter? Comparing the Performance of Public and Private Enterprises in Ghana' **Journal of Developing Areas** no 3, Western Illinois University, Macomb, IL

Beall, J (ed) **A City for All: Valuing Difference and Working with Diversity** Zed Books, London

Bennett, E B (1998) **Contract Procurement Solutions for Public–Private Partnerships** background paper for the Yale–UNDP Collaborative Program, Yale University, New Haven

Bennett, E B (1998a) **Public–Private Cooperation in the Delivery of Urban Infrastructure Services (Water and Waste)** background paper for the UNDP Public–Private Partnerships for the Urban Environment Programme Workshop, November, Lima, Peru

Bernard, A, Helmich, H and Lehning, P (1998) **Civil Society and International Development** OECD, Paris

Black, M (1994) **Mega-slums: The Coming Sanitary Crisis** WaterAid, London

Blair, H (2000) 'Participation and Accountability at the Periphery: Democratic Local Governance in Six Countries' **World Development** vol 28, no 1, pp21–39

Blokland, M, Braadbaart, O and Schwartz, K (eds) (1999) **Private Business, Private Owners: Government Shareholding in Water Enterprises** Ministry of the Environment, The Hague

Blore, I (1999) **Reclaiming the Wasteland: Market Systems and Governance of Household Waste in South Africa** University of Birmingham and DFID, Birmingham, UK

Britan, E and Serra, P (1998) 'Regulation of Privatized Utilities: The Chilean Experience' **World Development** vol 26, no 6, pp945–962

Brock, K (1999) **'It's Not Only Wealth that Matters – It's Peace of Mind Too': A Review of Participatory Work on Poverty and Illbeing** World Bank, Washington, DC

Brook Cowen, P J (1999) **Lessons from the Guinea Water Lease** Private Sector Note No 78, World Bank, Washington, DC

Brook Cowen, P J and Tynan, N (1999) **Reaching the Urban Poor with Private Infrastructure** Private Sector Note No 188, World Bank, Washington, DC

Brook Cowen, P (1997) **The Private Sector in Water and Sanitation: How To Get Started** Private Sector Note No 126, World Bank, Washington, DC

Brown, L D and Kalegaonkar, A (1998) **Addressing Civil Society's Challenges: Support Organisations as Emerging Institutions** vol 15, Institute for Development Research, Boston

Campbell White, O and Bhatia, A (1998) **Privatization in Africa** World Bank, Washington, DC

Caplan, K, Heap, S, Nicol, A, Plummer, J, Simpson, S and Wwiser, J (2001) **Flexibility by Design: Lessons from Multi-Sector Partnerships in Water and Sanitation Projects** prepared for BPD, Water and Sanitation Cluster , London

Caplan, K and Jones, D (2000) **Private Sector Workshop Report** The Workshop Series for BPD Water and Sanitation Cluster, London

Caplan, K and Payne, L (2000) **NGO Workshop Report** The Workshop Series for BPD Water and Sanitation Cluster, London

Caplan, K and Payne, L (2000) **Public Sector Workshop Report** The Workshop Series for BPD Water and Sanitation Cluster, London

Carney, D (ed) (1998) **Sustainable Rural Livelihoods: What Contributions Can We Make** DFID, London

Chisari, O and Estache, A (1999) **Universal Service Obligations in Utility Concession Contracts and the Needs of the Poor in Argentina's Privatizations** World Bank, Washington, DC

Cleaver, F (1999) 'Paradoxes of Participation: Questioning Participatory Approaches to Development' **Journal of International Development** vol 11, pp597–612

Coad, A (ed) (1997) **Lessons from India in Solid Waste Management**, WEDC, Loughborough, UK

Cointreau-Levine, S (1994) **Private Sector Participation in Municipal Solid Waste Services in Developing Countries, Volume 1: The Formal Sector** UMP Policy Paper 13, World Bank, Washington, DC

Cointreau-Levine, S (2000) **Guidelines Pack: Private Sector Participation in Municipal Solid Waste Management** SKAT, Geneva

Collignan, B and Vézina, M (2000) **Independent Water and Sanitation Providers in African Cities: Full Report of a Ten-country Study** World Bank, Washington, DC

Collignon, B, Taisne, R and Sie Kouadio, J-M (2000) **Water and Sanitation for the Urban Poor in Côte D'Ivoire** Hydroconseil, Paris

Dailami, M and Klein, M (1998) **Government Support to Private Infrastructure Projects in Emerging Markets** World Bank, Washington, DC

Davey, K J (1993) **Elements of Urban Management** UMP Discussion Paper No 11, World Bank, Washington, DC

Development Bank of Southern Africa (DBSA) (1998) **Infrastructure: A Foundation for Development** Development Report, DBSA, Midrand, South Africa

DBSA (2000) **Building Developmental Local Government** Development Report, DBSA, Midrand, South Africa

DBSA (2000a) **Impact of Public–Private Partnerships on the Poor: The South African Experience** DBSA, Midrand, South Africa

Devas, N (1999) **Urban Governance, The Poor and Access to Services** background paper for Influence and Access: Local Democracy and Basic Service Provision, One World Action seminar, London, May

Devas, N and Rakodi, C (eds) **Managing Fast Growing Cities** Longman, Harlow

Development Research Group (including Eskeland, G, Devarajan, S and Gaguet, J-P) (1998) **1998 Abstracts of Current Studies: Private Sector Development and Public Sector Management** Ref No 681-62C, World Bank, Washington, DC

Department for International Development (DFID) (1995) **Stakeholder Participation and Analysis** DFID, London

DFID (1997) **Water Policy Issues: Water Resources** Occasional Paper No 2, DFID and ODI, London

DFID (1998a) **Improving Water Services through Competition: Water Resources** Occasional Paper No 6, DFID, London

DFID (1999) **Guidelines for Sustainable Livelihoods** DFID, London

DFID (2000) **Meeting the Challenge of Urban Poverty** consultation document, DFID, London

DFID (2001) **Addressing the Water Crisis** strategy document, DFID, London

Dieng, A and Janssens, J G (1997) **The Management Lease Contract: The Western African Experience** Habitat/UNDP, Cape Town

Dillinger, W (1994) **Decentralisation and its Implications for Urban Service Delivery** UMP Policy Paper, World Bank, Washington, DC

Dorsch, J J and Yasin, M M (1998) 'A Framework for Benchmarking in the Public Sector: Literature Review and Directions for Future Research' **International Journal of Public Sector Management** vol 11, no 2/3, pp91–115

Dumol, M (2000) **The Manila Water Concession** World Bank, Washington, DC

Ecocuidad/GHK (2001) **The Lima Water Tankers** case study carried out for the Building Municipal Capacity for Private Sector Participation research project, unpublished report

Environment and Development Division, ECLAC (1998) **Progress in the Privatization of Water-related Public Services: A Country-by-country Review for Mexico, Central America and the Caribbean** ECLAC, Santiago, Chile

Estache, A, Gomez-Lobo, A and Leipeziger, D (2000) **Utilities Privatization and the Poor's Needs in Latin America: Have We Learned Enough To Get It Right?** paper to conference 'Infrastructure for Development: Private Solutions and the Poor' London, 31 May–2 June

Eyben, R (1999) 'How and What Can Social Anthropology Contribute to Development Policy?' **Development Anthropologist** vol 17, no 1–2, pp91–97

First National Bank (no date) **Building Communities from the Waste Up** First National Bank, Johannesburg

Foster, V (1998) **Considerations for Regulating Water Services While Reinforcing Social Interests** WSP, UNDP/World Bank, Washington, DC

Foster, V (2001) **Condominial Water and Sewerage Systems: Costs of Implementation of the Model. El Alto–Bolivia/Pilot Project, Economic and Financial Evaluation** discussion paper, Water and Sanitation Program – Andean Region, Lima, Peru

Fox, W (1994) **Strategic Options for Urban Infrastructure Management** UMP Policy Paper 17, World Bank, Washington, DC

Franceys, R (1997) **Private Waters? A Bias Towards the Poor** Private Sector Participation in the Water and Sanitation Sector: Water Resources programme, Occasional Paper No 3, DFID, London

Franceys, R (2001) **PPP Database**, May, unpublished, IHE

Franceys, R and Sansom, K (1999) **The Role of Government in Adjusting Economies, Paper 35 – India: Urban Water Supply** University of Birmingham and DFID, Loughborough, UK

Fröhlich, U (1999) **Private Sector: Just a (New) Hope?** report on the 15th AGUASAN Workshop, Swiss Centre for Development Cooperation in Technology and Management (SKAT), Gersau, Switzerland, June–July

Gentry, B (2000) **Historical Trends in Water Financing and Management** second part of a paper presented to the OECD, Yale University, New Haven

Gentry, B (1998) **Private Capital Flows and the Environment: Lessons from Latin America** Edward Elgar, Cheltenham

GHK International (1999) **Gaborone Housing Needs Assessment Final Report** unpublished report for DFID-SA, London

GHK International (2000) **Private Sector Participation in Tertiary Level Infrastructure in South Asia** GHK International, London (unpublished)

Goldin, I and Heymans, C (1999) 'Moulding a New Society: The RDP in Perspective' in G Maharaj (ed) **Between Unity and Diversity: Essays on Nation-building in Post-apartheid South Africa** David Philip, Cape Town

Gomez Echeverri, L (1997) 'Bridges to Sustainability: Business and Government Working Together for a Better Environment' **Yale Bulletin Series** no 101

Gordhan, K (1999) **PPP Presentation to Greater Johannesburg Metropolitan Council** Johannesburg, September

Gotz, G and Harrison, K (2000) **Case Study Research into MSPs in the Water Sector: Nelspruit and Dolphin Coast Concessions** unpublished draft, Johannesburg

Govender, P and Aiello, J (1999) **Johannesburg's Strategic Plan for Municipal Service Partnerships'** Development Southern Africa vol 16, no 4

Government of British Columbia (2000) **Public–Private Partnerships: The Challenges for Local Government** (www.marh.gov.bc.ca)

Goymen, K (2000) **Municipal Reforms in Turkey: The Case of Ankara** policy seminar paper, International Development Department (IDD), University of Birmingham, UK

Goymen, K (2001) **Metropolitan Project Management: Selective Observations Related to Ankara** research paper, Middle East Technical University, Ankara

Graham, P (1999) **Participatory Democracy: Some Lessons From a Constitutional Democracy Which Believes In It** background paper for Influence and Access: Local Democracy and Basic Service Provision, One World Action seminar, London, May

Gray, P (1997) **Colombia's Gradualist Approach to Private Participation in Infrastructure** Note No 113, Private Sector Development Department, World Bank, Washington, DC

Guijt, I and Shah, M K (ed) (1999) **The Myth of Community** IT Publishing, London

Haan, H C, Coad, A and Lardinois, I (1998) **Municipal Solid Waste Management Involving Micro- and Small Enterprises: Guidelines for Municipal Managers** ITC, Turin

Haarmeyer, D and Mody, A (1997) **Tapping the Private Sector: Reducing Risk to Attract Expertise and Capital to Water and Sanitation** Project Finance and Guarantees, World Bank, Washington, DC

Halcrow Group (2000) **PPP and the Poor in Water and Sanitation: PSP Strategy as Seen By a Consulting Firm** www.wedc.ac.uk

Halla, F and Majani, B (1999) 'Innovative Ways for Solid Waste Management in Dar-es-Salaam: Toward Stakeholder Partnerships' **Habitat International** vol 23, no 3, pp351–361

Halla, F and Majani, B (1999) 'The Environmental Planning and Management Process and the Conflict over Outputs in Dar-es-Salaam' **Habitat International** vol 23, no 3, pp339–350

Hazelton, D and Kondlo, S (1998) **Cost Recovery for Water Schemes to Developing Urban Communities: A Comparison of Different Approaches in the Umgeni Water Planning Area** WRC Report No 521/1/98, WRC, Pretoria

Hearne, R R and Jose, L T (1997) **Water Markets in Mexico: Opportunities and Constraints** Discussion Paper 97-01, International Institute for Environment and Development, London

Heymans, C (2000) **Proceedings of Workshop on Municipal Access to Capital Markets, Urban Lekgotla** Urban Futures Conference, Johannesburg, July

Heymans, C and Schur, M (1999) 'National and Provincial PPPs: Issues of Supervision and Accountability' **Development South Africa** vol 16, no 4, pp607–622

Hlahla, M (1999) interview transcript in **Partnerships** fourth quarter, vol 3

Hoornweg, D with Thomas, L (1999) **What A Waste: Solid Waste Management in Asia**, World Bank, Washington, DC

Idelovitch, E and Ringskog, K (no date) **Private Sector Participation in Water Supply and Sanitation in Latin America**, World Bank, Washington, DC

Institute of Development Studies (IDS) (1999) **Strengthening Participation in Local Governance** report of workshop, Brighton, 21–24 June

International Finance Corporation (IFC) (1997) **Managing Risks in Urban Water and Sanitation Projects in African Cities: Philippines – MWSS Privatization** IFC, Cape Town

IFC (1997) **Managing Risks in Urban Water and Sanitation Projects in African Cities: Senegal – Dakar Water BOT** IFC, Cape Town

IFC (1997) **Managing Risks in Urban Water and Sanitation Projects in African Cities: Gabon – SEEG Privatization** IFC, Cape Town

IFC (1999) **The Private Sector and Development: Five Case Studies** IFC/World Bank, Washington, DC

INTRAC (1999) **The Monitoring and Evaluation of Empowerment** unpublished document, INTRAC, Oxford

Jackson, B (1998) **Rural and Peri-Urban Water Supplies in South Africa: financing issues** paper presented at DWAF Workshop on Higher Levels of Service, Midrand, 10 February

Jackson, B (2000) **Privatisation of Water Services: Do Consumers Benefit?** presentation at Consumers International Congress, Durban, 13–17 November

Jackson, B and Hlahla, M (1999) 'South Africa's Infrastructure Service Delivery Needs: The Role and Challenge for Public–private Partnerships' **Development South Africa** vol 16, no 4, pp607–622

James, S (1998) **Creative Inter-Sectoral Partnering for Urban Water Supply Systems in Developing Countries** background paper for the UNDP Public–Private Partnerships for the Urban Environment (PPPUE) programme, Yale University, New Haven

Johnstone, N (1997) **Economic Inequality and the Urban Environment: The Case of Water and Sanitation** Discussion Paper 97-03, International Institute for Environment and Development, London

Johnstone, N and Wood, L (1998) **Private Sector Participation in Water Supply and Sanitation: Realising Social and Environmental Objectives** summary of proceedings of workshop, IIED, London, 26–27 November

Johnstone, N and Wood, L (eds) (2001) **Private Firms and Public Water** Edward Elgar, Cheltenham, UK

Johnstone, N, Wood, L and Hearne, R (1999) **The Regulation of Private Sector Participation in Urban Water Supply and Sanitation** Discussion Paper 99-01, IIED, London

Karasapan, O (1996) **Private Infrastructure – A Bibliography: A Guide to World Bank Publications on Private Participation in Infrastructure** Private Sector Note No 81, World Bank, Washington, DC

Kariuki, M (1997) **Water and Sanitation Services in Informal Settlements: Lessons Learned from Kibera, Nairobi** UNDP

Kariuki, M and Wandera, B (2000) **Regulation of Cesspit Emptying Services to Ensure Access for Low-income Urban Communities: A Case Study of Public-Private Initiatives in Dar-es-Salaam** conference paper from 'Infrastructure for Development: Private Solutions and the Poor', London, 31 May–2 June

Kathmandu Metropolitan City (2000) **Policy Statement on Private Sector Participation** unpublished document, Kathmandu

Kessides, C (1997) **World Bank Experience with the Provision of Infrastructure Services for the Urban Poor: Preliminary Identification and Review of Best Practices** TWU-OR8, World Bank, Washington, DC

Klein, M (1996) 'Economic Regulation of Water Companies' **Policy Research Working Paper** 1649, Policy Research Dissemination Center, World Bank, Washington, DC, September

Komives, K and Stalker Propky, L (2000) **Cost Recovery in the Focus Projects: Results, Attitudes, Lessons and Strategies** (draft) Research and Surveys Series, Business Partners for Development, London

Komives, K (1999) **Designing Pro-Poor Water and Sewer Concessions: Early Lessons from Bolivia** Private Sector Department, World Bank, Washington, DC

Komives, K and Mas, J-P (1999) **South Africa's BoTT Program: An Integrated 'One-stop Shop' Approach to Developing Sustainable Water and Sanitation Services in Rural and Peri-urban Communities** Water and Sanitation Services South Africa (WSSA), Johannesburg

Kotze, K, Ferguson, A and Leighland, J (1999) 'Nelspruit and Dolphin Coast: Lessons from the First Concession Contracts' **Development Southern Africa** vol 16, no 4, pp623–648

Lafont, J and Tirole, J (1990) 'The Politics of Government Decision-making : A Theory of Regulatory Capture' **Quarterly Journal of Economics** vol 106, January, pp1089–1127

Lardinois, I and Furedy, C (1999) 'Source Separation of Household Waste Materials Waste' **Urban Waste Series** 7, WASTE, Gouda

Lastarria-Cornhiel, S (1997) 'Impact of Privatization on Gender and Property Rights in Africa' **World Development** vol 225, no 8, pp1317–1333

Leach, M, Mearns, R and Scoones, I (1999) 'Environmental Entitlements: Dynamics and Institutions in Community-Based Natural Resource Management' **World Development** vol 27, no 2, pp225–247

Lee, T R (no date) **Improving the Management of Water Supply and Sanitation Systems in Latin America** ECLAC, Santiago, Chile

Lee, T R and Jouravlev, A (1997) **Private Participation in the Provision of Water Services: Alternative means for private participation in the provision of water services** Environment and Development Division, ECLAC, Santiago, Chile

Lindfield, M (1997) 'Planning for the Private Financing of Urban Infrastructure: Transaction Costs and Cross-Market Analysis' **Third World Planning Review** vol 19, no 1

Lobina, E and Hall, D (2000) 'Public Sector Alternatives to Water Supply and Sewerage Privatization: Case Studies' **Water Resources Development** vol 16, no 1, pp35–55

Loftus, A, and McDonald, D (2001) 'Lessons from Argentina: The Buenos Aires Water Concession' **Occasional Papers Series** no 2, Municipal Services Project, Cape Town, available at www.queensu.ca/msp

London Economics (1998) **Competition in Water** paper prepared for DFID, London

London Economics (1998a) **Improving Water Services through Competition** Water Resources Occasional Paper No 6, DFID, London

Lovei, L, Gurenko, E, Haney, M, O'Keefe, P and Shkaratan, M (2000) **Maintaining Utility Services for the Poor: Policies and Practices in Central and Eastern Europe and the Former Soviet Union** World Bank, Washington, DC, mimeo, September

LSHTM/WEDC (1998) Guidance Manual on Water Supply and Sanitation Programmes WEDC, Loughborough, UK

Lyons, M and Smuts, C (1999) 'Community Agency in the New South Africa: A Comparative Approach' **Urban Studies** vol 36, no 12, pp2151–2166

MacLeod, S (1997) **Managing Risks in Urban Water and Sanitation Projects in African Cities: Managing Investment Risks in the Water Sector** IFC, Cape Town

Marino, M, Stein, J and Wulff, F (1998) **Management Contracts and Water Utilities: The Case of Monagas State in Venezuela** Private Sector Note No 166, World Bank, Washington, DC

Masuko, L (1996) 'Zimbabwe' in P McCarney (ed) **The Changing Nature of Local Government in Developing Countries,** University of Toronto, Toronto.

Mazzucchelli, S A, Pardinas, M R and Tossi, M G (2001) 'Private Sector Participation in Water Supply and Sanitation: Realising Social and Environmental Objectives in Buenos Aires', in N Johnstone and L Wood (eds) **Private Firms and Public Water: Realising Social and Environmental Objectives in Developing Countries,** IIED, London, pp55–116

McCarney, P (ed) (1996) **The Changing Nature of Local Government in Developing Countries** University of Toronto Press, Toronto

Mearns, R (1995) **Environmental Entitlements: An Outline framework for Analysis** IDS Working Paper 15, Institute of Development Studies, Brighton

Mehta, M (1999) **A Review of Public–Private Partnerships in India: Draft Report for Water and Sanitation Office** DFID, New Delhi

Menard, C and Clarke, G (1999) **A Transitory Regime: Water Supply in Conakry, Guinea,** World Bank, Washington, DC

Menard, C, Clarke, G and Zuluaga, A M (2000) **The Welfare Effects of Private Sector Participation in Urban Water Supply in Guinea** World Bank, Washington, DC

Montgomery, R (1995) **Short Guidance Note on How to Do Stakeholder Analysis of Aid Projects and Programmes** Centre for Development Studies, Swansea

Moore, M, Choudhary, M and Singh, N (1998) **How Can We Know What They Want? Understanding Local Perceptions of Poverty and Ill-Being in Asia** IDS Working Paper 80, Institute of Development Studies, Brighton

Morales-Reyes, J I (1993) **Privatization of Water Supply** WEDC, Loughborough, UK

Mudege, N (1997) **The Role of Government in Adjusting Economies: Urban Water Supply in Zimbabwe** DAG Working Paper 18, University of Birmingham, Birmingham

Nankani, H (1997) **Testing the Waters: A Phased Approach to a Water Concession in Trinidad and Tobago** Note No 103, Private Sector Development Department, World Bank, Washington, DC

National Business Initiative (NBI) (2000a) **Democratic Local Government 2000–2001: A Guide for Local Councillors** NBI PPP Resource Centre, Johannesburg

NBI (2000b) **The Nelspruit Water Concession: A Public–Private Partnership Case Study** NBI PPP Resource Centre, Johannesburg

NBI and Municipal Infrastructure Investment Unit (MIIU) (1999) **Partnerships** 1st quarter, NBI and MIIU, South Africa

Neilson, L (2000) **Urban Governance and Management: Impacts on the Poor** World Bank Urban Forum: Urban Poverty Reduction in the 21st Century, Washington, DC

Nickson, A (1996) **The Role of Government in Adjusting Economies: Urban Water Supply Sector Review** DAG Working Paper 7, University of Birmingham, Birmingham

Nickson, A (1997) 'The Public–private Mix in Urban Water Supply' **International Review of Administrative Sciences** vol 63, p165–186

Nickson, A (1998) **Organizational Structure and Performance in Urban Water Supply: The Case of the Saguapac Co-operative in Santa Cruz, Bolivia** International Development Department Working Paper, University of Birmingham, Birmingham

Nickson, A (1999) 'Policy Arena: Does the NPM Work in Less Developed Countries? The Case of the Urban Water Supply Sector' **Journal of International Development** vol 11, pp777–783

Nickson, A (2000) **The Role of Government in Adjusting Economies, Paper 38: Organisational Structure and Performance in Urban Water Supply: The Case of the Saguapac Co-operative in Santa Cruz, Bolivia** The University of Birmingham and DFID, Loughborough, UK

Nickson, A (2001a) **Establishing and Implementing a Joint Venture: Water and Sanitation Services in Cartagena, Colombia** GHK Working Paper 442 03, GHK International, London

Nickson, A (2001b) **The Cordoba Water Concession in Argentina** GHK Working Paper 442 05, GHK International, London

ODA (1995) **Guidance Note on Indicators for Measuring and Assessing Primary Stakeholder Participation** Social Development Department, ODA, London

Ogus, A (1994) **Regulation: Legal Form and Economic Theory**, Clarendon Press, Oxford, pp38–41, 55–58

Ozkaya, M and Askari, H (1999) 'Management of Newly Privatized Companies: Its Importance and How Little We Know' **World Development** vol 27, no 6, pp1097–1114

Palmer Development Group (PDG) (2000a) **PPP and the Poor in Water and Sanitation, Case Study: Queenstown, South Africa** WEDC, Loughborough, UK

PDG (2000b) **PPP and the Poor in Water and Sanitation, Case Study: Durban, South Africa** WEDC, Loughborough, UK

Panos (1998) **Liquid Assets: Is Water Privatization the Answer to Access?** PANOS media briefing, London

Parnell, S (1998) **Social Reflections on the Implementation of Developmental Local Governance** in DBSA, Infrastructure: A Foundation for Development Development Report, DBSA, Midrand, South Africa

Petersen, J (2000) **Linkages Between Local Governments and Financial Markets** Municipal Finance Working Series, World Bank, Washington, DC

Petersen, J with Crihfield, J B (2000) **Linkages Between Local Governments and Financial Markets: A Tool Kit to Developing Sub-Sovereign Credit Markets in Emerging Economies** World Bank, Washington, DC

Pfammatter, R and Schertenleib, R (1996) **Non-governmental Refuse Collection in Low-income Urban Areas: Lessons Learned from Selected Schemes in Asia and Latin America** SANDEC Report No 1/96, Swiss Federal Institute for Environmental Science and Technology (EAWAG), Switzerland

Planact (1997) **Integrated Development Planning: A Handbook for Community Leaders** Planact, Johannesburg

Plummer, J (2000) **Municipalities and Community Participation: A Sourcebook for Capacity Building** Earthscan, London

Plummer, J (2000a) **Favourable Policy and Forgotten Contracts: Private Sector Participation in Water and Sanitation Services in Stutterheim, South Africa** GHK Working Paper 442 01, GHK, London

Plummer, J (2000b) **A Participatory Poverty Assessment of Urban Vientiane, Lao PDR**, unpublished report for Asian Development Bank, GHK, London

Plummer, J (2000c) **personal notes from an interview with the Queenstown Town Clerk**, March, South Africa

Plummer, J and Jones, S (1999) **Poverty in Gaborone: The Perceptions of the Poor** GHK, London

Plummer, J and Nhemachena, G (2001) **Preparing a Concession: Working Towards Private Sector Participation in Water and Sanitation Services in Zimbabwe** GHK Working Paper 442 04, GHK, London

Plummer, J and Slater, R (2001) **Just Managing: The Solid Waste Management Partnership in Biratnagar, Nepal** GHK Working Paper 442 02, GHK, London

PPIAF (2000) **Infrastructure for Development: Private Solutions and the Poor** papers for conference, PPIAF/DFID/World Bank, Washington, DC, 31 May–2 June

PPIAF/WSP (2000) **The Private Sector Serving the Poor: New Designs for Water and Sanitation Transactions** International Capacity Building Seminar, Paris, December

Racelis, M (1999) 'Anthropology With People: Development Anthropology as People-generated Theory and Practice' **Development Anthropologist** vol 17, no 1–2, pp72–78

Richardson, H (no date) **Efficiency and Equity Implications of Argentina's Privatization of Infrastructure Services** World Bank, Washington, DC

Rivera, D (1996) **Private Sector Participation in the Water Supply and Wastewater Sector: Lessons from Six Developing Countries** World Bank, Washington, DC

Rivera, D (no date) **Management Models for Small Towns** Management Contract in Marinilla, Colombia

Roger, N (1999) **Recent Trends in Private Participation in Infrastructure** Private Sector Viewpoint Paper Note No 196, World Bank, Washington, DC

Rondinelli, D and Vastag, G (1998) 'Private Investment and Environmental Protection: Alcoa-Kofem's Strategy in Hungary' **European Management Journal** vol 16, no 4, pp422–430

Republic of South Africa (RoSA) (1996) **National Training and Capacity Building Audit Project** concept paper, DWAF, Pretoria

RoSA (1997) **Contract Document Volume 2: Organisational Development – Programme Implementation Agent for Eastern Cape Water Supply and Sanitation Programmes** DWAF, Pretoria

RoSA (1997a) Municipal Infrastructure Framework, Department for Constitutional Development, Pretoria.

RoSA (1999a) **Training Needs Analysis**, National Public Private Partnerships Task Team: Guidelines and Regulatory Framework for Public Private Partnerships, Unpublished document South African National Treasury

RoSA (1999b) **Schedule of PPP Training Products**, National Public Private Partnerships Task Team: Guidelines and Regulatory Framework for Public Private Partnerships, unpublished document, South African National Treasury, Budget Office

RoSA (1999c) **Training policy and strategy**, National Public Private Partnerships Task Team: Guidelines and Regulatory Framework for Public Private Partnerships, unpublished document, South African National Treasury

RoSA (2000) **Guidelines for Public–Private Partnerships** Department of Finance, Pretoria, www.finance.gov.za

RoSA (2000a) **Municipal Services Partnerships White Paper** DPLG Pretoria, www.dplg.gov.za

RoSA (2000b) **Terms of Reference for ISD Consultants BoTT** DWAF, Pretoria

RoSA (2001) **Public–Private Partnerships: A Manual for South Africa's National and Provincial Government Departments** National Treasury, Pretoria

RoSA (no date) **Guidelines for Municipal Service Delivery** Department for Constitutional Development, Pretoria

Roth, G (no date) **The Private Provision of Public Services in Developing Countries** World Bank, Washington, DC

Ruel, M T, Haddad, L and Garrett, J L (1999) 'Some Urban Facts of Life: Implications for Research and Policy' **World Development** vol 27, no 11, pp1917–1938

Saghir, J, Sherwood, E and Macoun, A (1998) **Management Contracts in Water and Sanitation: Gaza's Experience** Note No 177, World Bank, Washington, DC

South African Local Government Association (SALGA) (1997/1998) **Annual Report 1997/1998: Towards a Viable and Sustainable Local Government** SALGA, Pretoria

SALGA (no date) **Strategic Business Plan: Transforming Local Government For A Better Life For All** SALGA, Pretoria

Schaeffer, M (2000) **Municipal Budgeting** World Bank, Washington, DC

Schneider, H (1999) 'Participatory Governance for Poverty Reduction' **Journal of International Development** vol 11, pp521–534

Schuebeler, P (1996) **Conceptual Framework for Municipal Solid Waste Management in Low Income Countries** UMP Working Paper No 9, SKAT, Geneva

Schusterman, R and Hardoy, A (1997) 'Reconstructing Social Capital in a Poor Urban Settlement: The Integral Improvement Programme, Barrio San Jorge' **Environment and Urbanization** vol 9, no 1

Schusterman, R, Hardoy, A and Hardoy, J E (1991) 'The History of a Squatter Settlement and Its People: How To Overcome the Mistrust and Apathy of Its Neighbours' **Environment and Urbanization** vol 3, no 2

Shafik, N (2001) **Issue Paper** prepared for the Third United Nations Conference on the Least Developed Countries LDCIII, Infrastructure Development Session, Brussels, 19 May

Silva, G, Tynan, N and Yilmaz, Y (1998) **Private Participation in the Water and Sewerage Sector: Recent Trends** World Bank Viewpoint Paper Note No 196, World Bank, Washington, DC

Sinclair, M D (1999) 'Regulation and Facilitation of Public–private Partnerships: The MSP Policy Framework' **Development Southern Africa** vol 16, no 4, pp585–606

Sindane, J (2000) **Public–private Partnerships: Case Study of Solid Waste Management in Khayelitsha, Cape Town in South Africa** National Business Initiative, Cape Town

Singha, D (1996) 'Can Pay, Will Pay – Securing A Slum Water Supply For Squatters' **Waterlines** vol 15, no 2

Slater, R (1997) 'Lessons From Sri Lanka: New Ways To Improve Local Government Performance' **Public Administration and Development** vol 17, pp251–265

Slater, R P and Phillips, S (1997) **Institutional Study: Visakhapatnam Slum Improvement Project** report to DFID, London

Smith, W (2000) **Regulating Infrastructure for the Poor: Perspectives on Regulatory System Design** paper delivered to conference on Infrastructure for Development: Private Solutions and the Poor, London, 31 May–2 June

Snell, S (1998) **Water and Sanitation Services for the Urban Poor: Small-Scale Providers' Typologies and Profiles** WSP, December, www.wsp.org

Solo, T M (1998) **Competition in Water and Sanitation: The Role of Small-scale Entrepreneurs** Private Sector Note No 165, World Bank, Washington, DC

Stoker G (1996) 'Governance as Theory: Five Propositions' **Enjeux des Debates sur la Gouvernance** Université de Lausanne, 29–30 November

Suez Lyonnaise des Eaux (1998) **Alternative Solutions for Supply of Water and Sanitation in Sectors with Low Financial Resources** LDE, Paris

Suez Lyonnaise des Eaux (no date) **Working Together for a Sustainable Future** LDE, Paris

Sweetsur, G (2000) **BOOT Waste Water Treatment Plant, Puerto Vallarta, Mexico** unpublished paper presented at World Bank Water and Sanitation Forum 2000: Investing in Sanitation, Washington, DC, Biwater Plc, Dorking, UK, April

Talen, E (1999) 'Sense of Community and Neighbourhood Form: An Assessment of the Social Doctrine of New Urbanism' **Urban Studies** vol 36, no 8, pp1361–1379

Tandy, P (1997) **The Role of Government in Adjusting Economies: Private Sector Participation in Urban Water Supply in South Africa** Working Paper 11 DAG, University of Birmingham, Birmingham

Tayler, K (2000) **Strategic Planning for Municipal Sanitation, Section 4: Guide to Sanitation Planning at the Municipal Level** GHK International, London

TEDCOR (2000) **personal communications** with marketing manager, TEDCOR, Johannesburg

Troyano, F (1999) **Small-scale Water Providers in Paraguay** Water and Sanitation Program Working Paper, January, available at www.wsp.org

UNCHS (1996) **Managing Water Resources For Large Cities and Towns** UNCHS, Nairobi

UNCHS (no date) **Privatization of Municipal Services in East Africa** UNCHS, Nairobi

United Nations Development Programme (UNDP) (1999) **Sustainable Livelihoods: Sustainable Livelihoods Documents** www.undp.org/sl/documents

Urban Sector Network (USN) (1998) **Developmental Local Government in South Africa: A Handbook for Urban Councillors and Community Members** USN, Braamfontein

Vaillancourt Rosenau, P (ed) (2000) **Public–private Policy Partnerships** MIT Press, Cambridge and London

Vanderschueren, F, Wegelin, E and Wekwete, K (1996) **Policy Programme Options for Urban Poverty Reduction** UMP Policy Paper 20, World Bank, Washington, DC

Villasenor, G B (2000) 'Understanding and Preventing Regulatory Capture' **CPBO Discussion Notes** No 02-2000, July, www.geocities.com/cbpo_hor/discussion/capture.html

Vivendi Water (2000) **Business Partners in Development KwaZulu Natal Pilot** Project Document, Vivendi Water, Durban, South Africa

Waddams Price, C (2000) **Subsidies and the Reform of Infrastructure Services** paper delivered to conference 'Infrastructure for Development: Private Solutions and the Poor', London, 31 May–2 June

Waddell, S (2000a) **Generating New Core Competencies For Systems Change Through Business: Civil Society Collaboration: The Emerging Mutual Gain Perspective** paper presented at 'Discovering Connections Conference', University of Michigan-Dearborn and Visteon, 24–27 September

Waddell, S (2000b) **Emerging Models for Developing Water Systems for the Rural Poor: From Contracts to Co-production** Research and Surveys Series, Business Partners for Development, London

Walker, J (1993) **Preparing for Private Sector Participation in the Provision of Water Supply and Sanitation Services** WASH Technical Report No 84, Water and Sanitation for Health Program, Washington, DC

Water and Sanitation Program (WSP) (East and Southern Africa Region) (1997) **The Water Kiosks of Kibera** Field Note, WSP-ESA, Nairobi

WSP (East and Southern Africa Region) (undated) **Small Service Providers Make a Big Difference** Field Note No 5, WSP-ESA, Nairobi

WSP (South Asia) (1999a) **Financing Community Investments** Field Note, WSP, Delhi

WSP (South Asia) (1999b) **Privatizing the Operation and Maintenance of Urban Water Supply: The Experience of Ajmer, Rajasthan, India** Field Note, WSP-SA, Delhi

WSP (South Asia) (1999c) **Villagers Treat Water as an Economic Good, Olavanna, Kerala, India** Field Note, WSP-SA, New Delhi

WSP (South Asia) (1999d) **Willing To Pay But Unwilling To Charge** Field Note, WSP-SA, Delhi

WSP (South Asia) (1999e) **Private Sector Participation in Provision of Water and Sanitation Services to the Urban Poor** WSP and DFID, Chennai, India

WSP (South Asia) (1999f) **Water Vending: Improving Water Services through Small Scale Private Providers in Chennai (Madras)** Field Note, WSP-SA, Delhi

WSP (South Asia) (2001a) **The Buenos Aires Concession: The Private Sector Serving the Poor** WSP-SA, Delhi, available at www.wsp.org

WSP (Andean Region) (2001b) **El Alto Condominal Pilot Project Impact Assessment** available at www.wsp.org

WSP (Andean Region) (2001c) **Lower Costs with Higher Benefits Water and Sewerage Services for Low Income Households: Lessons from EAPP** available at www.wsp.org

Water Research Commission (1995) **Private Sector Participation in Water Supply and Sanitation Services** Water Research Commission, South Africa

Webster, M and Sansom, K (1999) **Public–private Partnership and the Poor: An Initial Review** Task No 164, WELL Study, London

World Bank (1997) **Toolkits for Private Sector Participation in Water and Sanitation** World Bank, Washington, DC

World Bank (1997a) **The Private Sector in Infrastructure Strategy Regulation and Use** World Bank, Washington, DC

World Bank (1998) **Preparation of a Management Contract for the Urban Water Supply and Sanitation Services in the Kathmandu Valley: Legislative Review** Binnie Thames Water/World Bank, Washington, DC

World Bank (1999) 'What a Waste: Solid Waste Management in Asia' **Urban Working Paper Series** no 1, World Bank, Washington, DC

World Bank (2000) **Energy Services for the Poor** World Bank, Washington, DC

Worley International (2000) **Strategic Municipal Asset Management** World Bank, Washington, DC

Yepes, G (1999) **Do Cross–subsidies Help the Poor to Benefit from Water and Wastewater Services? Lessons from Guayaquil** WSP/UNDP/World Bank, Washington, DC

Zerah, M H (1999) **Private Sector Participation and the Poor Research Project** unpublished draft, WSP-SA and Lyonnaise des Eaux (LDE), Delhi

Zerah, M H (1999) **Report on the Documentation of Innovative Contracting Procedures in Hyderabad** unpublished report, WSP-SA, Delhi

Index

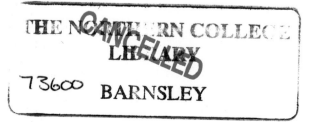